D1286511

THE PAPERS OF
BENJAMIN FRANKLIN

SPONSORED BY

*The American Philosophical Society
and Yale University*

Benjamin Franklin: Oil Painting by Benjamin Wilson

THE PAPERS OF

Benjamin Franklin

VOLUME 8 *April 1, 1758, through December 31, 1759*

LEONARD W. LABAREE, *Editor*

Helen C. Boatfield, Helene H. Fineman, and

James H. Hutson, Assistant Editors

New Haven and London YALE UNIVERSITY PRESS, 1965

The reprinting of this volume was made possible by a grant from the Charles E. Culpeper Foundation to the Friends of Franklin, and by a grant from the National Historical Publications and Records Commission.

Printed in the United States of America.

Library of Congress catalogue number: 59–12697
International standard book number: 0–300–00658–6

∞ The paper in this book meets the guidelines for permanence and durability of the Committee on Production Guidelines for Book Longevity of the Council on Library Resources.

10 9 8 7 6 5 4 3 2

Editor's Note

Ralph L. Ketcham, who had been associate editor for a little more than two years, resigned effective July 31, 1963. Before leaving he completed the preliminary editing of many of the documents from the first months included in the present volume. The editor gratefully records this help and acknowledges with sincere appreciation the important contributions of many kinds that Dr. Ketcham made to this edition during his period of service on the editorial staff.

L. W. L.

Contents

List of Illustrations

fourteenth, and the set-back story, substantially heightening the tower, was added in the fifteenth century. L. F. Salzman, ed., *The Victoria County History of Northampton*, IV (London, 1937), 124–6. From a photograph furnished by courtesy of The Mustograph Agency, London.

The Rectory at Ecton   117

In this house (but minus its porch and the lawn mower) were living in the summer of 1758 the Reverend Eyre Whalley and his wife, "a good natured chatty old lady," when Benjamin and William Franklin called on them during an ancestor-hunting tour through the Midlands. From here the rector sent to London a little later the record (printed on the pages adjoining this illustration) of the baptisms, burials, and deaths of all Franklins to be found in the parish registers. From a photograph furnished by courtesy of The Mustograph Agency, London.

The Graves of Thomas and Eleanor Franklin   117

The rector's wife guided the Franklins to the Ecton churchyard and pointed out there the gravestones of some members of their family. With "a hard brush and a basin of water" she had provided, Franklin's Negro servant Peter scrubbed the moss off the stones and William Franklin copied the inscriptions marking the graves of Benjamin's Uncle Thomas and Thomas' wife Eleanor (see below pp. 119, 137). These reminders of Franklin's family connection with the village and church remain legible two centuries and more after his pilgrimage to Ecton. From a photograph furnished by courtesy of *Life* Magazine.

Genealogical Chart of the Franklin Family   120

A much reduced facsimile of the chart Franklin prepared after returning to London from his journey to the Midlands in search of information about his English ancestors and surviving relatives. Reproduced by courtesy of the Historical Society of Pennsylvania. On the two following pages the contents of the chart are rendered in type and on the fourth page of the folio are explanatory notes.

Genealogical Charts of the White and Cash Families   140–141

These charts of two Birmingham and Philadelphia families to which Deborah Franklin was related through her mother conform in general to the method employed for the charts in the first volume of this series setting forth Benjamin Franklin's family connections.

These diagrams (Figures 1 and 2) to explain Franklin's invention appear on Plate I accompanying the description of it in James Ferguson, *Select Mathematical Exercises: Shewing how to construct different Clocks, Orreries, and Sun-Dials, on Plain and Easy Principles,* . . . (Second edition, London, 1778), Yale University Library. Figure 3 on this plate, not here reproduced, illustrates in profile a somewhat similar clock Ferguson himself devised later. The engraver is indicated as J. Lodge.

Oil painting, almost certainly executed in London by Benjamin Wilson in 1758–59, after a small original by an unidentified American artist. On Nov. 22, 1757, Franklin wrote Deborah asking her to have a miniature of their daughter Sally made and to send it over "with your small Picture, that I may here get all our little Family drawn in one Conversation Piece" (above, VII, 278). Sally's miniature never materialized, nor did the "Conversation Piece," but Deborah's "small Picture" reached London and on June 10, 1758, Franklin wrote that it was now "at the Painters, who is to copy it, and do me of the same Size" (below, p. 91). For many years the portrait was attributed to Matthew Pratt, but this statement, together with an analysis of the painting itself, almost conclusively establishes that the artist was Franklin's friend Benjamin Wilson and that the portrait was intended as a companion piece to that of Franklin reproduced as the frontispiece of this volume. Charles Coleman Sellers, *Benjamin Franklin in Portraiture* (New Haven, 1962), pp. 52–3, 64–5. "Serious paint losses in the lower third of the picture," according to Sellers, "were filled in as early as 1835 or 1836, though apparently without affecting the likeness or general coloring," but this action may have obliterated a signature and date comparable to what appears on the portrait of Deborah's husband. Upon its completion Franklin undoubtedly hung his wife's portrait in his Craven Street lodgings, but by the time of the American Revolution, after Deborah's death, it was in their Philadelphia home along with Wilson's portrait of Benjamin. When Major André carried off Franklin's picture in 1778 he left "that of its Companion, my Wife," in Franklin's later words, "by itself, a kind of Widow" (to Mme. Lavoisier, Oct. 23, 1788, Archives Nationales). The portrait continued in the possession of Benjamin and Deborah's descendants for several generations, but was acquired in 1953 by the American Philosophical Society, through whose courtesy it is here reproduced.

Contributors to Volume 8

The ownership of each manuscript, or the location of the particular copy used by the editors of each contemporary pamphlet or similar printed work, is indicated where the document appears in the text. The sponsors and editors are deeply grateful to the following institutions and individuals for permission to print in the present volume manuscripts or other materials which they own:

INSTITUTIONS

American Philosophical Society
Associates of the Late Rev.
 Dr. Bray
Boston Public Library
William L. Clements Library
Harvard College Library
Historical Society of
 Pennsylvania
Independence National Historical
 Park, Philadelphia
Library Company of
 Philadelphia
Library of Congress

The Maryland Archives
The James Monroe Memorial
 Foundation
Morristown National
 Historical Park
New-York Historical Society
New York Public Library
Pennsylvania Historical and
 Museum Commission
Princeton University Library
Public Record Office, London
The Royal Society, London
Yale University Library

INDIVIDUALS

Mrs. Ailsa Joan Mary Dick-
 Cunyngham, Prestonfield
 House, Edinburgh

John L. W. Mifflin, Middlebush,
 New Jersey

Method of Textual Reproduction

An extended statement of the principles of selection, arrangement, form of presentation, and method of textual reproduction observed in this edition appears in the Introduction to the first volume, pp. xxxiv-xlvii. A condensation and revision of the portion relating to the method of reproducing the texts follows here.

Printed Material:

In general Franklin's writings printed under his direction should be regarded as his ultimate intention and should therefore be reproduced without change, except as modern typography requires. In fact, however, newspapers and pamphlets were often set by two or more journeymen with different notions of spelling, capitalization, and punctuation. Although the resulting inconsistencies and errors did not represent Franklin s intentions, they are not eliminated by the editors. Again, in cases where Franklin's writings were printed by another, they were sometimes carelessly or willfully revised without his consent. He once complained, for example, that an English printer had so corrected and excised one of his papers "that it can neither scratch nor bite. It seems only to paw and mumble."[1] What was thus printed was obviously not what Franklin wrote, but, in the absence of his manuscript, the editors have no alternative but to reprint it as it stands. Still other Franklin letters are known only in nineteenth-century printings, vigorously edited by William Temple Franklin, Duane, or Sparks. Here, too, the editors follow the texts as printed, only noting obvious misreadings.

In reproducing printed materials, the following general rules are observed:

1. The place and date of composition of letters are set at the top, regardless of their location in the original printing.

2. Proper nouns, including personal names, which were often printed in italics, are set in roman, except when the original was italicized for emphasis.

1. BF to William Franklin, Jan. 9, 1768.

3. Prefaces and other long passages, though italicized in the original, are set in roman. Long italicized quotations are set in roman within quotation marks.

4. Words in full capitals are set in small capitals, with initial letters in full capitals if required by Franklin's normal usage.

5. All signatures are set in capitals and small capitals.

6. Obvious typographical errors are silently corrected. An omitted parenthesis or quotation mark, for example, is inserted when the other of the pair was printed.

7. Every sentence is closed with a period or other appropriate mark of punctuation (usually a question mark).

8. Longhand insertions in the blanks of printed forms are set in italics, with space before and after.

Manuscript Material:

a. *Letters* are presented in the following form:

1. The place and date of composition are set at the top, regardless of their location in the original.

2. The complimentary close is set continuously with the text.

3. Addresses, endorsements, and docketing are so labeled and printed at the end of the letter.

b. *Spelling* of the original is retained. When, however, it is so abnormal as to obscure meaning, the correct form is supplied in brackets or footnote, as: "yf [wife]."

c. *Capitalization* has been retained as written, except that every sentence is made to begin with a capital. When there is doubt whether a letter is a capital, it is printed as like letters are in the same manuscript, or, that guide failing, as modern usage directs.

d. Words underlined once in the manuscript are printed in *italics;* words underlined twice or written in large letters or full capitals are printed in SMALL CAPITALS.

e. *Punctuation* has been retained as in the original, except:

1. Every sentence ends with a period or other appropriate mark (usually a question mark), unless it is not clear where the sentence ends, when the original punctuation (or lack of it) is preserved.

2. Dashes used in place of commas, semicolons, colons, or periods are replaced by the appropriate marks; and when a sentence ends with both a dash and a period, the dash is omitted.

3. Commas scattered meaninglessly through a manuscript are eliminated.

4. When a mark of punctuation is not clear or can be read as one of two marks, modern usage is followed.[2]

5. Some documents, especially those of a legal character, lack all punctuation. This is supplied with restraint, and the fact indicated in a footnote. In some other, inadequately punctuated documents, it is silently added when needed for clarity, as in a long series of names.

f. *Contractions and abbreviations* in general are expanded except in proper names. The ampersand is rendered as "and," except in the names of business firms, in the form "&c.," and in a few other cases. Letters represented by the thorn or tilde are printed. The tailed "p" is spelled out as per, pre, or pro. Symbols of weights, measures, and monetary values follow modern usage, as: £34. Superscript letters are lowered. Abbreviations in current use are retained, as: Col., Dr., N.Y., i.e.

g. *Omitted or illegible words or letters* are treated as follows:

1. If not more than four letters are missing, they are silently supplied when there is no doubt what they should be.

2. The omission of more than four letters or one or more words is supplied conjecturally within brackets. The addition of a question mark within the brackets indicates uncertainty as to the conjecture.

3. Other omissions are shown as follows: [*illegible*], [*torn*], [*remainder missing*], or the like.

4. Missing or illegible digits are indicated by suspension points in brackets, the number of points corresponding to the estimated number of missing figures.

5. Blank spaces are left as blanks.

2. The typescripts from which these papers are printed have been made from photocopies of the manuscripts, and marks of punctuation are sometimes blurred or lost in photography. It has often been impossible to consult the originals in these cases.

h. *Author's additions and corrections.*

1. Interlineations and brief marginal notes are brought into the text without comment. Longer notes are brought into the text with the notation [*in the margin*].

2. Author's footnotes are printed at the bottom of the appropriate pages between the text and any editorial footnotes.

3. Canceled words and phrases are in general omitted without notice; if significant, they are printed in footnotes. The canceled passages of important documents, such as drafts of treaties, are brought into the text enclosed in angle brackets *before* the words substituted.

4. When alternative words and phrases have been inserted in a manuscript but the original remains uncanceled, the alternatives are given in brackets, preceded by explanatory words in italics, as: "it is [*written above* may be] true."

5. Variant readings of several versions are noted if important.

Abbreviations and Short Titles

Acts Privy Coun., *Col.*	W. L. Grant and James Munro, eds., *Acts of the Privy Council of England, Colonial Series, 1613–1783* (6 vols., London, 1908–12).
ADS	Autograph document signed.[1]
ALS	Autograph letter signed.
APS	American Philosophical Society.
Autobiog. (APS-Yale edit.)	Leonard W. Labaree, Ralph L. Ketcham, Helen C. Boatfield, Helene H. Fineman, eds., *The Autobiography of Benjamin Franklin* (New Haven, 1964).
BF	Benjamin Franklin
Bigelow, *Works*	John Bigelow, ed., *The Complete Works of Benjamin Franklin* . . . (10 vols., N.Y., 1887–88).
Board of Trade Journal	*Journal of the Commissioners for Trade and Plantations* . . . *April 1704 to* . . . *May 1782* (14 vols., London, 1920–38).
Cohen, *BF's Experiments*	I. Bernard Cohen, ed., *Benjamin Franklin's Experiments. A New Edition of Franklin's Experiments and Observations on Electricity* (Cambridge, Mass., 1941).
Colden Paps.	*The Letters and Papers of Cadwallader Colden.* New-York Historical Society *Collections* for 1917–23, 1934, 1935.
DAB	*Dictionary of American Biography.*
Dexter, *Biog. Sketches*	Franklin B. Dexter, *Biographical Sketches of the Graduates of Yale College* . . . (6 vols., N.Y. and New Haven, 1885–1912).
DF	Deborah Franklin.
DNB	*Dictionary of National Biography.*
DS	Document signed.

1. For definitions of this and other kinds of manuscripts, see above, I, xliv–xlvii.

Duane, *Works* William Duane, ed., *The Works of Dr. Benjamin Franklin* . . . (6 vols., Phila., 1808–18). Title varies in the several volumes.

Evans Charles Evans, *American Bibliography* (14 vols., Chicago and Worcester, Mass., 1903–59). Surviving imprints are reproduced in full in microprint in Clifford K. Shipton, ed., *Early American Imprints, 1639–1800* (microprint, Worcester, Mass.).

Exper. and Obser. *Experiments and Observations on Electricity, made at Philadelphia in America, by Mr. Benjamin Franklin,* . . . (London, 1751). Revised and enlarged editions were published in 1754, 1760, 1769, and 1774 with slightly varying titles. In each case the edition cited will be indicated, e.g., *Exper. and Obser.,* 1751 edit.

Gipson, Lawrence H. Gipson, *The British Empire before the American Revolution* (10 vols., to date: Vols. 1–3, Caldwell, Idaho, 1936; Vols. 4–10, N.Y., 1939–61; Vols. 1–3, revised edit., N.Y., 1958–60).
    British Empire

Hunter, *Forts* William A. Hunter, *Forts on the Pennsylvania Frontier, 1753–1758* (Harrisburg, 1960).

Johnson Papers *The Papers of Sir William Johnson* (13 vols. to date, Albany, 1921–62).

Lib. Co. Phila. Library Company of Philadelphia.

LS Letter signed.

Montgomery, *Hist.* Thomas H. Montgomery, *A History of the University of Pennsylvania from Its Foundation to A.D. 1770* (Phila., 1900).
    Univ. Pa.

MS, MSS Manuscript, manuscripts.

N.J. Arch. William A. Whitehead and others, eds., *Archives of the State of New Jersey* (2 series, Newark and elsewhere, 1880–). Editors, subtitles, and places of publication vary.

xxi

N.Y. Col. Docs.	E. B. O'Callaghan, ed., *Documents relative to the Colonial History of the State of New York* (15 vols., Albany, 1853–87).
Pa. Arch.	Samuel Hazard and others, eds., *Pennsylvania Archives* (9 series, Phila. and Harrisburg, 1852–1935).
Pa. Col. Recs.	*Minutes of the Provincial Council of Pennsylvania* . . . (16 vols., Phila., 1838–53). Title changes with Volume 11 to *Supreme Executive Council.*
Pa. Gaz.	*The Pennsylvania Gazette.*
Pa. Jour.	*The Pennsylvania Journal.*
Pargellis, *Lord Loudoun*	Stanley M. Pargellis, *Lord Loudoun in North America* (New Haven, 1933).
Pargellis, *Military Affairs*	Stanley Pargellis, *Military Affairs in North America 1748–1765* (N.Y., 1936).
Phil. Trans.	The Royal Society, *Philosophical Transactions.*
PMHB	*Pennsylvania Magazine of History and Biography.*
Sibley's Harvard Graduates	John L. Sibley, *Biographical Sketches of Graduates of Harvard University* (Cambridge, Mass., 1873–). Continued from Volume 4 by Clifford K. Shipton.
Smyth, *Writings*	Albert H. Smyth, ed., *The Writings of Benjamin Franklin* . . . (10 vols., N.Y., 1905–07).
Sparks, *Works*	Jared Sparks, ed., *The Works of Benjamin Franklin* . . . (10 vols., Boston, 1836–40).
Statutes at Large, Pa.	*The Statutes at Large of Pennsylvania from 1682 to 1801, Compiled under the Authority of the Act of May 19, 1887* . . . (Vols. 2–16, [Harrisburg], 1896–1911). Volume 1 was never published.
Van Doren, *Franklin*	Carl Van Doren, *Benjamin Franklin* (N.Y., 1938).
Van Doren, *Franklin-Mecom*	Carl Van Doren, ed., *The Letters of Benjamin Franklin & Jane Mecom* (Mem-

	oirs of the American Philosophical Society, xxvii, Princeton, 1950).
Van Doren and Boyd, *Indian Treaties*	Carl Van Doren and Julian P. Boyd, eds., *Indian Treaties Printed by Benjamin Franklin 1736–1762* (Phila., 1938).
Votes	*Votes and Proceedings of the House of Representatives of the Province of Pennsylvania, Met at Philadelphia . . . 1750, and continued by Adjournments* (Phila., 1751–). Each annual collection of the journals of separate sittings is designated by the year for which that House was elected, e.g., *Votes*, 1750–51.
WF	William Franklin
WTF, *Memoirs*	William Temple Franklin, ed., *Memoirs of the Life and Writings of Benjamin Franklin, LL.D., F.R.S., &c. . . .* (3 vols., 4to, London, 1817–18).

Genealogical references. An editorial reference to one of Benjamin Franklin s relatives may be accompanied by a citation of the symbol assigned to that person in the genealogical tables and charts in volume i of this work, pp. xlix–lxxvii, as, for example: Thomas Franklin (A.5.2.1), Benjamin Mecom (C.17.3), or Benjamin Franklin Bache (D.3.1). These symbols begin with the letter A, B, C, or D. Similarly, a reference to one of Deborah Franklin's relatives may be accompanied by a symbol beginning with the letter E or F, as, for example, John Tiler (E.1.1.2), or Mary Leacock Hall (F.2.2.3). Such persons may be further identified by reference to the charts of the White and Cash families printed in the present volume, pp. 139–42.

Chronology

April 1, 1758, through December 31, 1759

1758

April 1: William Smith's petition against the Pennsylvania Assembly laid before the King in Council.

April 20, 27: BF manages the defense of the Pennsylvania Assembly at hearings before the law officers of the Crown on Smith's petition.

May 10: BF defends Pennsylvania Acts at Board of Trade.

May 23?–30?: BF spends a week at Cambridge; performs evaporation experiments with John Hadley, professor of chemistry.

July 1?–25?: BF and WF take a "Ramble" through the English Midlands visiting their ancestral homes at Ecton and Banbury and DF's at Birmingham, collecting genealogical material on both families.

August 15?–30?: BF and WF at the fashionable resort of Tunbridge Wells.

October: BF and WF traveling with Richard Jackson in Suffolk and Norfolk.

November 25: British under Gen. John Forbes take Fort Duquesne.

November 27: Proprietors answer BF's Heads of Complaint; concede limited taxation of their estates.

December 1–7: BF has final interview with the Penns' agent, Ferdinand J. Paris.

1759

February 12: University of St. Andrews awards BF honorary degree of Doctor of Laws.

March 1?: BF sponsors the publication of Charles Thomson's *An Enquiry into the Causes of the Alienation of the Delaware and Shawanese Indians from the British Interest.*

April 30: BF petitions for Pennsylvania's share of £200,000 voted by Parliament for war expenses.

May 15: BF attends Board of Trade hearing on his "Teedyuscung Petition" of February 2.

May 29?: BF at Board of Trade hearing on Pennsylvania Indian Trade Act.

June 26: Privy Council declares Pennsylvania Assembly's proceedings against William Smith unwarrantable.

August 8?–November 2?: BF and WF traveling in the north of England and in Scotland; BF admitted burgess and guild brother of Edinburgh, (Sept. 5), Glasgow (Sept. 19), and St. Andrews (Oct. 2).

August 29: Order in Council appointing Sir William Johnson to investigate the complaints of the Delaware Indians.

September 13: Decisive British victory on the Plains of Abraham; Quebec surrenders, September 18.

September 29: BF authorized to receive Pennsylvania's share of the Parliamentary grant of £200,000.

THE PAPERS OF
BENJAMIN FRANKLIN

VOLUME 8

April 1, 1758, through December 31, 1759

From Thomas and Richard Penn[1]

Letterbook copy: Historical Society of Pennsylvania

Sir   London April 6th: 1758.

We did, as we before told you,[2] without any delay on our parts, cause Cases to be drawn up, stating the several Matters in Dispute, and laid before the Attorney and Sollicitor General,[3] intending to be governed by their opinions, in the answer we should give, to your heads of Complaint; We have since that several times applyed for them, and in particular just before the Hollidays, when the Attorney promised to take the Case into the Country, and consider it there. Our Agent[4] has attended at his Chambers since his return, but has not yet seen him, and til we receive both these opinions we cannot give an answer to your Paper, neither do we think it proper to submit the Case to your Consideration.[5]

We are much concerned at this delay, as no Persons can more earnestly desire a speedy determination of these unhappy differences than we do, the well being of our Country so much depend-

---

1. Thomas Penn (1702–1775), son of the founder of Pennsylvania, became one of the Proprietors in 1727, and after 1746, when he inherited his brother John's interest, owned three-quarters of the proprietorship and exercised dominant control. His brother Richard (1706–1771) owned the remaining one-quarter interest. BF's first meeting with them to discuss the disputes which had brought him to England occurred in the middle of August 1757. See above, VII, 250.

2. See above, VII, 279. The Proprietors are here replying to a letter from BF requesting an answer to the Heads of Complaint (above, VII, 248–52). BF's letter has not been found, but he sent copies of it (designated "No. 1") and this reply by the Penns (designated "No. 2"), to Isaac Norris on Jan. 19, 1759.

3. Charles Pratt (1714–1794), later lord chancellor and first Earl Camden, had become attorney general upon William Pitt's accession to power, July 1, 1757; and Charles Yorke (1722–1770) had been solicitor general since Nov. 1, 1756. *DNB*. See above, VII, 366 n, for Yorke's opinion, and below, p. 63 n, for an inference that they were slow in reaching decisions because they were "but young in Office." Both men were long members of Parliament and influential in the various ministries with which BF dealt during his agencies in England.

4. Ferdinand J. Paris; see above, VII, 247 n.

5. As BF later told Norris, he thought a joint state of the case, laid before the law officers by both parties, would have been "the fairest Way." See below, p. 235.

ing upon it.[6] If you think proper to lodge these Complaints before we receive the opinions, we shall on our parts do every thing in our power to bring it to a speedy issue, and with great satisfaction submit our conduct to the most publick examination. We are Your very affectionate Friends T:P:

Mr. Benjamin Franklin R:P:

From Richard Partridge: Receipt

DS: Historical Society of Pennsylvania

London, April 20, 1758.

Receiv'd of Benjamin Franklin, Esqr; the Sum of Forty Pounds, to be accounted for to the Province of Pennsylvania.[7]

per me. RICHD. PARTRIDGE

£40: 0: 0

[*Endorsed*] April 20, 1758 N. 82 Mr Partridge's Receipt, £40 for the Province 1758.[8]

6. Following the delay caused by BF's illness and the absence of most of the ministers from London in the fall of 1757, the opinions of the attorney and solicitor general were further delayed, as Thomas Penn and BF both alleged, by Robert Charles (BF's fellow agent, see above, VI, 230 n) having given Charles Pratt a retainer to represent the Pa. Assembly, prior to Pratt's appointment as attorney general and to BF's arrival in England. Pratt refused to submit an official opinion in adjudication of a dispute to which, in view of Charles's fee, he was technically a party. With BF's approval, Charles refused to accept a return of the retainer, thus impeding Pratt's decision. Unless BF had an intimation that Pratt's opinion would be adverse, it is strange to find him party to an obstructing procedure; generally BF had every reason to seek a speedy settlement. Penn, on the other hand, may have sought delay to try BF's patience, but probably neither BF nor Penn could have hastened the attorney general's opinion as long as Pratt feared the political consequences of *any* decisions over his name. See below, pp. 87 n, 234–5. The full official opinion of the King's legal advisors did not come until early November; Penn to Pa. Council, Nov. 10, 1758. Penn Papers, Hist. Soc. Pa.

7. BF recorded in his accounts that the £40 was "to be employ'd in Feeing Council and other Expences on Smith's Petition." "Account of Expences," p. 14; *PMHB*, LV (1931), 109. The receipt is in WF's hand except for the signature. See above, V, 11 n, for Richard Partridge, Pa. Assembly agent, and below, pp. 28, 31–40, for William Smith's petition.

8. In BF's hand. Another receipt at Hist. Soc. Pa. shows that Partridge received £30 more on May 2, 1758, "on account of the charges relating to

To Joshua Sharpe[9]

ALS: Boston Public Library

Sir   Craven Street, April 21. 58

I approve very much of engaging Dr. Hay.[1] I know not whether he will chuse to appear for us before the Attorney and Sollicitor General, but before the Committee of Council perhaps he may have no Objection.

If the Constitution of the Province is to be attack'd, as you intimate, the Cause is of so much greater Weight. If the Privileges of a single Englishman are of Importance, those of the Representative Body of a whole Province must be more so.

In the Royal Charter Sect. IV. and in W. Penn's Charter of Privileges Sect. II. and in the Act of Assembly 4to Anno, pag. 72.[2] you will see how the Privileges and Powers of the Assembly are founded, and what they are.

I am, Sir Your most obedient humble Servant   B FRANKLIN

Addressed: To / Joshua Sharpe Esqr / at his Chambers, Lincoln's / Inn New Square / No 4

Wm. Smiths Appeal against the Pennsylvania Assembly." This payment is recorded in the MS "Account of Expences," p. 31, but was omitted from the printed version, *PMHB*, LV (1931), 97–133.

9. Joshua Sharpe (c. 1716–1786), brother of Gov. Horatio Sharpe of Maryland and of William Sharpe, clerk of the Privy Council, had been admitted to Lincoln's Inn, 1740, and served as counsel for Pennsylvania (in 1755 and 1756) and other colonies before the Board of Trade and the Privy Council. *The Records of the Honorable Society of Lincoln's Inn* (Lincoln's Inn, 1896), I, 421; *Gent. Mag.*, LVI (1786), 441; *Board of Trade Journals, 1754–58, passim*.

1. George Hay (1715–1778), D.C.L. Oxon., 1742; at this time M.P., member of the Admiralty Board, vicar-general to the Archbishop of Canterbury, and King's advocate; knighted, 1773. *DNB*. Sharpe was to consult him about a hearing on the petition of William Smith to be held on April 27. See documents under that date for references to the matters mentioned by BF below. Hay is not recorded as counsel for the Assembly in any hearings at this time.

2. All three documents cited are quoted in the next document.

From David Hall   Letterbook copy: American Philosophical Society

Dear Sir   Philadelphia 24th April 1758
Yours of December the 9th.[3] I receiv'd per the Packet, by
which was glad to hear of your Recovery. I am sorry you can get
no good Hand to send over, and bad ones are not worth having.[4]
I have sent Mr. Strahan by this opportunity a Bill of Exchange,
out of which he will pay you One Hundred Pounds, which makes
the Eighth Hundred sent you since you left Philadelphia.[5] When
you have receiv'd the Money, you will please to notice the same
to me.
We have lately printed Four thousand Pounds for the lower
Counties; and this Day Week begin to print the £8000. for them
granted at their last Sitting.[6] I am Yours   D HALL
To Benjamin Franklin Esqr. Via New York per Packet
Copy per the Packet Via New York[7]

Robert Charles: Rights and Privileges of the Pennsylvania Assembly; and Richard Jackson: Answers to Questions Asked   MS:[8] American Philosophical Society

Perhaps stimulated by the sweeping attack on the privileges of the
Pennsylvania Assembly made by proprietary lawyers at the April 20th
hearing on William Smith's petition,[9] Franklin requested Robert Charles
to prepare extracts from the charters and laws of Pennsylvania setting

3. See above, VII, 287–8.
4. Hall (above, II, 409–10 n) had asked for help in finding a compositor
and William Strahan (above, II, 383–4 n) had explained that the great demand
for them in London had driven their wages so high that American employment was not attractive. He advised Hall to "breed up one of your own
people." Strahan to Hall, Feb. 22, 1758, APS.
5. See above, VII, 235–6, for a summary of Hall's remittances to BF in
England.
6. Hall was printing paper currency for the Delaware government.
7. Since an embargo was in effect at this time, the government packets were
virtually the only ships sailing for England. Hall recorded in his letterbook
that he also wrote WF on this date.
8. In a clerk's hand.
9. See below, pp. 28–51, 60–1.

6

forth the powers and privileges of its Assembly, to summarize the usages and rights which had developed under them, and to formulate some questions on how these powers and privileges might be altered under royal government. Most of the document printed here is what Charles prepared in response to this request. Franklin then asked for an answer to these questions from Richard Jackson, a lawyer "esteem'd the best acquainted with our American Affairs, and Constitutions, as well as with Government Law in general."[1] On April 24, three days before the second hearing on the Smith petition,[2] Jackson furnished the brief answers which conclude the document. This copy, containing the compositions of both Charles and Jackson, is among Franklin's own papers.

24th April 1758

KING CHARLES the second by Letters Patent under the Great Seal of England bearing date the 4th Day of March in the 33d Year of his Reign was pleased to grant unto William Penn Esqr. his Heirs and Assigns a large Tract of Land in America, to Erect the same into a Province and Seignorie by the Name of Pensylvania, and to create and constitute the said William Penn his *Heirs and Assigns* true and absolute Proprietary's of the Country aforesaid with divers great Powers and Authorities to him for the good Government thereof. Of which Grant or Charter be pleased to peruse the hereunto annexed Copy; and to attend particularly to the following Sections thereof which relate to the Powers wherewith the said Proprietary was invested for forming the Civil Government of this Province.[3]

Royal Grant
of Pensilvania
4th Mar 1682

Sect. 4th. "AND forasmuch as we have hereby made and ordained the aforesaid William Penn his Heirs and Assigns, the true and absolute Proprietors of all the Lands and Dominions aforesaid. Know ye therefore, that We reposing Special Trust and Confi-

1. See above, v, 148 n, for Jackson, and below, pp. 88–9, for BF's application to him for advice.
2. BF may have wanted the answers available for his lawyers' use at the hearing.
3. The verbatim extracts which follow this introductory paragraph can be found in *The Charters of the Province of Pensilvania and City of Philadelphia.* (Philadelphia: Printed and Sold by B. Franklin, 1741), where the royal charter and Penn's Charter of Privileges are printed in full, pp. 3–13, 17–22.

dence in the Fidelity, Wisdom, Justice, and provident Circumspection of the said William Penn, for us our Heirs and Successors do
grant free, full, and absolute Power by Virtue of
Power to make these Presents, *to him and his Heirs,* and to his
Laws with the and their Deputies and Lieutenants, for the good
Consent of the and happy Government of the said Country, to or-
freemen[4] dain, make, enact, and under his and their Seals to
publish any Laws whatsoever for the raising of
Money for the Publick Use of the said Province, and for any other
End appertaining either to the Publick State, Peace or Safety of the
said Country, or unto the private Utility of partic-
for raising ular Persons, according to their best discretions,
Money &c. by and with the Advice, Assent and Approbation
of the Freemen of the said Country, or the greater
Part of them or of their Delegates or Deputies, whom for the enacting of the said Laws, when and as often as need
and Assemblies shall require, We will that the said William Penn
to be convened. and his Heirs shall assemble in such Sort and Form,
as to him and them shall seem best, and the said
Laws duly to execute unto and upon all People within the said
Country and Limits thereof."

Sect. 5th. "AND We do likewise give and grant unto the said
William Penn, and his Heirs, and to his and their Deputies, and
Lieutenants, full Power and Authority to appoint and establish
any Judges and Justices, Magistrates and Officers whatsoever, for
what Causes soever, for the Probates of Wills, and
Power to make for the granting of Administrations within the Pre-
Judges and cincts aforesaid, and with what Power soever and
other Officers in such Form as to the said William Penn or his
for the Probate Heirs shall seem most convenient: Also to remit, re-
of Wills. lease, pardon, and abolish, whether before Judgment or after, all Crimes and Offences whatsoever
Power of committed within the said Country, against the said
Pardoning and Laws. Treason and Wilfull and Malicious Murder
Reprieving only excepted; and in those Cases to grant Re-
prieves untill our Pleasure may be known therein.
And to do all and every other Thing or Things, which unto the

4. The running captions are generally the same as in the printed version.

8

compleat establishment of Justice unto Courts and Tribunals, Forms of Judicature and manner of Proceedings do belong, although in these Presents express mention be not made thereof; And, by Judges by them delegated, to award Proc-

What may be done by the Judges. ess, hold Plea's and determine in all the said Courts and Tribunals, all Actions Suits and Causes whatsoever as well Criminal as Civil, Personal, Real, and Mixt; which Laws so, as aforesaid, to be published, Our Will and Pleasure is, and so we enjoyn require and command, Shall be most absolute and available in Law; and that all the liege People and Subjects of Us our Heirs and Successors, do observe and keep the same inviolably, in those Parts, so far

Obedience to the Laws enjoyned. as they concern them, under the Pain therein expressed, or to be expressed; provided nevertheless, That the said Laws be consonant to Reason, and be not repugnant or contrary, but as near as con-

Proviso that the Laws be not repugnant to the Laws of England. Hearing of Appeals reserved. veniently may be, agreeable to the Laws Statutes, and Rights of this our Kingdom of England; and saving and reserving to Us, our Heirs and Successors, the receiving, hearing, and determining of the Appeal and Appeals of all or any Person or Persons of, in, or belonging to, the Territories aforesaid, or touching any Judgment to be there made or given."

Sect. 7. "AND to the End the said William Penn, or his Heirs, or other the Planters, Owners or Inhabitants of the said Province, may not, at any time hereafter, by Misconstruction of the Powers aforesaid, through Inadvertancy or Design depart from that Faith and due Allegiance which by the Laws of this our Kingdom of England, they and all our Subjects in our Dominions and Territories always owe unto Us, our Heirs and Successors, by Colour of any Extent or Largeness of Powers hereby

Duplicate of all Laws to be transmitted to the Privy Council Within Five Years. given, or pretended to be given, or by force or Colour of any Laws hereafter to be made in the said Province, by virtue of any such Powers: Our further Will and Pleasure is, that a Transcript or Duplicate of all Laws which shall be so as aforesaid made and published within the said Province,

9

shall within Five Years after the making thereof,
if repealed be transmitted and delivered to the Privy Council
within Six for the time being, of Us, our Heirs and Succes-
Months to be sors: And if any of the said Laws, within six
Void. Months after that they shall be so transmitted
and delivered, be declared by Us, Our Heirs or
Successors, in Our or their Privy Council, inconsistent with the
Sovereignty or lawfull Prerogative of Us Our Heirs or Successors,
or contrary to the Faith and Allegiance due by the legal Government of this Realm, from the said William Penn, or his Heirs or
of the Planters or Inhabitants of the said Province; and that thereupon any of the said Laws shall be adjudged and declared to be
void by Us, Our Heirs or Successors, under Our
otherwise to or their Privy Seal: that then and from thenceforth,
be in full such Laws concerning which such Judgment and
Force. Declaration shall be made, shall become Void;
otherwise the said Laws so transmitted shall remain and stand in
full force, according to the true Intent and Meaning thereof."

Sect. 10. "AND We do further for Us, Our Heirs and Successors,
give and grant unto the said William Penn, his Heirs and Assigns,
free and absolute Power to divide the said Country and Islands
into Towns Hundreds and Counties, and to erect
The Proprietor and incorporate Towns into Boroughs into Cities,
may divide the and to make and constitute Fairs and Markets
Country into therein, with all other convenient Privileges and
Towns Immunities, according to the Merit of the Inhabi-
Hundreds tants, and the fitness of the Places, and to do all and
and Counties, every other Thing and Things touching the Prem-
incorporate ises, which to him or them shall seem meet and
Towns, requisite, albeit they be such as of their own nature
constitute might otherwise require a more especial Com-
Fairs, grant mandment and Warrant, than in these Presents is
Privileges, &ct. expressed."

Sect. 20. "AND further Our Pleasure is, And by these Presents,
for Us, Our Heirs and Successors, We do covenant and grant to
and with the said William Penn, and his Heirs and Assigns, That
We Our Heirs and Successors, shall at no time hereafter, set
or make, or cause to be set any Imposition Custom, or other

No Taxes to be impos'd on the People without their Consent or Act of Parliament. Taxation Rate or Contribution whatsoever, in and upon the Dwellers and Inhabitants of the aforesaid Province, for their Lands, Tenements, Goods or Chattels within the said Province; or in and upon any Goods or Merchandize within the said Province, or to be laden or unladen within the Ports or Harbours of the said Province unless the same be with the consent of the Proprietary, or chief Governor or Assembly, or by Act of Parliament in England."

Sect. 21. "AND Our Pleasure is, and for Us, Our Heirs and Successors, We charge and Command, that this Our Declaration shall from henceforward, from time to time be received and allowed in all our Courts, and before all the Judges of Us, Our Heirs and Successors, for a sufficient Discharge Payment and Acquitance; commanding all and singular the Officers and Ministers of Us, Our Heirs and Successors, and enjoyning them upon pain of Our high Displeasure that they do not presume, at any time, to attempt any thing to the contrary of the Premises, or that they do in any Sort withstand the same; but that they be at all times aiding and assisting, as fitting, unto the said William Penn and his Heirs, and to the Inhabitants and Merchants of the Province aforesaid, their Servants, Ministers, Factors and Assigns, in the full Use and Fruition of the Benefit of this Our Charter."

This Declaration shall be deemed an Acquittance.

Officers and Ministers to Aid the Proprietary and People &c. in the full enjoyment of this Charter.

Sect. 22. "AND Our further Pleasure is, and We do hereby for Us, Our Heirs and Successors, charge and require that if any of the Inhabitants of the said Province (to the number of Twenty) shall at any time hereafter be desireous, and shall by any writing or by any Person deputed for them signify such their Desire to the Bishop of London for the time being, that any Preacher or Preachers, to be approved of by the said Bishop, may be sent unto them for their Instruction, that then such a Preacher or Preachers, shall and may be and reside within the said Province, without any Denial or Molestation whatsoever."

Twenty Inhabitants applying to the Bishop of London may have a Preacher who shall reside in the Province unmolested.

11

MR. PENN to whom this Extensive Charter was
Mr. Penn a granted, was a known and professed Quaker, at
known Quaker the time of granting thereof, as appears by many
of his Writings which he Published in maintenance
of the Doctrines and Principles of that Body of
People. And the last recited Section of the Charter shews evidently, that the CROWN knew that the intended Establishment was
to be a Colony, principally, of such People.

As Mr. Penns Credit and Influence amongst those of his own
Perswasion was very considerable, he apply'd himself chiefly to
them in Brittain and Ireland, to promote the Settle-
Apply's ment of this new Colony, and likewise invited
himself to Sundry Forreigners from Germany, professing
those of his Principles somewhat Similar to those of the
own Perswasion Quakers, to come into this Province; And by his
to become ample and repeated Declarations for LIBERTY of
Settlers. CONSCIENCE, and for securing to all the Inhabitants the full Enjoyment of their CIVIL and RE-
LIGIOUS RIGHTS, and by adapting all his Schemes of Government,
rather to the restraint than extension of Power, many Persons of
good Character and considerable Substance transported themselves with their Families into this Province, and
his Success. became Purchasers of Lands for valuable Considerations.[5]

VARIOUS. were the Plans which Mr. Penn pro-
Various Schemes jected and essayed for the Government of this
of Government Province: till at last, he solemnly granted, and the
projected, at Representatives of the People in General Assembly
last, A Charter met solemnly, accepted of a CHARTER OF PRIVI-
of Privileges LEGES, bearing Date the 28th Day of October 1701.
granted 28th whereof be pleased to peruse the hereunto annexed
Octr. 1701. Copy and particularly to attend to the following
Clauses or Sections thereof, Vizt.

Sect. 1st. "BECAUSE no People can be truly happy, though under
the greatest Enjoyment of Civil Liberties, if abridged of the Freedom of their Consciences, as to their Religious Profession, and
Worship: And Almighty God being the only Lord of Conscience,

5. See above, VII, 361–2, for BF's quarrel with Thomas Penn over this point.

Father of Lights and Spirits; and the Author as well as object of all divine Knowledge, Faith and Worship, who only doth enlighten the Minds, and perswade and convince the understandings of People, I do hereby grant and declare, That no Person or Persons inhabiting in this Province or Territories, who shall confess and acknowledge One Almighty God, The Creator, Upholder, and Ruler of the World, and profess him or themselves obliged to live quietly under the Civil Government, shall be, in any Case, molested or prejudiced in his or their Person or Estate because of his or their consciencious Perswasion or Practice, nor be compelled to frequent or maintain any religious Worship, Place or Ministry, contrary to his or their Mind, or to do or suffer any other Act or Thing contrary to their religious Perswasion.

Sect. 2. "FOR the well governing of this Province and Territories, there shall be an Assembly yearly chosen by the Freemen thereof, to consist of Four Persons out of each County of most Note for Virtue, Wisdom and Ability, (or of a greater Number at any time as the Governor and Assembly shall agree) Assembly to be upon the First Day of October for ever; and shall chosen Annually. Sit on the Fourteenth Day of the same Month, at Philadelphia unless the Governor and Council for the time being shall see cause to appoint another Place, within the said Province or Territories: which Assembly shall have Power to chuse a Speaker and other their Officers: and shall their Powers be Judges of the Qualifications and Elections of and Privileges their own Members: Sit upon their own Adjournments: Appoint Committe's: prepare Bills in order to pass into Laws; impeach Criminals, and redress Grievances: and shall have all other Powers and Privileges of an Assembly, according to the Rights of the free born Subjects of England, and as is usual in any of the Kings Plantations in America."

Sect. 3. "That the Freemen in each respective County, at the time and Place of meeting for Electing their Representatives to serve in Assembly, may as often as there shall be Occasion, chuse a double Number of Persons to present to the Power to chuse Governor for Sheriffs and Coroners, to serve for Sherifs and Three Years if so long they behave themselves well: Coroners. out of which respective Elections and Present-ments, the Governor shall nominate and Commissionate One for each of the said Offices, the Third Day after such Presentment, or else the First named in such Presentment, for each Office as aforesaid, shall stand and serve in that Office for the time before respectively limited: And in Case of Death or Default, such Vacancies shall be supplied by the Governor to serve to the End of the said Term."

Sect. 4. "That the Laws of this Government shall be in this Stile, vizt. By the Governor, with the Consent and approbation of the Freemen in General Assembly Met, and shall be after Confirmation by the Governor, forthwith recorded in the Rolls Office, and kept at Philadelphia, unless the Governor and Assembly shall agree to appoint another Place."

Stile of the Laws.

Sect. 8th. "And no Act, Law or Ordinance whatsoever, shall at any Time hereafter be made, or done, to alter, change, or diminish the Form or Effect of this Charter, or of any Part of Clause therein, contrary to the true intent and meaning thereof without the Consent of the Governor for the time being, and Six Parts of Seven of the Assembly Met."

No Law shall alter this Charter without &c.

"AND LASTLY, I the said William Penn Proprietary and Governor of the Province of Pensilvania, and Territories thereunto belonging, for my Self, my Heirs and Assigns, have Solemnly declared granted and confirmed, and do hereby solemnly declare grant and confirm, That neither I my Heirs or Assigns, shall procure or do any Thing or Things whereby the Liberties in this Charter contained and expressed, nor any Part thereof, shall be enfringed or broken; and if any thing shall be procured or done by any Person or Persons, contrary to these Presents, it shall be held of no Force or Effect."

The Proprietors solemn Declaration and Confirmation of this Charter for himself and his Heirs.

IN CONFIRMATION of which Charter of Privileges divers Laws have been made and passed in Pensilvania which have received the Royal Approbation particularly.

Charter confirmed by divers Laws.

14

LIBERTY of CONSCIENCE stands confirmed by an Act passed in
4. Q. Anne   the 4th of Queen Anne Entituled, The Law con-
Body of Laws   cerning Liberty of Conscience.[6]
fol 4.

THE CONSTITUTION, Powers and Privileges of the Assembly's
of Pensylvania are declared and Confirmed by the
following Laws. Vizt.

4th. Q. Anne   AN ACT entituled "An Act to assertain the number
fol 67.   of Members of Assembly, and to regulate the
Elections.

12th K. Geo. 2d   A SUPPLEMENT to the Act for electing Members of
fol 514.   Assembly.

16th K. Geo. 2d   AN ACT for continuing and amending the Act of
fol 547.   Assembly Entituled A Supplement to the Act for
·electing Members of Assembly.

IN which Act of the 4th. Q. Anne, please to ob-
fol 72.   serve the following Clause touching the Rights
of the Assembly.

"And be it further enacted by the Authority aforesaid, That the
Representatives so chosen and Met, according to the Direction of
this Act, shall be the Assembly of this Province,
Powers and   and shall have Power to chuse a Speaker and other
Privileges of   their Officers, and shall be Judges of the Qualifica-
the Assembly.   tions and Elections of their own Members, Sit upon
their own Adjournments, appoint Committees,
prepare Bills in order to pass into Laws, impeach Criminals and
redress Grievances, and shall have all other Powers and Privileges
of Assembly, according to the Rights of the free-
4. Q. Anne.   born Subjects of England, and as is usual in any
fol 104.   of the Queens Plantations in America." The Elec-
3. K. Geo. 2d   tion of Sheriffs and Coroners is likewise confirmed
fol 392.   by Sundry Acts.
4. K. Geo 2d
fol 430.

6. This law and others mentioned below are printed, on the pages cited in
the side heads, in *A Collection of all the Laws of the Province of Pennsylvania:
Now in Force*. Philadelphia: Printed and Sold by B. Franklin. 1742; bound
with the collection of charters cited above, p. 7, n. 3.

15

By an Act passed 4th K. George 1st entituled, an Act for the advancement of Justice and more certain Administration thereof. All Crimes and Offences whatever are to be enquired of and determined by Judges Justices Inquests and Witnesses qualifying themselves according to their consciencious Perswasion respectively, either by taking an Oath, or the Solemn Affirmation allowed by Act of Parliament to those called Quakers in Great Brittain.

4 K. Geo.1 fol 157 Judges Justices Inquests and Witnesses to be qualified either on Oath or affirmation.

AND by an Act passed 11 K. George 1st Entituled An Act prescribing the Forms of Declaration of Fidelity Abjuration and Affirmation, instead of the Forms heretofore required in such Cases, all Quakers qualifying themselves according to the Forms of the said Act are declared capable of Serving in General Assemblies or to be Justices, Officers, Inquests or Jury Men.

11 K. Geo 1st. fol 310 Quakers qualifying as by this Act are capable of Serving as Members of Assembly, Justices &c. System of Government.

EVER since the granting of this Charter of Privileges

THE Government of PENSILVANIA has been Administered by a Deputy of the Proprietary or Proprietaries approved by the Crown and giving Security for the Observance of the Laws of Trade and Navigation in pursuance of the Act of Parliament of the 7th and 8th of K. William the 3d.

Deputy Governor. and Annual Assemblies

THE Assemblies have been annually chosen, who continue for the Year, May be called together as often as the Governor thinks fitt, but they contend that he has no Power, by the Constitution, of proroguing or dissolving them.

Are the Two Branches of the Legislature

THE Governor or Deputy with the Assembly, have together the whole Power of Legislation.

THERE is a Council composed of Persons named by the Proprietary or his Deputy, but without any Legislative Authority, being properly a Council of State, with whom the Deputy Governor is enjoyned to Advise and Consult.

A Council of State without Legislative Authority.

16

There are General Quarter Sessions of the Peace held, Courts of Common Pleas in the respective Counties of the Province, and Supreme Court for appeals, all established by Law which have had the Royal Sanction.

Courts of Justice

IT has likewise been customary for the Assembly to name a Person for the Office of Treasurer of the said Province, whose Accounts together with those of every other Officer employed in the management or Collection of the Public Revenue, are Yearly Submitted to the Assembly.

Nomination of a Provincial Treasurer in the Assembly.

THERE are Three different Revenues within this Province.

Three Revenues.

THE PROPRIETARY REVENUE which arises from the Sale of Lands, and reserved Quit Rents, and from the reserved Mannours of Ten Thousand Acres in Every Hundred Thousand purchased from the Indians and sold to the Settlers in this Province, all under the Collection and Management of Officers appointed by the Proprietary's.

Proprietors

THE GOVERNORS Revenue, which consists of Sundry Fees of Office and other Perquisites, and Emoluments, either given by Law or taken by Custom to his own Use for the Support of Government.

Governors

and

THE PUBLICK REVENUE for defraying the Ordinary and Extraordinary Expences of Government arising from

The Publick

AN EXCISE on Spirituous Liquors laid on by Act of Assembly.

Whence arising

INTEREST MONEY arising from Loans of a Paper Credit, which has been established for Thirty Years past within this Province.[7]

7. The bills issued under Assembly authority by the General Loan Office to applicants for credit circulated as currency in Pennsylvania. The interest on these loans, usually secured by real estate, had normally yielded a revenue sufficient for the conduct of government in the province. Since 1755, however, heavy taxes on real and personal property had been levied; see above, VII, 121.

APRIL 24, 1758

THE ACTS of Assembly establishing this Publick Revenue and
approved by the Crown, have constantly given
Disposal of the the Disposal of the Publick Money to the Assembly
Publick Money who yearly audit all Publick Accounts, and cause
in the Assembly. them to be Published in the Journals of their
Proceedings.

UNDER this System of Government Pensylvania has become
a great and flourishing Province. The Equity of
Pennsylvania it's Laws and the Moderation of it's Government
Flourishing and with the free Exercise of the Christian Religion
resorted to by persons of different Perswasions having
brought great numbers of People into this Province.

BUT of late, Differences have arisen between the Proprietaries
and the Assemblies occasioned by Instructions
Differences given by the said Proprietaries to their Deputies,
arisen by restrictive of the necessary Powers of Legislation,
means of and derogatory, as is conceived, of the Rights and
Proprietary Privileges which the Assemblies have hitherto en-
Instructions. joyed and exercised. And the Issue of those Disputes being uncertain.

IT may very possibly happen that the Circumstances of Affairs
in America may determine the Crown to resume
Possibility of a the Government of the said Province, or that the
Resumption or said Proprietaries may surrender the same to the
Surrender of the Crown, as a Treaty of that Nature was long since
Government set on Foot, and, it is said, part of the Consideration
Money actually paid to William Penn Esqr. the
first Proprietary.[8]

8. William Penn had proposed to give up his ruling powers in 1703. A
price of £12,000 was agreed upon in 1712 and he received £1000 on account
from the Crown pending surrender of the government, but the negotiations
stalled and the attempt was abandoned. William R. Shepherd, *History of
Proprietary Government in Pennsylvania* (N.Y., 1896), pp. 540–4; Winfred T.
Root, *The Relations of Pennsylvania with the British Government, 1696–1765*
(N.Y., 1912), pp. 349–65.

Now as the Settlement of this Province has been made under the Faith of a Royal Charter, the full Use and Fruition of the Benefit of which is promised unto the Inhabitants and Merchants of the Province aforesaid, their Servants Ministers Factors and Assigns. And under the Faith of the Charter of Privileges, which is in the Nature of a Pactum Cumpactum between the Proprietary and the People, the essential parts of which Charter have been confirmed by Laws that have obtained the Royal Sanction.

Province Settled under the Faith of these Two Charters.

AND as the Proprietary and People of this Province are authorized by the Royal Charter to make any Laws whatsoever for the raising of Money for the Publick Use of the said Province and for any other End appertaining either to the publick State Peace or Safety of the said Country, or unto the private Utility of particular Persons, Provided that the said Laws be consonant to Reason and be not repugnant or contrary, but as near as conveniently may be agreeable to the Laws Statutes and Rights of the Kingdom of England.

With Power to make Laws.

AND as the Sanction given by the Crown to sundry Laws in affirmance of the Establishment of the Constitution of Pensilvania proves their Consonancy to Reason, and that they are free from any Repugnancy or Contrariety to the Laws of England.

Which have had the Royal Sanction

IN case therefore of such Resumption of the Government of Pensylvania by the Crown or Surrendry thereof by the Proprietors. Your Opinion is earnestly desired in the following Points.

Can the Crown introduce or establish any other Mode of Government within the said Province than that now in Use there, and how can such alteration be legally attained?

Qu 1st

Can the annual Election of Assemblies be taken away, or the Rights and Privileges derived to them under the Two recited Charters be abolished?

2.

Can the annual Election of Sheriffs and Coroners be altered?

3.

19

4.   Can a Legislative Council be established, and how?

5.   Can the People professing themselves Quakers be legally abridged of any of their Rights they now enjoy in common with the other Inhabitants of being capable to be chosen Members of Assembly and to hold Places of Trust and Profit within the said Province?

AND in GENERAL.

WHAT are your Sentiments touching the Change and Alteration that may be legally made in the Constitution of this Province if it should come into the hands of The Crown.[9]

Ans. 1. I have perused the Royal Charter to William Penn, and the Charter of Privileges granted in 1701 to the Inhabitants of the Province of Pensilvania by the Proprietary, and think that the Crown cannot introduce or establish any other Mode of Government within that Province than that now in Use there, (as far as I am acquainted with the Government by the Case Stated, or otherwise) except by an Act of the Legislature of Great Brittain; or by the Consent of the Assembly and Proprietary or his Governor; And tho by the Charter of Privileges. S. 8. it is provided, that the effect of that Charter shall not be changed, altered or diminished, but by the Consent of the Governor and Six Parts in Seven of the Assembly, I should doubt whether an alteration made by a Majority would not be Sufficient. However by an Act of Parliament and by no other Authority in Great Brittain, I conceive, such alteration might be legally attained.

2. The Annual Election of Assemblies cannot be otherwise taken away; nor the Rights and Privileges derived to them under the two recited Charters be otherwise abolished.

3. Nor do I think the Annual Election of Sheriffs and Coroners can be altered by any other Authority: both this Privilege and the Subject matter of the last being founded on and confirmed by Laws made by Assemblies convened according to the Intention and Directions of the Royal Grantor and his Grantee, and both being as I conceive *consonant to Reason, appertaining to the Publick State, Peace, and Safety of the Country, and not repugnant to the Laws of*

9. Charles's "State of the Case" ends here. Jackson's response concludes the document.

England. The Office of Sheriff was Elective in England till 9 Ed. 2. Vid 28 Ed 1. C 8. That of Coroner is yet so. Besides these Laws have been transmitted to England in persuance of the 7th Clause of the Royal Grant without a disapprobation on the Part of the Crown. And tho' a Law void *for repugnancy to the Laws of England,* would not I think be made good by remaining thus not disapproved, (because the preservation of the Prerogative of the Crown and the allegiance of the Province only is here declared to be in view) yet this Circumstance furnishes a strong proof these Laws are not repugnant, as above, especially as their Subject matter so immediately concerns the State, and the administration of Publick Justice.

4. A Legislative Council, I think, cannot be established but by Act of Parliament.

5. Altho' the Rights the Quakers enjoy in Pensylvania are much more extensive than they enjoy in England, I think so far as they are Warranted and Supported by the Legislature of Pensylvania they cannot be legally abridged. And on this Head, had the Crown any objection to the Propriety of the Acts enabling them to be chosen Members of Assembly and to execute Offices of Profit and Trust, the Due Transmission of the Acts and their not having been declared inconsistent &c. within [five] Years seems to have waived them.

Should Mr. Penns Powers of Government by Surrender or otherwise come into the hands of the Crown, I do not think any considerable alteration can be made in the Constitution but by Act of Parliament: but should Publick Contention and personal Animosity render Resumption of the Powers by Act of Parliament Necessary, It is far from impossible the Legislature might think it fit somewhat to new model the present Constitution, but no Man can foresee what the Wisdom of Parliament will hereafter determine on this Point as Events shall arise.[1]   RD JACKSON

Endorsed: Province of Pensilv[ania] Case for Opinion on Charters &c.[2]

1. See the following document for a fuller analysis by Jackson of Parliament's probable course.
2. In BF's hand.

From Richard Jackson: Private Sentiments
and Advice on Pennsylvania Affairs[3]

Copy:[4] Yale University Library

[April 24, 1758?][5]

Copy, of private Sentiments and Advice on Pensilvania Affairs from R. J. Esqr. to B F.

I have considered the Royal Grant of Charles the 2d. to William Penn, the Charter of Privileges granted by him to the Province of Pennsylvania, and the present Constitution of that Province as it actually subsists, as well as the particular Disputes between the Proprietary and the Assemblies, which seems to have produced an irreconcileable Ill-will between the Parties; and have thrown together my Thoughts as they arose, on the several Subjects of those Disputes, and on the Consequences they may produce, should they admit of no amicable Termination.

1. It seems reasonable to me, that the Proprietary's Lieutenant Governor should reside there, tho', not uninstructed quite, yet free from any unreasonable Restraint, so that tho' it may be proper, he should be instructed to pass some Laws, and to refuse others; yet this Refusal should [not][6] be peremptory, and not with a View of subjecting the Province to the many Inconveniences that may attend the sending Home for the Result of the Proprietors Discretion, (except in some very particular Cases where no considerable Inconvenience can possibly happen). But with this Qualification, the Propriety of these Instructions will rest on the same Foundation, and must receive the same Determination as the Disputes the Subject of which I take to be the exceptionable Part of the Instructions: For if those Disputes should hereafter be by any Authority here, determined in favour either of the Proprietors or the Country, the Instructions will, so far, stand or fall by the

3. See below, pp. 88–9, for BF's explanation of how Jackson came to offer these "Sentiments and Advice."

4. In WF's hand, except for the title written by his father.

5. This undated document may have been written at any time between this date and June 10, 1758, when BF sent a copy of it (perhaps this MS) to the Pa. Assembly; it is printed at this point since it supplements the more formal opinion immediately above.

6. WF evidently omitted this word in copying.

Determination. But as the Practice of Instructing is originally a Practice of the Crown, I doubt the Council will not condemn it in a Proprietor.[7]

2. I think no Man in his Senses, at least no unprejudiced Man, will deny that Mr. Penn ought to bear his Share of the Taxes necessary for the Defence of the Province. It might certainly with a much greater Show of Reason be contended that Mr. Penn by the original Contract between him and the Grantees, ought to bear the whole Charge as well of the Defence as of the Civil Government, than that on the contrary the Inhabitants and Owners of Land by his Subinfeudation, ought to bear either without his Contribution. *The ancient Kings in Europe* subsisted in Times of Peace, and executed the ordinary Powers of Government without any other Revenue than what was similar to Mr. Penn's in Pennsylvania. 'Tis true in Time of War they had *extraordinary Aids* both *Personal* and *Pecuniary,* but the latter was altogether in Aid of the ordinary Revenue, which was first supposed exhausted, and the other was founded on an *Original Feudal Contract* that was mutual and bound the King as well as his Subject, for their reciprocal Benefit: And Wars have been often carried on without any Assistance on the Part of the Subject, but never without the King's bearing more than his Share of the Burthen. If this is not the Case at present in England, 'tis because of the New Model the Constitution received at the Revolution in this Point; and the Relation between the other Kings of Europe and their Subjects is very unlike that between Mr. Penn and the Inhabitants of Pennsylvania.

But I understand that, Mr. Penn is now dispos'd to submit to pay a Share of the Taxes necessary for the publick Service,[8] and that the Disputes on this Subject are reduced to two principal Ques-

7. Jackson appears to have meant that he did not believe the Council would condemn "the Practice of Instructing" in a Proprietor. The proprietary instructions had long been in dispute; see especially above, VI, 515–31, where the differences over taxation of the Proprietors' estates are also surveyed. The indexes of this and the three preceding volumes furnish additional references to these disputes.

8. Thomas Penn declared that "I . . . am determined to prove to the World that we will give as much in the pound out of [quitrents,] as other People do out of their Rents, and are very willing the Collectors or Assessors shall make the enquiry into the value of them by direction of the Commissioners." To Richard Peters, July 5, 1758, Penn Papers, Hist. Soc. Pa.

tions, the One, what Part of Mr. Penn's Property shall be liable to Taxation; the other, the Mode of assessing him.

As to the first, I am told, he insists on an Exemption for his located unimproved Lands, and for his Quitrents, at least those under 20s. in one yearly Payment. If the Preservation of the located unimproved Lands, or their Improvements, are Consequences of the Ends for which the Tax is laid, he certainly ought to contribute proportionably to their Value, the Pretence that the Quitrents were originally contracted for, thus exempted, is a Fact I am told so far from being true, that the Truth would probably rather show,* they are first to be, by that Contract, expended in the Publick Service. If Mr. Penn means to rely on a Comparison between his own Situation and that of the Crown of Great Britain, (which will be by no means admitted) this not only gives up his Claim to a general Exemption, but in Effect determines against him, on the present as well as the following Question, for tho' it may be literally true that the Located Unimproved Lands of the Crown pay no Land-Tax, it is because they are in no Sense, Improving Funds, and they are in some Measure Publick Estates, and the Fee Farm Rents of the Crown pay Land Tax down to the Sum of 10s.: and if they pay it no Lower, it is only to avoid the Confusion of small Fractions, where so immaterial an Interest is concerned, these being charged only by way of Deduction, whereas, were they charged in one gross Sum in the Hands of the Crown, there can be no Doubt but that the gross Sum would be charged to the full. Might it not be fairly insisted on, that Mr. Penn should be taxed even for his *Unlocated Rights?* If the Preservation and future Enjoyment of the Fruits of Mr. Penn's Patent that are to be expected, within the Unimproved Parts of Pennsylvania, depend altogether on the Defence of the Province, is it not some Moderation not to insist on a Valuation of them in the Assessment?

I say the Question on the Mode of Assessing Mr. Penn's Property, would likewise in Effect be determined by admitting a Comparison between his Relation to the Province, and that of the King to the Kingdom of Great Britain. The King does not interfere in the Nomination of Assessors of Taxes, that are directly or indirectly

---

*I allude to Mr. Penn's covenanting to discharge his Grantees from Indian Claims.

to affect him or his Revenue. The House of Commons without Controul frames all Revenue Laws, and tho' there are few Lawyers and fewer Statesmen in England who will allow the Constitution and Powers of the House of Commons and an Assembly to be perfectly analogous, the Civil Government in America can be supported on no other Basis. I have my Reasons however for thinking, that if this Question should singly be contested before the Council, it would be determined in favour of Mr. Penn, at present, upon the apparent Danger of Injustice, the Resentment of the People he has provok'd might subject him to, without its being consider'd that it is his own Fault that his Danger is greater than that of the Crown and Peers in Great Britain.

3. The Models of Bills, especially those for raising Money, sent over by Mr. Penn, are certainly improper in general, yet I doubt if they would be generally disapproved by the Council, as our Administration goes farther in framing Laws for Ireland. Should this Practice however render the Government of Pennsylvania impracticable, it will fall under what I mean to conclude with.

4. The Disposition of Publick Money, and a Militia, are Points on which tho' I intirely agree in my private Opinion with the Assembly of Pennsylvania, yet which I am convinced would be determined against them, both by the Privy Council and the Parliament, were they formally to be brought before either, on the Complaint of Mr. Penn or the Assembly; or should a Stoppage of the Current of Government in that Province make their Intervention necessary. And such a Determination I should not judge more probable, after Mr. Penn's Surrender or Sale of the Powers of Government than before, for tho' the Crown would then be more immediately interested, it might possibly be more tender and cautious in its Steps; it would certainly find it more difficult to bring the Matter, in a Manner agreeable to the Administration, before the Parliament, and the Censure of the Privy Council would not be any way decisive. I think therefore, that it is in many ways desireable that Mr. Penn should part with the Powers of Government, unless he can be won over by seeing his own Interests to espouse those of the Province: But I should not think it all adviseable to drive any of these Points, much less all at once to a formal Decision at present, if at all; the safest is the Dispute on the Tax Mr. Penn is to pay, the Mode of Fixing his Quantum of it, and

particular improper Models of Laws sent over by Mr. Penn, with a Prohibition to his Lieutenant Governor to pass any other.

Upon the whole, I do not think these Points ought to be determined against the Assembly of Pennsylvania, nor that the Constitution of Pennsylvania can be legally changed by any Authority but that of Parliament, nor do I think it can be altered or new modeled by Parliament without departing from Principles, that have singly long secur'd the Liberties of the English Nation, and without making a Precedent that will endanger the Constitution of the whole British Empire; but I think this, upon Grounds too refin'd to have much general Weight, when counterpois'd by Popular Opinion; and we may rest satisfy'd that an Administration will probably for the future always be able to support and carry in Parliament whatever they wish to do so; that they will almost always wish to extend the Power of the Crown and themselves both mediately and immediately; and that *the Opinion of the Bulk of Mankind without Doors* is the only Restraint that any Man ought reasonably to rely on for securing what a Ministry, or those that can influence a Ministry, wish to deprive him of. There are, 'tis true, Points which Ministers have carried, and will carry, against the Opinion of the Bulk of Mankind, but they are generally Points of some Consequence to themselves, and not merely to their Successors, or they are Points in which the People in general think themselves little concerned, and no particular Men or Body of Men respectable for Weight or Numbers, seem likely to be disgusted and raise a Clamour against them.

The principal Ministers in this Country wish to carry their great Points with as little Struggle and Opposition as possible. A formidable Opposition to them, either within Doors or without, they provide against in the first Place. They are secure against any evil Effects of it within Doors, except what may influence a Clamour without. Yet this is so far an Object of their Care, that they are not easily engaged to permit Contests in Parliament on other Points that People of Weight will interest themselves in, when they are sufficiently apprized before hand that this will be the Case, much less will they second those who make these Points; the former Step divides their Friends, and the latter stakes their own Credit. I think therefore it will be best for the Province to avoid a Formal Decision at least a speedy one, to keep up the Ball of Contention, 'till a proper Opportunity offers either to dispute, or amicably to determine; and in the mean Time *to remove the Prejudices that Art and Accident have spread among the People of this Country, and make themselves as respectable in the Eyes of the Ministry by Connections in England as possible.* If Mr. Penn continues to thwart the Province in their necessary Measures of Government, and thereby to make the Inhabitants as uneasy as he can, They should return him the same Treatment, and harrass him, from time to time, with Applications on every small Point that they are likely to succeed in. The Treaty with the Diahogo Indians[9] may be a very proper One to begin with. This Treaty has been made in Part by Mr. Penn's own Substitute, in Part by Sir Wm. Johnson's on Behalf of the Crown. It cannot be perfectly carried into Execution, but by Mr. Penn doing the Indians the Justice, or giving them the Satisfaction they demand; it is of the utmost Importance not only to the Inhabitants of Pensylvania but to the Rest of the King's Subjects in America that it be compleatly carried into Execution, and that with Speed; it is a Breach of the Royal Trust reposed in Mr. Penn if he neglects or refuses what he ought to do on this Occasion, and is therefore every way a Proper Case for the Interposition of the Crown on a Petition to the King in Council. It might likewise be proper to petition the King in Council another year should he refuse to pay a reasonable Tax on his Property in America, and thereby prevent a Bill passing to raise Money for the Publick Service; or even if he has refus'd it this last Session tho' the Bill be passed without it.

I think upon an Application to Parliament, concerted with the Treasury before Hand, Payment might be obtained for the Inlisted Servants,[1] tho' Vouchers are not now to be had within the Act passed here for that Purpose. But that in the mean Time the Masters should as soon as possible ascertain the Value of their Servants, and the Proofs of their being actually inlisted, if by no better means, by Affidavits of themselves and Neighbours before the Chief Justice of Pennsylvania.

9. For the Easton Treaty of July-August 1757 see above, VII, 264–8. There the Indians were promised satisfaction for alleged fraudulent land purchases by proprietary agents. BF petitioned the King on behalf of the Indians on Feb. 2, 1759; see below, pp. 264–76.

1. See above, VII, 224–8, for BF's earlier efforts to secure payment for indentured servants enlisted in the British Army.

Documents on the Hearing of William Smith's Petition

I. Copy: Penn Papers, Historical Society of Pennsylvania. II. MS: Boston Public Library.[2] III. AD: Historical Society of Pennsylvania (in Franklin's hand except as noted). IV. AD: New York Public Library. V. Copy: New York Public Library.

Following the imprisonment of the Rev. William Smith upon a writ of the Pennsylvania Assembly, and his "trial" before it for alleged contempt,[3] he addressed petitions for relief to the King in Council and to Parliament. The petition to the King, dated Feb. 6, 1758, from "Philadelphia County Goal" (printed in italics below as Part I), reached England in late March and was laid before the Privy Council on April 1. On the 10th the Council's Committee for Plantation Affairs ordered the attorney general and solicitor general to conduct hearings. These were set for April 20 and 27; Franklin and the other Assembly agents, their lawyers, the Penns and their lawyers, and observers from Pennsylvania were present.[4] The unusually full records of this case, the first managed by Franklin before officers of the Crown, show in detail both his and his opponents' procedures. The voluminous papers prepared by attorneys for Smith on both sides of the Atlantic are among the Penn Papers in the Historical Society of Pennsylvania. Long explanatory letters from Thomas Penn and from Ferdinand J. Paris are also among the Penn Papers. Documents gathered and prepared by Franklin and his associates are now at the New York Public Library, and his notes for the guidance of his lawyers are at the Boston Public Library. Further notes of his are at the Historical Society of Pennsylvania, and two letters from him, explaining his handling of the case, are printed below, pp. 60–3, 87–8. The documents printed here, under the date of the second hearing (April 27), though some were written earlier, include Smith's petition itself, Franklin's notes on it, and some other papers prepared by him or under his direction.

Smith's petition reached England under favorable auspices; it was

2. This document, in WF's hand except for the title, endorsement, and last two paragraphs in BF's, is now deposited with BF's letter to Joshua Sharpe, April 21, 1758 (see above, p. 5); probably it is the copy furnished to Sharpe, rather than that BF later sent to the Pa. Assembly (not found).

3. See above, IV, 467–9 n, for Smith and VII, 385 n, for his imprisonment.

4. *Acts Privy Coun., Col.,* IV, 375; summonses to counsel, Penn Papers, Hist. Soc. Pa.

carried by the influential and respected former governor, James Hamilton (above, III, 327 n), who had witnessed Smith's arrest and "trial" in Philadelphia. Furthermore, Jacob Duché, Jr., a student and admirer of Smith's, who accompanied Hamilton, had taken notes at the "trial" and was prepared to supply full, authentic details to support his mentor's appeal. At the same time, Franklin received letters and papers (not found) explaining the Assembly's conduct. The petition itself, which Franklin probably did not see until after its presentation to the Privy Council, he refuted point by point in a paper to guide his solicitor, Joshua Sharpe (printed in roman below as Part II interwoven with Part I). He also gave Sharpe extracts from the minutes of recent cases in Virginia, Massachusetts, and New York of breach of privilege arrests by colonial assemblies.[5] Council for Paris, who was managing Smith's case, bitterly attacked the Assembly and the Quakers at the first hearing (April 20), and Franklin prepared "Observations on the Reflections thrown on the Quakers" (printed below as Part III) for his lawyers to use in their response. At about the same time he drafted some leading questions they might ask James Hamilton, designed to show that Franklin and the Quakers had undertaken effective action for defense in Pennsylvania (printed below as Part IV). Though a brief had probably been ready for the April 20 hearing, Sharpe used both it and the papers drawn by Franklin to prepare a revised brief. Counselors William de Grey and George Perrot presented it the evening of April 27 in the attorney general's chambers at Lincoln's Inn.

5. BF's copy of the minutes of these cases (see below, p. 88) is lost, but a copy obtained by Smith's lawyers is among the Penn Papers, Hist. Soc. Pa. Three Virginia cases, 1752–56, involved interference with an election to the House of Burgesses, hindrance of burgesses traveling to a meeting of the House, and threats of bodily injury to a member. Though the speaker issued orders for arrest in each case, the men seem to have been released upon apology before the House. In Massachusetts in 1754 Daniel Fowle (see above, IV, 206 n) was arrested and committed for printing a libel against and behaving "very Contemptuously" before the House of Representatives. Though the House ordered his release after five days, it later adopted a report upholding its right to seize and hold persons for breach of privilege. The New York case involved the Rev. Hezekiah Watkins, whom the Assembly adjudged guilty of publishing a defamation of its conduct, but released upon his making an apology. The document consists merely of extracts from the printed records and thus, though it once existed in BF's hand, it is not printed here. The standard treatment of the general subject is Mary P. Clarke, *Parliamentary Privilege in the American Colonies* (New Haven, 1943). For the Smith-Moore case in particular see *ibid.*, pp. 220–2, 240–6, and the references cited above, VII, 385 n.

This fourteen-page revised brief began with a summary of the petition, extracts from the order committing Smith and from other documents, and a copy of the order from the Privy Council Committee to the attorney general and solicitor general to "Examine into the allegations [in the petition] and Report to this Committee what they conceive advisable for his Majesty to do for the Relief of the Petitioner." Then followed a summary of the case against Smith: an abstract of William Moore's offensive address Smith was said to have abetted; long abstracts from the Assembly Journal, Jan. 5–28, 1758, recording his conduct before the Assembly; and abstracts of the most material testimony against him by the Rev. Johann F. Handshue,[6] German printer Anton Armbrüster, clerk Robert Levers, Drs. Thomas and Phineas Bond, David Hall, and Smith himself. Then came legal justification of the Assembly's action; extracts from charters and laws granting powers to the Assembly, abstracts of cases where the House of Commons, 1675–1751, had committed persons for contempt and then denied release by writ of habeas corpus,[7] and a summary of the colonial precedents on breach of privilege that Franklin had supplied. The brief concluded with a summary of the Assembly argument, entitled "Observations," printed below as Part V.

6. The Rev. Johann Fredrich Handshue (Hanshew, Henshaw) (1714–1764), Lutheran minister and instructor in French and German at the Philadelphia Academy, had translated Moore's address into German at Smith's direction. Frederick L. Weis, "The Colonial Clergy of the Middle Colonies," Amer. Antiq. Soc. *Proc.*, LXVI (1956), 232. See above, V, 421 n, for Armbrüster, and II, 240 n, for the Bonds.

7. These cases, entitled "List of Authorities," refuted four specific parts of the charge that the House of Commons could not arrest, examine, and imprison persons for contempt:
"First. That the House of Commons Punish Libells against their own Members and Authority." [nine instances]
"Secondly. That a Sitting House may Punish Libels against the last House." [three instances]
"Thirdly. The Power of the House of Commons as to Commitments, and that no Court whatever can bail or discharge a person committed by it." [four instances]
"Fourthly. That the House of Commons hath directed the Administration of an Oath." [eight instances] Full extracts are among the Pa. Assembly Papers at the New York Public Library.

[April 27, 1758]

I. William Smith's Petition (in italics)
II. Franklin's Notes on the Petition (in roman)

To the King's most Excellent Majesty in Council.
The Petition, Complaint and Appeal, of William Smith of the
City of Philadelphia in the Province of Pensilvania, Clerk.
In humble Manner Sheweth.

[a] THAT *Your Petitioner on the 6th. Day of January, in the Year*
of Our Lord 1758, by Order of the Representatives of the People of the
said Province, in Assembly then sitting, was arrested by their Serjeant
at Arms, and by Vertue of that Order, held in close Custody, until the
25th. Day of the said Month; A great Part of that Time not being
permitted to speak to any Person, but in the Presence of the said Serjeant,
nor to hold any Correspondence, in Writing, but with his Privity and
Consent.[8]

a. It is acknowledged that the Petitioner was on the 6th. of January ordered into the Custody of the Serjeant at Arms, agreeable to the Practice of the Parliaments of Great Britain and Ireland, and the Representative Assemblies of all the British Colonies, in Cases which they deem Breaches of Priviledge, Contempts, false and libellous Charges, &c.

[b] THAT *during the Time of Your Petitioners Confinement, he was,*
in a formal Manner, brought to the Bar of the House of Assembly, and,
by them, charged with being a Promotor and Abettor, of the writing
and publishing a Libel, entitled, The humble Address of William
Moore, One of the Justices of the Peace, for the County of Chester.

b. Also, that according to such Practice he was brought to the Bar of the House, to answer such Questions as should be put to him touching a certain Address of William Moore, highly reflecting on the Justice of the late Assembly, and derogatory of the just

---

8. This sentence, following the semicolon, is marked "not proved" in a copy of the petition among the Pa. Assembly Papers, N.Y. Pub. Lib. When arrested, Smith was simply ordered into the custody of the sergeant at arms until his interrogation on the 13th, when the Assembly ordered that he have freedom to consult in private with friends and counsel until his "trial" began, January 17. *Votes,* 1757–58, pp. 12, 20–1, 27–8. How strictly Smith was guarded from the 6th to the 13th is not known, but see BF's observations at "g" below.

31

Priviledges and Powers of the House of Representatives, which the Petitioner was suspected to have written or abetted.

[c] THAT *Your Petitioner being One of the Trustees, under an Honourable private Society in London, for maintaining Charity Schools, to instruct Germans here;*[9] *And to that End, having the Care and Direction of a printing Press, to furnish them with a News Paper and other Matters, in their own language, doth acknowledge, and never did deny, That, when he found the said Address, which animadverted on the Proceedings of a former dissolved Assembly, printed and published in the Pensilvania Gazette, by Benjamin Franklin and David Hall, who are the known and publick Printers to the Assembly, and in the Pensilvania Journal, by William Bradford of the said City, he did, thô a considerable Time after such printing and publishing in the English Papers,*[1] *advise it to be translated, into the German Tongue, and published in the said German News Paper.*

c. That the Printers of the Pennsylvania Gazette and Pennsylvania Journal are not Officers of the Assembly tho' they sometimes print the Votes and Messages of the House by their special Order; and were call'd before the House as well as the Petitioner, but on discovering the Author, and behaving openly and properly to the House, were dismissed. See the Examinations of Hall and Bradford.[2]

[d] THAT *Your Petitioner answered to the Charge of the Assembly, That he was Not Guilty of any Matters, of which he stood accused, and protesting he never had the least Intention to violate the Privileges of that House, with great Humility prayed them to order him a Tryal, for his supposed Offence, in some Court of Justice, according to the Laws of England, and this Province;*[3] *For Reason alledging that, if he had*

9. On this society see above, v, 203–6; VI, 532–5. For recent differences among its members see below, p. 68 n.

1. Hall and Bradford printed Moore's address on Dec. 1, 1757, and the *Philadelphische Zeitung* printed it on the 31st.

2. Brief accounts of their examinations are in *Votes*, 1757–58, pp. 27–8, 36, and full transcripts are in the Penn Papers, Hist. Soc. Pa., and Pa. Assembly Papers, N.Y. Pub. Lib. See below, pp. 97–8, for BF's comment on David Hall's part in the Smith affair.

3. Marked "not proved" in Pa. Assembly Papers, N.Y. Pub. Lib., copy; no such appeal is recorded in printed or MS copies of Smith's statements before the Assembly, though according to a paraphrase of Smith's statement in Horace W. Smith, *Life and Letters of the Rev. William Smith, D.D.*, (Phila., 1880), I, 175, he asked for a trial in the regular courts.

committed the Crime, charged, it was cognizable in the established
Courts of Justice; And by the Assembly's imprisoning, trying, putting
him to great Charge in his Defence, and finally punishing him, if they
should so far proceed, he might be twice punished for One, and the
same, Offence.

   d. That no Representative Body in the King's Dominions, ever
orders a Trial in Courts of Justice for Offences that relate to
Breach of Priviledge, &c. and there could be no Danger of his
being punished by a common Court of Justice for such Offence.

   [*e*] THAT *the House rejecting Your Petitioners Prayer, did, by Vote,*
resolve to try Your Petitioner, themselves; And for that Purpose, did
direct him to bring his Witnesses before them, for summoning whom,
they gave their Orders; And did allow Your Petitioner Counsel, to
speak to Matters of Fact only; They, by another Vote, having resolved,
that neither Your Petitioner, or his Counsel, should be heard concerning
their Jurisdiction, or any other Matter of Law; and did appoint a Day
for Your Petitioners Tryal.

   e. The House, at the Petitioner's Request, gave him Leave to
bring Witnesses, and to use Council, and appointed a Day to hear
him: If in this they deviated from the usual Forms, 'twas in favour
of the Delinquent. [See Votes, Page 15][4] They also directed the
Clerk to furnish him with the Copies he ask'd and ordered that he
should be admitted to confer with his Council and such other of
his Friends as he desired to consult, in private. It is true they would
not suffer the Council to dispute their Authority, nor their Judgment of the Nature of the Offence, [See Votes, Page 18] but only
how far Mr. Smith was or was not concerned in it.

   [*f*] THAT *Your Petitioner being thus compelled to waive Points,*
which he judged very material, in his Defence, and to submit to the
Jurisdiction, Power and Direction of those, who did not scruple to
acknowledge themselves, principal Partys, yet hoping to mollify them
by this Submission, and by making it appear he had no Design of
violating their Privileges, did undertake to defend himself, and manifest
his Innocence, in the Manner prescribed to him; which he humbly ap-

---

   4. Probably a citation from a MS copy of the minutes; the citations in this
paragraph are on pp. 21 and 26 in *Votes*, 1757–58. Brackets in this and other
references among BF's notes are in the original.

prehends, he did so effectually, as must have given entire Satisfaction to all unprejudiced Judges, and have obtained his Discharge.

f. The House not being satisfied with his Defence, directed him to be committed till he should give Satisfaction to the House by proper Acknowledgments: This is no more than usual.

[*g*] THAT, *notwithstanding the Assembly's Proceeding, in all the Forms of an indifferent and legal Court of Judicature, by summoning Witnesses, examining them, on their Oaths, in and by the Authority of the House administered, terrifying some, who were not inclined to swear, or answer, with Imprisonment,*[5] *and hearing the Prisoner at the Bar, as they called Your Petitioner, in his Defence, still reserving to themselves the Conclusive Power, of declaring Your Petitioner Guilty, or Not Guilty, did, at last, very unjustly, by the Votes of a Majority, as their Verdict, find Your Petitioner Guilty, of Part of their Charge, against him, namely, the promoting and publishing the said Libel, intitled as above; And thereupon, intending to render Your Petitioner infamous, among the People, and to brand with Disgrace and Ignominy, the Character of a Clergyman, of the Church of England, who is placed at the Head of a Seminary of Learning, in the City aforesaid, and engaged in sundry other publick Undertakings, did by their final Sentence, adjudge that Your Petitioner should be committed to the Newgate, or Common Goal of the said County; The place for Thieves, Murderers and Felons, as well as Debtors, there to be detained, until further Orders, from the House; to which loathsome Goal he was committed, on the aforesaid 25th. of January and therein now lyes.*

g. If the House in the Enquiry into this Breach of Privilege went too much into the Forms, and used too much the Expressions proper to a Court of Justice, it was nothing more than an Impropriety in them, being in no sense any Prejudice to the Delin-

5. The Assembly had summoned for interrogation Drs. Thomas and Phineas Bond, who had encouraged circulation of Moore's libel; Michael Lovell, a friend of the Bonds' who testified in Smith's favor; Robert Levers, a clerk who had copied Moore's address for Smith; David Hall and William Bradford, printers of the libel in English newspapers; Rev. Johann F. Handshue; and Anton Armbrüster, printer of the libel in a German newspaper at Smith's direction. Handshue and Armbrüster, reluctant and evasive in their testimony, were probably the allegedly terrified witnesses. Full transcripts of the interrogations are in the Penn Papers, Hist. Soc. Pa., and in Pa. Assembly Papers, N.Y. Pub. Lib. On a copy of Smith's petition in this last collection, his characterization of the witnesses is marked "not proved."

quent, but rather in his Favour as he was in that Way allowed Council. He has no Charge as a Clergyman. His Character as such, or as a Schoolmaster, was not now to be hurt, by the Censure of the House for publishing a Libel, he having been long considered as a common Scribbler of Libels and false abusive Papers [both?] against publick Bodies and private Persons, and thereby keeping up Party Heats in the Province, on which Account he had been refused the Pulpit by the Minister, and denied a Certificate of Good Behaviour by the Vestry. [See the Depositions of Roberdeau and others; See Chattin's Deposition.]⁶ The Place of his Confinement is in a separate Building from the Criminals where only Debtors are confin'd, in airy commodious Apartments, where the Confinement is the only Inconvenience; and this (incurr'd by his Contumacy) he was told by the House might be prevented by his making proper Acknowledgments, which he refused.

[*h*] THAT *Your Petitioner did, imediately, read and tender, an Appeal, from this Judgment to Your Sacred Majesty in Council, and prayed to have the same entred, upon their Minutes, which they refused to do; Intimating that no Appeal lay, from any Judgment of theirs, to Your Sacred Majesty in Council.*

6. See above, VI, 52 n, 420–2 n, 457 n, for Smith's "scribbling" and his quarrel with Daniel Roberdeau. James Chattin, a printer, testified before the Assembly, Jan. 31, 1758, and four days later swore before William Allen that on Aug. 3, 1756, Smith had asked him to print a remonstrance signed "Obadiah Honesty," written by Smith and containing a quotation from a letter (dated Feb. 23, 1756) signed "W. Smith" printed in the London *Evening Advertiser*, April 20, 1756, violently attacking the Pa. Assembly and the Quakers. Chattin refused to include the offensive quotation; he printed "Obadiah Honesty" but he soon refused to sell it "partly by Reluctance in his own Mind, and partly by a friendly hint given [him] by a worthy member of the Assembly." Deposition in Pa. Assembly Papers, N.Y. Pub. Lib. Smith had been summoned before the Assembly on July 20, 1756, to answer questions about the *Advertiser* letter, but though he failed to give satisfaction, he was not prosecuted further at that time. *Votes*, 1755–56, pp. 119–20. The depositions by Roberdeau and others have not been found. Smith was not on good terms with the Rev. Robert Jenney, rector of Christ Church in Philadelphia, who wrote the Archbishop of Canterbury, Nov. 28, 1758, naming Smith as one who meddled in politics to the detriment of his religious profession. During Smith's quarrel with Roberdeau, a group of Christ Church vestrymen had testified, pointedly, to Roberdeau's good character. H. W. Smith, *William Smith*, I, 129–30, 185; *Pa. Jour.*, June 17, 1756.

h. It is true he demanded an Appeal to His Majesty; which he conceived he was entitled to by the Charter and Laws of the Province; and offered Bail to prosecute the Appeal; but the House on considering maturely the Words of the Charter and Laws, were of Opinion, "that no Appeals were intended to be directed by either to the King and Council from Judgments of the House of Assembly relating to Breach of Priviledge and Contempts to the House," and acquainted him that on making the Submission required by the House, Bail to prevent a Commitment would be unnecessary: This Submission he insolently refused, striking his Hand on his Breast, and saying he was determined his Tongue should never give his Heart the Lie. [See Votes, Page 24. 25.]⁷

[*i*] THAT *Your Petitioner in his said Appeal, did further pray that their Clerk should deliver to Your Petitioner attested Copys of all Papers, Minutes and Proceedings, relative to Your Petitioner's Tryal, humbly to be layd before Your Majesty; To which Prayer, although the Matters, therein mentioned, have been since specially desired, they have not yet vouchsafed to give Your Petitioner any Answer.*

i. It appears by the Votes, [Page 19, 20,] that Copies of all Papers necessary for his Defence were delivered to the Petitioner.⁸

[*k*] THAT, *thô by the Depositions, taken before the House, it appeared that very many Persons, Lawyers and Others, had seen, approved of, and advised the printing and publishing the Address of Wm. Moore before it was printed; That the Speaker and two other Members of Assembly, being consulted on the said Address, previous to it's Publication by the Printer to the House, and by him acquainted with the Contents thereof, did counsel and advise, and as far as in them lay, authorize the*

7. In printed *Votes*, 1757–58, pp. 32–3.
8. On Jan. 13, 1758, when the Assembly prescribed the rules for Smith's "trial," the clerk had been ordered to "furnish the said Smith with a Copy of the Minutes containing the Charge against him, and also a Copy of his own Examination before this House." This order, however, did not include many of the papers relating to his case, and of course took no notice of important depositions entered after January 13. On Jan. 31, 1758, the House ignored a further request from Smith for copies of relevant papers. *Ibid.*, pp. 21,36. On the other hand, Smith's lawyers seem to have had all relevant papers available to them at the April 20 and 27 hearings; copies are among the Penn Papers, Hist. Soc. Pa.

*printing and publishing the same;*⁹ *That David Hall the acting Printer of the Pensilvania Gazette, and Wm. Bradford, the Printer of the Pensilvania Journal, did also, before the House, acknowledge they had printed and published it, and that thô it appeared that the Paper, layd to the Charge of Your Petitioner, was only a Republication, in the Way of his Business, and that, of all those concern'd in it he was the least so. Yet no Person has, ever, been called in Question, as a Criminal, for any Matters relating thereto, but Your unhappy Petitioner, except Mr. Moore who declared himself the Author.*

k. The Address of William Moore speaks for itself, and will show whether it was such as good Lawyers ought to approve.¹ The Speaker and two other Members charg'd with authorizing the Publishing that Address, never saw it till it was printed, and only refus'd to assume to themselves any Authority of restraining the Press, and advis'd the Printer to Prudence and Caution. [See the Deposition of David Hall.]² The Printers of the Gazette and Journal were call'd in Question; but produc'd the Author, and as they were not concern'd in writing it, and behav'd properly before the House, as did the others who were concern'd in writing and publishing it, they were dismiss'd. Smith was an old Offender. See the Votes of 1756.³

9. Marked "not proved" on copy in Pa. Assembly Papers, N.Y. Pub. Lib.; see notes 2 and 3 below.

1. Moore's address accused the Assembly of shameful, virulent, slanderous conduct, oppressive injustice, revengeful malice, rancor, calumny, falsehood, usurpation, and scurrility, and was altogether a most intemperate document. The attorney general and the solicitor general agreed that "the paper in Question was a Libel" on the Assembly of which it spoke. *Acts Privy Coun., Col.,* IV, 383.

2. Hall had consulted speaker Isaac Norris, Joseph Galloway, and William Masters. He admitted he had not shown the address to them, but had related its contents, and that they had indicated no opposition to its publication. Hall very clearly thought he had their unofficial permission, and would not have printed the address without it, in fact the cautions about "restraining the Press" implied, he thought, an obligation to print it. He also consulted Assemblymen Daniel Roberdeau and John Baynton, who advised him "to be wary." Copies of his deposition, Penn Papers, Hist. Soc. Pa., and Pa. Assembly Papers, N.Y. Pub. Lib.

3. Smith's main offense, in 1756 and 1758, seems to have been a refusal to humble himself before the Assembly; he certainly was less blamable for circulating the libel than Hall and Bradford who had first printed it.

37

[*l*] THAT *Your Petitioner on the 4th. Day of February following in due Form of Law, applyed to the Chief Justice of the Province, to grant him his Majestys Writ of Habeas Corpus, in Order, that Your Petitioner, on the Return thereof, might either be discharged, or bailed, as the Nature of his Case should require; Whereupon, the said Chief Justice answered that, on a View of the Copy of Your Petitioners Commitment, it appearing to him, that, among other Things, Your Petitioner was committed for a Breach of Privilege, he did not think himself authorized in granting a Habeas Corpus, and bailing Your Petitioner during the Sitting of the House, and therefore, was obliged to reject the Prayer of the said Petition.*

1. The Chief Justices Answer, that the Petitioner being committed for Breach of Privilege, he did not think himself authorized to grant a Habeas Corpus, and bail the Petitioner, *during the Sitting of the House,* shows that the Confinement was not like to continue longer than the Sitting of the House, which probably is over before this Time, as the private Affairs of the Members call them Home on the first Approach of Spring, and the Winter Session rarely extends beyond the Middle of March. But if they should continue Sitting as long as possible, it could not be beyond September, when they are dissolved by Law; so that there is little Danger of the Petitioner's being imprisoned for Life.[4]

4. Smith's application to Chief Justice William Allen for a writ of habeas corpus, Feb. 4, 1758, and Allen's rejection of it the same day, are printed in H. W. Smith, *William Smith,* I, 179–80, and copies sent to England are in the Penn Papers, Hist. Soc. Pa. Allen, also a member of the Assembly, explained to Paris, March 18, 1758, that "Poor Smith and Moor, still remain in Gaol, and are like to continue so, till our Assembly *break up;* at which time I will grant a habeas corpus, and discharge them. Many of our Lawyers are of opinion, that I might have done it before now; but it would have answered no end; for, they would have recommitted them, the next day. I mean our pious Assembly, would have done it; for they seem to know no bounds, to their power and are resolved to crush every man that dares oppose them in their detestable measures. Upon the whole, it has been by all thoughtful men, among us, judged best, to let them lay in prison, *in hopes* of having *his Majestys determination,* in the matter, which will settle this mode of proceeding, in time to come. If our petty Assembly, can set up a new court of justice and try matters, cognisable in the courts of law, and imprison any of the Kings subjects, at their will and pleasure, we are, I think, the most unhappy of the Kings subjects." Penn Papers, Hist. Soc. Pa. Allen released the prisoners shortly after the Assembly adjourned, April 8, 1758, and protected their

[*m*] THAT *Your Petitioner verily believes the Words, in the said Commitment, which appear to the Chief Justice to imply a Breach of Privilege, were untruely incerted therein, on Purpose to exclude Your Petitioner from this legal Relief; As there was no Breach of Privilege, intimated in the Sentence passed against Your Petitioner by the House; And as he was never charged, even by the Assembly, with the least Indecency of Behaviour, or Mark of Disrespect, to the House, during the whole Process, nor with any other Matter, that could be construed a Breach of Privilege of the Assembly then convened.*

m. The House had voted it a Breach of Priviledge to assert, that the Assembly of the Province had no Right or Power, to hear the Petitions, examine into and redress the Aggrievances and Complaints of the People against publick Officers, or in any other Case where the Subject is oppressed; the same being one of their undoubted Rights and Privileges, and a fundamental and essential Power of the Constitution. [See Votes, Pag. 12.] Wm. Moore's Address, among other gross Abuses, charg'd the Assembly with *usurping Powers that did not belong to them,* in examining into the Complaints against him: Smith was concern'd in drawing this Address, and publish'd it; and contemptuously refus'd Submission to the House.[5]

[*n*] THAT *Your Petitioner did afterward, on the said 4th. Day of February petition the Honourable Wm. Denny Esqr.; Governor of the Province, Setting forth the peculiar Hardships of his Case, praying such Relief as his Honour thought suitable and just. To this Your Petitioner received for Answer, that the Governor with great Compassion, beheld*

---

freedom (except for Sept. 28–30, 1758) until the Assembly's dissolution, Sept. 30, 1758, ended the threat of imprisonment.

5. The Assembly's verdict had been "That the said William Smith is guilty of promoting and publishing the libellous Paper," Moore's address, but the order of commitment added that the address was "highly derogatory of and destructive to the rights of this House and the privileges of Assembly." Copies of the relevant documents sustaining Smith on this point, and copies of the Assembly's denial of habeas corpus, were attached to his petition to the King. The Assembly resolves cited by BF had to do with its verdict against Moore. *Votes,* 1757–58, p. 18. The Assembly's failure to prove that Smith had helped write Moore's address, and the belated addition of a clause to the charge against him suggest something of its irregular conduct. See below, pp. 62–3 n, for evidence that though BF did his best to support the Assembly cause in open hearings, he was in fact annoyed at its conduct.

Your Petitioners Afflictions, but, if he had any Power, to interfere in that Matter, the Exercise of it might, at this Critical Juncture, endanger the Safety of the whole Province.

n. Governors in the Colonies have no right to interfere in the Censure of the House for Breach of Privilege.[6]

[o] THAT *under these distressing and miserable Circumstances, destitute of any Aid, from Our Laws or Government, so that his Imprisonment may be continued during his Life. Your Poor Petitioner really unable to contend with so weighty a Body, who are in Possession of all the Publick Mony of the Province, is compelled to apply to Your Majesty, the last Resort from Your Colonys, and Fountain of all Justice, within Your Majestys Dominion for Redress,*

o. For several Years past, all new Laws for raising Publick Money, have plac'd the same in the Disposition of the Governor and Commissioners, none to be issued without the Governor's Assent. [See the Laws themselves][7]

MOST HUMBLY *imploring Your Majesty to afford Your unfortunate Petitioner and Subject, such Relief, as in Your Wisdom shall appear just and equitable.*

YOUR PETITIONER, *as in Duty bound shall ever earnestly pray &c.*
Philadelphia County Goal   WILLIAM SMITH

Febry. 6th. 1758.

The three principal Points of the Petition are contain'd in the Reference, and are answered under Letters, k, and c.[8]

Perhaps it may not be necessary to open the whole that can be said, in the Hearing before the Attorney and Solicitor General; as the Council on the other side may thence be better prepar'd when we come before the King in Council: Will it not be sufficient to

6. Smith's appeal and Denny's response are in H. W. Smith, *William Smith*, I, 180.

7. BF referred to the various supply acts under which he and other provincial commissioners had dispensed public funds. See above, VII, 131–2, 150, for the controversy over the governor's right to approve the expenditures.

8. The order of reference by the Privy Council Committee on Plantation Affairs to the attorney general and the solicitor general, dated April 10, 1758, and signed by its secretary, William Sharpe, summarized the points BF answered in parts "k" and "c" above. Copy in Pa. Assembly Papers, N.Y. Pub. Lib.

insist chiefly on these two Points; first, *that it is a Matter of not sufficient Importance for the King in Council to be troubled with, who if they encourage such trifling Appeals, may have much of their Time taken up with them.* 2. *That it being a Matter of Privilege the Crown will not be advised to interfere* and thereby bring a Branch of the Legislature, the House of Representatives, into Contempt, and weaken the Hands of Government, &c.

This is refer'd to Mr. Sharpe's Prudence. The Counsel however should be furnish'd with a compleat Brief, in Case it be necessary to go thro' the whole Affair.

Endorsed: Notes on W Smith's Petition.

III

Some Reflections being on this Occasion[9] unjustly thrown on the Quakers, will it be amiss to observe

That the Province was first settled by them, without any Expence to the Crown.

That they never received any Assistance from the other Colonies.

That this Colony on the contrary has afforded Assistance to the other Colonies; as, to New York in Queen Anne's Time a large Quantity of Provisions; to New-England in 1745, £4000 in Provisions and Gunpowder for their Forces at Cape Breton, and £10,000 in Provisions to New York, and the 4 New England Colonies of Massachusets Bay, Connecticut, Rhodeisland and New Hampshire, in 1755: for their Forces.[1]

That they have also from the first Settlement of the Province expended large Sums yearly in Presents for preserving Peace with the Indians, not for themselves only, but for the neighbouring Colonies also; the good Opinion the Indians had entertained of

9. The "Occasion" was the presentation on April 20, 1758, of the brief by Smith's lawyers. Paris argued that Smith had been imprisoned not for the offense with which he was charged, but for his consistent opposition to Assembly and Quaker policies and politics. He thus attacked Assembly "usurpation" of power and ridiculed Quaker pacifism which, Paris alleged, combined to put Pennsylvania in near treasonable opposition to the King and his ministers. Copy of the brief in Penn Papers, Hist. Soc. Pa. See below, pp. 60–2, for BF's account of Paris' assault and the response to it.

1. BF referred often to these instances of defense support and assistance by the Quaker-led Assembly, euphemistically labeled "money for the King's (Queen's) Use"; see above, III, 195, VI, 42–9, 170–1, 247.

them giving Weight to the Mediation of the Government; in particular this Colony was in 1744 at the Expence of the Treaty at Lancaster, in which the Six Nations were reconciled to Virginia, and a Bloody War just ready to break out against that Province happily prevented.[2]

That they have also at different Times granted considerable Sums to the Crown, their Principles never forbidding such Grants. They always thought it their Duty *to render to Cesar the Things that are his;* and when Money was demanded of them for military Purposes, their Method was, to grant a Sum absolutely *for the King's Use,* without Appropriation, and leave the Application to the Government.

In this Manner they granted £2000 to the Crown in Queen Anne's Wars, in the Infancy of the Colony; £3000 for the Expedition to Carthagena in 1739; £5000 in 1746 for the Expedition to Canada.

The Equity and Moderation always shown by the Quakers in the Exercise of the Powers they possess'd as Members of Assembly, never proposing or enacting any Laws for the Oppressing those of other Persuasions, induc'd great Numbers of different Religions and Nations to remove into Pensilvania with[3] their Families and Effects, thereby encreasing the Strength and Commerce of this Kingdom.

And tho' the Numbers of People of different Sects, have long since far exceeded the Quakers, yet the Respect of the People in general has been so great towards them for their prudent Conduct, that till 1756 there was always a great Majority of them chosen into the Assembly.

In June 1756, Six Quakers desired Leave to resign their Seats, which was granted, and Persons of other Persuasions chosen in their Stead.

At the Election of October 1756, on Account of the Clamours

2. See above, II, 160–1, V, 42–57, for earlier statements defending Quaker and Pennsylvania Indian policy. *In An Enquiry into the Causes of the Alienation of the Delaware and Shawanese Indians,* an MS copy of which was in England at this time, Charles Thomson described the 1744 treaty at Lancaster in detail; pp. 49–56 in the printed version.

3. The rest of this paragraph, and the next four, are in WF's hand, except for the insertion by BF noted below.

raised against them by the Proprietary Faction, the Quakers declin'd standing Candidates, and many of them even refus'd to vote; and many of those who did vote, voted for Members of other Persuasions, nevertheless some Quakers were chosen, but a large Majority of the Church of England and Presbyterians; and to make that Majority still greater 4 more Quakers who had been chosen without their Consent, desired Leave of the House to decline the Service, and their Seats were vacated accordingly, and filled with Churchmen by a new Election; so that at present, there are two to one in the House who are not Quakers; and those who are Quakers, are nevertheless for Defence.[4]

See the Votes of June 4, Page 101; June 28, Page 103; October 16, 1756, Page 5.[5]

See the Votes of Jan. 26. 1757. where, in the Remonstrance of the House, they UNANIMOUSLY demand the Governor's Assent to the Bill for granting £100,000 *for the Defence* of the Province, which Bill the Governor had refused on Account of Proprietary Instructions.

Since the beginning of the present War, the following Bills have at different times been pass'd by the Assembly and Sums granted for Service of the Crown and Defence of the Province viz.

May 10. 1754 A Bill granting £10,000 to the King's Use. Votes Page 56.

Dec. 12. 1754 A Bill granting £20,000 to the King's Use. Votes Page 21, 22.

Jan. 3. 1755. £5000 given to purchase Provisions for the King's Troops at their Arrival, then expected under General Braddock. Votes page 59.

March 28. 1755. A Bill granting £25,000 to the King's Use. Votes Page 78.

---

4. The last nine words added by BF. See numerous references in Vols. VI and VII above to the election and resignation of Quaker members of the Pa. Assembly.

5. I.e., *Votes*, 1755–56, pp. 101, 103; *Votes*, 1756–57, p. 5. The list of references below to Assembly passage of supply bills and other actions showing its promotion of the King's service are from the appropriate volumes of *Votes*, 1753–54 through 1756–57. The measures are all discussed in volumes v–vii of this series; see indexes. As a member of the Assembly, BF had played a major role in many of them.

April 2. 1755. £10,000 given to the King's Use and put into the Hands of Commissioners to be laid out in Provisions to victual the Northern Forces. Votes Page 80, 81, 82.

April. 9. The Expence of a Post from Philadelphia to Winchester voted, and that all Letters to and from the Army under Gen. Braddock should pass free of Charge. Page 87

May 15. 1755. A Resolve to defray the Expence of the new Roads to be cut for the Accommodation of Gen. Braddock's Army. Page 92.

June 21. 1755 A Bill granting £15,000 to the King's Use. Page 106

Augt. 2. 1755. A Bill granting £50,000 to the King's Use. Page 120.

Augt. 22. 1755. One Thousand Pounds put into the Hands of a Committee to buy Arms for the poor Inhabitants on the Frontiers. Votes page 155.

Page 175. See Extracts of Letters from the General (Braddock) and principal Officers, containing Thanks to the Assembly for their seasonable Services and Supplies. &c.

Sept. 29. 1755. Ten Thousand Pounds voted towards purchasing Provision and Blankets or other warm Clothing for the Troops on the Frontiers of New York. Votes page 177.

Nov. 8. 1755. A Bill for granting £60,000 to the King's Use. Votes Page 15.

Nov. 26. 1755 Another Bill for granting £60,000 to the King's Use. Page 46, 47.

Feb. 19. 1756. See General Shirley's Letter of Thanks for the warm Clothing.

July 3. 1756. A Bill for granting the Sum of £40,000 to the King's Use. Votes Pag. 114

Sept. 8. 1756. A Bill for granting £60,000 to the King's Use. Page 143. See the Governor's Refusal of this Bill, and the Resolves of the House thereupon, Page 150, 151.

Sept. 17. 1756 A Bill for granting £30,000 to the King's Use. Page 151.

Jan. 22. 1757 A Bill for granting to His Majesty the Sum of One Hundred Thousand Pounds for the Defence of this Colony, &c. Page 71.

Feb. 3. 1757. A Bill for granting the Sum of One hundred Thousand Pounds to the King's Use. Page 77.

Tis true that by Proprietary Instructions to their Governors, many of these Grants were refused, and the Province thereby reduced to great Distress, which Distress was cruelly made use of by the Proprietary Governors to extort from the Assembly their just Rights and Privileges, and among other Things to oblige them to tax their own Estates for the Defence of the Proprietary Estate and exempt the Proprietary Estate from any Part of the Burthen. When they refused to comply with this most unreasonable and wicked Demand, a Clamour was to be rais'd against them that they would do nothing for the Defence of the Province, numberless nameless Libels against them publish'd, disguising the true Cause of Disagreement between the Governor and Assembly, and charging it all on their being Quakers, as if it was a religious Dispute about the Lawfulness of Defence.[6]

See the Bill for granting £50,000 under Seal with the Governor's Amendments, in which where it was said the Sum should be "raised on all Estates real and Personal, the Proprietary Estate *not* excepted;" the Governor proposes this Amendment "dele the Word *not*, and insert the Word *only*;" and the House not agreeing to this Amendment, he refused to pass the Bill, notwithstanding the Dangerous Circumstances the Country was then in.[7]

And even the last Bill for granting £100,000 was refused on Account of its not complying with Proprietary Instructions, and would not have passed if Lord Loudon had not interpos'd his Influence with the Governor.[8] See Votes of 1757 Jany. 25. page 52.

Do these numerous Grants and Gifts look like the Acts of an Assembly who would be angry with Messrs. Moore and Smith for being zealous for the Defence of the Country?

But every Offender, who can make no better Defence, ascribes the Accusation to some Malice in his Prosecutors.

Smith is an old Offender, and was formerly treated with great Lenity by the Assembly on a like Occasion. See Votes July 20. 1756 page 119.[9]

He receives a Pension from the Proprietaries of £50 a Year, as

6. See above, VI, 238–84, for the events of November 1755, when this controversy was at its height.

7. See above, VI, 129–38.

8. See above, VII, 106–9, 145–53.

9. See above, p. 35 n.

Provost of the Academy and being a ready Scribbler is employ'd in all the dirty work of abusing and libelling the Assembly.[1]

This is the Secret of his being supported in the present Complaint by the Proprietary Faction. His Cause is to be made use of as one Battery against the Privileges of the Assembly, and Rights of the People.[2]

A Gentleman present at the first Hearing[3] said the Goal Smith was confin'd in was as bad as any Goal in England.

1. Though BF could not have known it, a long attack on Smith, dwelling on his supposed subservience to Thomas Penn, had appeared in *Pa. Jour.*, April 6, 1758. Written as an autobiographical letter, Smith is made to say "a *Salary* has ever since my infancy been the greatest joy *my Life has experienced*," and that since he had been pensioned by the Proprietors, he had "concluded for the future, to think as he [Penn] thinks, to act as he acts, and write as he commands. I have surrendered up my honesty to his hands, and my conscience to his keeping," etc. The satirical letter was part of a long controversy over Smith's case which filled large portions of *Pa. Jour.* from Feb. 2 to April 20, 1758. The articles on both sides show, among other things, that the contestants in Philadelphia recognized the Assembly's need to find precedents for its actions in the practices of the House of Commons.

2. The satire mentioned in the preceding note explained the privileges and rights under assault by having Smith describe what he would teach his students at the College of Philadelphia: "that *Liberty* is *Licenciousness;* that the assembly of an *American* colony is not entitled to the priviledge of the house of commons in respect to its constituents. Nor tho they are Brittons or the descendants of Brittons, to the rights of Englishmen. That the ancient maxim, *cujus est dare ejus est desponere,* is absurd and foolish. That a free people or their representatives ought not to have the power of disposing of their own properties, or of raising money as shall best suit their conveniency, but that they ought to be directed as the humour and interest of their *Superiours* shall dictate. That no American assembly ought to sit on their own adjournments, nor judge of their own elections, that tho annually elected it shou'd be subject to be dissolved every month, as caprice and passion shall direct. That private instructions ought to be implicitly obey'd tho ever so arbitrary and inconsistent with the good of the people, his Majesty's interest, or the defence of his colonies. I will teach them to spurn at *magna charta* charters of priviledges and the laws of the English constitution; and if ever I find Lock, Sidney, or *Cato's letters* within the walls of my jurisdiction, they shall be instantly condemned to the flames, their notions of the liberties of the English constitution carefully eradicated, and *machiavel* shall be the study of my pupils in their room. Thus will I instruct the rising generation in the principles of slavery, and in an implicit obedience to their superiours." *Pa. Jour.*, April 6, 1758.

3. Probably James Hamilton; see below, p. 48.

Enquire of Philadelphans present, whether the Prison of Philadelphia does not consist of two distinct Buildings? What they are and their Uses? Which of them Smith is confin'd in? Whether among the Felons or the Debtors?[4]

He asserts that the Assembly deny'd that an Appeal lay from *any Judgment* of theirs to his Majesty in Council.

Compare this with the Votes.[5]

See also David Hall's Deposition, concerning his consulting the Speaker and two other Members.[6]

If he presumes to come before his Sovereign with a LIE in his right hand, can he deserve to be favour'd with regard to his personal Liberty (which he might have had by a decent Submission) against the Liberties and Privileges of a whole People.[7]

A very unseasonable Time to call the Privileges of all the Assemblies of the Colonies in question; and employ them in defending those Privileges, when they are attack'd by foreign Enemies, and their utmost Attention necessary to defend their Countries, and by chearful and ready granting large Supplies, to secure the King's Dominions.

Hope his Majesty will be advis'd to reject the Petition.

The Petitioner[8] demanded an Appeal to be admitted by the Assembly, and that he should be in the mean-time bailed: This was not granted.

But he did not afterwards acquaint them that he intended to

4. Smith wrote the Bishop of London, Feb. 7, 1758, that "my Gaol is as comfortable as a Gaol can be, being crowded with Visitors from Morning to Night." He managed to conduct classes from his cell, and to court Rebecca, daughter of his fellow prisoner William Moore, whom he married in June. H.W. Smith, *William Smith*, I, 184, 186–7, 192–3.

5. The Assembly denied appeal (by implication) only from its judgments in cases of "Breach of Privilege and Contempt to the House." *Votes,* 1757–58, p. 33.

6. This sentence, squeezed in at the bottom of the page, may refer to one of the four or five preceding paragraphs.

7. This paragraph and the next seem to be BF's suggestions for concluding statements for his counsel rather than direct responses to charges made by Smith's lawyers.

8. The remainder of this paper, written at the bottom of the last sheet, seem to be random observations which in a more formal presentation BF would have placed earlier.

petition, nor furnish them with a Copy of his Petition and Complaint.[9]

There are many things charg'd in it as facts which possibly might have been set aside, and the Agents here furnish'd with proper Proofs to show the Falshood of such Charges, had a Copy been furnish'd of the Complaint, in America.

To decide therefore on his own Representation that the Proceedings against him were irregular, is to determine without full hearing of the opposite Side.

Endorsed: Smith and the Assembly of Pensilvania Observacons on the Reflections thrown on the Quakers.

IV

Mr. Hamilton late Governor of Pensilvania, will probably be present, as he was the first Night.[1] He might be ask'd

Whether Mr. Franklin was not always very zealous for the Defence of that Province?[2]

Whether he has known or heard of any Inhabitant of that Country that was more so?

Whether Mr. Franklin was not always among the foremost in pressing the Quaker Assembly to grant large Sums of Money for that purpose?

Whether he Mr. Hamilton ever heard of any Resentment they[3] had against Mr. Franklin, or Malice they bore him on that Account?

---

9. Smith first announced his intention of making this appeal before the Assembly's resolve denying he had a right to; he reiterated it in a letter of Jan. 31, 1758, which BF overlooked, and the Assembly chose to ignore, as "a farther Insult" to the House. *Votes,* 1757–58, pp. 32–3, 36.

1. That is, at the first hearing, April 20, 1758.

2. As provincial commissioners, BF and Hamilton had shared important and dangerous defense responsibilities; see above, VI, 284–5, 307–14, 342–3.

3. The Quakers. Hamilton might have answered this question affirmatively; Israel Pemberton and other strict Quakers resented the war measures BF promoted so successfully, and his "seduction" of many Friends into support of them. Theodore Thayer, *Israel Pemberton King of the Quakers* (Phila., 1943), pp. 117–18. See above, VII, 173 n, 376 n, and below, p. 100 n, for continuing mistrust of BF by some of the stricter Quakers.

V

OBSERVATIONS[4]

The Petitioner's Committment, is merely for a Contempt, and he might have been discharged so easily as upon a bare submission; Is this Mans Case then such as calls for an Enquiry into the privileges of the Representatives of the people in Pensilvania? nay in all the several Colonies in America, for they all must be affected by it—or ought not this Case rather to be got rid off upon some previous point.

We do not see how any Application can lye in this summary way to the Crown, no appeal lies in any Case from Committments for Contempts—nor a Complaint neither that we know of, to the Crown, or the King in his Courts, to release a party Committed for a Contempt, and, tho' an Habeas Corpus, or a proceeding in nature thereof, may lie as in the late Case of Murray Committed by the House of Commons in England, yet what was the Event when it appeared his Committment was for a Contempt? they never offered to Enquire further into it, but remanded the prisoner till he had cleared his Contempt,[5] so that We think the present application is wholly irregular and therefore ought to be dismissed.

And it is probable this Man has been released before now, if not upon his own Submission, as he is so obstinate yet upon some Adjournment of the House, for tho' there is no such thing as a prorogation used in pensilvania, yet they have adjournments that are always deemed there of the same nature, and put an end to a Session, as it is called and they begin that Business De novo, when they meet again, and the whole of an Assembly is only for a period of 12 months.

But if We are to go into a particular discussion of the Authority of Assemblys We then submit it to Consideration that the Representatives of the people Assembled, for the purpose of making Laws, in these large and distant provinces, and who are convened

4. One of the Assembly counsel, probably William de Grey, made notes for use in oral argument on the back of all the pages of this brief. See the headnote for the first portions of the brief of which these "Observations" are the concluding part.

5. The House of Commons had voted Alexander Murray guilty of dangerous and seditious practices, Feb. 6, 1750, and committed him to Newgate prison. His case was cited in the Assembly brief.

after the manner and for the same purpose and bear great resemblance to the parliament here, having a kind of like Legislative power and in the highest instance of it, that of levying money on the Subject—cannot be without so necessary a power as to commit for Contempts shewn them, incident to every Jurisdiction from the House of Lords down to the lowest Court of Justice—nay it is incident to every Magistrate, for even a single Justice of peace may Commit for a Contempt shewn him in Office—and without such power no Authority or decency can be preserved.

If the power of the Assembly to commit at all is at once established, and it must be strange Doctrine and policy too to deny it, We think it puts an end to all further discussion about the Cause of Commitment—for it is apprehended, if the Court of Kings Bench here, upon a prisoner being brought up by Habeas Corpus upon the return of the Writ, [know?] he has been committed by another Jurisdiction (having Authority so to do) for a Contempt, the Court of Kings Bench would not enter into a discussion whether he was guilty of a Contempt or not, it was sufficient the Jurisdiction who Committed him had determined it so, who are Judges of the Contempts offered them.

But it appears this Man's Contempt was for a most virulent Libel—which tho he was not the first Author of, yet he was next to him by Causing the Libel to be new dress'd and put on a new Garb, for the sake of introducing it into the Company of many, it could not otherwise have made its way to, and therefore he deserved punishment next to the Author himself, and more than any common inadvertent printer.

Those printers of the pensilvania Gazette and pensilvania Journal are not Officers of the Assembly tho they sometimes print the Votes and Messages of the House by their special Order; And were called before the House as well as the petitioner, but on discovering the Author, and behaving openly and properly to the House were dismissed.

The petitioner has no Charge as a Clergyman—his Character as such, or as a Schoolmaster was not now to be hurt by the Censure of the House for publishing a Libel, he having been long considered as a common Scribbler of Libels and false Abusive papers, both against publick Bodies and private Persons, thereby keeping up party heats in the province, on which account he had been refused the pulpit by the Minister and denied a Certificate of good behaviour by the Vestry. The place of his Confinement is in a seperate Building from the Criminals, where only Debtors are confined in Airy Commodious Apartments, where the Confinement is the only Inconvenience, and this (incurred by his contumacy) he was told by the House he might be prevented by his making proper acknowledgment, which he refused.[6]

It appears by the Votes that during the hearing, Copies of all papers necessary for his Defence were Delivered to the petitioner.

The address of Wm. Moore speaks for itself, and will shew whether it was such as good Lawyers ought to approve. The Speaker and 2 other Members, Charged with Authorizing the publishing that Address, never saw it till it was printed, and only refused to Assume to themselves any Authority of restraining the press and advised the printer to prudence and Caution.

We hope upon the whole that the Petition shall be dismissed.[7]

To Thomas Hubbard[8] Copy: Harvard College Library

Sir   London April 28th. 1758

In persuance of Mr. Winthrop's[9] memorandum, which I lately rece'd from you, thro' the hands of Mr. Mico,[1] I have procured and delivered to him the following things, viz.

6. Comparison of this paragraph and the two following with "f," "i," and "k" in BF's notes above shows how much the Assembly counsel depended on him.

7. The covering sheet of the brief is endorsed "1758 June 10th. N B—Copy made of the Brief and of the Addl. Instructions and of Mr. Franklin's notes on the petn. and of his Observations on the Reflections thrown on the Quakers which was sent to Mr. Franklin to forward to Pensilvania by his desire." See below, p. 87 n, for later action in Smith's case. Pratt and Yorke summoned the parties to further hearings for May 3, 1758, at 6 P.M., but then Pratt seems to have had the order canceled. Pa. Assembly Papers, N.Y. Pub. Lib.; Penn Papers, Hist. Soc. Pa.

8. Thomas Hubbard (1702–1773), Boston merchant, speaker of the Mass. House of Representatives, 1750–59, and treasurer of Harvard College. *Sibley's Harvard Graduates*, VI, 490–5. See above, VII, 69–71, for his father's belated romance.

9. On John Winthrop, professor of mathematics and natural philosophy; see above, IV, 261 n, and VI, 404 n.

1. Joseph Mico, merchant and London agent for Harvard College. He wrote

A Mahogany Case lined with lead containing 35 Square Glass Bottles, in 5 Rows, 7 in a Row.[2]

A Glass Globe of the same Size and kind with that I used at Philadelphia and Mounted in the same manner.

A large Glass Cylinder mounted on an Iron Axis with brass Caps, this form being most used here and thought better than the Globe as a long narrow Cushion will Electrify a greater surface at the same time.

The Bottles have Necks, which I think better then to be quite open, for so they would either be exposed to the dust and damp of the Air, if they had no Stoppers or the Stoppers would be too near together to admit of electrifying a single Bottle, or Row of Bottles, there is only a little more deficulty in lining the Inside with Tinfoil, but that is chiefly got over, by cutting it into narrow Stripes, and guiding them in with a Stick flatt at one end to apply the more conveniently, the pasted side to the Glass; I would have coated them myself if the time nad not been too short; I send the Tinfoyl which I got made of a proper breadth for the purpose. They should be coated nine Inches high which brings the Coating just even with the edge of the Case, the Tinfoyl is 10 Inches broad, which allows for lapping over the bottom.

I have bored the holes in all the Stoppers for the communicating Wires, provided all the Wires, and fixed one or two to show the manner, Each Wire to go into a Bottle, is bent so that the two ends go in and spring against the Inside Coating or Lining. The middle of the Wire goes up into the Stopper with an Eye, thro' which the long communicating Wires pass that connect all the Bottles in one Row.

To form occasional Communications with more Rowes, there must be on the long Wires of the 2nd. and 4th. Rows, four other moveable Wires, which I call Cross Wires about 2½ Inches long

---

Hubbard, May 13, 1758, that he had given Winthrop's memorandum to BF, and that he had sent the "Electrifying Instruments" (for which he had paid £10 3s. 7d.), together with some Hebrew psalters and this letter. Col. Soc. Mass. *Publs.*, x (1906), 234.

2. A "battery" of Leyden jars, similar to the one described here and once owned by BF, is at APS and is pictured in I. Bernard Cohen, *Franklin and Newton* (Phila., 1956), following p. 454. See earlier volumes of this series for BF's electrical experiments with globes and cylinders.

with a small Ball of any Metal about the size of a Pistol Bullet at each end, the Ball of one end to have a hole thro' the middle, so that it may be slipt on the long wire, and one of these Cross Wires is to be placed between the 3d. and 4th. Bottles of the Row at each end, and on each of the above mention'd Rows, that is, two to each Row, they must be made to turn easy on the Wires so that when you would charge only the middle Rowe, you turn two of them back on the first, and two on the fifth Rows, then the middle Row will be unconnected with the others, when you would charge more Rows you turn them forwards or backwards so as to have the communication compleated with just the number of Rows you want.

The Brass handles of the Case communicate with the outside of the Bottles when you want to make the Electrical Circuit.[3]

I see now I have wrote it, that the greatest part of this Letter, would have been more properly addressed to Mr. Winthrop himself, but probably you will send it him with the things, and that will answer the end. Be pleased to tender my best Respects to him and the rest of the Gentlemen of the College. I am with great Esteem and Regard Sir Your most obedient humble Servant

B. FRANKLIN

P. S. I beg the College will do me the favour to accept a Virgil I send in the Case, thought to be the most curiously printed of any Book hitherto done in the World.[4]

To Thomas Hubbard Esqr Boston

Endorsed: From B. Franklin Esqr April 28th. 1758 Dr. 70

3. That BF should take such obvious pleasure in writing a letter about electrical apparatus the day after the climactic hearing on the Smith appeal is another illustration of the continued variety of his interest.

4. Publii Virgilii Maronis *Bucolica, Georgica, et Aeneis.* Birminghamiae: Typis Johannis Baskerville. MDCCLVII. This is the first important publication by the new type-designer John Baskerville (1706–1775), usually regarded as one of his finest productions. Never losing his interest in the development of the printer's art, BF is listed in the front of the book as having subscribed to six copies. These cost him one guinea each. On June 5, 1758, he paid his stationer £6 2s. 1d. for having six copies bound in vellum and one in calf. "Account of Expences," pp. 13, 33; *PMHB,* LV (1931), 109, 112. The copy sent to Harvard is still there. See also below, pp. 79, 80.

From Isaac Norris

Letterbook copy: Historical Society of Pennsylvania

To B Franklin

My Dear friend,   Apl 29. 1758

The Assembly being fully Convinced by the Experence of the last year; that our forces, were, at a Great Expence Suffered to lye Ide [Idle] on the frontiers, and managed in such manner as to be of very little Service had Resolved[5] to reduce Their Numbers to Seven Hundred Men; Till Lord Loudoun made his Requisition from This Province and the Lower Counties, of Eight Hundred Men to Join the Regulars intended for a Western Expedition, upon which the first Resolve was alterd, and we Granted Seven Hundred (leaving the other one Hundred to be raised by the lower Counties,) To Join Lord Loudoun, and 300 to Remain in Garrison. This was the State of our Publick Affairs when I wrote last[6]—but Soon after Upon the Secretary of State's Letter to the Several Colony's by which it Appeared That Vigorous Efforts were designed to be Carried on and made from all the Colonies to Strike an Effectual Blow at the Same Time both to the Northward and Westward, the Assembly once more Resumed the Consideration of the Numbers of Men to be raised and Supported by us, for the Ensuing Campagne, and Agree'd "To Raise and Support Two Thousand Seven hundred Men," A great part of which Number are at this Time Ready, and in the Pay of the Province.[7] Thus After a long Tedious Sessions, we have at length Passed the Bill for Granting £100,000 More, with an Exemption of the Proprietary Estates, the Governor (as he Says) with the Unanimous Advice of his Council, having Absolutly Rejected the Bill by which Their Estates were Included, as will appear by the Bill which the Committee will Transmit under the Great Seal, to try At Home whether they alone of all the king's Subjects have a right to Such

5. Several times in his copy Norris wrote "Resloved"; it is silently corrected.

6. Feb. 21, 1758; see above, VII, 385–9. For the Earl of Loudoun, see above, VI, 453–4 n.

7. Gov. William Denny (above, VI, 489–90 n) had laid before the Assembly, March 8, 1758, William Pitt's letter of Dec. 30, 1757, outlining the men and materials he expected Pennsylvania to furnish for Gen. John Forbes's planned expedition against Fort Duquesne, and the House resolved to raise the additional troops on March 23. *Votes*, 1757–58, pp. 50–1, 56.

Exemptions for the Defence of their own Property, and the king's Colony Committed to their Care, for which purpose the House have Resolved to Address the Crown and Come into Some measure's, if Possible, to obtain the Decision, before we are Necessitated to Make other Grants to the Crown, on Such Unequal Terms, which in Time Must Leave our Estates at the Mercy of the Proprietors whenever the overburden of the Publick Debts and Taxes shall oblige the Poor or midling People to Sell their Lands.[8] Besides the Above Grants to the Crown we have another Bill for laying a Duty of Tonnage and other Duties for fiting out the Province Ship, which has been already Rejected by the Governor on Account of the Persons Named in the Bills, but as the Merchants have Petitiond the House to lower the Tonnage, the bill has been again Taken up and alterd in Some Parts of it, and now again Lyes with the Governor for his Assent.[9] These are large Sums, which the funds, I fear are Insufficient to Sink in the Time proposed, but the Acts provide for any Defects of those funds by Continuing the Acts till the whole is Compleated, as in the former Laws, but

8. The £100,000 supply bill taxing the proprietary estates passed the House on March 29, the resolves were approved on April 8, and the new supply bill exempting the proprietary estates became law on the 22d. *Ibid.*, pp. 60, 76, 80. The resolves reaffirmed Assembly protests against what it regarded as the governor's unconstitutional interference with money bills, and directed that "the said Bill, . . . together with the Governor's proposed Amendments thereon, be transmitted, by the Committee of Correspondence, under the Great Seal, to Benjamin Franklin, Esq; and the other Agents for this Province, to be by them immediately laid before the King and Parliament now sitting, if they shall receive the same in Time." Norris' account of the dispute may not be quite fair. Officially, Denny and the Assembly quarreled over the mode of assessing property, though Thomas Penn's latest instructions, which touched on this matter (see above, VII, 372–3 n), left Denny little choice beyond permission to reenact earlier tax measures which had exempted the proprietary estates.

9. A bill, passed on March 11, laid a duty, according to the tonnage carrying capacity, on vessels sailing to or from Pa. ports and laid an import duty on liquor and sugar. On the 20th, Denny objected to the collector (Hugh Davy) and to the five Assemblymen named in the bill as commissioners to construct and direct the ship of war proposed to protect Pa. shipping. A revised tonnage law, enacted April 29, provided for lower rates, appointed Assemblyman Richard Pearne collector, and substituted five Philadelphia merchants, some of them notable for their hostility to the proprietary party, as commissioners. *Votes*, 1757–58, pp. 51, 83; *Pa. Col. Recs.*, VIII, 41; *Statutes at Large Pa.*, V, 352–61.

These Debts Entailed Upon the Province for Several years to Come will make it Difficult to raise future Supplies out of an almost drained Country, for the taking of our Servants, the Evacuating our back Counties and Their Continual emigrations into North Carolinna, with the Other Distresses imposed Upon us by the Executive Part of Goverment Continue's to make Strange Changes in the Circumstances of the People from their late flourishing Situation, perhaps we may Obtain Some Assistance from the Parliament towards the Servants and Our last Supply, (which has Exceeded our Abilities) that we might fully Comply with our Part of the Intended Operations.[1] This year, and this Critical Circumstance has induced us once more To Exempt the Proprietors who have by their Deputy obstinatly Refused our Bill in which their Estates were included as I have Already informed you, which I presume, all Circumstances Considered, will put it upon as fair an Issue To be Try'd at home, Where it Must At last be Determined, as we Can expect or hope for, seeing the Nation seem in Earnest to Prosecute the American War Effectualy This year. I have duly recieved your Several letters to the 14th of January,[2] and whilst I am writing, a copy of the Last by General Abercrombie's Secretary,[3] who is, I presume arrived at N York with Some Men of war and Transports. These Early Supplies bid fair for a Successful Compaign if Properly Conducted, and May retrieve the Honour of the last Year, which has Justly alarmed the English Nation, at Such an Amazeing Expence for the Support of their American Colonies, to hear of Nothing but perpetual Loses. I hope the future Accounts from hence may be more Agreeable. I imagine it will be no Difficult Matter to find out that the Council are Joining their Utmost forces to Superceed our Governor. That Gentleman has the Misfortune to disoblige all Ranks and Parties Among us and Seems Not perfectly easy in his own family, So That in all Probability he has Occasion to Repent his hasty Acceptance of this

1. BF had been seeking for over a year to obtain compensation to masters of indentured servants enlisted in the British army (see above, VII, 224–8, and this vol., p. 27), and Pitt's letter of Dec. 30, 1757, had held out hope that Parliament would reimburse the colonies for their war expenditures. See below, p. 102, for the distress in Cumberland, one of the "back Counties."

2. See above, VII, 360–2, for the letter of Jan. 14, 1758; the "Several" earlier ones have not been found.

3. Possibly Joshua Loring; see above, VII, 363 n.

Goverment under his load of Instructions to which he was probably Almost a Stranger till After his Arrival among us. I realy pitty him and am Sorry for his Unhappy Situation but I fear he has neither Sufficient Resolutions or Abilities for Goverment and I Apprehend the Most we can Say in his favour, is That we like him better Than his Predecessor.[4] This letter will be a Convinceing proof That I write as I can get a little Time from Interruption. The Governor has enacted into a Law the Tonnage Bill, and the Act for Quartering the Soldiers, So That our Publick Bussiness of this session is Ended, and we only meet now, on Some reports and Messages we Think Necessary, before the House rises, and an Address to the Crown in hopes of Some releif against These Continual Proprietary Exemptions in our Mony Bills.[5] Tho' the Governor and Assembly are at Varience, He is not less So with his Council, by all Accounts but his Instructions bind him, or at least he apprehends himself So bound by Them, that it is apparent the Council, or Some of them oblige him To put his Hand To evry Thing they Dictate, and make him a meer Cypher in the Administration. I was in hopes To have Settled the Account of the Books before now,[6] but my whole Time has been Taken up by The Publick, to the Detriment of my Private Affairs So Continualy, That I have not been Able To do it. We are entering Upon a Recess, and I will Transmit the Account as I have carefully Taken it in Several Lists, the last Parcel were worthless both from the Contents, and the Miserable Condition which they were Sent To me in. I realy Think they have emptied your house of all your Old Books, for many of them were Primers out of your Own Printing

---

4. See below, pp. 89, 94–5, on proposals for a new governor. Richard Peters and other councilors had sought Denny's removal almost from the day of his inauguration. His predecessor was Robert Hunter Morris.

5. The Assembly approved a message and a report, both long, intemperate denunciations of Denny, before adjourning on May 3. *Votes*, 1757–58, pp. 84–94. There is no record of an address to the Crown at this session other than that implied in the resolves mentioned in note 8 above.

6. This book transaction is somewhat obscure, but apparently Norris received various lots of old books cleared out of BF's printing shop by William Dunlap. Some of the books came from Thomas Osborne, London bookseller, to whom BF paid £21 on Sept. 27, 1758 (see below, p. 169), and £40 on June 1, 1759, for remnants or parcels of old books consigned to Norris. "Account of Expences," pp. 34, 51; *PMHB*, LV (1931), 114, 120.

office, Whitefields Journals,[7] old used Grammars Spelling Books &c. &c., and many of the others Perfectly Rotten of which I have a Number, which you may have the Pleasure of Seeing at your Return—but I hope without the bad Effect I realy believe They had Upon me, for being willing to Take all that Could be used. The Sharpness and Acrid Salts Contracted by Their laying in some damp Place got into my mouth and stomach To such a Degree, that At the beginning of this Session I could not Attend the House, and it was like to have had worse Effects.[8] I now give my opinion of my Late severe attack, and mentiond it To my Friend James Wright[9] Some Time ago, but have not Tho't it Prudent to let any Body Else into the Secret—especially those of my own family who would be willing to persuade me to relinquish my Books, and use more Bodily Exercise, which I think would be no bad Advice, at my Time of life, but I may Take it and keep my own Council, as To the Injury recieved from an Inconsiderate poreing over Indifferent Books, in A very Indifferent, or rather bad, Condition to be handled, at all; I have done with this Subject, and shall only say, that I leave it intirely to your own Judgment to purchase the Couloured or other Copy of Those I have given you the Trouble to get for me, and thank you for the Pamphlets sent me, which I received a few days Since.[1] Your Account of the Interveiw and Conversation with our Proprietarys Agrees well with the Effrontry of their Agents at the last Easton Treaty with the Indians, after Seeing the One and hearing the other, nothing from that Quarter can or ought to Surprise us.[2] Tho' our Releif must be attended with Expence to the Province and the People Must have a Good stock of Patience, That your Patience and Mony may hold out till we can obtain Redress is my hearty Desire, but I Entreat you would let us know the State of both in Due time, for I am of Opinion we Should not Precipitate our Affairs to our Disadvantage, but by evry method endeavour, as we have been necessitated

7. See above, II, 269 n, for journals and other papers of George Whitefield printed by BF.

8. See above, VII, 385–6, for other comments by Norris on his illness.

9. See above, VI, 101 n.

1. BF sent bundles of pamphlets to Norris frequently; see above, VII, 176, for the books Norris asked BF to purchase.

2. See above, VII, 360–2, for BF's conversation, and 264 n, for the Easton treaty.

to begin, finish the Work effectually if it is in our Power, especially as we have a Righteous Cause, and an Agent Throly Acquainted with it equal to it, and willing to defend it.[3] I am your Assured friend

I NORRIS

If I should not have time to write to RC,[4] by this Packet pray my Complements to him and his family, I have Just received a letter via Liverpool from RP[5]—no publick News in it—but an Account of 11 Pensylvania Acts laid before the Privy Council,[6] and the Arrival of J. Hunt, and C. Wilson.[7] J. Hunt was at the Easton Treaty, pray desire them to send their Account with the Province.

Endorsed: B F recd the 7br. 16th[8]

3. Two days after Norris wrote these words, another Philadelphian extolled BF's virtues and talents even more glowingly. James Turner (above, III, 144–5 n), seeking DF's permission to copy a portrait of her husband (the miniature sent to Jane Mecom; see above, VII, frontispiece and p. 365), remarked upon "my grateful sense of the many instances of Mr. Franklin's goodness to myself, his benevolent endeavours in private life, to promote the interest of any person, though no way connected with his own, and to advance by his candid remarks and wise advice every useful art in America; the great obligations which the whole learned world confess themselves to be under to him for his important philosophical discoveries; his honest steady and undaunted zeal in the cause of Liberty; his knowledge of the true interests, and his wise counsels and unwearied labours for the real service of this province—of America in general—of his nation and his king—manifesting the invaluable friend, the eminent philosopher, the true patriot, the loyal subject, the honest, the truly great and good man—the boast of Boston, his native place—the blessing of Pennsylvania—the admiration of the world! ... [his fame] is already sufficiently extended, and will never be forgotten so long as the lightning's *flash* and thunder's *roar* continue to remind mankind who it was that explained to them the nature, and taught them how to guard against the effects of that terrifying meteor." Duane, *Works,* VI, 31–2.

4. Robert Charles.

5. Richard Partridge; letter carried by the ship *Philadelphia,* Capt. Charles Stewart, which arrived on April 29. *Pa. Gaz.,* May 4, 1758.

6. Presented on Jan. 20, 1758, referred by the Committee for Plantation Affairs to the Board of Trade, January 31, and by it to Sir Matthew Lamb on Feb. 10, 1758. *Acts Privy Coun., Col.,* IV, 341, 808; *Board of Trade Journal,* 1754–1758, p. 374. See below, pp. 63–7, for BF's attention to these acts.

7. John Hunt and Christopher Wilson; see above, VII, 376 n. No record of payment to them has been found in either the Assembly's or the commissioners' accounts.

8. In Norris' hand; see below p. 157, for the letter of Sept. 16, 1758, from BF.

To Thomas Leech[9] and Assembly Committee of Correspondence

LS with ALS postscript:[1] Yale University Library

Gentlemen,   London, May 13, 1758

I receiv'd yours of February 6.[2] with the Votes and other Papers relating to the Commitment of Moore and Smith. We immediately took Advice upon them, and engaged Counsel.[3] It was however some Time before we heard any Thing from the other Side. At length we had Notice from the Attorney and Sollicitor General,[4] that Smith's Petition was referr'd to them, and a Day appointed to hear the Affair, which was the 10th. of April. We got the Hearing postpon'd to the 17th.[5] when it came on at seven in the Evening. Paris was the Solicitor for the Petitioner, and he had engag'd two Counsel, vizt. Wilbraham and Forrester,[6] who opened the Case, that this was a Clergyman of the Church of England, who had made the Quakers angry by promoting Measures of Defence, and therefore they bore him Malice, &c. Much of their Pleading was Invective against the Assembly as Quakers, the Rest to show that

9. Thomas Leech (c. 1686–1762), clerk of the Assembly, 1723–27; member of the Assembly, 1730–50, 1756–62; an original trustee of the Academy; vestryman and warden of Christ Church. A short but conveniently timed illness led the Quaker Isaac Norris to resign as speaker and Leech was elected in his place, Jan. 2, 1758, in time to preside over the Assembly "trial" of his fellow Anglican William Smith. See above, VI, 456–7 n; VII, 360 n, 385. He occupied the chair for the rest of this Assembly, Norris being reelected in October 1758.

1. The body of the letter is in WF's hand.

2. Not found; see above, pp. 28–51, for lengthy documents on the petitions of William Smith and William Moore, and below, pp. 88–9, for papers BF sent to Pa. about them. BF's account here of the hearings on Smith's petition should be read in conjunction with those documents.

3. See above, pp. 5, 29.

4. Charles Pratt and Charles Yorke; see above, p. 3 n.

5. A mistake, the first hearing took place on April 20.

6. Randle Wilbraham (c. 1695–1770), D.C.L., Oxon., 1760, admitted to Lincoln's Inn, 1718, and M.P., 1740–68; and Alexander Forrester (c. 1711–1787), admitted to Lincoln's Inn, 1742, and M.P., 1758–74. Joseph Foster, *Alumni Oxonienses, 1500–1714*, IV (London, 1892), 1629; *The Records of the Honorable Society of Lincoln's Inn. Admissions*, I (London, 1896), 424; Gerrit P. Judd, IV, *Members of Parliament, 1734–1832* (New Haven, 1955), pp. 198, 376; *Gent. Mag.*, LVII (1787), 642.

they had erected themselves into a Court of Justice, without any Authority so to do, and that they ap'd the House of Commons tho' they had not the Powers of that House; that by presuming to order the Sheriff to disobey the King's Writ, they were guilty of a high and most flagitious Attempt against the Royal Authority, &c. and ending with praying that the King might be advis'd to issue his Mandate for the Discharge of the Prisoner. They took up the whole Evening with their Harangues; so that Day Se'nnight[7] was appointed for the Hearing of our Council in Reply. We had for Solicitor Joshua Sharpe, and for Council Parrot and De Grey,[8] two able and eminent Men in their Profession, who I took Care should be well instructed; they performed very well, showed that the present Assembly were not Quakers; that the Libel against them was a Breach of Privilege; that all Representative Bodies must have incident to them the Powers exercis'd by the Assembly, that if they had deviated in small Matters from the Practice of the House of Commons it was in favour of the Petitioner, at least it had not been to his Prejudice; that tho' their Clerk had inadvertently used some Expressions which more properly belong'd to Proceedings in Courts of Justice,* the Proceedings of the House had nevertheless been in themselves Parliamentary: That the Order forbidding the Sheriff to obey the Habeas Corpus had not prejudic'd the Petitioner, as the Writ never issu'd; and if it had, and the Prisoner brought before the Chief Justice in obedience to that Writ, he must have been remanded when it appeared he had been committed by the House for Breach of Privilege. That the Powers of the Assembly were granted by our Charters and confirm'd by our Laws; and that the Power in Question was, and always had been, exercis'd by all the Assemblies in America, of which Instances were produc'd, which I had furnish'd. And upon the whole hoping that His Majesty would not be advis'd to infringe

*The Expressions which had given a Handle to the Council for the Petitioner, were such as *Prisoner at the Bar*, *Trial found Guilty*, *Sentence*, &c.

7. A week later, April 27.

8. George Perrot (1710–1780), admitted to the Inner Temple, 1742, appointed King's counsel, 1759, and a baron of the Exchequer, 1763; *DNB*. William de Grey (1719–1781), admitted to the Middle Temple, 1742, highly successful as an advocate for and supporter of Lord North; appointed solicitor general, 1763; attorney general, 1766; knighted the same year; M.P., 1761–1780, and created first Baron Walsingham in 1780. *DNB*.

the Liberties and Privileges of a whole People in their Representative Body, to gratify a single factious Person, who was a common Dealer in Libels and Disturber of the publick Peace, contrary to the Duties of his Profession. The Council for the Petitioner reply'd with much ill Manners and Abuse of the Assembly, but no Argument; only Paris whispering them that the Act of the 4th. of Queen Anne was never presented to the Crown,[9] they insisted much on that, as if our Privileges could have no Existence without it, Penn not having Power to grant them. The Attorney and Sollicitor took the Matter under Consideration in order to form their Report, which as yet they have not made. Several Gentlemen of the Law who were present are of Opinion it must be in favour of the Assembly; but as Mr. Moore, a Member of Parliament[1] interests himself strongly for the Petitioner, his Brother's Case being involv'd with this, it is thought by others they will advise the Discharge of the Prisoner on Account of some alledg'd Irregularity of Procedure, but leave the Question of the Assembly's Authority undetermin'd. However we shall watch their Report, obtain a Copy of it before 'tis presented, and if unfavourable to us, oppose it before the Committee of Council. By Snead, who sails in a few Days, I propose to send Copies of Smith's Petition, and of the Remarks I furnish'd the Solicitor towards his Brief, and to the Council after the first Hearing towards their Reply.[2] Both the Proprietors were present, abetting this Attempt on our Privileges.[3]

9. Neither of the laws of the fourth of Queen Anne cited as evidence of the Assembly's powers and privileges (above, p. 15), was ever formally approved by the Privy Council. This failure is probably the foundation of Paris' charge; however, the acts were considered by the Council, Oct. 24, 1709, but not acted upon within six months, and so, under the terms of the Pa. Charter, they continued in full force and could not be disallowed thereafter. *Statutes at Large, Pa.*, II, 171, 212–21. See below, p. 400 n.

1. Daniel Moore, M.P. for Great Meadow (1754–61), was the brother of William Moore, Smith's fellow petitioner. On the Moore petition, see below, p. 149 n.

2. BF apparently did not send the copies until June 10; see below, p. 88. The *Betty Sally*, Capt. Edward Snead, did not reach Philadelphia until early October, following a voyage of about two months. *Pa. Gaz.*, Oct. 4, 1758. Since he had left London by June 10, he seems to have waited about two months for a westbound convoy.

3. On the same day BF made this report on the hearings, Thomas Penn wrote that in view of the sympathetic attention given Smith's petition, he felt

I have mention'd Mr. Moore's Influence as a Member of Parliament, for that is a Circumstance that gives great Weight here in all Applications to the Crown. Almost every Thing is granted to Members of Parliament, the Ministry being extreamly unwilling to disoblige them lest they should join in some Opposition, and therefore I think it would be Prudence in our Assemblies hereafter to chuse their Agents among the Members of the House of Commons, or at least to secure a Patron among them by all possible Means.

Mr. Penn but very lately laid before the Board of Trade a Number of Acts of Assembly made in 1755, 1756, and 1757. Their Lordships sent for the Agents on Wednesday last,[4] having some

sure "Mr. Franklin will give [the Assembly] strong cautions . . . not to seize either Persons or Papers" in the future. Penn to Richard Peters, May 13, 1758, Penn Papers, Hist. Soc. Pa. Paris described the hearings and what he thought was BF's reaction to them: "We have had two Hearings, before [the King's attorney and solicitor general], at which we, on our part, shewd that, even the Commons of Great Britain, had no such power as the Pensilvania Assembly had assumed, that the Assembly of Pensilvania was not a parliament, nor had any thing near so much power as the House of Commons had, that the Assembly had acted in a most arbitrary and unjust manner, (even if they had had a sufficient Jurisdiction) And that the King, by his Sovereignty, had full power to order Mr. Smith's Release, And had decreed that, and in much stronger Instances, in Pensilvania itself, and in Sundry other provinces, in America. Mr. Franklin had instructed his Counsell, to speak his usual Language, and to put the whole upon this single point, that the Assembly of Pensilvania had as full powers as the House of Commons had; A matter which, I dare to say, they would not have insisted on, nor would it have been endured, for a Moment, had we been heard, before a Superior Jurisdiction. I am in great hopes to obtain the Attorney and Solicitor General's Report, in our favour, after the Holidays. I have reason to believe they are both very clearly of Opinion, that Mr. Smith ought, instantly, to be released, (and whenever he is so, I hope he'l bring his Action against the Sheriff, for false imprisonment) but, these Gentlemen, who are but young in Office, are cautious, how they act, although I have layd before them precedents, of stronger advice given to the Crown, in Sundry Instances, by almost every Attorney and Solicitor General, from the time of the Revolution down to this present time, in Cases from the American Colonys." He added that he was informed that Franklin was "very uneasy at the Assemblys taking this most extravagant step," which "makes a good deal of Noise here." Paris to William Allen, May 13, 1758, Penn Papers, Hist. Soc. Pa. See below, p. 87 n, for Paris' account of delay on the petition by the law officers of the Crown.

4. The Board took up the acts, seventeen in all, on May 2, 1758, together with Sir Matthew Lamb's reports on them, and, in view of some doubts regarding the acts, requested the Proprietors to attend the Board the next

Objections to three of the Acts, vizt. To that in favour of Croghan and Trent, as it might be injurious to the Creditors who had not petition'd.[5] To that for regulating the Provincial Forces, as it contain'd a Clause concerning enlisting of Servants which seem'd to militate against an Act of Parliament.[6] To the Supplementary £100,000 Act,[7] as it made the Bills a legal Tender, contrary to the Spirit of the Act of Parliament, made for the New England Colonies, &c. Paris attended with the Proprietor, in Behalf of Mr. Hockley; a poor Man as he said who was ruin'd by the first Act, since by being Croghan's Partner he was oblig'd to pay his Debts.[8] He endeavour'd to show that the Act was partially made to favour Friends of the Assembly, that it was hurried thro' the House in an unprecedented Manner, lest the other Creditors should have Notice; that it did not appear any Proof had been made that the petitioning pretended Creditors had really any Thing due to them; and a good deal more of the same kind, tending to throw an Odium on the Assembly. In Answer, I alledg'd that the Assembly were quite indifferent and without any Partiality in favour of the Persons to be reliev'd; that if the Bill went quick thro' the House, it was owing to the Shortness of Time, being near the End of a

---

day, when, after "some discourse," the Proprietors and the Assembly agents were summoned to appear on May 10. The Board's journal for that date records simply that Thomas Penn and the agents appeared, that there was "some discourse" on several laws, and that a report to the Privy Council Committee was ordered, which was signed two days later. *Board of Trade Journal,* 1754–1758, pp. 400–5.

5. See above, VI, 295 n, for the Pa. act, passed Dec. 2, 1755, which, upon petition from fifteen of the "principal Creditors," relieved George Croghan and William Trent from the threat of imprisonment for debts for a period of ten years.

6. See above, VI, 437, for the offending clause in the Pa. law enacted April 15, 1756; and VI, 400 n, for the act of Parliament.

7. Of March 23, 1757; see above, VII, 151–2 n, and IV, 495–8, for the paper currency dispute.

8. Richard Hockley (d. 1774), Thomas Penn's protégé, had been in partnership in the Indian trade with Croghan and Trent, 1748–52, but the firm ended in insolvency. He had been a silent partner, however; and when Croghan and Trent mixed their disordered private dealings with those of the partnership, Hockley was caught unwittingly, because the law in favor of Croghan and Trent stated that their partners were not to be similarly favored. Nicholas B. Wainwright, "An Indian Trade Failure. The Story of the Hockley, Trent and Croghan Company, 1748–1752," *PMHB,* LXXII (1948), 343–75.

Session when the Petition was presented; that, however, the Bill had been considered by the Governor and his Council, one of whom was himself a Petitioner,[9] and another a near Relation and Friend of one of the Petitioners, and Amendments propos'd by the Governor which were agreed to. That the Petitioners in general were Merchants of the greatest Note and Reputation in the City, who had in view chiefly that Croghan and Trent by their Acquaintance with the Indian Languages and Interest among them, might if at Liberty be of Service to the Province in Treaties, &c. and therefore were willing to postpone their private Claims for Ten Years; which was also a principal Inducement with the House. That none of the other Creditors had either oppos'd the Bill or complain'd of it since it passed; if they had petitioned against it, I was persuaded the House would either not have gone into it, or would have repeal'd it. That I was surpriz'd after Three Years to hear it said that Mr. Hockley was injur'd by it. That he was on the Spot when it pass'd, and I never heard that he oppos'd it; if he did, it must have been before the Governor and Council;[1] for it could not pass without his Knowledge, as he was a great Officer in the Province, Receiver of the Proprietary Quit Rents, and Keeper of the Great Seal. That Mr. Hockley being a Partner and not a Creditor,[2] must of Course be accountable for Partnership Debts, whether the Bill had pass'd or not, but if he was injur'd I wonder'd he had never before apply'd to their Lordships, and that the

9. Benjamin Shoemaker. Councilor Joseph Turner was an uncle of another petitioner, Buckridge Sims.

1. The Council minutes record that Governor Morris did show the bill to Hockley, who claimed to have had no earlier notice of it and then proposed an unspecified amendment to which both Morris and the Assembly agreed. *Pa. Col. Recs.*, VI, 744. Hockley wrote Thomas Penn substantially the same story, but added that Benjamin Chew had suggested the amendment to protect Hockley, and that before "the last Form [of the bill's enactment] . . . Mr. Lawrence had enough influence" to get it changed again, apparently not to Hockley's liking. Thomas Lawrence 2d and Edward Shippen sought to collect £702 from Hockley on a debt perhaps due from his partnership with Croghan and Trent. Hockley to Penn, Dec. 18, 1755, Penn Papers, Hist. Soc. Pa.; Nicholas B. Wainwright, *George Croghan: Wilderness Diplomat* (Chapel Hill, 1959), p. 87.

2. The improper imposition by Croghan and Trent of their private affairs on the partnership made Hockley their creditor; he later pressed claims against them and eventually collected £2000 from Croghan. *Ibid.*, p. 279.

Proprietor had kept the Bill so long without presenting it. To which he answer'd, that he had indeed receiv'd the Bill soon after it pass'd, but perceiving it to be of an extraordinary Nature, he wrote over to enquire into the Circumstances relating to it,[3] and kept it till he should receive the Information he wanted; and afterwards till he should have some other Bills to present with it. I then desired he would speak out if in Consequence of the Enquiry he made, he had or had not receiv'd Information of any Complaint of the other Creditors against the Bill. To this he made no Answer. Paris intimated that Mr. Hockley might not know of the Passing of the Bill, having come to the Offices I mention'd since that Time;[4] and said the poor Man had been so cruelly oppress'd by the Creditors, who as soon as the Act pass'd, fell upon him, and had oblig'd him to pay above £1500 that he had not Spirit before to apply for a Repeal of the Act, &c. What the Board will do in it I know not, but believe they will advise the Repeal of it, for they seem'd to entertain strong Prejudices against it.[5]

In Answer to the Objection against the other Acts, I said that the Clause relating to Enlisting of Servants, regarded only our own Provincial Troops and not the King's regular Forces; and that it had never been us'd to prevent Enlisting Servants in those Forces, and could be of no Consequence at present, because the Servants were now almost all inlisted, and that by Authority of the Act of Parliament without complying with the Directions of the Act in paying for them; at which their Lordships seem'd much surprized. As to the legal Tender of our Bills, I said they had always been issued under that Sanction; that no body in the Colony, or trading to it, complain'd of it; and that to issue them with a Declaration that they were not a legal Tender, would naturally produce

3. No particular inquiry has been found, but Hockley besought Penn's protection incessantly, and Penn would have liked nothing better than to embarrass the Assembly while helping his protégé.

4. Paris was mistaken; Hockley had been receiver general since 1753.

5. Upon receipt of reports from Board of Trade and its own committee, the Privy Council repealed the act on June 16, 1758. The committee declared "that to suffer the continuance of an Act so unjust and partial in its nature, passed so irregularly, and without observance of any of those Rules which justice requires in all Cases which effect private property would be a precedent of the most dangerous consequence in the Colonies. . . ." *Acts Privy Coun., Col.,* IV, 340–2.

a Depreciation. I believe they will not venture to advise the Repeal of that Act on that Account, and for the others I suppose we need not be much concern'd.[6]

The Board of Trade tho' they have had the Treaty of Easton so long before them, in which Tedyuscung refers his Claims to the Determination of the Crown, have not yet call'd on Mr. Penn, or taken any Step to bring the Matter to a Hearing before the King and Council, nor has Mr. Penn made any Proposals to them of satisfying the Indians.[7] I went Yesterday to Lord Halifax's[8] to press that Matter, and to Lord Granville's. The latter only I found at Home;[9] and he says it should by all means be expedited; it is

6. After some grumbling by the committee about Pennsylvania's legal-tender acts, the Privy Council approved the other measures presented. *Ibid.*, pp. 341–2, 808.

7. Although both Penn and Paris professed an eagerness to settle the charges of land fraud, Paris took refuge as usual in procedural niceties; he observed to William Allen, June 10, 1758, that he did not "see how the Forms of business admit" of any action by the Proprietors. Penn Papers, Hist. Soc. Pa. BF presented a petition on behalf of Teedyuscung (see above, VII, 16 n) to the King in Council, Feb. 2, 1759; see below, pp. 264–76.

8. George Montagu Dunk, 2d Earl of Halifax (1716–1771), was president of the Board of Trade, 1748–61, during part of which period he was able to strengthen substantially the authority and effectiveness of the Board in handling colonial affairs. He was lord lieutenant of Ireland, 1761–63, first lord of the Admiralty, 1762, and a principal secretary of state, 1762–65. He was an uncle of Lord North, in whose ministry he served briefly as lord privy seal, 1770, and secretary of state, 1771. *DNB*; Arthur H. Basye, *The Lords Commissioners of Trade and Plantations, Commonly Known as the Board of Trade, 1748–1782* (New Haven, 1925). On Granville, lord president of the Privy Council, see above, VII, 249 n.

9. Penn tried hard to keep BF from seeing the important ministers (Penn to Peters, May 13, 1758, Penn Papers, Hist. Soc. Pa.) and for this or other reasons BF made little progress at this time in establishing personal contact with them. In 1775, while recounting his negotiations with Pitt (by then Lord Chatham), he recalled that "When I came to England in 1757, you may remember I made several Attempts to be introduc'd to Lord Chatham (at that time first Minister) on Account of my Pensilvania Business, but without Success. He was then too great a Man, or too much occupy'd in Affairs of greater Moment. I was therefore oblig'd to content my self with a kind of non-apparent and un-acknowledg'd Communication thro' Mr. Potter and Mr. Wood his Secretaries, who seem'd to cultivate an Acquaintance with me by their Civilities, and drew from me what Information I could give relative to the American War, with my Sentiments occasionally on Measures that were proposed or advised by others. I afterwards considered Mr. Pitt as an In-

not yet properly before the Council, but ought to be brought there and settled as soon as possible; so I am preparing a Petition for the Purpose to be presented next Week; having no longer any Hopes of a private Accommodation with the Proprietors, who still pretend they cannot answer our Complaints for want of the Attorney and Sollicitor's Opinion, (as you will see by the inclos'd Copies of Letters)[1] and openly abet every Attack upon and Abuse of the Assembly.[2]

Mr. Charles and Mr. Partridge assisted in all these Affairs with great Zeal and Diligence, and were very serviceable on many Accounts; as was also my Son.

I hope this Summer may establish my Health, and enable me to bear, if it be necessary another Winter here in your Service; for how much soever I desire to be at home with my Family and Friends, I would not by Precipitation or Impatience, prejudice your Affairs; but endeavour to reconcile myself to this uncomfortable Absence as long as my Services seem acceptable, and the Assembly shall think my Stay here of Use to my Country.

I am, Gentlemen, with great Esteem and Respect, Your obedient, and faithful humble Servant   B FRANKLIN

---

accessible: I admired him at a distance, and made no more Attempts for a nearer Acquaintance." Account of Negotiations in London, March 22, 1775, Lib. of Cong.

1. Probably copies of an unlocated letter from BF, and a reply by the Penns, April 6, 1758; see above, pp. 3–4.

2. BF's quarrel with the Proprietors had been exacerbated at a recent meeting of the German Society (see above, V, 203–6, and VI, 532–5) attended by BF, James Hamilton, Dr. Samuel Chandler, Thomas Penn, and perhaps others. Following discussion of how the Society's charitable schools for the Germans might be kept out of politics, BF read a letter (not found) he had received from Michael Schlatter, the superintendent of the schools in Pennsylvania, complaining of the Rev. William Smith's "haughtiness." Penn concluded an account of the meeting by observing to Peters: "I was not pleased that [Schlatter] chose Franklin to make these Complaints to, and think he acted a very weak, and not an honest part in doing it, he must know how Franklin stands in the opinion of all the Trustees in Pennsilvania, as well as myself, and should certainly have applied to Mr. Hamilton or you—I find Smith and he different on one material point,—Smith would oblige some of the Germans to learn English, and Mr. Slater would have let them go on in their own way, in this the Society agreed with Mr. Smith, which Mr. Franklin was not so well pleased with." To Richard Peters, May 13, 1758, Penn Papers, Hist. Soc. Pa.

To Thomas Leech, Esqr. Speaker of the Honble. House of Representatives, with the Committee of Correspondence.

PS. May 19. The above is a Copy of mine per Pacquet.[3] The Attorney and Solicitor General have not yet made their Report, and are out of Town for the Holidays, as are all the Ministry even Lord Granville, who seldom leaves the City, so that nothing can be done till their Return. I sent the Copy of Smith's Petition per Pacquet: Nothing new has since occur'd; but perhaps before this Ship sails I may have something farther to add.   B F

Endorsed: Benja. Franklin's Letter May. 13 1758.

From Charles Thomson[4]   ALS: New-York Historical Society

Dear Sir   Philada. May 14th: 1758

This is the third Letter I have lately wrote you. With the two last, one dated the 5th: the other the 16th: of April I sent you a Copy of two Conferences between Teedyuscung and this Government.[5] Whether they are gone in the Man of War in which Lord Loudon went, or whether they are kept to go in the Packet I cant say.[6] We are told here that his Lordship is much blamed with

3. The original of this letter, not found, went on the packet *General Wall*, which sailed from Falmouth on May 20 and reached New York on July 3. This copy probably went on the *James and Mary*, Capt. James Friend, aboard which BF sent several other letters and boxes. She reached the Downs on May 20 to wait for a westbound convoy, but did not arrive in New York until early October. *N.-Y. Mercury*, July 10 and Oct. 9, 1758; *London Chron.*, May 22, 1758; "Account of Expences," p. 15; *PMHB*, LV (1931), 108.

4. See above, VII, 266 n.

5. The letters of April 5 and 16 have not been found. The Indian conferences were probably those of March 15–25 and April 12–13, minutes of which are printed in *Pa. Col. Recs.*, VIII, 32–5, 86–96. A MS copy of the minutes of the second conference, probably the one sent to BF, and a letter from Thomson to WF, March 12–16, 1758, telling of events through the 15th, are at APS.

6. Lord Loudoun, succeeded by Maj. Gen. James Abercromby (see above, VI, 459 n) as commander-in-chief and recalled to England, embarked on board H.M.S. *Hampshire* in New York, April 28, 1758, and reached Portsmouth on May 31. The packet was probably the *Earl of Halifax* which, though scheduled to depart in early May, did not leave New York until June 3. *N.-Y. Mercury*, May 1 and June 5, 1758; *Pa. Gaz.*, May 4, 1758; Gertrude S. Kimball, ed., *Correspondence of William Pitt*, (N.Y., 1906), I, 263.

you for detaining the Packets,[7] and yet the present General seems to be treading in his Steps. I really believe the truth of the Matter is, they do so little, that they have nothing to write but what they are ashamed should be known. The Embargo is continued,[8] the Packets delayed so that I fancy you will have the same Irregular Intelligence this year as last. But these things are out of my Province. These great Men have, no doubt, Reasons for their Conduct. I have without asking your Leave, assumed the Task of informing what I know of Indian Affairs. Immediately upon Teedyuscung's Return to Bethlehem from the last Conference I sent you; he sent Capt. Harrison his Sister's Son and four other Indians up to Fort Allen, there to be joined by a Party of Capt. Ornd's Men[9] to scour the Frontiers and try if they could fall in with any of those who had been doing the Mischief. He like wise sent his two Sons with a Message[1] to the three Indians Nations over the Allegheny and about the Ohio, viz. the Delawares, Shawanese and Quahana-

7. DF might have complained to her husband about British officers' interference with the mails; she had written Lord Loudoun of being "insulted in my own House" by Sir John St. Clair, and that though "Mr. Franklin had at a considerable expence" established twice weekly postal service between Philadelphia and New York, the delay caused by Loudoun's orders utterly disrupted the arrangement. She asked that the posts be "regularly discharged," and wanted "to know how the Charges of Expresses may be defrayed." Ignoring DF's requests, Loudoun said in reply that though he did not intend "to offend anyone much less Mrs. Franklin," he insisted "on the [franking] Priviledges of a Peer," and hoped DF would direct postmasters to cooperate with him lest he be compelled "to disagreable Measures." DF to Loudoun, Jan. 20, 1758, Public Record Office; Loudoun to DF, Jan. 24, 1758, APS.

8. Proclaimed March 18, 1758, and in effect until lifted by Abercromby on May 22. *Pa. Col. Recs.*, VIII, 37–8; 1 *Pa. Arch.*, III, 392.

9. Jacob Arndt; see above, VI, 343.

1. The Indians sent to range the woods and the messengers lingered at Fort Allen, drunk and carousing. Teedyuscung's inflated status as "king" and pacifier of the Indians was soon to end; the planned attack on Fort Duquesne, again extending English power into the Ohio Valley, would undercut his alleged influence in the west by making it appear that he had backed English peace efforts at a time when they were in fact preparing to invade Indian lands. *Pa. Col. Recs.*, VIII, 98; Anthony F. C. Wallace, *King of the Delawares: Teedyuscung 1700–1763* (Phila., 1949), pp. 172–5. The rest of this paragraph is an almost verbatim copy of an "Extract of a Letter dated Tuesday, April 18th, 1758," perhaps written by Thomson, printed as a supplement to the minutes of the April 12–13 conference in *Pa. Col. Recs.*, VIII, 96–7.

quesie, of which last Castaruga is Chief.[2] 1. he delivered four Strings to acquaint those Nations that he had twice received good News from them, and lately heard that they inclined to be at Peace with the English, but now he hears of fresh Murders being committed, which two contraries he cannot reconcile or see thro and therefore desires to know the Reason. 2. he delivered a large black belt with 5 strokes across made of white wampum at which he said. Hark! Men of Allegheny, you sent me word, you had laid hold of the two Ends of the Peace Belt and desired that I and the English should lay hold of the Middle. We have done it and have held and do hold it still fast. Therefore I must desire all your Captains to sit quiet at home and not partake of these Evils or murder the English any more. For indeed we are many Indians that live here amongst them. By such doings you may hurt the Chain of Peace. 3. A White Belt with black strokes across, set with black wampum, at which he said My friends and Brethren Shawanese and Delawares, you live near the others and if any of you live too nigh the French, move a little further from them and take each other by the hand and let all your Chiefs come and I will take them by the hand and go with them to the Governor where they shall hear words with their own Ears for themselves. 4. A White Belt set with black wampum across and he said; Hereby I require and charge all Indians here and there not to acquaint the French anything of Transactions here: But to stop their Ears and Eyes that they may neither hear nor see what passes amongst us.

This Message we are in hopes will have some Effects in drawing off some of the Indians about Fort duQuesne from the French Interest. Soon after the date of my last we received Advice from Shamokin what Indians they were that had been doing the Mischief on this Side of Susquehannah. I send you an Extract of the Letter which was dated April 13th: "On the 9th. Instant Job Chillaway and his Brother left this on a Message in the Service of the Government and on the 12 returned from his hunting Cabbin about 8 Miles up the River. He saw Nepenose a Munsey and four

2. Probably Custaloga (Cashtaloga, etc.), a French-aligned Indian of the Muncey or Unami (or Wanami; perhaps a variation on Quahanaquesie) tribe of Delaware living on Beaver Creek near Venango. Hunter, *Forts,* pp. 24–5; Nicholas B. Wainwright, *George Croghan Wilderness Diplomat* (Chapel Hill, 1959), pp. 125, 153–4.

other Indians returning to the Allegheny. He told Job that there were 35 Indians crossed the River on the Rafts; 25 of which number were then his Company and that they had ten Scalps and five Prisoners, that the three Indians, that fired on the Party was of their Company and during the Skirmish there were 3 Indians on the Mountains on the west Side of the River reconnoitring the Fort. He told Job several Circumstances that confirmed it. He also further informed Job that the French intended to attack the Fort in about 21 Days, that the big Island was the Place of Rendezvous, and that this Party was sent out for Intelligence and that they should be joined by about 2000 Men two thirds of which were Indians."[3] The Reason of this Party's coming so far down seems to have been to revenge a private Injury. The Indians you know are a revengeful People, and what Injury they received you will best know by an Extract of another Letter from your friend S. Wright,[4] 23 April "The Destruction of McCords family on Conewago[5] seems probably to have been a Piece of private Revenge; we heard a good many flying Stories to that Purpose, but two Days ago we saw a sober sensible Man, who lives about 7 Miles from that Place and seems not under any great apprehensions of Dangers. He told us McCord was a morose rash Man; that for some years past great Numbers of Indians had Cabbins about the heads of Swatara and some other Creeks viz. Conewago and Chickus, for the Convenience of hunting; that soon after Braddocks defeat about 100 Delawares and Nanticokes had cabins near McCord's Place; that he went to them and bid them be gone, for he would burn their Cabins: they refused to leave the Place as it was so convenient for hunting, said they would not hurt any thing, nor so much as come near his House. Upon which he set fire to their Cabins and burned them all down with whatever little things were in them; the Indians still unwilling to shift their Quarters, put up other Cabins, these he served in the same Man-

3. This letter appears to have been written from Fort Augusta (at Shamokin). See above, VI, 444, 501 n, for the fort and earlier rumors of attacks on it.

4. Probably Susanna Wright; see above, IV, 210–11 n.

5. The home or "fort" of William McCord near Shippensburg had been destroyed, and twenty-seven persons including McCord's family killed or captured, by Delaware Indians on April 1, 1756. Hunter, *Forts*, p. 561. The belated explanation of the attack (below) suited the belief of Thomson and the Quakers that foul play by whites had caused the Indian attacks.

ner and laid them all in ashes, upon which the whole body of Indians quitted those parts but told him, they would one time or other take a proper Revenge, of which Menace he lived in continual fear, till it was put in Execution. Now these who destroyed McCord and his family passed several Plantations, where they might as easily have perpetrated their barbaritys as there: they lodged one night in a Man's barn as the People found by their tracks &c. in the Morning, but did no damage nor injured any person in that Neighbourhood except that one single family." By some Indians who lately came down from the six Nation Country we learn; that the six Nations with all the tribes in Friendship with them have been collecting and holding Councils for 6 months past, and that the Result of them is, that they will send some of their Chiefs to the French and some to the English and demand to have boundarys fixed betwixt each Nation and themselves, and if the French on their part refuse to comply with this Demand, they will then join their whole Force with the English against them. They do not say it, but doubtless the same is their Resolution in Regard to the English. These Indians also confirm that of the Tweghtwees and other distant Nations entring into the Confederacy.[6]

The securing a Country and fixing Boundaries is undoubtedly the grand Scheme of the Indians and to effect this they will use their utmost Endeavours, nor do I think it is possible to secure their Friendship without agreeing to this. They see themselves cooped up between two powerful Nations who are daily encreasing upon them and squeezing them into a narrower Compass; so that unless they now exert themselves they see plainly they will be quickly crushed, or deprived of their Country. Indeed the late advices are no more than a Confirmation of what Teedyuscung told us in the first Easton Treaty with Gov: Morris. He then expressly declared that whoever would secure and guarantee the Land to the Indians, him they would join; and whoever refused Peace on that Condition, him they would strike. To this they still adhere and I fancy will adhere. And considering the Method how we have hither to dilly dallyed with them and the Measures we at present

6. This news is taken from a letter from James Wright to Governor Denny, May 4, 1758, read in Council on May 8. Some Conestoga Indians from near Lancaster, in Philadelphia for conferences, May 8–12, confirmed the reports. *Pa. Col. Recs.*, VIII, 116–23.

seem to pursue I am afraid we shall lose all Interest with the Indians and that all will be overset that has hitherto been done towards procuring Peace and by that means the Expedition now on foot to the westward[7] be rendered more precarious. At a gloomy Season I sometimes fear a second Monaungahela Action, which may God prevent. By the Minutes I send,[8] you will see the Governor has agreed to the Settlement at Wyoming and to Morrow Mr. Hughes sets out to see it done. He takes with him about fifty Men he has hired but no Soldiers. And unless Pawling goes none of the other Commissioners joined with him will go.[9]

Since the Coming in of the Cherokees, little Regard is paid to the Northern Indians and particularly the Delawares. At first there seemed a general Desire to set the Cherokees upon the six Nations: And no sooner had we advice that a Number of the Delawares, Munseys &c. were coming down from Diahoga to settle at Wioming in Confidence of the Promises made by this Government, than a Party of Cherokees were ordered to Shamokin to range there abouts. A good deal of pains was taken to convince the General[1] and others in Authority, of the ill judged Policy of

7. Gen. John Forbes's planned expedition against Fort Duquesne.

8. Not found, but probably those referred to in *Pa. Col. Recs.* in the following note.

9. On May 2, Teedyuscung had asked for the completion of the Indian houses begun at Wyoming the previous fall; see above, VII, 282 n. Prodded by Forbes's recommendation and urging from the Assembly, Denny agreed, May 4, to dispatch builders led by provincial commissioner John Hughes. Commissioners Edward Shippen, James Galbreath, and Francis Tomlin did not go, but Shippen forwarded supplies and Henry Pawling, an erstwhile opponent of the Quaker party but now apparently friendly to it, did go. *Pa. Col. Recs.*, VIII, 101–2, 110–14; 1 *Pa. Arch.*, III, 394; [Thomas Balch], *Letters and Papers Relating Chiefly to the Provincial History of Pennsylvania* (Phila., 1855), pp. 117–20. See below, p. 103, for the return of the expedition.

1. John Forbes (1707–1759), son of a Scottish laird, studied medicine but left it in 1735 for a successful army career, rising to colonelcy and adjutant general to Lord Loudoun by 1757. He arrived in Philadelphia in mid-April 1758 as brigadier general and commander of the expedition against Fort Duquesne. Though critically and painfully ill, he got an army and supplies together in ten weeks, moved slowly but steadily westward, and on November 25 occupied the fort, abandoned and destroyed by the French. Still ill, he returned to Philadelphia and died the following March. *DAB*; Alfred P. James, ed., *The Writings of General John Forbes* (Menasha, Wis., 1938), pp. ix–xii, 301.

such a Step and the fatal Consequences that must necessarily ensue. Whereupon Orders were sent to stop them so that they got no farther than Carlisle. Since as I just now learn from undoubted Authority they have sent out a party of seventy Cherokees against Venango which is one of the Indian Towns to which Teedyuscung's two Sons are gone with the Message in the beginning of my Letter; so that all the good Effects expected from that Message are, it is to be feared, or will be blasted by this Step; and what other Consequences will ensue must be left to time to manifest. There are two things now apushing with great earnestness one by a Set of Men in this government and the other by some in Virginia and Maryland. And it seems more than probable that for the more effectually executing their several purposes they will both unite and assist each other.What our people aim at is getting Teedyuscung deposed or removed out of the Way. His boldly charging the Proprietors with Fraud and Forgery they cannot stomach and they are in hopes were he removed, they could by some Means or other get that Charge withdrawn or have it represented only as a Calumny of Teedyuscung. In order to accomplish their End every thing is attempted and they are doing all in their Power to raise a Party against him among the Indians. It is a sufficient Recommendation to the most worthless Indian to rail at Teedyuscung. This seems like a drowning Man catching at a Straw.

All the Times that Teedyuscung was in Town this Winter, neither he nor any of the Messengers were once invited to Dinner by the Governor or any of the Party, or treated with any Civility except at the publick Conferences, but no sooner was it known that an Indian was come to Conestogo who spoke ill of Teedyuscung than he was sent for, caressed and entertained, tho a fellow of a bad Character and of no weight or Influence among the Indians. But anything will do to flourish with at home. But the setting aside Teedyuscung is not the worst. The Scheme of a considerable Number in Virginia and Maryland and what our people will be far from discouraging, is the setting the Cherokees against the Delawares and others in Alliance with them or at least preventing a Peace between them. There are many I understand who are concerned in the Ohio Company and many more who have an Itch for Land jobbing. These are eager for settling a Colony on the Ohio but are afraid it cannot be done with the Consent of the Indians, or at least that the Consent of the Northern Tribes cannot be obtained, they therefore think it necessary in order to weaken the Indians and thereby prevent their opposing a Settlement there to set one against another. And tho our people have nothing to do with the Land there yet as they think a new Broil with the Delawares would prevent any farther Inquiry into their past iniquitous Practices, they would be well enough pleased to see it. Besides these two parties there is another to the Northward that greatly thwarts the Measures taken in this Province for obtaining and securing Peace. This is no other than Sir William, who for fear of shewing his own want of Influence is unwilling any other should have an Influence, and rather than any thing should be done with the Indians without passing thro his hands he would chuse it should be undone. He is now about assembling a Number at Onondago. This Meeting of his will I suppose delay that which is expected with this Government. The Chief of the Senekas is to be down at our next Meeting; And a great number of the principal Men from many Tribes intended to come: unless this precipitate Step of sending the Cherokees against Venango prevent them. I realy think that a very imprudent Step in the present Situation of Affairs, but it tends to promote the Scheme before mentioned; And no other purpose can it answer. Had they wanted to employ the Cherokees; or to prevent the Incursions of the Enemies, why was not the lower Shawanese Town attacked, which has done the Virginians more mischief than all the other Indians on the Ohio?[2]

2. This paragraph and the preceding one relate to a double threat to the Quaker-Assembly policy of restoring peace with the Indians by redressing the grievances of the main Pa. tribes, the Delaware and Shawnee, through negotiations with Teedyuscung, recognized as their "king." A formidable band of nearly 900 Cherokee warriors had rendezvoused on the Potomac, eager to join the campaign against Fort Duquesne (so the English hoped)— or to attack their traditional foes, the Delaware and Shawnee (so those Indians feared). If the restless Cherokee assaulted the Pa. Indians, the frontier would be in flames and the Delaware and Shawnee would again be driven into the arms of the French. At the same time, the Iroquois, with the approval of Sir William Johnson, moved to reassert their power over the Pa. tribes and to deflate once and for all Teedyuscung's exaggerated claims of leadership. British military authorities sought Cherokee, Delaware, Shawnee, and Iroquois support for the summer campaigns against Forts Duquesne and Ticonderoga, an aspiration which appeared hopeless until news arrived that the French were unable to supply the Indians with the necessaries of life. The

You see in the Minutes I now send you Teedyuscung offered to go himself or to send one of his Counsellors to the Indians on Ohio to know if they were concerned in the late Mischiefs done in this Province; and recommended it to the Governor to send a White Man with him who might be depended on and who could see and hear with his own Eyes and Ears. But this the Governor did not see fit to comply with. Is it not strange, or can any thing more plainly demonstrate a want of Zeal or a careless Negligence in the present Affair, than this, that during these two Years that we have been treating with these Indians, tho so many Messages have come and gone into the Indian Country no White Man has ever been sent. And exept what we have from the Indians themselves we know no more of the Situation of Affairs with these People, their Numbers or Strength than we did at first. This cannot be for want of Persons who would chearfully undertake the Service. I myself know one who offered to go and who is still ready. One to whom I believe no Objection could be offered as to his Ability or faithfulness in executing the Task, except that he has not been a very warm friend of the Proprietors or their Measures.[3]

Virginia officers with the Cherokee, insistent that the warriors have free reign regardless of the fears and possible alienation of the Pa. tribes, may very well have acted with the interests of the Ohio Company and other land speculators in mind, as Thomson charged, but it is unlikely that responsible Pennsylvanians, even bitterly partisan proprietary leaders, would have connived to inflame their own frontier and to thwart the Forbes expedition. In any case, tension eased when later in May most of the Cherokee, disgusted with the British, returned southward. Essential documents are printed in 1 *Pa. Arch.*, III, 367–71; *Pa. Col. Recs.*, VIII, 56–7; *Johnson Papers*, II, 824–30; James, ed., *Writings of Forbes*, pp. 84–6; and John C. Fitzpatrick, ed., *The Writings of George Washington*, II (Washington, 1931), 198–200, 215–18. *Pa. Jour.*, June 15, 22, and 29, 1758, carried short arguments by advocates of "hard" and "soft" Indian policy, the latter probably written by Thomson.

3. Thomson and Christian Frederick Post went to Wyoming in June to confer with Teedyuscung and other Indians there, but the hazardous journey to interview the hostile Indians around Forts Duquesne and Venango was undertaken by Post alone, July 17–Sept. 22, 1758. His journal is printed as an appendix to Thomson's *An Enquiry into the Causes of the Alienation of the Delaware and Shawanese Indians* ..., which BF had printed in London in 1759. Thomson himself was almost certainly the "one who offered to go"; two months later Denny refused to send him west with Post, obviously for political reasons. *Pa. Col. Recs.*, VIII, 147.

The people thro the Country seem to shew a readiness to enter into the Service of the present Campaign. The Commissions for raising the additional 1400 Men were made out about two Weeks ago and at this Time several Companies are quite full and most that I hear of are pretty near. Mr. Jackson has left the Academy and got a Captain's Commission. He has taken with him for his Lieutenant one White who was a Writing Master in the Academy. To supply Mr. Jackson's Place the Trustees have for the present brought down Mr. Allison from the College to take Care of the Latin School.[4] There is as I am informed no very good understanding between the Masters. The Removal of one Man[5] might be a Blessing to the Institution, to which I sincerely wish well.

Budden and Lyon and one or two other Vessels are arrived from London. Duncan not yet.[6] I hope my friend William is well.

You will no doubt hear by this Packet of Boscawen's Arrival[7] and the forwardness our Expeditions are in. We look here as if we should be ready to set out by the beginning of October next.[8] The highland Regiment at Carolina was to sail from thence the twelfth of this Month for this Place.[9]

I am now got down to the 16th: of the Month, as I have observed little order thro the whole of this Letter it would be in vain to attempt it now. I shall therefore without further ceremony add that I am informed by Mr. Bryan[1] who left York a few Days ago, that the Province of New York have got their Levies compleat, tho with very great Difficulty. Before they could raise their num-

4. Paul Jackson (1731–1767), professor of languages, and John White had received commissions in the Third Pa. Battalion. Francis Alison discharged Jackson's duties until June when John Beveridge was appointed. Montgomery, *Hist. Univ. Pa.*, pp. 292–3, 341; 5 *Pa. Arch.*, I, 185.

5. William Smith.

6. The ship *Myrtilla*, Capt. Richard Budden; the snow *Chippenham*, Capt. Charles Lyon; and the ship *Carolina*, Capt. Robert Duncan, all from London, were listed as having arrived in Philadelphia in *Pa. Gaz.*, May 18, 1758.

7. Adm. Edward Boscawen arrived in Halifax with a fleet, May 9, to take part in Amherst's successful assault on Louisbourg.

8. Sarcasm aimed at Forbes' laborious preparations which had already detained him in Philadelphia over a month.

9. The Highland (63rd) Regiment, commanded by Col. Archibald Montgomery, disembarked in Philadelphia on June 8. James, ed., *Writings of Forbes*, pp. 110, 116.

1. Probably George Bryan; see above, VI, 386–7 n.

ber which was 2683 they were obliged to pass some very severe Laws, which shews their want of Men. By one Law they gave Liberty to all Servants and Apprentices to enlist, enjoining the Masters under Penalty not to prevent them. By another they appointed the Number of Men which each County should raise, and ordered that if they were not raised by a certain Day, what were wanting should be draughted out of the Militia. And if any Person thus draughted refused to go or to furnish an able bodied Man in his Room he was to be shot. New Jersey gave £12 Bounty and as their quota is only 1000, they soon raised them; and both they and the New York Provincials are gone to Albany, where they may be by this Time.

I just now saw one of the Virgils you sent over. It is a most charming Letter and neatly done. It is indeed an Edition worthy of Virgil. I have with Mrs. Franklin's leave taken one. I hope it will be agreeable to you. I shall now read Virgil with double pleasure.[2]

The General disavows the sending the Cherokees against Venango and says it was done contrary to his express Orders.[3]

We wait with Impatience the Event of that Matter.

My Letter is already too long and to appologize for it would be only adding to that Fault. I shall therefore put an End to it by assuring you that I am with the highest Esteem Dear Sir Your affectionate Friend and humble Servant CHAS. THOMSON

P.S. Duncan is arrived. Could I by any Means know in what Light Indian Affairs appear to you it would give me very great Satisfaction.

To Benjamin Franklin Esquire.

Endorsed: Cha Thompson May 14. 58 Indian Affairs[4]

2. The Baskerville edition of Vergil; see above, p. 53 n. Apparently BF later made this copy a present, for a vellum-bound copy inscribed "The Gift of Doctr. B. Franklin to Chas. Thomson," is in Yale Univ. Lib.

3. In early May, Forbes, desperate to keep the impatient Cherokee busy until they could join his march to Fort Duquesne, had encouraged their scouting and scalping parties to the Ohio Valley (where Fort Venango was located), but he had also sought to prevent them from attacking Pa. Indians; the designs were not wholly compatible. James, ed., *Writings of Forbes*, pp. 81–8.

4. In BF's hand.

From Isaac Norris

Letterbook copy: Historical Society of Pennsylvania

Dear Friend Franklin   Philada. May 26. 1758

Comming into town I hear by Accident that a Vessel is to sail for Liverpoole either this Evning or to Morrow,[5] as this is the first Notice I have had of it I can only acknowledge the Receipt of your Letters by Budden and the rest of the Books the Day after by Captain—I forget his Name.[6] Baskerville's Virgil is certainly a curious performance of the Press for which I return my thanks to the Donor. I think I once saw a Sheet as a Specimen of the Work about a Year ago and if it had not been put out of my Mind by other Affairs I would have been a Subscriber. Please to let me know whether Baskerville [has] any other Classical Authors in the same Letter and which of them that I may have an Opportunity of contributing my Mite to encourage such a curious and Ingenious Man as Baskerville who has done an Honor to the English Press.[7] I dare no begin on our Affairs at this Time but as I hear there will be another Vessel in a few Days I propose to write by her but could not let this Vessel sail without a Line of thanks from your Assured Affectionate Friend   I N

Endorsed: Recd ackd. by BF. 7br. 16 1758

From the Earl and Countess of Macclesfield[8]

MS note: American Philosophical Society

St. James's Square [London] May the 28th [1758][9]

Lord and Lady Macclesfield Compliments to Mr. Franklin and Desiers the favour of his Company to Diner on Sattarday Next[1] at 3 o'clocke.

Addressed: Craven Street

5. *Pa. Gaz.*, June 1, 1758, listed the ship *Philadelphia,* Capt. Charles Stewart, as cleared for Liverpool.

6. See above, p. 78 n, for these ship arrivals.

7. See above, pp. 53 n, 79, for Baskerville's Vergil and below, p. 229, for Norris' "Mite" to encourage him.

8. See above, IV, 448 n.

9. So dated because 1758 was the only year of BF's adult life in the May of which he was in England prior to his honorary doctorate at St. Andrews,

From Hugh Roberts[2] ALS: Historical Society of Pennsylvania

My worthy friend Ben: 1st June 1758 Philada

If I was to attempt an Excuse for my delay of writing, 'twould be, that no person can reasonably expect me to undertake a new employ at these advanced years, for I have not held an Epistolary Correspondence with any, nor has it fell in my way to write three Letters of this kind in my Life where Friendship was the only motive; but as I am convinced that no excuse can justly extenuate the omission therefore that thy Censure may fall feather-Edged, I confess my Self guilty of a neglect I could scarce pardon in another, nor hope it from any but one of thy generous Temper.

Thy late indisposition[3] allarm'd thy Friends as the news of thy recovery gave new Life in proportion (when I say thy Friends I mean every Freeman in the province, for thou hast the happiness to have no Enemies but what arise from Envy or a Servile dependence, and they are few among us). And if I have any Interest with thee let me entreat that thou would study to preserve that Health which is of so much Consequence to thy Friends Relatives and Country. I sometimes Visit thy small Family where renewing the rememberance of thy presence and hearing some Account of thy wellfare gives a fresh and Lively Joy.

Thou must not expect much information of our publick Affairs from one who never enquires concerning the fluctuating News of the day, for as I am convinced I can be of little service, find most peace of mind in a disengagement but will just observe that the Confining SMITH AND MOOR,[4] employ'd the time of the trifling Emissaries about the City, but the proceedings of the Assembly therein has had this happy effect to make the Scots Clan[5] who were very public in their Clamours against the Conduct of the House,

---

Feb. 12, 1759. Any one as conscious of BF's scientific achievements as Lord Macclesfield would hardly have addressed him as "Mr." after that date.

1. June 3, 1758.
2. See above, II, 153 n; V, 11 n.
3. See above, VII, 271, 272–4.
4. See above, pp. 28–51.
5. William Smith and other Scots on the College and Academy faculties were active in the proprietary party, as were, increasingly, leaders of the Presbyterians in Pa., many of whom were also Scots. See above, VII, 386 n, for "Presbyterian Politicks."

now communicate their thoughts to each other in whispers under the Thistle.[6] Since they find the Representatives claim some right to their motto Nemo me impune Lacessit.

I believe the general Treaty of Peace with the Indians will have a happy effect unless the proprietary Brokers should be determin'd to risq all to retrieve his Reputation 'tho I believe there's scarce a man of them but what thinks with me that his Avarice has long since eclipsed that Glory, And yet to support their designs they Labour to Spin Threads which are too fine to bear any weight.

The Hospital near the time of closing the Accounts with the Tradesmen was almost out of Credit but now revives with fresh Vigor, partly by the Gentlemen who sign'd the late Bills of Credit continuing their additional Labours for that Service. And I believe but few good and Charitable Institutions have faild of a support where Harmoney remain'd among the Managers and party Views were discouraged:[7] I have been Obliged to apply to thy good Wife to make 150 wafers for the Seal, and when I inform'd her, that I had fix'd them all and that each would produce at least Ten pounds she acknowledged full Satisfaction but to prevent my giving her the trouble again please to send me a Box of good Wafers

6. I.e., *sub rosa*. See below, p. 159, for BF's pleasure at Roberts' clever substitution of the Scots flower for the English in the pun on the Latin phrase when applied to the "Scots Clan."

7. Roberts' accounts as treasurer of the Pa. Hospital, audited by an Assembly committee, March 28, 1759, show £360 received from fees earned by the official signers of bills of credit and contributed to the Hospital. *Votes,* 1758–59, p. 48; above, v, 319–20. On March 28, 1757, the Hospital minutes had recorded that "The President of the Board, Benjamin Franklin, being appointed Provincial Agent to England and is about to sail in a short time, he is requested after his arrival there, to use his interest in Soliciting Donations to the Hospital whenever he may have a Prospect of Success therein." Thomas Hyam and Sylvanus Bevan (above, v, 291 n) were asked to assist BF in the mission. Thomas O. Morton and Frank Woodbury, *The History of the Pennsylvania Hospital, 1751–1895* (Phila., 1895), p. 42. The only evidence that BF was soon active on the Hospital's behalf is a printed program containing "A Short Account of the Westminster Hospital or Publick Infirmary," describing its fund-raising efforts, endorsed by BF "Give this to Mr. Rhoads from BF," now among BF's papers at APS. Samuel Rhoads (above, II, 406 n), as well as Roberts, would have been interested in the "Account," which also included a program of anthems (two by Handel) presented on April 7, 1758, to benefit the Westminster Hospital, perhaps attended by BF.

near 2 Inches diameter, note they should be thickest in the Middle as the Inscription is deepest there.[8]

I cannot give any particular Account of the old junto,[9] for I have not been there since thy departure nor is it agreable to meet where one must be under a continued restraint; for what I might Call reason grounded on freedom, would be deem'd petulance or a turbulant disposition. The major[ity] not attending to anything that deviates from the last prevailing Rules they have had the imaginary happiness to receive from their feeble Dictator who still remains their primum Mo BILLY vel primum MOB ILLE and they doubt every thing but what springs from that Fountain, so that they appear allmost degenerated into a state of SEPTYCISM tho I would not ROBHISON[1] nor the son of any man living to explain my thoughts where nature readily dictates, aided by thy early example. And for this latter freedom I have less occasion to ask pardon when I consider the Gentleman to whom I scribble has sometimes slipt in the same way.[2]

Our old Friend William Parsons has departed this Life and its said has bequeath'd more than his Estate (and Left the remainder for Support of his wife and Children) to raise a Fame after Death

8. Wafer: a thin disk of dried paste to be moistened and placed on a document, then covered with a small piece of paper. When a seal is pressed upon this "sandwich" the design is embossed on the top paper. BF sent the wafers (see below, p. 160), which Roberts wrote in 1760 had been of great service.

9. See above, I, 255–6.

1. Written ROB ISON with H above the space and a caret below: "rob his son."

2. On Roberts' love of punning see above, V, 12. His offerings in this paragraph, while perfectly understandable to BF, are somewhat less than obvious to the present-day reader. Since the only surviving "Billy" of the old Junto, William Coleman, was a particular friend of BF's and doubtless known as such to Roberts, he is an unlikely object of Roberts' shaft. William Allen, the acknowledged dictator of the proprietary party and a prominent Presbyterian as well, is probably the "first mover" (*primum mobile*), who directed the sentiments of the remaining old juntoists, most of whom were in the proprietary interest. The condition of "SEPTYCism" (scepticism) into which they had fallen is certainly an allusion to the timid, servile conduct of former sheriff Septimus Robinson who had failed ignominiously to arrest Israel Pemberton, Jr., in 1750, and, in a memorable affair well known to Roberts and BF, had connived with Allen to permit rioting sailors (MOB ILLE) to interfere with Assembly elections in 1742. *Pa. Col. Recs.*, IV, 391–4; *Votes*, 1742–43, pp. 62–8, 75–114; *An Historical Account of the Origin and Formation of the American Philosophical Society* (Phila., 1914), pp. 58–9; above, II, 363–4.

which he had the unhappiness to fail of gaining in the Conduct of Life.[3]

Stephen Potts[4] is also lately deceasd at a small publick House or rather ORDINARY he kept near the Soldiers Barracks and when I consider the unhappy exit of some of our old Members, I am convinced that a little Speculative knowledge on various Subjects 'tho it tends to give a short elevation and some small esteem with a part of Mankind, does not Essentially Contribute to happiness, or even the prospect of it; but after all our deepest Searches into Matters that do not amount to a certainty nor produce real Tranquility; we must Confess that a Steady Conduct and well establish'd habits of real wisdom and Virtue with an humble dependance on the Omnipotent Ruler of the Universe, fixes our Multiform Ideas on the surest Basis.

I should have been pleas'd to have received any Orders at thy departure or Since, wherin I could ha' done thee or thine any Service, and as I know 'twould have given me a pleasure tis but reasonable to confer it on my Friend when in my power. Therefore I intend per my next to favour thee with orders to purchase a few Books.

I have had less leasure of late than in many years past tho I expected as Age advanced to have enjoy'd more, but find the removal from my own Business is like jumping from Earth into Water that closely surrounds one again. But my present confinement has been cheifly occasion'd by my Son George's Sickness who was suddenly attack'd early this spring with what the Physicians call a Rheumatic Fever but he now makes slow advances towards a Recovery.[5]

Our friend Philip Syng has lately lost his Steady and valuable Son John[6] who by poking into a Kitchen Sink with a stick in one

3. William Parsons (above, I, 359 n) had died on Dec. 17, 1757. He left £200 to help poor scholars at the Academy of Philadelphia, various legacies to relatives, and a perhaps inadequate residue of his estate to his wife. *PMHB*, XXXIII (1909), 343.

4. Another old Junto friend; see above, II, 209 n, for Potts, and below, pp. 159–60, for BF's reply.

5. George Roberts (1737–1821), recovered and visited BF in England in 1760, while studying iron manufacturing there. Hugh Roberts to BF, May 15, 1760; BF to Roberts, Feb. 26, 1761; *PMHB*, XVIII (1894), 35–42.

6. John Syng (1735–1758); see above, I, 209–10 n, for his father.

hand and holding a Candle in the other the Vapour Assending, instantly took Fire and burnt or penetrated him to such a degree as in a few days to deprive him of his Senses and Life.

I wish thy Son Billy every improvement and Advantage in this Embassy that a Close application to Business could possably produce And if I was to undertake the Admonition of Youth, part of my Advice would be to endeavour to Choose those enjoyments that admit of a tranquil reflection and that when they are inclin'd to be merry, be this allways annex'd, to be Merry and Wise. From thy old Friend   H ROBERTS

To Benja Franklin at London

To John Kirke[7]   LS:[8] The James Monroe Memorial Foundation

Sir   London June 3, 1758

Yours of the 1st. of April[9] I received, with a Bill enclos'd for £25 Sterling, which when paid I shall dispose of as the Directors of the Union Library Company desire: But it will fall far short of discharging Mr. Keith's Account,[1] who says the Orders he has receiv'd for Books will amount to about £100, and seem'd surpriz'd that a larger Bill was not sent. I told him the Company might possibly be unacquainted with the Prices of some of the Books, and had not imagined they would come to so much Money; but that if he sent them he need not doubt the Honour of the Directors, in taking care to make him a speedy Remittance; for it was the Custom in our Company, (and I suppos'd it might be the

7. John Kirke, treasurer of and subscriber to the Union Library Company, which, founded in 1747, by 1758 had a room on Chestnut Street, a membership of 100, and a collection of 317 titles. It merged with BF's Library Company of Philadelphia in 1769. *PMHB*, XLII (1918), 196; Carl and Jessica Bridenbaugh, *Rebels and Gentlemen, Philadelphia in the Age of Franklin* (N.Y., 1942), pp. 87–8.

8. In WF's hand, but with one insertion (noted) and the address sheet in BF's.

9. Not found.

1. George Keith, bookseller of No. 2 Talbot Court, Gracechurch Street. *Kent's Directory for the Year 1770* (London, 1770), p. 102; H. R. Plomer et al., *A Dictionary of the Printers and Booksellers . . . from 1726 to 1775* (Oxford, 1932), p. 144.

same in yours) in case a Parcel of Books amounted to more than the Subscription Monies in the Treasurer's Hand would discharge, a Number of the Subscribers advanc'd one or two Years Payment of their Subscriptions and by that Means ballanced the Account immediately with their Correspondent in England. I advis'd him also to call on Mr. Titley[2] who perhaps long before this has re-ceiv'd Mr. Clifford's[3] Order: I never ask'd Mr. Titley for the Money for the Microscopes and other Optical Glasses, because I was not sure they would be acceptable; but I sent them per Budden, and hope they got safe to Hand.[4] Please to present my Respects to the Directors, and assure them of my Readiness to Serve the Company in what I may. I am, Sir, Your very humble Servant   B FRANKLIN
To Mr. Kirke

Addressed: To / Mr Kirke / Treasurer of the Union Library / Company / Philadelphia

[*Memorandum:*][5] In answer to this Letter, remark G. Keith has not writ any Letter, to the Directors. That our Estimate was chiefly taken from the Monthly Review. That we have rece'd the Microscope &c.
Write to Keith

2. A Benjamin Titley was a merchant of Nicholas Lane, Lombard Street. *A Complete Guide to . . . the City of London . . .* (London, 1752), p. 177. The next fifteen words were inserted by BF in the margin.

3. Thomas Clifford (1722–1793), merchant of Philadelphia, probably re-lated to and agent for George Clifford, merchant of Lime Street, London. *PMHB*, v (1881), 26 n; *Kent's Directory*, p. 40.

4. BF's accounts, Aug. 30, 1758–April 14, 1759, contain several entries for books bought of Keith and for optical instruments bought for the Union Library. "Account of Expences," pp. 22, 24, 33; *PMHB*, LV (1931), pp. 107–17. See above, p. 78 n, for Capt. Richard Budden's arrival in Phila-delphia. Because of his frequent and safe passages, his ship was called the "bridge" between London and Philadelphia. *PMHB*, XXXIX (1915), p. 380.

5. On another page, presumably in Kirke's hand. The address sheet con-tains miscellaneous ciphering probably added by him.

To Thomas Leech and Assembly
Committee of Correspondence

LS: Yale University Library; draft (incomplete): American Philosophical Society[6]

Gentlemen,   London June 10, 1758

In mine of May 13.[7] I gave you a particular Account of the Hearing before the Attorney and Sollicitor General, on a Reference of Smith's Petition; they have not yet made their Report, and would now I hear excuse themselves from doing it, as unnecessary, since they have heard that the Prisoners are discharged. But they are still solicited by Mr. Penn and Mr. Moore[8] to report, on an Allegation that they have Letters advising that Warrants are issued for taking them up again. None of my Letters from Pennsylvania mentioning any Thing of this, I have ventured to say I doubt the Truth of it. Whether they will report or not is uncertain: But if they should report against us, I am determined to dispute the Matter again before the Council.[9]

6. Signature and postscript of LS and all of surviving draft are in BF's hand; main text of LS is in WF's hand.

7. See above, pp. 60–8, for the letter, and pp. 28–51, for the hearings on William Smith's petition referred to below.

8. Daniel Moore; see above, p. 62 n.

9. Penn's solicitor, Ferdinand J. Paris, fully explained the delay to William Allen, June 10, 1758: He had applied "Incessantly" to Charles Pratt (the attorney general) and to Charles Yorke (the solicitor general) for their opinions, and found Yorke "most ready, and most clear, in his Opinion, that the Comittment was arbitrary, and illegal, but he doubted how and in what manner the King could order Mr. Smith's Release." Pratt, however, "found many doubts, he was ill, he was busy; he agreed, also, that the King could release the prisoners, but he was very unwilling, that that should be order'd, upon a written Report of *his*. . . . This Gentleman is a very good Lawyer, and has been Suddenly promoted, first, to be of Counsell for the King, and, presently after that, to the Office which he now holds, and to which he was raised, over the Head of the present Solicitor General. Althô such his promotion was very agreeable to *Some*, Yet it was not so to All, of our Grandees, And it is whisperd, that there is an intention, to put another Gentleman into his Offices; And I am the most mistaken, that ever I was in my life, if he does not entertain some Suspition, that this [matter?] was referred to him, as a means to found or assist, his own Removal; And, for that Reason, the various delays, doubts, and shifts, which he has given, were made use of by him." Pratt had also noted that Paris' lists of precedents for royal release of prisoners

I send you herewith a Copy of the Notes I furnish'd our Sollicitor with, when drawing his Brief, a Copy of the Brief itself; a Copy of some Remarks on the Reflections thrown upon the Assembly by the Council at the first Hearing, as being Quakers and therefore against Defence, and as bearing Malice against Smith because a Clergyman of the Church of England, and against Moore because he petition'd for Defence, &c. These I gave to our Council before the 2d. Hearing when they were to speak, and they made a good Use of them. I furnish'd also a Number of Cases from the Votes of Assemblys in the other Colonies, showing that they all claim'd and exercis'd a Power of committing for Breach of Privilege, &c. but of this Paper of Cases, I have no Copy by me.[1]

Mr. Charles at my Request has drawn the State of a Case in order to obtain Opinions of eminent Lawyers how far our present Privileges would be affected in case of a Change of Government by our coming immediately under the Crown. I send you a Copy of this Case, with the Opinion of one Council upon it, who is esteem'd the best acquainted with our American Affairs, and Constitutions, as well as with Government Law in general: He being also thoroughly knowing in the present Views of the leading Members of the Council and Board of Trade, and in their Connections and Characters, has given me withal, as a Friend, some prudential Advice in a separate Sheet distinct from his Law

---

irregularly held (fourteen cases, from 1680 to 1756; Penn Papers, Hist. Soc. Pa.) all had to do with acts of governors and courts; Paris confessed he had been unable to find precedents involving imprisonments *by an Assembly*. (BF's optimism about the case's result depended principally on that fact.) Paris then threatened to appeal the case directly to the Privy Council, whereupon Pratt promised to "consult his Superiors, whether he should, or should not, make a Report." Two days later, Paris and the Pa. agents learned that the prisoners had been released. Richard Partridge then argued that no opinion was required, and Pratt readily concurred. On June 2, however, on learning that Smith had been recommitted (the Assembly had issued a warrant on April 26, but it was not executed), Paris renewed the threat to take the case to the Privy Council. See below, p. 296, for BF's explanation of the delay. Eventually Pratt and Yorke delivered an opinion, approved by the Privy Council, June 26, 1759, condemning the Assembly for its irregular, tyrannical conduct toward Smith. *Acts Privy Coun., Col.,* IV, 375–85; *Pa. Col. Recs.,* VIII, 438–46.

1. All these documents are printed or explained above, pp. 28–51.

Opinion, because the Law Opinion might necessarily appear where he would not care the Advice should be seen. I send you also a Copy of this, and should be glad of your Sentiments upon it.[2] One Thing that he recommends to be done before we push our Points in Parliament, viz. *removing the Prejudices that Art and Accident have spread among the People of this Country* against us, and obtaining for us *the good Opinion of the Bulk of Mankind without Doors;* I hope we have in our Power to do, by Means of a Work now near ready for the Press, calculated to engage the Attention of many Readers, and at the same time efface the bad Impressions receiv'd of us: But it is thought best not to publish it till a little before the next Session of Parliament.[3]

The Proprietors are determin'd to discard their present Governor, as soon as they can find a Successor to their Mind. They have lately offer'd the Government to one Mr. Graves, a Gentleman of the Temple, who has for some time had it under Consideration, and makes a Difficulty of accepting it: The Beginning of the Week it was thought he would accept, but on Thursday Night I was told he had resolved to refuse it. I know not, however, whether he may not yet be prevail'd on. He has the Character of a Man of good Understanding and good Dispositions.[4] The Intention to appoint a new Governor was to have been kept a Secret, that Mr. Denny might not hear of it too soon; but it was not well kept.[5]

Here is a Prospect of a great Harvest, and Corn falls in Price; if the Grain is well got in, 'tis thought His Majesty may be pre-

2. See above, pp. 6–27, for Robert Charles's "State of a Case," and Richard Jackson's legal opinion and private sentiments.

3. The work referred to, *An Historical Review of the Constitution and Government of Pensylvania. . .*, written by Jackson with assistance from the Franklins, appeared in London, May 29, 1759. Thomas Penn was disdainful of the Franklins' propaganda efforts: "I suppose you will hear that Mr. W. Franklin has said many imprudent things, but no body will answer him yet tho' he should write again. Appealing to the Publick will always displease the Administration and for that reason I shall not practice it but let them write what they please." To Richard Peters, May 13, 1758; Penn Papers, Hist. Soc. Pa.

4. The last page of the draft is missing, hence earlier printed versions, all taken from it, end here.

5. See below, pp. 94–5, for the proposed appointment of William Graves as governor of Pennsylvania.

vail'd on to grant Leave by Proclamation for Exporting Corn from the Colonies to Neutral Countries.[6]

I should be glad to know what is intended to be done with Regard to the Loss of the Servants.[7] If we are to make any Application here for Redress, the Lists and Proofs should be sent.

Please to present my best Respects to the Assembly, and believe me to be, with sincerest Regard and Esteem, Gentlemen, Your most obedient humble Servant   B FRANKLIN

To the Speaker, and Committee of Correspondence

June 26. The Notice I had of this Opportunity is too short, to get Copies ready of the Papers mention'd, but I hope Robinson will arrive safe with them.[8]

Endorsed: Benja. Franklin's Letter June 10th. 1758.

To Deborah Franklin   ALS: American Philosophical Society

My dear Child,   London, June 10. 1758
    I was down at Cambridge[9] with Billy when Snead sail'd,[1] so did not write again by him as I intended. His sailing so soon was unexpected to me. I am somewhat out of the Way of Vessels, and Mr. Partridge by Mistake wrote me Snead was not to sail that Week; so being very kindly entertain'd there in the Colleges, we did not hurry so soon home as we might have done. However, this Vessel[2] perhaps may be there about the same time.

I think nobody ever had more faithful Correspondents than I have in Mr. Hughes and you. I have now before me your Letters

6. No such proclamation was issued; see above, VII, 373, and below, p. 106.
7. On indentured servants in the army, see above, VII, 224–8.
8. See n 2, this page, for Captain Robinson.
9. See below, p. 108.
1. See above, p. 62 n.
2. Probably the ship *Speedwell,* Capt. Anthony Robinson, which left London shortly after June 8, 1758 (it was in the Downs by June 15, *London Chron.,* June 15–17), and arrived in Philadelphia on October 6; BF called the ship the *Mercury* writing to DF on Sept. 6, 1758, perhaps having in mind the vessel of that name commanded by Capt. Thomas Robinson, captured by the French but later retaken. *Pa. Jour.,* May 4, 1758.

of Jany. 15, 22, 29, and 31. Feb. 3, 4 and 6. March 12. April 3, 9, 17, and 23, which is the last. I suppose I have near as many from Mr. Hughes.[3] It is impossible for me to get or keep out of your Debts.

I receiv'd the Bill of Exchange you got of Mr. Nelson and it is paid. I received also the Proprietaries Account.[4]

It gives me Concern to receive such frequent Accounts of your being indisposed; but we both of us grow in Years, and must expect our Constitutions, tho' tolerably good in themselves, will by degrees give way to the Infirmities of Age.

I have sent in a Trunk of the Library Company's, some of the best Writing Paper for Letters, and best Quills and Wax,[5] all for Mrs. Moore,[6] which I beg she would accept; having receiv'd such Civilities here from her Sister and Brother Scot, as are not in my Power to return. I shall send some to Sally per next Opportunity.

By Capt. Lutwidge I sent my dear Girl a newest fashion'd white Hat and Cloak, and sundry little things which I hope will get safe to hand. I now send her a pair of Buckles, made of French Paste Stones, which are next in Lustre to Diamonds, they cost 3 Guineas, and are said to be cheap at that Price.[7] I fancy I see more Likeness in her Picture than I did at first, and look at it often with Pleasure, as at least it reminds me of her. Yours is at the Painters, who is to copy it, and do me of the same Size; but as to Family Pieces, it is said they never look well, and are quite out of Fashion; and I find the Limner very unwilling to undertake any thing of the kind. However, when Franky's comes, and that of Sally by young

3. The numerous letters from DF and from John Hughes have not been found. On Hughes, see above, VI, 284 n.

4. See above, VI, 223 n, for John Nelson, and VII, 157–8, for the Proprietors' account, still unpaid.

5. BF paid 13s. for a ream of paper, 7s. for 200 large quills, and 9s. for two lbs. of "superfine" wax on May 20, 1758. "Account of Expences," p. 17; *PMHB*, LV (1931), 111. See also below, pp. 323–4.

6. Hannah Hill Moore (wife of Samuel Preston Moore; see above, IV, 295 n), whose sister, Harriet, had married John Scott, merchant of London, in 1755. Charles P. Keith, *The Provincial Councillors of Pennsylvania* (Phila., 1883), pp. 31, 74.

7. BF paid £9 1s. 6d. for these gifts to Sally. "Account of Expences," pp. 19, 31, 33; *PMHB*, LV (1931), 111, 112.

Hesselius, I shall see what can be done.[8] I wonder how you came by Ben. Lay's Picture.[9]

You are very prudent not to engage in Party Disputes. Women never should meddle with them except in Endeavours to reconcile their Husbands, Brothers and Friends who happen to be of contrary Sides. If your Sex can keep cool, you may be a means of cooling ours the sooner, and restoring more speedily that social Harmony among Fellow Citizens that is so desirable after long and bitter Dissensions.

Cousin Dunlap has wrote me an Account of his Purchasing Chattin's Printing House.[1] I wish it may be advantageous to him without injuring Mr. Hall. I can however do nothing to encourage him as a Printer in Philadelphia, inconsistent with my Pre-Engagements to so faithful a Partner. And I trust you will take Care not to do any thing in that way that may draw Reflections on me; as if I did, underhand, thro' your means, what I would not care to appear in openly. I hope he will keep a good Understanding with Mr. Hall, and am pleas'd to hear he ask'd his Advice and Friendship. But I have thought it right and necessary to forbid the Use of my Letters by Mr. Dunlap without Mr. Hall's Consent. The Post Office, if 'tis agreable to you, may be removed

8. The portrait of Sally BF had brought to England, done by Benjamin West, no longer exists nor does the later one by John Hesselius. The picture of DF, probably also done by Hesselius, is missing too, but a copy of it made by Benjamin Wilson in 1759, is now at APS. The picture of Francis Folger Franklin, probably that painted by Samuel Johnson (?) in 1736–1737, is now owned by Mrs. James Manderson Castle, Jr., of Wilmington, Del. On the proposed "Conversation Piece" of the whole family and individual pictures see above, VII, 278, and Charles C. Sellers, *Benjamin Franklin in Portraiture* (New Haven, 1962), pp. 47, 52–3, 316–17, 409–10.

9. See above, II, 357 n, for Benjamin Lay. William Williams painted Lay's portrait (now lost); Henry Dawkins later engraved it. William Sawitzky, *Antiques*, XXI (1937), 240–2.

1. James Chattin, a Quaker printer, had lived with BF in 1747 and probably was helped by him. Chattin had advertised in *Pa. Gaz.* as late as Feb. 23, 1758, but by June 15 William Dunlap (see above, V, 199 n) sought business at Chattin's former address. Albert C. Myers, ed., *Hannah Logan's Courtship* (Phila., 1904), p. 100; Thomas, *Printing*, II, 55–9; Carl and Jessica Bridenbaugh, *Rebels and Gentlemen, Philadelphia in the Age of Franklin* (N.Y., 1942), p. 83. Franklin's partnership agreement with Hall forbade him to be concerned in any other printing business.

to Mr. Dunlap's House, it being propos'd by our good Friend Mr. Hughes.[2]

I wrote to you lately to speak to Armbruster not to make Use of my Name any more in his News Paper, as I have no particular Concern in it, but as one of the Trustees only.[3]

I have no Prospect of Returning till next Spring, so you will not expect me. But pray remember to make me as happy as you can, by sending some Pippins for my self and Friends, some of your small Hams, and some Cranberries. Billy is of the Middle Temple, and will be call'd to the Bar either this Term or the next.[4] I write this in answer to your particular Enquiry.

I am glad you like the Cloak I sent you. The black Silk was sent by our Friend Mr. Collinson. I never saw it.[5]

Your Answer to Mr. Strahan was just what it should be; I was much pleas'd with it. He fancy'd his Rhetoric and Art would certainly bring you over.[6]

Cousin Burkmaster[7] has suffered much, and had a narrow Escape; I am concern'd for his double Misfortune. A Ship and a Mistress are too much to lose at once; but let him think, if he can,

2. Dunlap announced removal of the post office, formerly at BF's house on Market Street, to his house for the winter season, *Pa. Gaz.*, Dec. 21, 1758. See above, VII, 169 n.

3. See above, V, 421–2 n, for BF's printing venture with Anton Armbrüster. BF's disclaimer was unnecessary; the paper seems to have expired after its Dec. 31, 1757, publication of William Moore's attack on the Pa. Assembly; see above, p. 32 n.

4. See above, IV, 78 n.

5. See above, VII, 278, 381–3, for presents sent DF from London.

6. See above, VII, 295–8, for William Strahan's letter urging DF to come to England. Her reply has not been found but he wrote David Hall, June 10, 1758, that "I have received Mrs. Franklin's Letter; to whom I beg you would give my sincere Respects, and tell her I am sorry she dreads the Sea so much, that she cannot prevail on herself to come to this fine Place, even tho' her Husband is before her. There are many Ladies here that would make no Objection to sailing twice as far after him; but there is [no] overcoming Prejudices of that kind." APS.

7. Capt. George Buckmaster (*c.* 1722–1791), of Newport, R.I., had married Abiah Franklin (C.11.1), daughter of BF's brother James. She died in 1754, and Buckmaster married Rebecca Taylor, June 15, 1758; thus he either rewon his mistress or quickly found another. James N. Arnold, *The Vital Records of Rhode Island*, IV (Providence, 1893), 12; VIII (1896), 401, 414, 459; XII (1901), 41.

that whatever is, is best. You mention sending a Letter of Caty's,[8] but it did not come.

I have order'd two large print Common Prayer Books to be bound on purpose for you and Goodey Smith; and that the largeness of the Print may not make them too bulkey, the Christnings, Matrimonies, and every thing else that you and she have not immediate and constant Occasion for, are to be omitted. So you will both of you be repriev'd from the Use of Spectacles in Church, a little longer.[9]

If the ringing of the Bells[1] frightens you, tie a Piece of Wire from one Bell to the other, and that will conduct the lightning without ringing or snapping, but silently. Tho' I think it best the Bells should be at Liberty to ring, that you may know when the Wire is electrify'd, and, if you are afraid, may keep at a Distance.

I wrote last Winter for Josey Croker to come over hither, and stay a Year, and work in some of the best Shops for Improvement in his Business, and therefore did not send the Tools: But if he is about to be married I would not advise him to come, I shall send the Tools immediately.[2]

You have dispos'd of the Apple Trees very properly. I condole with you on the Loss of your Walnuts.

I see the Governor's Treatment of his Wife makes all the Ladies angry.[3] If 'tis on Account of the bad Example, that will soon be remov'd, for the Proprietors are privately looking out for another, being determin'd to discard him, and the Place goes abegging. One to whom it was offer'd sent a Friend to make some

8. Not found, but Catharine Ray (above, v, 502 n) was probably announcing her forthcoming marriage to William Greene, Jr., Apr. 30, 1758. William G. Roelker, ed., *Benjamin Franklin and Catharine Ray Greene: Their Correspondence, 1755–1790* (Phila., 1949), p. 30.

9. The Prayer Books cost 13s. "Account of Expences," p. 43.

1. See above, v, 69, for BF's description of the electric-bell warning system at his house.

2. Joseph Croker did not go to England, marry, or need tools; he had been killed by Indians, May 27, 1758; see above, VIII, 218 n.

3. Mrs. Denny arrived in Philadelphia in August 1757 bringing the governor's mistress, to be introduced as her "niece." Denny kept his wife a prisoner, spent her money, circulated stories of her "misconduct," and otherwise mistreated her. Philadelphians evidently came to disbelieve the story of the aunt-niece relationship. Nicholas B. Wainwright, "Governor William Denny in Pennsylvania," *PMHB*, LXXXI (1957), 188, 195.

Enquiries of me. The Proprietor told him he had there a City House and a Country House which he might use Rent free; that every thing was so cheap he might live on £500 sterling a Year, keep a genteel Table, a Coach, &c. and his Income would be at least £900. If it fell short of that, the Proprietor would engage to make it up. For the Truth of his being able to live genteely and keep a Coach for £500 a year, the Proprietor refer'd him to Mr. Hamilton, who it seems told him the same Story; but on Enquiring of Mr. Morris,[4] he had quite a different Account, and knew not which to believe. The Gentleman is one Mr. Graves,[5] a Lawyer of the Temple; He hesitated a good while, and I am now told he declines accepting it. I wish that may not be true; for he has the Character of being a very good sort of Man; tho' while the Instructions continue, it matters little who is our Governor. It was to have been kept a Secret from me, that the Proprietors were looking out for a new one, because they would not have Mr. Denny know any thing of it, till the Appointment should be actually made, and the Gentleman ready to embark. So you may make a Secret of it too, if you please, and oblige all your Friends with it.[6]

I need not tell you to assist Godmother[7] in her Difficulties; for I know you will think it as agreable to me, as it is to your own good Disposition.

I could not find the Bit of Thread you mention to have sent me of your own Spinning: perhaps it was too fine to be seen.

4. James Hamilton and Robert Hunter Morris (above, v, 527–8 n), both former governors, were in England at this time. Hamilton returned to Pa. as governor in November 1759.

5. William Graves (b. *c.* 1724), admitted to the Inner Temple, 1747, was also offered appointment as chief justice in North Carolina in 1758, but he seems to have declined all colonial offices; in 1762 he was a master in the High Court of Chancery. *A Calendar of the Inner Temple Records,* v (London, 1936), 87, 148, 164–5; *Gent. Mag.,* XXVIII (1758), 612. Thomas Penn told Richard Peters he had rejected one prospect as too young (34) and inexperienced. July 5, 1758; Penn Papers, Hist. Soc. Pa.

6. News that Denny was to be replaced seems to have been current in Philadelphia at this time; Israel Pemberton wrote, May 31, 1758, that he preferred "the present weak and corrupt man" to James Hamilton, considered a strong-willed man hostile to the Quakers. Pemberton hoped William Shirley (above, III, 319 n) might be the new governor. To John Hunt; Pemberton Papers, Hist. Soc. Pa.

7. Not identified.

I am glad little Frankey[8] begins to talk, it will divert you to have him often with you.

I think I have now gone thro' your Letters, which always give me great Pleasure to receive and read, since I cannot be with you in Person. Distribute my Compliments, Respects, and Love, among my Friends, and believe me ever my dear Debby Your affectionate Husband   B FRANKLIN

Mrs. Stevenson and her Daughter[9] desire me to present their Respects and offer their Service to you and Sally. I think of going into the Country soon, and shall be pretty much out this Summer, in different Parts of England.[1] I depend chiefly on these intended Journeys for the Establishment of my Health.

To Joseph Galloway[2]   ALS: Yale University Library

Copy; Original per Robinson[3]
Dear Sir,   London, June 10. 1758
I have been so full lately in my Letters to the Committee,[4] which you of course must see, that I need not trouble you particularly with a Letter of any Length.

I find myself engag'd in an Affair that will take much more time than I expected. God knows when we shall see it finish'd, and our Constitution settled firmly on the Foundations of Equity and English Liberty: But I am not discourag'd; and only wish my Constituents may have the Patience that I have, and that I find will be absolutely necessary.

I receiv'd your Favour of Feb. 4. at the same time with the Letter from the Committee.[5] It has been represented here, (as you had been told it would be) that the Speaker did not like the Warmth of the House, and pretended Sickness to be out of the Way;[6] but I have heard of no particular Reflections on you: I know that the

8. Francis, son of William Dunlap, born Feb. 8, 1755.
9. See below, p. 122 n, for Mary Stevenson and BF's correspondence with her.
1. See below, pp. 133–46.
2. See above, VII, 29 n.
3. See above, p. 90 n.
4. See above, pp. 60–8, 87–90.
5. Neither letter has been found.
6. See above, VII, 385, and this vol., p. 58, for Norris' "diplomatic illness."

Cannon and Small Arms of the Party consist of great and little Calumnies and Falshoods, and you may depend on my endeavouring to shield your Reputation wherever I find it attack'd, as I rely on the like Defence in the same Case from your Friendship.

The Letters you mention to be wrote per Capt. Gmelin never came to hand.[7]

I hear nothing of Mr. Hamilton's Application for a Charter for Philadelphia from the Crown. It is no easy Matter here to get Alterations made in Constitutions either for the better or the worse. The Ministry don't care for the Trouble of these Things. I believe he will hardly attempt it. The Proprietors, I imagine, will be against the Application, as it will seem to call their Power of granting Charters into Question. However I shall enquire, and if I find any Steps taking towards a new Charter, endeavour to get some Alterations for the better. To be sure there is room enough for Amendment.[8]

Billy tells me he will write, but joins in sincere Respect and Esteem for you, with Dear Sir, Your affectionate Friend and humble Servant   B FRANKLIN

Mr. Galloway

Addressed: To | Joseph Galloway Esq | Philadelphia | Free | B FRANKLIN

Endorsed: B. Franklins Letter June 10. 1758.

To David Hall   LS:[9] American Philosophical Society

Dear Mr. Hall   London June 10, 1758

I have receiv'd yours of February 6 and February 20.[1] containing a full Account of your Trouble in the Affair of Moore and

7. Probably Capt. Gmeling of the British army, suspected of theft; perhaps returned to England to answer charges. Pargellis, *Military Affairs,* pp. 354–5.

8. Galloway had been appointed, March 3, 1757, to a committee "to consider the Charter of the City of Philadelphia, and Conduct of the Mayor and Commonalty of the said City." *Votes,* 1756–57, p. 97. Nothing is known of the committee's deliberations or of Hamilton's application, if indeed he made any.

9. The signature, last paragraph of the postscript, and address are in BF's hand, the rest in WF's.

1. See above, VII, 371, 384, but neither letter, as it survives in Hall's letterbook, contains "a full Account" of his part in the Smith-Moore affair, nor has it been found elsewhere. See above, however, p. 32.

Smith. I make not the least Doubt of your having acted uprightly in consulting the Members, and from mere Motives of Prudence, without the least Influence of Mr. Allen or any others, and in no other Respect can I think you have been to blame; for as to the Use made by the opposite Party of your inadvertently calling yourself the Province Printer, it was what you could not foresee. I hope that little Cloud is quite blown over before this Time, and that you stand clear in the Opinion of the Assembly, whose good Will I would have you by all Means cultivate and preserve.[2]

In two of my late Letters I mention'd my having received in all £600 from you by Bills; but one of them drawn by Wm. Cooper of Boston on Yoldin and Company for £100 endors'd by Mifflin and Saunders to you, is protested, and I sent you the Protest.[3]

Mr. Strahan undertook to send you Bodkins, and to write to you on the Impossibility of getting good Hands to go over on reasonable Terms.[4]

I enclose you one of the last Papers by which you will see our Troops are landed in France. I pray God they may act with Spirit, and return with Honour.[5]

I hope to send you what is necessary for the Almanack by the next Pacquet.[6]

My Love to Couzin Molly and your Children. I am Yours affectionately   B FRANKLIN

2. Hall apologized, Feb. 2, 1758, for his inadvertent use of the title "Provincial Printer," and the Assembly resolved that there never had been such an office, though "occasionally" a printer had been employed to print the journal. *Votes*, 1757–58, pp. 14, 28, 37. The resolve was technically correct, but BF, with his partners, had been the Assembly's sole printer since 1730, and on at least five occasions, in printing governors' proclamations, he called himself "Printer to the Province." He sought, of course, to retain the profitable public business.

3. See above, VII, 236 n, for the protested bill, there listed as drawn on Messrs. Yeldin, White & Smith.

4. See above, p. 6 n, for Hall's need of a new compositor. A bodkin is a printer's tool used for correcting set type; alternatively, a thick needle or straight awl used in bookbinding.

5. News that a large British force had landed near St. Malo, June 2 and 3, appeared in the *London Chron.* June 10, 1758. After destroying many ships and stores in small adjacent ports, the troops re-embarked, June 12, without capturing well-fortified St. Malo. Gipson, *British Empire*, VII, 132–4.

6. This material was not sent and Hall prepared the almanac for 1759 himself. See below, p. 319.

P.S. Miller is here, and has set up in St. Martin's Lane. He talks of removing to Philadelphia however, but not before the War is over. He has got a compleat Printing House English and Dutch.[7]

I have receiv'd no Papers from you lately, and but twice or at 3 Times since my being in England. The Reason I cannot conceive as I make no doubt of your sending them. Put them for the future under Cover to Henry Potts, Esqr. comptroller of the General Post Office.

Billy desires to be kindly remember'd. Mr. Strahan sends you the Paper I intended.[8]

Addressed: To / Mr. Hall / Printer / Philadelphia

Endorsed: B. Franklin June 10. 1758.

To Israel Pemberton

ALS: Princeton University Library

Sir   London, June 10. 1758

I receiv'd your Favour of the 16th. of March[9] but a few days since, which is the first I have had, except a Copy of the Enquiry that came to hand some time ago, but without a Letter, so that I did not know who sent it. I think it well drawn up; and since there seems to be no farther Hopes of accommodating Matters with the Proprietaries, I see no reason to favour them longer by secreting it, and think to put it to Press to morrow.[1]

7. John Henry Miller (1702–1782), German born, BF's former journeyman, returned to Prussia in 1741, worked in Pennsylvania again, 1751–54, then in England, and came back to Philadelphia, 1760, where he established a successful German printing house. *DAB.*

8. William Strahan wrote Hall this same day that "Messrs. Franklin are in good Health," and that BF "still kept his Money by him" since favorable war news had driven stocks too high for profitable investment. Strahan also apologized for not having warned BF about "such an insignificant Fellow as [William] Smith [who had] turned out such an Incendiary." APS.

9. Not found.

1. Charles Thomson's *An Enquiry into the Causes of the Alienation of the Delaware and Shawanese Indians* ... was not published until March 1759, with documents dated as late as Dec. 11, 1758, appended. See above, VII, 376 n, on Quaker unwillingness for BF to see the MS *Enquiry.* Pemberton wrote John Hunt, May 31, 1758, that he feared "your not communicating the Enquiry to Franklin before you did to Granville is not well received [?] by the former nor by his friends here." Hunt replied, July 8, that "B.F. has not

The obtaining Justice for the Indians is, to be sure, a Matter of the utmost Importance, and I make no doubt we shall be able to effect it; tho' the Proprietaries are at present on the high Ropes, make loud Declarations of their Innocence, all the Indian Complaints are father'd on the Malice of the Quakers, and they are determin'd to have Justice done to their Characters, &c.[2]

discovered any dislike or distance" on that account. Both letters in Pemberton Papers, Hist. Soc. Pa.

2. Indian policy in Pa. and in London was in a confused state; see above, pp. 69–80, for events and quarrels in Pa. Following the long series of conferences in January–February 1758 among Quakers, the Penns, and the King's ministers, from which BF had been excluded, the Quakers went ahead with their plans to reform Indian policy. Wealthy Quakers subscribed £800 to underwrite an Indian trade to be conducted, according to a plan approved by Lord Granville, by the "fittest" persons (Quakers) under a special "charter." They also urged their transatlantic brethren to restrain their dispute with the proprietary and royal officials. Though the Pa. Trade Act (see below, p. 399 n) fell "vastly short" of their hopes, London Quakers, urged on by Pemberton, pressed their views. They were so careful to avoid the appearance of working in concert with BF that their leaders, including Dr. Fothergill, apparently did not even see him from May through August 1758. Hunt, Fothergill, and others to the Trustees of the Friendly Association, May 26, 1758; Pemberton to Hunt, May 31, 1758; Hunt to Pemberton, July 8 and Aug. 3, 1758; all in Pemberton Papers, Hist. Soc. Pa.

Other strains were apparent, too. Isaac Norris and many other Pennsylvania Quakers were as much concerned with Assembly rights as BF, and thus shared his differences with Pemberton and the Friendly Association. A dispute among proprietary officials over a report by the governor's Council on Indian grievances held up its entry into the Council minutes for a year, and probably caused Thomas Penn to wonder what information he could depend on. With divided counsels within nearly all parties on both sides of the Atlantic, it is little wonder that Penn told Peters "we should not be too forward to settle" Indian grievances, and that at the same time he badgered the Pa. agents to act on the claims. To Peters, July 5, 1758 (Penn Papers, Hist. Soc. Pa.), and to Richard Partridge, July 6, 1758 (APS). BF delayed a formal petition to the Privy Council on behalf of the Indians until Feb. 2, 1759. With these difficulties in mind, and remembering that prejudices persisted in England against Quaker government in Pa., Fothergill told his American friends: "B. Franklin has not yet been able to make much progress in his affairs. Reason is heard with fear: the fairest representations, are considered as the effects of superior art; and his reputation as a man, a philosopher and a statesman, only seem to render his station more difficult and perplexing. ... You must allow him time, and without repining. He is equally able and sollicitous to serve the province, but his obstructions are next to insurmountable: Great pains had been taken, and very successfully to render him odious

I was afraid before I left Pensilvania that your Friends plac'd too much Confidence in Croghan. He is now known better. The Account you give me of our People's Management at the Treaties with the Indians is shocking! What a Mixture of Madness, Folly and Knavery!³

I shall write you more fully soon, and request a Continuance of your Correspondence. My Respects to the Gentlemen of your Friendly Association,⁴ and believe that I am, with great Esteem, Sir Your most obedient Servant   B FRANKLIN

Mr. Pemberton

Addressed: To / Mr Israel Pemberton / Mercht / Philadelphia

Endorsed: London June 10. 1758 From Benja. Franklin.

From Isaac Norris

Letterbook copy: Historical Society of Pennsylvania

My Worthy Friend   Pensyla. June: 15th: 1758.

The Repeatd Exemptions of the Proprietary Estate, from Bearing a part in our Present Heavy Taxes,⁵ Apears so unreasonable That I Think They Cannot long Support That Cause to the Nation, Who Bear the Burthen of An American War, (where our Proprietarys have so large an Interest to Defend) as well as for the more Immediate Defence of their own Estates. The Taxing the Proprietary Estate in Maryland has appeard so Essential To the Assembly of that Province, That After making Several Concessions on Their Part, They have Adjourn'd, without doing any Thing, Rather Than depart from that Article, upon which, and Several Other[s] the Council, were Inflexible.⁶ I should be pleas'd To know

and his integrity suspected, to those very persons to whom he must first apply. These suspicions can only be worn off by time, and prudence." Fothergill to Pemberton, June 12, 1758, Etting-Pemberton Papers, Hist. Soc. Pa.

3. See above, VII, 265–6 n, for Quaker disappointment in George Croghan.

4. See above, VII, 18 n.

5. See above, p. 55 n, for the most recent tax exempting proprietary estates.

6. Governor Sharpe had written William Pitt, May 18, that the impasse persisted in spite of General Forbes's indignant reproach of the Maryland legislature for its failure "to act as good and Loyall Subjects ought to do."

What Grounds There are for a Suspicion of my own That the Government wink for a While, at the Irregularities of some Proprietors in order to Resume All such American Grants into their hands at a proper Juncture.[7] As for the Offers made by our Proprietarys, They are so evasive, and so well known to Such as have any knowledge of the Situation of their Estate here, That it is useless To say any Thing on That Head; A Great part of our last Grant is already Expended, my Brother[8] Told me lately That the Commissioners had drawn for about £60,000, of it, but Then out of this, the old arrears, are I Suppose paid off, and a considerable advance to each Soldier of the new Levies, To be hereafter Deducted out of their Pay, of which and the State of our Finances, 'Tis probable Some of the Commissioners will write more Correctly,[9] but it is very easy to foresee, that if the War Continues A little longer, as it probably will, we shall be under Difficulties To know where To Raise our future Supplys, for the lower People, of which, we are sensible, the Bulk of the Province is Compos'd, Can bear no more, the Back Counties Supply little or nothing, and Cumberland has Refus'd to Tax Their County alledging They rather Stand in need of Assistance from the other Counties. This is true with regard To a part of its Inhabitants, but many of the Others are in the Way of making Great Estates, and realy do so, and these ought to be Taxed, as well as the Prodigious Tracts of Located Lands, Taken Up in That County by a few persons in Philadelphia, who I persume would be willing to be exemptd under the General Calamity of the County, and these Probably have had Influence enough with the Comissioners and Assessors, To refuse laying any Tax There, for which purpose and to excuse Themselves, They, Just before the Rising of the Assembly wrote a letter To the Treasurer which was laid before the Governor, (who would give no Answer to it) and a copy Deliverd to the Assembly, who order'd the Treasurer to do his Duty, in which the law was his Sole Guide, but I have not since heard Whether they have laid

Gertrude S. Kimball, ed., *Correspondence of William Pitt* (N.Y., 1906), I, 243–4; Alfred P. James, ed., *Writings of General John Forbes* (Menasha, Wis., 1938), p. 80.

7. See below, pp. 157–8, for BF's response to this hint.
8. Charles Norris, trustee of the General Loan Office.
9. See the next document.

the Tax, and as for the Excise, they have evaded That laid by the Collectors Refusing to Qualify, upon which, the House were Obligd to Name another, but this is a favourite County with Some;[1] I Shall leave the Particular Account of J Hugh' late Journey to Wyoming to himself, who will, no doubt, Send a more minute Account,[2] than is in my power to do, he was so kind as to Call at my house on his Return, but did not Chuse to alight from his Horse, and finding him Sufficiently fatugued, and so near the End of his Journy, I could not Think it reasonable To press him. I. Zanes,[3] who also went to Wyoming, Calld upon me a few days ago, and from both These Gentlemen I find they were in Some Danger from a Party of Skulking Indians very near them whilst they were at work upon the Houses They were Building for Teedyuscung and the Delawares, They lost one of their Company in whom I hear your Family has Some Concern,[4] in which I Can Sincerly Joyn; Tho' he was unknown to me. That undertaking was a Publick Spirited Concern with the Gentlemen who performd it. Whilst some proposd by the Governor, Declined the Danger, and still Sleep securly at Home. Our friend Thompson has left his School for a while, Upon A Message To These Delawares At

1. Tax collections in Cumberland Co. had been negligible since the Indian attacks began there in 1755. As collectors were paid a percentage of the taxes they gathered, and forfeited bond if they failed in their duties, it was not easy to keep offices in the county filled. Nathaniel Wilson had resigned as excise collector, and on May 3 the Assembly appointed Benjamin Chambers in his place, but he too seems to have declined. *Votes*, 1757–58, p. 94; 1758–59, p. 106. Norris' insinuations about "Great Estates" in the county probably refer to the many large grants of land Thomas Penn had made to his friends (the Allens, Peterses, Shippens, Armstrongs, and others), and to his own vast holdings there. When the county always elected proprietary men to the Assembly, and evaded Assembly-laid taxes, Norris was quick to suspect illegalities. Chambers' appointment may have arisen from the political differences; after he had resisted efforts by proprietary officials to remove two cannon from his homestead to a safer place, Denny ordered his arrest. Of Chambers' successful defiance of the warrant John Armstrong remarked that "he has the Brass and Malice of the Devil." 1 *Pa. Arch.*, III, 12, 79, 105, 192.

2. No letter from Hughes to BF on the expedition has been found; his letter to the governor is in *Pa. Col. Recs.*, VIII, 134–5. See also above, p. 74 n.

3. Isaac Zane (fl. 1733–1799), had joined Hughes at Wyoming with more workmen and supplies sent by the Friendly Association. His journal is in *PMHB*, XXX (1906), 417–26.

4. Joseph Croker, see above, p. 94 n.

Wyoming, and from Thence, I am Told, To Tiahoga, with a friendly Message from the Cherokee's to the Delawares,[5] and an Invitation from this Goverment to the Seneka's, which is at this time well Judg'd, and has been sent, as I am informd, by the Influence of General Forbes, Who had some warm Difference upon these messages, with the Council, if my Information is True, but as this Comes to me at Second hand, I shall refer to Such other Accounts, as may be More fully depended upon of which no doubt, there will be Authentick Accounts Transmitted by these Vessels.[6] The Situation of Indian Affairs must be very Critical at this Time, as well with Regard to themselves, as the Europeans now heming them in on both Sides, Their friendship is of the utmost Consequence to the french, and They know it, and act accordingly, whilst the Colonies are divided in their Int[erest] and it will be hard to unite Them. The Method proposd by Appointing Superintendants for the Districts to the Northward and Southward is better in Theory Than Practice, Till they can find Sutible Men, under the present management, we can only Judge by the fruit, of which I know of none worth recommending, but I fear the Southern District is worst Supplyd.[7] The Troops are marching off to the frontiers of the Province. I am told the Highlanders[8] (who arrived a few days ago from Carolina) march to day, or to morrow, and that Colonel Washington is at Rays Town[9]—except

5. See above, pp. 74–7, for Charles Thomson's work in Indian affairs, and the alarm caused by the arrival of Cherokee warriors in Pennsylvania. Thomson and his companion, Christian Frederick Post, had negotiated near Fort Allen with Teedyuscung and other Indians, but it was far too dangerous for them to go to Wyoming and Tioga. They presented their report to Denny and Forbes on June 16, 1758. 1 *Pa. Arch.,* III, 412–22.

6. See the next document for a first-hand report of dealings with Forbes.

7. Norris probably objected to the way southern Indian agent Edmund Atkin had sent needy, restless Cherokees to Pa., and Assembly leaders had long objected to Sir William Johnson's conduct of Indian affairs in the Northern District; e.g., he opposed Pa. officials holding conferences with the Seneca as Norris had urged. General Forbes also criticized the agents; James, ed., *Writings of Forbes,* pp. 135–8.

8. See above, p. 78 n.

9. George Washington at this time commanded Virginia troops gathering to join Forbes's expedition at Fort Loudoun, 35 miles east of Raystown. John C. Fitzpatrick, ed., *The Writings of George Washington,* II (Wash., 1931), 204–11.

a very few skulking Parties now and then in Small Numbers, we have not had much Damage on the frontiers, but it is probable, we may hear of more, during the harvest, unless the large Bodies of Soldiers now dispersd Thro' the back Counties should deter the Enemy from the attempt, which is not probable. I can only Recommend Patience and perseverance, To my Good friend in the Honorable Comission the Province has intrusted him with, in an honest Cause. I shall not Distrust his Abilities against All the bad Governors we have ever had, or can have sent for, to oppose him, but in Conversing with These or their Masters, Common prudence Will Direct him to Judge of Sutible evidence upon all publick Transactions to Guard against misrepresentations, for after the Numberless Instances where our publick affairs have been misrepresentd under the Same Influence, it Cannot Surprize us, That the Same Politicks Should be pursue'd to the fountain head, of which I have now before me, in your last letter a Glaring Instance.[1] I know nothing more of the fleet against Lewisburg Than what is in the Pub[lick] Papers, and if I did, the Conveyance from Thence will be so much shorter, that it would be unnecessary to send the Intellegence from hence, but there is great hopes of succeeding in That Enterprize under Such Commanders, and Such a force as the Brittish Nation has There.[2] I hear Just now That Chas. Thompson, with a few Indians are returnd, but can give no Intellegence of the Sucess of his Journy. If these Vessels Stay long enough, Those Concern'd in Town, will Take Care to Transmit the Account. The Store Ships arrived two, or Three days ago, to the Great Satisfaction of the Gentlemen Concern'd in the Westren Expedition.[3] I am your Affectionate friend   I N

Pray make my Complements to Billy to whom I wrote some time ago.

Copy

In margin: Recd & ackd by BF 7br. 16. 1758

1. Norris wrote Richard Partridge on this date that he had letters (not found) from BF "to the latter end of feby. last." Hist. Soc. Pa.

2. Thirteen thousand British and colonial troops under Amherst and Wolfe captured the French fortress at Louisbourg on July 26, 1758. *Pa. Gaz.*, Sept. 7, 1758.

3. The store ships, anxiously awaited by Forbes, had arrived on June 13. James, ed., *Writings of Forbes*, p. 113.

From Joseph Galloway

AL (incomplete): American Philosophical Society

Dear Sir   Philadelphia June 16th. 1758

I received your favour of the 17th. of February.[4] I am Sorry the Affair of Obtaining Permission to export Grain &c. from the Colonies to the European Neutral Ports meets with Difficulties. It certainly can only arise from the Ministrys being so much engaged as not to be able to give that Attention to it as to see clearly the great Benefit that woud accrue to the Trade of the Nation, and the Little prejudice the Enemy must suffer by it. I perceive it will have the Common Effect of all unnecessary and ill judged Prohibitions, That of giving the dishonest Trader an Opportunity of making his Fortune while the honest man alone remains a Sufferer. The Several heads of a remonstrance you Sent me a Copy of are so full and the facts so well stated, One woud conclude the first perusal woud carry conviction with it. I hope you will not desist from the Application untill you receive an Answer; The merchants here are very uneasy and solicitous about it.[5]

Your Patience with the Proprietaries, has been very great. They seem determined to try your Philosophy. Notwithstanding their large Professions of Sincerity, and of Settling things with the Assembly on Reasonable Terms, I cannot help Suspecting them. I heartily wish those that Profess to be the Friends of Pennsylvania[6] may not through a Mistaken Attachment to a form of Government the worst in the world (I mean a Proprietary one) Oblige you to Slip the Opportunity of Releiving us from Slavery and Thraldom. Your Story of the Goose in Chesapeak Bay often recurs to my mind.[7] It gives me high Pleasure to hear Mr. Pitt, that Friend to Liberty and Public Virtue is so firmly establish'd, under his Administration it is to be hoped we shall be heard with

4. See above, VII, 373–7.

5. See above, VII, 373 n, for the restriction on the export of grain from North America. The remonstrance sent by BF has not been found; it was probably on the Flour Act of 1757 (30 Geo. II, c. 9) and originally addressed to Parliament. During 1757–58 British magazines and newspapers printed articles about the act. See also, below, pp. 334–5.

6. Probably Philadelphia or London Quakers.

7. Unfortunately, it does not recur to the editors.

impartiality and redress'd with Justice. His being at the Head of the Ministry is no small Damp to the Spirits of our Proprietary Party.

The Minutes of our last Session is not yet printed tho' almost ready for the Press.[8] In my last I informed you the Assembly had passed a Law granting £100,000 to his Majestys use for raising Cloathing and Paying 2700 Men to Act for conjunction with [the] Kings Troops to the Westward under Brigadier General Forbes.[9] The Men have been since raised with astonishing Expedition. A great Spirit was Shewn in the People to Defend their Country. The new Levies are all marched to Carlisle the Place of Rendevous. Col. Bouquett with a Battalion of the Royal Americans has march'd towards Rays Town; Colonel Armstrong with his Battalion and the Virginia Forces are also in Motion. We have now here 1300 Highlanders commanded by Col. Mongomery—who will move westward in a few Days. In the whole including about 1000 Cherakees now in Virginia the Troops against Fort d'Quesne will be between 6 and 7000 Men.[1] A very good Understanding has Subsisted between the General and the Commissioners, tho he hath requested many things of us we cou'd not grant. Every thing has been done by this Province that cou'd be expected of it. No kind of Obstruction, but every kind of Assistance has been given to the Service, that our Circumstances wou'd permit so that tis hoped Pennsylvania will regain her lost Credit[2]—and the Quaker

8. Proceedings for the session which had ended May 3, 1758, were not advertised in *Pa. Gaz.* until Sept. 14, 1758.

9. See above, pp. 54–5.

1. The forces gathering for Gen. John Forbes's expedition against Fort Duquesne included Pa. provincials under Col. John Armstrong, Va. provincials under Col. George Washington (see the preceding document), a battalion of the Royal American Regiment commanded by Col. Henry Bouquet, and a battalion of the 63rd (Highland) Regiment commanded by Lt. Col. Archibald Montgomery. Most of the Cherokee went home before the expedition left Carlisle. Alfred P. James, ed., *The Writings of General John Forbes* (Menasha, Wis., 1938), pp. 65–128, presents a full record of Forbes's organizing efforts in Philadelphia.

2. Forbes, however, complained bitterly of obstruction. He found Pennsylvanians "the most perverse generation of mortalls that ever breathed Air," and declared "I meet with rubbs and hindrances in every thing depending on the Commissioners, and they meddle, and give orders in the meerest trifles." To Gen. John Stanwix, May 29, 1758; *ibid.*, p. 102.

Government and Quaker influence be Terms buried in Oblivion and no more remembred. The French on the Ohio, tis said are in great want of Provisions and have differd with the two Principal Captains of the Delawares who with the other River Indians on Susquehannah wou'd join the English but through the Influence of the P——y Party they have never been requested so to do, under a foolish expectation [*remainder missing*].[3]

To John Lining[4]

MS not found; reprinted from Benjamin Franklin, *Experiments and Observations on Electricity* (London, 1769), pp. 363–8.[5]

Dear Sir, London, June 17, 1758.

In a former letter[6] I mentioned the experiment for cooling bodies by evaporation, and that I had, by repeatedly wetting the thermometer with common spirits, brought the mercury down five or six degrees. Being lately at Cambridge,[7] and mentioning this in conversation with Dr. Hadley, professor of chemistry there,[8] he proposed repeating the experiments with ether, instead of common spirits, as the ether is much quicker in evaporation. We accord-

3. This sentence probably concluded "that the Six Nations would pacify the Delawares," or words to that effect. Galloway, other Assemblymen, and Quaker leaders persuaded Forbes that proprietary agents had bungled Indian affairs; he wrote Pitt, June 17, that had "those Indians who were friends, been manadged with *common* prudence and honesty," they would have remained in the English interest. Kings Beaver and Shingas, leaders of Delaware war bands which had been ravaging the Pa. frontier, later joined the Forbes expedition when they learned how powerful it was and that the French could no longer supply them with necessaries. *Ibid.,* pp. 118, 251–3. Israel Pemberton had sought since Forbes's first arrival in Philadelphia to persuade him to seek peace with the Indians, especially the Seneca, but proprietary officials thwarted action until June 2 when messages arrived which convinced Forbes "he had been imposed upon." Pemberton to John Hunt, June 18, 1758, Pemberton Papers, Hist. Soc. Pa. He then began negotiations, though his goal was military alliance with the Indians, not peace.

4. On Dr. John Lining, see above v, 521 n.

5. Letter XXXII in 1769 and 1774 editions of *Exper. and Obser.*

6. See above, VII, 184–90, esp. 184–5.

7. See below, pp. 133–4, for BF's report on this trip.

8. John Hadley (1731–1764), F.R.S., 1758, and a physician in London from 1760 until his death. *DNB.*

ingly went to his chamber, where he had both ether and a thermometer. By dipping first the ball of the thermometer into the
ether, it appeared that the ether was precisely of the same temper-
ament with the thermometer, which stood then at 65; for it made
no alteration in the height of the little column of mercury. But
when the thermometer was taken out of the ether, and the ether
with which the ball was wet, began to evaporate, the mercury
sunk several degrees. The wetting was then repeated by a feather
that had been dipped into the ether, when the mercury sunk still
lower. We continued this operation, one of us wetting the ball,
and another of the company blowing on it with the bellows, to
quicken the evaporation, the mercury sinking all the time, till it
came down to 7, which is 25 degrees below the freezing point,
when we left off. Soon after it passed the freezing point, a thin
coat of ice began to cover the ball. Whether this was water
collected and condensed by the coldness of the ball, from the
moisture in the air, or from our breath; or whether the feather,
when dipped into the ether, might not sometimes go through it,
and bring up some of the water that was under it, I am not certain;
perhaps all might contribute. The ice continued increasing till we
ended the experiment, when it appeared near a quarter of an inch
thick all over the ball, with a number of small spicula, pointing
outwards. From this experiment one may see the possibility of
freezing a man to death on a warm summer's day, if he were to
stand in a passage thro' which the wind blew briskly, and to be wet
frequently with ether, a spirit that is more inflammable than
brandy, or common spirits of wine.

It is but within these few years, that the European philosophers
seem to have known this power in nature, of cooling bodies by
evaporation. But in the east they have long been acquainted with
it. A friend tells me, there is a passage in Bernier's travels through
Indostan, written near one hundred years ago,[9] that mentions it
as a practice (in travelling over dry desarts in that hot climate)

9. François Bernier, *Histoire de la dernière révolution des états du Grand
Mogol* (4 vols., Paris, 1670–71); translated and printed in English a year
later. BF may have used the reprinting in *A Collection of Voyages and Travels
... compiled from the curious and valuable Library of the late Earl of Oxford
... Printed by ... Thomas Osborne* (London, 1745), where Bernier's work
is in II, 101–236. The stories BF relates below appear on p. 215 of this volume.

to carry water in flasks wrapt in wet woollen cloths, and hung on the shady side of the camel, or carriage, but in the free air; whereby, as the cloths gradually grow drier, the water contained in the flasks is made cool. They have likewise a kind of earthen pots, unglaz'd, which let the water gradually and slowly ooze through their pores, so as to keep the outside a little wet, notwithstanding the continual evaporation, which gives great coldness to the vessel, and the water contained in it. Even our common sailors seem to have had some notion of this property; for I remember, that being at sea, when I was a youth, I observed one of the sailors, during a calm in the night, often wetting his finger in his mouth, and then holding it up in the air, to discover, as he said, if the air had any motion, and from which side it came; and this he expected to do, by finding one side of his finger grow suddenly cold, and from that side he should look for the next wind; which I then laughed at as a fancy.

May not several phaenomena, hitherto unconsidered, or unaccounted for, be explained by this property? During the hot Sunday at Philadelphia, in June 1750,[1] when the thermometer was up at 100 in the shade, I sat in my chamber without exercise, only reading or writing, with no other cloaths on than a shirt, and a pair of long linen drawers, the windows all open, and a brisk wind blowing through the house, the sweat ran off the backs of my hands, and my shirt was often so wet, as to induce me to call for dry ones to put on; in this situation, one might have expected, that the natural heat of the body 96, added to the heat of the air 100, should jointly have created or produced a much greater degree of heat in the body; but the fact was, that my body never grew so hot as the air that surrounded it, or the inanimate bodies immers'd in the same air. For I remember well, that the desk, when I laid my arm upon it; a chair, when I sat down in it; and a dry shirt out of the drawer, when I put it on, all felt exceeding warm to me, as if they had been warmed before a fire. And I suppose a dead body would have acquired the temperature of the air, though a living one, by continual sweating, and by the evaporation of that sweat, was kept cold. May not this be a reason why our reapers in Pensylvania, working in the open field, in the clear hot

1. See above, IV, 336, for earlier reference to this day, actually Sunday. June 18, 1749.

sunshine common in our harvest-time,* find themselves well able to go through that labour, without being much incommoded by the heat, while they continue to sweat, and while they supply matter for keeping up that sweat, by drinking frequently of a thin evaporable liquor, water mixed with rum; but if the sweat stops, they drop, and sometimes die suddenly, if a sweating is not again brought on by drinking that liquor, or, as some rather chuse in that case, a kind of hot punch, made with water, mixed with honey, and a considerable proportion of vinegar? May there not be in negroes a quicker evaporation of the perspirable matter from their skins and lungs, which, by cooling them more, enables them to bear the sun's heat better than whites do? (if that is a fact, as it is said to be; for the alledg'd necessity of having negroes rather than whites, to work in the West-India fields, is founded upon it) though the colour of their skins would otherwise make them more sensible of the sun's heat, since black cloth heats much sooner, and more, in the sun, than white cloth. I am persuaded, from several instances happening within my knowledge, that they do not bear cold weather so well as the whites; they will perish when exposed to a less degree of it, and are more apt to have their limbs frost-bitten; and may not this be from the same cause? Would not the earth grow much hotter under the summer sun, if a constant evaporation from its surface, greater as the sun shines stronger, did not, by tending to cool it, balance, in some degree, the warmer effects of the sun's rays? Is it not owing to the constant evaporation from the surface of every leaf, that trees, though shone on by the sun, are always, even the leaves themselves, cool to our sense? at least much cooler than they would otherwise be? May it not be owing to this, that fanning ourselves when warm, does really cool us, though the air is itself warm that we drive with the fan upon our faces; for the atmosphere round, and next to our bodies, having imbibed as much of the perspired vapour as it can well contain, receives no more, and the evaporation is therefore check'd and retarded, till we drive away that atmosphere, and bring dryer air in its place, that will receive the vapour, and

*Pensylvania is in about lat. 40, and the sun, of course, about 12 degrees higher, and therefore much hotter than in England. Their harvest is about the end of June, or beginning of July, when the sun is nearly at the highest.

thereby facilitate and increase the evaporation? Certain it is, that mere blowing of air on a dry body does not cool it, as any one may satisfy himself, by blowing with a bellows on the dry ball of a thermometer; the mercury will not fall; if it moves at all, it rather rises, as being warmed by the friction of the air on its surface? To these queries of imagination, I will only add one practical observation; that wherever it is thought proper to give ease, in cases of painful inflammation in the flesh, (as from burnings, or the like) by cooling the part; linen cloths, wet with spirit, and applied to the part inflamed, will produce the coolness required, better than if wet with water, and will continue it longer. For water, though cold when first applied, will soon acquire warmth from the flesh, as it does not evaporate fast enough; but the cloths wet with spirit, will continue cold as long as any spirit is left to keep up the evaporation, the parts warmed escaping as soon as they are warmed, and carrying off the heat with them. I am, Sir, &c.   B.F.

From David Hall   Letterbook copy: American Philosophical Society

Sir   Philadelphia 22d July. 1758.

Inclosed you have the third Copy (in Case of Miscarriages) of a Bill for £149. 12s. 5d., and the first Copy of another Bill for £100. which makes in all sent you £1049. 12s. 5d. One Hundred pound of which protested, for which you have Credit.[2] The Exchange for the £100. to be paid you by Mr. Strahan was 60 as was that of £149. 12s. 5d. and this last 57½.[3] You will please advise me of their coming to hand, and of being paid when you have got the Cash. Yours   D HALL

To Benjamin Franklin Esqr. via Liverpool Capt. Stiles
2d Copy via Liverpool per Capt. Moore Augt. 26th[4]

2. See above, VII, 236, for Hall's remittances to BF, including a record of the protested bill.

3. That is, in the first case £100 sterling equaled £160 Pa. currency and in the second £157 10s.

4. *Pa. Gaz.*, July 27, 1758, reported clearance of the brig *Shirley*, Capt. Henry Styles, and on August 24 clearance of the schooner *Pitt*, Capt. Francis Moore.

From Isaac Norris

Letterbook copy: Historical Society of Pennsylvania

My Dear friend (B F)   Pensyla. July 25th 1758

If I Could hear the News by this Days post, I might Possibly Send Some Intellegence from our Westren Expedition and Ticonderoga, but there is no probability of transmitting from hence, any thing Relateing to Cape Breton, which will not be Sooner known by A direct Conveyance from thence.[5] The Politicians in Town are in full Expectation of Success in that Quarter and with great reason. Our forces under General Forbes Seem to fortify Themselves At particular places to perserve a Communication and Secure A Retreat in Case of Necessity, and by moveing forward Slowly, to Ensure Success against fort DuQuesne, or at least to preserve themselves in the Neigh[bor]hood of the Enemy and guard the frontiers of These Colonies, except against Some Small Indian excursions, which will probably Continue during the War, unless we Can find Some means of Reconcileing them to our Interests. The Delawares of Vinango and About the Ohio, I realy believe are well dispos'd to a peace, and to Come into our alliance Cordialy, if they Are not prevented by our New Politicks,[6] Tho' I am informd that General Forbes has Interested himself in Indian Affairs and been of Good Service. I shall enclose a late Message from the Cherokee's to the Delawares, As I received it from Chas. Thompson about a Month ago, Since which a Deputation from the Ohio has been in Philadelphia, who held a Treaty There in Company with Several Delawares who accompanied them from Wyoming.[7] Chas. Thompson offerd his Service on

5. The three main British military campaigns in North America in 1758 were against Fort Duquesne (captured Nov. 25, 1758), Louisbourg on Cape Breton Island (captured July 26, 1758), and Fort Ticonderoga, where the British under Abercromby were repulsed in a bloody engagement, July 8, 1758. News of the last event was known in Philadelphia (and so by Norris) by July 20, but the full extent of the defeat was not yet realized.

6. See above, pp. 69–79, for Indian affairs. The "New Politicks" may have been efforts by proprietary officials to suppress Indian complaints about land purchases or efforts to have outside Indians (Cherokee or Iroquois) subdue the Delaware and other Pa. tribes.

7. The Cherokee message to the Delaware, June 20, 1758, peaceful but condescending, is in *Pa. Col. Recs.*, VIII, 135–8, and minutes of a conference

their return but was refused by the Governor, by which means, one Post A Moravian went alone.[8] 'Tis Clear, that uncommon endeavors are used to Induce the Indians to forego their Complaints Concerning the Injustice done them on Account of their lands. What Success they may meet with, by perseverance, I cannot Say, but the lands Cannot be easily Eradicated from the Minds Of those Tribes who have been Disposess'd of them, as they Think, Iniquituously. The Committee bro't me your last letter to them A few days Since, but I have forgot the Date.[9] It will give me great Pleasure to hear the Summer Contributes to the Return of a Good State of health, which we all Sincerly wish you, pray remember me kindly to Billy, and I Must Also desire My Complements to My friend R C[1] and his good family, My Brother[2] Shiped him a pipe of Wine by ———. I Suppose the Committee will Send a Copy Of the Votes So far as they are printed. I am your Assured friend   I N
Copy
B Franklin recd ackd 7br 16 1758[3]

From Eyre Whalley[4]   ALS: Historical Society of Pennsylvania

In July 1758 Franklin, accompanied by his son William, took the first of the extended journeys in the British Isles or on the Continent that

in Philadelphia with Teedyuscung and other Indians, July 8–12, 1758, are in 1 *Pa. Arch.*, III, 456–69. After the conference, 30 Quakers and assemblymen protested the "very general and uncertain terms" Governor Denny used in speaking about Indian grievances.

8. See above, p. 77 n.
9. Probably that of May 13, 1758; see above, p. 69 n.
1. Robert Charles.
2. Charles Norris.
3. See below, pp. 157–9.
4. Eyre Whalley (1704–1762), A.B., Oxford, 1726; rector of Ecton Parish, Northamptonshire, 1743–62. BF had visited him at Ecton shortly before this letter. Various Whalleys, kinsmen of Eyre and descendants of Peter Whalley (d. 1656, M.P. and mayor of Northampton), served as rectors in Cuckney (Cogenho, Cooknoe) and Broughton Parishes as well as in Ecton. Marriages between them and the family of Archdeacon John Palmer of Ecton (see below, p. 137 n) strengthened the links between the neighboring parishes. John Bridges, *The History and Antiquities of Northamptonshire* (Oxford, 1791), I,

became his annual practice during his London residence except when his official duties prevented. He thought that these travels contributed greatly to his health, as they certainly did to his pleasure and to the number of his friends and acquaintances. The first of these trips was to the English Midlands, where he visited the ancestral homes of his and Deborah's families, looked up such relatives as he could find there, and pursued the genealogical inquiries he so greatly enjoyed. This document and several of those which follow show the principal results of his quest. For the most complete account of the journey, see his letter to Deborah, September 6, below, pp. 133–46, and for the English Franklins, see above, I, l–liii, lxviii–lxix.

Ecton July 25th. 1758

The Register of Ecton in the County of Northampton begins September 25th. 1559. Those contained in it of the Name of Franklin are taken out in the Words and Spelling of the Register; and are as followeth, viz.

Baptized.

Ap. 8. 1563. Robeart Son of Thomas Franckline.[5]

Augst. 1. 1565. Jane daughter of Thomas Franckline.

May 16. 1567. John Son of Thomas Francklyne.

May 9. 1570. James Son of Thomas Francklyne.

May 26. 1573. Henry[6] Son of Thomas Francklyne.

Feby. 28. 1595. Thomas Son of Henry Francklyne.

Octr. 8. 1598. Thomas[7] Son of Henry Francklin.

Mar. 11. 1637. Thomas Son of Thomas Francklin.

Nov. 7. 1641. Samuel Son of Thomas Francklin.

Mar. 23. 1650. Benjamin Son of Thomas Francklin and Jane his wife.

Octr. 29. 1654. Hannah daughter of Francklin and Jane his wife borne 23d.

Jany. 3. 1657. Josia[8] Son of Thomas Francklin and Jane his wife born Decr. 23.

347–9; II, 85–8; John Cole, *The History and Antiquities of Ecton* (London, 1825), pp. 15–17.

5. Thomas Frankline (or Franklyne; Genealogy, A) was BF's great-great-grandfather.

6. BF's great-grandfather (A.5).

7. BF's grandfather (A.5.2).

8. BF's father (A.5.2.9).

Octr. 24. 1673. Mary[9] daughter of Thomas Francklin Junr. and Helen his wife

Mar. 10. 1677. Elizabeth[1] daughter of Josias Franklin and Anne his wife.

Buried.

Augst. 29. 1565. Jane daughter of Thomas Francklyne.

Augst. 11. 1598. Thomas Son of Henry Francklyne.

Octr. 23. 1631. Henry Francklyn, Husbandman.

Jany. 29. 1646. ——Franklin, an aged Widow.[2]

Octr. 30. 1662. Jane[3] wife of Thomas Franklin Senior.

Feby. 3. 1663. Awdrey wife of Nicolas Franklin.

Septr. 1. 1696. Elizabeth Franklin Widow aged 79.[4]

Jany. 7. 1702. Thomas Franklin,[5] Clerk to the Commissioners for Taxes.

Mar. 16. 1711. Helen Widow of Thomas Franklin.

Married

Feby. 5. 1561. John Walsh and Margerye Francklyne.

Octr. 30. 1595. Henry Francklyne and Agnes Joanes.[6]

Feby. 4. 1630. Nicolas Francklyn and Awdrey Bett.

Sir

I have very carefully examined the Registers of this Parish, and the above are all I can find either Baptized, Married, or Buried, of the Name of Franklin: you, Sir, are descended from Henry the youngest Son of the first Thomas mentioned in the Register. Thomas, the only Surviving Son of which Henry was your Grandfather. Elizabeth daughter of Josias Franklin and Anne his wife,

9. Mary Franklin Fisher (A.5.2.1.1), BF's first cousin.

1. BF's eldest half-sister (C.1), the "Sister Douse" for whose welfare he had shown much concern before sailing to England; see above, VII, 190, 199, 221. She died Aug. 25, 1759.

2. This was Agnes Joanes (or James), widow of Henry Franklin and BF's great-grandmother; for her marriage to Henry see the entry in this record under date of Oct. 30, 1595.

3. BF's grandmother.

4. Second wife of BF's grandfather Thomas. In preparing the Genealogy in Volume I the editors failed to establish her dates from this and other now available information.

5. Josiah's eldest brother and BF's uncle (A.5.2.1).

6. BF's great-grandparents.

The Tower of Ecton Church

The Rectory at Ecton

The Graves of Thomas and Eleanor Franklin

Baptized 10th of Mar. 1677. I Suppose was the eldest Child of your Father. The Omissions from the year 1641. to the year 1650. common in most Registers, were probably owing to the Confusions of those times. If I can give you any farther Light or Satisfaction in anything, you may command me. With Compliments to you and your Son, I am, Sir, your most obedient Servant

EYRE WHALLEY

Addressed: To / Benjn. Franklin Esq / at / Mrs. Stevenson's / in / Craven Street / London

To Mary Fisher[7]   Draft: Historical Society of Pennsylvania

Dear Cousins,   London; July 31. 1758

We have been return'd but a few Days from our Ramble thro' a great Part of England.[8] Your kind Letter for which we thank you, is come to hand,[9] acquainting us of the finding of my Son's Ring. He has since receiv'd it. Your Entertainment of us was very kind and good, and needed no Apology. When we left you, we went to Ecton, where, by the Help of good Mrs. Whalley,[1] we found the Gravestones plac'd for my Uncle Thomas[2] and my Aunt, his Wife, expressing that he died the 6th of January 1702 in the 65th Year of his Age, and she the 14th of March 1711, in the 77th of her Age. Mr. Whalley has been so obliging as to search the Register of Ecton Church for us, and send me an Extract from it, by which I find, that our poor honest Family were Inhabitants of that Village near 200 Years, as early as the Register begins. The first mentioned is in 1563, when Robert Son of Thomas Franklin was baptized. This Thomas Franklin was our Great-Great Grandfather: He had also a Daughter Jane, baptized Augt. 1. 1565, which

7. Mary Franklin Fisher (1673–1758), BF's first cousin (A.5.2.1.1); see below, pp. 134–5, for BF's comments on her and her husband. He was Richard Fisher (d. 1758), scion of a prosperous Wellingborough (Northamptonshire) family which had endowed the town with £40 per year to support a charity school and other civic enterprises. John Bridges, *The History and Antiquities of Northamptonshire* (Oxford, 1791), II, 152–3.

8. See below, pp. 133–46, for the details of BF's trip.

9. Not found.

1. Wife of the Ecton rector; see preceding document.

2. Thomas Franklin (A.5.2.1), Mary Fisher's father; see below, p. 137.

died an Infant; a Son John, May 16. 1567. a Son James May 9. 1570. a Son Henry, May 26. 1573. Whether Robert, John, and James left any Posterity I do not find; but the youngest Son Henry married Agnes Joanes the 30th of October 1595. and had one Son Thomas, which died August 1598, and another son born October 8. the same Year, which he also call'd Thomas; and this youngest Son of Henry was our Grandfather. Josiah my Father was the youngest Son of my Grandfather, and I am the youngest Son of Josiah; so that I am the youngest Son of the youngest Son of the youngest Son of the youngest Son for five Generations; whereby I find that had there originally been any Estate in the Family none could have stood a worse Chance for it.[3] God, however, has blest me, with Augur's Wish, and what is still more, with Augur's Temper,[4] for which double Blessing I desire to be ever thankful.

When we return'd from the North we call'd at Banbury, and there found Robert Page, who had married our Cousin Jane Daughter of John Franklin; she is dead and left no Children. In the Church Yard we found a Gravestone expressing that Thomas Franklin was buried there March 24. 1681/2, and also John the Son of the said Thomas Franklin, who died June 11. 1691.[5] by which I find that our Grandfather remov'd from Ecton in his Old Age to Banbury, perhaps to live with his Son John; His first Wife and Mother of his Children, was named Jane; she was buried at Ecton Oct. 30. 1662. but I think he married again, for I find in the Register a Widow Elizabeth Franklin, who was buried at Ecton Sept. 1. 1696. aged 79. Perhaps she return'd to Ecton after his Death. I do not remember ever to [have] heard of her, but suppose

3. At this point BF first wrote: "but by God's Blessing on my own Industry I find I have far'd as well or done tolerably as most of them. His Name be praised for all his Goodness and Mercies." Then, remembering the Biblical Agur, he crossed out these words and substituted the remainder of this paragraph as printed above.

4. Proverbs 30: 7–9; Agur, son of Jakeh, asks: "Two things have I required of thee; deny me them not before I die: Remove far from me my vanity and lies: give me neither poverty nor riches; feed me with food convenient for me: Lest I be full, and deny thee, and say, Who is the Lord? or lest I be poor, and steal, and take the name of my God in vain."

5. Thomas Franklin (A.5.2) and John Franklin (A.5.2.3), BF's grandfather and uncle.

my Father nam'd his first Child, after her, Elizabeth, who is yet living; she was born Mar. 10. 1677.[6] If this Widow Elizabeth was our Grandfathers second Wife, you probably may remember her.[7]

Endorsed: Letter to Cousin Fisher

Gravestone Inscriptions at Ecton and Banbury

MS: Historical Society of Pennsylvania

When Franklin visited Ecton in Northamptonshire and Banbury in Oxfordshire seeking the remains and records of the English Franklins, he had his son copy the gravestone inscriptions of Uncle Thomas Franklin (A.5.2.1) and his wife Eleanor at Ecton, and of Grandfather Thomas Franklin (A.5.2) and his son John at Banbury. The inscriptions, as transcribed by William and printed below from the manuscript in his hand, vary in some unimportant respects from the capitalization, abbreviations, and use of Arabic numerals on the stones themselves.

Ecton Church Yard

Here lyeth the Body of Thos. Franklin who departed this Life January the 6th. Anno Domini 1702, in the 65th. Year of his Age.

Here lyeth the Body of Eleanor Franklin the Wife of Thos. Franklin who departed this Life the 14th. of March 1711, in the 77th. Year of her Age.[8]

Banbury Church Yard

Here lyes the Body of Thos. Franklin who was buried March 24, 168½. And also the Body of John the Son of the abovesaid Thos. Franklin who was buried June the 11th.⎱ 1691
or 9th ⎰

6. BF's eldest half-sister, Elizabeth Douse (C.1). She died about thirteen months after BF wrote this letter.

7. The draft breaks off here. At the bottom of the page, upside down and crossed out, BF had written: "Mr. Franklin's Compliments to Dr. Heberden and will wait on him tomorrow at Dinner: but Mr. F's Son cannot have that Pleasure being gone into the Country." See below, pp. 281 n, 393, for Dr. William Heberden and BF's first known letter to him. The dinner took place in August or September 1758.

8. The parish register, as copied by Eyre Whalley for Franklin, gives her name as Helen and the date of her death as March 16, not 14.

Genealogical Chart of the Franklin Family

AD: Historical Society of Pennsylvania

Soon after returning to London from his July visit to Ecton and Banbury, Franklin made an elaborate genealogical chart in which he brought together both the information he had gathered on this trip and his own previous knowledge. He drew circles to represent individuals and inserted in each (sometimes spilling over the edges) such vital data as he had accumulated. He then connected the circles by double lines to show the descent of each person, going back as far as the earliest known ancestor, his great-great-grandfather, Thomas Franklyne. The chart is on a sheet of about 15 by 20 inches.[9] On the back is the endorsement "Memor. of the Family." A much reduced facsimile, showing its appearance, is printed facing this page; it is followed by a reproduction in type, necessarily somewhat conventionalized, but arranged as nearly as possible as is the original. The manuscript is torn and several entries are partially or wholly lost; in the printed version the missing data, derived from other sources, have been supplied within brackets.

This chart and the genealogical tables and charts in the first volume of this edition (pp. l–liii, lvi–lxii, lxviii–lxix, lxxii–lxxv) each include some information not contained in the other, and some data in Franklin's chart differ from what the editors provided. Notes appended to the printed chart explain conflicting points and supply additional comment on some details.

From Mary Fisher

ALS: Historical Society of Pennsylvania

Dear Sir!   Wellingborough, Augst. 14th. 1758

We have received your kind Letter[1] as also your Present of most excellent Madeira, which was the more agreeable to us as Mr. Fisher was seized with an Illness soon after you left these Parts, under which his Physicians have obliged him to drink a greater Quantity of generous Wine than before he was used to. His ail is a Mortification in his Foot, which considering his Age will I fear prove fatal: It has hitherto got the better of all Medicines that have been applied, and we have not wanted for the best Physicians and Surgeons this Country affords.[2] Tho' in this Distress we are pleased

9. It is reproduced in full size (but with the blank lower portion of the sheet omitted) in *PMHB*, XXIII (1899), facing p. 4.

1. See above, pp. 117–19.

2. In spite of the improvement mentioned in the postscript to this letter, Richard Fisher died Dec. 12, 1758.

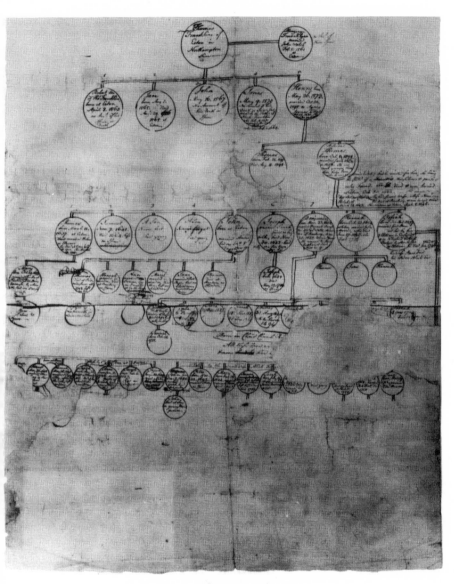

Genealogical Chart of the Franklin Family

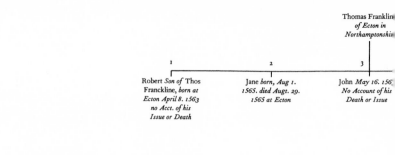

Thomas Franklin
of Ecton in
Northamptonshire

1	2	3
Robert *Son of* Thos Franckline, *born at Ecton April 8. 1563 no Acct. of his Issue or Death*	Jane *born, Aug 1. 1565. died Augt. 29. 1565 at Ecton*	John *May 16. 156_ No Account of his Death or Issue*

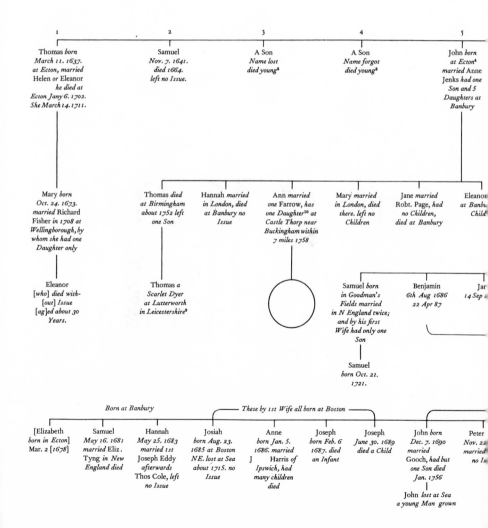

1	2	3	4	5
Thomas *born March 11. 1637. at Ecton, married* Helen *or* Eleanor *he died at Ecton Jany 6. 1702. She March 14.1711.*	Samuel *Nov. 7. 1641. died 1664. left no Issue.*	A Son *Name lost died young[a]*	A Son *Name forgot died young[a]*	John *born at Ecton[4] married* Anne Jenks *had one Son and 5 Daughters at Banbury*

| Mary *born Oct. 24. 1673. married* Richard Fisher *in 1708 at Wellingborough, by whom she had one Daughter only* | Thomas *died at Birmingham about 1752 left one Son* | Hannah *married in London, died at Banbury no Issue* | Ann *married one* Farrow, *has one Daughter[10] at Castle Thorp near Buckingham within 7 miles 1758* | Mary *married in London, died there. left no Children* | Jane *married* Robt. Page, *had no Children, died at Banbury* | Eleanor *at Banbu_ Child* |

| Eleanor *[who] died with-[out] Issue [ag]ed about 30 Years.* | Thomas *a Scarlet Dyer at Lutterworth in Leicestershire[9]* | | | Samuel *born in Goodman's Fields married in N England twice; and by his first Wife had only one Son* | Benjamin *6th Aug 1686 22 Apr 87* | Jar _ *14 Sep _* |

| | | | | Samuel *born Oct. 21. 1721.* | | |

	Born at Banbury			These by 1st Wife all born at Boston				
[Elizabeth *born in Ecton] Mar. 2 [1678]*	Samuel *May 16. 1681 married Eliz. Tyng in New England died*	Hannah *May 25. 1683 married 1st Joseph Eddy afterwards Thos Cole, left no Issue*	Josiah *born Aug. 23. 1685 at Boston NE. lost at Sea about 1715. no Issue*	Anne *born Jan. 5. 1686. married J Harris of Ipswich, had many children died*	Joseph *born Feb. 6 1687. died an Infant*	Joseph *June 30. 1689 died a Child*	John *born Dec. 7. 1690 married Gooch, had but one Son died Jan. 1756*	Peter *Nov. 22 married no Is_*

John *lost at Sea a young Man grown*

Margerye Francklyne[1]
married John Walsh
Feb. 5. 1561 at Ecton
No Acct of their Issue

4

James *May 9. 1570. No*
ount of his Death or Issue,
ght be the Father of Nicholas
lin who Feb. 4. 1630 married
y Bett, who died Feb. 3. 1663.

5

Henry, *born May 26. 1573.*
married Oct. 30. 1595 to Agnes
Joanes, *he died Oct.*
23. 1631. She died
Jan. 29. 1646

Thomas
born Feb. 28. 1595
died Aug. 11. 1598

A *Second* Thomas, *born Oct. 8. 1598.*
married Jane White in 1636. She was
much younger, than him, being born
when he was at Man's Estate; but he
waited for her, she being the Child
of a Neighbour and particular Friend.
She died and was buried at Ecton,
Oct. 30. 1662. He married again but
had no Children by his second Wife,
whose Name was Elizabeth
He died at Banbury, and was buried
there March 24. 168½. His Widow at
Ecton, Sept. 1. 1696.[2]

6

Joseph
married Sarah[5]
. lived in
Suffolk, died
Nov. 30. 1683.
had only one Son
born after his
Death

7

Benjamin *born*
Mar. 23. 1650.
married Hannah
Daughter of
Samll. Wells, Min-
ister of Banbury,
Nov. 23. 1683.
When in Years He
removed to New
England and died
there in 17[6]

8

Hannah *born*
Oct. 23. 1654.
at Ecton, married
John Morris, *who*
died June 17. 1695.
she died 1716[7]

9

Josiah *born*
Dec. 23. 1657.
married first
Anne   *and*
had by her 3 Chil-
dren in England and
4 in N England; 2d
Abiah Foulger, *by*
whom he had 10 Chil-
dren. he died Jan.
1745 or 1746 his Wife
Anne *died   his*
Widow Abiah *died*[8]

Joseph
born 1683
ied May 10. 1704
no Issue

Eleanor   Jane   Hannah

nah   Thomas   Elizabeth   [Mary   [John   Joseph   Josiah
. 1689   *31 Aug 1692*   *27 [Oct] 169[4]*   *23 April 1696*   *8 April 1699]*   *[27 Jan. 1700]*   *3 Jan 1702*
1710   *2 March 1694*   *[date of death*   *27 Aug. 1696]*   *died 10 Jan*
                             (after 1717) torn
                             off and not known]

in Christ Church Par[ish Southwark]
ese died 've[ry young] and none had [Issue]

————— *These by the second Wife Abiah Folger* —————

born   James *born*   Sarah *born*   [Ebenezer   [Thomas   [Benjamin   [Lydia *born*   Jane *born*
. 1694.   *Feb. 4. 1696*   *July 9. 1699.*   *born 1701*   *born 1703]*   *born Jan. 6.*   *Aug. 8.] 1708.*   *Mar. 27 1712.*
d Capt.   *married* Anne   *married* James   *died 1703]*   *died young*   *1706. married]*   *married* Robt   *married* Edwd
Home   *left 4 Children*   Davenport   *a Child being*   Debora Read   Scot. *died*   Mecom
ut 1730   *died 1733*[12]   *died*   *drowned in a*   *at Philad*   *1758*
                                                Tub.   *in 1730*

1. BF probably guessed that Margerye was Thomas' sister; her marriage is recorded among the extracts from the Ecton parish register BF received from the Rev. Eyre Whalley; see above, p. 116.

2. By an oversight the editors failed to include this date in their genealogical table.

3. For discussion of the order of birth of these unnamed twin sons among the children of Thomas and Jane, see above, 1, li n.

4. BF's chart leaves a blank for this date. The editors followed Benjamin Franklin the Elder, who gives it as Feb. 20, 1643, but whether he intended this to be Old Style or New Style is not known. "A short account of the Family of Thomas Franklin of Ecton in Northamptonshire. 21 June 1717." Yale Univ. Lib.

5. Benjamin Franklin the Elder gives her maiden name as Sawyer. "A short account."

6. The editors' table supplied the date of death as March 17, 1727, from *New-England Weekly Journal*, March 27, 1727.

7. The year of death is inserted in pencil. The editors followed Benjamin Franklin the Elder in giving the date of birth as Oct. 29, 1654 (though it now appears that this was probably the date of baptism; see above, p. 115), and the date of death as June 24, 1712. "A short account."

8. Anne's maiden name, Child, is found in Benjamin Franklin the Elder's "A short account"; her date of death, July 9, 1689, is entered on an undated MS in BF's hand listing the birthdays of Josiah Franklin's children (below, p. 454); Abiah's death, May 8, 1752, is recorded in Jane Mecom's "Book of Ages," Van Doren, *Franklin-Mecom*, p. 101.

9. BF fails to show here Thomas' daughter Sarah (A.5.2.3.1.1.1), in 1758 a child of about five, who resided with BF in London at various times during 1766–70.

10. The daughter, whom BF showed here only as an empty circle, was named Hannah; she married Thomas Walker and in 1758 had two sons, John and Henry.

11. Benjamin Franklin the Elder recorded the birth of his daughter Jane as Feb. 14, 1687; "A short account."

12. James Franklin died on his thirty-eighth birthday, Feb. 4, 1735. See George P. Winship, "Newport Newspapers in the Eighteenth Century," Newport Hist. Soc., *Bulletin*, No. 14 (Oct. 1914), p. 5; Howard M. Chapin, "Ann Franklin of Newport, Printer, 1736–1763," *Bibliographical Essays A Tribute to Wilberforce Eames* ([Cambridge, Mass.], 1924), p. 339.

to hear that your Ramble (as you call it) has been agreeable to your Self and Son; and particularly that Mr. and Mrs. Whaley gave you so kind a Reception at Ecton. You have taken more Care to preserve the Memory of our Family, than any other Person that ever belonged to it, tho' the Youngest Son of five Generations. And tho' I believe it never made any great Figure in this County, Yet it did what was much better, it acted that Part well in which Providence had placed it, and for 200 Years all the Descendants of it have lived with Credit, and are to this Day without any Blot in their Escutcheon, which is more than some of the best Families i: e. the Richest and highest in Title can pretend to. I am the last of my Fathers House remaining in this Country, and you must be sensible from my Age and Infirmities, that I cannot hope to continue long in the Land of the Living.[3] However I must degenerate from my Family not to wish it well; and therefore you cannot think but that I was well pleased to see so fair Hopes of its Continuance in the Younger Branches, in any Part of the World, and on that Account most sincerely wish you and Yours all Health Happiness and Prosperity, and am Dear Sir Your most Affectionate Kinswoman   MARY FISHER.

Turn over

P.S. This Letter has been wrote above a Month but was neglected to be sent to You on the Account of Mr. Fisher's Illness, who has been so bad that we expected nothing but Death for some Weeks; tho' now have the Pleasure to inform You that his Mortification is entirely stopp'd, and on that Account have Hopes of his Recovery. Your Last is come to Hand[4] and I hope you'll Excuse the Delay in Answering your Former for the Reason mentioned before. Mr. Holme our Minister[5] begs to return his Compliments to you and Son.

Sepr. 18th. 1758.

Addressed: To / Mr. Benjamin Franklin / at Mrs. Stevenson's / in Craven Street. Strand. / London

3. Mary Fisher died on Christmas Day, 1758, thirteen days after her husband. She was 85 years of age.

4. Not found.

5. Thomas Holme, vicar of Wellingborough for eighteen years, master of the school there, and clerk of Lancashire. *Victoria History of Northampton,* II, 268; John and J. A. Venn, *Alumni Cantabrigienses,* Part I (Cambridge,

To Mary Stevenson[6]

ALS: American Philosophical Society

Dear Polley,   Tunbridge Wells,[7] Augt. 20. 1758

My Son I know intended writing to you this Morning, so as to send per this Days Post; but sundry unexpected Hindrances have

1922–27), II, 399, *sub* "Thomas Holme," his son. See Holme's letter of Jan. 9, 1759 (below, pp. 224–5) regarding the deaths of the Fishers and the settlement of her estate.

6. Mary (Polly) Stevenson (1739–1795), daughter of BF's landlady, Mrs. Margaret Stevenson (see above, VII, 273–4 n), was one of the charming, intelligent girls to whom BF gave the long and affectionate friendship for which he had such a talent (Catharine Ray and Georgiana Shipley were others). Polly's almost filial devotion to him was a major influence in her life. She had acquired an unusually good education and by the time BF arrived at Craven Street in 1757, she was spending most of her time as companion to an elderly aunt, a Mrs. Tickell, in Wanstead, a village about ten miles from London, apparently with the understanding that the aunt would leave her a comfortable estate. Nothing came of BF's hope of having her as a daughter-in-law; in 1770 she married William Hewson, a brilliant young physician and anatomist, who four years later died from an infection incurred while dissecting. Polly devoted the rest of her life to the care and education of her two sons and daughter. From 1775 BF had tried to persuade her to move to America and in 1784–85 she and the children visited him in Passy. Finally in 1786 she brought her family to Philadelphia, and was at BF's bedside when he died (1790), five years before her own death at her son's home near Bristol, Pa.

About 170 letters between the bright, spirited woman, remarkable in her own right, and the fatherly philosopher survive. They are full of humor and good will, and range from science and the phonetic alphabet to marriage counseling and public affairs, not to mention a stream of reports on growing children and grandchildren. Eight of his letters to her appear in the 1769 edition of *Experiments and Observations on Electricity*. In 1783 he wrote: "In looking forward,—Twenty-five Years seems a long Period; but in looking back, how short! Could you imagine that 'tis now full a Quarter of a Century since we were first acquainted! It was in 1757. During the greatest Part of the Time I lived in the same House with my dear deceased Friend your Mother; of course you and I saw and convers'd with each other much and often. It is to all our Honours, that in all that time we never had among us the smallest Misunderstanding. Our Friendship has been all clear Sunshine, without any the least Cloud in its Hemisphere." Many of their letters are in James M. Stifler, *"My Dear Girl" The Correspondence of Benjamin Franklin with Polly Stevenson, Georgiana and Catherine Shipley* (N.Y., 1927). Whitfield J. Bell, Jr., " 'All Clear Sunshine': New Letters of Franklin and Mary Stevenson Hewson," APS *Proc.*, C (1956), 521–36, describes the extent and character of the full correspondence.

7. See below, p. 131 n, for the visit to Tunbridge Wells.

prevented him as well as me. He is gone to dine abroad, and I doubt will hardly be able to disengage himself before the Post goes. Therefore, as well as to acknowledge the Receipt of your kind Favour of the 18th.[8] I snatch a Moment from Company, and write this Line to let you know that we are well, and that you will hear from us both by Tuesday's Post. 'Till then I shall only say, that I find my self, with greater Esteem and Regard than ever, Dear Child, Your sincerely affectionate Friend and Servant

B FRANKLIN

Endorsed: Aug 20 –58

A Letter from Father Abraham to His Beloved Son

Printed in *The New-England Magazine*, I, no. 1 (August 1758), 20–8.

About a year after Franklin's nephew, Benjamin Mecom, had set up his press in Boston,[9] he launched upon the ambitious plan of publishing a magazine. The first of the three issues (all that ever appeared) of this journal, the *New-England Magazine*, was dated August 1758.[1] Among its contents are Mecom's dedication to "a good old Gentleman" (possibly his uncle), the epitaph from the stone Franklin had erected over his parents' graves the year before,[2] and "A Letter from Father Abraham, to his beloved Son."

Jack C. Barnes thinks that Franklin probably wrote this last piece and has advanced substantial arguments for the attribution.[3] Franklin's interest in, and the help he gave to, his sister's son make his supplying Mecom with such a piece for the first issue seem plausible.[4] The use of "Father Abraham" as the ostensible writer of the letter may well relate directly to the "plain clean old Man, with white Locks," whose speech appeared so conspicuously in *Poor Richard* for 1758.[5] The em-

8. Not found.
9. See above, IV, 355–6 n; VII, 68, 94, 134.
1. Holman S. Hall, "The First New England Magazine," *New England Magazine*, new series, XXXIII (1905–06), 520–5.
2. See above, VII, 229–30.
3. Jack C. Barnes, "A Moral Epistle: A Probable Addition to the Franklin Canon," *New England Quarterly*, XXX (1957), 73–84.
4. In June 1758 BF "sent Benny a Trunk of Books and wrote to him," as he told Jane Mecom, Sept. 16, 1758 (below, p. 152). He might have sent the Father Abraham piece at that time.
5. Mecom reprinted this speech in pamphlet form, March 30, 1758; see above, VII, 326–50, esp. 329.

phasis on self-examination and the quotation of the "Golden Verses" of Pythagoras parallel and anticipate a passage on the same point and a reference to the same verses in Part II of Franklin's autobiography, written in 1784.[6] The style in the first and last parts of the letter is reminiscent of Franklin's, and the general subject of the pursuit of virtue is one on which he wrote a good deal. Even the vulgar analogy introduced near the end, Barnes believes, "has a Franklinian flavor."[7]

Against this attribution may be cited the entire absence of any direct evidence, any surviving acknowledgment that he had made a contribution to his nephew's magazine, or any suggestion of his authorship by relatives or other contemporaries. Franklin was far from being the only eighteenth-century writer who preached the pursuit of virtue; didactic pieces in the same vein abound; Pythagoras' verses in Nicholas Rowe's translation were printed and reprinted many times; and the value of self-examination was a theme of numerous writers. The inserted *"golden Extract* from a favourite OLD BOOK," which occupies almost half the whole, seems much too unctuous (as well as impractical) for Franklin to have quoted it at such length, much less to have written it himself. Neither the extract nor the verses with which it closes have been identified. If Franklin did write the first and last parts of the whole, it is not impossible that Mecom himself interpolated this middle section to pad his uncle's contribution and fill more space in the magazine.

On balance it is quite possible, though not necessarily "highly probable," as Barnes puts it, that the author of Father Abraham's Speech also wrote the first and lasts parts of Father Abraham's Letter; for that reason it is included here in its entirety.

A LETTER from Father Abraham, to his beloved Son.

Dear Isaac,   [August, 1758]

You frequently desire me to give you some *Advice*, in Writing. There is, perhaps, no other valuable Thing in the World, of which so great a Quantity is *given,* and so little *taken*. Men do not generally err in their Conduct so much through Ignorance of their

6. *Autobiog.* (APS-Yale edit.), pp. 151–60.

7. It should be pointed out, however, that in this middle period of his life BF wrote *for publication* almost nothing of this sort, whatever may be said of some of his private letters, his earlier contributions to *Pa. Gaz.* and *Poor Richard Almanacs,* or a few pieces he wrote for the amusement of friends in his later years. Even his "Old Mistresses Apologue," written in 1745, the most recent of his "naughty" pieces, was not intended for publication, and first appeared in print only in the 1880s; see above, III, 27–31.

Duty, as through Inattention to their own Faults, or through strong Passions and bad Habits; and, therefore, till that Inattention is cured, or those Passions reduced under the Government of Reason, *Advice* is rather resented as a Reproach, than gratefully acknowledged and followed.

Supposing then, that from the many good Sermons you have heard, good Books read, and good Admonitions received from your Parents and others, your Conscience is by this Time pretty well informed, and capable of advising you, if you attentively listen to it, I shall not fill this Letter with Lessons or Precepts of Morality and Religion; but rather recommend to you, that in order to obtain a *clear* Sight and *constant* Sense of your Errors, you would set apart a Portion of every Day for the Purpose of *Self-Examination,* and trying your daily Actions by that Rule of Rectitude implanted by GOD in your Breast. The properest Time for this, is when you are retiring to Rest; then carefully review the Transactions of the past Day; and consider how far they have agreed with *what you know* of your Duty to God and to Man, in the several Relations you stand in of a Subject to the Government, Servant to your Master, a Son, a Neighbour, a Friend, &c. When, by this Means, you have discovered the Faults of the Day, acknowledge them to God, and humbly beg of him not only Pardon for what is past, but Strength to fulfil your solemn Resolutions of guarding against them for the Future. Observing this Course steadily for some Time, you will find (through God's Grace assisting) that your Faults are continually diminishing, and your Stock of Virtue encreasing; in Consequence of which you will grow in Favour both with GOD and Man.

I repeat it, that for the Acquirement of solid, uniform, steady Virtue, nothing contributes more, than a daily strict SELF-EXAMINATION, by the Lights of Reason, Conscience, and the Word of GOD; joined with firm Resolutions of amending what you find amiss, and fervent Prayer for Grace and Strength to execute those Resolutions. This Method is very antient. 'Twas recommended by Pythagoras, in his truly *Golden Verses,* and practised since in every Age, with Success, by Men of all Religions. Those golden Verses, as translated by Rowe, are well worth your Reading, and even getting by Heart. The Part relating to this Matter I have transcribed, to give you a Taste of them, *viz.*

Let not the stealing God of Sleep surprize,
Nor creep in Slumbers on thy weary Eyes,
Ere ev'ry Action of the former Day,
Strictly thou dost, and *righteously* survey.
With Rev'rence at thy own Tribunal stand,
And answer justly to thy own Demand.
Where have I been? In what have I transgrest?
What Good or Ill has this Day's Life exprest?
Where have I fail'd in what I ought to do?
In what to GOD, to Man, or to myself I owe?
Inquire severe whate'er from first to last,
From Morning's Dawn till Ev'nings Gloom has past.
If Evil were thy Deeds, repenting mourn,
And let thy Soul with strong Remorse be torn:
If Good, the Good with Peace of Mind repay,
And to thy secret Self with Pleasure say,
Rejoice, my Heart, for all went well to Day.

And that no Passage to your Improvement in Virtue may be kept secret, it is not sufficient that you make Use of *Self-Examination* alone; therefore I have also added a *golden Extract* from *a favourite* OLD BOOK, to instruct you in the prudent and deliberate Choice of some disinterested Friend, to remind you of such Misconduct as must necessarily escape your severest Inquiry: Which is as follows;

Every prudent Man ought to be jealous and fearful of himself, lest he run away too hastily with a Likelihood instead of Truth; and abound too much in his own Understanding. All Conditions are equal, that is, Men may be contented in every Condition: For Security is equal to Splendor; Health to Pleasure, &c. Every Condition of Life has its Enemies, for *Deus posuit duo et duo, unum contra unum.* A rich Man hath Enemies sometimes for no other Reason than because he is rich; the poor Man hath as poor Neighbours, or rich Ones that gape after that small Profit which he enjoys. The Poor very often subsist merely by Knavery and Rapine among each other. Beware, therefore, how you offend any Man, for he that is displeased at your Words or Actions, commonly joins against you, without putting the *best* Construction on (or endeavouring to find out a reasonable Excuse for) them. And be sure you *hate* no Man, though you think him a worthless or unjust Person. Never *envy* any one above you: You have Enemies enough by the common Course of Human Nature; be cautious not to encrease the Number; and rather procure as many Friends as you can, to countenance and strengthen you. Every Man has also an Enemy within himself. Every Man is choleric and covetous, or gentle and generous by Nature. Man is naturally a beneficent Creature: But there are many external Objects and Accidents, met with as we go through Life, which *seem* to make great Alterations in our natural Dispositions and Desires. A Man naturally passionate and greedy, may, to all Appearance, become complaisant and hospitable, merely by Force of Instruction and Discipline; and so the Contrary. 'Tis in vain for a passionate Man to say, *I am pardonable* because *it is natural to me,* when we can perhaps point out to him an Example in his next Neighbour, who was *once* affected in the very same Manner, and could say as much to defend himself, who is now exceedingly *different* in his Behaviour, and quite free from those unhappy Affections which disturbed his Repose so often, not long ago, and became a chearful, facetious, and profitable Companion to his Friends, and a Pattern of Humility to all around him.

Nothing was ever well done or said *in a Passion.* One Man's Infirmities and bad Inclinations may be harder to conquer than another Man's, according to the various and *secret* Circumstances that attend them; but they are all capable of being conquered, or very much improved for the better, except they have been suffered to *take Root in* OLD *Age;* in this Case it is most convenient to let them have their own Way, as the Phrase is.

The strongest of our natural Passions are seldom perceived by us; a choleric Man does not always discover when he is angry, nor an envious Man when he is invidious; at most they think they commit no great Faults.

Therefore it is necessary that you should have a MONITOR. Most Men are very indifferent Judges of themselves, and often think they do well when they sin; and, imagine they commit only small Errors, when they are guilty of Crimes. It is in Human Life as in the Arts and Sciences; their Plainest Doctrines are easily comprehended, but the finest Points cannot be discovered without the closest Attention; of these Parts only the wise and skilful in the Art or Science, can be deemed competent Judges. Many Vices and Follies resemble their opposite Virtues and Prudence; they border upon, and seem to mix with each other; and therefore the exact Line of Division betwixt them is hard to ascertain. Pride resembles a generous Spirit; Superstition and Enthusiasm frequently resemble true Religion; a laudable worthy Ambition resembles an unworthy Self-Sufficiency; Government resembles Tyranny; Liberty resembles Licentiousness; Subjection resembles Slavery; Covetousness resembles Frugality; Prodigality resembles Generosity; and so of the Rest. Prudence chiefly consists in that Excellence of Judgement, which is capable of discerning the MEDIUM; or of acting so as not to intermingle the one with the other; and in being able to assign to every Cause its *proper* Actions and Effects. It is therefore necessary for every Person who desires to be a wise Man, to *take particular Notice of* HIS OWN *Actions*, and of HIS OWN *Thoughts and Intentions* which are the Original of his actions; with great Care and Circumspection; otherwise he can never arrive to that Degree of Perfection which constitutes the amiable Character he aspires after. And, lest all this Diligence should be insufficient, as Partiality to himself will certainly render it, it is very requisite for him to *chuse a* FRIEND, or MONITOR, who must be allowed the greatest Freedom to advertise and remind him of his Failings, and to point out Remedies. Such a One, I mean, as is a discreet and virtuous Person; but especially One that does not creep after the Acquaintance of, or play the Spaniel to, *great* Men; One who does not covet Employments which are known to be scandalous for Opportunities of Injustice: One who can bridle his Tongue and curb his Wit; One that can converse with himself, and industriously attends upon his own Affairs whatever they be. Find out such a *Man;* insinuate yourself into a Confidence with him; and desire him to observe your Conversation and Behaviour; intreat him to admonish you of what he thinks amiss, in a serious and friendly Manner; importune his Modesty till he condescends to grant your Request. Do not imagine that you live one Day without Faults, or that those Faults are undiscovered. Most Men see that in another, which they can not or will not see in themselves: And he is happiest, who through the whole Course of his

Life, can attain to a reasonable Freedom from Sin and Folly, even by the Help of *Old Age,* that great Mortifier and Extinguisher of our Lusts and Passions. If such a Monitor informs you of any Misconduct, whether you know his Interpretations to be true or false, take it not only *patiently,* but *thankfully;* and be careful to reform. Thus you get and keep a Friend, break the inordinate and mischievous Affection you bore towards your Frailities, and advance yourself in Wisdom and Virtue. When you consider that you must give an Account of your Actions to your vigilant Reprover; that other Men see the same Imperfections in you as he does; and that it is impossible for a good Man to enjoy the Advantages of Friendship, except he first puts off those Qualities which render him subject to Flattery, that is, except he first cease to flatter himself. A good, a generous Christian Minister, or worthy sensible Parents, may be suitable Persons for such a difficult Office; difficult, though it should be performed by *familiar* Conversation. And how much more meritorious of Entertainment are People of such a Character, than those who come to your Table to *make Faces,* talk Nonsense, devour your Substance, censure their Neighbours, flatter and deride you? Remember that if a Friend tells you of a Fault, always imagine that he does not tell you the whole, which is commonly the Truth; for he desires your Reformation, but is loth to offend you. And *nunquam sine querela ægra tanguntur.*

> I know, dear Son, *Ambition* fills your Mind,
> And in Life's Voyage, is th' impelling Wind;
> But, at the Helm, let sober Reason stand,
> To steer the Bark with Heav'n directed Hand;
> So shall you safe *Ambition's* Gales receive,
> And ride securely, though the Billows heave;
> So shall you shun the giddy Hero's Fate,
> And by her Influence be both good and great.
>
> She bids you first, in Life's soft vernal Hours,
> With active Industry wake Nature's Pow'rs;
> With rising Years still rising Arts display,
> With new-born Graces mark each new-born Day.
> 'Tis now the Time *young Passion* to command,
> While yet the pliant Stem obeys the Hand;

Guide now the Courser with a steady Rein,
E'er yet he bounds o'er Pleasure's flowry Plain;
In Passion's Strife no Medium you can have;
You rule, a Master; or submit, a Slave.[8]

To conclude. You are just entering into the World: Beware of the *first Acts* of Dishonesty: They present themselves to the Mind under *specious Disguises,* and *plausible Reasons* of Right and Equity: But being admitted, they open the Way for admitting others, that are *but a little* more dishonest, which are followed by others *a little* more knavish than they, till by Degrees, however slow, a Man becomes an *habitual* Sharper, and at length a *consummate Rascal* and Villain. Then farewel all Peace of Mind, and inward Satisfaction; all Esteem, Confidence, and Reputation among Mankind. And indeed if *outward* Reputation could be preserved, what Pleasure can it afford to a Man that must *inwardly* despise himself, whose own Baseness will, in Spite of his Endeavours to forget it, be ever presenting itself to his View. If you have a *Sir-Reverence* in your Breeches, what signifies it if you *appear* to Others neat and clean and genteel, when you *know* and *feel* yourself to be b----t. I make no Apology for the Comparison, however coarse, since none can be too much so for a defiled and foul Conscience. But never flatter yourself with *Concealment;* 'tis impossible to last long. One Man may be too cunning for another Man, but not for *all Men:* Some Body or other will smell you out, or some Accident will discover you; or who can be sure that he shall never be heard to talk in his Sleep, or be delirious in a Fever, when the working Mind usually throws out Hints of what has inwardly affected it? Of this there have been many Instances; some of which are within the Compass of your own Knowledge.

Whether you chuse to act in a public or a private Station, if you would maintain the personal Character of a Man of Sincerity, Integrity and Virtue, there is a Necessity of becoming *really good,* if you would *do good:* For the thin Disguises of *pretended* private Virtue and Public Spirit, are easily seen through; the Hypocrite detected and exposed. For this Reason then, *My*

8. The "*golden Extract* from a favourite OLD BOOK" ends here. Neither the extract nor the concluding verses have been identified.

dear ISAAC, as well as for many others, be sincere, candid, honest, well-meaning, and upright, in all you do and say; be *really* good, if you would *appear* so: Your Life then shall give Strength to your *Counsels;* and though you should be found but an indifferent *Speaker* or *Writer,* you shall not be without Praise for the Benevolence of your Intention.

But, again, suppose it possible for a Knave to preserve a fair Character among Men, and even to approve his own Actions, what is that to the Certainty of his being discovered and detested by the all-seeing Eye of *that righteous* BEING, who made and governs the World, whose just Hand never fails to do right and to punish Iniquity, and whose Approbation, Favour, and Friendship, is worth the Universe?

Heartily wishing you every Accomplishment that can make a Man amiable and valuable, to HIS Protection I commit you, being, with sincere Affection, *dear Son,* Your very loving Father,

ABRAHAM.

From William Franklin   ALS: American Philosophical Society

Honoured Father   Tunbridge Wells,[9] Septr. 3, —58

I miss'd writing on Friday and Yesterday no Post went from hence, otherwise I should before have acknowledgd the Receipt of your Favour of the 30th. Ulto.[1] Mr. Jackson[2] is prevented from

9. For about two weeks at the end of August BF and WF vacationed at fashionable Tunbridge Wells, 36 miles southeast of London, described in 1766 as "in a most flourishing state, with a great number of good houses for lodgings, and all necessary accomodations for company; its customs are settled, its pleasures regulated, its markets and all other conveniences fixed, and the whole very properly adapted to the nature of a place, which is at once designed to give health and pleasure to all its visitants. . . . A place where town and country are so happily blended, as to afford all the advantages of retirement, whithout any of the inconveniences of solitude." The daily routine included drinking the waters, concerts, country excursions, tea, visiting the bookshops, chapel, lectures, gambling, cards, horse-racing, balls, and endless promenading on the walks to "see and be seen" and engage in conversation. Thomas B. Burr, *The History of Tunbridge-Wells* (London, 1766), pp. 64–5, 111. BF returned to London before the end of the month, leaving WF at Tunbridge Wells with friends whom he planned to accompany on further travels.

1. Not found.

2. Richard Jackson.

setting off from here so soon as he intended by reason of the matrimonial Affair he mentioned to us not being quite settled. He says he has Letters from the Parties almost every Day, and was he to leave this Place they would not know where to direct to him; however he expects by Wednesday next to have Matters quite adjusted.[3] Mr. Bridges goes with us as far as Mr. Rose Fuller's,[4] where it is intended to stay a Day or two. In a Fortnight from hence Mr. Jackson thinks it will be proper we should set off on our Norfolk Tour, and therefore proposes being in London some Days before.[5] I am extremely oblig'd to you for your Care in supplying me with Money, and shall ever have a grateful Sense of that with the other numberless Indulgencies I have receiv'd from your paternal Affection. I shall be ready to return to America, or to go any other Part of the World, whenever you think it neccessary. We have chang'd our Lodgings to the House next adjoining, but much for the worse, tho' somewhat cheaper. Mr. Hunter[6] is now acquainted with a pretty many Persons, and is as fond of this Place as he was before averse to it.

Your Letter of Yesterday, with the agreeable News of the King of Prussias having defeated the Russians was very acceptable. It contain'd some Particulars which no one else had, and I had an Opportunity of obliging several by communicating them. There has been a Contribution of 1s. from each Gentle-

3. The "matrimonial Affair" was not Jackson's own, but one he was handling as a lawyer.

4. Thomas Bridges (d. 1768), was married to Anne, Richard Jackson's sister. William Berry, *County Genealogies ... of Kent* (London, 1830), p. 494; New Haven Colony Hist. Soc., *Papers*, IX (1918), 277–9 n, 421. Rose Fuller (1716–1777?), of Sussex, studied at Cambridge and Leyden, M.D., F.R.S., M.P. from 1756 to 1777. Gerrit P. Judd IV, *Members of Parliament, 1734–1832* (New Haven, 1955), p. 202; John and J. A. Venn, *Alumni Cantabrigienses*, Part I (Cambridge, 1922–27), II, 185. By coincidence, Fuller was first cousin of Ambrose Isted, owner of the manor and the "Franklin House" in Ecton.

5. Richard Jackson had estates in Norfolk. BF accompanied Jackson and WF on this tour "thro' Suffolk into Norfolk," as he called it to DF, June 27, 1760. The party probably left London during the first week of October and returned before the end of the month.

6. William Hunter, BF's associate in the colonial post office; see above, V, 18 n.

man and Lady towards Bonfires, firing of Guns, &c. for this Evening.[7]

Tomorrow I accompany Mr. Bridges's Family to Penshurst.[8] We went yesterday to survey the Roads when Mr. B's Horse getting into a deep Slough threw him off, but he received little Damage except being much dirty'd. He with the rest of the Family desire to be kindly remember'd to you, as does Mr. Hunter. I am, Honoured Sir Your ever dutiful Son   WM. FRANKLIN

P.S. Please to give my best Respects to Miss Hunter,[9] Mrs: Stevenson and such others as do me the Honour of enquiring after my Welfare.

Addressed: To / Benjamin Franklin, Esqr / at Mrs. Stevenson's / Craven Street / London

To Deborah Franklin

MS not found; reprinted in part from Duane, *Works*, VI, 36–9; in part from *The Pennsylvania Magazine of History and Biography*, VIII (1884), 403–6; remainder missing.[1]

My Dear Child,   London, September 6, 1758.

In mine of June 10th, by the Mercury, captain Robinson,[2] I mentioned our having been at Cambridge. We staid there a week,

7. News of Frederick the Great's victory at Zorndorf, Aug. 25, 1758, appeared in *London Chron.*, Sept. 2, 1758. The celebration was noisy enough to frighten a Miss Seare, causing a versifier to write in *London Chron.*, Dec. 12–14, 1758:

> Tho' Fred'rick's name, to every friend
> Of Liberty, be dear;
> No more such victories let him send,
> If they give pain to Seare.

8. The seat of the illustrious Sidney family, five miles from Tunbridge, at this time owned by William Perry. "Excursions to the noblemans and gentlemans seats . . . furnish another pleasurable employment of time at Tunbridge Wells. . . . Through the polite hospitality of the worthy proprietors, [they] are always open to the inspection of the curious." Burr, *Tunbridge-Wells*, pp. 169–97, 124–5.

9. William Hunter's sister Mary (Polly).

1. No contemporary manuscript of any part of this long letter about BF's visit to his and DF's ancestral homes survives; perhaps its parts were separated

(*Footnotes 1 and 2 continued on following page*)

being entertained with great kindness by the principal people, and shown all the curiosities of the place; and, returning by another road to see more of the country, we came again to London.[3] I found the journey advantageous to my health, increasing both my health and spirits, and therefore, as all the great folks were out of town, and public business at a stand, I the more easily prevailed with myself to take another journey and accept of the invitation. We had to be again at Cambridge at the commencement, the beginning of July. We went accordingly, were present at all the ceremonies, dined every day in their halls, and my vanity was not a little gratified by the particular regard shown me by the chancellor and vice chancellor of the university, and the heads of colleges.[4] After the commencement, we went from Cambridge, through Huntingdonshire into Northamptonshire,[5] and at Wellingborough; on inquiry we found still living Mary Fisher, whose maiden name was Franklin, daughter and only child of Thomas Franklin, my father's eldest brother: she is five

and finally lost as they were passed around and copied by members of both families (see, for example, below, p. 152 n). The first part of its text, dealing chiefly with the homes and relatives of the Franklins, was printed in 1817 by William Duane (allied by marriage to the family; see Genealogy D.3.1 and D.3.6) with a notation at the end: "The leaf of the manuscript book containing the remainder of this letter torn out." The second part, concerned with DF's English relatives, was contributed to *PMHB* in 1884 by John M. Cowell, a Pennsylvania descendant of her great-grandfather Abraham Cash, who explained that he had found the extract among his father's papers. Another text of this part, differing only in minor details, is in a typescript among the George Simpson Eddy Papers in Princeton Univ. Lib., sent to him in 1933 by Franklin Bache, great-grandson of BF's grandson Benjamin Franklin ("Benny") Bache (D.3.1). Mr. Bache called his transcript "my copy of a copy probably of the copy in the 'Cash family.' It is almost certainly authentic." The text as printed in *PMHB* is used here as it seems a little more directly descended from the original and conforms somewhat more closely to BF's normal usage. In both parts a few obvious errors in transcription have been in minor cases silently corrected. How extensive the missing final part of BF's letter may have been cannot now be determined.

2. See above, p. 90 n.

3. See above, pp. 108–9.

4. Degrees were conferred at Cambridge July 6, 1758. The Duke of Newcastle (1693–1768) was chancellor; the vice chancellor was Dr. John Green (1703–1779), Regius professor of divinity, 1748–56, master of Corpus Christi College, 1750–64, and bishop of Lincoln, 1761–79. *DNB*.

5. Duane incorrectly printed "Northumberlandshire."

years older than sister Douse, and remembers her going away
with my father and his then wife, and two other children to New
England, about the year, 1685.[6] We have had no correspondence
with her since my uncle Benjamin's death,[7] now near 30 years.
I knew she had lived at Wellingborough, and had married there
to one Mr. Richard Fisher, a grazier and tanner, about fifty years
ago, but did not expect to see either of them alive, so inquired for
their posterity; I was directed to their house and we found them
both alive, but weak with age, very glad however to see us; she
seems to have been a very smart, sensible woman. They are
wealthy, have left off business, and live comfortably. They have
had only one child, a daughter, who died, when about thirty years
of age, unmarried; she gave me several of my uncle Benjamin's
letters to her, and acquainted me where the other remains of the
family lived, of which I have, since my return to London, found
out a daughter of my father's only sister, very old, and was never
married. She is a good clever woman, but poor, though vastly
contented with her situation and very cheerful.[8] The others are

6. See above, I, xlix–lxxvii, for genealogical tables and charts of the Franklin
family. BF's father Josiah moved to Boston in 1683 with his first wife, the
former Ann(e) Child, their daughter Elizabeth (C.1; BF's "sister Douse"),
then aged five, and two younger children, Samuel (C.2) and Hannah (C.3).
Writing to BF in 1739, Josiah had mentioned his niece Mary Fisher (A.5.2.1.1)
and her husband Richard but said he did not know if they were still living;
see above, II, 231. For BF's visit with them see above, p. 117.

7. For the uncle (A.5.2.7) for whom BF was named, and some of his verses,
see above, I, 3–6. The elder Benjamin Franklin died in 1727.

8. Eleanor Morris (A.5.2.8.1), daughter of Hannah Franklin and her husband John Morris. The elder Benjamin Franklin wrote in 1717 that his sister
Hannah "had several good offers" of marriage, but being somehow "a
hinderance in brother Johns closing with several good offers, soe she her
selfe refused severall and took up with what proved the worst." Her husband,
a rag dyer, went into housebuilding, overreached himself, and died leaving
his wife and daughters £600 in debt. The daughter Eleanor, wrote Uncle
Benjamin, "Has a charming tongue, is of a very obliging cariage free in her
promises but far from endeavours to perform them." "A short account of the
Family of Thomas Franklin of Ecton in Northampton shire. 21 June 1717,"
Yale Univ. Lib. In the letter of 1739 mentioned in the second note above,
Josiah Franklin told BF that he had also lost touch with the children of his
brother John and sister Hannah. For BF's considerate treatment of Eleanor
Morris and John's daughter Anne Farrow in connection with Mary Fisher's
estate, see below, pp. 224–5, 288, 302, 414.

in different parts of the country: I intend to visit them, but they were too much out of our tour in that journey. From Wellingborough we went to Ecton,[9] about three or four miles, being the village where my father was born, and where his father, grandfather, and great-grandfather had lived, and how many of the family before them we know not.[1] We went first to see the old house and grounds; they came to Mr. Fisher with his wife, and after letting them for some years finding his rent something ill paid, he sold them.[2] The land is now added to another farm, and a school kept in the house: it is a decayed old stone building, but still known by the name of Franklin House. Thence we went to visit the rector of the parish,[3] who lives close by the church,

9. Here and later Duane misprinted "Ecton" as "Eaton."

1. Benjamin Franklin the Elder composed these nostalgic verses about his birthplace while living in London:

On Ecton 1702

This is the Church Whose preacher I did fear
These are the Bells I did Delight to Hear
This is the Yard Where I did often play
And this the Ile I katechize did say
Here Lyes the Dust I did so often Dread
There live'd the Baker that did make the bread
But Where's the Boyes that Higher did me Lead
    Here stands the stones that did my Haste Retard
There Lyes the Mother I did Disregard
That is the street Which I could nere Abide
And These the Grounds I play'd at seek and Hide
This is the pond Whereon I caught a fall
And that the Barn Wherein I play'd at ball
There Runs the River Where I oft did Fish
And Either had good sport or did it Wish
And these the Long broad pleasant Medows Where
Noe bouling-Green more Even can Appear
On these fair Leyes Ectons fair Daughters Dance't
When Charming Martyn his high straines Advanc't
Here Nappy Ale was sould brew'd by a Friend
Here in Excess I first of all offend
And He that Wrote this, here does make an End.

Benjamin Franklin (the Elder) MS Commonplace Book, Amer. Antiq. Soc.

2. At an uncertain date the property was acquired either by Thomas Isted (1677–1731), who had bought the manor of Ecton in 1712, or by his son and successor Ambrose Isted (1718–1781). *Autobiog.* (APS-Yale edit.), p. 46.

3. Eyre Whalley; see above, p. 114 n.

a very antient building. He entertained us very kindly, and showed us the old church register, in which were the births, marriages, and burials of our ancestors for 200 years, as early as his book began. His wife a goodnatured chatty old lady, (grandaughter of the famous archdeacon Palmer,[4] who formerly had that parish, and lived there,) remembered a great deal about the family; carried us out into the church-yard, and showed us several of their grave stones, which were so covered with moss that we could not read the letters till she ordered a hard brush and basin of water, with which Peter scoured them clean, and then Billy copied them.[5] She entertained and diverted us highly with stories of Thomas Franklin, Mrs. Fisher's father, who was a conveyancer, something of a lawyer, clerk of the county courts, and clerk to the archdeacon, in his visitations; a very leading man in all county affairs, and much employed in public business.[6] He set on foot a subscription for erecting chimes in their steeple, and completed it, and we heard them play.[7] He found out an easy method of saving their village meadows from being drowned, as they used to be sometimes by the river, which method is still in being; but when first proposed, nobody could conceive how it could be; but however they said if Franklin says he knows how to do it, it will be done. His advice and opinion was sought for on all occasions,

4. John Palmer (1612–1679), rector of Ecton, 1641–79, and archdeacon of Northampton, 1665–79. A succession of Palmers and Whalleys were rectors of Ecton from 1641 until into the nineteenth century. John Cole, *The History and Antiquities of Ecton* (London, 1825), pp. 15–17; John Bridges, *The History and Antiquities of Northamptonshire* (Oxford, 1791), II, 144.

5. Peter was BF's Negro servant. For WF's copies of the inscriptions see above, p. 119.

6. The elder Benjamin Franklin had written that this Thomas (his brother and BF's uncle, A.5.2.1) "was a black thin man of very mean appearance, but of great understanding and quick apprehension, very passionate, soon reconciled, and just in his dealings, Highly for the church of Eng. yet wanted a cordial love for its Ministers and toward his end had almost turn'd dissenter." As a youth he had left farming and for a time "kept a school and sold tobacco," but as his work of preparing legal documents increased he sold his school and "at length became a Noted scrivener." "A short Account," Yale Univ. Lib.

7. The bells, put up in 1690, played "the *4th Psalm* on Sunday, and *Britons strike home* on the other days, at the hours of four, six, eight, and twelve." Cole, *History of Ecton*, p. 9.

by all sorts of people, and he was looked upon, she said, by some, as something of a conjurer. He died just four years before I was born, on the same day of the same month.[8]

Since our return to London I have had a kind letter from cousin Fisher, and another from the rector, which I send you.[9]

From Ecton we went to Northampton, where we staid part of the day; then went to Coventry, and from thence to Birmingham—here, upon inquiry, we soon found out yours, and cousin Wilkinson's, and cousin Cash's relations:[1] first we found one of the Cash's, and he went with us to Rebecca Flint's,[2] where we saw her and her husband: she is a turner and he a buttonmaker; they have no children; were very glad to see any person that knew their sister Wilkinson;[3] told us what letters they had received, and showed us some of them; and even showed us that they had, out of respect, preserved a keg, in which they had received a present of some sturgeon. They sent for their brother Joshua North, who came with his wife immediately to see us, he is a turner also, and has six children, a lively active man. Mrs.

8. This coincidence apparently impressed BF greatly; he mentioned it again thirteen years later in the opening pages of his autobiography (ostensibly addressed to WF), and added: "The Account we receiv'd of his Life and Character from some old People at Ecton, I remember struck you, as something extraordinary from its Similarity to what you knew of mine. Had he died on the same Day, you said one might have suppos'd a Transmigration." *Autobiog.* (APS-Yale edit.), pp. 47–8.

9. The letter from Mary Fisher was probably the lost one of July 1758; see above, p. 117. For the letter from Whalley see above, pp. 114–17.

1. The identity of the various members of DF's large and ramified family mentioned in the rest of this letter can best be shown by the accompanying genealogical charts. The White Family chart (designated "E" in sequence after the charts in the Introduction to Volume I of this series) shows persons related to DF through her mother's paternal grandfather; the Cash Family chart (designated "F") shows persons related through her mother's maternal grandfather. Individuals are assigned letter and numeral symbols according to the same system as in the earlier genealogical lists and charts (for explanation, see above, I, xlix–lx). Many persons in both family groups who are not mentioned in this letter or in later Franklin correspondence are omitted from the charts as printed here. For the "cousin Wilkinson" and "cousin Cash" mentioned here, see E.2.3 and F.2.3.

2. E.2.4, a first cousin of DF's mother.

3. Elizabeth North Wilkinson (E.2.3), was living in Philadelphia with her husband Anthony as early as 1721. *PMHB*, XVII (1893), 365.

Genealogical Charts of the White and Cash Families

On the following pages are two charts showing Deborah Franklin's family connections through her mother's parents. They supplement the lists and charts of Benjamin Franklin's relatives included in the first volume of this series (pp. xlix–lxxxvi), are arranged in the same manner, and like the earlier charts, omit the names of numerous persons who do not appear in the Franklin correspondence. To aid in identification each individual has been assigned a letter and numeral symbol according to the same system as used before, explained in detail above, I, xlix–l, with the letters "E" and "F" indicating the White and Cash charts respectively.

For much of the data the present editors are heavily indebted to Francis James Dallett, director of the Newport Historical Society, Newport, Rhode Island. His article "Doctor Franklin's In-Laws," *Pennsylvania Genealogical Magazine*, XXI (1960), 297–302, and its accompanying chart, must be taken as a starting point for any investigation of this subject. In the course of his researches he accumulated a large number of miscellaneous notes on the Cash, Leacock, and related families, including material from Birmingham parish registers and other English sources. These notes are now in the possession of Mrs. Elizabeth Parker Fitler of Gladwyne, Pa., who has graciously made them available to the editors. In addition, extensive use has been made of records of burials and baptisms at Christ Church, Philadelphia, published in *Pennsylvania Magazine of History and Biography*, I–VII, XII–XVII, and of marriages there, published in 2 *Pennsylvania Archives*, VIII, 11–296.

WHITE FAMILY

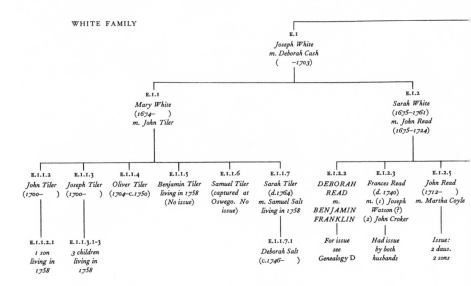

E.I
Joseph White
m. Deborah Cash
(–1703)

E.I.1
Mary White
(1674–   )
m. John Tiler

E.I.2
Sarah White
(1675–1761)
m. John Read
(1675–1724)

E.I.1.2
John Tiler
(1700–   )

E.I.1.3
Joseph Tiler
(1700–   )

E.I.1.4
Oliver Tiler
(1704–c.1750)

E.I.1.5
Benjamin Tiler
living in 1758
(No issue)

E.I.1.6
Samuel Tiler
(captured at
Oswego. No
issue)

E.I.1.7
Sarah Tiler
(d.1764)
m. Samuel Salt
living in 1758

E.I.2.2
DEBORAH
READ
m.
BENJAMIN
FRANKLIN

E.I.2.3
Frances Read
(d. 1740)
m. (1) Joseph
Watson (?)
(2) John Croker

E.I.2.5
John Read
(1712–   )
m. Martha Coyle

E.I.1.2.1
1 son
living in
1758

E.I.1.3.1–3
3 children
living in
1758

E.I.1.7.1
Deborah Salt
(c.1746–   )

For issue
see
Genealogy D

Had issue
by both
husbands

Issue:
2 daus.
2 sons

CASH FAMILY

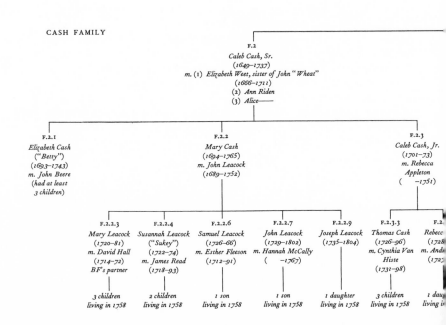

F.2
Caleb Cash, Sr.
(1649–1737)
m. (1) Elizabeth Weet, sister of John "Wheat"
(1666–1711)
(2) Ann Riden
(3) Alice——

F.2.1
Elizabeth Cash
("Betty")
(1693–1743)
m. John Beere
(had at least
3 children)

F.2.2
Mary Cash
(1694–1765)
m. John Leacock
(1689–1752)

F.2.3
Caleb Cash, Jr.
(1701–73)
m. Rebecca
Appleton
(–1751)

F.2.2.3
Mary Leacock
(1720–81)
m. David Hall
(1714–72)
BF's partner

F.2.2.4
Susannah Leacock
("Sukey")
(1722–74)
m. James Read
(1718–93)

F.2.2.6
Samuel Leacock
(1726–66)
m. Esther Fleeson
(1712–91)

F.2.2.7
John Leacock
(1729–1802)
m. Hannah McCally
(–1767)

F.2.2.9
Joseph Leacock
(1735–1804)

F.2.3.3
Thomas Cash
(1726–96)
m. Cynthia Van
Histe
(1731–98)

F.2.
Rebecc
(1728
m. And
(172

3 children
living in 1758

2 children
living in 1758

1 son
living in 1758

1 son
living in 1758

1 daughter
living in 1758

3 children
living in 1758

1 dau
living i

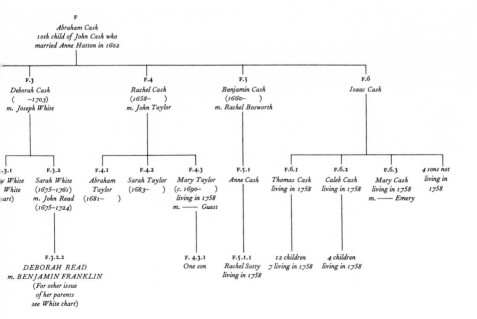

E
—— *White*
First name unknown

E.2
(dau.) White
First name unknown
m. John North

E.2.1	E.2.3	E.2.4	E.2.5	E.2.6	E.2.7
Mary North *1690–)*	*Elizabeth North* *(living in 1758)*	*Rebecca North* *m. William (?)*	*Thomas North* *(1696–)*	*John North* *(1701–69)*	*Joshua North* *(1703–)*
—— Edes *before 1758)*	*m. Anthony* *Wilkinson*	*Flint* *both living in*		*m. Sarah* *Merryweather*	
	(—1765)	*1758*			

E.2.1.1
One child
living in London
in 1758

Issue:
4 daus.
1 son (he
d. 1737)

E.2.5.1
John North
living in 1758

E.2.6.1	E.2.6.2	4 other
Sarah North *(1725–)*	*John North* *(b. & d. 1726)*	*children;* *names and* *dates not known*

Issue:
6 children

E.2.5.1.1	E.2.5.1.2	E.2.5.1.3
William North	*John North*	*Mary North*

F
Abraham Cash
10th child of John Cash who
married Anne Hatton in 1602

F.3	F.4	F.5	F.6
Deborah Cash *(—1703)* *m. Joseph White*	*Rachel Cash* *(1658–)* *m. John Taylor*	*Banjamin Cash* *(1660–)* *m. Rachel Bosworth*	*Isaac Cash*

.3.1	F.3.2	F.4.1	F.4.2	F.4.3	F.5.1	F.6.1	F.6.2	F.6.3	4 sons not
w White *White* *art)*	*Sarah White* *(1675–1761)* *m. John Read* *(1675–1724)*	*Abraham* *Taylor* *(1681–)*	*Sarah Taylor* *(1683–)*	*Mary Taylor* *(c. 1690–)* *living in 1758* *m. —— Guest*	*Anne Cash*	*Thomas Cash* *living in 1758*	*Caleb Cash* *living in 1758*	*Mary Cash* *living in 1758* *m. —— Emery*	*living in* *1758*

F.3.2.2
DEBORAH READ
m. BENJAMIN FRANKLIN
(For other issue
of her parents
see White chart)

F.4.3.1
One son

F.5.1.1
Rachel Sotty
living in 1758

12 children
7 living in 1758

4 children
living in 1758

Flint desired me to tell her sister that they live still in the old house she left them in, which I think she says was their father's.[4] From thence Mr. North went with us to your cousin Benjamin[5] Fillers [Tiler][6] where we suppd that night, he is a button maker, employs a great number of hands and lives very genteely, his wife is a very sensible, polite, agreeable woman, but they have no children, he told us Oliver[7] had lived at Canterbury, married a second wife and was in good business, getting money apace, but died eight years since, his eldest brother John[8] was living and had one son, his brother Joseph[9] also living, had three children and his sister Sarah[1] married to Mr. Salt, had one child, Samuel,[2] was in the Army and had no child, I think they said he was among the forces taken at Oswego and had not since heard of him.[3] They invited us to dine with them another day, which we did, when all the brothers and sisters were met together with one Mrs. Guest,[4a] another own cousin of Mother Read's her maiden name was Mary Taylor, she had a sister whose name was Sarah and a brother Abraham, she is a grand daughter to Abraham Cash,[5a] a widow about 68 years of age and has only one son, she remembers father Read and mother; mother and she are sister's children. She is a very sensible, smart, old lady, reads a great deal and is well acquainted with books, and her conversation

4. John North (E.2).

5. Duane's text ends here; the rest of the letter that survives is from the Cowell transcript.

6. "Filler" in both the Cowell and the Bache-Eddy versions is certainly an earlier transcriber's error for "Tiler" or "Tyler." Benjamin Tiler (E.1.1.5) was DF's first cousin, and the brothers and sisters of whom he gave news to BF could only be members of this family group.

7. E.1.1.4.

8. E.1.1.2. The eldest child in this family, Mary (E.1.1.1), had apparently died earlier.

9. E.1.1.3.

1. E.1.1.7.

2. Samuel Tiler (E.1.1.6), Benjamin's younger brother. The punctuation here leaves something to be desired; the Bache-Eddy version substitutes a semicolon. Sarah Salt's one child was Deborah, a girl of twelve, as becomes clear a few lines below.

3. The French captured Oswego, Aug. 14, 1756; see above, VI, 493 n.

4a. F.4.3.

5a. F; the common ancestor of most of those mentioned in this part of BF's letter.

very agreeable, she seems to be the scholar of the family, she made me a present of a pencil case and a Clezzel (?)[6] for Sally. Mrs. Salt is a jolly, lively dame, both Billy and myself agree that she was extremely like you, her whole face has the same turn, and exactly the same little blue Birmingham eyes. I think her name is Sarah, and she has one daughter named Deborah, about 12 years old. We had a very genteel dinner, and were very cherry, drinking mother's health, yours, Sally's and all our relations in Pennsylvania, they talk of the presents they had received from mother, of buckskins and the like and one had still preserved, a pair of gloves, sent them thirty years ago. I breakfasted twice at Mrs. Salt's and was to have dined there but had not a spare day, being engaged at different houses, we spent a week in and about Birmingham, continually on the foot, from one manufactory to another and were highly entertained in seeing all the curious machines and expeditious ways of working. Every morning we were visited at our Inn by some or other of the relations, whose names I entered in my book. There were two own cousins of Caleb Cash[7] being the sons of Isaac Cash,[8] the eldest Thomas has had twelve children, seven of whom are alive, the other named Caleb Cash has four children, the eldest remembers our kinsman John North[9] before he went to Pennsylvania, they are button makers and sent a present of their work, there was also Mrs. Mary Edes,[1] Cousin Wilkinson's eldest sister. She is a widow, has but one child who lives in London. There was also Mary Emery,[2] eldest daughter of Isaac Cash who was brother to old Mr. Cash that went to Philadelphia, with her came Caleb Cash her brother, who had been with us before,[3] they and their brother Thomas are all

6. Thus in both transcripts; probably a misreading of "chizzel" (chisel) and to be used for sharpening pencils.

7. Caleb Cash, Jr. (F.2.3), DF's mother's first cousin, a Philadelphia merchant and a founding member (1732) of the fishing club, The Colony (State) in Schuylkill, famous, among other reasons, for its Fish House Punch.

8. F.6.

9. E.2.6, DF's mother's first cousin, who had moved to Philadelphia at least as early as 1725; *PMHB*, XVII (1893), 110.

1. E.2.1, DF's mother's first cousin.

2. F.6.3, DF's mother's first cousin.

3. Isaac Cash (F.6) and Caleb Cash, Sr. (F.2), DF's great uncles; and Caleb Cash (F.6.2), DF's first cousin once removed, the man of that name mentioned

in the button business, four of the brothers of this family are dead. There was also Sarah Jones the daughter of Sarah Wheat, who was the daughter of John Wheat, who was brother to Caleb Cash's wife, that went into Pennsylvania with her daughters Mary and Betty.[4] Also there came a daughter of Sarah Jones, she has five children living, has had fourteen and seems very poor. At Cousin Tilers we heard of Rachel Sotty,[5] but did not see her, she is the daughter of Ann Cash, who was the daughter of Benjamin Cash, who was the son of Abraham Cash, her husband is a merchant at Rotterdam, in good circumstances—when we were coming away they brought us their letters, and little presents of their workmanship for their relations, all the letters and presents are in a little box and two parcels which I send under the care of Mr. John Schutz, Conrad's brother.[6] There are some for Sally, so if mother is well enough to get all the relations together some day to dinner, let Sally read part of this letter to them, and drink the health of your Birmingham friends, for we often drank at Birmingham our friends in Philadelphia. From Birmingham we went into Worcestershire to see Hagly Park, Lord Lyttleton's[7] and some other fine streets [seats?] and gardens and returned through Birmingham we went to Warwick to see old Guy's

most closely above. The profusion of Calebs in the Cash family is somewhat confusing; at least seven are found in Birmingham and Philadelphia church records by 1758.

4. The first wife of Caleb Cash, Sr. (F.2), was Elizabeth Weet or Wheat. Her brother John "Wheat," merely mentioned on the accompanying chart, was the father of Sarah Wheat and grandfather of Sarah Jones. None of these three were blood relatives of DF. Caleb and Elizabeth Cash's two eldest children were Elizabeth ("Betty") Beere (F.2.1) and Mary Leacock (F.2.2), DF's mother's first cousins.

5. F.5.1.1. Her maiden name is not known.

6. Between July 28 and Sept. 11, 1758, BF advanced a total of 33 guineas to John Shütz at the request of his brother Conrad (a Philadelphia papermaker; see above, II, 363 n), and on September 12 took Shütz's note for this amount, "which Note is to be sent over for Payment in Pensilva." Three days later he loaned Shütz 2 guineas more. "Account of Expences," pp. 19, 22, 34; *PMHB*, LV (1931), 112–13.

7. George Lyttelton (1709–1773), first Baron Lyttelton, author and politician, whose ancestral home Hagley, was admired by Horace Walpole and the poet James Thomson. *DNB*. In both versions of this part of the letter "Lord" is given as "long."

Castle[8] &c.—and while we were here John North[9] came from Birmingham, twenty miles on foot to see us, a little angry with his Uncle Joshua[1] for not informing him of us when we were in town, he is the son of Thomas North who is a brother to John North[2] of Pennsylvania, he has two sons William and John and a daughter Mary and is a button maker, he seems an honest hearty fellow, did not hear of us till we were gone and then followed us, being resolved, he said, to have his name put down in my book among the rest of the family, they are industrious, ingenious, working people and think themselves vastly happy that they live in dear old England. [*Remainder missing.*]

To Joseph Galloway

ALS: Yale University Library

Dear Sir   London, Sept. 6. 1758

I have been much in the Country this summer, travelling over great Part of the Kingdom, partly to recover my Health, and partly to improve and increase Acquaintance among Persons of Influence. Being just come to Town, I find this Ship on the Point of Sailing; so can only now say, that I have receiv'd your Favour of July 28.[3] with the Papers enclos'd which I am very glad to see; and that no Report on Smith's Affair has yet been made, nor any now expected; nor any thing new occur'd since my last.[4] No new Governor is yet appointed that I can hear of; but Mr. Partridge tells me Gen. Shirley seems willing to accept of it, if offer'd to him.[5] By the Mail that goes hence on Saturday

8. Guy of Warwick, a legendary hero of the Anglo-Saxon battles against the Danish invasion, left his wife, who was heir to the Warwick title and occupant of the famous Warwick Castle, out of remorse for his violent life. He later lived as a hermit near the castle, revealing himself again to his wife only on his deathbed.

9. E.2.5.1.

1. E.2.7.

2. E.2.6. The Johns in the North family are somewhat less numerous than the Calebs among the Cashes; only five have been identified.

3. Not found.

4. Probably that of June 10, 1758 (above, pp. 96–7); for "Smith's Affair" see above, pp. 28–51, 60–3, 87–8.

5. Instead, William Shirley was appointed governor of the Bahamas in November 1758. *Gent. Mag.*, XXXVIII (1758), 557. See above, p. 95 n, for

for the Pacquet, I shall write to the Committee and all my Friends fully; also per another Ship that I hear is to sail in a few Days, Capt. Duncan.[6] Billy is still in the Country.[7] I fear this will hardly get on board if I add more than that I am, with great Esteem Dear Sir, Yours affectionately   B FRANKLIN

Addressed: To / Joseph Galloway Esqr. / Philadelphia

Endorsed: 1758 Anno Dom
          Letter Septr. 6. 1758. Benjamn. Franklin

Accounts with Isaac Norris

MS account: American Philosophical Society; MS account book: Library Company of Philadelphia

During Franklin's first English residence he carried out numerous financial transactions for Isaac Norris. At his friend's request he bought and sent to Philadelphia a telescope,[8] several books and pamphlets, medicines, and a surprising number of decanters and other forms of glassware; he advanced money to other people on Norris' orders; and, above all, he invested substantial sums in England for the speaker's account. For all these services Norris sent to England a series of bills of exchange and also received credit for interest on the investments.

Among the papers of the two men are records of these transactions. A document in Franklin's hand in the American Philosophical Society Library is headed "Isaac Norris Esqr in Account with B. Franklin," in which he recorded in debtor and creditor columns his expenditures and receipts from Jan. 3, 1759, to Feb. 16, 1762. Norris' manuscript account book, 1735–65, in the Library Company of Philadelphia, contains on facing pages an identical series of entries, but terminating July 5, 1761. On another page are entered records of three shipments

---

Quaker proposals that he be named governor of Pa. His acceptability to the Quakers and to BF may have militated against his appointment by Thomas Penn, and his age (64) may have made him seem more suitable for the relatively quiet post in the islands. John A. Shutz, *William Shirley King's Governor of Massachusetts* (Chapel Hill, [1961]), pp. 249–50.

6. BF did not send his letters on the packet; they were carried by Capt. Robert Duncan on the *Carolina,* which did not reach Philadelphia until early January 1759. *Pa. Gaz.,* Jan. 11, 1759.

7. In Tunbridge Wells; see above, pp. 131–2.

8. See above, VII, 284, and below, pp. 158, 226.

of goods Franklin sent to Norris. The last two record, though in fuller detail, transactions included in the general account; the first, dated Sept. 15, 1758, shows the shipment of a 24-foot refracting telescope, which cost with its packing case £17 7s. 6d. With three possible exceptions, every transaction recorded in the documents here described is also entered, sometimes with considerably more detail, in Franklin's "Account of Expences"; see above, VII, 164–5.[9]

Nine of the entries relate to investments Franklin made for Norris in stocks and annuities, either purchased from others or transferred from his own holdings.[1] Their total face value was £5350, but there were discounts for advance payment of installments on the subscriptions and others resulting from market fluctuations, so he paid only £4324 14s. 2½d., including broker's commissions. Interest at 3 percent totaled £345 7s. 6d. during the period of these accounts.

These accounts are not printed in full here, but as transactions are mentioned in later correspondence, reference will be made to this summary.

9. Also in Lib. Co. Phila. is Norris' "Journal Beginning 1747," in which he recorded as they occurred various transactions with BF, the earliest on May 16, 1748, many of them duplicating entries in these accounts.

1. In British financial parlance the word "stock" applies, not only to holdings of capital shares of business corporations, but especially to money loaned to the government on a funded debt. By the 1750s most such "stocks" took the form of "annuities," that is, of loans for which the government promised "to pay a fixed rate of interest for the money advanced till re-payment of the principal, but without stipulating to make such re-payment at any particular time, or even any express agreement to ever re-pay it, and, sometimes, on condition that the money should *not* be re-paid till after a certain period." J. J. Grellier, *The Terms of All the Loans Which Have Been Raised for the Public Service during the Last Fifty Years* . . . (London, 1799), pp. 1–2. Many of these annuities also included a lottery feature as an added inducement to investors. For example, BF's first investment for Norris recorded in these accounts was for £525 face value of the Annuity of 1759, purchased from another investor, May 30, 1759. It allowed "for every £100 advanced a capital of £105, bearing interest at 3 per cent. per ann. commencing from January 5, 1759, and a lottery ticket, entitling to a farther capital of £10, bearing the same interest, but commencing from January 5, 1760." *Ibid.*, p. 16. Discounts allowed by the seller, and by the Bank of England for advance payment of installments of the subscription not yet due, reduced the net cost to £414 14s. 10d. "Account of Expences," p. 28; *PMHB*, LV (1931), 118–19. Some of BF's other transactions in government stock will appear in later volumes.

To Joseph Galloway

ALS: Yale University Library

Dear Sir,   London, Sept. 16. 1758

I wrote you a few Lines on the 6th Inst. in which I omitted acknowledging the Receipt of your several Favours of April 17. May 9. and June 16.[2] They all got safe to hand with the several Papers as mention'd; but the Votes, except what related to Smith's Affair, I have not yet received. No Report has yet been made by the Attorney and Solicitor General, nor any now expected. The Expence to Smith must have been considerable. Moore's Petition, tho' talk'd of, was, I believe, never presented.[3]

I heard, with great Pleasure, that the Assembly had pass'd a Bill for so large a Supply and raising so great a Body of Men for the Service of the current Year. God send your Forces Success. For if this Year's Service proves as fruitless as the last, I know not how you will bear such a Burthen for another. You have however shown your Zeal for the King's Service; and the Proprietor, by the first Refusal of the Bill has shewn, that all is to be risqu'd rather than his Purposes not serv'd.[4]

The Commissioners I think fully justify'd themselves, from the Governor's mean Accusations.[5] I believe there never was a Set

2. See the document next but one above for BF's letter of September 6, and above, pp. 106–8, for Galloway's of June 16; the others have not been found.

3. The records of the Privy Council show that Smith's and Moore's petitions were both presented to that body and referred to its committee on April 1, 1758, and that the committee referred both to the attorney general and solicitor general on April 10. *Acts Privy Coun., Col.*, IV, 375. Ferdinand Paris stated, however, that only "Many days after Mr. Smith's petition had been presented, and referred" had Daniel Moore brought his brother's petition to Paris. "With some difficulty I got that put into the same Channel, as Mr. Smith's, And at length, got sight of Mr. Moore's Case and paper." He was surprised to find that it was accompanied by no supporting papers and so he could not bring it to a hearing at the same time as Smith's. Later he did procure some facts, since both cases were closely related, and hoped to bring the Moore petition to a hearing. Paris to William Allen, May 13, June 10, 1758. Penn Papers, Hist. Soc. Pa. The Privy Council acted finally on the Smith case, June 26, 1759 (for the report of its committee, see *Acts Privy Coun., Col.*, IV, 375–85), but no evidence has been found that Moore's petition was ever pressed to a conclusion.

4. For the Supply Act of April 22, 1758, see above, pp. 54–5.

5. Denny had accused the provincial commissioners of ignoring him in spending public funds. *Pa. Col. Recs.*, VIII, 42, 64, 67–8. Galloway and four

of Commissioners since the Time of the old Romans, that acted with more Integrity and Uprightness, and less Regard to private Interest.

Mr. Thomson has, as you desired, sent me constantly Copies of the Treaties with Tedyuskung.[6] They are very Satisfactory, and must be of great Use when the important Affair of doing those People Justice comes under Consideration here. Sundry Circumstances have prevented it for some time, but it will now speedily be brought on.[7]

You will probably soon have a Change of Governors, (as I wrote you the 10th. of June last, when I wrote also to the Committee)[8] but as to a Change of Government, that perhaps is at some Distance, unless the Province, heartily tir'd of Proprietary Rule, should petition the Crown to take the Government into its own Hands.[9]

I have not lately seen the Proprietaries. Their Conduct in Smiths Affair, abetting the Abuses thrown on the Assembly at the Hearing, and soliciting in favour of his Cause, was look'd upon by every body as an open Declaration of War; and having no longer any Hopes of an Accommodation, I have never since desired an Audience of them.[1] Some Ship before Winter will probably bring me full Directions from the Assembly as to my future Proceedings. How far the Cause may be drawn into Length, is impossible to foresee; but you need be under no Apprehension of its suffering for want of Money; when I see any likelyhood of that, I shall give you timely Notice; and in the mean time, on occasion, could advance of my own; for the Remittances I have received since my being here, have greatly exceeded my Expences.[2]

---

of his colleagues published a long report in defense of their conduct in *Pa. Gaz.*, April 27, 1758. This report was probably one of the "several Papers" which BF acknowledged receiving from Galloway.

6. See above, p. 69.

7. "The important Affair" was a petition to the King on Teedyuscung's behalf; see below, pp. 264–76.

8. See above, p. 89.

9. See below, p. 157, for BF's own remarks on "a Change of Government."

1. See below, pp. 178–88, for BF's final dealings with the Proprietors.

2. How much BF had available in London at this time is not clear, but a memorandum of April 12, 1759, records that on that day he completed payment on an investment of £1480 19s. 8d. in government stock and the associ-

The Taking of Louisburg gave great Joy here, and to me the more, as it will tend to rivet the Patriot Minister[3] in the Seat of Power.

It is said the Proprietor has taken great Offence at some Letter of my writing into Pensilvania.[4] I know not what it is, but Copies are somehow obtain'd for him of such of my Letters as are laid before the Assembly; which must make me cautious how I speak freely of Persons and Measures here, lest he should have a Handle to create me Enemies. But as to his own Resentment against me, it gives me very little Concern.

Billy is gone to Portsmouth, so cannot write to you per this Opportunity. I have sent him your Letter which came with yours of July 28 to me. The Affidavits mention'd in the Council's Defence of the Proprietor, are not annext to the Copy you favour'd me with. If you have any Affidavits on the other side of the Question, I should be glad to have them with the others.[5] The Proprietor's E[stimate] of his Estate is a curious Paper, and will be of good Use.[6] I thank you for the Account of the Forces in North America.[7]

I long to hear the Event of your Expedition against Fort Duquesne. Since the Repulse at Ticonderago, I have been in pain for my Countrymen.[8]

---

ated lottery tickets with a total face value of £1725. "Account of Expences," p. 26; *PMHB*, LV (1931), 117. For details of this stock issue, see above, p. 148 n.

3. William Pitt. News of the capture of Louisbourg, July 26, 1758, appeared in *London Chron.*, Aug. 19, 1758.

4. See above, VII, 360–4.

5. Galloway's letter of July 28 has not been found; for BF's low opinion of the Council's defense of proprietary land purchases, see below, p. 158.

6. This is the paper entitled "My Estimate of the Province, T. Penn," printed in the appendix of Richard Jackson's *An Historical Review of the Constitution and Government of Pensylvania* in May 1759 with BF's remarks upon it; see below, pp. 360–79. Apparently Galloway had included it with his letter of July 28, 1758, to BF.

7. Galloway may have sent a private account of all the forces, but information about particular groups appeared frequently in colonial newspapers. For example, on June 8, 1758, *Pa. Gaz.* named the ships of the Royal Navy in the Louisbourg expedition and on June 15 listed the regiments taking part in the same attack with the number of men in each.

8. News of the British defeat at Ticonderoga, July 8, was in *London Chron.*, Aug. 22, 1758.

Present my best Respects to the rest of the Committee[9] and the Members of the House, and believe me, with great Esteem, Dear Sir, Yours affectionately   B FRANKLIN

Mr. Galloway

Sept. 19. I enclose you one of the latest Papers, communicate it to the Speaker.[1]

Endorsed: Letter Sept. 16. 1758 Benjamn. Franklin.

To Jane Mecom   Copy: Historical Society of Pennsylvania[2]

Dear Sister   London Sept 16 1758

I received your Favour of June 17. I wonder you have had no Letter from me since my being in England. I have wrote you at least two and I think a third before this;[3] And, what was next to waiting on you in Person, sent you my Picture.[4] In June last I sent Benny a Trunk of Books and wrote to him. I hope they are come to hand, and that he meets with Incouragement in his Business.[5] I congratulate you on the Conquest of Cape Breton, and hope as your People took it by Praying the first Time, you will now pray that it may never be given up again, which you then forgot.[6] Billy is well but in the Country. I left him at Tun-

9. The Assembly Committee of Correspondence.

1. Probably *London Chron.,* Sept. 19, 1758, containing BF's "A.B." letter, see below, pp. 162–8.

2. This copy, in an unknown hand, follows BF's usual spelling, capitalization, and punctuation much more closely than does the earliest printed version in Duane, *Works,* VI, 39–42. It also bears every appearance of being a contemporary one; copies circulated in Philadelphia as early as Jan. 2, 1759, when Hannah Callender recorded in her diary that "Able James and Doctor Evans drank tea here. Some passages of Ben: Franklin's droll humor related. In a letter to his sister in New England, a strong Presbyter [here follows, somewhat modified, the passage about Cape Breton]." *PMHB,* XII (1888), 434.

3. None of these letters between BF and his sister have been found.

4. See above, VII, frontispiece and pp. xv, 365.

5. Benny was to receive "20 per cent for his trouble" in selling this shipment, worth £52 10s. 4½d. BF recorded it May 19, 1758; and the next day sent Mecom £6 1s. 6½d. worth of printing supplies. "Account of Expences," p. 16; *PMHB,* LV (1931), 111.

6. A reference to the capture of Louisbourg by New England forces in 1745 and its return to France in the peace treaty of 1748. See above, III, 26–7, for his letter about the prayers for that expedition.

bridge Wells, where we spent a fortnight, and he is now gone with some Company to see Portsmouth.

We have been together over a great part of England this Summer; and among other places visited the Town our Father was born in and found some Relations in that part of the Country Still living. Our Cousin Jane Franklin, daughter of our Unkle John, died but about a Year ago.[7] We saw her Husband Robert Page, who gave us some old Letters[8] to his Wife from unkle Benjamin. In one of them, dated Boston July 4. 1723 he writes "Your Unkle Josiah has a Daughter Jane about 12 years Old, a good humour'd Child" So Jenny keep up your Character, and don't be angry when you have no Letters.

In a little Book he sent her, call'd *None but Christ*,[9] he wrote an Acrostick on her Name, which for Namesakes' Sake, as well as the good Advice it contains, I transcribe and send you

> Illuminated from on High,
> And shining brightly in your Sphere
> Nere faint, but keep a steady Eye
> Expecting endless Pleasures there
> Flee Vice, as you'd a Serpent flee,
> Raise Faith and Hope three Stories higher
> And let Christ's endless Love to thee
> N-ere cease to make thy Love Aspire.

7. Jane Franklin Page (A.5.2.3.5) and her father John (A.5.2.3); see Genealogy (I, li-lii); see also above, facing p. 120, for BF's chart showing his and Jane Mecom's relationship to these people. Uncle John Franklin seems to have been a good, genial, but rather hapless fellow who practiced the dyer's trade in Banbury for most of his life, and died "Much lamented . . . for he was a peace maker and a friend of the poor." He had bad luck in marriage: "he lived a batchelor long and was a sutor to many young women whose love he seldom miss'd gaining . . . at last he married Ann Jeffs [Jenks ?]. . . . She proved neither capable nor carful" as a helper in his business. He confessed that he had indeed taken up with "the Worst at last" and said "If my Wife was but like other women . . . I should ever Adore her, but he checkt himself and said: but, May be, It is best it should be as it is, for I should a been apt to set her in the first place." His daughter Jane trained as a lace maker and for a time a resident of Ashton (Northamptonshire), was a sister of Anne Farrow (see below, p. 222 n). "A short account of the Family of Thomas Franklin of Ecton in Northamptonshire. 21 June 1717." by the elder Benjamin Franklin, Yale Univ. Lib.

8. Not found.

9. Not identified.

Kindness of Heart by Words express
Let your Obedience be sincere,
In Prayer and Praise your God Address
Nere cease 'till he can cease to hear.[1]

After professing truly that I have a great Esteem and Veneration for the pious Author, permit me a little to play the Commentator and Critic on these Lines. The Meaning of *Three Stories* higher seems somewhat obscure, you are to understand, then, that *Faith, Hope* and *Charity* have been called the three Steps of Jacob's Ladder, reaching from Earth to Heaven. Our Author calls them *Stories*, likening Religion to a Building, and those the three Stories of the Christian Edifice; Thus Improvement in Religion, is called *Building Up,* and *Edification. Faith* is then the Ground-floor, *Hope* is up one Pair of Stairs. My dearly beloved Jenny, don't delight so much to dwell in these lower Rooms, but get as fast as you can into the Garret; for in truth the best Room in the House is *Charity.* For my part, I wish the House was turn'd upside down; 'tis so difficult (when one is fat) to get up Stairs; and not only so, but I imagine *Hope* and *Faith* may be more firmly built on *Charity,* than *Charity* upon *Faith* and *Hope.* However that be, I think it a better reading to say

Raise Faith and Hope *one Story* higher

correct it boldly and I'll support the Alteration. For when you are up two Stories already, if you raise your Building three Stories higher, you will make five in all, which is two more than there should be, you expose your upper Rooms more to the Winds and Storms, and besides I am afraid the Foundation will hardly bear them, unless indeed you build with such light Stuff as Straw and Stubble, and that you know won't stand Fire.

Again where the Author Says

Kindness of Heart by Words express,

Stricke out *Words* and put in *Deeds.* The world is too full of Compliments already; they are the rank Growth of every Soil, and Choak the good Plants of Benevolence and Benificence, Nor do I pretend to be the first in this comparison of Words and Actions to Plants; you may remember an Ancient Poet whose Words we have all Studied and Copy'd at School, said long ago,

1. For Uncle Benjamin's somewhat similar acrostic on BF's name, see above, I, 4–5.

A Man of Words and not of Deeds,
Is like a Garden full of Weeds.[2]
'Tis pity that *Good Works* among some sorts of People are so little
Valued, and *Good Words* admired in their Stead; I mean seemingly
pious Discourses instead of *Humane Benevolent Actions*. These they
almost put out of countenance, by calling Morality *rotten Mor-*
ality, Righteousness, *ragged Righteousness* and even *filthy Rags;*
and when you mention *Virtue*, they pucker up their Noses as
if they smelt a Stink; at the same time that they eagerly snuff up
an empty canting Harangue, as if it was a Posie of the Choicest
Flowers. So they have inverted the good old Verse, and say now
A Man of Deeds and not of Words
Is like a Garden full of ——
I have forgot the Rhime, but remember 'tis something the very
Reverse of a Perfume. So much by Way of Commentary.

My Wife will let you see my Letter containing an Account
of our Travels,[3] which I would have you read to Sister Douse,[4]
and give my Love to her. I have no thoughts of returning 'till
next year, and then may possibly have the Pleasure of seeing
you and yours, take Boston in my Way home. My Love to Brother
and all your Children, concludes at this time from Dear Jenny
your affectionate Brother   B Franklin

a Copy

To Charles Norris   ALS: Library of Congress

Dear Sir,   London, Sept. 16. 1758.
    I received your Favours of May 17. and June 15.[5] and am glad the
Books on Husbandry and Gardening got safe to hand. I shall send
the others you write for per Bolitho, if I can get them on board.[6]
    I hope the Crab Apple Trees you have planted will grow, and
be propagated in our Country. I do not find that England any
where produces Cyder of equal Goodness with what I drank

2. James Howell, *Proverbs* ... (London, 1659), p. 20, and doubtless in
many other such compilations.
3. See above, pp. 133–46.
4. Elizabeth Franklin Douse (C.1); see above, VII, 190–1.
5. Not found.
6. See above, VII, 176 n, for two of the books sent to Norris; below, p.
158, for the others.

frequently in Virginia made from those Crabs. They are also said to be plentiful Bearers, and seldom fail. I should be glad to see the Industry of our People supplying the Neighbouring Colonies with that Cyder. I think it would even be valued here.

It is as you say surprizing to find such Opinions prevailing here, of the Wealth and Populousness of Pensilvania. This, among other Prejudices to our Disadvantage, propagated by our Enemies, I hope will be removed by a Piece to be published next Winter, which I have now under Correction;[7] and then I have reason to believe our Affairs may more easily be put into a better Situation than they have been for some Years past.

Be pleased to present my best Respects to your Sister.[8] I send her some Colliflower seed, which Mrs. Charles[9] procur'd for 'me, said to be of an excellent kind. Remember me also affectionately to the Brothers and Sister at Sasquehanah,[1] when you have Occasion to write to them. I shall send them some more Pamphlets when the season comes on.

The Spirits of the People here seem at present a good deal elated with our late Successes, and that of the King of Prussia.[2] I long to hear that you have succeeded at the Ohio, being in pain for the Forces gone thither.[3]

With great Esteem, I am, Dear Sir, Your most obedient Servant

B FRANKLIN

Mr. Cha. Norris

Endorsed: Lond: Septr. 16th. 1758 Benjamin Franklin Esqr recd Janry. 11th. 1759

7. Richard Jackson's *Historical Review* (London, 1759).

8. Probably Deborah Norris, unmarried sister of Charles and Isaac, who at this time was living with the widowed Charles at his home on Chestnut Street. She was almost as much interested in gardening as he was. Edward Armstrong, ed., *Correspondence between William Penn and James Logan,* 1 (Phila., 1870), xliii n.

9. Mrs. Robert Charles, eldest daughter of Patrick Gordon, governor of Pa., 1726–36. Mabel P. Wolff, *The Colonial Agency of Pennsylvania 1712–1757* (Phila., 1933), p. 121.

1. James, John, and Susanna Wright; see above, IV, 210–11; VI, 101–2. They and Norris were close friends.

2. The British capture of Louisbourg and the defeat of the Russians at Zorndorf by Frederick II of Prussia on Aug. 25, 1758. The latter was reported in *London Chron.,* Sept. 7–9, 1758.

3. The Forbes expedition which captured Fort Duquesne, Nov. 25, 1758.

To Isaac Norris: "Separate Notes"[4]   AD: Library of Congress

Separate Notes

London, Sept. 16. 1758

Baskerville is printing Newton's Milton in two Volumes, 8vo. I have inserted your Name in his List of Subscribers, as you mention your Inclination to encourage so deserving an Artist.[5]

It is certain that the Government here are inclin'd to resume all the Proprietary Powers, and I make no doubt but upon the first Handle they will do so. I only think they wish for some Advantage against the People's Privileges as well as the Proprietary Powers. I believe a Petition from either of the Assemblies,[6] expressing their Dislike to the Proprietary Government, and praying the Crown to take the Province under its immediate Government and Protection, would be even now very favourably heard. Tumults and Insurrections, that might prove the Proprietary Government insufficient to preserve Order, or show the People to be ungovernable, would do the Business immediately; but such I hope will never happen. I know not but a Refusal of the Assembly to lay Taxes, or of the People to pay them, unless the Proprietary Estate be taxed, would be sufficient: But this would be extreamly improper before it is known whether Redress may not be obtained on Application here. *I should be glad to know your Sen-*

4. Though clearly part of a letter to Isaac Norris, this document, headed "Separate Notes" by BF and bearing a long endorsement in Norris' hand, has no salutation, complimentary close, or signature. The endorsement by Norris shows it is not an extract of a letter BF made and kept for himself; instead it is probably the private, confidential accompaniment of a longer letter the rest of which (not found) was a report from BF as agent to the Pa. Assembly.

5. See above, pp. 53, 80, for earlier praise of John Baskerville. Thomas Newton (1704–1782), rector of St. Mary-Le-Bow and later bishop of Bristol, had published Milton's *Paradise Lost* in 1749 with a life and elaborate notes, and the rest of Milton's poetry in 1752. *DNB.* Baskerville's reprinting of the work (1758) lists "Isaac Norris Esq. Speaker of the Assembly of Pennsylvania" and "Benj. Franklin Esq. Philadelphia" among the subscribers.

6. Pennsylvania and probably Maryland, not Delaware. There seems to be no evidence that the "Newcastle Assembly" was interested in attacking proprietary government, but in Maryland there was agitation for the taxation of Lord Baltimore's estates. See above, p. 101.

timents on the Point of getting rid of the Proprietary Government, and whether you think it would be generally agreable to the People.[7]

I was much concern'd to hear of your Indisposition, and for the Occasion of it. They have certainly made some Mistake about the Books, and sent you a Box or two that were not of the Parcel and not intended to be sent you. Osborne teazes one to have the Account closed, but let not that induce you to run the like Hazard, or fatigue yourself to the Prejudice of your Health, which I hope you have long before this time perfectly recovered.[8]

Your Telescope is at length finished, and I shall have it in a few Days, tho' I doubt too late to be sent per this Ship. I would willingly have it examin'd too per Mr. Short, a Friend of mine, and the great Optician here,[9] before I ship it. I shall send it with your Brother's Books and yours, on Gardening &c. per next Ship, perhaps per Bolitho.[1]

The Defence made by the Council of the Indian Walk Purchase, seems to me a miserable one. I observe the Secretary's Prevarication about his Discourse at Easton, &c. How comes the Report to be sign'd only by L. Lardner?[2]

7. Norris had hinted about this project on June 15 (see above, p. 102), and speculated further in replying to this letter, Jan. 15, 1759 (below, p. 228). The decision to seek royal government in Pa., taking shape during 1758 as negotiations with Penn proved futile, was a major factor in BF's loss of his Assembly seat in 1764, and became the main reason for his second agency to Great Britain until 1770, when the dispute between all the colonies and the mother country submerged other issues.

8. See above, p. 58, for Norris' illness, and below, pp. 169–70, for his book account with Thomas Osborne.

9. See above, V, 233 n, for James Short, and VII, 284 n, for the telescope.

1. See the preceding document.

2. At the Easton conference of November 1756 the Indians asserted that they had been cheated by proprietary land agents in the Walking Purchase of 1737 and other treaties; see above, VII, 15–23, 111–14. On Dec. 14, 1756, Governor Denny directed the Council to look into the whole matter, naming three members to whose care the inquiry was "more immediately committed." The investigation dragged on for more than a year and then, at a meeting on Jan. 6, 1758, at which none of the three specially named councilors was present, other members submitted a report which Denny and the Council unanimously approved. It exonerated the proprietary agents, blamed the Indian defection directly on the Assembly for refusing to grant funds to arm the Delaware against the French, and by innuendo accused the Quakers of instigating the complaints at Easton. Apparently the three specially named

Endorsed: London Septr. 16. 1758 Benja Franklin Seperate Notes recd Janry. 1759 The Ministry would chearfully join in Resuming the Governmt on an Applicatn from the Assembly or &c[3]

To Hugh Roberts

ALS: Historical Society of Pennsylvania

Dear Friend,   London, Sept. 16. 1758

Your kind Letter of June 1.[4] gave me great Pleasure. I thank you for the Concern you express about my Health, which at present seems tolerably confirm'd by my late Journeys into different Parts of the Kingdom, that have been highly entertaining as well as useful to me. Your Visits to my little Family in my Absence are very obliging, and I hope you will be so good as to continue them. Your Remark on the Thistle and the Scotch Motto, made us very merry, as well as your String of Puns. You will allow me to claim a little Merit or Demerit in the last, as having had some hand in making you a Punster; but the Wit of the first is keen, and all your own.

Two of the former Members of the Junto you tell me are departed this Life, Potts and Parsons.[5] Odd Characters, both of them. Parsons, a wise Man, that often acted foolishly. Potts, a Wit, that seldom acted wisely. If *Enough* were the Means to make a Man happy, One had always the *Means* of Happiness without ever enjoying the *Thing;* the other had always the *Thing* without ever possessing the Means. Parsons, even in his Prosperity, always fretting! Potts, in the midst of his Poverty, ever laughing! It seems, then, that Happiness in this Life rather depends on Internals than Externals; and that, besides the natural Effects of Wisdom and

---

councilors had been critical of one or another part of this report as drafted by their colleagues and it was entered on the Council minutes only on Jan. 20, 1759, signed by Lynford Lardner and four other councilors not including any of the three. *Pa. Col. Recs.*, VII, 354, 776; VIII, 244–59; 1 *Pa. Arch.*, III, 299–300. Why the copy BF received bore only Lardner's signature is not clear. For Secretary Richard Peters' "prevarication" about what had been said at Easton and discussed in the report, see above, VII, 112 n.

3. In Norris' hand.

4. See above, pp. 81–5, for the letter and for other matters mentioned below by BF and not otherwise explained here.

5. Stephen Potts and William Parsons; see above, II, 209 n; I, 359 n.

Virtue, Vice and Folly, there is such a Thing as being of a happy or an unhappy Constitution. They were both our Friends, and lov'd us. So, Peace to their Shades. They had their Virtues as well as their Foibles; they were both honest Men, and that alone, as the World goes, is one of the greatest of Characters. They were old Acquaintance, in whose Company I formerly enjoy'd a great deal of Pleasure, and I cannot think of losing them, without Concern and Regret.

Let me know in your next, to what Purposes Parsons will'd his Estate from his Family; you hint at something which you have not explain'd.[6]

I shall, as you suppose, look on every Opportunity you give me of doing you Service, as a Favour, because it will afford me Pleasure. Therefore send your Orders for buying Books as soon as you please. I know how to make you ample Returns for such Favours, by giving you the Pleasure of Building me a House.[7] You may do it without losing any of your own Time; it will only take some Part of that you now spend in other Folks Business. 'Tis only jumping out of their Waters into mine.

I am grieved for our Friend Syng's Loss. You and I, who esteem him, and have valuable Sons ourselves, can sympathise with him sincerely. I hope yours is perfectly recovered, for your sake as well as for his own. I wish he may be in every Respect as good and as useful a Man as his Father. I need not wish him more; and can now only add that I am, with great Esteem, Dear Friend, Yours affectionately   B FRANKLIN

Mr. Roberts

P.S. I rejoice to hear of the Prosperity of the Hospital, and send the Wafers.

I do not quite like your absenting yourself from that good old Club the Junto: Your more frequent PRE SENCE might be a means

6. In printing this letter in 1838 Sparks silently omitted this paragraph and the last one of the postscript; *Works*, VII, 180–2. His instructions to his copyist, written in ink, remain on the MS. Later editors have copied from Sparks.

7. When BF was building his house in 1764–65, he assigned the supervision to another friend, Samuel Rhoads, but he asked Roberts, an ironmonger, to oversee the installation of an oven with a contrivance to carry off steam and smoke, and to give advice on the completion of the "Habitation."

of keeping them from being ALL ENgag'd[8] in Measures not the best for the Publick Welfare. I exhort you therefore to return to your Duty; and, as the Indians say, to confirm my Words, I send you a Birmingham Tile.

I thought the neatness of the Figures would please you.[9]

Pray send me a good Impression of the Hospital Seal in Wax. 2 or three would not be amiss, I may make a good Use of them.[1]

Addressed: To / Mr Hugh Roberts / Philadelphia

Endorsed: Letter from Benja Franklin dated London sept 16. 1758 recd per Capt Duncan Janry 1759

From Eyre Whalley

ALS: Historical Society of Pennsylvania

Sir, Ecton Sept. 16th. 1758

I return you my most Sincere thanks for your very kind Presents to me and my wife, which have done, and will afford very agreeable Entertainment to each of us:[2] our acknowlegments for them Shou'd have been much earlier, had I not waited to see, if I cou'd meet with any Letter or other Composition of Mr. Thomas Franklin; in which Inquiry I have hitherto in a great Measure been unsuccessful. The Inclosed is a Lease of his drawing, of which kind I have Several now in my Possession; it is in his own Handwriting, and Signed by him and his wife.[3] I am told, by a very good Lawyer, he has Seen Several Conveyances that were made by him, and that they were very well done: and I believe he had a good deal of Business of that Sort in this Neighbourhood. He had

8. William Allen, the proprietary leader.

9. Roberts acknowledged receipt of the tile, May 15, 1760, remarking on its fine painting, "a great curiosity."

1. BF probably hoped to raise some funds for the hospital from British friends.

2. BF's presents have not been identified and his letter (if one accompanied them) has not been found. See above, pp. 114–17, for Whalley's services to BF.

3. The document, remaining with the letter, is an indenture dated May 1, 1682, between Peter Whalley and Francis Smith for the lease of some glebe lands; it is signed by Peter Whalley and witnessed by "Thos Franklin" and "Eleanor Franklin." BF wrote on it "Old Lease of Uncle Thomas's Drawing." See above, pp. 137–8, for Thomas Franklin and his renown in Ecton.

a Natural Turn and Genius for Musick, he put up the Chimes in our Church, made a House-organ, and, I am informed by Some now in the Parish that remember him, used frequently to amuse himself with playing upon it. If I can pick up any thing of his worth your Notice, during your Stay in this part of the world, I will certainly transmit it to you. My wife joins in best Compliments to you and your Son with Sir, your most obliged and most humble Servant   E WHALLEY

To the Printer of The London Chronicle

Printed in *The London Chronicle: or, Universal Evening Post,* September 16–19, 1758.[4]

Partly on the testimony of Lord Baltimore's uncle and secretary, Cecilius Calvert, and partly from internal evidence, Verner W. Crane attributed these "Queries" to Franklin.[5] Although he was not officially connected with any group in Maryland, Franklin's intervention in the disputes of that province is easily explained. Like Pennsylvania, Maryland was a proprietary province whose proprietor refused to consent to the taxation of his estates. Therefore, anything which could be done to discredit the proprietary government in Maryland was likely to weaken the Penns as well. By assailing the conduct of Lord Baltimore and his deputy, Franklin was, as Professor Crane has remarked, mounting a "flank attack" upon Thomas Penn.[6]

4. Also reprinted in Verner W. Crane, ed., *Benjamin Franklin's Letters to the Press 1758–1775* (Chapel Hill, [1950]), pp. 3–7. Students of BF's political writings are much indebted to Professor Crane for this volume. In it he thoroughly examines the public prints of the period and not only lists contributions previously recognized as by Franklin, but identifies and reprints a large number never before correctly attributed to him in earlier compilations. The present editors are happy to acknowledge how greatly Professor Crane has simplified this part of their work.

5. Calvert wrote Gov. Horatio Sharpe of Md., Dec. 5, 1758, that the "supposed Author is Mr. Franklyn by Correspondent from Maryland." *Archives of Maryland,* XXXI (1911), 507. Sharpe wrote a rebuttal, not published at the time, but printed in *Md. Hist. Mag.,* XXXIII (1938), 233–47. Crane points out that the signature used in this letter, A.B., was the same that BF used in his "Cool Thoughts" pamphlet, April 12, 1764, which also linked the Md. and Pa. cases; and that BF seems to have sent the September 19 issue of the *Chronicle* to the leaders of the Assembly as soon as it came off the press (see above, p. 152 n). Crane, *Letters to the Press,* p. 7, notes 8, 10.

6. *Ibid.,* p. 4 n.

To the PRINTER, &c.

SIR,

I have seen in the papers lately, the following article of news, viz.

"They write from Maryland, that their Assembly had passed a bill for raising 1000 men, and £45,000 to pay them, as the quota of that Province towards the expedition against Fort Duquesne, in obedience to his Majesty's Commands signified in a letter from Mr. Secretary Pitt; but that the said bill had unfortunately miscarried, having received a negative, chiefly on account of its proposing to tax the Proprietary Estate as well as the other Estates of the Province; which the Government there will not permit. That two other bills for raising considerable sums for his Majesty's service, had miscarried on the same account within this last year; and so the Virginia and Pennsylvania forces are gone by themselves, without the expected assistance from Maryland.[7] It is hoped, however, that they may be strong enough to effect the service: though, since General Abercrombie's repulse,[8] people are in some pain for them, lest the French should spare a force sufficient to intercept and defeat them."[9]

And afterwards in the *Public Advertiser* of Monday, Sept. 11, the following paragraph, viz.

"The paragraph inserted in the Chronicle of the 6th instant, and from thence published in other News Papers, throwing a reflection on the Proprietor of Maryland, and the Government of that Province, as if a negative had been put on some supply bills for his Majesty's service, chiefly because the Government there would not permit the Proprietary Estate to be taxed; we are assured is a malicious insinuation, void of truth, and it is well known the Proprietary Estates are already taxed equally with the Estates of

7. In response to William Pitt's letter of Dec. 30, 1757, urging the colonies to increase their exertions, Sharpe convened the Md. Assembly on March 28, 1758. The lower house passed the supply bill on April 8. For the political setting, see Charles A. Barker, *The Background of the Revolution in Maryland* (New Haven, 1940), pp. 237–48. For the Pa. response to Pitt's letter, see above, pp. 54–5; and for Norris' comment on the Md. situation, p. 101.

8. At Ticonderoga, July 8, 1758.

9. This paragraph appeared in *London Chron.*, Sept. 5–7, 1758, perhaps written or inspired by BF.

any of the inhabitants in Maryland; and that the Proprietor has no objection thereto."[1]

When I read the first, I had not the least doubt of the truth of it, as it agreed perfectly with letters I myself had received from correspondents of credit in that Province.[2] I was therefore surprized to find the facts flatly contradicted in the second, and with that air of confidence that is usually inspired by a good cause, and a clear knowledge of the truth. So I recurred again to my letters; and as I have a respect for the Proprietor, and would be far from joining with any malicious person, in throwing reflections void of truth, I shall rather give an opportunity to his Lordship's friend to remove them, by letting him know in what light things are seen and represented here by the people of that Province to their correspondents, of which, perhaps, he may not be fully apprized. This I shall do in the following Queries, which the gentleman may answer if he thinks proper.[3]

1. Whether the only tax in Maryland, of which his Lordship pays any part, be not the tax of *One Shilling* only, for every hundred acres of surveyed or occupied land?

2. Whether the tax of one shilling per hundred acres on all the surveyed lands in Maryland, subject to that tax, is any considerable sum; as, whether it amounts to £1500 or 2000 per annum, more or less, paid by the whole Estates of the Province, including the Proprietor's.

3. Whether the Proprietor's share of this small sum, be not very small, as he only pays for his manor lands, and they but a small part of the Province?[4]

1. Cecilius Calvert may have been responsible for this paragraph.

2. Not identified.

3. No reply appeared in any of the London papers. In his letter to Sharpe attributing this paper to Franklin, Dec. 5, 1758, Calvert called it "Impertinent and ridiculous not worthy answer tho' easy of confute." *Archives of Maryland,* XXXI (1911), 507.

4. In answering these three queries Sharpe admitted that this tax was the only one which the proprietor would pay, but argued that Baltimore's share was unduly high, partly because for various reasons his manor lands produced less income than those of the inhabitants in general. The governor stated that the total proprietary income was about £16,500 Maryland currency (£11,000 sterling) per annum, but he undertook to determine Baltimore's proper share of the tax by comparing this personal *net* income with the *gross* produce of the province, which he estimated at about £1,070,000 currency. He concluded

4. Whether the Proprietor has not other ways very large incomes or revenues from the Province?[5]

5. Whether his share of the said one shilling tax be a penny, a farthing, or even half a farthing per pound, more or less, per ann. on those revenues?[6]

6. Whether the act of 1756, by which that tax was laid, does not, for raising the supply of forty thousand pounds thereby granted, lay several heavy taxes on the people, of which the Proprietor, by his residence in England, can pay little or no part; such as an excise on liquors; a particular tax on batchelors, proportioned to their estates; a duty on horses; a duty on writs, conveyances, leases, and other instruments and law proceedings; a duty on negroes; a duty on pitch, tar, turpentine, &c. And whether, this being the case, it can properly and *truly* be said, "that the Proprietary Estates are already taxed *equally* with the Estates of any of the inhabitants of Maryland?"

7. Whether the sum granted by the said act and struck in paper bills, has not been, some time since, totally expended, and the said funds mortgaged for years to come, to sink the bills and discharge the debt?

8. Whether it did not become necessary last year to pass a new bill for raising more money, and providing additional funds; which being accordingly done by the Assembly, the same received a flat negative?

9. Whether the Assembly did not then pass another bill to raise £25,000 by an equal assessment on all estates, faculties, and incomes, the Proprietary's not excepted?

10. Whether this bill did not, during the debates upon it in the House, receive all the opposition the influence of the government could give it, both within and without doors; notwithstanding which it passed by a majority of forty to ten?

---

that Baltimore would be paying about £390 too much. This and Sharpe's other answers to BF's queries are from *Md. Hist. Mag.*, XXXIII (1938), 233–47.

5. Barker, who has made a thorough analysis of proprietary revenues in Maryland, shows that during the 1750s the proprietor's net income transferred to England varied from about £10,600 sterling to about £15,000. Of the total about £1000 sterling was derived from the rental of manor lands. *Background*, pp. 139–44.

6. Three pence in the pound, said Sharpe.

11. Whether this bill did not also receive, when it came up, a flat negative?

12. Whether on Mr. Pitt's letter, recommending vigorous measures against the enemy, the House did not last winter resolve on a grant of £45,000 for the current year, and to raise 1000 men, and send up a third bill for that purpose on the same equitable plan?[7]

13. Whether this third bill did not also receive a flat negative?

14. Whether about this time the militia were not forced out from their homes to the frontiers in a very severe season?

15. Whether it is not a prevailing opinion in Maryland, that this was done to distress the people, and cause them to urge their representatives to come into any terms of raising money, rather than they should be obliged to leave their stocks of cattle perishing for want of care, and have no opportunity of making preparation for another crop?

16. Whether the Assembly did not resolve, that this unnecessary measure was *without Law to warrant it?*[8]

17. Whether they were not, however, prevailed on to depart from the usual forms, and agree to a conference on the latter bill, though a money bill?

18. Whether one of the principal points of conference was not, *the taxation of the Proprietary estate?*

19. Whether the Council did not particularly and zealously contend for the Proprietor against that taxation?[9]

20. Whether the Council of Maryland are not appointed, without the least concurrence of the Crown, *solely by the Proprietor,* and removeable at his will?

7. Sharpe's comments on this bill conclude: "Let it suffice here to say that His Majesty's Attorney General Mr. Pratt thinks it unjust and unreasonable and hath given it as his opinion that the Bill was such a One as could not have been enacted into a Law without a Breach of Publick Faith and a Violation of the Maryland Constitution."

8. Sharpe held that the militia call was legal and justified, that those who opposed it did so to weaken his authority over the militia, and that when he next called out the militia "several hundred . . . readily marched and served under the Governor's Command."

9. Sharpe responded that the objection to the bill was not so much the taxation of the Proprietor as the Assembly's effort to control expenditures by naming commissioners in the bill for that purpose, a usurpation of prerogative. See above, VI, 284, 290; VII, 131–2, 150, for the Pa. Assembly's handling of this problem.

21. Whether most of its members, or their families, do not enjoy posts, not only of honour, but of *great profit,* under the Proprietor, and during his pleasure?[1]

22. Whether therefore it is not probable—they have never been well informed "That the Proprietor had no objection to being taxed equally with any of the inhabitants of the Province for its defence;" or otherwise they would not have dared to act a part so prejudicial to his honour?

23. Whether if the taxing of their offices was the principal thing they were averse to, and they presumed to use his Lordship's name and concerns as a screen for their own selfishness, and thereby defeated a bill so necessary for the King's service, they do not deserve some mark of his Lordship's displeasure?

24. Whether the people of Maryland do not at present stand in an unfavourable light, as not having contributed to this year's service?

25. Whether they have any Agent here to present their complaints and justify their conduct?[2]

26. Whether the Assembly did not, in the last session, present a bill to raise money for the payment of an Agent, which received a negative, as other bills of the like kind have heretofore done?

27. Whether a negative to such a bill was a measure as honest as it was politic?

28. Whether this may not justify any friend of that Province, though only a trader thither, in laying a true state of their affairs before the Publick, as far as they come to his knowledge?[3]

My last query is more general, viz.

Whether the frequent clashings of interests between the Proprietors and people of our colonies, which of late have been so

1. Sharpe responded, quite correctly, that a similar practice existed in the neighboring colonies under direct control of the Crown.

2. Baltimore's secret instructions to Sharpe had forbidden him to pass any agency bill unless it named Secretary Calvert as agent. Barker, *Background,* p. 238. Sharpe replied to this query by saying that the Lower House "want an Agent to serve themselves, only, to insert Queries in London Chronicles, ... or to harrass the Proprietary whenever he may happen to disoblige a Leading Member."

3. Sharpe was "pretty sure that the Querist is no Trader to the province," because British merchants feared the proposed bill would adversely affect their business with Maryland.

prejudicial to his Majesty's service, and the defence of his dominions, do not at length make it necessary for this nation to enquire into the nature and conduct of these Proprietary Governments, and put them on a better footing?[4] I am, Sir, yours, &c.

A.B.

To Deborah Franklin ALS: American Philosophical Society

My dear Child, London, September 21. 1758

I have wrote you a long Letter of 3 Sheets per Duncan, and sent also in a large Pacquet directed to you, a great Number of Letters for my Friends. By Bolitho I shall send you some Stuff for Chair Bottoms, and an Iron Oven if I can get it on board.[5] Seal the enclos'd before you forward it. I have this Day got a most violent Cold, but hope it will wear off without any Sickness.[6] Billy not yet return'd from the Country. We have lately met with a small Rebuff in France. The Troops are return'd.[7] Mr. Shutz's Brother

---

4. To raise this issue was obviously the author's chief reason for writing the letter. As Crane has pointed out, the case for BF's authorship is greatly strengthened by comparing this passage with his "Separate Notes" to Norris of Sept. 16, 1758, above pp. 157–8. Sharpe replied to this query at length, commenting that in royal as well as proprietary governments "a few ill disposed persons of but common Abilities" in the elective branches of the assemblies will impose on "the inferiour Class of People." One could not be surprised if at elections "their Choice falls for the most part on such as are fit Tools for Demagogues to work with." Could the querist "point out a Remedy for the Evil without depriving the People of their Liberty and Priviledges? or will he insist that neither the People nor their Representatives can be ever in the wrong."

5. See above, pp. 133–46, for the long letter, and below, p. 226 n, for the arrivals of Captains Duncan and Bolitho in Philadelphia. The "Pacquet" probably contained the several letters of the 16th. BF paid £1 10s. 8d. for eight yards of cotton, perhaps for chair bottoms, on Sept. 21, 1758, and on October 26 paid £5 7s. 8d. for the oven. "Account of Expences," pp. 34, 36; *PMHB*, LV (1931), 114–15.

6. William Strahan wrote David Hall, Sept. 26, 1758, "Mr. Franklin I saw yesterday. He has got a little Cold, which has obliged him to keep at home this two or three Days. He is really a most sensible and amiable Man." APS.

7. A poorly led British force at the Bay of St. Cas, Brittany, suffered heavy casualties in re-embarking on Sept. 11, 1758. Gipson, *British Empire*, VII, 136–7.

has the Birmingham Things in his Care.[8] I am, Dear Debby Your ever loving Husband   B FRANKLIN

Addressed: To / Mrs Franklin / at the Post Office / Philadelphia / per the Carolina / Capt. Duncan

Thomas Osborne:[9] Bill and Receipt

ADS: Historical Society of Pennsylvania

I.N.
Benja. Franklyn Esqr.   Bought of T. Osborne
pd

1757

Decr. 6.	Compleat Body of Gardening[1]	1. 16	–
	Philiders fr. Book of Chess[2]	– 3.	6
	Compleat Body of Husbandry	1. 15	–
7.	Journals of the H. of Commons vol. ⎱ 21. 22. 23[3] ⎰	10. 10	–

1758

Sept. 15.	Body of Gardening	1. 16	–
	2 Body of Husbandry	3. 10	–
	2 Lisles Observations on Do.	1. –	–

£20. 10. 6

To The Remainder of a parcell of ⎫
New Books sent to Mr. James Read ⎬   21   – –
now in the Hands of Mr. Dunlap[4] ⎭

41: 10. 6

8. See above, pp. 144–5.

9. For Thomas Osborne, the bookseller, see above, VII, 176 n.

1. The titles of the books on gardening and husbandry in this bill, bought for Charles and Isaac Norris, are given above, VII, 176 n. Invoices for those sent to Isaac are in BF's accounts with him; see above, pp. 147–8.

2. A.D. Philidor (pseud. of François André Danican), *L'Analyze des échecs, containant une novelle méthode pour apprendre en peu de tems à se perfectioner dans ce noble jeu* (London, 1749). BF probably bought this book for his own use.

3. BF bought these volumes for the province, as shown in his statement of disbursements for the public account submitted to Isaac Norris, Feb. 15, 1763, Hist. Soc. Pa.

4. Probably Osborne had sent these books to Read, and when DF's relative William Dunlap began selling books in Philadelphia (above, VII, 169 n), he took over this unsold stock from Read, who was notoriously delinquent in

N.B. there are parcell of Old Books still to be setled now in the Hands of Mr. Norris[5]

Recd Septr. 27th. 1758 of Benja. Franklyn Esqr forty one pounds 10s. 6d. in full of this bill. (Excepting the Old Books in Mr. Norris Hand still to be setled)[6]

THO OSBORNE

Endorsed: T. Osborne Bill £41. 10. 6

From David Colden[7]

ALS: American Philosophical Society; draft (incomplete): New-York Historical Society

Sir   Coldengham October 26th. 1758

About the time you left America, I was employd in endeavouring, with my Fathers assistance, to form an explication of the phenomena of Electricity, on his Principles of action in matter:[8] some conceptions had occur'd to me in pursuing the Experiments made by you and Mr. Canton, which gave me reason to hope it might be effected on very simple principles. When I had compleated this attempt, a Copy of it was designed to be sent to Lon-

---

paying his English debts, and had given up bookselling in 1747; see above, III, 175 n, 316–17, 329–30, 377–9, 394; IV, 142; V, 191.

5. Probably also some of Read's former stock in trade, which had been stored with BF and had been turned over to Norris along with some of BF's own old publications. Norris complained, April 29, 1758, that "The Sharpness and Acrid Salts Contracted by Their laying in some damp Place got into my mouth and stomach To such a Degree, that At the beginning of this Session I could not Attend the House, and it was like to have had worse Effects"; see above, p. 58. As Norris asked him to do, Jan. 17, 1759 (below, pp. 228–9), BF paid Osborne £40 "in part for a Parcel of old Books," June 7, 1759, and charged Norris accordingly. The payment is included in BF's accounts with Norris (above, pp. 147–8) and recorded in "Account of Expences," p. 41; *PMHB*, LV (1931), 120.

6. On this date BF recorded the payment to Osborne and the fact that the Norris brothers owed him £9 17s. for the books on gardening and husbandry. "Account of Expences," pp. 34–5; *PMHB*, LV (1931), 114.

7. Son of Cadwallader Colden and the author of a defense of BF's electrical theories; see above, V, 135–44. He had written a letter very similar to this, Sept. 18, 1757, but, as he explains here, it never reached BF; see above, VII, 263–4.

8. Cadwallader Colden, *The Principles of Action in Matter, the Gravitation of Bodies, and the Motion of the Planets* (London, 1751). See above, II, 416–18.

don last September was a Year, but being unfortunately taken by the French on board the Irene, Captain Jacobson, was carried into Lewisburgh.[9]

Had not your absence from America prevented your seeing those papers before they were finished, I doubt not but they would have been much more correct; however I am so unwilling to have them appear in publick before you have had an oppertunity of judging them, that I have desired my Cousin Alexander Colden (as I formerly did) to leave the Copy I now send, some time with you, for your consideration.[1] The favour which I have formerly had of corresponding with you on this subject, gives me assurance that you will take the trouble of considering it, and of leting me know your sentiments of it. I shall esteem it a great favour Sir, that you make corrections in any part which may appear to want it. I had much rather not have it publishd, than that it should afterwards appear unworthy the notice of the Judicious: but if it meet with your approbation I shall reckon myself very safe in the publication. I must beg you to let my Cousin see what you write me on this occasion, that he may know how to order the Printing; for I shall desire him to delay it, in case you make any material objections, till I have an oppertunity of obviating them, or recalling my error.[2]

9. David Colden had directed that the paper sent in 1757 be delivered to the Academy of Sciences in Paris in case of its capture by a French ship. There is no evidence, however, that this was done. In May 1759, Alexander Colden saw some extracts from the *Histoire* of the Academy reprinted in *Gent. Mag.* and jumped to the erroneous conclusion that they were pirated from his cousin's work. They were, in fact, on the controversy between Nollet and LeRoy over BF's electrical theories. *Gent. Mag.*, XXIX (1759), 220–3; *Colden Paps.*, V, 254, 259, 301–2.

1. The paper which Colden now sent was revised and hence "more correct" than the one of the preceding year. *Colden Paps.*, V, 259–60. A copy of a paper by David Colden, "Supplement to Principles of Action in Matter," extending his father's theories of matter and gravitation to the electrical phenomena, is in N.-Y. Hist. Soc. Another copy of the "Supplement" is appended to a manuscript revision of his father's work in the University of Edinburgh Library. Probably, but not certainly, both these documents are copies of the 1758 revision, which was never published.

2. Colden sent his paper to Peter Collinson for delivery to Alexander Colden. Collinson reported, March 6, 1759, that he had carried out these instructions and that next Franklin is to see David's paper. "It happens very Suiteable for Him for he has Just finish'd an Electrical Machine on his own

My Father desires his sincere Complements to you.

Your advice to my Cousin, in any thing concerning this peice, shall be most gratefully acknowledgd by, Sir Your most Obedient and most Humble Servant   DAVID COLDEN

To Benjm. Franklin Esq.

Addressed: To / Benjamine Franklin Esqr / att / London

To Jane Mecom   ALS: American Philosophical Society

Dear Sister   London Nov. 11. 1758

I wrote you a long Letter of Sept. 16. and again I wrote to you Oct. 2. since which I have receiv'd your Favour of Augt. 15.[3] You mention its being sent by the Son of our good Friend Dr. Perkins.[4] I have not seen him yet, but shall endeavour to find him out. I hope my Health is now pretty well established by the frequent Journies I have made this Summer, and that I shall be able to go pretty well thro' another Winter. In our last Journey stopping at a Place call'd Attleborough, I think it was in Suffolk,[5] we found in the Church Yard the following Inscription on a large handsome Stone

"*In Memory of Thomas Foulger, late of Illington Hall, who died Dec. 23d. 1754. aged 51 Years.*"

As I have never in my Life met with or heard of any Foulgers but

place [plan?]—which is remarkly Different from any I have Seen." Alexander wrote twelve days later that he had "not yet had time to examine my Cousins theory of Electricity with the attention it deserves, but shall convey it to Mr. Franklyn, who will probably be able either to confirm or illustrate it by his Experiments." BF wrote Cadwallader Colden, Dec. 3, 1760, expressing his regret that the "valuable Work" of the "very ingenious young Gentleman . . . has not yet been made publick." *Colden Paps.,* V, 297, 298–9, 376. Some of David's work has not been entirely unnoticed, however; *The American Magazine,* I (January 1758), pp. 164–6, published his "New Experiments in Electricity"; and descriptions of some other experiments, sent to his father, March 2, 1758, were printed in 1923 in *Colden Paps.,* V, 220–7.

3. See above, pp. 152–5, for the "long letter" of September 16. The letters of October 2 and August 15 mentioned here have not been found.

4. For John Perkins, Boston physician and BF's scientific correspondent, see above, IV, 267 n. Nothing is known about his son.

5. Attleborough is in Norfolk. For "our last Journey" see above, p. 132 n.

those of our Family, I made Billy copy it, intending to enquire after them when we return'd, but we came another Way.[6] Pray ask Cousin Abisha Foulger[7] if he or any in Nantucket can tell what Part of England our Grandfather Peter Foulger came from. I think I have heard our Mother say he came out of Suffolk, but am not certain.[8] In Dr. Mather's Magnalia,[9] I find that in Bishop Laud's Time a great many eminent Ministers with Numbers of their Friends and Hearers went out of Suffolk, Norfolk, and Lincolnshire, to New England, flying from the Persecution then on foot against the Puritans. It is possible he might be among them. The Dr. mentions him in Page 54 of Book VI. in the Terms of "an able and godly Englishman, well learn'd in the Scriptures," who about the Year 1647 was employ'd as an Assistant to Mr. Mayhew, the same that converted the Indians of Marthas Vineyard.[1]

I never expected much from the Germantown Affair, so am not disappointed.[2] I took Lots and built there in Complaisance to my Brothers, but the Expence was not great. I wish the Glasshouse you mention may have all the Success the Undertakers can desire.

Mr. Strahan has sent a very large Cargo to Benny, which I hope will turn out to his Advantage.[3] I have also order'd him a Cargo of Stationery which will go per the next Ship.[4] I am glad to hear he is industrious and frugal, and that you like his Wife: I make no doubt, that with those Qualities, and the Advantage of so discreet

6. BF did, however, request his friend David Edwards of Bury St. Edmunds (see above, VII, 275 n) to inquire about the Foulgers (Folgers) of Illington. See below, p. 277.

7. B.1.4.6.1, BF and Jane's first cousin once removed.

8. Peter Folger (B.1) was born in Norwich, Norfolk, and came to New England in 1635.

9. Cotton Mather, *Magnalia Christi Americana* (London, 1702).

1. Thomas Mayhew (1593–1682) acquired title to Martha's Vineyard and nearby islands in 1641. His son Thomas (c. 1621–1657) and he were the pioneer missionaries to the Indians in New England and achieved great success in converting the natives of their islands. *DAB*.

2. For the glass works at Germantown in Braintree, Mass., and the Franklins' real estate ventures there, see above, v, 119 n.

3. See above, p. 152.

4. BF paid £67 11s. 4d. for the stationery, Dec. 19, 1758; "Account of Expences," p. 37; *PMHB*, LV (1931), 115.

a Partner, he will do well in the World, which will give me great Pleasure.

Billy presents his Duty to you and Brother, and joins with me in Love to you all. He last Week put on the Gown as a Lawyer; being call'd to the Bar in Westminster Hall. He was enter'd of the Middle Temple some Years before we came over.[5] I am, my dear Sister, Your affectionate Brother   B FRANKLIN

From David Hall   Letterbook copy: American Philosophical Society

Sir   Philadelphia 20th November 1758
Inclosed I have now sent you a Bill of Exchange for one Hundred Pounds Sterling;[6] the second Copy of which I sent by the Dragon Capt. Hammit the Receipt of which you will please to acknowledge, and advise me of its being paid when you have received the Money, which will much Oblige Yours &c.
                                                              D HALL

To Benjamin Franklin Esqr. per Cornelia Capt. Patton

Copia per Capt. Hammit
3d per Capt. Ritchie Via Bristol

From Isaac Norris

Letterbook copy: Historical Society of Pennsylvania

Dear Friend [BF][7]   Pensylva Novr. 21st. 1758
It is easy to perceive the Disposition of the People by the last Election under the Burthen of their heavy Taxes and several severe Losses upon particulars from the Conduct of some of the

---

5. At BF's request, William Strahan had entered WF's name in the Middle Temple, Feb. 11, 1751; he was called to the bar Nov. 10, 1758; see above, IV, 78 n.

6. This bill went in the brig *Cornelia*, Robert Patton, which cleared Philadelphia Nov. 16; the second copy in the ship *Dragon*, Francis Hammet, clearing Nov. 23; the third in the brig *Grace*, John Richy, clearing Dec. 7. BF entered it on Jan. 3, 1759, in "Account of Expences," p. 23; *PMHB*, LV (1931), 115; he acknowledged it on April 8 (below, p. 317).

7. Brackets in the original.

Military Gentlemen towards such as have supplied Our Western Army with Carriages,[8] they are yet willing to bear these and every Thing else in their Power in hopes of preserving their Priviledges as Englishmen.

The Art and every other Means used towards the Electors on One Side; The perfect Indifference in those who are chosen, and indeed the Difficulty of getting them to serve on the other, shew, that the Attack upon what the People apprehend their Just Rights, is carried to great Lengths and without the political Disguises necessary on these Occasions. Are not then Our Rulers egregious Bunglers here who manage this Affair with such Ill Success, and so likely to continue, during their weak Administration. And I heartily wish them no better on that Side of the Water notwithstanding any Inclination to infringe the Rights of their Countrymen in America.

We are now daily expecting to hear the Event of our Western Army who Left Loyalhannen[9] about ten days ago in order to attack Fort du Quesne; This Expedition has cost the Crown a surprizing Sum of Mony and the Colonies not Less in proportion to their Abilities and I wish the Success may in some Manner answer the Expence of which I have no sanguine Expectations.[1] The House is now sitting upon a Call from the Governor in pursuance of a Letter from General Forbes requesting to know what this Province will do towards supporting twelve Hundred Men to garrison the Forts and Entrenchments the Army has made in their Advances towards the Ohio; but I shall refer to the Answer a Com-

8. According to General John Forbes, commander of the expedition against Fort Duquesne, "several Waggoners" had been "abused," presumably for tardiness and carrying light loads. Incidents may also have arisen from an act of the Pa. Assembly, Sept. 20, 1758 (*Statutes at Large, Pa.*, V, 372–4), which offered large inducements for carrying supplies to Raystown. The teamsters who responded would not drive their teams west of Raystown, and Forbes resorted to impressment to get his expedition moving. Forbes to Denny, Sept. 9; to Abercromby, Oct. 8; to Bouquet, Oct. 10, 1758, in Alfred P. James, ed., *Writings of General John Forbes* (Menasha, Wis., 1938), pp. 207, 225, 228.

9. Loyalhanna, the site of Fort Ligonier, was an Indian town forty miles east of Fort Duquesne.

1. On Nov. 24, 1758, the French demolished Fort Duquesne and departed; Forbes's troops occupied its ruins the next day.

mittee are now preparing by order of the House which I hope will be finished Time enough to go by this Conveyance[2] as well as the Minutes of the last Indian Treaty at Easton[3] all which we intend to Authenticate to enable you to act according to the Situation of Affairs during the sitting of the Parliament either before the Parliament or wherever the Application is to be made on Account of the Province.

Several Members of the House were with me fearing we might be deficient in the Necessary Supplies of Mony but as this Sitting of the House is like to be Short and I have already wrote on this Head, I hope you will be free either with my Self or the Committee on this necessary Article, in the Mean time I shall inclose an Order for two Hundred Pounds Sterling to be paid into your Hands which use freely if necessary 'till we can learn the Situation of Our Finances Here and of the Mony wanted there.[4] As for Our other

2. Governor Denny received Forbes's letter of Oct. 22, 1758, on November 6 and summoned the Assembly to meet on November 15. On the 22d the House adopted a committee report which evaded Forbes's request by postponing the consideration of "the raising of Supplies" until its next meeting. On December 6, the Assembly adjourned until February 5. *Votes,* 1758–59, pp. 5, 10–11, 16. BF seems not to have received a copy of the committee report; see below, p. 236.

3. Over 500 Indians, including representatives from all the Six Nations, attended the conference at Easton, Oct. 7–26, 1758. Foremost among their complaints was the Albany Purchase of 1754, by which the proprietary agents had acquired title to all the lands in Pa. west of the Alleghenies; see above, v, 349–50 n and (map) p. 225. On October 20 Denny, in the name of the Proprietors, restored these western lands to the Indians and settled all other disputes except that over the Walking Purchase. This action helped to draw the Indians away from the French and contributed materially to the demise of French power in the Ohio Valley. For this conference see "Benjamin Chew's Journal of a Journey to Easton, 1758," Carl Van Doren and Julian P. Boyd, eds., *Indian Treaties printed by Benjamin Franklin, 1736–1762* (Phila., 1938), pp. 312–18, and the biographies of Croghan, Weiser, Pemberton, and Teedyuscung cited earlier in these volumes. The minutes of the conference were published, Nov. 17, 1758, and went through a second edition the next February. On Jan. 19, 1759, BF complained that he had not yet received them, although he had seen their publication advertised in *Pa. Gaz.;* see below, pp. 236–7.

4. Immediately following this letter in Norris' letterbook is a copy of an order on Giles Baily and Archibald Drummond of Bristol, Nov. 21, 1758, to pay BF £200 sterling from funds due to Norris' daughters Mary and Sarah

Agents I have procured an Order from the Last Assembly for their Salary &c. which will come within our next Supply Bill at our next Sitting.[5] I am your Assured Friend   I N

Endorsed: BF recd [?] ackgd 18 Jan 1759.

From Isaac Norris

Letterbook copy: Historical Society of Pennsylvania

Dear Friend Benjamin Franklin   Philada. Novr 23d. 1758
    Be pleased to receive the inclosed Bill of Exchange John Hunter[6] on Messrs. Thomlinson, Hanbury, Colebrooke & Nisbitt Merchants in London No. 732 for Three Hundred Pounds Sterling. for my Account[7] till further Order from Your Assured Friend
                                                    I N

Wrote [a Seperate Letter][8] at W Griffitts's and Sent by his Young Man who went down after the Vessels.

Endorsed: recd by BF ackgd Janry. 18 1759

---

under the will of their great uncle Dr. William Logan (1686–1757) of Bristol. BF received this order and another for £300 Norris sent him two days later (see the next document), on Jan. 3, 1759. "Account of Expences," p. 23; *PMHB*, LV (1931), 115; Accounts with Isaac Norris, above, pp. 147–8.

5. On Sept. 30, 1758, the House voted Robert Charles and Richard Partridge £100 each. *Votes*, 1757–1758, p. 122. The "next Supply Bill" was passed April 17, 1759. *Votes*, 1758–1759, p. 63.

6. Col. John Hunter of Virginia; see above, VI, 223 n.

7. For BF's receipt of this bill see the next to last footnote to the preceding document.

8. Brackets in the original. Norris presumably meant by the memorandum that he wrote this as a separate letter from that of November 21, immediately above, while at the house of William Griffitts (see above, VII, 174 n) and sent it after the departing convoy by Griffitts' servant.

Ferdinand John Paris: Answer to Heads of Complaint; Thomas and Richard Penn: Message to the Assembly

Printed in *Votes and Proceedings of the House of Representatives,* 1758–1759, pp. 28–31; copy: Maryland Archives; also printed in *Minutes of the Provincial Council of Pennsylvania* (*Pa. Col. Recs.*), VIII, 276–81.[9]

On Aug. 20, 1757, Franklin presented to Thomas and Richard Penn the "Heads of Complaint," a summary of the Pennsylvania Assembly's major grievances against the Proprietors.[1] The Penns refused to answer it, however, until they received the opinions of the attorney general and solicitor general upon it. They submitted the paper, together with a series of queries, to the law officers early in November 1757, but it took a "whole Year (wanting eight Days only)" to get both opinions.[2] On Nov. 27, 1758, the Penns' agent, Ferdinand Paris, drew up an answer for the Proprietors, based in part on the law officers' opinions, and sent it to Franklin. It is printed below as Number I. It made one major concession, as the solicitor general had advised: the Proprietors were now willing "to have the annual Income of their Estate enquired into" and to contribute their fair share, but no more than that, to the public service. The next day, the Penns signed a message to the Assembly in which, besides covering some of the same ground as Paris had, they criticized the procedures the Assembly and its representatives in England had used in presenting these grievances, misrepresented the circumstances under which Franklin had prepared the "Heads of Complaint," abused him personally, and indicated their unwillingness to deal further with him. This message is printed below as Number II. There is no evidence that the Proprietors sent Franklin a copy.

On the same day, November 28, Franklin wrote the Penns asking

9. The Md. Arch. MS copy differs in minor details from the text in *Votes.* It was probably made because the Md. Assembly had a controversy with Lord Baltimore over taxation very similar to that of the Pa. Assembly with the Penns. The text in the Pa. Council minutes has several differences in phraseology from the other two. All three give the Proprietors' message to the Assembly first and Paris' Answer to the "Heads of Complaint" last; they are reversed here in order to follow the correct chronological order. The two printed versions also insert BF's "Heads of Complaint" between the other two papers; it is printed above, VII, 251–2.

1. For the circumstances of the writing, as well as the text, of the "Heads of Complaint," see above, VII, 248–52.

2. Solicitor General Charles Yorke delivered his opinion on Jan. 13, 1758 (see above, VII, 366 n). It was Attorney General Charles Pratt for whose opinion the Proprietors waited until the first week of November 1758. Thomas Penn to Pa. Council, Nov. 10, 1758, Penn Papers, Hist. Soc. Pa.

178

for clarification of certain points in the "Answer" of the 27th (see below, pp. 186–7), and the exchange closed with a message Paris delivered personally "a few Days after" (below, pp. 193–4). On December 8 and 9 Thomas Penn wrote letters to his leading supporters in Pennsylvania, Richard Peters, Benjamin Chew, and William Allen (quoted or cited in appropriate footnotes) and sent them copies of most, if not all, of the documents in the case, of which the two printed here were to be given to the Assembly. Franklin's long letter to Isaac Norris, Jan. 19, 1759 (below, pp. 232–7), also enclosing documents, related his side of the story.

I
ANSWER *to* HEADS *of* COMPLAINT.

London, November 27. 1758.

The Proprietaries of Pennsylvania have well considered the Paper laid before them, called "*Heads of Complaint.*" They have also taken the best Advice they could procure upon the same; and some Answer would have been given long since, had not one of the Agents prevented the Proprietaries from obtaining their Counsel's Opinion and Advice thereon.[3]

The Proprietaries could have wished, in order to that Harmony which they most sincerely desire, that the House of Representatives had sent some Address, Representation, or Memorial, pointing out clearly and distinctly any Grievances they thought themselves under; and that they had given as full Powers, as the Nature of such a Case would admit, to some Person of Candour,[4] to enter into the Detail and full Discussion of those several Matters, which seem to be alluded to in the Heads of Complaint.

Had those Things been done, which the Proprietaries conceive to be the common and ordinary Methods of proceeding in such Cases, many Points might have been speedily adjusted to mutual Satisfaction, and particularly all such, wherein the Questions arise between the Proprietaries personally, and the House of Representatives; in which Instances the House may assuredly rely on the utmost Indulgences that can, with Justice or Reason, be desired.

3. The agent referred to was Robert Charles. For his Fabian tactics see above, p. 4 n. BF explained his patience with Charles' strategy to Isaac Norris, Jan. 19, 1759, below p. 233.
4. A hit at BF.

As to others, wherein the Rights and Prerogatives of the Crown, intrusted to the Proprietaries, may be affected, it is hoped the House would not, for their own Sakes, desire the Proprietaries to attempt to give up any of those.

It admits of Observation, that the Heads of Complaint begin by transposing some Parts of the Royal Charter, as if that had, in explicit Terms, prescribed the Discretion of the Assembly to be made use of in making Laws; the Proprietaries desire to be perfectly understood in this Matter; they do not so much as imagine, but that the Representatives of the People will, and must use a Discretion in choosing, whether they will, or will not, give their Advice and Assent to any Law; but the Charter (when read in its own Language) gives the Power to make Laws to the Proprietary, and his Deputy or Lieutenant, according to their best Discretions (always with the Advice and Assent of the Representatives) and does not run in the Terms set forth in the Paper of Complaint.[5]

5. In the Royal Charter of Pa., Charles II granted "free, full and absolute power" to William Penn and his heirs and "to all his and their Deputies, and Lieutenants" to make "any Lawes whatsoever . . . according unto their best discretions, by and with the advice, assent and approbacon of the freemen of the said Countrey." *Pa. Col. Recs.,* I, 19. In the "Heads of Complaint," BF began by observing that "the reasonable and necessary Power given to Deputy Governors of Pennsylvania by the Royal Charter, Section 4th. and 5th. of making Laws with the Advice and Consent of the Assembly, for Raising Money for the Safety of the Country and other Publick Uses, 'according to their best Discretion,' is taken away by Proprietary Instructions enforced by penal Bonds, and restraining the Deputy from the Use of his best Discretion." In his letter to Norris, Jan. 19, 1759, BF quite properly observed that Paris' strictures on his "transposing" some parts of the Royal Charter were "mere Cavilling," because he "neither meant, nor had Occasion to mean in that Place, anything but what related to the Discretion of the Deputies as restrained by Proprietary Instructions, contrary to the Charter" (below, p. 235). The phraseology of the Royal Charter of 1681 certainly suggests that the initiative in legislation was to rest with the Proprietors or their deputies and that the Assembly had only the right to give or withhold its "advice, assent and approbacon" of measures proposed to it. A comparable formula appeared in the enacting clause of all legislation in England and the colonies, but the power of the initiative had passed in fact to Parliament, and especially to the House of Commons, early in the seventeenth century, and the British government recognized and accepted a similar development in the colonies in 1680. Wallace Notestein, "The Winning of the Initiative by the House of Commons," British Academy *Proc.,* 1924–25, p. 175; Leonard W. Labaree, *Royal Government in America* (New Haven, 1930), pp. 219–22, 422, 429.

Persons not well inclined to Governors, or Government, may indeed desire that all Matters whatsoever should be left to the Discretion of a Lieutenant, on the Spot, whom the House might supply, or not, just as he should yield up that Discretion of his, more or less, to them;[6] but as long as Instructions are constantly given to every Person intrusted with the Government of any British Colony (and Bonds also required from every such Person for Observance of such Instructions) as long as Instructions are constantly given to all Persons whatsoever, executing even the regal Government of His Majesty's Kingdoms during the Royal Absence; as long as these Proprietaries are repeatedly commanded by the Crown, upon the Nomination of each successive Lieu-tenant-Governor, to give Instructions to such Lieutenant; and as long as a Lieutenant-Governor may, by his Misbehaviour (if left intirely to his Discretion) bring the Proprietaries Estate and Franchises into Danger; so long the Proprietaries must contend to give Instructions to, and take Bonds from, their Lieutenant-Governor.[7]

The particular Matters wherein a Lieutenant-Governor should be instructed, make a very different Consideration, wherein the Proprietaries, and such Persons authorised as aforesaid, might surely put the same upon a reasonable Footing; the Proprietaries, however, cannot be of Opinion, that their Instructions were such as would have made it impossible to have raised Sums sufficient for the Defence of the Country, in Addition to the Forces sent from Great-Britain, supposing those Sums applied in a proper Manner.[8]

6. In the "Heads of Complaint" BF had contended that the deputy governor, "being on the Spot," could "better judge of the Emergency State and Neces-sity of Affairs" than the Proprietors and that therefore the instructions by which they were bound were unreasonable.

7. In discussing the propriety of instructions, Paris was relying on and, in some cases, paraphrasing the opinion of Solicitor General Yorke, Jan. 13, 1758, Penn Papers, Hist. Soc. Pa.

8. Paris intended that this paragraph should answer the second paragraph of the "Heads of Complaint," in which BF had contended that the "Modes, Measures, and Times" of raising money prescribed in the governor's instruc-tions reduced the Assembly "to the Necessity of either losing the Country to the Enemy, or giving up the Liberties of the People, and receiving Law from the Proprietary."

The Proprietaries conceive, that the last Paragraph of the Complaint is extremely injurious to them, and very unjust,[9] as it insinuates, that they would not contribute their Proportion to the Defence of the Province. It is true, they did instruct their Lieutenant-Governor not to assent to any Law, by which their Quit-Rents should be taxed; this they did, because they thought it not proper to submit the Taxing their chief Rents, due to them as Lords of the Fee, to the Representatives of their Tenants; but that there might not be the least Shadow of Pretence for accusing them of Cruelty and Injustice, they ordered Five Thousand Pounds to be paid for the public Service, out of the Arrears of that very Fund;[1] and they leave it to the World to judge, whether it was not unjust and cruel in the late Assemblies, to tax them with refusing to contribute, only because it was not done in the Manner the Representatives of the People insisted on having it done: However, to take off all Pretence of Clamour, they are very ready to have the annual Income of their Estate enquired into, and are as ready to contribute whatever the said Sum shall fall short of their Proportion of what has been laid on the Inhabitants in general, for every Part of their Estate, that is in its Nature taxable; but as an Equality is contended for, they do expect, if they have contributed more than their Proportions (which they believe they have very greatly) that the Overplus shall be returned to them; and as the House of Representatives contend for their Right in disposing of their Property, and do not represent the Proprietaries, so the Proprietaries conceive, and are advised, they themselves, and they only, have a Right to judge when, and how, to dispose of their Estates and Properties.[2]

9. In the third paragraph of "Heads of Complaint" BF charged that instructions were "both unjust and cruel" which forced the governor to refuse consent to tax bills "tho' ever so necessary for the Defence of the Country, unless the greatest Part of their [the Proprietors'] Estate is exempted from such Tax."

1. For the Proprietors' gift of £5000, see above, VI, 257 n. It may not be unfair to note, however, that as Norris reported as late as April 5, 1759, more than three years and four months after word of the gift had reached the governor, some £600 of the total still remained unpaid; see below, p. 304.

2. It was with the intention of divining the meaning of the proposals in the last part of this paragraph that BF wrote the Penns on November 28; see below, pp. 186–8.

The Heads of Complaint conclude well with Expressions of a Desire that Harmony may be restored between the several Branches of the Legislature, and the public Service be provided for;[3] Propositions most desireable, and which the Proprietaries most willingly embrace with open Arms, and with open Hearts: The Rights and Powers of the Crown, and the executive Part of Government being preserved, and the Proprietaries reserving to themselves the Right of disposing of their Estate, there seems to be no such great Difference in Opinions as to other Matters, but what might be adjusted in a reasonable Manner with cool, temperate Persons, fully authorised for the Purpose: Had such Power been lodged here, it is probable many of the seeming Differences would have been settled; but as the Agent, who delivered the Heads of Complaint, declined the Settling here, of the Draught of one single Bill for raising a Supply, on Account of Want of Power so to do; as he alledged,[4] the Proprietaries find themselves obliged to write to the House of Representatives, that in case they are so well and happily disposed, they will forthwith authorise and impower, in as good a Manner as the Case will admit, some Persons of Candour to enter into free Conferences, and adjust those other Matters in the most agreeable Manner;[5] in which the Proprietaries assure the Representatives, and all the good People of the Province, they shall meet with the most cordial and affectionate Concurrence of the Proprietaries, as far as can, with Reason, be desired of them.

FERDINAND JOHN PARIS,
*Agent for the Proprietaries
of Pennsylvania.*

3. The final, unnumbered paragraph of "Heads of Complaint" expresses a hope for the speedy redress of the grievances and concludes in the exact words Paris uses here.

4. For BF's explanation of his "Want of Power" to treat with the Proprietors, see below, pp. 233-4. It is not clear what kind of supply bill to the "Settling" of which he had refused to agree, but he had discussed one with the Penns the last week of January 1758 at some length, so it is likely that the incident Paris refers to here took place then or early in February. See above, VII, 366, 370–1 n, 372–3 n.

5. Yorke had recommended that the Proprietors "turn their Thoughts, to some Plan" to compose the dispute with the Assembly. He had held that it was "agreeable to Reason, and Justice, to tax the Quit Rents," providing the Assembly consented to an equitable method of assessment.

II

A MESSAGE *from the Honourable the Proprietaries* THOMAS *and* RICHARD PENN, *Esquires, to the House of Representatives of the Province of Pennsylvania.*

GENTLEMEN, London, November 28, 1758.

In the Month of August, in the last Year, Mr. Franklin delivered to us a Note or Billet, entituled, "*Heads of Complaint.*" When first delivered, it was a blank Paper, neither dated, signed, or addressed to any Person; but a few Days after he did sign it, and set a Date to it of the Twentieth of August.

It appeared to us to be very short and general, and to allude to sundry Transactions in Pennsylvania, which were to be sought for in your Votes, and without the Aid whereof, it was not possible to guess at the Meaning of Mr. Franklin's Note.

Whether such a Paper was delivered by him of his own Choice, or by Direction, he best knows; but we believe it is the First of the Kind, on any such great Occasion; and you will give us Leave to acquaint you, that the Importance of the Matter, the Preservation of Order and Decency between the Assembly and us, and the Necessity and Usefulness of a free Intercourse between us and them, seemed to require a very different Representation.[6]

However, we overlooked that Piece of Disrespect, and applied ourselves to select, from all your public Votes and Transactions, what we judged might be the Intent and Meaning of the said Paper; and as we found the most material Parts thereof consisted of Matters, wherein the Powers of Government, and the Rights and Prerogatives of the Crown (intrusted to us) were concerned, we thought it right, and so acquainted Mr. Franklin, to take the Opinions and Advice of His Majesty's Attorney and Sollicitor-General thereon, that we might act with the greatest Caution and Security in Matters of such great Importance.

At the Time Mr. Franklin delivered us his Paper, the long Vacation was begun, and the Lawyers gone into the Country, but the first Day they returned to Town, we laid all those Matters before those Gentlemen for their Opinions, which were so long delayed

6. This disingenuous statement of the origin and dubious nature of the "Heads of Complaint" hardly does justice to BF and ignores the fact that he wrote the paper at the Penns' specific request, as Thomas Penn explained to Peters, Sept. 5, 1757; see above, VII, 250–1.

by Means of an Obstruction given by one of your Agents, that we could not obtain the same for a whole Year (wanting eight Days only) after the Papers had been laid before them.

As soon as we had been advised by those Gentlemen, we returned our Answer in Writing, signed by our Agent, to Mr. Franklin, and now send you hereto annexed a Copy of the said Heads of Complaint, and our Answer thereto.

We are always ready to receive Representations from the House of Representatives, on any Matter that requires Redress. As to the legal Rights of Government, or the Powers and Prerogatives of the Crown, we must support them, as a Duty which we owe to the Crown, to the Nation in general, and to the Inhabitants of the Province in particular.

As to those Matters which concern our Property, we have a Right, and are so advised, to prevent any Injury being done thereto, and are not to be deterred from taking the necessary Care therein, by those Misrepresentations of, and unjust Charges against, us, which have been repeatedly printed, and are even glanced at in the Heads of Complaint presented to us,[7] as if we had refused to contribute a reasonable Proportion to the Defence of the Country; an Injury the greater, because those who uttered it, knew that we had contributed a very considerable Sum to the Expence of the War, and, in the Opinion of many People, and from all the Information we can procure, more in Proportion than any Person in the Province.

As to any Matters which may relate to yourselves, we are ready to receive the fullest Information, and also to enter into free Conferences on all these several Subjects with any Persons of Candour, whom you shall authorize and impower for that Purpose; which Matter, we the rather mention to you, in regard that we having offered to settle the Draught of a Supply Bill with Mr. Franklin, he excused himself from joining therein, as not having Power to enter into Terms with respect to that one single Measure.

We shall always be open to Representation and Conviction, and we see no Matters remaining, but such as may, by the desirable Methods of free Conferences with Persons of Candour, and empowered for the Purpose, be well settled to mutual Satisfaction

7. The Penns, echoing Paris, were complaining about paragraph three of the "Heads of Complaint."

on both Sides, and to the Welfare and Happiness of the Province, which we have most affectionately at Heart.

As Mr. Franklin's Paper contained an Expression of Desire that Harmony might be restored between the several Branches of the Legislature, and we are certain you cannot wish it more ardently than we do, we choose to mention what appears to us to be the readiest, the easiest, and the most desirable Method of attaining that happy End. THOMAS PENN,
RICHARD PENN.

To Thomas and Richard Penn

Copy: Pennsylvania Historical and Museum Commission[8]

Gentlemen London Novr. 28th. 1758.

I yesterday receiv'd a Paper from Mr. Paris, containing your Answer to the Heads of Complaint, wherein I am inform'd that the Proprietaries, "to take off all pretence of Clamour, are very ready to have the annual Income of their Estate enquired into, and are as ready to contribute whatever the said Sum [viz. £5000 by them formerly ordered to be paid][9] shall fall short of their Proportion of what has been laid on the Inhabitants in general, for every part of their Estate that is in its Nature Taxable; but, as an Equality is contended for, they do expect, if they have contributed more than their Proportions (which they believe they have very greatly) that the Overplus shall be return'd to them; And, as the House of Representatives contend for their Right in disposing of their Property, and do not represent the Proprietaries, so the Proprietaries conceive, and are advised, they themselves, and they only, have a Right to judge, when, and how, to dispose of their Estates and Propertys."

As the Money granted last year is probably expended before this time, and a new Supply Bill must come under Consideration in the ensuing Winter Session, it seems necessary, for preventing

8. The ALS has not been found. This copy, in the hand of Thomas Penn's clerk, is one sent to the proprietary supporters in Pa. and read at the council, March 26, 1759. *Pa. Col. Recs.*, VIII, 299–300. The endorsement is in Peters' hand.
9. Brackets in the MS copy.

Delays prejudicial to his Majesty's Service, that this proposal shou'd be clearly understood by the Assembly: I therefore beg to be inform'd more explicitly of the following particulars.[1] 1. In what Manner you are willing the Annual Income of your Estate should be enquired into, and whether you will consent to a Law that shall direct such enquiry, and the Mode of it.[2] 2. What Parts of your Estate you look upon to be in their Nature taxable, and what Parts not taxable.[3] 3. Whether the proportion you propose to contribute, is to relate only to the Taxes that have been heretofore laid on the Inhabitants, and the Sums already raised and spent, or to those also that shall hereafter be found necessary to be laid and raised for the Defence of the Province in the insuing

1. According to his next letter to Peters, Thomas Penn did not reply directly or in writing to BF in answer to the queries that follow here. Instead, he sent Paris to him with a verbal message, not thinking it "necessary to keep up a Correspondence with a Gentleman who acknowledged he is not impowered to conclude proper Measures; so that I hope we have ended all Correspondence with him, which we could not carry on after knowing how he treated us." Penn gave almost identical accounts in letters to Benjamin Chew and to William Allen. To Allen he added that Paris told BF that the Proprietors had written directly to the Assembly "and should be ready to receive any application from them," but "did not see it could answer any good purpose to continue correspondence" with BF. "Mr. Paris gave him the words in writing to prevent mistakes, to which he answered not a word, look'd as if much disappointed, and took no notice of him when he went out." Penn to Peters, Dec. 8; to Chew, Dec. 9; to Allen, Dec. 9, 1758, Penn Papers, Hist. Soc. Pa. In the letter to Peters he indicated what his answers to BF's questions really were; they are summarized in the notes below.

2. As to the "annual Income" from proprietary estates, Penn wrote Peters, he intended that the inquiry should be confined to income from "all Rents and Quit Rents," should be conducted by the Constables, either with or without a law to direct them, and their returns "may afterwards be checked by the Receiver General." Penn thought that a law regulating the assessment of proprietary estates would not "be at all improper, if it regards only Rents of the several Denominations."

3. In obedience to Yorke's opinion, Penn conceded that proprietary rents were taxable, but he stipulated that the taxes were to "be paid by the Tenants, and to be allowed by us, to them, at such times as they do really pay their Rents to us, provided the Sum we have already paid, shall be allowed by the Public in part of it." On the other hand, "our vacant land we are advised is not Taxable, nor our Fines or Purchase Moneys." Yorke had written that the Proprietors had "rightly instructed their Governor, not to consent to tax the unoccupied, and unimproved, Lands; whether surveyed and reserved, or not," and had held that fines and purchase money were likewise not taxable.

and future years.[4] 4. Whether it is proposed that the Assembly for the future, do dispose of what the People pay for his Majesty's Service, and the Proprietaries separately dispose of their Proportion, and that otherwise they will not contribute; or what is the plain Intention of those Expressions that relate to the Disposition of the Money.[5]

As a Ship is just departing for Pennsylvania, I request as speedy an Answer as may be to these Points, they being of immediate Importance. The rest of the Matters contain'd in the Paper[6] may be considered at another time. Mean while, with due Respect, I am, Gentlemen Your most obedient and most humble Servant

B FRANKLIN

Thomas Penn and Richd. Penn Esqrs. Agent for the Assembly of Pennsylvania

Endorsed: 28th Novr 1758 Copy Mr Franklins Letter to the Proprs after receiving their answer to the Heads of Complaint. reced from Mr Allen by Packet 18th Febry 1759 at 10 o Clock at Night Enterd. in Minutes 26th. March 1759. No 214

Ebenezer Kinnersley[7] to [William Smith]

Printed in *The Pennsylvania Gazette*, November 30, 1758.

William Smith, provost of the College and Academy of Philadelphia, wrote an account of the institution which appeared at the end of November 1758 in a publication of which he was the principal editor, *The American Magazine and Monthly Chronicle for the British Colonies*, 1

4. Penn told Peters: "There is one point Mr. Franklin has mentioned I have not given you my sentiments upon, which is, whether we propose to contribute in proportion only of the Sums already given, or to those still necessary for the defence of the Country; no doubt we mean to both."

5. Penn wrote Peters that the Proprietors agreed to this tax contribution, "provided a fair Tax is laid and the Money put into such hands, as shall best lay it out for the purposes, the King's Service requires, and we do expect none of the Money, paid by the People, or by us, shall be disposed of but with the approbation of the Governor, or by order from the Crown."

6. Paris' answer to the "Heads of Complaint."

7. On Kinnersley and his work in electricity see above, IV, 192 n, and the indexes of III, IV, and V.

(1757–58), Supplement, 630–40.[8] In describing the members of the faculty, Smith had this to say about Ebenezer Kinnersley, professor of English and Oratory and chief master of the English School, who had been Franklin's principal collaborator in electrical experimentation: ". . . he is well qualified for his profession; and has moreover great merit with the learned world in being the chief inventor (as already mentioned) of the *Electrical* apparatus, as well as author of a considerable part of those discoveries in *Electricity*, published by Mr. Franklin to whom he communicated them. Indeed Mr. Franklin himself mentions his name with honor, tho' he has not been careful enough to distinguish between their particular discoveries. This, perhaps he may have thought needless, as they were known to act in concert. But tho' that circumstance was known here, it was not so in the remote parts of the world to which the fame of these discoveries have extended."

Immediately upon reading these remarks, Kinnersley sent the *Pennsylvania Gazette* the following statement exonerating Franklin from Smith's aspersions. Franklin's partner David Hall printed it conspicuously as the first item in the issue of the *Gazette* then just going to press. It was possibly owing to this letter that, when Smith revised his "Account" for inclusion in a volume of *Discourses on Several Public Occasions During the War in America* (London, 1759), pp. 215–33, he omitted the entire passage describing the individual members of the faculty.

To the AUTHOR of the Account of the College and Academy of Philadelphia, published in the *American Magazine* for October, 1758.

Sir,   [Nov. 30, 1758]
I was very much surprized and concerned to see the Account you have been pleased to give of my electrical Discoveries, in Page 639 of the *American Magazine*. If you did it with a View to procure me Esteem in the Learned World, I should have been abundantly more obliged to you, had it been done, so as to have no Tendency to depreciate the Merit of the ingenious and worthy Mr. Franklin, in the many curious and justly celebrated Discoveries he has made in Electricity. Had you said that, being honoured with Mr. Franklin's Intimacy, I was often with him when he was making Experiments, and that new Discoveries were

8. On this magazine, which lasted only a year, see Frank L. Mott, *A History of American Magazines, 1741–1850* (N.Y., 1930), pp. 80–2; and Albert Gegenheimer, *William Smith* (Phila., 1943), pp. 62–7.

sometimes made when we were together, and at other Times some were made by myself at Home, and communicated to Mr. Franklin, this would have been really true, though it is what I never desired to have published. But to say, "That I am the Author of a *considerable* Part of those Discoveries in Electricity, published by Mr. Franklin;" the Expression, from whomsoever you might have the Intelligence, appears too strong; it may be understood to comprehend *more* than is strictly true, and therefore I thought myself obliged to take this public Notice of it. If you will please, Sir, to examine what Mr. Franklin has published on Electricity, I think you will no where find that he appropriates to himself the Honour of any one Discovery; but is so complaisant to his electrical Friends, as always to say, in the plural Number, *we* have found out, or, *we* discovered, &c.[9] As to his *not being careful to distinguish between the particular Discoveries of each;* this perhaps was not always practicable; it being sometimes impossible to recollect in whose Breast the Thought first took Rise, that led to a Series of Experiments, which at length issued in some unexpected important Discovery. But had it been always practicable to distinguish between the particular Discoveries of each, it was altogether unnecessary; as, I believe, none of Mr. Franklin's electrical Friends had the least Thought of ever appearing as Competitors for any of the Honours that they have beheld, with Pleasure, bestowed on him, and to which he had an undoubted Right, preferable to the united Merit of all the Electricians in America, and, perhaps, in all the World. I am, Sir, Your most obedient humble Servant,   EBENEZER KINNERSLEY.

9. This use of the first person plural is found repeatedly in BF's letters to Collinson describing the Philadelphia electrical experiments. In addition, in his own copy of the 1751 edition of *Exper. and Obser.* (Yale Univ. Lib.), BF often wrote the names or initials of Kinnersley, Philip Syng, or Thomas Hopkinson in the margin to show responsibility for particular experiments. Perhaps as a consequence of Smith's criticisms, he inserted several footnotes acknowledging these men's work in the editions of 1769 and 1774, in the preparation of which for the first time he took an active part himself.

Benjamin Franklin and Richard Jackson:
Opinion on the Expedition to Fort Duquesne

Copy: Public Record Office, London[1]

This undated document was probably written in the latter part of November or in December 1758, or possibly as late as the first two weeks or so of January 1759, although it has previously been assigned to the last half of 1757.[2] No "Winter Expedition" against Fort Duquesne had been undertaken, or even definitely planned, for late 1757 or the first months of 1758, whereas General John Forbes's expedition, which had been planned for the summer of 1758, was unable to begin its major advance until September, as Forbes explained in a letter which reached William Pitt November 14.[3] He had promised to continue his march in spite of difficulties and, so far as Londoners knew some months later, it might still be under way. News that the French had evacuated and destroyed the fort on November 24 and Forbes had occupied the ruins the next day reached London Jan. 20, 1759.[4] From November 14 to January 20, then, Forbes's march might well have been regarded as a "Winter Expedition." Pitt's receipt of the general's earlier dispatch may have led him to seek from Franklin, Jackson, and others familiar with the American situation advice as to how Forbes's troops could best be employed after they had attained their initial objective.

[November–December 1758]

Mr. Franklin and Mr. Jackson have consider'd the Points propos'd to them, and are of Opinion, That.

In case the Winter Expedition against Fort Duquesne prove effectual, the two Forts of Beef River and Presqu'isle[5] should be

1. In a volume of Chatham Papers dated 1758–1763.
2. Alfred Owen Aldridge, "Franklin and Jackson on the French War," APS *Proc.*, XCIV (1950), 396–7.
3. Alfred P. James, ed., *Writings of General John Forbes* (Menasha, Wis., 1938), pp. 202–6.
4. *London Chron.*, Jan. 18–20, 1759, printing news from Forbes at Fort Duquesne dated Nov. 26, 1758, and received in London via New York. His dispatch to Pitt of the same date arrived only on March 11; James, ed., *Writings of Forbes*, pp. 267–9.
5. Fort Le Boeuf on the portage between Rivière aux Boeufs (French Creek) and Presqu' Isle (the present Erie) on Lake Erie; see map, above, v, 225. The French retained both posts, and also Fort Machault (Venango, the present Franklin) at the junction of Rivière aux Boeufs and the Allegheny River, until early in August 1759, evacuating them only after the surrender

taken early in the Spring; and, (if we do not intend a Naval Force on Lake Erie) they should be both destroy'd; if we do, they should be both Strengthen'd. They are Posts of no great Strength at present, and without Cannon, unless Supply'd since the Summer 1756. The Garrison in each consisted then but of 30 Men. Battoes can go up, during the Spring Freshes, quite to Beef River Fort, and there is only 15. Miles Land Carriage from thence to Presqu'isle on Lake Erie; a very good Road.

If Certain Intelligence is obtain'd at Presqu'isle, that the French have Left only a weak Garrison at Niagara, as expecting the English at Quebeck or Montreal; (which is Likely, for in 1756. they drew off the Garrison that had been plac'd there to defend that Fort against General Shirley, and left only 50 Men:) in that Case, Niagara might be attempted from Presqu'isle, and those Forts preserv'd till that Expedition is over.[6] If Niagara is taken, they should both be preserv'd to keep up the Communication; for Niagara itself should be kept and maintained by a Strong Garrison and well Supply'd, it being a better Harbour for Naval Force than Oswego. Presqu'isle should also be Strengthen'd and made a Port for Naval Force on Lake Erie. The taking and keeping Fort Niagara would give us great Reputation and Influence with the Six Nations.

If this be not attempted, at Least strong Ranging Parties should be sent out from Fort Duquesne to annoy the Shawnese and other Indians that have join'd the French against us,[7] Destroy their Towns, and Oblige them to Sue for Peace or quit the Country; and to destroy the French Posts between Lake Erie and Ohio. Much of this kind may be done this Summer by the Forces that take Duquesne, if they have diligent and Active Officers.

As the Frontiers of Virginia, Maryland, Pensilvania and New Jersey will be render'd pretty Secure and quiet by the Taking of Duquesne, the Provincial Forces of those Colonies, amounting to

---

of Fort Niagara on July 25 made them untenable. Hunter, *Forts,* pp. 77–8, 96–7, 164–5.

6. The successful attack on Fort Niagara in the summer of 1759 came from the east via Lake Ontario, not from the west via Lake Erie.

7. The Shawnee Indians had defected to the French in 1755; see above, VI, 238. Though they were no longer as actively hostile as at first, their reliability remained uncertain.

above 2000 Men, might be almost all employ'd in those small Subsequent Expeditions.

Means should also be used to open again our Intercourse with the Twigtwees, and engage them to declare for us.[8] They are Numerous and Strong, and enclin'd to the English. The Destroying the French Posts in their Country is Necessary to this End. Their Trade with us would soon be very Considerable and beneficial. If we take the Fort at Pontchartrain, or Detroit, all the Tribes of the Twigtwees will be secured to us, and must depend upon us.

From Ferdinand John Paris

Copy: Historical Society of Pennsylvania[9]

This undated, unsigned document, in the hand of Thomas Penn's clerk, is undoubtedly a copy of the "words in writing to prevent mistakes" Paris gave to Franklin in the interview described above, p. 187 n and mentioned as "No. 5" in Franklin's letter to Norris, Jan. 19, 1759 (see below, p. 233). Since that interview took place "a few Days after" Franklin's letter to the Proprietors of November 28, and before Penn wrote about the affair to Peters on December 8, this paper was apparently written during the first week of December 1758. It effectively ended the correspondence between Franklin and the Penns during this mission to England. Thereafter his efforts on behalf of the Assembly had to be directed to the British government, not the Proprietors.

Sir   [December 1–7?, 1758]

The Readyness with which the Proprietarys of Pennsylvania receive any application, which is but sayd to come from the House

---

8. The Twightwee Indians, living in the Ohio region to the west of Fort Duquesne, had been cut off from intercourse with the British by the French advances. BF had met some of their chiefs at the Treaty of Carlisle in 1753; see above, v, 84–107.

9. Neither the Paris original nor the copy BF sent Norris Jan. 19, 1759 ("Message No. 5"), has been found. From the "No 214" which appears in the endorsements of both this and the copy of BF's letter to the Penns, Nov. 28, 1758 (above, p. 188), it appears that this was also one of the copies of papers Penn sent to his Pa. supporters in December 1758. The endorsement is in Peters' hand.

of Representatives, induced them to accept and to send an Answer, to a very extraordinary Paper,[1] which You deliver'd to them.

In that Answer, which you have been pleased to call Proposals, You have been acquainted with the Proprietarys Intention, to write to the House of Representatives, from whom the Proprietarys will always, be willing to receive any Representation, and to give it a full, and candid Consideration.

They have, since, wrote to the House, what seemed to them to be proper, on this Occasion, and therefore cannot conceive it will answer any good purpose, to continue a Corrispondence with a Gentleman, who has already acknowledged his Want of Power to conclude proper Measures.

Endorsed: Copy Proprietary Answer to Mr Franklins Letter of the 28th Novr 1758 desiring an Explanation of their Answer to the Heads of Complaint. No 214.

To James Bowdoin[2]

MS not found; reprinted from Benjamin Franklin, *Experiments and Observations on Electricity* (London, 1769), pp. 369–74.

The problem of "augmenting the Benefit of Fire"[3] and cutting expenditures for fuel compelled Franklin's attention throughout his life. The Pennsylvania fireplace represents his earliest and most famous attempt to solve it. A less familiar contrivance, conceived for the same purpose, was the "simple machine" which he described in this letter to Bowdoin. Either Franklin did not give Bowdoin a full description of this "machine," which he preferred to call his "Sliding Plate,"[4] and we should call a damper, or he improved it in the years immediately following 1758, for in describing it to Sir Alexander Dick in 1762 he explained that the sliding plate was hinged. When it was pulled forward to the hinge the front section could be dropped to "hang perpendicular," thereby closing the upper part of the fireplace opening and permitting the fire to be "speedily blown up" by the increased draft.[5] For a time,

1. The "Heads of Complaint."
2. Boston merchant and scientific correspondent of BF; see above, IV, 69 n.
3. "An Account of the New-Invented Fire-Places," above, II, 422.
4. BF to Lord Kames, Feb. 28, 1768, Scottish Record Office; to Jan Ingenhousz on smoky chimneys, Aug. 28, 1785, N.Y. Pub. Lib.
5. In producing this effect BF was adapting to some extent the shutter from his Pennsylvania fireplace; see above, II, 431, 434.

Franklin's sliding plate enjoyed a considerable vogue in London and "many Hundreds" were "set up in Imitation of it."[6] He recommended it to his Scottish friends, Dick and Lord Kames, and mentioned it in 1785 in his celebrated essay "On the Causes and Cure of Smoky Chimneys."[7]

Dear Sir,   London, Dec. 2, 1758.

I have executed here an easy simple contrivance, that I have long since had in speculation, for keeping rooms warmer in cold weather than they generally are, and with less fire. It is this. The opening of the chimney is contracted, by brick-work faced with marble slabs, to about two feet between the jambs, and the breast[8] brought down to within about three feet of the hearth. An iron frame is placed just under the breast, and extending quite to the back of the chimney, so that a plate of the same metal may slide horizontally backwards and forwards in the grooves on each side of the frame. This plate is just so large as to fill the whole space, and shut the chimney entirely when thrust quite in, which is convenient when there is no fire; drawing it out, so as to leave a space between its farther edge and the back, of about two inches; this space is sufficient for the smoke to pass; and so large a part of the funnel being stopt by the rest of the plate, the passage of warm air out of the room, up the chimney, is obstructed and retarded, and by that means much cold air is prevented from coming in through crevices, to supply its place. This effect is made manifest three ways. First, when the fire burns briskly in cold weather, the howling or whistling noise made by the wind, as it enters the room through the crevices, when the chimney is open as usual,

6. BF to Dick, Jan. 21, 1762.

7. The next to last sentence and the first part of the last should be read as correcting a statement in the headnote on the Pennsylvania fireplace, above, II, 420. There the editors said that it was the fireplace which was imitated in London by the hundreds and that BF sent a model to Sir Alexander Dick and recommended it to Lord Kames. It now appears most probable, however, that it was his sliding damper that attracted most attention in Great Britain, and that he installed it in his Craven Street lodgings in 1757 or 1758 after contending with the coal-burning fires of London, so different in many of their characteristics from the wood fires of Philadelphia for which he had designed the Pennsylvania fireplace. Furthermore, as he explained to Kames in 1768, the version of the Pennsylvania fireplace produced in England had been so "improved" that he declined to recommend it to friends.

8. The wall between the chimney flue and the room and above the fireplace opening.

ceases as soon as the plate is slid in to its proper distance. Secondly, opening the door of the room about half an inch, and holding your hand against the opening, near the top of the door, you feel the cold air coming in against your hand, but weakly, if the plate be in. Let another person suddenly draw it out, so as to let the air of the room go up the chimney, with its usual freedom where chimneys are open, and you immediately feel the cold air rushing in strongly. Thirdly, if something be set against the door, just sufficient, when the plate is in, to keep the door nearly shut, by resisting the pressure of the air that would force it open: Then, when the plate is drawn out, the door will be forced open by the increased pressure of the outward cold air endeavouring to get in to supply the place of the warm air, that now passes out of the room to go up the chimney. In our common open chimneys, half the fuel is wasted, and its effect lost, the air it has warmed being immediately drawn off. Several of my acquaintance having seen this simple machine in my room, have imitated it at their own houses, and it seems likely to become pretty common. I describe it thus particularly to you, because I think it would be useful in Boston, where firing is often dear.

Mentioning chimneys puts me in mind of a property I formerly had occasion to observe in them, which I have not found taken notice of by others;[9] it is, that in the summer time, when no fire is made in the chimneys, there is, nevertheless, a regular draft of air through them; continually passing upwards, from about five or six o'clock in the afternoon, till eight or nine o'clock the next morning, when the current begins to slacken and hesitate a little, for about half an hour, and then sets as strongly down again, which it continues to do till towards five in the afternoon, then slackens and hesitates as before, going sometimes a little up, then a little down, till in about half an hour it gets into a steady upward current for the night, which continues till eight or nine the next day; the hours varying a little as the days lengthen and shorten, and sometimes varying from sudden changes in the weather; as if, after being long warm, it should begin to grow cool about noon, while the air was coming down the chimney, the current will then change earlier than the usual hour, &c.

9. Apparently BF had not committed his observations to paper; this is the earliest of his writings on chimney ventilation that has been found.

This property in chimneys I imagine we might turn to some account, and render improper, for the future, the old saying, *as useless as a chimney in summer*. If the opening of the chimney, from the breast down to the hearth, be closed by a slight moveable frame, or two in the manner of doors, covered with canvas, that will let the air through, but keep out the flies; and another little frame set within upon the hearth, with hooks on which to hang joints of meat, fowls, &c. wrapt well in wet linen cloths, three or four fold, I am confident that if the linen is kept wet, by sprinkling it once a day, the meat would be so cooled by the evaporation, carried on continually by means of the passing air, that it would keep a week or more in the hottest weather. Butter and milk might likewise be kept cool, in vessels or bottles covered with wet cloths. A shallow tray, or keeler, should be under the frame to receive any water that might drip from the wetted cloths. I think, too, that this property of chimneys might, by means of smoak-jack vanes,[1] be applied to some mechanical purposes, where a small but pretty constant power only is wanted.

If you would have my opinion of the cause of this changing current of air in chimneys, it is, in short, as follows. In summer time there is generally a great difference in the warmth of the air at mid-day and midnight, and, of course, a difference of specific gravity in the air, as the more it is warmed the more it is rarefied. The funnel of a chimney being for the most part surrounded by the house, is protected, in a great measure, from the direct action of the sun's rays, and also from the coldness of the night air. It thence preserves a middle temperature between the heat of the day, and the coldness of the night. This middle temperature it communicates to the air contained in it. If the state of the outward air be cooler than that in the funnel of the chimney, it will, by being heavier, force it to rise, and go out at the top. What supplies its place from below, being warmed, in its turn, by the warmer funnel, is likewise forced up by the colder and weightier air below, and so the current is continued till the next day, when the sun gradually changes the state of the outward air, makes it first as

1. A smoke jack is a machine for turning a roasting-spit using the power generated by the ascending current of heated air in the flue. Vanes in the jack's shaft set in the flue are turned by the current and a simple transmission system conveys the motion to the spit before the fire.

warm as the funnel of the chimney can make it, (when the current begins to hesitate) and afterwards warmer. Then the funnel being cooler than the air that comes into it, cools that air, makes it heavier than the outward air; of course it descends; and what succeeds it from above, being cool'd in its turn, the descending current continues till towards evening, when it again hesitates and changes its course, from the change of warmth in the outward air, and the nearly remaining same middle temperature in the funnel.

Upon this principle, if a house were built behind Beacon-hill, an adit[2] carried from one of the doors into the hill horizontally, till it met with a perpendicular shaft sunk from its top, it seems probable to me, that those who lived in the house, would constantly, in the heat even of the calmest day, have as much cool air passing through the house, as they should chuse; and the same, though reversed in its current, during the stillest night.

I think, too, this property might be made of use to miners; as where several shafts or pits are sunk perpendicularly into the earth, communicating at bottom by horizontal passages, which is a common case, if a chimney of thirty or forty feet high were built over one of the shafts, or so near the shaft, that the chimney might communicate with the top of the shaft, all air being excluded but what should pass up or down by the shaft, a constant change of air would, by this means, be produced in the passages below, tending to secure the workmen from those damps which so frequently incommode them. For the fresh air would be almost always going down the open shaft, to go up the chimney, or down the chimney to go up the shaft. Let me add one observation more, which is, That if that part of the funnel of a chimney, which appears above the roof of a house, be pretty long, and have three of its sides exposed to the heat of the sun successively, *viz.* when he is in the east, in the south, and in the west; while the north side is sheltered by the building from the cool northerly winds. Such a chimney will often be so heated by the sun, as to continue the draft strongly upwards, through the whole twenty-four hours, and often for many days together. If the outside of such a chimney be painted black, the effect will be still greater, and the current stronger. I am, dear Sir, yours, &c.   B.F.

2. A tunnel. Bowdoin had acquired his mansion on Beacon Hill, Boston, in 1756. Justin Winsor, *The Memorial History of Boston* (Boston, 1882), II, 522.

From Charles Thomson

MS not found; reprinted from extract in [Charles Thomson], *An Enquiry into the Causes of the Alienation of the Delaware and Shawanese Indians from the British Interest,* . . . (London, 1759), pp. 172–82.

Lawrence Wroth first identified Thomson as the author of this letter, Pemberton as the author of that which follows next, and Franklin as the recipient of both, on the strength of a statement in Franklin's letter to Pemberton, March 19, 1759.[3] When Franklin received them, Thomson's *An Enquiry into the Causes of the Alienation of the Delaware and Shawanese Indians* was probably already in the printer's hands. This was an examination of proprietary Indian policy and negotiations and related matters from the Treaty of Conestoga, 1722, through the conference at Easton, July-August 1757, which Thomson had undertaken at the instance of the Friendly Association.[4] Apparently Franklin had also received a copy of the journal of the Moravian Christian Frederick Post on an official mission to the Ohio Indians in the summer of 1758 to persuade them not to oppose General Forbes's expedition against Fort Duquesne. Franklin sent Post's journal and these extracts of Thomson's and Pemberton's letters to the printer to be added as an appendix to the *Enquiry.* In some respects they were sequels to Thomson's original account and Post's journal, he thought, would add to the popular interest in the work as a whole.

William Strahan printed 1000 copies of the pamphlet; it was probably one of the "sundry Pieces in Defence of the Province" the cost of which, amounting to £213 13s., Franklin charged to the provincial account.[5] He also paid Thomas Jefferys, geographer to the Prince of Wales, £4 19s. for the engraving, printing, and paper of the map of Pennsylvania showing Indian lands and claims, which appears in the front of the *Enquiry.*[6] The pamphlet was published about March 1,

3. Lawrence C. Wroth, *An American Bookshelf 1755* (Phila., 1934), p. 128.

4. On the Friendly Association for Regaining and Preserving Peace with the Indians by Pacific Measures, see above, VII, 18 n; and on the transmission of a MS copy of Thomson's *Enquiry* to English Quakers early in 1758, see above, VII, 376–7 n. The copy of the *Enquiry* used for printing was almost certainly another one that BF mentioned to Pemberton, June 10, 1758, as having come "to hand some time ago, but without a Letter, so that I did not know who sent it." See above, p. 99.

5. Verner W. Crane, ed., *Benjamin Franklin's Letters to the Press 1758–1775* (Chapel Hill, [1950]), p. xlvii; BF to Isaac Norris, Feb. 15, 1763, Hist. Soc. Pa.

6. Bill and receipt dated May 11, 1759, Hist. Soc. Pa.

1759, and in April Franklin sent 300 copies to Pennsylvania: 50 to the Assembly, 25 to Pemberton and Thomson, and 225 to David Hall.[7]

Philadelphia, Dec. 10, 1758

I attended the late Treaty at Easton.[8] I wish I could say the same Conduct as usual was not pursued. During the whole Treaty two Things were laboured with the utmost Diligence; to lessen the Power of Teedyuscung, and to save, if possible, a certain Character.[9] In both they[1] failed; for Teedyuscung, instead of losing has increased his Power, and established himself at the Head of five Tribes. The Indians that lie to the North of us, between us and the Lakes, consist of three Leagues: The Senekas, Mohawks, and Onondagoes, who are called the Fathers, compose the first: The Oneidas, Cayugas, Tuscororas, Nanticokes, and Conoys, (which are united into one Tribe) and the Tuteloes, compose the second League; and these two Leagues make up what we call the Six Nations. The third League is formed of the Chihohocki, (or Delawares) the Wanami, the Munseys, Mawhiccons, and Wapingers. From all these Nations, except two or three, we had the chief Sachems with us at Easton. The whole Number of Indians, by the best Account we could get, amounted to 501. I send you a Copy of what I there took down from Day to Day; it may give you some Notion of the Proceeding at Easton, and inform you of several Things which I doubt not will be misrepresented. I was careful to set down nothing but what I heard or saw myself, or received from good Authority. The Intimacy I had with several of the Indians, and the Confidence they have been pleased to re-

7. See below, p. 322.

8. For "the late Treaty at Easton," Oct. 7–26, 1758, see above, p. 176 n. The official minutes of the conference are reprinted in facsimile in Van Doren and Boyd, *Indian Treaties*, pp. 213–43. Page references will be to this reprinting. The journal of Benjamin Chew, one of the Pa. Council, at Easton is also printed *ibid.*, pp. 312–18. These two will be cited hereafter in the notes to this document as "Official Minutes" and "Chew's Journal."

9. On Teedyuscung, the Delaware chieftain, see above, VII, 16 n. The "certain Character," whom Thomson never clearly identifies, was probably George Croghan, Sir William Johnson's deputy superintendent of Indian affairs (above, v, 64 n), or possibly Secretary Richard Peters, long identified with the management of proprietary relations with the Indians.

1. The supporters of the Proprietor.

pose in me, gave me an Opportunity of being acquainted with what passed at the private Council.[2]

On Saturday, Oct. 8,[3] the Governor had the first Interview with the Indians, at which very little more passed than the Compliments usual at a first Meeting. Monday and Tuesday the Indians were in close Consultation among themselves. The Place of their Meeting at Croghan's. And here let me observe, that it affords some Matter of Speculation, why Croghan, who is here in no public Capacity, should be honoured with a Guard at his Door.[4] The Reason of the Indians meeting at his House is more easily accounted for, as he treats them with Liquor, and gives out that he himself is an Indian. The Subject in Debate these two Days, is, Whether what Teedyuscung has done shall stand, or they are to begin anew? The grand Thing aimed at by our Proprietary Managers, is to get Teedyuscung to retract the Charge of Fraud and Forgery.[5] In order to gain this Point the Senekas and Six Nations are *privately* treated with and prompted to undo what has been done, in order, as is pretended, to establish their own Authority and gain the Credit of the Peace.[6] Teedyuscung, and his People, absolutely refuse to retract any Thing they have said. He insists, that what was done in the Beginning of the War, was done by and with the Advice and Consent of the Senekas; that the Reasons he had assigned to the Governor for his striking the English, are the true and only Reasons. The Debates were warm. At Length it is agreed, that

2. Thomson had served as Teedyuscung's secretary at the Easton Treaty in the summer of 1757. As Pemberton mentions in the letter which follows this, Thomson was not present at the beginning of the 1758 conference.

3. An error for Sunday, October 8. On the day before Teedyuscung and Governor Denny and his Council had met and exchanged greetings but did not begin formal sessions of the conference.

4. Croghan attended this treaty only "in an advisory capacity." Nicholas B. Wainwright, *George Croghan Wilderness Diplomat* (Chapel Hill, 1959), p. 147.

5. At Easton in November 1756 Teedyuscung had accused the Proprietors of forging a copy of a deed of 1686, on the basis of which the Walking Purchase was made; see below, p. 267 n.

6. At Easton this charge was openly pressed against the proprietary agents by the members of the Assembly present. When the proprietary men denied that they had tampered with the Indians, the assemblymen explained that it was the "rascal" Croghan whom they suspected of being "at the bottom" of efforts to get Teedyuscung to change his position. Chew's Journal, p. 314.

every Thing already transacted between Teedyuscung and the English shall stand; that at the opening the general Council, Teedyuscung shall make a short introductory Speech, after which the Seneka and other Chiefs, without invalidating any Thing already done, shall proceed to Business.

Matters thus settled, they break up on Tuesday about 11 o'Clock, and expect to meet the Governor immediately, but the Meeting is deferred till next Day.

On Wednesday Morning some of the Quakers got together the Chiefs and old Men of the several Tribes, in order to smoke a Pipe with them.[7] After they had broken up, Mr. Chew of the Council, came to invite the Committee of Assembly to a Conference, in order to shew them the Speech the Governor intended to make to the Indians, and to take their Advice thereon; it being before agreed on, that Nothing should be said to the Indians, but what the Committee of Assembly and Commissioners should be previously made acquainted with. The Council and Commissioners being agreed, the Indians are desired to meet; while the Chiefs were calling them together the Governors agree to go to Dinner, and desire the Meeting may be deferred till four o'Clock. As the Indians were met when they received this, that they might not scatter, they agree to sit down and wait at the Place of Meeting till the Time appointed. At four the Governors came, when they had taken their Seats, Teedyuscung arose and made a Motion to speak, but the Governor of New Jersey[8] said, as he had not yet welcomed the Indians, he desired to be heard first, and after welcoming the Indians in the Name of his Province, he recapitulated what he had done to obtain an Interview with them, confirmed what he had said in the Messages he had sent them, professed his Desire to do them Justice, and live at Peace with them, but insisted upon their delivering up those of his People they had Prisoners among them, without which, he could never be convinced of their Sincerity. He farther added, that as the Senekas

7. This gathering, at which Thomson was present, took place in the Lutheran church at Easton. Chew's Journal, p. 313.

8. Francis Bernard (1712–1779) was governor of New Jersey, 1758–60, and of Massachusetts, 1760–69; he was created a baronet at the end of the latter administration; *DAB*. He participated in the Easton Treaty in order to settle disputes with the Munsey and Minisink Indians and to obtain the return of prisoners taken by the Indians.

and Cayugas had undertaken to answer his Message to the Munseys, he was ready to hear what they, or any other Indians there, had to say respecting his Province.

As soon as he had done, Teedyuscung arose, and addressing the Governors said, that as he had been desired to invite down the several Nations of Indians he had any Intercourse with, he had done it; that here they were now met, and if they had any Thing to say to the Indians, or the Indians to them, they might now speak to each other; that for his own Part he had Nothing to do but to sit and hear; he had already told the Governor of Pensilvania the Cause why he had struck him, and had concluded a Peace with him, for himself and his People, and that every Thing which could be done at present was concluded and agreed upon, in order to secure a lasting Peace.   *With this he gave a String.*

Then Tagashata the Seneka arose and said, That he was very glad the Most High had brought them together with such good Countenances; but that the Day was now far spent, that the Business they were about was weighty and important; he therefore desired it might be deferred for the present, and that he might be heard To-morrow Morning early. On Thursday they met; the Conference was at first interrupted by Teedyuscung coming in drunk, and demanding of the Governor a Letter that the Alleghenians had sent by Pisquetumen. This Letter contained the Speech of the Alleghenians, in Answer to the Message delivered to them by Frederic Post. The Indians entrusted Post with the Carriage of it; but as he went from Shamokin to meet the General, he sent it down by the Indians, and by some Mistake inclosed it in a Packet to Bethlehem; so that when the Indians came to Philadelphia and met the Governor, in order to deliver their Speech and Belts, they found they had none. This gave them great Uneasiness, but the Governor informing them he expected Post at the Treaty, they agreed to go up to Easton and wait his Coming; and this they did the readier, as they had some Messages for Teedyuscung. But now being informed, that the Governor had received from Bethlehem the Letter containing their Speech, they desired Teedyuscung to request it of the Governor that it might be read, as they were eager to return, and a great deal depended on the Answer they were to carry back. As Teedyuscung was too drunk to do Business, Mr. Peters told him that the Letter should be read at another Time, and begged him to have a little Patience.[9] This Bustle being over, Tagashata arose and spoke, approving what had been said by the Governor of the Jerseys, and declaring that the Minisinks had listened to the Advice of the Senekas, and laid down the Hatchet; and that they, the Senekas, had also sent the same Advice to the Delawares and Minisinks on the Ohio, and hoped they would regard it. After the Indians had finished their Speeches, just as the Council was going to break up, Mr. Norris, Speaker of the Assembly, arose, and craved the Ear of the Governors, letting them know that he understood Reports were propagated among the Indians to his Prejudice, and that tended to raise Uneasiness among them, and set them against the People of the Province. He then called upon Moses Tetamy, a noted Indian, to declare whether he had heard of any Person spreading a Report among the Indians, that he was concerned in the Purchase of Lands at or near Wyoming. Tetamy observed, that Teedyuscung was too drunk to enter upon that Matter now. Mr. Norris then said, that as that was the Case, and as he was obliged to go Home Tomorrow, and could not attend another Meeting, he took this Opportunity, in the Presence of both the Governors, and of all the Gentlemen present, to declare that he was neither directly nor indirectly engaged in the Purchase of any Lands at or near Wyoming; and that whoever asserted the contrary erred against Truth; and he desired Moses Tetamy would inform the Indians of this.[1]

This Speech was levelled against G. Croghan, who had been spreading some false Reports among the Indians, and endeavouring to set Teedyuscung against the People of the Province. As Mr. Norris had no Opportunity of canvassing the Matter publickly, in order to know what Croghan had said, he next Morning sent for Teedyuscung, who being asked what had passed between him and George Croghan respecting the Wyoming Lands, declared,

9. The Official Minutes are silent as to Teedyuscung's drunken demand for the letter Post had brought back from the western Indians. According to Chew, the Delaware chieftain interrupted the conference, not to demand the letter from the "Alleghenians," but to boast and threaten, proclaiming that he was "King of all the nations and of all the world" and to advise his brethren that "the way to be well used" by the English was "to make war on them and cut their throats." Chew's Journal, p. 314.

1. Both the Official Minutes and Chew's Journal are silent on Norris' attempt to defend himself and the altercation with Croghan that followed.

That in the Beginning of this Week, G. Groghan came to him and told him, that Isaac Norris and a Quaker who lived in Philadelphia, had been concerned with the New-England People in purchasing the Lands at Wyoming, and that they had paid the Money for the said Lands; that though they endeavoured to make the Indians easy and satisfied about it, yet whenever the Indian Claim to these Lands was mentioned, they could not bear it, and were very uneasy about it; that the said G. Croghan desired him (Teedyuscung) to say nothing about this Affair to any Body at this Treaty, and that if he did not, it was in the Power of him the said George, who acted by Virtue of a Commission from Sir W. Johnson, to set that Affair right, and to settle the Indians on the said Lands, notwithstanding what these Purchasers could do. And Teedyuscung declared, that if this should prove true, neither he, nor any other Indians, would settle on these Lands, but would resent the Injury.

This was interpreted by Moses Tetamy, in the Presence of Amos Strickland, James Wharton, James Child, and Abel James, who subscribed their Names as Evidences. And Mr. Norris, in order to satisfy Teedyuscung that the whole was a groundless Falsehood, wrote and signed and delivered to Teedyuscung a solemn Declaration, that neither he, nor any one for him, to his Knowledge, was either directly, or indirectly, concerned in the Purchase of any Lands at or near Wyoming.

This done, he sent for G. Croghan, and read to him what Teedyuscung had charged him with; which Croghan positively denied, and appealed to another Indian who was present at the Conversation: The other Indian being called upon, confirmed every Word that Teedyuscung had said. Croghan still persisted in denying it, and told a plausible Story which he said was the Subject of their Conversation, as he could shew from his Diary. Mr. Norris told him, it was possible the Indians might have misunderstood him, and desired him to produce his Diary; but Croghan refused that, and said he would shew it to the Governors at a convenient Time, and that it should be read in public before the Conference broke up. On this one of the Indians observed, that it would be easy for him to go Home and write down what he pleased, and afterwards pretend he had done it before; that the best Way was to shew it now, and then it might have some Credit paid to it. This he was pressed to do, in Vindication of himself, and to avoid Suspicion. But he persisted in refusing, for a Reason, I suppose, you will think too obvious to mention, and went away in a Passion.

It is evident from the Countenance and Favour Croghan meets with that he does not act of himself, in these his Endeavours to embroil Affairs among the Indians.

On Friday, October 13, a Conference was held, at which the Governors spoke, and the Allegheny Letter was read. At the Close of the Conference, one Nichos a Mohawk made a Speech, which at Con. Wieser's[2] particular Request was not then interpreted in public.[3] The Substance of the Speech, we were soon after informed, was to disclaim Teedyuscung's Authority. This Nichos is G. Croghan's Father-in-Law, and him 'tis thought Croghan now makes use of to raise Disturbance among the Indians, as he found himself baffled in his other Scheme. He could not prejudice Teedyuscung and set him against the People of the Province; he therefore now labours to set the Indians against him by the same Methods, I suppose, that he attempted the former.

On Sunday, October 15, there was a private Conference at Scull's[4] but neither Teedyuscung nor any of his People were there. Next Day a Conference was held in public, at which were read the Minutes of what had passed: When they came to what was said Yesterday they stopped; but at the Request of the Six Nation Chiefs it was read. What concern'd Teedyuscung there, seemed little more than whether he should be considered as a King or an Emperor.[5] They did not deny his Power over his own Nations, and he never claimed (except in his Cups, if then) any Authority over the Six Nations; nay, as the Governor observed, he expresly declared they were his Superiors, and that tho' he acted as Head for his own four Tribes, he acted only as a Messenger from his Uncles.

2. Conrad Weiser (above, III, 89 n) was the official provincial interpreter.

3. It was interpreted, however, on October 15 at a private conference between N.J. and Pa. officials and the chiefs of the Six Nations.

4. A public house in Easton.

5. In fact, the Six Nations deflated Teedyuscung's pretensions to being a "great man"; they denied emphatically his ridiculous claim to authority over them and inquired who had made the Delaware a great man. Official Minutes, pp. 224–5.

On Wednesday, October 8th,[6] when the Six Nation Indians come to return an Answer, they gave us a Specimen of their Finesse in Politics. We had been harrassed with an Indian War; the Governor called upon them to declare the Causes of it. The Chiefs disclaimed all Concern in it, and declared that it was not done by the Advice or Consent of the Public Council of the Nations, tho' they frankly owned some of their young Men had been concerned in it. As Counsellors they would not undertake to assign the Causes of their Uneasiness, or what had induced them to strike the English, lest it should appear as if they had countenanced the War, or at least had not been at due Pains to prevent it. They therefore left the Warriors to speak for themselves. The Causes they assigned were the same that had been assigned before. Our Managers were very earnest to have the Six Nations Speaker say he spoke for the Delawares.[7] However, Teedyuscung maintained his Independancy; and as soon as Tomas King sat down, he arose and said, that as his Uncles had done, he would speak in Behalf of his own People; and as his Uncles had mentioned several Causes of Uneasiness, he would now mention one in Behalf of the Opines, or Wapings, &c. This I find differently represented in the printed Treaty; but as there are several other Places liable to Objections, I shall, if I have Leisure, send you one with some Notes.[8]

You see by Tomas King's Speech, that what was conjectured in the Enquiry relating to the Purchase of 1754, was not groundless, and that that Purchase was one main Cause of the War.[9]

6. Either Thomson's or the printer's error for October 18.

7. The Oneida chieftain, Thomas King, was chosen to speak for the warriors and declared that he spoke not only for those "of the Elder and Younger Nations, but of our Cousins the Delawares and Minisinks." He attributed the war to the mistreatment of certain Shawnee in South Carolina and of Seneca in Virginia, to the failure of the governors of Va. and Pa. to support the Indians against the encroachments of the French on the Ohio, and to dissatisfaction with the Albany Purchase of 1754. Official Minutes, pp. 228–30.

8. According to the Official Minutes (p. 230), Teedyuscung complained that in 1755 nine Wappinger (Opine, Pompton) Indians had been murdered at Goshen (in N.Y., close to the N.J. boundary) and that no attempt had been made to satisfy the Indians who complained. What Thomson had in mind is not clear; no copy of the treaty with his notes has been found.

9. In his *Enquiry* (p. 82) Thomson had cited the Albany Purchase of 1754 (above, v, 349–50 n) as one of the causes of war.

I find the same Effect may be attributed to different Causes; for the going away of the Six Nation Chiefs, which I, who was not so clear-sighted as to discover the great Dissatisfaction said to have been visible in the Countenances of the Indians, attributed to the Coldness of the Day and the Fatigue of long sitting, I find in the printed Treaty ascribed to their Aversion to Teedyuscung and Disapprobation of what he was saying. The next Day the Munseys, dissatisfied with some Part of the Six Nations Conduct, demanded and received back the Belt by which they had put themselves and their Affairs under their Direction, and gave it to Teedyuscung. The Close of the Conference on Friday, October 20th, was nothing but Confusion. After the Governor had done, Nichos the Mohawk said the Governor left Things in the Dark; that neither he nor any of the Chiefs knew what Lands he meant; if he spoke of the Lands beyond the Mountains, they had already confessed their having sold them; but the Governor had their Deeds, why were not these produced and shewn to their Cousins the Delawares? Here C.Weiser went and brought the Deed of 1749. Nichos acknowledged the Deed. It was shewn to Teedyuscung; but he could not readily be made to understand why it was now brought, all Matters relating to Land being as he thought referred to the Determination of the King.[1] Governor Bernard of the Jerseys, who had something to say, had several Times desired to be heard; but the Affair of the Deed so engrossed the Attention of our Governor, his Council, and Interpreter, that no Regard was paid to what Governor Bernard desired. In short their Behaviour on the Occasion was so very unpolite, that many could not help blushing for them.[2] And at the last, the producing the Deed raised such a Commotion among the Indians, that they broke up without giving Governor Bernard an Opportunity to speak a Word.

Next Day a private Conference was held with the Chiefs of the

1. There appears to have been a misunderstanding as to whether lands beyond the Kittatinny Hills which the Six Nations had sold to the Proprietors in 1749 were rightfully theirs to sell or belonged to Teedyuscung and the Delaware Indians. Denny called upon both groups to confer and decide who owned the lands in question. Official Minutes, pp. 233–4; Chew's Journal, pp. 317–18.

2. The Official Minutes (p. 233) indicate that it was the Indians, not the whites, who opposed Bernard's speaking when they were so confused about the land question.

Indians. As our People have not thought fit to publish it, I shall give it to you as I had it from some who were present.[3]

Teedyuscung taking out a String of white and black Wampum, told the Council and Commissioners (the Governor was not there) that he had made Enquiry concerning the Deed produced Yesterday, and was satisfied his Uncles had sold the Land describ'd therein; he saw likewise that Nutimus the Delaware Chief had signed the Deed, and found upon Inquiry that he had received forty four Dollars, part of the Consideration-Money. This being the Case, he would make no Dispute about that Deed, but was ready to confirm it; for he wanted to be at Peace with his Brothers the English. But he observed, that his confirming that Deed would not affect the Claims he had formerly made; for the Lands he thought himself principally wronged in, lay between Tohiccon and the Kittatinny Hills. On this he gave a String. After he had delivered the String, Tokahayo, a Cayuga Chief, arose, and in a very warm Speech commended the Conduct of Teedyuscung, and at the same Time severely reprehended that of the English. He told Teedyuscung, "That he himself and the other Chiefs were obliged to him for his Candour and Openness; that they plainly perceived he spoke from the Heart, in the same Manner they used to do in ancient Times, when they held Councils together. They wished they could say as much of the English; but it was plain the English either did not understand Indian Affairs, or else did not act and speak with that Sincerity and in the Manner they ought. When the Indians delivered Belts, they were large and long; but when the English returned an Answer or spoke, they did it on small Belts and trifling little Strings.* And yet the English made the Wampum, whereas the Indians were obliged to buy it. But the Reason was, the Indians spoke from the Heart, the English only from the Mouth. Besides, how little the English attended to what was said appeared from this, that several of the Belts and Strings they (the Indians) had given them, were lost." [That is *unan-*

*Among the Indians the Size of the Belts they give with their Speeches, is always in Proportion to their Ideas of the greater or less Importance of the Matters treated of.[4]

3. Thomson apparently overlooked the account of this private conference which appears in the printed minutes, pp. 237–8.
4. BF probably added this note.

swered; for you'll please to observe no Answer was returned to the Complaints the Indians made respecting Carolina, the Ohio Affair, or the Opines.]⁵ "If the English knew no better how to manage Indian Affairs, they should not call them together. Here they had invited them down to brighten the Chain of Peace, but instead of that, had spent a Fortnight wrangling and disputing about Lands. What must the People of Allegheny think of this Conduct when they are informed of it by their Messengers?"

On Tuesday a public Entertainment was given to the Indians,⁶ and in the Evening the Chiefs were called together by R. Peters and C. Weiser. Hitherto the Indians, tho' several Times pressed to it, had deferred giving an Answer to the Proposal made on Behalf of the Proprietors to release back to the Indians the Lands of the Purchase of 1754, West of the Allegheny Mountains, provided the Indians would confirm to them the Residue of that Purchase.⁷ But the Deeds being drawn up agreeable to what the Proprietors proposed, it now remained to persuade the Indians to sign them as drawn. And To-night 'tis said that is done.⁸ I wish this may not be a Foundation of fresh Uneasiness. In public Council they declared they would confirm no more of that Land than what was *settled* in the Year 1754, for which *only* they had received the Consideration; but all the rest they reclaimed. Yet now by the

5. Brackets in the original. Denny did, in fact, promise to inquire from the governor of Virginia about one of these complaints and Bernard pointed out that the massacre at Goshen had taken place in the province of New York but that he would report the complaints to the governor there. Official Minutes, pp. 232, 240. Only about the South Carolina affair was nothing further said at the conference.

6. The public entertainment on Tuesday, October 24, is not mentioned in the Official Minutes, and Chew's Journal stops with the 21st.

7. Sir William Johnson had written the Board of Trade, Sept. 10, 1756, that he believed jealousies over land were at the heart of Indian grievances. With regard to the Albany Purchase of 1754 by the Pa. Proprietors he stated: "I conceive the most effectual method of producing tranquillity to that Province, would be a voluntary and open surrender of that Deed of Sale, fix with the Indians in the best manner they can the bounds for their settlement, and make them Guarantees to it." *N.Y. Col. Docs.,* VII, 130. The present action was, at best, only a partial compliance with that suggestion.

8. Thomson must have copied this passage directly from his notes at Easton. The deed of release (printed in *Johnson Papers,* X, 43–8) is dated Oct. 23, 1758. It was delivered at a private conference on the 24th and exhibited at the public session on the 26th. Official Minutes, pp. 241, 242.

Deed as drawn, ten Times, nay I may say twenty Times as much Land is conveyed as was then settled. For the English Settlements in 1754 extended but a little Way up the Juniata and Sherman's Creek, whereas the present Grant reaches to the Allegheny Mountains. May not the Warriors to whom the Lands have been given for hunting Grounds disapprove this Grant as they did before, and maintain their Right by Force of Arms? I wish this Fear may be groundless. Besides, I could have wished that another Time than the *Close of an Entertainment* had been chosen for executing the Deeds, considering the Indians Fondness for Liquor.

But I have already too much transgressed upon your Patience; I shall therefore only add that I am, &c.

From Israel Pemberton[9]

MS not found; reprinted from extract in [Charles Thomson], *An Enquiry into the Causes of the Alienation of the Delaware and Shawanese Indians from the British Interest,* . . . (London, 1759), pp. 183–4.

December 11, 1758

At the late Treaty Teedyuscung confirmed the Purchase of 1749;* his Motives for this Confirmation, were to engage the Six Nations to confirm the Wyoming Lands to him and his People;[2] but such Measures were pursued, by our proprietary Managers, to prevent it, and to set the Indians at variance with each other, that all our

*This was a Purchase made by the Proprietors from the Six Nations, of Lands claimed by the Delawares.[1]

9. For the identification of the author and addressee of the letter from which this extract was taken and the circumstances of its first printing, see headnote to the document immediately above.

1. By the purchase of 1749, the Proprietors acquired title to a rectangular area bounded on the south by the Kittatinny Hills, on the west by the Susquehanna River, on the east by the Delaware River, and on the north by a line drawn "from Mahoniahy Creek on Susquehannah to Leheighwochter Creek on Delaware." "Benjamin Chew's Journal of a Journey to Easton, 1758," Van Doren and Boyd, *Indian Treaties,* p. 317. This note was probably written by BF. Toward the end of the Easton Treaty Teedyuscung admitted that this had been a legitimate sale. *Ibid.,* p. 237.

2. Teedyuscung wished to settle his people permanently in the Wyoming Valley. See above, VII, 282 n.

Arguments, Persuasions and Presents were scarce sufficient to keep them from an open Rupture.

The Business was shamefully delayed from Day to Day, which the Minutes are calculated to screen; but it well known to us who attended, that the Time was spent in attempting Teedyuscung's Downfal, and silencing or contradicting the Complaints he had made; but he is really more of a politician than any of his Opponents, whether in or out of our proprietary Council; and if he could be kept sober, might probably soon become Emperor of all the neighbouring Nations.

His old Secretary not being present, when the Treaty began,[3] he did not demand the Right of having one, and thought it unnecessary, as he was determined rather to be a Spectator than active in public Business, so that we are imposed on in some Minutes of Consequence.[4]

General Forbes's proceeding with so much Caution has furnished Occasion for many imprudent Reflections; but I believe he pursued the only Method, in which he could have succeeded.[5] Whether he is a Soldier or not I cannot judge, nor is it my Business; but I am certain he is a considerate understanding Man; and it is a Happiness to these Provinces, that he prudently determined from the entrance on the Command here, to make use of every rational Method of conciliating the Friendship of the Indians, and drawing them off from the French;[6] so that since we had his Countenance and Directions, our pacific Negotiations have been carried on with some Spirit, and have had the desired Effect.

The Express left the General at Fort Duquesne (now Pitt's-burgh)[7] on the 30th ult. and says he would stay to meet the Indians,

3. Charles Thomson arrived, however, no later than October 11. Chew's Journal, p. 313.

4. Thomson had also complained of the untrustworthiness of the official minutes; see the preceding document.

5. Gen. John Forbes's army captured its objective, Ft. Duquesne, on Nov. 25, 1758.

6. For Forbes's assiduous efforts to conciliate the friendship of the Indians, see esp. Alfred P. James, ed., *Writings of General John Forbes* (Menasha, Wis., 1938), pp. 81–2, 109, 127, 137, 180–1.

7. "I have used the freedom of giving your name to Fort DuQuesne, as I hope it was in some measure the being actuated by your spirits that now makes us Masters of the place." Forbes to William Pitt, Nov. 27, 1758, James, ed., *Writings of Forbes,* p. 269.

of whom he expected five hundred in a Day or two, having heard they were near him on the other Side the River.[8] He will, no doubt, provide for divers Matters shamefully neglected at Easton, where our proprietary Agents wisely releas'd to the Indians all the Lands westward of the Mountains,[9] without so much as stipulating for the keeping a trading House in any Part of that extensive Country.

This Neglect is now much noticed; and as we are assur'd there will be a great Want of Goods there this Winter, I am fitting out two Waggons with about £5 or 600 worth of Strouds,[1] Blankets, Matchcoats, &c. which shall be sent to the General either to be sold or given away in such Manner, as may most effectually promote the public Interest: The Weather being pleasant and mild, and the Roads good, I am in hopes they will be conveyed to Ray's-Town in a few Days. Our Friendly Association have, out of their Fund, expended upwards of £2000 but the Cost of these Goods must be paid (if they are given away) out of the Contributions of the Menonists and Swengfelders, who put about £1500 into my Hands for these Purposes.[2] I am, &c.

8. The express reached Philadelphia on or a little before December 11. Forbes enclosed a letter to Denny, dated November 26, in which he announced his intentions of conferring with the Indians. The General "also sent word to Philadelphia describing the need of goods" with which to supply the Indians. *Pa. Col. Recs.*, VIII, 232–4; Theodore Thayer, *Israel Pemberton* (Phila., 1943), p. 171.

9. See the preceding document.

1. Coarse warm cloth.

2. Although Pemberton dispatched the two wagons from Philadelphia on December 13, they did not reach Pittsburgh until April 30, 1759. While the goods were in transit, the trustees of the Friendly Association objected to his use of the Mennonite and Schwenkfelder funds; so he returned the money to the Friendly Association, paid for the goods himself, and traded them to Indians at Pittsburgh. Thayer, *Pemberton*, pp. 171–4; John W. Jordan, ed., "James Kenny's 'Journal to the Westward,' 1758–59," *PMHB*, XXXVII (1913), 395–449.

To the Printer of the London Chronicle

Printed in *The London Chronicle: or Universal Evening Post*, December 28–30, 1758; draft: American Philosophical Society.[3]

Sir,

When people consider the supply of Twelve Millions as necessary for the service of the ensuing year, the greatness of the object astonishes;[4] and they are apt to say, Whence can so vast a sum arise?[5] Can England possibly bear the continuance of a war at so enormous an expence?

But when this *great whole* is divided into its parts, and each considered separately; when the burthen is divided by the number of shoulders that are to bear it, and that number is well considered, our terrible apprehensions may in some degree diminish.

Suppose that Britain contains six millions of inhabitants,[6] and that four millions of these are able to do something for a livelihood. Let these four millions but retrench a little of the idle time they spend, and increase their industry only to the amount of twelve-pence a week per head, one with another during the year, and there is your Twelve Millions.[7]

Or, Let the superfluous expence in living of these six millions be retrenched, by greater frugality, to the amount only of eight-

3. The draft shows interestingly BF's revisions of style and substance. Some of these are described below in footnotes.

4. At the opening of Parliament on Nov. 23, 1758, the budget for 1759 was presented; it amounted to £12,705,339. Albert von Ruville, *William Pitt, Earl of Chatham* (London, 1907), II, 216–18.

5. The draft contains another sentence here, with its last three words struck out: "If the War is long continued at this Expence England must be ruined."

6. This phrase underwent considerable revision before it assumed its final form. BF first wrote "British Dominions including the Colonies" and estimated their population at twelve million. When he substituted Britain for British Dominions, he estimated her population at eight million and then revised it downward to six million.

7. BF erred in these calculations and those in the following paragraph. If four million people "increased their industry . . . twelve pence a week per head," in one year they would add £10,400,000 and not £12,000,000 to the national income. The annual savings of six million people at eight pence each per week would similarly be £10,400,000 not £12,000,000. BF's corrected figures are very close to the 1758 budget, £10,486,000, and it may be that he inadvertently based his figures on it.

pence a week per head, one with another; and there again is your Twelve Millions; or, if you please, another Twelve Millions.

Methinks I hear the reader say, Habits are hard to break, and those who have been accustomed to idleness or extravagance do not easily change their manners. I allow it, I believe they seldom do but when they are obliged to it. However, this is certainly one good that springs out of the evil of taxes; when they are heavy, they oblige people to be more industrious and more frugal. And so the evil, if indeed it be an evil, contributes naturally to its own cure.

Let it be farther considered, that through the plenty of our last harvest, corn is fallen to less than half the price it bore this time twelvemonth. Supposing, then, that your people will neither be more industrious nor more frugal, yet, compared with their last year's expence, they must, one with another, save, this year, in the price of their bread alone, at least eight-pence a week per head; which amounts again to your Twelve Millions.[8]

So that bountiful Heaven, smiling on the Protestant cause, seems to have thrown twelve millions into the lap of Britain, which she may spend in pursuance of this just war, without being a penny poorer at the end of the ensuing year than she is at the end of the present.

It is to be hoped then, that these bug-bear terrors will not precipitate a peace which shall be either *unsafe* or dishonourable to the nation. I am, yours, &c.   CHEARFUL.[9]

8. £10,400,000 is the correct figure.
9. In the draft, BF used the letter N as his signature. There also appears in the draft the following postscript: "Let me only add, That our Trade upon the whole (tho' some particular Branches may possibly suffer) was never in a more flourishing State than at present, the Exports this Year exceeding what has been ever known in the Memory of Man; and our Money sent to the Colonies must inevitably return in a short time for Manufactures."

James Ferguson:[1] Account of Franklin's Three-Wheel Clock

Printed in James Ferguson, *Select Mechanical Exercises: Shewing how to construct different Clocks, Orreries, and Sun-Dials, on Plain and Easy Principles,* ... (Second edition, London, 1778), pp. 1–4.

Apparently Franklin never wrote a description of the three-wheel clock he devised, nor does he seem to have known that his friend James Ferguson published an account of it. He told Jan Ingenhousz in 1785, however, that he had seen several of his clocks in Paris, made by John Whitehurst of Derby, England.[2] In the absence of any account of the construction and operation of this timepiece by its inventor, there is here reprinted Ferguson's description, first published in 1773.[3] It is placed with documents of 1758 (though no specific date can be assigned to this invention), on the basis of a statement by Ferguson's biographer, who wrote: "The Clock usually called '*Ferguson's Clock,*' appears to have been invented and made by Ferguson in 1758, and is often alluded to in works on Horology, &c. It was contrived by him as an improvement on a singular Clock which had then been recently invented by the celebrated Dr. Franklin;—now known as '*The Franklin Clock.*'"[4]

A Clock shewing the Hours, Minutes, and Seconds, having only three Wheels and two Pinions in the whole Movement. Invented by Dr. FRANKLIN *of Philadelphia.*

The dial-plate of this clock is represented by Fig. 1. of Plate I. The hours are engraven in spiral spaces, along two diameters of a circle containing four times 60 minutes. The index *A* goes round in four hours, and counts the minutes from any hour it has passed by, to the next following hour. The time, as it appears in the figure, is either 32½ minutes past XII, or past IIII, or past VIII;

1. James Ferguson (1710–1776), astronomer, mathematician, and horologist, also published some of BF's magic squares and his magic circle; see above, IV, 392–402.

2. To Ingenhousz, April 29, 1785, Lib. Cong. Ingenhousz had asked permission to publish an account of the clock and BF replied that he did not know that his contrivance "has ever been publish'd. ... You are welcome to do what you please with it."

3. When the first edition of Ferguson's *Select Mechanical Exercises* appeared.

4. E[benezer] Henderson, *Life of James Ferguson, F.R.S., in a Brief Autobiographical Account and Further Extended Memoir* (Edinburgh, London, and Glasgow, 1867), p. 231.

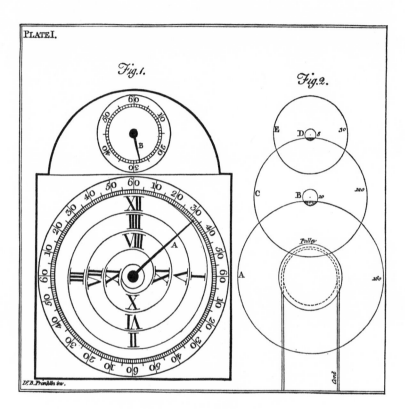

Fig. 1.

Fig. 2.

Franklin's Three-Wheel Clock

and so on in each quarter of the circle, pointing to the number of minutes after the hours the index last left in its motion. Now, as one can hardly be four hours mistaken in estimating the time, he can always tell the true hour and minute, by looking at the clock, from the time he rises till the time he goes to bed. The small hand *B*, in the arch at top, goes round once in a minute, and shews the seconds as in a common clock.

Fig. 2. shews the wheel-work of this clock. *A* is the first or great wheel, it contains 160 teeth, goes round in four hours, and the Index *A* (Fig. 1.) is put upon its axis, and moved round in the same time. The hole in the index is round, it is put tight upon the round end of the axis, so as to be carried by the motion of the wheel, but may be set at any time to the proper hour and minute, without affecting either the wheel or its axis. This wheel of 160 teeth turns a pinion *B* of 10 leaves; and as 10 is but a 16th part of 160, the pinion goes round in a quarter of an hour. On the axis of this pinion is the wheel *C* of 120 teeth; it also goes round in a quarter of an hour, and turns a pinion *D*, of 8 leaves, round in a minute; for there are 15 minutes in a quarter of an hour, and 8 times 15 is 120. On the axis of this pinion is the *second-hand B* (Fig. 1.) and also the common wheel *E* (Fig. 2.) of 30 teeth, for moving a pendulum (by pallets) that vibrates seconds, as in a common clock.

This clock is not designed to be wound up by a winch, but to be drawn up like a clock that goes only 30 hours. For this purpose, the line must go over a pulley on the axis of the great wheel, as in a common 30 hour clock. Several clocks have been made according to this ingenious plan of the Doctor's, and I can affirm, that I have seen one of them, which measures time exceedingly well. The simpler that any machine is, the better it will be allowed to be, by every man of science.[5]

5. Ferguson went on to criticise BF's clock on two counts: 1. it had to be rewound more than once a week; 2. "if a person wakes in the night, and looks at the clock, he may possibly be mistaken four hours in reckoning the time by it, as the hand cannot be upon any hour, or pass by any hour, without being upon or passing by four hours at the same time." In his modification only the minutes of one hour were shown on the single dial, but small segments of revolving plates, set behind the dial and bearing numbers for the hours and seconds, appeared through small apertures in it. Ferguson readily admitted a major defect in his invention: for technical reasons it could not be

From John Hughes[6]   ALS: Public Record Office, London

Dear Sir   Philada. January the 1st 1759

As I am Just now Inform'd that a vessel is going from New York to London I Embrace the Opertunity of Letting You know Your friends are Generally in health Especially Mrs. Franklin and Family whom I Continue to visit frequently in Your Absence and if Occation Required shou'd be fond of an Oppertunity to Serve You or Yours, but Mrs. Franklin's Good Oeconomy Renders friends I think almost Unecessary however I believe we Shall keep up a friendly Correspondence Untill Your Return.

As You will have heard of General Forbes Success at fort Duquesne before this Comes to hand it is Unnecessary to Say any thing on that head only that at General Amherst Request we have kept the 14,00. [*sic*] old Troops in pay in hopes of another Effort the Next Season to Root the french out of this part of North America at Last.[7]

If You have Interest Enough to have a Guard Ship Order'd here next Spring it will be Doing us Good Service as M: Chatelau is Gone off Safe after Taking about 30 of our Ships or vessels And no Doubt Several will be on the Coast next Summer and Ruin our Trade.[8]

---

as accurate as either a conventional clock or BF's unless the device for showing the seconds were to be eliminated. Nevertheless, he recorded in his commonplace book that "I showed this Clock to Dr. Franklin, who approved very much of the alteration." Ferguson, *Select Mechanical Exercises*, pp. 4–11; Henderson, *Life of Ferguson*, p. 235. Ferguson also devised a clock showing motions of the sun and moon and the times of high and low tide, and BF later had Whitehurst construct clocks for him on this design.

6. Although few of his letters have survived, Hughes was one of BF's most faithful correspondents; see above p. 90.

7. With the recall of the incompetent Abercromby in September 1758, Maj. Gen. Jeffery Amherst (1717–1797) was appointed commander-in-chief of the British forces in North America. On Dec. 13, 1758, Amherst wrote Governor Denny asking him to recommend that the Assembly continue the 1400 Pa. provincial troops "in their Pay during the Winter." Denny sent this request to the Assembly on December 21, and agreement was reached two days later. *Pa. Col. Recs.*, VIII, 236, 240–1.

8. Captain Sebière du Chateleau appeared off the Capes of the Delaware in the beginning of October 1758 in the *Prince Edward* frigate of St. Malo "pierced for 36 Guns but mounted only 26." *Pa. Gaz.*, Oct. 26, 1758. The Frenchman created so much havoc in the shipping lanes that on Nov. 23,

Every thing now is Quiet, and our River partly full of Ice so that Navigation is partly stopt at present and no Londoners Arived Except Bolitha.⁹ Sir be pleased to Except the Compliments of the Season and believe me Yours Affectionately   JON HUGHES

P:S the post waits.

Addressed: For / Benjamin Franklin Esqr / in / London / via New York

Endorsed: Letter from Mr Hughes one of the Assembly of Pensilvania, to B Franklin Mentioning the Continuance of 1400 Pensilvanians in pay thro' the Winter at the Request of General Amherst.

Mr. Hughes's Lettrs. from Jan 1. to Feb. 5 1759 Answer'd.¹

From Richard Quinton²   ALS: Historical Society of Pennsylvania

Sir   Wellingb[orough] 4th. Janry. 59
  Your Relation Mrs. Fisher was Bury'd last week, and Mr. Fisher about A Week before,³ of which I should certainly have

---

1758, the Pa. Assembly directed BF to petition the Admiralty for a vessel of superior force "to be stationed at our Cape, for the more effectual Protection of Trade." *Votes*, 1758–59, p. 11. This BF did, and sometime between March 19 and April 7, 1759, he was advised by the Admiralty that the Assembly should apply directly to the naval commander in North America for a ship. See below, pp. 297, 315. It does not appear, however, whether an application was ever made. For BF's collaboration with Thomas Penn, on an earlier occasion, to get a ship stationed in Delaware Bay, see above, VII, 285.

9. *Pa. Gaz.*, Dec. 14, 1758, reports that the *Myrtilla,* John Bolitho, Captain, entered at the Philadelphia customs house.

1. These endorsements, in BF's hand, are on different pages. The other letters have not been found; nor has BF's answer.

2. Described as "gentleman" of Wellingborough in Joseph Foster, ed., *Alumni Oxonienses, 1715–1886* (London, 1888), III, 1168. This letter appears to have been written in answer to one of BF's (not found) about Mary Fisher's estate, in which he particularly mentioned Eleanor Morris (A.5.2.8.1), a first cousin of BF and Mary Fisher and so another heir-at-law. For BF's and his Uncle Benjamin's impression of Miss Morris, see above, p. 135 n. The genealogy of the English Franklins (above, I, l–liii, lxviii–lxix) will be found helpful to an understanding of this and later letters concerning the settlement of Mrs. Fisher's estate.

3. Mary Franklin Fisher (A.5.2.1.1), BF's first cousin, died at Wellingborough on Christmas Day, 1758, at the age of 85. Her husband, Richard

given You advice, had I suppos'd You yet in Town. I went last night to the Executors[4] who inform'd me they had wrote to the person You mention and was surpris'd they had not had an Answer (therefore would write again this post both to Her and You which I presume will be Satisfactory).[5] Our Ministers Name is Thos. Holmes[6] who I am inform'd made Mr. Fisher's Will, wherein I am informed He left only one Hundred pound at Her disposall,[7] out of which His Heirs insist upon the funerall Charges being paid, and also Her being buryd in the same manner as Her Husband, at Her desire, [I] fear it will not amount to fourscore to be divided between the person You mention and another relation who was sent for on the occasion and is still here.[8] You cannot oblige me more than by comanding me, who am with the Compliments of the Season to Your Son and Self Your Most Obedient Servant   RICHD. QUINTON

Addressed: To / Mr. Francklin at Mrs. / Stevensons in Craven Street / Strand / London

Endorsed: Mr Quinton. Jan 4. 59

––––––

Fisher, had died thirteen days earlier. BF made their acquaintance on his "Ramble" through the English Midlands in the summer of 1758 and afterwards corresponded with his cousin Mary. See above, pp. 117 n, 120–1, 134–5.

4. Rev. William Fisher (d. 1778), rector of Newton Bromswold and nephew of Richard Fisher, was executor of his will. Mary Fisher died intestate and Anne Franklin Farrow (A.5.2.3.3), a first cousin of hers and BF's, was appointed administratrix of her estate. See below, pp. 224, 239. But because Mrs. Farrow was 73 years of age and lived at some distance from Wellingborough, William Fisher assumed in large part the work of settling Mary Fisher's estate as well as that of her husband. For William Fisher, see Henry I. Longden, *Northamptonshire and Rutland Clergy from 1500,* v (Northampton, 1940), 47–9.

5. No letter from William Fisher has been found.

6. Rev. Thomas Holme (above, p. 121 n), vicar of Wellingborough and master of the school there, assisted William Fisher in administering Mrs. Fisher's estate.

7. On the terms of Richard Fisher's will, see below, p. 224.

8. Anne Farrow, the administratrix. For the final distribution of Mrs. Fisher's estate, see below, pp. 288–9, 302.

From Anne Farrow[9]

ALS: Historical Society of Pennsylvania

Dear Sir   Castle Thorp, January the 8 1759

I hope you will not think it bold though I Present you with a few Lines being So near a Relation. Hearing you was not gone out of England[1] I thought I could do no less When I was informed in Summer[2] you was come over into England to see all your Relations I fanced my Self with great Pleasures of seeing you and your offspring. Which Pleasure would have been the greatest I could have had in this world to think that I had lived to see my Dear Uncle Josiahs Son and his offspring[3] as was my Dear Fathers first Prentence.[4] If I had not been of low Circumstance I would have gone to New England many years agone to have seen my Relations and what a Pleasent Place it was for my good Uncle Benjman sent me the heads of it and if my age and circumstance would Answer I would see you still before you went out of England but I am a Poor Widow being now in my Seventy four. But Dear Sir I hope you will be so good as to grant a Poor widows request as to Answer my Letter[5] but I Should have joy without measure to see you I having Neither Brother nor Sisters alive only a Daugh-

9. BF's first cousin (A.5.2.3.3); see the preceding document. Mrs. Farrow used no punctuation in this letter or that of Jan. 19, 1759 (below, pp. 237–9). Periods and capitals have been added sparingly where the sense seems absolutely to require.

1. Mrs. Farrow was in Wellingborough during the last week of December 1758, and for a few days at the beginning of January 1759, serving as the administratrix of Mary Fisher's estate. She probably learned that BF was still residing in London from his letter (not found) to Richard Quinton. See the preceding document.

2. Possibly by Mary Fisher, whom Mrs. Farrow visited on occasion (below, p. 237); possibly by Mrs. Farrow's brother-in-law, Robert Page, whom BF visited at Banbury in the summer of 1758. See above, p. 118.

3. Although Mrs. Farrow's home at Castlethorpe near Stony Stratford, Bucks, was only about twenty miles from Banbury, through which BF and WF passed on the last leg of their Midlands journey in the summer of 1758, it was on a different road to London and they did not go to visit her. The cousins did see each other, however, before she died. BF to Jane Mecom, July 17, 1771.

4. Josiah Franklin was apprenticed to his brother John (A.5.2.3), a silk dyer, when they both lived at Banbury. For their brother Benjamin's comments on John, see above, p. 153 n.

5. BF lost no time in granting this request; see below, p. 237.

ter.[6] I thank God I have a good Bed to Lodge you if you was to come that is all my comfort I live wihin two Miles of Stony Strafford. My Daughters complements and mine wait on you and your son though unknown so I remain your ever affectionate and Loving Coussin to Command ANNE FARROW

Direct for me at Castle Thorp near Stoney Strafford

Addressed: To Mr / Franklin in Craven / Street Strand / London

Endorsed: Ann Farrow Jan. 8. 1759

From Thomas Holme[7]   ALS: Historical Society of Pennsylvania

Sir   Jan: 9th. 1759.

As I am inform'd that you are still in London, I therefore take the Liberty to acquaint you with the Death of Mr. Richard Fisher of this Town on the 12th. Ulto. He left his whole Estate Real and Personal to the Amount of about £5000 between his three Neices:[8] except a clear Rent Charge of £45 per Annum to his Wife for Life, and £100 in Cash to be paid to her in three Months after his Decease; She survived him only Thirteen Days, and was never during that Time capable of making a Will; So that the said £100 devolves to her Administrators and accordingly Administration has been granted to Ann Farrow of the Parish of Castlethorpe in the County of Bucks, but subject to Distribution to all of equal Degree in Kindred: We know of no Relations so near as own Cousins besides your Self, Ann Farrow aforesaid and Eleanor Morris in London;[9] and as the two last, as we are informed here, are but in poor Circumstances; and the said £100 after Deduction of Funeral and other Charges will be reduced to about £70[1] it is expected you will not insist upon you Share in the Distribution,

6. Hannah Farrow Walker (A.5.2.3.3.1) of Westbury, Northamptonshire.

7. See above, p. 121 n. Many of the matters dealt with in this letter are elucidated in other letters, above, pp. 221–2, and below, pp. 237–9, 288–9.

8. Not identified. In contradiction to this statement, a published summary of Richard Fisher's will records that he left his house and land in Wellingborough to his nephew and executor, Rev. William Fisher. Henry I. Longden, *Northamptonshire and Rutland Clergy from 1500,* v (Northampton, 1940), 49.

9. BF, in his missing letter to Richard Quinton, had called attention to his cousin Eleanor Morris, whose kinship to Mary Fisher, however, appears to have been already known at Wellingborough.

1. The exact figure was £79 18s. 4d.

but let them take the Benefit of it.[2] But if not, or if you know of any other Relations of equal Degree,[3] it will be esteem'd a Favour if you'll send such Intelligence either to the Revd. Mr. William Fisher the sole Executor of Richd. deceased, or to Sir Your very humble Servant   THO: HOLME. Vicar of Wellingborough.

P.S. I had wrote the above before I received Yours,[4] and which in a great Measure will I hope answer your Enquiry: the £100 was bequeath'd to Mrs. Fisher in such Terms as to rest in Her on his Decease, tho not payable till 3 Months after, so that there is not the least Doubt of its belonging to her Representatives. Mr. Fisher beside what I mention'd above, gave his Wife the Use of all his Houshold Goods, Linnen and Plate for her Life and the Dwelling House to live in Rent and Tax free; but ordered the said Goods &c. after her Decease to be divided equally between his Neices and the Legacies to Mrs. Fisher were on this Express Condition that she relinquished all Claim to Thirds.[5] And he Left no other Legacies whatsoever except to his Neices to the Value of so much as a Shilling. Mrs. Fisher's wearing Apparrel (Which as I am told were of no great Value)[6] have been divided between Mrs. Farrow and Mrs. Morris, and her Share[7] is in the Hands of One Mrs. Whitebread who was a very intimate Acquaintance of the late Mrs. Fishers. I shall be very ready to give you any further information with Regard to this Affair that you may think necessary and am Sir Yours very sincerely   THO: HOLME.

Jan: 11th. 1759.

Endorsed: Revd Mr Holme Jan 9. and 11 1759 answerd

2. As Holme expected, BF divided his share between his elderly cousins.

3. In answer to this query, or to a similar one by Anne Farrow on Jan. 19, 1759, BF supplied the names of Mary Fisher's four surviving first cousins in New England: Samuel Franklin (A.5.2.7.1), Elizabeth Douse (C.1), Peter Franklin (C.9), and Jane Mecom (C.17).

4. Not found, but obviously prompted by Richard Quinton's letter of Jan. 4, 1759.

5. At common law, a wife, upon the death of her husband, got "the third of all the lands and tenements whereof he was seized during coverture, to hold to herself for the term of her natural life." William Blackstone, *Commentaries on the Laws of England* (4th edit., Oxford, 1770), II, 129.

6. Her apparel was valued at £11 0s. 6d.

7. Presumably Eleanor Morris' share, she not having been in Wellingborough as Anne Farrow was.

From Isaac Norris

Letterbook Copy: Historical Society of Pennsylvania

Dear Friend BF   Janry 15. 1759

I refer to the above Copies and enclose Duplicates of the Bill and Order for £500 0s. that is to say An Order on Giles Bailey and Archibald Drummond for £200 and a Bill as above No. 732 for £300[8] and having dispatched these Mony Matters I am to acknowledge the receipt of yours of the 16th of 7ber last[9] by Captain Duncan a few Days ago, for tho' Captain Bolitho got in very fortunatly before our Weather set in very cold (by whom I received the Telescope) yet Duncan and the others were kept out long by a Succession of clear frosty Weather and N West Winds.[1]

The Telescope came in damp so that it swelled and I could not open it when I was in Town, where I have left it and therefore have not yet examined it.[2] I may possibly give you some Account hereafter of the Optician for I do not expect to make any new Discoveries. But as Telescopes of this Length are not common in America we shall not be so ready at making or contriving Machines to hang it upon.

When I wrote for the State of our Mony in your Hands I had no thoughts of a minute Account of particulars, but a general Estimate when a further Supply would be necessary[3]—however— I have, above taken care against any Defect of that kind, and if you have any Occasion of it pray use it freely 'till the Assembly can make a further Provision.

I mentioned in my last (of which a Copy goes herewith) that I had no sanguine Expectations of our Army's march against Fort du Quesne and I had good Reason, but Accidents have favoured us and the Dispositions of the Indians so that the French have

8. See above, pp. 176, 177.

9. See above, pp. 157–9.

1. Capt. John Bolitho had brought the *Myrtilla* into Philadelphia by December 14, but by January 4 the river was so full of ice that no vessel could stir. Some passengers from the *Carolina*, Capt. Robert Duncan, managed to reach the city before the 11th, but the ship itself did not come up until the following week. *Pa. Gaʒ.*, Dec. 14, 1758; Jan. 4, 11, 18, 1759.

2. On the telescope, see above, VII, 284, and this volume, p. 158. In 1769 it was used to observe the transit of Venus. APS *Trans.*, I (1771), 44, 48.

3. See above, p. 176.

226

been necessitated to evacuate the Fort after demolishing it in the Manner the Public Papers set forth.[4]

This Acquisition will be acceptable in England as tis said here General Forbes had Orders to march and fortify as he advanced and that the Ministry did not expect to be in Possession of that Fort this Year and had accordingly given Directions not to attack it without a Moral certainty of Success. But the Disposition of the Indians especially since the last Treaty at Easton and the destroying the Fort and Magazine the French had collected at Cadraqui have very fortunatly made Du Quesne an easy Conquest.[5]

It is now a considerable Time since we have had any Accounts from the K of Prussia or the Hannoverian Army[6] but should they prove successful the English Nation may have it in their Power to procure good Terms in America and an Opportunity of showing their political Abilities in giving us an honourable Peace or the prospect of a successful as well as a just War as in my Opinion the present War really is. I have given Orders to the Clerk to get ready all necessary Papers to be transmitted by this Vessel which I hope he will be able to do in time, and among the Rest, the best List of the Servants with their Vouchers, for this is a heavy Burthen upon many Masters—who have suffered much by the Losses of their Servants and some Compensation ought to be made them somewhere.[7]

R Patridge some time since wrote to me that he knew General Shirley would accept of this Government if offered to him—it goes a begging at a strange Rate, but who would accept it with the

4. The French evacuated and destroyed Fort Duquesne November 24 and the British occupied the ruins the next day. Governor Denny had expressed misgivings about the expedition similar to those of Norris. *Pa. Col. Recs.*, VIII, 227.

5. On the Easton Treaty of October 1758, at which many Indian grievances were adjusted, see above, pp. 176 n, 200–11. Lieut. Col. John Bradstreet captured Fort Frontenac at Cadaraqui, the outlet of the St. Lawrence from Lake Ontario (now Kingston, Ontario), on Aug. 27, 1758. This achievement effectively cut off Fort Duquesne from much-needed supplies. Gipson, *British Empire*, VII, 236–46.

6. A few days after Norris wrote this, news reached Philadelphia of the defeat of Hanoverian and allied forces at the hands of the French, October 10, and of the Prussians by the Austrians, October 14. *Pa. Gaz.*, Jan. 18, 1759.

7. On the efforts of Pa. to get compensation for masters of indentured servants enlisted in the British Army, see above, VII, 141, 214–15, 224–8.

227

Conditions,[8] as for the present Gentleman he appears among us as A Cypher of no Importance but in respect of the Side of the Figure upon which it is placed—he does not seem inclined to quarrel with the House unless he is bid to do it. The Petition to the Crown was actually wrote and I yet have it but being at the latter End of the Year it dropped by a kind of tacet Consent.[9] I own the Thought in your Paper was in my Mind that an Application of that kind from the House would give the Ministry a handle against the Proprietors but might likewise operate against the People or at least that it would be better to let it lye for Consideration especially as Maryland had given a Handle of the same kind against Proprietary Government by refusing their Supplies unless their Proprietor would suffer his Estate to be taxed in common with their own for the Defence of that Colony and I cannot learn that the Assembly of that Province receed from their former Resolutions.[1] And when they begin with Proprietary Governments ours will probably come likewise under Consideration for we now begin to make too great a Figure to be totally neglected. I am your Affect Friend   I N[2]

January 17. 1759. I was going to close my Letter when One of the Passengers called at my House and informed me he thot the Vessel was not quite ready and I might depend upon 2 or 3 Days. I have therefore deferrd till this date and now propose to add what I had intended as a P.S. of two or three Words—That I have not yet been able to settle the Account of Osborns Books by the frequent Interruptions I have met with—but that want of Leisure on my Side ought not to keep him out of his Mony therefore I

8. Rumors about a successor to Denny had been circulating for months. On one early candidate, see above, pp. 89, 94–5.

9. Probably a petition for royal assumption of the government of Pa., but no draft of such a document has been found.

1. For BF's paper in *London Chron.* supporting the Maryland House of Delegates' position, see above, pp. 162–8. See also his comments to Norris, above, pp. 157–8.

2. In Norris' letterbook this letter ends here but with a note to see a postscript on an earlier page "entered out of place." At the point indicated, which follows immediately the entries of his letters to BF of Nov. 21 and 23, 1758, appears a notation "Sent a Copy of the above to BF and Duplicates of Bills and added viz." Then are entered the two postscripts printed here, the second undated.

desire you would pay him Forty Pounds Sterling on my Account which as well as I can estimate will about close with him. But will endeavour as soon as I can to settle that Account with Care.[3]

I would also request the troublesome Task of getting me the value of half a Guinea or a Guinea in a few black and Red Pencils sorted of the best Sort they make some flat for protracting and drawing, which I have not been able to purchase in Town, and I would have them all Small or the smaller Sort. My Friend R Charles sent me, some time since, of the larger Sort but the Lead is coarse and they do not answer my Purpose—likewise a small Quantity of Camels Hair Pencils[4] and an Assortment of Water Colours made up in Pastels or Crayons [I think these are the Technical Terms] for mine and my Daughters Use and a pound of best Sealing Wax.[5]

These important Affairs being adjusted I would add American News, if I knew any worth communicating, but as the Military Gentlemen are got into Winter Quarters, and General Forbes to Philadelphia, tho' in a very bad State of Health,[6] I know nothing beyond the publick Intelligence which from the peaceable and Friendly Dispositions of the Indians seems to contain little more than the Captures of our Own and the Enemys Privateers. The rest of the Campagne last Year we are now expecting from Europe where the Miserable Devastations of War in Germany and the Constant Danger that Hero and Friend of Liberty must necessarily be exposed to, give evry well wisher to Humanity and the British Interest, at times an anxious Concern for the King of Prussia and the Settlement of an honourable and durable Peace between the contending Powers. I am &c.   I N

3. On Thomas Osborne's books that Norris had bought and BF's settlement of this account, see above, p. 169 n.

4. Small artist's brushes.

5. Brackets in this sentence are in the MS. These purchases are duly recorded in BF's account with Norris described above, pp. 147–8, and in "Account of Expences," pp. 38, 42, but are omitted from *PMHB*, LV, (1931), 97–133. BF paid 12s. for 2 doz. "Lead Pensils," £1 7s. 9d. for "Hair Pensils and Crayons" (quantity not specified), and 7s. for 1 lb. "finest Wax."

6. Forbes had been ill almost continuously throughout his campaign against Fort Duquesne; he died in Philadelphia, March 11, 1759, and was buried in Christ Church.

I am obliged to you in joining me in the Subscription to Basker-villes Milton—please to pay him.[7] The Subscription to the Report of Council which I have seen subscribes Lynford Lardner &c.—I am told they were ashamed of it when twas known a Copy had got abroad here.[8] Post's Journal is very long but I have it, and would send it if I thought some other of your Correspondants from hence had not already transmitted it.[9] 'Tis important and the Message was well timed. The Indians complain there was no more than One sent—but that was the Governors (I should say Councels) Fault in refusing Charles Thompson who offered to go on that fatiguing and hazardous Embassy which was the kinder in him as he had at that Time the great Affair of Matrimony in his Head which he has since reduced to practice and permanency.[1]

[*In margin:*] BF recd this ackd Mar. 19th

From David Hall   Letterbook copy: American Philosophical Society

Sir   Philadelphia 18th Janry. 1759

Yours by Duncan[2] I received with the Account of what Bills you have received for me since you left Philadelphia, wherein you told me you was afraid that some Bill had miscarried, as the whole Sum received by you was £100 less than that mentioned by me in mine of 22d July 1758.[3] Upon which I looked over my Book and

7. See above, p. 157. On March 10, 1759, BF paid 16s. for Norris' copy of this work and charged him accordingly in his running account. "Account of Expences," p. 38.

8. See above, p. 158 n, for BF's query about Lardner's name alone appearing on a copy of the Pa. Council's report on the "Walking Purchase."

9. BF had indeed received a copy of Christian Frederick Post's journal of his journey to the Ohio Indians in the summer of 1758 and, long before this letter from Norris reached him, had sent the journal to the printer to be added to Thomson's *Enquiry* as part of the appendix. See above, p. 199, and below, pp. 297–8. Just possibly, however, Norris may have been referring here to the journal of Post's second journey to the Ohio Indians (Oct. 25–Jan. 10), a copy of which BF had received by March 19, 1759. See below, p. 298.

1. The date of Thomson's marriage to Ruth Mather of Chester, Pa., has not been found.

2. Not found; probably one of a group of letters BF had written to Philadelphia correspondents in September 1758.

3. See above, p. 112, where Hall told BF that he had now sent a total of

found the Amount of the Bills sent to be right.[4] I then looked over
the Thirds and the Fourths[5] of the Bills sent that I had by me, and
found the inclosed three Thirds, one of which you are Debited
with, but which I cannot tell, as I happened not to indorse all the
Setts at the same Time, which I should have done, nor did I
minute the Number of the Bill sent to you, You will see by the
Date of the Bill, and the Place where drawn, that it is not among
the List you sent me. Two hundred Pounds of the three I remitted to Mr. Strahan, the Third to you. The first Copies of all
which I sent per the Industry Capt. Nuttle for Liverpool, who was
taken by a French Privateer, and of Course, his Letters, I suppose
all lost.[6] The second Copies were sent per the Carolina Capt.
Duncan, who arrived safe and Mr. Strahan received the Money
of the two Bills sent him, and credited me for them accordingly.
Now, that his should come safe to hand, and not yours tho' sent
by the same Ship, to me is a Mystery and what I cannot account
for, but am afraid it must have happened through the Neglect of
Some Person, you may have entrusted to receive and forward my
Letters that might come for you when you happened to be in the
County [Country?].[7]

I have advised with some of our Merchants about the Affair,
who told me to get the three Bills registred to sign my Name as
close as I could to John Nelson's, and to send them all to you; and
to desire you to go to the Gentlemen on whom they are drawn,
tell them what has happened, know which of the three is not paid,
and get the Money. The two that were paid to Mr. Strahan, you

---

£1049 12s. 5d., of which one bill for £100 had been protested and for which
BF had received credit in Hall's accounts.

4. For the account book in which Hall recorded his remittances to BF, see
above, VII, 235–6.

5. The buyer of a bill of exchange customarily received up to four copies,
of which he would send two or three to his overseas correspondent by different ships, retaining the others for record or for later transmittal in case those
he had first sent failed to arrive. This procedure was especially important in
time of war.

6. On the capture of the *Industry*, Capt. Samuel Nuttle, his release, the
stranding of his ship on Guernsey, and his return as a passenger to Philadelphia, see *Pa. Gaz.*, Mar. 16, 1758.

7. Replying April 8, 1759, BF acknowledged that the error had been his and
that the £100 had been duly received; see below, p. 320.

will please return. If, by any Accident, it should have gone into a wrong Hand, and the Money paid, it will be a great loss, and a Thing that I believe seldom, or never happened before. However, I shall hope for a better Account of it, till I know otherwise; The Third of the three Bills you have inclosed.

Inclosed you have likewise the first Copy of a Bill of Exchange for £100. more No. 920 for which you will please give me Credit.[8] Yours &c.   D H[9]

To Benjamin Franklin Esqr per the Severn Capt Hatton

2d Copy by Myrtilla, Capt. Bolitho.
3d Copy per the Carolina Capt Duncan

To Isaac Norris   Duplicate[1] Yale University Library

Dear Sir,   London, Jan. 19. 1759.

When I first began to treat with the Proprietors, they desired I would put down in Writing the principal Points of Complaint which were to be the Subjects of Conference between us, that they might previously consider them. I accordingly deliver'd them the Paper herewith enclos'd, called *Heads of Complaint*,[2] in which I confin'd myself to those that related chiefly to his Majesty's Service and the Defence of the Province, as being of more immediate Importance, and omitted the Appointment of Judges during Pleasure, and some other things,[3] as Points that might afterwards come into Discussion, if we could by any means get over the former.

This Paper was deliver'd in August 1757: They receiv'd it with

8. BF acknowledged receipt of this bill in his letter of April 8, and recorded it in his "Account of Expences," p. 24; *PMHB*, LV (1931), 116. From this time on he became more systematic in noting the number of each bill of exchange he recorded as having received.

9. BF's reply of April 8, 1759, mentioned that this letter contained a postscript dated February 5, but Halls's ALS has not been found and there is no postscript in his letterbook copy.

1. In BF's hand; marked by him "Copy" at the top.

2. See above, VII, 248–52.

3. The tenure of judges and "some other things" were included in the Assembly Committee's Report on Grievances, Feb. 22, 1757, which was a foundation of BF's mission to England; see above, VII, 136–42.

Pretensions to great Candour and real Intention of seriously considering it and giving a speedy Answer. We had several subsequent Conferences on those Heads, an Account of which I have given in former Letters. The Result was, that they said there were some Points in which the Royal Prerogative was concern'd, and it was therefore necessary, for the greater Safety in Proceeding, to have the Opinion of the Attorney and Solicitor General. This they would endeavour to obtain as soon as possible, having already stated a Case and laid it before those Gentlemen for their Consideration. After some Months Delay on this Head, I wrote them a Letter, of which I now send you another Copy, No 1. together with their Answer, No 2.[4] Our Friends here were generally of Opinion that these Delays were not affected; and therefore, that I might not incur the Charge of Rashness and Precipitation in an Affair of so great Consequence, I still patiently waited for the Answer which was to depend on the expected Report, often sending or calling to know if it was yet ready. At length, after Fifteen Months, I received the Paper I here inclose No 3.[5] The next Day I wrote the Letter No 4.[6] and a few Days after, Mr. Paris came and delivered me the Message No 5.[7] Thus a final End is put to all farther Negociation between them and me.

I need not point out to you the studied Obscurity and Uncertainty of their Answer, nor the mean Chicanery of their whole Proceeding. The Reason given for declining any farther Treaty with me, to wit, "That I had acknowledged a Want of Power to conclude proper Measures,"[8] is of a Piece with the rest: The Truth is, I did refuse to take upon me to settle a Money Bill with the Proprietors, as having no Power to do an Act of that kind that should be obligatory on the Assembly, for that they neither had given nor could give me such a Power, it being no less than giving me a Power of making Laws for the Province; a Power which, tho' the Assembly are trusted with by the People, they cannot

4. BF's letter (No. 1) has not been found; for the Penns' reply, April 6, 1758 (No. 2), see above, pp. 3–4.
5. Paris' "Answer to the Heads of Complaint," Nov. 27, 1758; see above, pp. 179–83. BF did not receive a copy of the Penns' message to the Assembly, November 28, printed above immediately following Paris' "Answer."
6. Above, pp. 186–8.
7. Above, pp. 193–4.
8. Quoted from No. 5 above.

delegate to another.[9] But I never acknowledged any want of Power to treat and confer with them, and to endeavour accommodating the Differences with them agreable to my Instructions. They say they have now wrote to the Assembly, and it is given out, that their Proposals to the House are so fair, that it is not doubted they will be agreed to. I wish you may find them so. In the mean time, tho' I am advis'd to make no Application to Parliament till I hear farther from the House, yet I shall immediately permit the Publishing a Work that has been long in hand, containing a true History of our Affairs and Disputes;[1] from which I have reason to hope a good Effect, if those Disputes must at length come under the Consideration of the Legislature here.

Seven or eight Months after the Heads of Complaint were delivered to the Proprietors, Mr. Paris came to me with a Message from them, purporting "that it was Mr. Charles's Fault they had not yet obtain'd the Attorney and Solicitor's Opinion, he, Mr. Charles restraining the Attorney by means of a retaining Fee formerly given him, which Mr. Charles would not take back again tho' desired so to do by the Attorney, and until that was done, the Attorney did not think himself at Liberty to consider Mr. Penn's Case."[2] Speaking to Mr. Charles of this, he told me, that on hear-

9. This passage probably refers to negotiations (partly in writing, perhaps partly oral) in the latter part of January and the beginning of February 1758 with regard to a future supply bill. See above, VII, 366, 370, 372. At some point in the discussion BF had proposed that the Proprietors authorize the governor to approve a new bill on the same terms as the £100,000 Act of March 1757 (see above, VII, 121–33, 145–53) and they had reluctantly agreed. They refused, however, his other proposal to withdraw their standing instructions on the detailed terms of supply bills "or at least to give more general Power to the Governor to agree with the House if they should desire to amend the Bill in any particular." Instead they told Peters to advise Denny and the Council to consent only to a change, including one on the method of assessments, which might be "more constitutional, in favour of Government, or conformable to our Instructions." Thomas Penn to Richard Peters, Feb. 2, 1758, Hist. Soc. Pa. From BF's present statement it would appear that the Penns had wanted BF to sit down and work out with them the exact terms of a supply bill which the Assembly and the governor would then be expected to pass. BF quite properly refused for "Want of Power."

1. Richard Jackson's *An Historical Review of the Constitution and Government of Pensylvania*, published at the end of May 1759; see below, p. 360.

2. This message was probably oral; it is not found in any of the surviving

ing of my coming over, before my Arrival, he had retain'd the Attorney General in Behalf of the Province, and he did not think it consistent with his Duty to the Province to withdraw that Retainer. In which I thought him right. The Proprietors might either have got their Advice elsewhere; or, which would have been the fairest Way, have agreed with me on a joint State of the Case, to be laid before those Gentlemen in Behalf of all Parties concern'd: But they would never so much as let me see the Case they had stated.[3] This Conduct of Mr. Charles is what they complain of in the first Paragraph of their Answer.

The Observation about the transposing some Parts of the Royal Charter to introduce the *Discretion of the Assembly* as necessary to the Making of Laws, is likewise mere Cavilling. I neither meant, nor had Occasion to mean in that Place, anything but what related to the Discretion of Deputies as restrained by Proprietary Instructions, contrary to the Charter.[4]

I need make but little Observation on their Complaint of Injustice in the Assembly, in charging them with refusing to contribute &c. when they have given £5000. It is well known that they first declar'd in their Answer to the Assembly concerning Indian Expences, that being Governors they ought not to contribute to publick Expences anymore than any other Governor.[5] The same Doctrine makes the first Part of their Deputy's Disputes with the Assembly. And tho' being beat out of that Argument, they afterwards gave £5000 that Sum was expressly declar'd in the Act to be in Lieu of their Share of the £60,000 Tax. And ever since that Act they have *refus'd* to contribute anymore; unless their Instructions, forbidding their Lieutenants to pass any Tax Act in which the greatest Part of their Estates is not exempted, can be construed to be no *Refusal*.

Upon the whole, the House will see, that if they purpose to continue Treating with the Proprietors, it will be necessary to recall me and appoint another Person or Persons for that Service,

---

documents. In their letter of April 6, 1758, mentioning the delay (above, p. 3), the Penns gave BF no hint that it was caused by such a conflict of interest.

3. In their letter of April 6, 1758, the Penns told BF flatly that they did not "think it proper to submit the Case to your Consideration."

4. See above, p. 180 and note.

5. In 1753, see above, v, 42–57.

who are likely to be more acceptable or more pliant than I am, or, as the Proprietors express it, Persons of Candour. Whether my Conduct towards them, or theirs towards me, has exhibited most or least of that Quality, I must submit to my Judges. But if the House, grown at length sensible of the Danger, to the Liberties of the People, necessarily arising from such growing Power and Property in one Family with such Principles, shall think it expedient to have the Government and Property in different Hands, and for that purpose shall desire that the Crown would take the Province into its immediate Care, I believe that Point might without much Difficulty be carried, and our Privileges preserved; and in that I think I could still do Service.[6]

Smith the Libeller has been arriv'd here some Weeks, but as yet I hear nothing of him.[7] If he attempt anything against the Province, either in the way of Petition or public Scribbling, I shall take care to do what may be proper for our Justification.

I received your Favours of Nov. 21. and 23. with Bills for £200 and £300 Sterling,[8] which I have put into the Hands of my Banker to procure Acceptance. I thank you for your Permission to use the Money freely on Occasion; but as I brought with me, and have had remitted to me since my Arrival, considerable Sums of my own, I do not see that I shall want it, and therefore pray that you would not on that Supposition refrain ordering it out of my Hands when your Occasions require it.

The Answer of the Committee you mention as preparing by Order of the House, relating to the Demand of 1200 Men for Garrisons per General Forbes,[9] is not come to hand; Nor, which

6. BF here reverts to a topic he had discussed with Norris and others before (see above, pp. 20–1, 88, 101–2, 157–8) and which became the initial objective of BF's second mission to England in 1764.

7. Provost William Smith arrived in London to prosecute his appeal, Jan. 1, 1759. Horace W. Smith, *Life and Correspondence of the Rev. William Smith, D.D.* (Phila., 1880), I, 204.

8. See above, pp. 174–7.

9. See above, pp. 175–6. In answer to Forbes's "Demand," the Assembly had informed Denny, Nov. 22, 1758, that the people of Pa. could not reasonably be expected "to bear the additional Burthen of defraying the extraordinary expence" of such garrison troops in addition to their existing heavy taxes. But after receiving news of the taking of Fort Duquesne, the House voted to continue the 1400 old troops in service. *Pa. Col. Recs.*, VIII, 229–30, 241.

I wonder at, the late Indian Treaty, tho' I see it advertis'd in the Papers as printed. The latter I very much want.[1]

I am extreamly oblig'd to the Assembly for the repeated Instances of the Confidence they place in me. I beg you would present my dutiful Regards to the House, and assure them of my inviolable Fidelity and Zeal in their Service. With the greatest Esteem and Respect, I am, Dear Sir, Your most obedient Humble Servant   B FRANKLIN

Isaac Norris Esqr.

Endorsed: London Janry 19th. 1759 Benjamin Franklin

From Anne Farrow   ALS: Historical Society of Pennsylvania

Dear Sir   Castle Thorp, Jan the 19. 1759

The Joy I had in receiving your Letter[2] was beyond Measure. To think as you granted my Desire and return you thanks for Paying the Post and very glad to hear you and your Son is well hoping your Spouse and Daughter is the Same and I am very glad to hear of them not doubting But the[y] are Endowed with all the Qualifications to render your Lifes happy and to see you will be the greatest of Joy.[3] That was our Granfather in Banbury Church yard.[4] As to my Fathers been Born at Ecton I always thought he was till 2 years ago I was at Wellingbourgh and our Cousin Fisher said som'thing of his coming from some other Town to Live at Ecton and Named the Place but I quit forgot[5] for my Memory has failed me some years but my Eye Sight is good. I

1. The Easton Treaty had been published on November 17, 1758; *Pa. Gaz.*, Nov. 16. BF needed it for his petition on Indian affairs.

2. Not found, but evidently in reply to Mrs. Farrow's letter of Jan. 8, 1759, as she had asked (see above, p. 223), and containing information about his branch of the family and inquiries about hers.

3. Apparently BF had promised to visit Mrs. Farrow when possible.

4. BF had probably told her about the gravestone of their mutual grandfather Thomas Franklin (A.5.2) in Banbury Churchyard, the inscription on which WF had copied the previous July; see above, p. 119.

5. Benjamin Franklin the Elder (A.5.2.7) specifically stated that his brother John was "born and brought up" in Ecton. "A short account of the Family of Thomas Franklin of Ecton in Northamptonshire. 21 June 1717." Yale Univ. Lib. The same stone marked his grave at Banbury as his father's.

bless God for it so I make a Shift to keep a Little School for my Living. I cant Remember my Uncle Josiah because my Father kept a Batchelors house when he was first Prentice [Apprentice] and my aunt Morris kept his house and I was the 3 child but my Mother and Uncle Franklins talking of him.[6] As to my own age I cant tell it no other ways than I was in my 5 years old when my Father died and my aunt Franklin told me I was 01 [10?] years old if I lived till the Michealmas after my Mother died and so I count I was seventy 3 last Mich[ealmas].[7] It was a great loss for 6 children to Lose Father and Mother so soon but I hope it was their gain for I can Remember some of my Fathers Heavenly ways though I was so little. He died of a Mortification or else if he had Lived he Designed going into New England. My Daughter Hannah[8] was Born July the 21 1724 and she is maried and has 2 Sons one of my Fathers Name and one of my Husbands. John Walker was Born March the 4 1755. Hennery Walker was Born November the 29 1756. My Daughter was at Lutterworth Last Summer and She belives he[9] Lives very well for he goes on with the Dying Bussinese and has only one Child Living. He was well a little while ago. My Daughter Lives at a Place called Westbury

6. That is, Mrs. Farrow cannot remember BF's father Josiah (A.5.2.9), because her father John was still a bachelor when Josiah served as his apprentice and his only sister Hannah (later Mrs. John Morris; A.5.2.8) kept house for him. Anne Farrow was John Franklin's third child and she remembers her mother and either her Uncle Thomas (A.5.2.1) or Uncle Benjamin the Elder (A.5.2.7) talking about Josiah.

7. This sentence appears to mean that her birthday was on or about Michaelmas (September 29). If she was five when her father died, June 7, 1691, she became six at the end of the following September and seventy-three in September 1758. Since the date of her mother's death is unknown, it is impossible to do more than guess at what she meant by the figure (which appears to be "01") she gave as her age at her mother's death. Her "aunt Franklin" must have been the wife of either her Uncle Thomas or Uncle Benjamin.

8. Hannah Farrow Walker (A.5.2.3.3.1), whose name appears below as a joint author of this letter.

9. Probably Thomas Franklin (A.5.2.3.1.1), Mrs. Farrow's nephew and BF's first cousin once removed. BF may have inquired about him in his now-missing letter to her. The "one Child" mentioned here was Sarah Franklin (A.5.2.3.1.1.1), who resided with BF in London at various times in 1766–72. In letters of 1766 and 1767 BF noted that Thomas and "Sally" were the only descendants of Grandfather Thomas in England then bearing the Franklin name.

within tow Miles of Braekly in Northampton Shire. But She came to see me this Christmas and is not gone yet for our Cousin Fisher is dead and their is a Small matter to come amongst us First cousins so the[y] fetch me over to Administer being I Lived the nearest but Mr. Fisher.[1] Mr. Fishers Executor Pays all charges for when I come the[y] would have her buried as grand as her Husband. So my Daughter was force to Stay to Look after my School the while. The Sum was a hundred Pound But the Funeral Charges before I came away came to between thirty and forty Pound[2] for Mr. Fisher Paid the Bills for it was not in my Power to do it and I Should be glad to know how many first Cousins thier is.[3] I would have buried her in a Neat Manner but the[y] complled me to Buirey her as her Husband was. My Daughter Joynes in affectionate Regards to you and your Son So we remain till Death Dear Sir   HANNAH WALKER and ANNE FARROW

Addressed: To Mr / Franklin at Mrs / Stevensons in Craven / Street Strand / London

Endorsed: Mrs Farrow

Comments on Hoadly and Wilson's Electrical Pamphlet

AD: American Philosophical Society; italicized text summarized from Dr. [Benjamin] Hoadly and Mr. [Benjamin] Wilson, *Observations on a Series of Electrical Experiments* (London, 1756). (Yale University Library)

In August 1756 Benjamin Hoadly and Benjamin Wilson, English electrical experimenters, published a 76-page pamphlet entitled *Observations on a Series of Electrical Experiments*. In it they developed a "doctrine of resistances" to explain the resistance any material substance or body offers to electrification, whether positive or negative, or to an increase or decrease in the body's electrical potential. They described the "electrical fluid" as subtle, elastic, and all-pervasive, and in the final pages announced their conclusion that it was the identical all-pervasive fluid that Newton had propounded and to which he had given the name "aether."

1. For the estates of Richard and Mary Fisher and their administration by William Fisher and Anne Farrow, see above, pp. 221–2, 224–5.

2. The exact sum was £31 2s. 2d.; see below, p. 288.

3. Thomas Holme had asked BF the same question ten days earlier; see the preceding document.

When Franklin learned of this pamphlet's publication he told Collinson of his interest[4] and he ultimately secured a copy, probably sometime after reaching England in the summer of 1757. His own major contributions to electrical science were all in the past, yet he always managed to find time in his busy life to keep track of new developments, and he obviously read the Hoadly and Wilson pamphlet with great care. Some things in it he found perplexing, others he thoroughly disapproved, and he undertook in his methodical way to set down his reservations and objections. In his own copy he carefully numbered the 301 paragraphs of the pamphlet and then, using the appropriate numbers, wrote an eight-page memorandum containing his questions and comments. In the margins of his copy opposite more than half of these debated paragraphs he also drew short parallel lines to call attention to particular phrases or sentences to which his comments were directed.[5]

Franklin's memorandum of criticisms is unintelligible when read without immediate access to what Hoadly and Wilson had previously written. To reprint here the full seventy-six pages of their pamphlet would be an inappropriate assignment of space, hence the editors have undertaken a compromise. The Hoadly and Wilson text is reproduced in summarized or abstracted form, set in italic type. Each section in the summary is preceded by inclusive numbers representing those Franklin assigned in his copy to the corresponding paragraphs of the original. Whenever Franklin's memorandum has a comment, this is set in roman type immediately following the summary of the questioned passage. The summaries are rather longer than the editors would have preferred, but this length has seemed necessary both for the sake of clarity and in order to do as much justice as possible to the authors' ideas and findings.[6]

As Franklin's note at the end of his memorandum shows, he first

4. See above, VII, 25. BF probably saw the listing of the publication in *Gent. Mag.*, XXVI (Aug. 1756), 406.

5. Franklin's copies of this pamphlet and of the second edition of 1759, mentioned below, bound with other pamphlets on electricity, including marked copies of his own *Exper. and Obser.*, 1751 and 1754 editions (see above, III, 118), are in Yale Univ. Lib. In marking the Hoadly and Wilson pamphlet old habits asserted themselves and he scrupulously corrected the printer's errors he detected.

6. The editors confess to some diffidence in offering this condensed version of the original; Hoadly and Wilson's pamphlet lacks some of that simplicity and clarity of style that was a hallmark of BF's scientific prose. They take comfort, however, from the fact that in 1767, when Joseph Priestley summarized a part of this pamphlet in his *History of Electricity* (pp. 450–1), he concluded by observing: "On this theory I shall make no particular remarks, because I cannot say that I clearly comprehend it."

read it to Wilson and then, on Jan. 28, 1759, gave him a copy. For this reason the paper is included in this edition as of that date. Dr. Hoadly had died, Aug. 10, 1757, so was not involved in the oral discussions that must have taken place when Wilson received Franklin's criticisms. Later in 1759 the surviving author published a revised edition of the pamphlet.[7] In the prefatory note he explained that he had "thought it expedient to make some alterations, and to add some new experiments." Comparison of the two editions shows that of Franklin's twenty-eight specific criticisms Wilson ignored all but seven. In five instances he made relatively small changes or incorporated explanatory footnotes; twice only he made major changes. These are all described below in footnotes at the appropriate places, as are a few additional revisions involving Franklin's writings, but no attempt is made here to discuss other changes or additions in the second edition.

[January 28, 1759]

1–2. The authors cite Newton's theory of an all-pervading "fluid" called "aether," which is "much rarer within the dense Bodies of the Sun, Stars, Planets, and Comets, than in the empty celestial space between them," and becomes denser the farther away it gets from these bodies. By causing each body to try to go "from the denser parts of the aether towards the rarer," this aether causes gravity.

2. How is it discovered that the Ether grows denser in proportion to its Distance from the Sun Planets, &c.[8]

3–13. The earth is surrounded by aether, causing gravitation towards it; aether pervades the "pores" of all bodies, its density in inverse ratio to the density of each body; hence we may conclude that some resistance will arise to efforts to alter the density in any body and some force will be necessary. It is agreed that electrical phenomena are caused by a similar elastic fluid, and the term "electrified" means that the amount of this "electrical fluid" in a body has been either increased over or decreased below the amount "that naturally belonged to it." There is

7. *Observations on a Series of Electrical Experiments.* By Dr. Hoadly, and Mr. Wilson. . . . The Second Edition. With Alterations and the Addition of some Experiments, Letters, and Explanatory Notes. By B. Wilson. (London, 1759).

8. In the 1756 edition "aether" was stated flatly as existing "according to Sir Isaac Newton." In the 1759 edition Newton "has supposed" there is such a fluid, and a footnote calls attention to the modification. While BF had not directly challenged the phraseology in this particular, it is possible that in conversation with Wilson he had advised some modification.

resistance to such change and "a limit, beyond which we cannot encrease or diminish the natural quantity of this electrical fluid, in each particular body."

13. Is this an Effect of Resistance in the Body, or is it a Consequence of the Atmosphere's being extended beyond the Distance at which it can be retain'd by the Attraction of the Body? An Experiment will easily determine this, viz. When the Prime Conductor is fully charg'd, try if any Electricity is to be obtain'd from the Back of the Globe, which has pass'd by the Points.

14–36. There is also resistance to the return of the electricity in a body to its natural state after electrification, and some external force is required to effect the return. Bodies differ in this resistance to electrical change: glass, wax, etc., and above all, air, resist the most; metals, water, animals, etc., the least. In the latter group, polished and extended surfaces resist most; rough surfaces, edges, and sharp points resist least. An experiment is devised to prove this theory of resistance: a highly polished iron bar with rounded ends and suspended in air by silk threads is electrically charged. This is to be discharged by advancing towards it a pointed body made of a low-resistance substance, bringing it constantly closer even until contact is established. But as this is being done the bar is discharged gradually without the violent discharge the experimenters want, because as the pointed body approaches the bar there is so little air between the two that there is little resistance to the discharge. So they substitute a blunt-ended, highly polished body and approach it to the bar "with some degree of quickness" so that the discharge will take place "at once, and not gradually; violently, and not with ease."

35. Is there not as much Air in Proportion between a Point presented to the prime Conductor, and its opposite Point of the Surface of the prime Conductor, as between a blunt Body presented, and an equal Part of the Surface of the P.C. opposite to it?

37–63. The authors wish to determine the circumstances [shape, nature of surface, etc.] which affect the ease and speed with which a body is charged, discharged, or recovers to its "natural state." They have devised a series of experiments involving a long iron bar tapered at both ends and balanced on a tall drinking glass. If they bring a charged tube close (about six inches) to its mid-point, it is electrified minus; if they bring the tube close to an end of the bar, it is electrified plus. If

*a second similar bar balanced on a glass is placed in line with the first
with the points touching and the tube is brought close to the mid-point
of the first, the first bar will be electrified minus and the second bar
plus. If a third bar is placed at the other end of the first and the tube
advanced to the first as before, this middle bar will be electrified minus
and both end bars electrified plus. All this shows that the first bar has
discharged through its tapered ends some of its natural quantity of
electricity. Now cover its pointed ends with close-fitting glass caps.
When the charged tube is again brought close to the mid-point the bar
"will be electrified plus, instead of minus: which shews how much more
strongly the extended surface of the bar, opposite to the excited tube,
resists the fluid's escape, than the tapered ends did."*

63. Will the Bar remain electrified plus when the Tube is withdrawn?[9]

*64-68. Set two or all three bars in line as before and advance the
charged tube to one end, not the mid-point, of the first or middle bar. All
three will be electrified plus, the middle bar the most, the nearer end bar
next in amount, and the further bar least of all. It would seem that if
a fourth, fifth, and sixth bar, etc., are added, ultimately the most distant
would not be affected at all, and "consequently that the virtue of the
tube is limited, and can affect the fluid in these bars to a certain distance
only."*

67. Is the Effect mention'd in this and the following Section
[pars. 67 and 68],[1] any other than a necessary Consequence of a
certain limited Quantity of Electricity, being divided among a
greater Number of Bodies, or extended over a greater Surface?

*69-74. Consider the air surrounding the bars in these experiments.
Though air strongly resists being electrified, the excited tube can and
does overcome that resistance when it succeeds in electrifying the bar
minus through the intervening air [a distance of about six inches] and,
in the experiment with a single bar, forces electrical fluid into the surrounding air. The fluid seemingly stands in the air near the points of*

9. In response to BF's question Wilson inserted in the 1759 edition after
"*minus*" in the quoted passage the words "even though the tube be withdrawn." In BF's copy of this edition he underlined the added words and wrote
"Quy" in the margin.

1. BF inserted his parallel-line check marks opposite both pars. 67 and 68,
but numbered his question "67" only.

the bar and when the excited tube is withdrawn, most, but not all, of the electrical fluid returns into the bar. What remains "forms itself into a kind of atmosphere every way surrounding the bar with a nearly equal degree of density."

74. How is it found that any of it returns in again? If any of it remains out, how does it appear that it forms an Atmosphere round the Body?[2]

75–77. *When the single bar was electrified plus, there was enough fluid to electrify two bars applied at its other end; it follows that when a single bar is electrified plus by itself and continues so after the tube is withdrawn, the expelled fluid similarly forms an atmosphere around the bar. Therefore, whenever a body is electrified either plus or minus and remains so after the experiment is over, there are "similar atmospheres of the electrical fluid"[3] surrounding them, ready to expand into any approaching body less resistant than air. This is why "bodies give very nearly the same signs" when electrified either plus or minus.*

77. How does it appear that the Atmospheres surrounding Bodies electrified plus and minus, are similar? If they are both plus Atmospheres, how do they destroy each other on being brought together?

78–80. *I say "very nearly" the same signs because on accurate observation there are enough differences to enable us to say which bodies are electrified plus and which minus. Consider the different circumstances the fluid is in around a body electrified plus or minus. When a bar is electrified plus the electrical atmosphere formed around it lies between the air and bar and both resist the fluid's entry, the bar more forcibly. So the fluid exerts its effort at expansion outwardly and it gradually dissipates into the air. "Whilst it is doing this, and no longer, the bar will remain electrified plus."*

80. If the Electrical Atmosphere round a Body electrified plus, lies between the Body and the Air, must not the Air be push'd off, a Vacuum of Air created, and the Space occupied by the electrified Atmosphere be unfit to breathe in? But none of these Things happen. Put an Iron Rod into an empty Bottle; electrify the Rod,

2. As will be seen below, this concept of an "atmosphere" surrounding an electrified body is central to the authors' whole theory. Yet Wilson ignored this question in the second edition.

3. In his copy BF underlined the words here directly quoted.

and none of the Air is driven out of the Bottle by the electrical Atmosphere of the Rod. This I have try'd by an accurate Experiment. I have also often breath'd in an electric Atmosphere, without perceiving any Unfitness in the Air for Respiration.[4]

81. *"When a bar is electrified* minus, *the atmosphere formed round it, which during the action of the tube that electrified it, lies in the same manner between the air, and the bar," will when the tube is withdrawn, try to expand in a contrary direction, that is, from the air into the bar. It will gradually flow into the bar and restore its "natural degree of density." Only while this is going on will the bar remain electrified minus.*

81. When a Bar is electrified minus, by having Part of its Quantity forc'd out on its Surface, and you draw off that Quantity by a Point or otherwise, how does it appear that any electrical Atmosphere remains between the Bar and the Air?[5]

82. *When two balls both electrified plus are suspended and brought near each other, they repel each other and stand for some time at a distance, because the two atmospheres, each trying to expand, want more room to do it in. When the weight of the balls is insufficient to prevent it, they are driven apart until the atmospheres are dissipated and the weight of the balls brings them back to their natural position.*

82. Are not the two Atmospheres confined to the Balls, not only by the surrounding Air, but by a mutual Attraction between each Atmosphere and its Ball? If not, why does the Atmosphere accompany the Ball in its swiftest Motion? Must it not then be one Effect of such an Attraction to keep each Atmosphere spherical; and then if the two Atmospheres are brought near together by the Weight of the Balls, would they not, by endeavouring to preserve their Sphericity keep the Balls at a Distance?

4. In the 1759 edition Wilson changed the text to read "When a bar is electrified *plus,* the atmosphere found round it is extended in the air to a considerable distance," instead of as formerly "lies between the air . . . and the bar." He added as a footnote: "The electric atmosphere is not to be understood as lying between the air and the bar, as it is exprest in the former edition, but extended in the air all the way from the bar."

5. In the 1759 edition Wilson changed the opening lines of the text to read: "When a bar is electrified *minus,* the atmosphere formed round it, which during the action of the tube that electrified it, is extended in the same manner in the air to a considerable distance from the bar." He also added as a footnote: "This alteration was in consequence of the former."

83. *When two balls both electrified minus are suspended and brought near each other they similarly repel each other because "the condensed electrical fluid in the air, in order to force itself in at the surfaces of the balls between their two centers, crouds in, and forces them asunder," until the atmospheres get all inside the balls and weight restores them to their natural position.*

83. Two Balls suspended by silk Strings may be electrify'd minus, by touching them with the Coating of a charg'd Bottle, which you hold by the Hook. In that Case the Electrical Fluid which quits the Balls does not go into the Airs, but into the Coating of the Bottle, an equal Quantity at the same time passing from the Hook thro' your Body to the Earth. Whence then arises the condensed Electrical Fluid supposed to be in the Air surrounding the Balls?

84. *When two balls, one electrified plus and the other minus, are similarly suspended, "they will gradually come together and unelectrify each other." The atmosphere of the ball electrified plus is trying to dissipate itself outwards and that of the other "to dilate itself from the air inwards to the center of the ball." So the two atmospheres exert their forces in the same direction and the flow of the electrical fluid in each facilitates the flow in the other, and the two balls and the air between "very readily return to their natural states."*

84. The Word *gradually* seems not the most proper as the Balls rush together with double Quickness, compar'd to that with which either would fly to a Body in its natural State.

Query. One of the two Atmospheres being suppos'd to enter the Ball electrified minus, what is suppos'd to become of the other?[6]

85–89. *Following this train of reasoning we can obtain a method of determining whether a body is electrified plus or minus, "even without unelectrifying it." Fasten two cork balls to the ends of an 8-inch thread*

6. There is no parallel-line check mark in BF's copy here, but the word "gradually" is underlined in pencil (BF's markings are regularly in ink). In response to BF's "Query," Wilson added a long note in the 1759 edition, saying in part: "But this seems to follow from the principles we have already deduced, that a quantity, equal to what was in the ball electrified *plus*, is at the end of the experiment diffused in the balls electrified *minus*; and the remaining quantity which form'd the atmospheres is diffused in the air, or the bodies from whence it at first flow'd, in order to crowd into the body electrified *minus*."

246

and double it over a bar before electrifying it so that the balls are hanging below it as near together as possible. Bar, thread, and balls then become in effect one body ready to be electrified. Suppose, first, we electrify it minus; the balls will repel each other. Now bring an excited tube a certain distance under the balls; "they will at first repel each other more," because the force of the excited tube will condense their atmospheres more (till the resistance at their surfaces is overcome), and these atmospheres being increased, the mutual repulsion will increase.

89. How does condensing the Atmospheres more, make the Balls repel each other more, since it should seem that Atmospheres being condens'd would take up less Room, and thereby suffer the Balls to approach nearer? How is it known that the Atmospheres encrease while they are condensing? May not the Approach of the Balls, on bringing the Tube nearer to them, be rather ascrib'd to their receiving some Electricity which they wanted, and thereby recovering their natural State. See 90, 92. See also 97.[7]

90–93. As soon as this initial resistance is overcome, the tube drives the atmospheres into the balls "and consequently begins to unelectrify them," that is, they become "less forcibly electrified minus." On withdrawing the tube the balls will hang nearer together than before [par. 90]. Now suppose we electrify the bar-and-ball combination plus; the balls again repel each other. When an excited tube is brought under them as before, they will come nearer together, because air resistance cannot prevent the electrical fluid escaping from the balls electrified plus and creating an atmosphere around them. Then, the excited tube, acting "in concert with the air," forces this atmosphere back into the balls [par. 92]. This appearance will continue as long as the bar-and-ball combination can be increasingly electrified plus by the tube; when the tube is withdrawn the balls will repel each other more forcibly than before because of their increased electrification.

93. Is not the Balls being electrify'd more forcibly than at first, owing to their having receiv'd an Addition from the Tube?

97–102. In the case of a bar electrified minus, if the tube is held under the balls long enough for them to cease repelling each other when it is withdrawn, and the tube is then again presented to them, it will electrify both balls and bar plus [par. 97]. It is reasonable to conclude from this

7. For the pertinence of the paragraphs BF cites at the end of this comment see below where these paragraphs are summarized.

that in the first experiment [see above, pars. 37–63], *if the tube had been brought nearer and nearer to the mid-point of the tapered bar and finally made to touch it, the bar would have been electrified plus (instead of minus). Testing proves this conclusion correct. There must therefore be some middle distance at which the tube, instead of electrifying the bar either minus or plus reduces it to its natural unelectrified state. "This would appear a most amazing paradox . . . to any one, who did not know that bodies were capable of being electrified* plus *and* minus,*" that is, that the same excited tube brought towards the bar first electrifies it, then ceases to electrify it, and finally electrifies it again.*

103–109. *The cork-ball experiment is also useful to prove that the power of the excited tube (or other electrifying machine) to electrify bodies at a certain distance is limited. The comparative force with which the balls repel each other provides an index to the degree of electrification of the bar to which they are attached. Hang the balls at the end of the bar and bring the excited tube to the middle of it at a distance to electrify it minus. However long it is kept at that distance it can electrify the bar only to a fixed degree. This is shown by the fact that the balls will repel each other only to a certain distance and remain in that position as long as the tube is unmoved. This proves that the power of the tube is limited and is confirmed by a further set of experiments.*

110–114. *Hermetically seal a glass tube at one end; cement to the other end a brass contrivance to which an air pump for creating a vacuum in the tube may be attached and then removed without destroying the vacuum. Before the air pump has been attached, the outer and inner surfaces of the tube are equally exposed to the air and are in equilibrium. Attach the pump and exhaust the air from the tube; the outer surface is now exposed to the air and the inner surface exposed to the electrical fluid, "which I will suppose to be naturally dispersed in empty spaces void of all gross bodies, (as the vacuum is thought very nearly to be) as well as in the pores of gross bodies."*

114. Upon what is this Supposition founded?

Can we suppose the Airs to be exhausted, and the electrical Fluid left behind in just the same Quantity as before? Or, does some electrical Fluid enter during that Operation, to supply the Vacuity made by exhausting the Air?

115–119. *The equilibrium is still preserved between the powers at these surfaces, there being no observable evidence to the contrary. We*

*may conclude that the air in its natural condition does not affect the tube
at its outer surface more than the electrical fluid does at the inner. Now
take the air-exhausted glass tube off the air pump and have a person
grasp it by the brass end while standing on the ground. Let another
person bring an excited tube near the outer surface, say near to the
hermetically sealed end. Immediately "lucid rays of light" will appear
proceeding from the inner surface of that part of the exhausted tube which
is nearest the excited tube and darting through the vacuum to the brass
grasped by the hand.*

119. If the electrical Fluid was dispers'd in the Vacuum as in
114, would it not be put in Motion by this Experiment, and appear
at both Ends at the same Time? See 124.

*120–125. If the tubes are kept steady at the same distance for some
time, the light will disappear. After a further interval of time, if the
excited tube is removed the rays of light will reappear, this time darting
from the brass through the vacuum to the point on the inner surface from
which they had first appeared. This light, too, will in time disappear.
When the excited tube is brought nearer and nearer the exhausted tube,
a fresh darting of rays appears, similar to the first, again continuing for
a time only. When the excited tube is removed the returning flow of rays,
stronger and in greater quantity, reappears and then ceases. Apparently,
when any electrical force is offered to the outer surface of the exhausted
tube, the electrical fluid on the inside flows to the brass and hand, "where
it finds the resistance to its escape is the weakest." Yet there is some
resistance even there, hence some force must be given the electrical fluid,
condensing it enough to overcome that resistance* [124]. *Furthermore, the
inside surface of the tube must be losing some of its natural quantity of
the fluid into the vacuum and thence into the brass, etc., unless more is
supplied it from the excited tube.*

*126–144. Here follows an extended discussion to show that no
electrical fluid passes from the excited tube through the glass of the exhausted tube onto its inner surface to replace that driven off. The conclusion is that this inner surface has now been electrified minus and remains so until the return flow of rays signals the restoration of the
natural state to that inner surface. A further experiment demonstrates
the correctness of this conclusion. An excited tube gradually loses its
power, but we know that an iron bar suspended in air by silk threads
can be kept uniformly electrified for an indefinite period by means of an*

electrifying machine kept uniformly in motion.[8] *Therefore, approach the exhausted tube to an "excited bar" (steadily charged by such a machine) close enough "to make the lucid appearance begin" and keep it steadily there. The rays continue only for a time, then die away as before, but upon removing the exhausted tube from proximity to the excited bar the return flow of rays again takes place. The situation here is the same as in the series of experiments with tapered bars: the second bar brought in contact with the first is here represented by the brass at the tube's end and the person holding it and standing on the ground. The excited tube (or excited bar) has power "to dilate the electrical fluid" in the first bar in the one case, and on the inner surface of the exhausted tube in the other case, and to drive it into the second bar and the brass end of the tube respectively. In both experiments this power is limited; while it is effective, this electrical fluid will flow, but "when the electrical fluid in the brass, hand, &c. is sufficiently condensed to ballance the force of the dilating fluid in the vacuum," no more will flow and the lucid light will disappear.*

144. As the Brass and Hand communicate with the Earth, how does it appear that the Electrical Fluid is condens'd in them? See 229, 230.

145–146. *So long as the exciting tube is held at the same distance the electrical fluid in the vacuum and the brass, etc., will be kept in equilibrium, for the same power that drove it to its present position can hold it there while the force remains unchanged. But when the tube is withdrawn "the force of the condensed part of the fluid in the brass drives that in the vacuum back again to the inner surface of the glass, where the tube had been applied," and is in turn replaced by fluid from the brass, all this being manifest by light shooting from the brass to the glass until equilibrium is restored."*

146. Is not the Electrical Fluid rather attracted back by the minus side of the Glass, and drawn thro' the Brass?

147. *This effect is similar to what happened to the two tapered bars when the tube was withdrawn: equilibrium was "restored by the condensed part of the fluid in one bar's gradually flowing into the dilated part in the other."*

8. Machines for creating an electric charge less laboriously than by rubbing a glass tube had come into common use both in Europe and America. For BF's description of an early electrical machine devised in Philadelphia, see above, III, 134.

147. Is it not rather *drawn* than *press'd* back?

148–165. *It has been found that in order to electrify glass with considerable force it is necessary to cover its two surfaces with metal or some similar easily electrified material; but why these coverings are necessary has not hitherto been satisfactorily explained. Cover the middle of both sides of an oblong pane of glass with leaf gold but leaving two or three inches of uncovered glass at all edges. When any spot on the upper covering is electrified, the entire covering is equally electrified and the glass surface immediately below it is equally exposed to the electrical fluid with no air intervening. An electrifying machine brought into direct communication with the upper gold covering by means of a wire will exert its full force against the whole extent of the glass immediately under the covering. Another wire from the under covering to the ground will remove much of the resistance to the escape of electrical fluid through the under side of the glass. The uncovered areas of glass at the rims prevent electrical leakages around the edges from one covering to the other. Place a drinking glass under each corner of the pane; let one person standing on the ground hold a finger within an inch of the under covering; bring a wire ending in a knob from the electrifying machine to within an inch of the upper covering; now set the machine in motion. A spark will jump from the wire to the upper covering and at the same time one from the lower covering to the finger. Repeated sparks will appear for a time and then cease, even though the machine is kept in motion. It would seem that whatever had been "thrown in" at the upper covering had passed out in equal quantities at the lower, and that the electrical fluid had a free passage through the glass, which remained unelectrified. Indeed, after the wires are removed one may touch either covering without producing more than very slight signs of electrification. But if one touches both covers at once with fingers of different hands "he will receive so severe a stroke, as will convince him that the glass was very strongly electrified." It is certainly true that as much fluid is thrown out at the under surface into the finger as was thrown into it at the upper surface from the wire; "but the reasoning upon this fact is evidently false, as it contradicts experiment."*[9]*

166–173. *Can our doctrine of resistances help us resolve this difficulty?*

---

9. A footnote here in the 1759 edition reads: "See Dr. Franklin's letters upon this subject." Wilson doubtless referred especially to *Exper. and Obser.*, pp. 2, 23–4, 72, reprinted above, III, 157, 355–6; IV, 27.

Suppose we give the resistance of each surface of the glass the numerical value of six, and the power of the electrifying machine the value of nine. Electrical fluid will be forced into the glass with the net force of three and condensed there to that force and no more. It cannot escape around the uncovered edges of the glass. As much fluid as force three can throw into the upper surface will be thrown out at the lower one at the under-covering (where the resistance is least because of the ground wire) until the resistance at this surface is gradually reduced to three, and then all forces will be in equilibrium. As we saw was the case in the experiment of the exhausted tube, it was possible for the excited tube, though at a distance, to drive electrical fluid out of the inner surface of the glass, though none passed through. We may therefore here imagine it possible that the fluid penetrating to a certain distance into the upper surface may similarly act at a distance and force out some of that near the under surface until the resistance on the under surface is reduced to three and an equilibrium is reached. Sparks may therefore appear until then in the experiment as described, but not thereafter.

174–183. How can we conceive a quantity of elastic fluid lying in one part of the glass while "its neighbouring fluid in another part is attenuated"? Following the precedent of the experiment of the exhausted tube, withdraw the wire which communicated from the electrifying machine to near the top covering, but leave the finger in place near the bottom covering; no sparks jump from the finger to the lower covering. "This therefore seems to be an experimental Proof that there is some power remaining in the glass itself" to prevent a return flow of the fluid previously thrown into the finger.[1] The machine had apparently condensed the fluid in the upper surface of the glass, causing the dilation of that in the under surface and its consequent passing out into the finger; if now the condensed fluid could dilate itself and pass out again at the upper surface, the fluid would likewise return from the finger to the lower surface, but the resistance at the upper surface prevents this from happening. It is the condensed fluid in the upper surface which prevents

1. A footnote here in the 1759 edition explains that Wilson conceived the condensation of the electrical fluid as being "made *at* or exceedingly near the surface" of the glass, but whether inside or outside he could not say without further experimentation. This view, he pointed out, differs considerably from BF's, and he cited *Exper. and Obser.*, 1751 edit., pp. 72–5 (above, IV, 27–30), to show that BF conceived "a kind of partition" of denser glass running through the middle of its thickness, through which the particles of electrical fluid in one half could not pass to reach the other half.

the return of the sparks. In the case of the exhausted tube, the excited tube did not have enough power to condense fluid in the glass, and when the excited tube was withdrawn the excited fluid in the atmosphere surrounding it was likewise withdrawn, permitting the return of the lucid appearance; hence the difference in the two experiments.

184–189. We know that the pane of glass has remained electrified and "we have all the reason in the world" to believe that as much fluid had passed out at one cover as had entered in the other. Hence the electrification of the glass does not arise from an increase or decrease in the whole quantity of electrical fluid as in the case of metals, etc. The only possible explanation is the continued condensation of fluid at the upper surface after the wire is withdrawn, and the continued attenuation at the under surface. That is, the upper surface is electrified plus and the under surface minus. There is some similarity here to the experiment of the tapered bars when the excited tube was applied to the middle of the center of three bars. Yet in that case, when the excited tube was withdrawn the three bars returned to their natural state, while in the present case some resistance remains in each surface of the glass preventing a similar return. Here, because the respective plus and minus electrification of the two glass surfaces continues after wire and finger are both withdrawn, there must be two atmospheres left standing on these surfaces, which are now surrounded with air,[2] as in the case of the cork balls, and these atmospheres are endeavoring to dilate into the air. Whenever they can communicate, the plus atmosphere will drive the minus atmosphere into the glass surface electrified minus, as in the case of the cork balls.

189. There is, I imagine, seldom more than one of the Atmospheres subsisting at the same time, and that not 100th part, perhaps, of the Quantity contain'd in the positive Surface of the Glass. So that the Communication is to be formed between the positive and negative Surfaces, rather than between positive and negative Atmospheres.

When the Pane of Glass is charg'd, touch the positive side with your Finger, and you draw a small Spark and with it all the Atmosphere of that Side; but you create a Negative Atmosphere on the other side. Then touch the Negative Side, and by giving a Spark you destroy the negative Atmosphere, but at the same time

2. At this point in par. 189 BF placed his parallel-line mark, and he added the numbers "82, 83, 84," to refer back to those paragraphs.

a quantity flows out of the positive side of the Glass, and spreads on that Surface, creating a positive Atmosphere. This you may draw off in a Spark as before, and repeat by alternate Touches on the opposite sides 100 times running.[3]

190–191. *The broad column of air in immediate contact with all uncovered surfaces of the glass separates these atmospheres, and we know that a pane of glass, properly covered, will remain electrified much longer than metals. There is only one way of unelectrifying the glass with violence: open a direct communication between the two surfaces, as was done when a person touched them simultaneously with fingers of his two hands. However quickly he does it a strong spark will appear.*

192. *To form a communication between the two surfaces gradually instead of suddenly, bend a wire in circular form so that the two ends may be brought to within two or three inches of the covers of the glass; taper the ends to fine points and afix a piece of sealing wax to the midpoint of the wire to hold it by. With this device "the glass will quietly and gradually return to its natural state," and at the end the wire will not be electrified. If this experiment is done in the dark "a very visible stream of light" will appear at each end of the wire during the action. May we not conclude: 1. That nothing more has been done but gradually restore the equilibrium in the glass? 2. That the excess of electrical fluid on one side of the glass had exactly balanced the deficiency on the other, and that, therefore, during the electrification as much had been thrown out of the glass as thrown in? 3. That in the simultaneous touching of both covers by the fingers the violence was due only to the increased*

3. This comment led to the first of Wilson's major revisions in the 1759 edition. He inserted the following footnote: "The reader will please to observe, that in the other edition, the reasoning upon the electric atmospheres, is not altogether agreeable to experiment. I say, *not altogether*, because though there are really such electric atmospheres extended over each surface of the glass, yet they are neither so powerful nor so extensive, as they are there supposed to be. I have therefore chose to vary and illustrate that part, which relates to the experiment, by a farther analogy between the exhausted tube and the pane of glass, as it appears to be the clearest and most satisfactory method. And I do think if my worthy friend [Hoadly] had now been living, he would readily have concurred in this alteration." He then entirely omitted pars. 189–191 of the first edition and substituted two full pages of text to show parallels between what happens when the relative positions of the excited and exhausted tubes are variously changed and what happens when some or all of the positive charge on the upper surface of the pane of glass is drawn off.

velocity of the movement of the fluid? 4. That this velocity had been great enough to kindle a strong spark, while by the new method there will be only a "continued stream of faint bluish light"?

193–201. We may make further observations on this subject: 1. If the wire from the electrifying machine is brought into contact with the upper covering but the ground wire left off from the lower, the glass cannot be electrified, because of the combined resistance of glass, cover, and surrounding air, and this is true however great the power of the machine. 2. If the ends of the bent wire are brought into direct contact, or nearly so, with the two coverings, the glass cannot be electrified, because the fluid has a free passage from one covering to the other. 3. Without such a communicating wire the two atmospheres will come together if the coverings come too close to the edges of the glass, and it cannot be electrified. 4. There is a great resemblance between the two atmospheres lying at the two surfaces of the glass, electrified respectively plus and minus, and the two atmospheres surrounding the cork balls in a previous experiment.

201. It seems this Resemblance does not hold as to Atmospheres in the two Cases. The different States of the opposite sides of the Glass, being within its Substance, and not depending on Atmospheres subsisting without. Thus a Number of Glass Plates ground truly flat, and coated, may be laid one on another, and electrified, so that every other two Faces in contact shall be positive, and every other two negative, and the whole Forces united be very great and give a terrible Blow when discharg'd proportion'd to the Quantity of Surface coated;[4] and yet no Atmosphere could subsist, unless on the two outside Plates; for the Plates being in close Contact, exclude any Atmosphere.

202–208. Electrify two panes of glass coated as before and each supported by drinking glasses at the corners, and let them stand. 1. Connect the two upper surfaces by a wire; no alteration will occur because the two atmospheres act upon their respective upper coverings with no more force than before they were connected. Thus, when two balls both

4. It was for such a device as this that BF and his Philadelphia friends had invented the name "electrical battery" in or before 1749 (see above, III, 357), almost certainly by analogy to the artillery battery (a number of cannon at one emplacement under a single command) which he had been instrumental in erecting for the defense of Philadelphia at the time of the Association of 1747.

electrified plus are brought together they do not unelectrify each other but merely repel each other, as the two panes of glass would do if the force were strong enough. The same is true if the two under surfaces are connected by wire. 2. But if by "a cross communication" one wire connects the upper cover of one pane with the under covering of the other and another wire connects the two remaining coverings to each other, "the condensed atmospheres will neither of them be confined, but a free passage will be opened to them to dilate into the panes of glass." The electrical fluid will circulate around and be reduced to the natural state in both glasses and wires.

208. The Change is here hinted to be in the Glass.

209–214. Numerous experiments might be made confirming the "uncommon appearances" occuring in the electrification of glass, but I stop here with a mere caution not to carry too far the comparison of the atmospheres on the electrified pane with those on the cork balls. We have seen that the variety in resistance to electrification of different bodies leads us to know why bodies act so differently in different situations according to the nature of the bodies they are contiguous to, and enables us to explain "the most amazing appearance of all," that of the Leyden bottle. Our success so far encourages us to inquire where this resistance is exerted and from what power within the body it arises. We know by experiment that every body resists electrification, though some do it with greater force than others. We may reasonably conclude that resistance to the entry of electrical fluid is exerted at the surface where the attack is made, but resistance to the fluid's exit is exerted at all internal surfaces at once, and if the force at any point is greater than the resistance there, then it will always enter or leave at that point.

215–220. There is an exact analogy to this resistance in the resistance of glass to the entrance of light at one surface and to its going out at the opposite surface; at both surfaces their resistance drives off great numbers of rays that might otherwise have passed through. The rays reflected back into the glass in their endeavor to get out are again resisted when they return to the first surface. Newton has shown that this force of resistance begins to operate on rays of light before they arrive in contact with either surface. We have reason to believe that the resistance to electrification, either plus or minus, of all bodies is of the same nature as that which not only prevents the entrance and exit of rays of light but throws them off with the same velocity with which they tried to enter or leave, and that the two kinds of resistance probably arise from the same cause. The experiments in Newton's Optics serve greatly to confirm this opinion, and we have tried to establish it by electrical experiments.

221–234. *Whence does this power arise? "Let a person standing on wax electrify a tube, and let another person standing on the ground take as many snaps, as he can from the tube." Soon he can get no more. But if, when this happens, the person on the wax sets one foot on the ground and keeps it there, the other person "may take snaps from morning to night, if he pleases." The following conclusions may be drawn: 1. The person standing on the wax has "naturally" a quantity of the electrical fluid in him, which in the experiment is thrown into the other person on the ground. 2. But the person on the wax has only a limited quantity of the fluid. 3. Therefore, the cause of the fluid's passing out and causing the snap is that the fluid is condensed in the hand which touches the tube in rubbing it, and so long as this condensation can be made with a degree of force superior to the resistance against escape, it will continue to produce snaps. 4. The person standing on the ground must be considered as one body with the earth and will not be sensibly electrified however many snaps he takes* [229]. *5. When the person on the wax touches his foot to the ground, he too becomes one body with the earth and the degree of density in his body cannot be sensibly altered however many snaps are taken* [230]. *6. In these circumstances, therefore, neither of these persons can be electrified. 7. It follows that all animals, vegetables, water, minerals, and metals on or in the earth partake "of this common stock in the general course of nature": without being sensibly electrified. 'Whence therefore arises their resistance to being* sensibly *electrified?" Any body sensibly electrified, whether plus or minus, is surrounded by an atmosphere strong enough to balance every power endeavoring to electrify it beyond a certain degree; otherwise it might be electrified without limit. It is this atmosphere surrounding bodies when artificial force electrifies them that resists their being electrified* more, *and when it absolutely prevents such electrification, it must be equally as strong as the electrical fluid flowing from the excited tube or machine.*

234. All Fluids naturally seek an Equilibrium. If the Body electrified receives no more after a certain Quantity, is it not owing to an Incapacity, in the Globe, of having more than a certain Quantity at one Time on its surface, rather than to any Resistance in the Atmosphere already communicated? Increase the Surface

of the Body electrified, and you may give it an Additional Quantity from the Globe *ad infinitum*.

235–239. *"In the ordinary and quiet manner, in which the imperceptible works of the Author of nature are carried on"* this subtile, active, all-pervasive electrical fluid cannot be idle, but must be in constant, if imperceptible, action; i.e., it must be electrifying all bodies plus or minus, though not forcibly enough to give sensible signs of it. We may conclude therefore that all bodies have surrounding electrical atmospheres sufficient to balance the smaller force attacking them. In these atmospheres is placed the power which occasions the resistance to the bodies being electrified to a higher degree. That power is the elasticity of the electrical fluid—everywhere dispersed when "gross bodies" are not in the way, but likewise confined within bodies according to their different situations and neighborhood to other bodies. These atmospheres may be increased or diminished to a certain degree by art, and when this is done with violence "the natural contexture of the bodies is altered in proportion to the violence." Thus we see, even with the small force of our electrical machines, not only bodies parting with their natural share of the fluid, but of many of their component particles, "which may be perceived by the smell they yield on being electrified, and the rays of light they throw out, which, mixing with the air, occasions real Fire."*

239. Since the Smell occasion'd by Electricity is the same, whatever be the Body electrify'd, is it not probably occasion'd by some other thing than the component Parts of those Bodies?[5] May not real Fire be produc'd by Electricity without mixing with Air?

240. *These are proofs that the atmospheres have been increased, since they can only happen by the "sudden dissipation of them by art" after an increase. Before this they kept the enclosed body "compact and entire"; if the force that increased them had been gradually withdrawn, the atmospheres would have gradually returned to their natural density and the bodies to their natural state "both with regard to their component particles, and their natural share of this fluid and of the rays of light within them, which were all disturbed and in action before."*

240. What is meant by the natural Share of Rays of Light in Bodies? See 278 and 283, and 286, and 288.[6]

5. For BF's earlier discussion of this matter, see above, IV, 32–4.
6. In the 1759 edition Wilson made a small concession to BF by omitting the words "rays of" in the expression "and of the rays of light within them,"

241–248. *The above remarks on the increase of density in atmospheres may be criticized as arising from theory, but this theory "has been very carefully raised from experiments"; it can be destroyed only by showing a fallacy in the reasoning or an experiment to contradict it. Further experiments are now offered in support of the doctrine. Glass is the most difficult of the common substances to electrify; it has the most resisting atmosphere on its surfaces, that is, the densest atmospheres. Metals resist electrification much less; their atmospheres are not the densest. Heat rarefies bodies and increases conductivity: when glass is heated it resists electrification no more than metals do, and when melted, no more than water. A subtle and elastic fluid must be rarefied sooner than such a dense body as glass, and it seems most probable that the resisting atmosphere around glass is rendered as weak as that of metals by heat, and therefore resists the passage of electrical fluid no more than metals do. This seems confirmed by the fact that, as glass gradually cools, its resistance to electrification increases until, when quite cold, it resists as forcibly as ever. Wax resists electrification perhaps as much as glass, certainly more than metals when its surface is smooth and polished; it can be melted with a small degree of heat, so its atmospheres are readily brought down to the same degree of rarity as those of metals and when heated only by friction it seems to become an electrical conductor.*

249–250. *The same is true of brimstone (sulfur); hence the results of the following experiment. Place a glass globe so as to communicate with one end of a metal bar suspended by silk strings and a sulfur globe to communicate with the other end of the bar. If both globes are equally rubbed, the bar will not be electrified at all: we cannot get a single spark from it.*

250. This experiment seems mistaken. The rubbed Brimstone electrifies negatively; or, at least, differently from Glass. It is doubted, whether Brimstone warmed to any Degree by Friction, short of a melting Heat, will conduct.[7]

---

near the end of the paragraph. The references are to other paragraphs in which Hoadly and Wilson had used the same or a similar expression, but Wilson made no corresponding changes in them.

7. In the 1759 edition Wilson beat a full retreat on this experiment and made his second major change in the text. He omitted entirely pars. 249–256 dealing with sulfur and added the following note at the end of par. 248: "In the other edition, there is an experiment or two with a sulphur globe, which

251–256. Brimstone is classed with glass, wax, resin, etc., in its resistance to electrification, but like wax does not resist heat of friction as glass does; therefore its surface atmosphere can be more easily reduced by friction to the same weakness as that of metals. When rubbing the sulfur globe has heated, and so attenuated, the atmosphere on its surface, the globe and the machine that moves it become conductors and carry off the electrical fluid thrown into the bar by the glass globe. It is the heat caused by friction on the sulfur globe that causes the effects described [in par. 250]; hence if the sulfur globe is kept unrubbed but the glass globe is rubbed, the bar will be electrified and a spark obtained from it. All this is strong confirmation of what we have been saying, that the resistance of all bodies to being electrified is exerted at their surfaces and is caused by atmospheres of electrical fluid which lie at these surfaces and differ in density according to the different nature and quantity of the bodies immediately surrounding them. It shows us that heat arising from rubbing attenuates the electrical atmosphere of the sulfur globe and takes off the sulfur's natural resistance to electrification.

258–259. Set on glass an electrified Leyden bottle that has a hook in its coating; attach a clean chain to the hook; let a person grasp the coating with one hand and with the other hand bring the other end of the chain, and his finger and thumb that holds it, into contact with the wire of the bottle. There will be two possible courses for the electrical fluid to pass from the wire to the coating: the person's body or the chain. If the links of the chain hang loosely the person feels the shock; if the chain is stretched taut the fluid will pass through it and he will feel no shock, however long the chain may be. It follows that the electrical fluid does not always pass from one body to another by the shortest way, *but by the way of the* least *resistance, even if that is more roundabout.*[8]

---

was taken from the works of Dr. Franklyn: But as the experiments were never repeated either by Doctor Hoadly or myself, and the reasoning upon them was liable to objections, and not necessary in the present case, I have chose to leave that part out in this 2d edition." The reference to BF's works in this note is to a letter from Ebenezer Kinnersley to BF, Feb. 3, 1752, proposing certain experiments with a sulfur globe, and to BF's report back, March 16, 1752, confirming Kinnersley's anticipated result with one of the experiments; *Supplemental Experiments and Observations on Electricity, Part II*, pp. 99–106; above, IV, 263–5, 275–6.

8. BF made no comment here, but in the 1759 edition Wilson added the following note: "Doctor Watson and Doctor Franklyn are therefore mistaken

260–70. If the chain alone forms the communication and is spread on the table so loosely that the links barely touch each other, not only will there be a spark at the end where the chain touches the wire, but if the room is dark, a number of sparks will appear at places where the links do not absolutely touch each other. When the chain is stretched tight enough to make absolute contact between all links, only the spark at the end will appear. The appearance or non-appearance of these sparks shows us whether the fluid is passing through the chain. We may conclude that the resistance in the chain arises from the sum of the resistances at the different surfaces of the several links where the fluid had to break its way through. When the links were forced into contact with each other the chain acted as a single piece of metal and no such series of resistances arose, the person holding it was not affected on the discharge of the bottle, and no sparks appeared between the links. Now, fasten a wire of whatever length to the hook of the bottle as well as the chain; then let a person, grasping the bottle as before and leaving the chain loose on the table, bring the other ends of both the wire and the chain (and also his fingers) into contact with the wire of the bottle. Now we have three ways of discharging the bottle: the person, the chain, and the wire. We find that the fluid does not go through the person: he feels no shock. It does not go through the chain: there are no sparks between its links. It must be passing through the wire; there it had only one surface to break through: the one at the end where it met the wire of the bottle. No one who has not tried this experiment can imagine how taut the chain must be stretched to avoid having sparks appear between the links; its own weight is not enough. This confirms Newton's assertion about the pressure needed to bring a piece of convex glass into absolute contact with a plane glass on which it is laid. From all these observations and experiments we conclude that the power which produces resistance to electrification, either plus or minus, "is the elasticity of these small atmospheres of the

---

in regard to the Leyden experiment, where they advance that the electric fluid always makes the *shortest circuit*." Actually, as early as September 1753 BF had suggested that lightning goes "considerably out of a direct course" on its way to the ground, "taking in all the best conductors it can find." This letter was published in 1754 in *New Experiments and Observations on Electricity, Part III*, p. 124 (above, v, 76–7), and so was available to Wilson. Writing to John Lining, March 18, 1755, BF had given Kinnersley credit for proving experimentally that the charge from a Leyden jar followed the better conductor, not the shortest course (above, v, 523), but this letter was not published until the 1769 edition of *Exper. and Obser.*, p. 322.

electrical fluid, which are formed at all their surfaces by the action be-
tween the particles of this fluid (both within and without bodies) and
the component particles of the bodies: and therefore must be different at
the surfaces of different bodies."

270. Do Bodies in Vacuo resist being electrified? May not the Resistance arise rather from Airs, adhering closely to the Surfaces of Bodies.

271–274. *Now we shall try to explain how light bodies* [i.e., light in weight], *at considerable distance from an electrified body, are drawn to and from that body. The electrical fluid surrounding an excited tube in the air is dilated to a certain distance; beyond that it must be con-*
densed; that is, the fluid is rarer the nearer it is to the excited tube, and grows denser until at the limit of the tube's influence it returns to its natural state. Any light body within this distance will be forced from the denser to the rarer part of the fluid surrounding the tube, but when in its approach it becomes sufficiently electrified to have an atmosphere around it similar to that of the tube, it will be driven back again. Whenever afterwards it comes near any body more easily electrified than itself and communicating with the ground, its electrical atmosphere will be dissipated and it will immediately return to the tube as before.

275–278. *From all the above experiments it appears that the electrical fluid is as universal and powerful an agent at or near the earth's surface as that fluid Newton calls aether. It is as subtle and elastic, it similarly pervades the pores of all bodies, is dispersed through whatever vacuum we can create, and from the appearance of thunder and lightning seems to be extended to great distances in the air. "We shall make no scruple therefore now to affirm, that these two fluids are one and the same fluid."*
It is much more philosophical to do so than to suppose two such fluids equally present everywhere and equally capable of producing the same effects. The word electrical *is much too confining a meaning for so universal an activity as this is found to be.* "Electricity *means no more than the power we give bodies by rubbing them, to attract and repel light bodies"* near them, as amber does when rubbed. *This fluid not only does so but it heats them by putting their component particles and the particles of light and air within them into vibration, "and makes them throw out the rays of light that before lay hid," and part with their sulfurous and volatile particles which, with the rays of light, on mix-*
ing with the air, "burst out into sparks of real culinary *fire," as the*

chemists call it. Furthermore, in passing through animals it occasions convulsions, tremors, pain, and sometimes death, and it even fuses glass and gold into an enamel.[9]

278. What is meant by Rays of Light that before lay hid? See, 240, 283, 286, 288, 289.[1]

279–301. *It is as improper to call this fluid "fire" as it is to call air "sound." When sound is produced the particles of air are put into vibrations which convey the idea of sound through the ear. So when this fluid throws the particles of a body into such agitations in the air that it grows hot, shines, glows, and is consumed away, we say the body is on fire, but this fluid is not fire, nor can* fire *indeed be called a* Principle or Element *in the chemist's sense any more than* sound *can. The authors conclude with various arguments and illustrations of their theory of the identity of the "electrical fluid" with aether; they quote Newton twice at length in support, and end with a postscript asking the reader's indulgence because of the difficulty of finding satisfactory terminology for the discussion of their subject, and referring the reader to Wilson's treatise on electricity for some of the experiments mentioned here.*[2]

Jan. 28. 1759
Gave these Hints to Mr. Wilson, a Copy of which I had formerly read to him.

9. In the 1759 edition Watson changed the last part of par. 278. He dropped the statement that the gold and glass became incorporated and formed "an enamel," and substituted the statement that they became "so closely united, that Aqua Regia [a mixture of nitric and hydrochloric acids used to dissolve gold] itself, has no effect upon the metal." He added in a footnote that he had made the original statement on the strength of BF's reported experiment (*Exper. and Obser.*, 1751 edit., pp. 64–6; above, IV, 21–3), but upon later repeating it himself he concluded that the gold was not actually vitrified but brought into such close contact with the surface of the glass and by such a great force as to support his point about the strength of the electrical fluid at the surface of all bodies.

1. These references are to other paragraphs mentioning the rays of light within bodies.

2. In 1752 Collinson had sent BF a copy of Benjamin Wilson, *A Treatise on Electricity* (2d. edit., London, 1752). BF later sent it to Cadwallader Colden and Colden had returned it with critical comments on Newton's and Wilson's concepts of "Aether." See above, IV, 333, 355, 374–5.

Petition to the King in Council

I. Draft: American Philosophical Society. II. Copy: Historical Society of Pennsylvania; also two additional copies: Historical Society of Pennsylvania[3]

During the Indian conference at Easton in November 1756, the Delaware chieftain Teedyuscung, dramatically accused the Proprietors of having defrauded his people of lands in northeastern Pennsylvania.[4] Governor Denny promptly relayed this charge to the Penns, who proposed to the Board of Trade that Sir William Johnson, superintendent of Indian Affairs in the Northern District, be empowered to investigate Teedyuscung's charges and to "settle all matters" between the Proprietors and the Delaware. On March 10, 1757, the Board of Trade sent a recommendation to this effect to Johnson and, on the same day, the Proprietors ordered Denny to refer the Delaware to Sir William.[5] This

3. The draft, written with widely spaced lines to accommodate alterations, is in a clerical hand, but has been extensively revised in a hand which may be that of Richard Jackson. On a separate page from the original endorsement is written (inaccurately): "Rough Draught of the Petition of Benja. Franklin Esqr. agent of Pennsylvania in his Autograph 1758." At the top of the first page is a later notation: "Phillipps MS 35872." All three copies of the petition as actually submitted are among the Penn Papers. The one printed here is in the hand of Thomas Penn's secretary and is used primarily because of the endorsement in Penn's own hand. One of the others was written by the same secretary and appears to be identical in textual details with the first; it has no endorsement. The third copy is in an unidentified clerical hand, has some differences from the other two in punctuation, and carries an endorsement written by Ferdinand John Paris. Also among the Penn Papers (Hist. Soc. Pa.), but not printed here, are two lists dated respectively Feb. 21 and March 27, 1759, of other documents used by Paris in preparing the Proprietors' case for the hearing. They include Indian treaties, deeds, Council minutes, depositions, maps, etc.

4. For the conference at Easton, Nov. 8–17, 1756, which BF attended, see above, VII, 15–24. According to Teedyuscung, fraud had been committed at the Walking Purchase of 1737 (above, VII, 19 n), and at a purchase in 1749 at which the proprietary agents had bought from the Six Nations land above the Kittatinny Hills which the Delawares claimed as their own. At the Easton conference of Oct. 7–26, 1758, Teedyuscung acknowledged that the purchase of 1749 had been properly made, but he never admitted that the Walking Purchase had been fairly performed; he did, however, withdraw his complaints about it at a hearing before Sir William Johnson in 1762. Van Doren and Boyd, *Indian Treaties*, pp. 157, 237, 317; *Johnson Papers*, III, 786.

5. Van Doren and Boyd, *Indian Treaties*, p. 199; Proprietors to Denny, Feb. 12 and March 10, 1757; *Johnson Papers*, II, 684; Board of Trade to Sir William Johnson, March 10, 1757, *N.Y. Col. Docs.*, VII, 221–2.

the governor did at a conference with the Indians at Easton, July 31, 1757, but Teedyuscung refused to submit his case to Johnson's determination, declaring instead that he wanted George II to judge it.[6] The Pennsylvania Assembly supported Teedyuscung and on Sept. 29, 1757, ordered its committee of correspondence to transmit to its agents in London the minutes of the Indian conference of July–August, 1757, copies of several deeds which the proprietary agents had produced at that conference, and such other papers as were "necessary to a true Representation of the Complaints of the said Indians against this Province, that the same may be laid before His Majesty for His Royal Determination."[7] On Nov. 28, 1757, Robert Charles, Franklin's fellow agent, wrote the Board of Trade, desiring that he might lay before it the minutes of "the late Indian treaty at Easton," but on December 21, the Board informed him that this would be unnecessary, because Sir William Johnson had already sent them a copy.[8]

The minutes, in which Teedyuscung referred "his Claims to the Determination of the Crown," did not, however, bestir the Board to action, so that on May 13, 1758, Franklin informed Thomas Leech, the speaker of the Pennsylvania Assembly, that he was "preparing a Petition . . . to be presented next Week" to bring "the Matter to a Hearing before King and Council."[9] It is possible, though by no means certain, that Franklin composed a petition at this time. By the following September 20, however, a long draft was in existence. The original text of the surviving copy, written in a clerk's hand, probably represents Franklin's first intention. It has been heavily revised in another hand, possibly that of Richard Jackson, and it bears a notation that a fair copy had been made for Franklin. This paper, in its revised form, is printed below as Number I. During the months that followed, Franklin apparently decided on a further drastic revision:[1] the aspersions on the Proprietors were much toned down and most of the background narrative and quotation were eliminated, resulting in a document only about half as long as the draft. In this form (Number II below) the petition was presented to the Privy Council and on Feb. 2, 1759, the Council referred it to its committee for report.[2] Since the petition itself is undated

6. Van Doren and Boyd, *Indian Treaties,* pp. 199, 201, 206.
7. *Votes,* 1756–57, p. 161.
8. *Board of Trade Journal,* 1754–58, pp. 353, 357.
9. See above, pp. 66–8.
1. Toward the end of September BF and Jackson began an extended tour through Suffolk and Norfolk (see above, p. 132 n) and they would have had plenty of time to discuss the matter further.
2. *Acts Privy Coun., Col.,* IV, 402.

and the day on which it was filed is unknown, the petition, together with the preliminary draft, is placed here at the date of this reference to the committee.

I

[September 20, 1758]
To the Kings most Excellent Majesty in Council
   The Humble Petition of Benjamin Franklin Esquire
   Agent Appointed by the Assembly of Pensilvania.
Sheweth.

That the Indians who were formerly possessed of the Lands, now Enjoyed by Your Majesty's Subjects, along the Extensive Coast of North America, having been found to be easily prevailed on, for small Considerations paid them, to Cede Amicably to Your Majesty, Your Royal Predecessors and the Proprietary Grantees under the Crown, Large Tracts of those Lands for the Use of your Majesty's Subjects.

It has allways been thought advisable and good Policy, to make purchases thereof from the Native Indian Possessors from time to time, as the British Settlements have been extended. These Indians at the same time Retiring further back into the Country, there forming a kind of Frontier, where they are Capable whilst Maintained in Friendship of doing great Service to the English and of Contributing to the Prosperity of their Settlements Whereas, if they are deprived of these Lands without their consent, no formal cession is made thereof by them for considerations received or if fraud or deceit is used towards them therein. It proves The greatest Cause of Discontent, amongst them which they harbour in their Breasts, and upon any Opportunity offering thereto especially if excited by an Enemy breaks out into the greatest Violencies.

That William Penn Esquire, the late Proprietary of Pensilvania, and his Representatives, have agreable to the aforesaid good Policy at several times for small concessions purchased and obtained cessions and Conveyances from the Native Indians, of Sundry Large Tracts of Land within that Province and [the] Indians Right and claim to the same which Purchases so far as they were made fairly, without fraud, and the Lands duly Run out according to the true intent of the parties, The Indians have been forced peaceably and Quietly to acquiesce therein.

But complaints having been made of late years by the Indians and repeatedly confirmed particularly by the Delawarr Indians so called, from their Situation on the Great River of that Name, which runs along the Province of Pensilvania, that several of the Lands they had possessed have been taken from them by the Proprietarys of Pensilvania without Purchases thereof being made of them[3] and that where Purchases were made more Lands have been taken than was agreed for, and that Deceit and Circumvention has been used in the describing and running out of their Lands whereby they have been defrauded of large Quantities Contrary to their true intent and meaning,[4] and those Injuries in respect of their Lands having been assigned by the Indians as one great Cause for the Violences they have during the Present French Warr offered to your Majesties Subjects in the Outsettlements of Pensilvania,[5] where the cruelest Murthers and most horrid Devastation has been comitted by them and the Lands and propertys of your Majestys Subjects as well as the Welfare of Pensilvania being concerned therein Your Petitioner as Agent appointed by the assembly of that Province begs leave to Represent those Complaints of the Indians to your Majesty as it is the Indians desire and they have requested the Assembly to do that they may be enquired into by Your Majesty and be Redressed.

That amongst other Transactions complained of by the Indians is the following, very singular Instance. By a Deed say'd to have been made in 1686 but which from its not being Extant, nor Recorded amongst the other Public Writings of the Province lyes under Suspicious Circumstances.[6] The Indians in Consideration of

3. The reference here is especially to the purchase of 1749, mentioned in an earlier footnote.

4. Here the reference is to the Walking Purchase of 1737.

5. At Easton, Nov. 13, 1756, Teedyuscung asserted that land fraud was not the principal cause of hostilities between his people and the English, but that resentment over it had caused that blow to come "harder." Van Doren and Boyd, *Indian Treaties*, p. 156.

6. The validity of the deed of Aug. 28, 1686, on the basis of which the Walking Purchase was made, was contested by the Indians and the anti-proprietary faction and defended by the Penns and their supporters. Both sides acknowledged that no original of the deed existed. The issue was what weight should be given to a paper which the Penns asserted was a copy of the original deed. At Easton, in November 1756, Teedyuscung accused the Proprietors of forging this copy, a charge which Charles Thomson seconded

certain Small Quantities of Merchandize, are mentioned[?] to Sell and Confirm to the said Wm. Penn and his Heirs a Tract of Land in Pensilvania, beginning at a certain Mark by the said River Delawar and within certain Limits of Mountains and Creeks Extending itself into the Woods by the Vague and fallacious description—As far as a Man could goe in a Day and Half, and from whome it has acquired the Name of the Walking Purchase.[7]

The description of the premises in that Deed (if it was Real) was such that the said Wm. Penn, by whose Wisdom the Province of Pensilvania was made to Flourish, never thought fitt in his Life time to run it out, But after his Death and it's having lain Dormant for above 50 Years, His Two Sons John Penn and Thomas Penn Esquires the present proprietarys of Pensilvania in 1737 by Representing it to the Indians as a Real Subsisting good and binding Contract having Obtained a Confirmacion,[8] thereof caused it to be carried into Execution and the Day and Halfs Walk to be performed tho' it were to be wished that such confirmation had waited till after the Tract had been run out and the contents thereof known or at least that it had been [illegible.] For the Two persons appointed by the said proprietaries to perform the same[9] were so

___

in his *Enquiry* (p. 48). On behalf of the Proprietors, a committee of the Pa. Council submitted to that body on Jan. 6, 1758, a lengthy refutation, which was not entered on the minutes until Jan. 20, 1759. See above, p. 158 n. At a hearing before Sir William Johnson in 1762, Teedyuscung admitted that the charge of forgery "was a Mistake." *Johnson Papers*, III, 786.

7. The description of the land granted by the deed of 1686 was, indeed, vague. As quoted in the Council committee's report the tract was to be bounded by a line drawn from a spruce tree on the Delaware River to a "White Oak marked P" and then *"back into the Woods as far as a Man can go in One Day and an Half,* and bounded on the Westerly Side with the Creek called Neshameny, *or the most Westerly Branch thereof so far as the said Branch does extend, and from thence by a Line* [blank in the deed] to the utmost Extent of the said One and Half Day's Journey, and from *thence by a Line* [blank] *to the aforesaid River Delaware, and from thence down by the Several Courses thereof to the first-mentioned Spruce Tree."* Pa. Col. Recs., VIII, 251–2.

8. On Aug. 25, 1737, the Penns signed a deed of confirmation with the Delaware chieftains Monokykickan, Lappawinzoe, Tishekunk, and Nutimus. Van Doren and Boyd, *Indian Treaties,* p. 206; *Pa. Col. Recs.,* VIII, 249; Thomson, *Enquiry,* p. 33.

9. James Yeates and Edward Marshall. They each received £5 for making the walk and Marshall was also paid a half-crown "for his good performance of the Journey." *PMHB,* XXXII (1908), 116.

Chosen Trained and Instructed as without regard to the Indians Walkers appointed on the part of the Delawares, who called out to the Proprietaries Walkers not to Run and to goe by the Course of the River and not by the Compass which they did not understand nor could have meant by the Contract the Proprietary Walkers pressed on in such manner and at such a Rate that the Indians totally dissatisfyed therewith and unable to keep up with them gave out protesting against their proceeding, but the Proprietaries Agents still kept on and went with such Celerity and Dispatch and Traversed such an Extent of ground that however it might have gained them Applause from the Spectators on a Race Course, was greatly to the Disatisfaction not only of the Indians but of all Sober and Sensible People then present;[1] and the Proprietaries Extending that Tract of Land agreed for in Terms so Vague by such Arts of Jockeyship[2] gave the Indians the worst of Opinions of the English, and even of the Chiefs amongst them the Proprietaries themselves; and which with other Injustices they complain the Proprietaries having done them with respect to their Lands lost this Nation their Friendship and Esteem and exposed your Majesty's Subjects to their Resentment and Revenge which will best appear as also will the Complaints of the Indians as from their own words delivered as follows. Att a Conference had at Easton in Pensilvania on the 13th. November 1756 By the Lieut. Governor several Commissioners appointed by the assembly[3] and others with the King of the Delawarrs and several other Indians The Delawar King Teedyuscung's Speech contained the following expressions as then interpreted into English vizt.

"This very Ground that is under me (Striking it with his foot) was my Land and Inheritance, and is taken from me by Fraud, when I say this Ground I mean all the Land lying between Tohiccon Creek and Wioming on the River Susquehanna;

"All the Land extending from Tohiccon over the great Mountain to Wioming has been taken from me by Fraud for when I had

1. BF may have relied on Thomson's *Enquiry* for this account of the walk, or he may have been using accounts of it which he had heard at Easton in 1756.

2. BF knew that this term would infuriate Thomas Penn; see above, VII, 362.

3. Of whom BF was one; see above, VII, 15–24.

agreed to Sell the Land to the Old Proprietary by the Course of the River, The Young Proprietarys came and got it run by a Streight Course by the Compass and by that means took in double the Quantity intended to be Sold."[4]

Upon which the Commissioners appointed by the assembly on the 29th of January 1757 Reported to the House That they apprehended it of importance to the Province, that the Complaints made by the Indians whether Justly founded or not should be fully represented and took Notice That the Indians insisted on the Wrongs that had been done them in the Purchases of Lands with Warmth and Earnestness, and that the Transaction of the Walking Purchase had at the said Conference at Easton been universally given up as unfair and not to be depended [defended], and that it was unworthy of any Government.[5]

That at another Conference held at Lancaster on the 12th of May 1757 By the Lieut. Governor of Pensilvania, The Speaker and several Members of the Assembly and others with the Indians[6] The Lieut. Governor in his Speech to the Indians having taken Notice of the unhappy Differences that had Subsisted between the People of Pensilvania and the Delawarr and the Shawness Indians, and that having desired to know what was the Cause of their Committing Hostilities on the English Tweedyuscung, The Delawarr King had acknowledged that their foolish Young Men had been deluded by the Enemy the French, who had persuaded them to take up the Hatchett against the English, *But that one Reason why the Blow fell the heavier* on the English, was that their Brother Penn (called Onas by them) had fradulently possessed himself of some of their Lands without having first purchased or given any cons[iderati]on for the same.[7] To which another Chief

4. Quoted by BF from the minutes of the Easton conference of November 1756, Van Doren and Boyd, *Indian Treaties,* p. 157.

5. Here BF partly paraphrased, partly quoted, from the commissioners' report, which he himself had helped to prepare; see above, VII, 111–12.

6. For this conference, see Van Doren and Boyd, *Indian Treaties,* pp. 176–86.

7. This passage reads as if a dialogue about the causes of Indian hostilities had taken place at Lancaster between Denny and Teedyuscung. Such was not the case, however, since the Delaware chieftain had boycotted the conference, probably because he feared that the representatives of the Six Nations present would cut him down to size. BF is here summarizing from Denny's speech at

of the Indians in his Answer delivered the next Day, said that those were the true Causes from whence their differences had arose.[8] And at a Subsequent Conference a few Days after Vizt. the 19th of the same May The same Chief who was of the Mohawk Indians say'd their Forefathers Conquered the Delawarrs, and that a long time after they lived among the Pensilvanians, but upon some differences between the Pensilvanians and the Delawarrs The Mohawks had removed them giving them Lands to Plant and Hunt on Wyoming and Juni[a]ta on Susqu[e]hannah, But that the Pensilvanians had made Plantacons there which the Mohawks had inspected, and found true.[9]

That at another Conferrence held at Easton in July 1757 By the Lieut. Governor, the Speaker, and several Members of the Assembly and others with the Indians[1] The said Delawarr King Teedyuscung on the 28th of that Month delivered himself as follows.

"The Complaints I made last Fall,[2] I yet continue. I think some Lands have been bought by the Proprietary, or his Agents, from Indians who had not a right to Sell, and to whom the Lands did not belong.[3] I think also, when some Lands have been Sold to the proprietary by Indians who had a Right to Sell to a certain place, whether that purchase was to be Measured by Miles or Hours Walk, that the Proprietaries have, contrary to Agreement or Bargain taken in more Lands than they ought to have done, and Lands that belonged to others. I therefore now desire that you will

the opening of the conference in which he described Teedyuscung's complaints at the Easton conference of November 1756. Van Doren and Boyd, *Indian Treaties*, p. 176.

8. In this speech Thomas King, an Oneida, actually expressed no more than his satisfaction that the Proprietors had learned from Teedyuscung what his grievances were. *Ibid.*, p. 177.

9. Van Doren and Boyd, *Indian Treaties*, pp. 181–2. While the plantations in the Wyoming Valley may have been established by Pennsylvanians, Little Abraham may also have been referring to Connecticut's Susquehannah Co. (above, v, 22–1 n, 350 n), which had sent surveyors to the Wyoming Valley in 1755. Julian P. Boyd, ed., *The Susquehannah Company Papers* (Wilkes-Barre, Pa., 1930–33), II, xv.

1. For this conference, July 25–Aug. 7, 1757, see Van Doren and Boyd, *Indian Treaties*, pp. 191–212.

2. That is, at the Easton conference of November 1756.

3. Teedyuscung was referring to the purchase of 1749.

produce the Writings and Deeds by which you hold the Land,[4] and let them be read in Publick, and Examined, that it may be fully known from what Indians you have bought the Lands you hold, and how far your purchases extend, that Copies of the whole may be laid before King George and published to all the provinces under his Government. What is fairly bought and paid for I make no further Demands about: But if any Lands have been bought of Indians to whom these Lands did not belong, and who had no Right to sell them, I expect a satisfaction for these Lands. And if the Proprietaries have taken in more Lands than they bought of true Owners, I expect likewise to be paid for that. But as the persons to whom the Proprietaries may have Sold these Lands which of Right belonged to me, have made some Settlements, I do not want to disturb them, or to force them to leave them, but I expect a full Satisfaction shall be made to the true Owners for these Lands though the Proprietaries, as I said before, might have bought them from persons that had no right to Sell them."[5]

In Answer to which the Lieut General of Pensilvania[6] on the 31st of the same Month of July 1757 Acquainted the Delawar King, that his Complaint had been Laid before Your Majesty's Ministers who looking on it as a Matter of great Importance Determined that it should be carefully Enquired and Examined into, and had Appointed Sir Wm. Johnson to hear the particulars of the Charge and the Proprietaries Defence and lay the whole Matter before Your Majesty for Your Royal Determination in

4. This was done over Richard Peters' strenuous objections, on Aug. 3, 1757, and again the following day. Charles Thomson, Teedyuscung's secretary, was careful to take copies of all the documents which the proprietary officials produced: a copy of the deed of Aug. 28, 1686; "A Release, from the Delaware Indians," Aug. 25, 1737; "A Release of the Indians of the Five Nations, of the Lands on Sasquehannah River," Oct. 11, 1736; "A Release from the Six Nations of Lands Eastward [from the Susquehanna River] to the Delaware," Oct. 25, 1736, with another endorsed on it, dated July 9, 1754; and the deed of 1749. Thomson laid these documents before the Assembly and on Sept. 29, 1757, it ordered its Committee of Correspondence to transmit them to the agents in London. See above, VII, 266.

5. Quoted from the conference minutes; see Van Doren and Boyd, *Indian Treaties*, p. 197.

6. That is, Governor Denny. This and the concluding paragraphs, comprising the last page of the MS text, are in a different clerical hand.

order that your Majesty might do him Justice if Injured, and that in that Case Your Majesty would Determine it your Self.[7]

THAT your Petitioner conceives Sir Wm. Johnson has made some Report to Your Majesty, how these Matters have Appeared to him.[8]

YOUR Petitioner therefore humbly prays Your Majesty would be pleased to take the Premises into Your Royal Consideration, and Grant the Indians such Relief in the Premises as to Your Majesty in your great Wisdom and Justice shall seem meet.

AND your Petitioner shall ever pray &c.

Endorsed: Drt Petition Of the Agent Appointed by the Assembly of Pensilvania Representing the Complaints of the Indians of the Injuries done them in respect to their Lands.

1758 Sepr. 20th Copied fair for Mr. Franklin[9]

II

[February 2, 1759]

To the King's most Excellent Majesty in Council

The humble Petition of Benjamin Franklin Esquire

Agent appointed by the Assembly of Pennsylvania.

Sheweth,

That the Indians who were formerly possessed of the Lands, which form the extensive Countries, now enjoyed by your Majesty's Subjects in North America, having been found willing, for small Considerations, to cede Amicably large Tracts of those Lands, to Your Majesty, Your Royal Predecessors, and the Proprietary Grantees under the Crown, it has always been thought good Policy to make Purchases thereof from time to time, as the British Settlements have been extended; and the Indians at the same time retiring further back into the Country, have formed a kind of Frontier, where, while they continue upon Terms of Friendship, Trade, profitable to this Nation, is carried on with

7. A paraphrase of Denny's speech from the conference minutes; see Van Doren and Boyd, *Indian Treaties*, p. 199.

8. On Sept. 28, 1757, Johnson informed the Board of Trade that because of Teedyuscung's reluctance, he had declined to press his "Mediation upon the Indians." *N.Y. Col. Docs.*, VII, 277.

9. This and the foregoing endorsement are in the hand of the same clerk but appear to have been written at different times.

them, by exchanging British Manufactures for their Peltry,[1] they
contribute to the Prosperity of the British Settlements in Time of
Peace, and are the Chief and best protection of them from the in-
roads of Enemies in time of War.

But if they entertain any Suspicion that they have been deprived
of their Lands without their consent, and that no Consideration
has been paid for them, or that any Fraud or Deceipt hath been
practiced towards them therein, they usually conceal their Discontent until an opportunity offers of revenging themselves; and
then, especially if excited by an Enemy, commit the most out-
rageous Acts of violence, by small Parties who plunder and
Murder, without regard to Condition, Age, or Sex, and always
fly before a Superior force to Places where their knowledge of
the Country renders it almost impossible to discover and reduce
them.

That as the Calamities of a War thus carried on, are not easily
prevented, it is almost equally difficult to put a stop to them by
Treaty, these Natives being unwilling to disclose the Cause of
their Resentment, 'til they have attained what they deem sufficient
Vengeance for the supposed Injury; And when the Secret is drawn
from them, and Peace is made by a Satisfaction promised, the
delay of that satisfaction is frequently the Cause of their renewing,
without warning, the same Ravages.

That the Delaware Indians, and other Neighbouring Nations
having for some time carried on a cruel War against Your Majesty's
Subjects in North America, and having spread Desolation and
Terror through Your Majesty's Provinces of Virginia, Maryland,
Pennsylvania and New Jersey, and thereby unpeopled a great
part of those Countries, a Treaty was at length set on foot for the
putting an end to these Devestations, during the Course of which
Treaty several Conferences were held between George Croghan
Esquire the Deputy Agent of Sir William Johnson Bart.[2] (whom

1. This reference to British trade and manufactures, not found in the draft,
was certainly added as an appeal for support from mercantile interests at
home, which enjoyed substantial influence with the Board of Trade and Privy
Council.

2. George Croghan was not present at Easton in November 1756. It was
Teedyuscung's complaints, aired there for the first time, which caused Sir
William Johnson to send Croghan to the conferences in 1757 and 1758.

Your Majesty had been pleased to appoint Sole Agent for Indian Affairs within the District of these Provinces) and William Denny Esquire Lieutenant Governor of Pennsylvania, on the behalf of Thomas and Richard Penn the Proprietaries, and also on behalf of the said Province, and Teedyuscung, Chief of all the Delaware and many other Confederated Indian Nations, who had been properly empowered by them to make their Demands and conclude a Peace.

That at some of their Conferences, particularly at one holden at Easton in Pennsylvania, the 13th of November 1756, Teedyuscung complained that the Indians had been unjustly dispossessed and defrauded of large Quantitys of Land by your Majesty's Subjects, particularly of the Lands which are included within the Forks of the River Delaware, and also of other Lands on both sides the said River.

That at another Conference holden at Easton in July 1757 Teedyuscung having earnestly desired that all Differences between the Indians and Your Majesty's Subjects might be referred to Your Majesty's Royal Determination; and that the same might be published throughout all Your Majesty's Provinces,[3] It was finally agreed (amongst other things) by the said George Croghan, the said Lieutenant Governor and Teedyuscung, That all the Purchase Deeds and Writings, by which the said Thomas and Richard Penn, or their Ancestors, or the Grantees of their Ancestors, now hold any Lands within the back parts of the Province of Pennsylvania, should be examined and Copies thereof laid before your Majesty for Your Royal Decision of the Bounds and Limits between the Lands heretofore bought of the Indians and those yet unpurchased.[4]

3. On July 28, 1757, Teedyuscung had requested that the "Writings and Deeds" by which the Proprietors held former Indian lands be laid before "King George and published to all the Provinces under his Government." Van Doren and Boyd, *Indian Treaties*, p. 197.

4. The agreement was reached Aug. 2, 1757. The "back parts" of the province involved in this agreement were understood to mean lands in northeastern Pa. Van Doren and Boyd, *Indian Treaties*, pp. 197, 205. On May 15, 1759, at a hearing on this petition before the Board of Trade, BF handed over the copies of the deeds which the Assembly had sent him. *Board of Trade Journal*, 1759–63, p. 36; BF to Norris, June 9, 1759, below, p. 398.

That Your Petitioner, as Agent appointed by the Assembly of the Province of Pennsylvania (in which as well as in Your Majesty's adjacent Provinces the Lives and Properties of many Thousands of Your Majesty's Subjects will be in the utmost Danger, should the Hostilitys of the Indians be renewed) begs leave humbly to represent the Premises to Your Majesty, AND PRAYS

That Your Majesty would be pleased to take the Premises into Your Royal Consideration, and to do therein as to Your Majesty in Your great Wisdom shall seem meet

And Your Petitioner shall ever Pray &ca.

Signed B. FRANKLIN

Copy.

Endorsed: Petition of Benjamin Franklin on Teedyuscungs Complaint presented Feby. 1759.[5]

It comes very ill from Mr. F to suggest that delay of satisfaction is dangerous when the papers delivered the 4 of Augt. 1757 are not yet laid before his Majesty. After an appeal the proprietors could not take any measures but wait for the appellant they had used their utmost endeavours to bring it on.[6]

5. The Privy Council referred the petition to its committee, Feb. 2, 1759, and the committee in turn referred it to the Board of Trade, April 12. *Acts Privy Coun., Col.,* IV, 402. In a letter to Galloway, April 7, 1759, BF anticipated this customary and routine action by reporting that the petition had already been sent to the Board of Trade (see below, p. 313). The Board conducted a hearing on May 15, at which BF, the Proprietors, the solicitors of both parties, "and several other persons" attended and the parties were heard. On May 16, 23, and 29, the Board considered its report and the members signed it on June 1, 1759. *Board of Trade Journal,* 1759–63, pp. 36, 37, 40–1, 42. For the text of the report, see below, pp. 379–89.

6. This endorsement is in Thomas Penn's hand. By "the papers delivered the 4 of Augt. 1757" he could only have meant the deeds the proprietary officials had produced at the Easton conference on that date. Van Doren and Boyd, *Indian Treaties,* p. 206. Since BF laid copies of these deeds before the Board of Trade on May 15, 1759, Penn must have endorsed this copy of the petition before then.

M. Foulger to David Edwards[7]

ALS: Historical Society of Pennsylvania

Sir   Illington,[8] Feb. the 5 1759

As you have Testified so particularly a desire, in being better Informd in your Affair, with Mr. Franklin we took an Oppertunity of meeting Mr. Foulger, who could give little Intelegence more than we have Acquainted you, the before mention'd Peter Foulger, went when he was a Lad with a Neighbouring Gentleman the Name unknown to us, As a Servant to New England,[9] After his Arrival, he Frequent Convers'd with his Relations, who lived at, or near, Windham in Norfolk his Letters cannot be Produce'd by none of the Family that we can Learn. If it suits with my Husbands Conveinency he will meet you; at your Appointment. Which Concludes Me, Your Humble Servant   M: FOULGER
Accept United Compliments and Dispose of that to your worthy Friend, Mr. Franklin as you Express him if Agreeable.

Addressed: To / Mr David Edwards / at Mr Grigsbys Attorney at Law / At / St Edmunds Bury / Suffolk
Endorsed: Reced Feb. 7th. 1759. DE.

The University of St. Andrews:
Degree of Doctor of Laws

DS: American Philosophical Society; Latin copy and English translation: American Philosophical Society; two Latin copies: Yale University Library[1]

Little can be established with certainty about the circumstances under which Franklin received his first honorary degree in Great Britain and

7. Neither the writer of this letter, her husband, nor the other "Mr. Foulger" mentioned in it has been identified. On David Edwards, see above, VII, 275 n.

8. A small village in the Hundred of Shropham, Norfolk, about nineteen miles from Norwich and four miles from Attleborough, where BF had found the grave of a Thomas Foulger, to whom he believed he must have been related. He apparently asked his friend David Edwards of Bury St. Edmunds to make inquiries in that neighborhood. See above, pp. 171–2.

9. BF's maternal grandfather, Peter Folger (or Foulger; B.1), was born in Norwich and had migrated to New England in 1635 with his parents and one sister.

1. The two copies in Yale Univ. Lib. are in the College Records and the

first doctorate. The minutes of the Senatus of the University of St. Andrews contain the following entry dated Feb. 12, 1759: "Sed[erun]t Rector, prin[cipa]l Murison, profr. Brown Mr. Gregory, Mr. Jon Young, Dr. Hadow, Mr. Morton, Mr. Watson Mr. Wilson. Conferr'd the Degree of Doctor in Laws on Mr. Benjamin Franklin famous for his Writings on Electricity, And appoint his Diploma to be given him gratis, The Clerk and Arch Beadles dues to be paid by the Library Quaestor." There is no contemporary evidence to show who proposed the honor, though it would be reasonable to suppose that it was one of the more scientifically oriented professors, possibly David Gregory (mathematics), David Young (natural and experimental philosophy), or Thomas Simson (medicine and anatomy), who, although absent from this meeting, signed the diploma, and whose brother Robert had corresponded with Franklin (above, VII, 184).

At this time Franklin was in London and the degree was conferred *in absentia*. How he was notified of the honor is not clear for no letter from the rector or any other university official can be found,[2] and no letter of response survives in which he acknowledges receipt of the diploma. But that he and his friends were highly gratified is certain; it soon became customary for associates and correspondents, when addressing him formally or referring to him, to call him "Doctor Franklin." This was his usual title during the rest of his life.[3]

Stiles Papers, respectively. BF probably provided Stiles with the text, together with information on his other honors, at Stiles's request, during a visit to Newport in July 1763.

2. In the course of an address in 1938 Sir James Irvine, then principal and vice chancellor of St. Andrews, mentioned such a letter in terms implying that he had seen it (*Journal of the Franklin Institute*, CCXXVI, 271–9), but Mr. R. N. Smart, Keeper of the MSS at the University Library, has informed the editor by letter, Dec. 11, 1963, that he has "been unable to find any evidence for its existence." Sir James's account of a ceremony at which the degree was actually conferred, when BF visited St. Andrews the following October, is wholly imaginary. In a letter to Principal T. M. Knox, April 25, 1964, R. G. Cant, Keeper of the Muniments, has commented: "There was no need for him [Franklin] to attend in person—indeed the University only began to insist on it for Honorary Graduates in 1887. Consequently, there was no occasion for any Graduation Ceremony when he visited St. Andrews in October, 1759."

3. With the original diploma in the Franklin Papers, APS, are a Latin copy and an English translation, both contemporary. The translation reads as follows (omitting the signatures at the end): "We the Rector, Provost, Presidents of the Colleges, Dean of the Faculty of Arts, and other Orders of Professors in the University of St. Andrews in Scotland, to our Readers Greeting Whereas it is just and reasonable, that they who by great Study have

[February 12, 1759]

Nos Universitatis St. Andreae apud Scotos Rector Promotor, Collegiorum Praefecti, Facultatis Artium Decanus, caeterique Professorum Ordines, Lectoribus Salutem

Quandoquidem aequum est et Rationi congruens, ut qui magno Studio bonas didicerunt Artes, iidem referant Praemium Studiis suis dignum, ac prae inerti Hominum vulgo propriis quibusdam fulgeant Honoribus et Privilegiis, unde et ipsis bene sit, atque aliorum provocetur Industria; Quando etiam eo praesertim spectant amplissima illa Jura Universitati Andreanae antiquibus concessa, ut, quoties respostulat, idoneos quosque in quavis facultate viros, vel Summis qui ad eam Facultatem pertinent, Honoribus amplificare queat; Quumque ingenuus et honestus Vir Benjaminus Franklin, Artium Magister, non solum Jurisprudentiae Cognitione, Morum Integritate, Suavique Vitae Consuetudine, Nobis sit commendatus, Verum etiam, acute inventus, et exitu felici factis Experimentis, quibus Rerum Naturalium, et imprimis Rei Electricae parum hactenus exploratae, Scientiam locupletavit, tantum sibi conciliaverit per Orbem Terrarum Laudem, ut summus in Republica Literaria

---

learned the Arts, should also receive a Reward worthy of their Studies, and outshine the slothful Herd of Mankind by some peculiar Honours and Privileges, both to reward them and excite the Industry of others; And whereas the Design of those very extensive Privileges granted in antient times to the University of St. Andrews is, that as oft as Occasion requires they may have it in their Power to dignify Men excelling in any Faculty with the highest Honours appertaining to that Faculty; and whereas the ingenuous and worthy Benj: Franklin has not only been recommended to us for his Knowledge of the Law, the Rectitude of his Morals and Sweetness of his Life and Conversation, but hath also by his ingenious Inventions and successful Experiments with which he hath enriched the Science of natural Philosophy and more especially of Electricity which heretofore was little known, acquired so much Praise throughout the World as to deserve the greatest Honours in the Republic of Letters; For these Reasons and from a willingness as far as in us lies to bestow the Rewards due to Virtue we create constitute and declare the above named Mr. Benjamin Franklin Doctor of Laws and will that for the future he be treated[?] by all as the most Worthy Doctor, and we grant to him with a liberal Hand all the Privileges and Honours, which are any where granted to Doctors of Laws. In Testimony of which we have given these our Letters signed with our Hands and sealed with the common Seal of the University at St. Andrews the 12th of February 1759."

mereatur Honores: Hisce nos adducti, et praemia Virtuti debita, quantum in nobis est, tribuere volentes, Magistrum BEN- JAMINUM FRANKLIN supra nominatum, UTRIUSQUE JURIS DOCTOREM Creamus, Constituimus et Renunciamus Eumque deinceps ab universis pro Doctore dignissimo haberi volumus; adjicimusque Ei, plena manu, quaecunque uspiam gentium. Juris utriusque Doctoribus competunt Privilegia et Ornamenta. In cuius Rei testimonium hasce nostras Privilegii, Literas, Chirographis singulorum confirmatas, et communi Almae Universitatis Sigillo munitas DEDIMUS ANDREAPOLI duo- decimo Die Mensis Februarii Anno Domini millesimo Septin- gentesimo quinquagesimo nono.

AND. SHAW S.T.P. Univers. Rector et Promotor[4]
THOS. TULLIDEPH Coll: St. Salvat: et St. Leonar: Praefectus
JA. MURISON Coll. Mar: Praefectus
ROBTUS WATSON P.P. Fac. Art. Doc.
THOMAS SIMSON Med. et Anat. p. candosensis
DAVID YOUNG P.P.
JOANNES YOUNG P.P.
DAVID GREGORIE Math: P.
GUIEL: BROWN S.T et H.E.P.
ALEXR. MORTON H.L.P.
GUAL. WILSON G.L.P.
GEOR: HADOW M. D. Ling. Heb. P.

4. The signers with their titles were: Andrew Shaw, professor of sacred theology [divinity] and Biblical criticism, university rector provost; Thomas Tullideph, principal of the [United] Colleges of St. Salvator and St. Leonard; James Murison, principal of the College of St. Mary's; Robert Watson, pro- fessor of philosophy [logic, rhetoric, and metaphysics]; Thomas Simson, Chandos professor of medicine and anatomy; David Young, professor of [natural and experimental] philosophy; John Young, professor of philosophy [ethics and pneumatics, i.e., spiritual philosophy or psychology]; David Gregory, professor of mathematics; William Brown, professor of sacred theology [divinity] and ecclesiastical history; Alexander Morton, professor of humanity [humane letters]; Walter Wilson, professor of Greek; and George Hadow, M.D., professor of Hebrew and Oriental languages. James M. Anderson, ed., *The Matriculation Roll of the University of St Andrews 1747– 1897* (Edinburgh and London, 1905), pp. lxxiv–lxxxiii.

Preface to Dr. Heberden's Pamphlet on Inoculation

Printed in [William Heberden], *Some Account of the Success of Inoculation for the Small-Pox in England and America. Together with Plain Instructions, By which any Person may be enabled to perform the Operation, and conduct the Patient through the Distemper.* London: Printed by W. Strahan, M,DCC,LIX. (Historical Society of Pennsylvania)

Since at least 1730, Franklin had advocated inoculation for smallpox as "a safe and beneficial Practice."[5] His suggestion for Dr. William Heberden's[6] pamphlet and his own preface to it may be regarded as further efforts to persuade the people to use "a discovery God in his mercy has been pleased to bless mankind with."

London, Feb. 16, 1759.

Having been desired by my greatly esteemed friend Dr. William Heberden, F. R. S. one of the principal Physicians of this city, to communicate what account I had of the success of Inoculation in Boston, New-England, I some time since wrote and sent to him the following paper, viz.

About 1753 or 54, the Small-pox made its appearance in Boston, New-England.[7] It had not spread in the town for many years before, so that there were a great number of the inhabitants to have it. At first, endeavours were used to prevent its spreading, by removing the sick, or guarding the houses in which they were; and with the same view Inoculation was forbidden; but when it was found that these endeavours were fruitless, the distemper breaking out in different quarters of the town, and increasing, Inoculation was then permitted.

5. See above, I, 186–7, 214; II, 154; III, 79, 445. James Franklin's *New-England Courant* had opposed the method when it was introduced in Boston in 1721; whether his younger brother then shared the prejudice against it is unknown.

6. William Heberden (1710–1801), "one of the most eminent English physicians of the eighteenth century." A prolific writer about diseases and their cure, he was also a philanthropist, a classical scholar, and a patron of learning. So impressive was his erudition that Samuel Johnson called him "Ultimus Romanorum, the last of our learned physicians." *DNB*. BF may have made his acquaintance at the Royal Society, or Dr. John Fothergill may have introduced the two men. It is not clear when Heberden asked BF for an account of the inoculation for smallpox in Boston nor when BF replied.

7. BF is here referring to the epidemic of 1752. John Duffy, *Epidemics in Colonial America* (Baton Rouge, 1953), p. 35. For BF's correspondence with Dr. John Perkins of Boston about this epidemic and others in Philadelphia, see above, IV, 336–7, 340–1.

Upon this, all that inclined to Inoculation for themselves or families hurried into it precipitately, fearing the infection might otherwise be taken in the common way; the numbers inoculated in every neighbourhood spread the infection likewise more speedily among those who did not chuse Inoculation; so that in a few months, the distemper went thro' the town, and was extinct; and the trade of the town suffered only a short interruption, compar'd with what had been usual in former times, the country people during the seasons of that sickness fearing all intercourse with the town.

As the practice of Inoculation always divided people into parties, some contending warmly for it, and others as strongly against it; the latter asserting that the advantages pretended were imaginary, and that the Surgeons, from views of interest, conceal'd or diminish'd the true number of deaths occasion'd by Inoculation, and magnify'd the number of those who died of the Small-pox in the common way: It was resolved by the Magistrates of the town, to cause a strict and impartial enquiry to be made by the Constables of each ward, who were to give in their returns upon oath; and that the enquiry might be made more strictly and impartially, some of the partisans for and against the practice were join'd as assistants to the officers, and accompany'd them in their progress through the wards from house to house.[8] Their several returns being received, and summ'd up together, the numbers turn'd out as follows,[9]

Had the Small-pox in the common way,		Of these died		Received the distemper by Inoculation,		Of these died	
Whites	Blacks	Whites	Blacks	Whites	Blacks	Whites	Blacks
5059	485	452	62	1974	139	23	7

It appeared by this account that the deaths of persons inoculated, were more in proportion at this time than had been formerly observed, being something more than one in a hundred. The favourers of Inoculation however would not allow that this was

8. This inquiry was made by the selectmen, overseers of the poor, and several "principal Inhabitants" on July 23–24, 1752. *Boston Evening Post*, July 27, 1752.

9. Although there are minor differences, BF appears to have taken these statistics from William Douglass, *A Summary, Historical and Political, of the ... British Settlements in North-America* (London, 1755), II, 398.

owing to any error in the former accounts, but rather to the Inoculating at this time many unfit subjects, partly through the impatience of people who would not wait the necessary preparation, lest they should take it in the common way; and partly from the importunity of parents prevailing with the Surgeons against their judgment and advice to inoculate weak children, labouring under other disorders; because the parents could not immediately remove them out of the way of the distemper, and thought they would at least stand a better chance by being inoculated, than in taking the infection, as they would probably do, in the common way. The Surgeons and Physicians were also suddenly oppress'd with the great hurry of business, which so hasty and general an Inoculation and spreading of the distemper in the common way must occasion, and probably could not so particularly attend to the circumstances of the patients offered for Inoculation.

Inoculation was first practised in Boston by Dr. Boylstone in 1720.[1] It was not used before in any part of America, and not in Philadelphia till 1730. Some years since, an enquiry was made in Philadelphia of the several Surgeons and Physicians who had practis'd Inoculation, what numbers had been by each inoculated, and what was the success. The result of this enquiry was, that upwards of 800, (I forget the exact number) had been inoculated at different times, and that only four of them had died.[2] If this account was true, as I believe it was, the reason of greater success there than had been found in Boston, where the general loss by Inoculation used to be estimated at about one in 100, may probably be from this circumstance; that in Boston they always keep the distemper out as long as they can, so that when it comes, it finds a greater number of adult subjects than in Philadelphia, where since 1730 it has gone through the town once in four or five years,[3]

1. BF misdated this courageous experiment. It was on June 26, 1721, during a severe epidemic in Boston, that Zabdiel Boylston (1679–1766) introduced the practice in colonial America, inoculating his son and two slaves, and provoking such widespread and violent indignation that for a time, his life and that of Cotton Mather, who had encouraged him, were in danger. Success vindicated the two men, and in 1726 Boylston was elected Fellow of the Royal Society.

2. BF himself had undertaken this inquiry in the winter of 1751–52; see above, IV, 340.

3. There were smallpox epidemics in Philadelphia in 1736–37, in which BF

so that the greatest number of subjects for Inoculation must be under that age.

Notwithstanding the now uncontroverted success of Inoculation, it does not seem to make that progress among the common people in America, which at first was expected. *Scruples of conscience* weigh with many, concerning the *lawfulness* of the practice: And if one parent or near relation is against it, the other does not chuse to inoculate a child without free consent of all parties, lest in case of a disastrous event, perpetual blame should follow. These *scruples* a *sensible Clergy* may in time remove. The *expence* of having the operation perform'd by a Surgeon, weighs with others, for that has been pretty high in some parts of America; and where a common tradesman or artificer has a number in his family to have the distemper, it amounts to more money than he can well spare. Many of these, rather than own the *true motive* for declining Inoculation, join with the scrupulous in the cry *against it,* and influence others. A small Pamphlet wrote in plain language by some skilful Physician, and publish'd, directing what preparations of the body should be used before the Inoculation of children, what precautions to avoid giving the infection at the same time in the common way, and how the operation is to be performed, the incisions dress'd, the patient treated, and on the appearance of what symptoms a Physician is to be called, &c. might by encouraging parents to inoculate their own children, be a means of removing that objection of the expence, render the practice much more general, and thereby save the lives of thousands.

The Doctor,[4] after perusing and considering the above, humanely took the trouble (tho' his extensive practice affords him scarce any time to spare) of writing the following PLAIN INSTRUCTIONS,* and generously, at his own private expence, printed a

---

*To make them the plainer and more generally intelligible, the Doctor purposely avoided, as much as possible, the *medical terms* and *expressions* us'd by Physicians in their writings.[5]

---

lost his son Francis (above, II, 154), in 1746, in 1750, and in 1756. See above, III, 77–79; IV, 63; VI, 452.

4. That is, Heberden.

5. The *Instructions,* to which BF's paper served as a preface, suggested that inoculation could be performed with safety the year round. They described certain infirmities which would disqualify one from being inoculated; they

very large impression of them, which was put into my hands to be distributed *gratis* in America.[6] Not aiming at the praise which however is justly due to such disinterested benevolence, he has omitted his name; but as I thought the advice of a nameless Physician might possibly on that account be less regarded, I have without his knowledge here divulg'd it. And I have prefix'd to his small but valuable work these pages, containing the facts that gave rise to it; because *facts* generally have, as indeed they ought to have, great weight in persuading to the practice they favour. To these I may also add an account I have been favoured with by Dr. Archer, physician to the Small-pox Hospital here, viz.[7]

There have been inoculated in this Hospital since its first institution to this day, Dec. 31, 1758 — Persons 1601

Of which number died — — 6

Patients who had the Small-pox in the common way in this Hospital, to the same day — — 3856

Of which number have died — — 1002

By this account it appears, that in the way of Inoculation there

discussed the process of inoculation itself; and they described measures to be taken during periods of preparation, illness, and recuperation.

6. Two thousand copies of the pamphlet were printed. BF himself paid £4 2s., the added cost of his own introductory pages. William Strahan's bill, receipted Dec. 31, 1759, below, p. 453. On July 12, 1759, BF noted that he had sent 1500 of the pamphlets to David Hall "to be given away." "Account of Expences," p. 43; *PMHB*, LV (1931), 123. Evidently some of them were still on hand in 1764, because on February 24 of that year BF sent some copies to Jonathan Williams, Sr., to be distributed gratis in Boston and on the following September 24 Dr. Thomas Moffat of Newport thanked him for sending a copy.

7. Dr. Edward Archer (1718–1789) was elected physician to the Smallpox Hospital in 1747. "Under his leadership the Hospital became the center for teaching and research in inoculation methods in England and was visited by all continental physicians interested in the practice." So great was Archer's devotion to the institution that, after serving it for 42 years, he chose to die within its walls. The London Smallpox and Inoculation Hospital was founded in 1746, largely through the efforts of Isaac Maddox, Bishop of Worcester. It provided free inoculation and furnished lodgings at a modest charge. In 1752, in order to accommodate more patients, the hospital moved from Windmill Street to Cold Bath Fields, where its capacity was 130 patients, but even this did not meet the demand and there were always long waiting lists. Genevieve Miller, *The Adoption of Inoculation for Smallpox in England and France* (Phila., 1947), pp. 146–56.

has died but *one* patient in 267, whereas in the common way there had died more than *one* in *four*. The mortality indeed in the latter case appears to have been greater than usual, (one in seven, when the distemper is not very favourable, being reckon'd the common loss in towns by the Small-pox, all ages and ranks taken together) but these patients were mostly adults, and were received, it is said, into the Hospital, after great irregularities had been committed. By the Boston account it appears, that, Whites and Blacks taken together, but about one in eleven died in the common way, and the distemper then was therefore reckon'd uncommonly favourable. I have also obtain'd from the Foundling Hospital,[8] (where all the children admitted, that have not had the Small-pox, are inoculated at the age of five years) an account to this time of the success of that practice there, which stands thus, viz.

Inoculated, boys 162, girls 176, in all   338
Of these died in Inoculation, only   —   —   2
And the death of one of those two was occasioned by a worm fever.

On the whole, if the chance were only as *two* to *one* in favour of the practice among children, would it not be sufficient to induce a tender parent to lay hold of the advantage? But when it is so much greater, as it appears to be by these accounts (in some even as *thirty* to *one*) surely parents will no longer refuse to accept and thankfully use a discovery GOD in his mercy has been pleased to bless mankind with; whereby some check may now be put to the ravages that cruel disease has been accustomed to make, and the human species be again suffered to increase as it did before the Small-pox made its appearance. This increase has indeed been more obstructed by that distemper than is usually imagin'd: For the loss of one in ten thereby is not merely the loss of so many persons, but the accumulated loss of all the children and childrens children the deceased might have had, multiplied by successive generations.   B. FRANKLIN,
of Philadelphia.

8. The Hospital for the Maintenance and Education of Exposed and Deserted Young Children, commonly known as the Foundling Hospital, was incorporated in 1739 and opened its doors on March 25, 1741. Between that date and March 1756, it provided a home for 1384 children. R. H. Nichols and F. A. Wray, *The History of the Foundling Hospital* (London, 1935).

From David Hall Letterbook copy: American Philosophical Society

Sir.   Philadelphia February 27th. 1759.

According to Promise,[9] I have now, by Captain Finglass, sent you the first Copy of another Bill of Exchange for £100. Sterling more,[1] which makes in all remitted you, since you left Philadelphia (besides the £100. protested)[2] £1249 12s. 5d.

If I had known that Captain Finglass would have sailed so soon after Capt. Duncan, I believe I should not have given you any Expectation of a Bill by him;[3] but I did not care to be worse than my word.

This comes under Cover to Peter Collinson Esqr., to whom I have Apologized for the Trouble of conveying it to you. The Reason of my sending it under his Cover, is, I have heard from your Friends that you hinted to them, you had Room to think, some of your Letters were intercepted, the Substance of a Letter of theirs to you having come to Philadelphia, tho' not to them, nor from you.[4] If so, it may have been the Case with the missing Bill,[5] and not paid to a wrong Hand, which I was afraid of; as I imagine if any Directions had been given to stop your Letters, it was more on Account of the Intelligence they might contain, than any thing else. I design to continue sending your Letters to this Gentleman till I shall hear from you to the contrary; and am, Sir Yours &c.

                                                          D H

To Benjamin Franklin Esqr. per the London Capt. Finglass

Copy per Arnold Capt. Cozzin

9. Evidently made in the missing postscript of Hall's letter of Jan. 18, 1759; see above, p. 232 n.

1. This bill, dated Dec. 1, 1758, was drawn by John Hunter on Messrs. Thomlinson, Hanbury, Colebrooke, and Nesbitt, London merchants. "Account of Expences," p. 26; *PMHB*, LV (1931), 117.

2. A bill sent Nov. 12, 1757, had been protested; see above, VII, 236 n.

3. On March 1, 1759, *Pa. Gaz.* reported the clearance of Duncan's ship, the *Carolina;* on March 8, that of Finglass' ship, the *London.*

4. On Sept. 16, 1758, BF had complained to Joseph Galloway that friends of the Proprietors in Philadelphia had sent copies of some of his letters to the Penns in London. See above, p. 151. A garbled version of this complaint was probably the basis of Hall's supposition that letters from Philadelphia to London had been intercepted.

5. For the missing bill, see above, pp. 230–1, and below, p. 320.

Sir   Wellingborough March 17th. 1759.
   I have communicated Yours of the 8th Instant to Mr. Fisher,[6]
who gave me the inclosed Bill of Funeral and other necessary
Expences, to be sent to you for your Satisfaction with regard to
the Distribution of your late Cousin Fishers Estate which according to my Calculation will stand as follows—
Dr.   Administratrix to the Estate late Mrs. Fisher's.   Credr.

	£ s. d.		£ s. d.
To a Legacy be- queathed. by the late Mr. R:Fisher	100:0:0	By necessary Ex- pences.	31: 2:2
To Mrs. Fishers wearing Apparel divided between Mrs. Morris and Mrs. Farrow valued at	11:0:6	By four equal 7th Shares at £11 8s. 4d. each	45:13:4
		By three more at Do.[7]	34: 5:0
	£111:0:6		£111: 0:6

Mr. Fisher (as he gave Bond with Mrs. Farrow for the due Distribution of this personal Estate) approves of your Proposal to
receive the four Shares due to your Relations in America, and will
directly pay £45 13s. 4d. to your Order, on sending a proper Discharge for the Same, and will also pay your Share, which you are
so good as to give them, to Mrs. Morris and Mrs. Farrow.[8] If I

   6. Not found. Rev. William Fisher superintended the administration of
Mary Fisher's estate for Anne Farrow, the administratrix. For matters connected with that estate and identification of other persons mentioned in this
letter, see above, pp. 221–5.
   7. Mary Fisher's estate was divided equally among her seven living first
cousins: four in New England (Samuel Franklin, Elizabeth Douse, Peter
Franklin, and Jane Mecom) and three then in England (Anne Farrow, Eleanor
Morris, and BF).
   8. On July 14, 1759, BF wrote his sister, Jane Mecom, asking her to suggest
in what form he might most satisfactorily send the legacies to her and Elizabeth Douse; see below, p. 415. Mrs. Douse died Aug. 25, 1759, in debt to BF,
so he may never have sent her share; Mrs. Mecom apparently drew on her son
Benjamin, who was also indebted to BF, so that the transfer could become
merely a bookkeeping arrangement. BF to Jane Mecom, Jan. 9, 1760. How

can be of any further Service to You in this, or any other Affair here, I beg you would make no Scruple of sending your Commands to Sir Your very humble Servant THO HOLME.

The Expences of the Funeral of Mrs. Mary Fisher, who was buried Decr. 30. 1758.[9]

	£	s.	d.
Pd. for the Administration for Mrs. Farrow	01	19	04
Gave the Under-bearers	00	06	00
Pd. the washwoman for laying Mrs. Fisher out and for Gloves	00	07	02
Pd. a Woman for helping to lay Her out, and for Gloves	00	07	02
Gave the Servant Jenny for a pair of Gloves	00	01	02
Pd. Mr. Day for five Bottles of Wine	00	09	04
Pd. Mr. Maules Draper's Bill for the Funeral	13	13	00
Pd. the Glazier's Bill for a lead Coffin	07	00	00
Pd. the Carpenter for Coffins and Furniture &c.	04	01	06
Pd. Mr. Lucas the Apothecary	00	18	00
Pd. the Sexton for taking up and laying down the Grave-Stone	00	02	03
Pd. the Sexton for digging the Grave, the Bell and cleaning the Church	00	07	06
Pd. Mr. Holme for the Grave in the Church and a Mortuary	00	16	08
Pd. the Church-Wardens for opening the Grave in the Church	00	06	08
Charges in bringing and carrying Mrs. Farrow home	00	06	06
	31	02	02

These Expences were approved of
by the Administratrix Mrs. Farrow,
and defrayed by me   WM. FISHER sole Executor
                          of the late Mr. Richd Fisher

Addressed: To | Mr. Benjamin Franklin | at Mrs. Stephenson's in Craven Street | Strand | London | Free | WM CARTWRIGHT
Endorsed: Revd Mr Holme March 17. 1759 answd the 27th

the other two American heirs were paid does not appear. On the amounts to which the two elderly English cousins became entitled, see below, p. 302 n.
9. This statement is in a different hand from that of the letter it accompanies.

From Isaac Norris

Letterbook copy: Historical Society of Pennsylvania

Respected Friend B Franklin   March 17th. 1759.

I now enclose Second Bills of Exchange amounting to £362 5s. 2d. Sterling which I request you would be pleased to receive for my Account.[1] This goes by way of Ireland[2] which is One Reason of my sending the Second instead of the First, but the cheif Reason is to get one of the first Bills endorsed which was omitted by oversight and I have not time to stay till it is done without Danger of loosing this Conveyance.

As I may probably lodge some mony in England to lye there some time I leave it to you to place it in the Bank if it gives Interest after making Use of what you may have Occasion for,[3] till our Publick Mony can replace it to me which now is, I presume, near at Hand as we are upon the Supply Bill for the Current Year.

I should be sorry to give any unnecessary trouble on my Account but if it falls in your Way to enquire and let me know the best Manner of placing some Mony in England and the limitation of time in calling it out again it would much oblige &c. I cannot enter on publick News at this Time.   I N

Anthony Stocker on Geo Campbell Mercht in Liverpoole payable in London			£200. 0.–
Ditto	On	Ditto	131. 8.–
Ditto	On	Ditto	30.17.2
55 per Ct Exchange[4]	Sterl payable at 30 Days Sight		£362. 5.2

Endorsed: BF received this acknowledgd 9 June 1759[5]

---

1. BF recorded the receipt of three bills totaling this amount on May 17, 1759. "Account of Expences," p. 27; *PMHB*, LV (1931), 118.

2. The brig *Boscawen,* Capt. Thomas Marshall, cleared for Cork, March 22. *Pa. Gaʒ.*, March 22, 1759.

3. On BF's investments for Norris, see above, p. 148.

4. That is: £155 Pa. currency equaled £100 sterling.

5. No such acknowledgement is found in BF's letter of June 9.

To Isaac Norris

This unusually full and explicit letter describes more clearly than virtually any other contemporary document the attitude of leading members of the ministry on some of the constitutional questions which were to become increasingly important in the relations between the colonies and the mother country during the next fifteen or sixteen years. In the light of what Franklin here reported it is perhaps surprising that he should have believed, five years later, that direct royal government of Pennsylvania would be a substantial improvement over continued control by the Proprietors. On the other hand, his understanding, as early as 1759, of the position which leading British politicians took about fundamental constitutional relationships was almost certainly one factor in conditioning his own thinking when the issue became acute during the years immediately before the American Revolution.

Sir   London, March 19, 1759

In mine of January 19, I acknowledg'd the Receipt of your Favours of November 21. and 23. with the Bills for £500. I have now before me your farther Favours of January 15. and 17.⁷ I heartily congratulate you on the Reduction of Fort Duquesne,⁸ and the Establishment of Peace on your Borders, which I pray God may long continue. To that End I hope the Fort on the Ohio will not be abandon'd; whatever the Indians may propose; for we know by Experience they are not able to keep the French out; and if they return again the Indians will be again debauch'd from our Interest. I hear there are some Pacquets for me on board Bolitho,⁹ I suppose they are the Publick Papers you mention, as ordered to be transmitted to me. I hope to get them tomorrow, and shall be glad to find among them the List of Servants, and Accounts of the Province Disbursements in the last Campaign, pursuant to Mr. Secretary Pitt's Letters; for these will be very necessary in the Application for Reimbursement.¹

---

6. Apparently in WF's hand.

7. For these and the foregoing letters, see above, pp. 174–7, 226–30, etc.

8. The British took Fort Duquesne on Nov. 25, 1758.

9. That is, on board the *Myrtilla*, Capt. John Bolitho.

1. In his letter of Jan. 15, 1759 (above, p. 227), Norris informed BF that he had ordered the clerk of the Pa. Assembly to send him "all necessary Papers," including a list of indentured servants taken into the British army, for whom their masters claimed compensation. On Dec. 30, 1757, and again on Dec.

The Work I mention'd in one of my last Letters, as preparing for the Press, is well nigh finished. It will make near 30 Sheets in 8vo: 23 of which are already printed. It is called *An Historical Review of the Constitution of Pensylvania*, &c. The Dedication is to the Speaker of the House of Commons; and I flatter myself we shall after its Publication, stand in a much fairer Light. I hope by the next Ships to be able to send you one of them.[2]

I long to hear what the Proposals are which the Proprietaries have made to the Assembly.[3] I expect to find them ambiguous, obscure, evasive and empty. But perhaps I am too much prejudic'd; I wish I may find myself mistaken, and that they are really come to their Senses.

They have by some Means or other, obtain'd Copies of some of my Letters to you. One of them they were greatly offended at; it is that wherein I exprest my great Contempt for Thomas, on occasion of his meanly giving up his Father's Honour in the Affair of the Charter.[4] He read it with much Anger to Dr. Fothergill,[5] who blam'd me for writing it, as it gave them a Handle to justify their Refusing to treat farther with me. Yet it is fit that I should give you my Opinion of Persons and Things here, that you may

9, 1758, William Pitt had written the colonial governors that he would recommend that Parliament compensate the colonies for their war expenditures. *Pa. Col. Recs.*, VIII, 27–8, 272–3.

2. This book of Richard Jackson's, written with BF's assistance (see below, p. 361, and BF to Hume, Sept. 27, 1760), was published at the end of May 1759. The speaker to whom it was dedicated was Arthur Onslow (1691–1768). It was an edition of 2000 copies, of which BF sent 500 to David Hall with orders to deliver 50 to the Assembly. He also sent 25 to his nephew Benjamin Mecom and 25 to James Parker in N. Y. "Account of Expences," p. 43; *PMHB*, LV (1931), 121.

3. BF is here referring to the Penns' message to the Assembly of Nov. 28, 1758, which he had not been permitted to see during his exchanges with the Proprietors about the Heads of Complaint. See above, p. 178.

4. The offending letter was BF's to Norris of Jan. 14, 1758 (above, VII, 360–62). Responding to the present letter on July 31, 1759, Norris disclaimed any responsibility for the miscarriage of BF's letters. See below, p. 421.

5. For Dr. John Fothergill, Quaker physician and sometime political adviser to BF, see above, IV, 126 n. Evidently Fothergill wrote Norris about the incident and Norris responded, Aug. 9, 1759, deploring some "exceptional Expressions" that had been used during the controversy but wishing the Proprietors would see that their "True Interest" was "inseperable from the Good of the People." Hist. Soc. Pa.

form right Judgments in your Affairs; tho' if what I am now going to say should be handed back hither, great Inconveniences might ensue, both to those Affairs and me. I confide therefore, that Care will be taken of this Letter, and that it will only be shewn to prudent Persons.

The Prevailing Opinion, as far as I am able to collect it, among the Ministers and great Men here, is, that the Colonies have too many and too great Privileges; and that it is not only the Interest of the Crown but of the Nation to reduce them. An absolute Subjection to Orders sent from hence in the Shape of Instructions, is the Point to be carried if possible. L—d G——[6] who you know is President of the Council told me frankly in a Conversation he honour'd me with on that Head, "Your People in the Colonies refuse Obedience to the King's *Instructions,* and treat them with great Slight, as *not binding,* and *no Law,* in the Colonies; whereas, says his L—p, those Instructions are not like little Pocket Instructions given to an Ambassador or Envoy, in which much may be left to Discretion; they are first drawn up by grave and wise Men learned in the Laws and Constitutions of the Nation; they are then brought to the Council Board, where they are solemnly weigh'd and maturely consider'd, and after receiving such Amendments as are found proper and necessary, they are agreed upon and establish'd. The Council is *over all* the Colonies; your last Resort is to the Council to decide your Differences, and you must be sensible it is for your Good, for otherwise you often could not obtain Justice. The King in Council is THE LEGISLATOR of the Colonies; and when his Majesty's Instructions come there, they are the LAW OF THE LAND; *they are,* said his L—p, repeating it, the Law of the Land, and as such *ought to be* OBEYED."[7] The whole of this Conversation was curious, of which, if I live to have the Pleasure of seeing you again, I will show you the Minutes;[8] they are too

6. John Carteret, first Earl Granville (above, VII, 249 n).

7. There are similar versions of this conversation with Lord Granville in BF to James Bowdoin, Jan. 13, 1772, and in BF's *Autobiography,* APS-Yale edit., p. 261. In both of these places, BF sets the date of this conversation soon after his arrival in England in 1757. Writing to John Adams, April 29, 1781, BF recalled as one of the British "Court Maxims or Assertions" Granville's remark "that *the King is the Legislator of the Colonies,*" and he warned of the danger of trusting British peace offers. Adams MSS, Mass. Hist. Soc.

8. Not found.

long for a Letter. L—d Hardwike,[9] is next at the Council Board; than whom no one is suppos'd to be for carrying the Prerogative higher in all Respects even on this Side the Water; all his Actions they say, on all Occasions, have shown this; and he makes little less Scruple than the President[1] in declaring his Opinions of this kind. These two govern at that Board, so that one may easily conjecture what Reception a Petition concerning Privileges from the Colonies may meet with from those who are known to think that even the People of England have too many. As to the Board of Trade,[2] you know who presides and governs all there,[3] and if his Sentiments were no other ways to be known, the fruitless Experiment he has try'd at the Nation's Cost, of a military Government for a Colony, sufficiently shows what he thinks would be best for us.[4] The Speaker of the House,[5] indeed, is look'd on as a stanch Friend to Liberty; and so is the Secretary Mr. Pitt;[6] the Attorney General[7] is likewise *inclin'd* to that Side in all Questions, tho' the Nature of his Office requires him to be something of a

9. Philip Yorke, first Earl of Hardwicke (1690–1764), was an eminent lawyer who, during his term as lord chancellor, 1737–1756, "transformed equity from a chaos of precedents into a scientific system." *DNB.* The name was originally written "L—d H—" and "Council" as C——L." The blanks were filled in later, probably by Norris.

1. Originally written "P—t" and filled in later.

2. Originally written "B— of T—" and filled in later.

3. George Montagu Dunk, Earl of Halifax (1716–1771), was president of the Board of Trade, 1748–61.

4. In 1749, Halifax had sponsored the colonization of Nova Scotia with British subjects and the establishment of a civil government there. The new colony had a distinctly military flavor, most of its early governors were army or navy officers, and it had no elective assembly until October 1758—an omission which led some settlers to leave in discontent. Yet the colony was not ruled by martial law and its settlers were promised "all the liberties, privileges and immunities enjoyed by His Majesty's Subjects in any other of the Colonies and Plantations in America." Thomas B. Atkins, ed., *Selections from the Public Documents of the Province of Nova Scotia,* I (Halifax, 1869), 709–42; John B. Brebner, *New England's Outpost Acadia before the Conquest of Canada* (N.Y., 1927), chap. 7.

5. Arthur Onslow. Jackson's *Historical Review* was dedicated to him.

6. With one eleven-week interruption in 1757, William Pitt (1708–1778), the "Great Commoner," was secretary of state for the Southern Department, Dec. 4, 1756, to Oct. 5, 1761. As such he had supreme direction of the war, the American colonies, and foreign affairs. *DNB.*

7. Charles Pratt; see above, p. 3 n.

Prerogative Man; but the Sollicitor General[8] who is L H—'s *Son* is wholly and strongly tinctur'd with high Notions of the Prerogative, imbibed from his Father, and may be said to be dy'd in grain.

From this Sketch of Leading Characters, you will judge, that if the Proprietor does not agree with us, our best Chance in an Application is directly to Parliament; and yet that at this Time is something hazardous, for tho' there are many Members in both Houses who are Friends to Liberty and of noble Spirits, yet a good deal of Prejudice still prevails against the Colonies, the Courtiers think us not sufficiently obedient; the illicit Trade from Holland, &c. greatly offends the Trading and Manufactoring Interest; and the Landed Interest begin to be jealous of us as a Corn Country, that may interfere with them in the Markets to which they export that Commodity:—I wish indeed that the illicit Trade could be wholly prevented, for it is not to be justified.[9] As to other Things, I am meditating a Pamphlet[1] that I hope may help to introduce less partial, more generous, and sounder Politicks.

Smith is here, and by the Help of Paris worries the Attorney and Solicitor General for a Report on his Case, who did not intend to make any. The Attorney is greatly perplex'd, angry with the Council for referring the Affair to them, and with Smith for urging a Report;[2] He has open'd his Mind to a Friend of mine[3] on this Head; says, "the Council he knows are for Clipping the Wings of Assemblies in their Claims of all the Privileges of a House of Commons;[4] the House of Commons are thought to claim too many,

8. In the margin: "Mr. Yorke," probably added by Norris. This was Charles Yorke (1722–1770), second son of the Earl of Hardwicke, lord chancellor; see above, p. 3 n.

9. In later years BF condemned smuggling, not only by Americans but by Englishmen as well. In a letter to *London Chron.*, Nov. 24, 1767, he attacked evasion of the customs laws and argued that the colonists who smuggled were less at fault, since they had no share in passing those laws, than Englishmen, who were represented in the Parliament that enacted them.

1. Possibly *The Interest of Great Britain Considered, With Regard to her Colonies, And the Acquisitions of Canada and Guadeloupe,* published in 1760.

2. William Smith reached England on Jan. 1, 1759, to expedite his petition to the King against the Pa. Assembly which had arrested him for allegedly promoting and abetting a libel against it. See above, pp. 28–9.

3. Probably Richard Jackson.

4. The Assemblies of all the colonies, West Indian as well as Continental,

some very unfit and unreasonable, and not for the common Good; but the Council have let the Colonies go on so long in this Way that it will now be difficult to restrain them; and the Council would now make the Attorney and Sollicitor the first Instruments of so odious a Measure; that they (the Council) should have carried it into Parliament, but they are afraid the Parliament would establish more Liberty in the Colonies than is proper or necessary, and therefore do not care the Parliament should meddle at all with the Government of the Colonies; they rather chuse to carry every Thing there by the *Weight of Prerogative,* which by Degrees may bring Things to a proper Situation. Most Attorney Generals (he said) would immediately do what they knew would be pleasing to the Council; but he could not: He must however make some kind of Report." This is the Substance of his Discourse to my Friend, who communicated it to me with Leave to mention it to you and the Committee, as it contains some Hints that are of Importance, but it is to go no farther. It is some Comfort that the Council are doubtful of the Parliament. The West India Interest in the House,[5] in any general Attack on the Colonies would doubtless be of use to us, and perhaps that may be a little apprehended, and it may be thought not proper to disoblige those Members as they make a considerable Body: But at the same Time it is known here, that if the Ministry make a Point of carrying *any thing* in Parliament, they can carry it. On the whole, it is conjectur'd the Attorney and Sollicitor General's Report, will be of a special kind; some Censure perhaps pass'd on Modes and Expressions in your Proceeding; but the general Authority of an Assembly not impeach'd. This, however, is only Conjecture.

Last Tuesday I attended the Funeral of our old Agent Mr.

---

modeled themselves as far as possible on the House of Commons in organization and procedure and especially in their claims to parliamentary privilege. In this last respect they were particularly zealous in punishing outsiders for alleged contempt, as the Pa. Assembly did in the case of William Smith. Mary P. Clarke, *Parliamentary Privilege in the American Colonies* (New Haven, 1943).

5. Numerous West India planters lived in England for long periods and some of them gained seats in the House of Commons. Together with British merchants, both in and out of the House, interested in the sugar trade, these absentee planters constituted a politically strong group: "the West India Interest."

Patridge.[6] I hear some Application will be made from this Side, to have another appointed in his Stead; but I own I do not see the Necessity of it at least for the present. If indeed we could get a Member of Parliament to patronize us and our Affairs, (which I know will be in our Power after the next Election) it might be of great Service;[7] but any Thing that is to be done at the Offices, one Person can do as well as 20. The House however will do what they find best.

My Petition concerning the Indian Lands is refer'd by the Council to the Board of Trade,[8] who as yet have not appointed any Hearing, or taken any other Step in it; but I shall press it forward.

I have also lodg'd a Petition at the Admiralty for a Guard Ship;[9] and hope to obtain some Answer before this Ship sails, that you may know whether you are to expect one or not.

With the greatest Respect and Esteem, I am Dear Sir, Your most obedient and most humble Servant   B FRANKLIN[1]

To Isaac Norris, Esqr.

Endorsed: London Mar 19th. 1759 Benjamin Franklin Esqr. recd July 13th. 1759

To Israel Pemberton   LS:[2] Boston Public Library

Dear Sir,   London, March 19, 1759.

I received your Favour of December 11, and January 19.[3] By those Ships you will receive some of the printed Enquiries,[4] to

6. Richard Partridge (above, v, 11–12 n) died on March 6, 1759.

7. BF had Richard Jackson in mind for the agency, as he wrote Galloway, April 7, 1759; see below, p. 309. What other possible applicant BF may have heard of is not known.

8. See above, pp. 264–76.

9. See above, p. 220 n.

1. Immediately below BF's signature Isaac Norris wrote: "C N brought to Fairhill July 13 1759"; that is, his brother Charles Norris had brought the letter to Isaac's estate on that day.

2. Apparently in WF's hand.

3. For the letter of Dec. 11, see above, pp. 211–13; that of Jan. 19, has not been found.

4. On Charles Thomson's *An Enquiry into the Causes of the Alienation of the Delaware and Shawanese Indians from the British Interest* and BF's part in its publication, see above, pp. 199–200.

which Post's first Journal is added, which being more generally interesting, occasions the other to go into more Hands and be more read. Extracts of your and Mr. Thomson's Letters are also added to make the Thing more compleat. Mr. Hall has Orders to deliver 25 to you and Mr. Thomson;[5] and I hope you will promote the Sale of the rest, that the Charges of Printing &c. may be lessen'd.

I congratulate you heartily on the Re-establishment of Peace on your Borders, in which the Endeavours of your Association[6] have had so large a Share. I pray that it may long continue: But if we abandon Pittsburg at the Instances of the Indians, I think the French will not fail to return; the Indians are too much divided and irresolute to prevent them; and they will easily again be debauch'd from our Interest. I hope therefore that Place will be retain'd; and at least a small Tract distinctly mark'd out round it, from which those who inhabit the Fort may raise their Provisions, but not suffered to extend Settlements beyond such Bounds as are agreed on; till future Treaties shall make farther Agreements. A Hunting Country ought without Doubt to be secur'd to our Friends; but a strong Place and a small compact Settlement there of sober orderly People, must I think, in the Nature of Things, contribute greatly to the Security of the Colonies; by retaining the Friendship of the Indians thro' the Benefits of Trade and Neighbourhood of Arts; and by bridling them if they are seduc'd by our Enemies; or at least standing in the Gap and bearing the Blows as a Shield to our other Frontiers.

I have just receiv'd the Copy of Post's second Journal which will be of good Use;[7] and I am extremely oblig'd to you for your Care in sending every Thing that is necessary to give us proper Information of the present State of Indian Affairs.

5. See below, p. 322.

6. The "Friendly Association for Regaining and Preserving Peace with the Indians by Pacific Measures," a group founded in 1756 by Pemberton and other Quakers. See above, VII, 18 n.

7. BF saw to the publication of Post's "second Journal." Strahan's press issued it on June 5, 1759, under the title *The Second Journal of Christian Frederick Post, on a Message from the Governor of Pensilvania to the Indians on the Ohio.* Five hundred copies were published at a cost of £6 15s. On July 12, 1759, BF noted that he had sent David Hall 300 copies of the second Journal. "Account of Expences," p. 43; *PMHB*, LV (1931), 123.

My Petition relating to Teedyuscung's Claims[8] lay long in the Council Office before there was a Council to consider it. As soon as a Council met, it was read and referr'd to the Board of Trade.[9] As yet they have done nothing in it, but I understand they intend to appoint Commissioners out of the neighbouring Provinces to make Enquiry, examine Evidences, and report what they can find to be the Truth of the Case.[1]

It is every where represented here by the Proprietor's Friends, that this Charge of the Indians against him, is a mere Calumny, stirr'd up by the Malice of the Quakers, who cannot forgive his deserting their Sect.[2] I expected he would be imprudent enough to publish the Report of his Council in his Justification;[3] but I hear Nothing of it, and suppose he does not quite like it. There are some shameless Falshoods in it that are easily expos'd. The Affidavits mention'd in it are not come to hand;[4] I wish I could see them.

I believe it will in time be clearly seen by all thinking People, that the Government and Property of a Province should not be in the same Family. 'Tis too much Weight in one Scale. I am of

8. See above, pp. 264–76.

9. This statement is not wholly accurate. The Privy Council referred the petition to its Committee on Plantation Affairs, Feb. 2, 1759, but the Committee did not refer it to the Board of Trade in turn until April 12, more than three weeks after BF wrote this letter. *Acts Privy Coun., Col.,* IV, 402; *Board of Trade Journal,* 1759–63, p. 32. These two steps were routine procedure in such matters; BF apparently thought of them as a single, already completed action.

1. The source of this rumor is not known; on the Board of Trade's recommendation the Privy Council, Aug. 29, 1759, ordered Sir William Johnson, superintendent of Indian affairs, to conduct the inquiry. *Acts Privy Coun., Col.,* IV, 402–3.

2. The Delaware Indians had charged the Proprietors with forgery and land fraud. Thomas Penn had given up Quaker dress and opinions on defense as early as 1743, and after his marriage in 1751 regularly attended the Church of England, in which his children were baptized, though he never received the Sacrament. Howard M. Jenkins, "The Family of William Penn," *PMHB,* XXI (1897), 339, 343.

3. This report, purporting to exonerate the Proprietors, was completed by a committee of the Pa. Council, Jan. 6, 1758, but was not entered in its minutes until Jan. 20, 1759. *Pa. Col. Recs.,* VIII, 246–61. BF, who had received a copy, called it a "miserable" performance. See above, p. 158.

4. Several of these were by men who had in some way participated in the Walking Purchase of 1737.

Opinion, the Crown would not be displeas'd with an Application to be taken under its immediate Government, and I think our Circumstances would be mended by it.[5]

My Son joins in best Respects and Wishes for you and yours, with, Dear Sir, Your affectionate Friend and humble Servant

B FRANKLIN

Mr. Pemberton

Addressed: To | Mr Israel Pemberton | Mercht | Philada | per Pacquet | via N. York

Endorsed: London March 19th. 1759. From Benjn. Franklin.

Josiah Franklin Davenport[6] to Deborah Franklin

ALS: American Philosophical Society

Honoured Aunt   March. 22d. 1759

I have been Confin'd since Saturday last with a fever, altho now abated I am advised by Doctor Redman[7] not to go abroad, Which is the Occasion I now write my Business.

I have sold my House to Mr. Waiscott,[8] and he has just been here and tells me the deeds are finish'd, and that he is to undertake a Journey on Saturday morning from Which he Shall not return for some time, and Withal has agreed with Workmen to repair the House in his Absence, And as there is a Ballance due to Uncle on it,[9] we want that Settled before the deed is executed. I left with Uncle the Lease &c. and when he went away I Told him I should sell the House before his return, to which he approv'd and told me

5. Since the spring of 1758, at least, BF had been contemplating royal government as a solution of the difficulties in Pa. See above, pp. 6–21, 88.

6. BF's nephew (C.12.4). He was now secretary to the Pa. Indian commissioners.

7. John Redman was a leading Philadelphia physician; see above, v, 356 n.

8. Not identified.

9. Davenport had conveyed the rent of this house to BF to repay the principal and interest on a loan from his uncle. In his will of 1757 BF directed his executors to pay the interest towards the support and education of one of Davenport's children, recently blinded by smallpox. In the same will he made his nephew a contingent beneficiary of the income of his printing house and bequeathed each of Davenport's children outright the sum of £10. See above, VII, 202–3.

he should leave the papers With You, and that you and I could settle as Well as if he was Present.

I should be Glad if you'd please to look them up, as the Deed must be executed tomorrow, and if it don't suit you to Come here perhaps you can Get Mr. Dunlap;[1] The money is ready to discharge it. It will be a detriment to Mr. Waiscott if it is not finished to morrow. I am Honoured Madam Your Dutifull Nephew

J. F. DAVENPORT

Instrument to Uncle. Bond's two £100 each one for Security one from Dr. Kearsley.[2] Waiscotts Lease.

Addressed: To / Mrs. Deborah Franklin / Per Pent[3]

From David Hall   Letterbook copy: American Philosophical Society

Sir   Philadelphia 24th March. 1759

Inclosed you have the second Copy of a Bill of Exchange for One hundred Pounds Sterling No. 945[4] Likewise the first Copy of another Bill for the same Sum;[5] which makes in all remitted you by me, since you left Philadelphia Thirteen Hundred Forty Nine pounds twelve Shillings and five pence Sterling, which as usual, you will give me Credit for, and advice of the Payment. I am Yours &c.   D HALL

To Benjamin Franklin Esqr per Arnold Capt Cuzzins

This Letter sent under Cover to Peter Collinson Esqr.[6]

NB the Number of the Bill is 4410. Exchange 55.

Second Copy by the General Wall Packet Captain Lutwyche April 9. 1759.

1. William Dunlap, husband of one of DF's nieces and postmaster of Philadelphia; see above, V, 199 n; VII, 168–9.

2. Either Dr. John Kearsley (above, V, 20 n) or his nephew of the same name (above, VII, 110 n).

3. Not identified.

4. On Feb. 27, 1759, Hall advised BF that he was sending him the first copy of this bill, and BF recorded its receipt, April 9, 1759. See above, p. 287; "Account of Expences," p. 26; *PMHB*, LV (1931), 117.

5. BF recorded the receipt of this bill, number 4410, drawn by Leonard Jarvis of Boston on Messrs. William and Richard Baker, London merchants, on May 29, 1759. "Account of Expences," p. 27; *PMHB*, LV (1931), 118.

6. For Hall's use of Collinson as a cover, see above, p. 287.

To Thomas Holme

Draft: Historical Society of Pennsylvania

Reverend Sir   London, March 27. 1759

I received your Favour of the 17th. Instant,[7] with the Accounts, which are clear and satisfactory. And as you are so kind as to offer any farther Service in this Affair, may I take the Freedom to request you would make and send me a Draft of such a Discharge for me to sign, as will be proper and satisfactory to Mr. Fisher? If the Money could be paid by an Order or Bill on some Person here in London, it would be most convenient to me. Mrs. Morris was with me on Saturday, and desires, as she cannot go down to Wellingborough, her Share may be paid to me with the others, and She will receive it here of me. I am, with great Esteem, Reverend Sir, Your most obedient humble Servant,   B F

[*On the back:*][8]

34.	5.			31.	2.	2
11.	0.	6		45.	13.	4
23.	4.	6		23.	4.	6
11.	7.	3		100.	0.	0

From Isaac Norris

Letterbook copy: Historical Society of Pennsylvania

My Friend B Franklin   March 28. 1759

This serves to cover Bills of Exchange as per List hereunder and to inform you that our Supply Bill lyes with the Governor now the

7. See above, pp. 221–5, 288–9, for the persons mentioned and the matters treated in this letter.

8. The left-hand column is obviously BF's attempt to determine how much Anne Farrow and Eleanor Morris should each receive in cash from Mary Fisher's estate. Their two one-seventh shares of the total estate after the payment of funeral expenses, plus his own share that he was dividing between them, totaled £34 5s. (3 times £11 8s. 4d.). Deducting £11 0s. 6d., the value of the clothing already given them as part of their inheritance, he found they should together receive £23 4s. 6d. in cash. He divided this amount by two and got a figure of £11 7s. 3d., but here he slipped, for the result should have been £11 12s. 3d., as the cash distribution to each woman. His right-hand column shows the disposition of the £100 cash in the estate: the funeral expenses, the shares of the four cousins in America, and the amount to be divided between the two women in England.

24 Inst including the Proprietary Estates[9] and granting £100,000 for the Raising &c. of 2,700 Men but I shall refer to another Letter for further Particulars on that Head[1] and propose this as a seperate Cover to the Bills of Exchange. I am &c.

Anthony Stoker on Geo Campbell 1st Bill	£200.0.
Do Do	131.8
Do Do	30.17.2
	£362.5.2[2]

By Captn Cuzzens

BF. recd this Letter ackd. June 9th. 1759[3]

From Isaac Norris

Two Letterbook copies:[4] Historical Society of Pennsylvania

Dear Friend B Franklin   Philada. Aprl. 5. 1759

I have already wrote by Captain Cuzzins inclosing Bills of Exchange.[5] So that I now only inclose a First Bill which I have since purchased drawn by John Hunter[6] on Messrs. Thomlinson Hanbury Colebrooke and Nesbit Merchants in London No. 1049 for £200. Sterling[7] which I have ordered payable to your Self or Order which please to reserve for my Account.

I dined Yesterday with Col. Hunter who informs me that Mony may be lodged in the Bank on Parliamentary Interest for any Time and drawn out as it is wanted without any previous Notice, if this is so as I think it is, pray be so kind as to lodge the Monies arising

9. On March 24, the Pa. Assembly passed and sent to Governor Denny a supply bill containing the customary and controversial provision for the taxation of proprietary estates. *Votes,* 1758–59, p. 46.

1. See below, pp. 304, 326–7.

2. BF recorded the receipt of these bills on May 17, 1759. "Account of Expences," p. 27; *PMHB,* LV (1931), 118.

3. BF's letter to Norris of June 9, 1759, contains no such acknowledgement; see below, pp. 396–404.

4. The longer of the two versions, on p. 103, has been used, rather than that on pp. 97–8.

5. See immediately above.

6. For Col. John Hunter, agent for Thomlinson & Hanbury, see above, VI, 223 n, VII, 254 n.

7. BF recorded the receipt of this bill on May 29, 1759. "Account of Expences," p. 27; *PMHB,* LV (1931), 118.

from the Bills I have remitted in the Bank for further Orders as Occasion may require.[8] Our Supply Bill for granting £100,000 and 2,700 Men to his Majesty[9] has been refused in plain Terms because the Governor is restricted by Proprietary Orders and cannot pass it, but adds that he will be willing to pass such a Bill as he gave his Assent to the last Year (which exempts the Proprietary Estate).[1] I am of Opinion that if our present Supply Bill does not pass; The House will frame a new Bill exempting the Proprietors granting about £80,000 and 2,000 Men instead of the Number and Sum in the present Bill to make up for the Proprietary Deficiency.[2] The House, I think will not come into the Governor's Proposals as they have already declared by an Unanimous Resolve,[3] but have agreed to a Bill which will be ready to be sent up this Day granting the Men and Mony as in their former Bill with an Additional Clause declaring that the Proprietary free Gift of £5,000 (about £600 of which is Still unpaid)[4] shall be accounted for as part of the Grants heretofore made by this Province since the Excise Act[5] and shall accept it as a proportion of the £55,000 and the two £100,000 Grants[6] and if it exceeds the proportion the Proprietaries ought to pay upon the Several Acts he shall take Credit for the Overplus upon the present Grant, and on the Other Hand if it falls Short of this equitable proportion they are to make up the Deficiency. What Success this Bill, thus framed, will meet

8. These first lines of the paragraph are marked in the margin with a line and the notation: "See p. 97 a loose small paper inclosed viz." The lines are not included in the other letterbook copy. For BF's investments on Norris' behalf, see above, p. 148.

9. For fuller details on this supply bill, see below, pp. 326–7.

1. For the supply bill enacted on April 22, 1758, see above, pp. 54–5.

2. This sentence is inserted in the margin and does not appear in the other letterbook copy.

3. On April 2, 1759, the Assembly resolved "unanimously in the Negative" to a proposal for exempting the proprietary estates from taxation. *Votes,* 1758–59, p. 55.

4. For the proprietary gift of £5000, see above, VI, 257 n.

5. While Norris may be referring to the Excise Act passed on May 26, 1744, it seems more likely that the reference here is to the Excise Act, raising £30,000 "for the King's service," passed on Sept. 21, 1756. *Statutes at Large, Pa.,* IV, 395–407; V, 243–61.

6. For the three grants referred to, see above, VI, 257 n; VII, 152–3, and this volume, pp. 54–5.

with, I have not heard but as it seems probable that the different Instructions from what they formerly were may yet be continued with sufficient precautions against having their Estates taxed in any Manner an Assembly regardful of the Rights of their Constituents can pass I presume it may meet the Fate of our Other Supply Bills of which we shall be able to send an Account in a very few Days for the Season presses and we cannot sit much longer.[7] I shall give Directions to the Clerk to Copy these Minutes if they can be got ready for Captain Cuzzins or at least to go by the Packet.[8] We were a little disappointed on the Arrival of the Packet to hear nothing from you as She brought Advices to near the Middle of February but we have received the Letters by Capt. Nicholson dated in November last which I will endeavour to Answer more fully by the Packet.[9] In the mean Time that I may not loose this opportunity I shall Conclude Your Assured Friend

I N

Endorsed: B F acknowled the receipt of this Letter June 9. 1759

To Deborah Franklin

LS (incomplete):[1] American Philosophical Society

[*c.* April 7, 1759][2]

[*First part missing*] By the same I shall write to dear Precious, Cousin Debby,[3] and some other Friends. I have now only to let

7. On the final passage of this bill, see below, p. 327 n.

8. Norris presumably means the exchanges between Denny and the Assembly, concerning the supply bill; they may be found in *Votes,* 1758–59, pp. 52, 55. The *General Wall* packet, Capt. Walter Lutwidge, arrived in New York, March 15, and sailed again, April 16, 1759. *New-York Mercury,* March 19, April 16, 1759.

9. On April 5, 1759, *Pa. Gaʒ.* records the arrival of Capt. George Nicholson of the *Rebecca and Susanna* the day before. None of BF's November letters to Pa. have been found.

1. Only two pages (one leaf) from the middle of a longer letter have been found. Most of what survives is in WF's hand, though BF signed it and made several insertions, some of which are noted as such below.

2. The note following the signature, together with the dated postscript, indicates that the first part of this letter was written no later than April 7, when BF wrote the letter to Galloway which is printed immediately following this one.

3. Deborah Croker Dunlap, DF's niece. She was the wife of William Dun-

you know what I have sent in these Ships. There are two or 3 Boxes; Mr. Neate shipt them, but I know not on board which Ship, as he has not sent me the Bills of Lading. They were shipt on board [the] Cornelia Capt. Smith two Boxes and a Leaden Case, mark'd BF No 1. 2. 3.[4] The Contents are[5]

A Parmesan Cheese, at 20*d.* per Pound cost [I believe this is put in a Box by itself, tho' first cover'd with a Lead Case: If so there are 3 Boxes][6]		£7:10:6

In the square Box.

Norden's Egypt, 2 Vols. Folio, for Mr. Wright[7]	4: 4:0
A small Book of Husbandry, and Madam Maintenon's Letters[8] } for Do.	0: 6:0
New System of Husbandry, Fol. for Mr. Galloway	1:15:0
Pamphlets for Mr. Norris and Mr. Galloway about [*illegible*]	1: 1:0
Cruels[9] for Sally	0:16:10½
Shoes 2 Pair for Debby Franklin[1]	1: 5:6
Pins and Needles for Ditto	0:17:6½
Piece of rich Tabby[2] for Do. at 9*s.* per yard about	6:15:0

lap, whom BF had appointed postmaster of Philadelphia before leaving for England; see above, VII, 168–9.

4. This sentence, in BF's hand, is added in the margin with marks for insertion here.

5. Nearly all the articles in this shipment are recorded in "Account of Expences," pp. 37, 38, either individually or lumped together with the entry: "Sent sundry things to Mrs. Franklin that cost £33 10*s.*" A notation with these entries in the account book reads: "Sent per Capt. Smith in the Cornelia." The entries were omitted by Eddy in *PMHB*, LV (1931), 97–133.

6. Brackets in the original.

7. Friderik Ludvig Norden, *Travels in Egypt and Nubia . . . Translated from the Original . . . and Enlarged . . . by T. Templeman* (2 vols., London, 1757). BF bought the work for James Wright of Hempfield, Pa.; see below, p. 411.

8. Probably *Letters of Madame de Maintenon. Translated from the French* (2 vols., London, 1759). Just which books on husbandry BF was sending to Wright and Galloway (immediately below) is uncertain, but see above, VII, 176 n.

9. Yarns for crewel embroidery.

1. That is, for DF.

2. Any of several fabrics in plain, or taffeta, weave.

Deborah Franklin

Persian Lining for Do. 12 yards at 2*s*.	1: 4:0
Gloves for Do.	1: 4:0
Court Plaster for Sally	0: 1:0
2 Gilt Silver Cups, fit for nothing but to give Drams in to Indian Kings: They were struck off to me unexpectedly at an Auction	0:18:8
A Candle Screen to save Debby's Eyes[3]	0: 7:6
Milton for I. Norris Esqr.[4]	0:16:0
Some Colliflour and Brocoliseed	
In the long Box	
1 lb. Sealing Wax for I. Norris Esqr.	0: 7:6
Arnold on Music for C. Cash 2 vols.[5]	0: 5:6
Female Conduct[6] for Sally, from her Brother	0: 4:6
2 Pieces of Ticks	4: 0:0
1 Piece of rich Pink and Green ¾ Sattin strip'd Lutestring,[7] 15 Yards at 9*s*. Newest Fashion for Sally	6:15:0
A Sponge for BF. put it in his Room	0: 1:0
A Barometer and a Thermometer for Mr. Hughes:	3: 7:6
Thermometer for C. Norris, Esqr. about 17*s*. but have mislaid the Acct [*In margin,* BF *hand:*] It is 18[8]	0:17:0
Ditto for James Wright	1:11:6
2 Canvas Patterns in a Marble Case	0: 6:9
Newton's Milton for B.F. put it in his Room	0:16:-
Reading Glass and Labels for Mrs. Franklin	0:15:0

The Reading Glass is set in Silver and Tortoise Shell; the Pattern pretty and I imagine the Glass may suit your Eyes: If not, you can present it to some Friend.

3. The last four words are in BF's hand.

4. This and the next to last item on the list refer to copies of [John Milton], *Paradise Lost . . . From the Text of Thomas Newton.* Printed by John Baskerville, for J. and R. Tonson in London: Birmingham, 1758. See above, pp. 157, 230.

5. Probably John Arnold, *The Compleat Psalmodist. In 4 Books* (4th edit., London, 1756). Caleb Cash (F.6.2) was DF's first cousin once removed.

6. Not identifiable among many popular works on this theme.

7. A plain, stout, lustrous silk.

8. So recorded in "Account of Expences," p. 38.

God be with you, my dear Child, and give us once more a happy Meeting. My Love to my dear Sally; for whose Recovery I am very thankful.[9] My Duty to Mother, and Love to all our Relations and Friends. I am Your ever loving Husband   B FRANKLIN

Per Pacquet I shall write to the Speaker, Mr. Galloway and Mr. Hughes.[1]

P.S. April 11. I have now time to answer the rest of your Letters.[2] I received no Gammons by Bolitho, and suppose they are to come by Cuzzins. All that I had before are gone; they were much admired: I have still a Piece of one of the Pieces of Beef from which we now and then get a Bit. I never receiv'd any Cranberry's from Boston.

I think the old Present of Buckskins or best Buckskin Gloves would be acceptable to your Birmingham Friends.[3] I wish you had sent some of them. I forwarded your Letter but have not since heard from them.

My Love to Cousin Spofford:[4] I forwarded her Letter in to the Country when I first came to England, but have forgot how or where it was directed.

I received your Letter by Mr. North.[5] I should have ask'd him to dine here with Capt. Bolitho, but found there was some Difference between them.

I lament the Death of our Friend Mifflin![6] by all outward Appearances, one might have expected a long Life for a Man of his Constitution and Temperance, but there is no Dependance on Appearances.

9. Nothing is known of this illness.

1. The letters to Norris and Hughes have not been found; that to Galloway follows this document.

2. This sentence inserted in BF's hand above the line.

3. For DF's Birmingham relatives BF had met during the previous summer, see above, pp. 138–46.

4. Not identified; probably a relative of DF.

5. DF's letter not found. The letter carrier may have been John North (E.2.6), DF's first cousin once removed, a resident of Pa. If so, he must have voyaged to England with Capt. John Bolitho in the *Myrtilla,* which reached Deal on March 12 on its way to London; *London Chron.,* March 10–13, 1759.

6. John Mifflin; see above, 1, 373 n; he was seven years younger than BF. William Logan wrote in his interleaved copy of *A Pocket Almanack* for 1759 opposite the page for February: "11. Jno Mifflin buried." Yale Univ. Lib.

I have receiv'd the State of Mr. Smith's Account.[7] There are some Mistakes in it, which I shall endeavour to get rectify'd when I see Mr. [*remainder missing*].

To Joseph Galloway   LS: Yale University Library

Mr. Galloway
Dear Sir,   London April 7, 1759
I have your Favours of November 18 and February 9.[8] Since my last[9] our old Agent Mr. Patridge is deceas'd.[1] You see something of my Friend Mr. Jackson in his Opinion and private Paper of Advice on our Affairs, which I last year transmitted to you.[2] He is a Gentleman of considerable Fortune, and no Man in England has a greater Regard for the Colonies. He has made American Affairs his Study for some Years past, and is extreamly well acquainted with them. He has made considerable Purchases of Lands in the Colonies,[3] so that in point of Interest he is in some Degree an American. He will undoubtedly be chosen a Member in the next Parliament, it being settled that he is to come in by the ministerial Interest.[4] If this should happen, I think we could not make a more happy Choice of a Patron in that House, to act as our principal Agent, for he will certainly have great Weight in the House, being already in high Esteem with many of the present leading Members. I mention this to you because I fancy some Proposals will be made from this Side to have another appointed immediately in Mr. Patridge's Room, which I do not think necessary; and am of Opinion that if we continue to employ two Agents,

7. Not identified.

8. Neither letter has been found.

9. That of Sept. 16, 1758 (above, pp. 149–52), is the last letter that has been found, although others may have been written in the meantime.

1. Richard Partridge (v, 11–12 n) died on March 6, 1759.

2. See above, pp. 20–7.

3. Jackson owned a farm in Kent, Connecticut. Carl Van Doren, ed., *Letters and Papers of Benjamin Franklin and Richard Jackson 1753–1785* (Phila., 1947), p. 6.

4. Jackson was returned to Parliament at a special election in 1762 by the conjoint borough of Weymouth and Melcombe Regis. *DNB*. It would appear that he was disappointed by his failure to win a seat in the general election of 1761. Jackson to BF, April 4, 1763, APS.

one should be a Member of Parliament,[5] whose Weight and Influence with the Ministry may stand us in good Stead on Occasion; and as no considerable Member, tho' he might esteem it an Honour to be consider'd as the Patron of a great Province, would care to submit to the Drudgery of running about and attending the Offices with every little Solicitation, there should be an Assistant Agent for that Purpose, which I think Mr. Charles under good Direction will execute very well. This you will consider of: I have hinted it to Mr. Jackson, and find him not averse to it.[6] He has propos'd to get me elected on the same Interest, and is sure he can effect it; but I am too old to think of changing Countries, [I?] am almost weary of Business, and languish after Repose and my America.

I am now in daily Expectation of hearing from you what kind of Proposals the Proprietor has made the Assembly for an Accommodation, and what Resolutions the House take thereupon.[7] I wish I may be wrong in my Opinion, that you will find them obscure, uncertain and evasive, like his Answer to the Heads of Complaint,[8] of which I have sent Copies. In the meantime we are just on the point of publishing a Piece, intitled A Review of the Constitution of Pensylvania;[9] it will make an 8vo. Volume, and is all printed but the Appendix, which will be done in a few Days, tho' perhaps not Time enough to send any Copies by these Ships. I hope this Work will put a finishing Stroke to the Prejudices that have prevail'd against us, set the Proprietary Character and Conduct in their proper Lights, and without expresly taking Notice of

5. BF had suggested this to Norris, March 19, 1759, above p. 297.

6. On April 2, 1763, the Pa. Assembly appointed Jackson its agent at "the Court of Great Britain for the ensuing Year." *Votes,* 1762–63, pp. 41–2. Robert Charles had resigned his agency in 1761 because the Assembly had refused to honor an agreement, designed to insure the equitable assessment of the proprietary estates, which he and BF had made with the Proprietors on Aug. 28, 1760. Nicholas Varga, "Robert Charles: New York Agent, 1748–1770," 3 *William and Mary Quar.,* XVIII (April, 1961), 214.

7. For the Proprietors' message to the Assembly, Nov. 28, 1758, see above, pp. 184–6. Gov. Denny laid it before the House on Feb. 27, 1759, which studiously ignored it in later addresses and in transmitting a supply bill on March 24. 8 *Pa. Arch.,* VI, 4923–5, 4932–4; *Pa. Col. Recs.,* VIII, 276–81, 299–301.

8. See above, pp. 179–83.

9. See below, pp. 360–1.

the infamous Libellers they have employ'd or encourag'd, fully expose and confute their Falshoods and Calumnies.

Smith (now we talk of Libellers) is here, dancing Attendance on the Attorney and Sollicitor General to obtain a Report. They are very unwilling to make one,[1] but perhaps may at length be teas'd into it by Paris, who is a most malicious and inveterate Enemy to our Province. I have reason to believe, however, that if they censure any Thing in the Conduct of the Assembly, it will be Modes and not Essentials: But of this I cannot yet be certain; and am determin'd to renew the Contest in a Hearing before the Council, if the Report appears likely to prejudice our Privileges.[2] This may perhaps keep Smith longer an Expence to his Supporters with you than they will care to bear, tho' 'tis said they have sub-scrib'd largely: He represents himself as a Clergyman persecuted by Quakers, for the Services done the Church in opposing and exposing those Sectaries, and in that Light a Bishop recommended him to Oxford for a Degree of Doctor of Divinity, which it seems he has obtain'd;[3] and if he can get a Benefice here, as possibly he may, it is not unlikely he will desert poor Philadelphia and by re-moving his Candlestick leave the Academy in the Dark.[4]

We shall do everything that is necessary to obtain a Share this Year of the Parliamentary Grant to the Colonies, to be made in Pursuance of the Expectations given them by Mr. Pitt; but the Treasury is really so distress'd by the vast Expence of the War, that our Expectations must not be very high.[5] The List of Servants

1. For Attorney General Charles Pratt's reluctance to make a report on William Smith's petition, see above, pp. 295–6.

2. For the law officers' report, see below, p. 403 n.

3. On March 12, 1759, the Archbishop of Canterbury and the Bishops of Durham, Salisbury, St. Asaph, Gloucester, and Oxford recommended Smith for a degree at Oxford. He was awarded a Doctorate in Divinity on March 27, 1759. Horace W. Smith, *Life and Correspondence of the Rev. William Smith, D. D.* (Phila., 1880), I, 197–202.

4. Smith was provost of the College of Philadelphia.

5. See above, p. 291 n, for Pitt's offer to reimburse the colonies for ex-penses incurred in the war. On April 30, 1759, the House of Commons ap-proved a resolution of its committee of the whole, granting the several colonies £200,000, which resolution was embodied in a supply bill passed by the House on June 1, 1759. *Votes of the House of Commons,* 1758–59, pp. 436–7, 523. For BF's efforts to obtain a share of this grant, see below, pp. 333–8.

is not come.[6] Nor have the Parliament yet determin'd what to allow.

I rejoice to hear of the Establishment of Peace with the Indians, and the Repose now enjoy'd by our Frontiers. Our Province has certainly great Merit, both with its Neighbours and the Mother Country, in pursuing and accomplishing that Measure. But I fear, if the present Expedition against Canada, should, as most Expeditions do, fail of Success,[7] the French will return to the Ohio, and debauch the Indians again from our Friendship, if they are not retain'd in that Friendship, and the French discourag'd from the Attempt, by our keeping Possession of Fort Duquesne and the other Forts erected to secure our Communication with it: For tho' I believe that our Negotiations of Peace contributed greatly to Forbes's Success,[8] I cannot but think at the same Time that his Approach with such a Force facilitated the Negotiations. The Indians may promise to keep the French out of that Country if we desert it; they did so at the Treaty of Carlisle;[9] but they were not able to effect it; and whenever a French Army shall again appear on the Ohio, the French Party among the Indians will again hold up their Heads, their Hands will be strengthen'd, and they will overawe or influence the English Party and carry them all over as before. I hope, therefore, Pittsburg will not be abandon'd. But by establishing a Trade with the Indians on the fairest Terms, giving them the strongest Assurances that no Encroachment shall be made on their Lands; no Settlements attempted without fair Purchase, and those only in a small Compass round the Forts just to supply them Provisions; the Indians may be thoroughly reconcil'd to our abiding there.

You may depend upon it that the Proprietor has found some

6. On Jan. 15, 1759, Isaac Norris had promised to send BF a list of indentured servants enlisted in the British Army for whom their masters claimed compensation; see above, p. 227, and also p. 291.

7. The references here are to Amherst's projected invasion of Canada via Lake Champlain and to Wolfe's expedition up the St. Lawrence against Quebec. Gipson, *British Empire*, VII, 360, 370.

8. BF is alluding to the conference held with the Indians at Easton, Oct. 7–26, 1758 (above, pp. 176 n, 200–11), and to General Forbes's capture of Fort Duquesne, Nov. 25, 1758.

9. For this treaty, held in the fall of 1753, at which BF served as one of the Pa. commissioners, see above, V, 84–107.

Means of obtaining Copies of the Letters you receive from me. He read one of them to Dr. Fothergill, who gave me an Account of it; it was a long one to the Speaker or Committee dated January 14. 1758,[1] wherein I gave an Account of a Conference between him and me on the Charters, and the Contempt I felt for Thomas when he so readily gave up his Father's Character as an honest Man, and allow'd that he had pretended to grant Privileges which were not in his Power to grant, in Deceit of the People who came over and settled on the Faith of those Grants, &c. He was extreamly exasperated at this Letter, and produc'd it to justify himself in refusing to treat farther with me. Dr. Fothergill blam'd me for writing such harsh Things; but I still see nothing in the Letter but what was proper for me to write, as you ought to be acquainted with every thing that is of Importance to your Affairs, and it is of no small Importance to know what Sort of a Man we have to deal with, and how base his Principles. I might indeed have spar'd the Comparison of Thomas to a *low Jockey*, who triumph'd with Insolence when a Purchaser complain'd of being cheated in a Horse; an Expression the Dr. particularly remark'd as harsh and unguarded; I might have left his Conduct and Sentiments to your Reflections, and contented myself with a bare Recital of what pass'd; but Indignation extorted it from me, and I cannot yet say that I much repent of it. It sticks in his Liver, I find; and e'en let him bear what he so well deserves. By obtaining Copies of our private Correspondence, he has added another Instance confirming the old Adage, That Listners seldom hear any Good of themselves.

The Enquiry into the Causes of the Alienation of the Shawanese and Delaware Indians, has been some time publish'd and is more read than I expected.[2] It will, I think, have a good Effect. The Proprietary Interest must lessen as they are more known. My Petition in Behalf of the Indians is refer'd by the Council to the Board of Trade, where I shall prosecute it and endeavour to obtain a Report, as soon as possible.[3] Mr. Thomas Penn, had artfully

1. See above, VII, 360–2.
2. For Charles Thomson's *An Enquiry into the Causes of the Alienation of the Delaware and Shawanese Indians from the British Interest*, see above, p. 199.
3. See above, pp. 264–76, 276 n, for BF's petition to the King in Council on behalf of the Indians and for the date of its referral to the Board of Trade.

waited on Lord Granville and Lord Halifax,[4] and left with each a Copy of the last Easton Treaty,[5] with a Note requesting his Lordship would turn to and read the 5th. Paragraph of the last Page,[6] where he would find how highly satisfy'd the Indians were with Onas; so that when I spoke with them on the Petition, Lord Granville told me he understood all Matters were settled between the Proprietor and the Indians to their Satisfaction, and ordered the Treaty to be brought him, and read the Note and the Paragraph mention'd, to me. On which I explain'd that Matter to him, and set him right, by showing him, that what was there mention'd related only to the Purchase at Albany,[7] and that the Delawares still understood their Complaint to be before the King, being told that it was so by the Governor in another Part of the Treaty, which I pointed out.[8] My Lord then saw the Mistake he had been led into, and said it ought to be immediately settled; and accordingly the next Council Day it was referr'd as above. Lord Halifax seem'd to be under the same Mistake till I show'd him those Passages of the Treaty, where the Governor says, the Proprietors had press'd a Decision, but that the King was busy being engag'd

---

The Board of Trade completed its report on June 1, 1759. *Board of Trade Journal,* 1759–63, p. 42. For the text of the report, see below, pp. 379–89.

4. For these two officials, see above, pp. 293, 294.

5. The minutes of the "last Easton Treaty," that of Oct. 7–26, 1758, are reproduced in facsimile in Van Doren and Boyd, *Indian Treaties,* pp. 215–43.

6. Wherein Thomas King, an Oneida chieftain, declared that the Indians had always found Onas (the governor of Pa. and by extension the Proprietors) "ready to grant all their Requests; with him we never had any Difference, he has always settled our Affairs without giving us any Trouble, and to our Satisfaction. We heartily thank Onas. This Act confirms us in the good Opinion we have always had of him." *Ibid.,* p. 243.

7. For the Albany Purchase of 1754, given up by the proprietary agents at Easton in October 1758, because it had antagonized the Indians, see above, v, 349–50 n.

8. On Oct. 23, 1758, Gov. Denny, replying to Teedyuscung's queries about what action the King had taken on the "Dispute about Lands," declared that "His Majesty lives at a very great Distance from us, is now engaged in a War with the French, and the Business of War takes up a great deal of Time and Attention. . . . As yet I have had no answer relative to your Affairs. You may depend upon it, as soon as I receive one, it shall be communicated to you. And I can assure you, the Proprietaries have pressed Dispatch, and will do every Thing they can to bring it to a speedy Determination." Van Doren and Boyd, *Indian Treaties,* p. 239.

in a great War, &c. at which his Lordship smil'd. I am inclin'd to think, from what the Secretary[9] told me, that they purpose to appoint Commissioners in America to make Enquiry; but I shall urge an immediate Determination here; as the Question seems to be chiefly this, Whether certain Lands are convey'd by certain Deeds; those Deeds being to be laid before their Lordships by the Proprietor; particularly whether the Walking Purchase was duly run out according to the Direction of the Deed (supposing that Deed a good one) on which it was founded?[1] This I should think may be decided here on the Face of the Deeds and Maps; and I do not well see what farther Lights Commissioners can obtain.

It is thought Mr. Hamilton will return our Governor; but it is not yet declared.[2] For my part, I must own, I am tired of Proprietary Government, and heartily wish for that of the Crown.

I petition'd the Admiralty for a Ship, and received the Answer which I enclose to you.[3] I think it will be scarce worth while to apply to the Admiral in America for a Ship, since probably he will, as Boscawen did, make Demands that you cannot comply with[4] or if you do, you have no Security that such Ship shall continue on your Station, and while he is on it, he will not be directed by your Government. New York and Boston have so often found the Inconvenience of these Station Ships that they are very indifferent about having them: The Pressing of their Men and thereby disappointing Voyages, often hurting their Trade more than the

9. The secretary to the Board of Trade at this time was John Pownall, brother of Thomas Pownall (above, V, 339–40 n).

1. See below, p. 385, for the Board of Trade's recommendation that Sir William Johnson, superintendent of Indian Affairs, investigate the matter. BF appears somewhat naive if he sincerely believed that such a complicated issue, with so many persons or groups directly or indirectly interested, could be satisfactorily settled by the examination of a few documents in London.

2. James Hamilton (above, III, 327–8 n), who had been governor of Pa. from 1748 to 1754, was reappointed on July 21, 1759, this time serving until 1763.

3. For BF's petition for a ship to protect the trade of Pa. against French depredations, see above, p. 297. The Admiralty's answer, the tenor of which can be inferred from BF's next sentences, has not been found.

4. On Aug. 5, 1758, apparently in response to requests from Pa. for a guard ship, Admiral Edward Boscawen promised to dispatch "the Eccho of Thirty-two Guns," provided the colony raised 300 seamen for his fleet, lying at that time off Louisbourg. *Pa. Col. Recs.*, VIII, 164.

Enemy hurts it. I represented that the Garrison of Louisburgh, Halifax, &c. might have their Provisions intercepted, but the Secretary[5] said the Admiral must want common Sense, if he did not take care of that. The Truth is, the British Trade is so extensive and lies so wide, that they have not yet Ships enow to protect it everywhere, tho' our Navy at present is the greatest and most formidable that the World ever saw.

Mr. Pitt hitherto holds his Ground, tho' 'tis thought his Adversaries are secretly sapping his Foundation. His indisputed Character for Integrity and Disinterestedness, support him strongly, and Success if God grants it will probably establish him.

The Armies are all in Motion on the Continent, and this is like to be as bloody a Summer as the two last. All the Contending Parties[6] there seem to be making such great Efforts, as indicate a speedy End to the War, since the vast Expence must make a Continuance of it impossible. If the wonderfully great King of Prussia can keep them at Bay one Year more, it is thought his Enemies will be tired of the fruitless Attempt to destroy him; and he really bids fair for it, having opened the Campaign with as fine an Army, notwithstanding all his Losses, as he has had at any Time during the Year.

I suppose Billy writes to you. By one of these Ships he has sent you a System of Husbandry and some Pamplets.[7] With great Esteem, I am, Dear Friend Yours affectionately   B FRANKLIN

To Joseph Galloway Esqr.

Endorsed: Benjamin Franklins Letter April. 7. 1759

5. John Clevland (above, VII, 285 n) was secretary to the Admiralty.

6. In 1759, Frederick II of Prussia, assisted by British troops and those of Hanover, Brunswick, and Gotha, was fighting France, Austria, Russia, Sweden, and several of the smaller German principalities.

7. On Aug. 9, 1759, Galloway wrote WF, acknowledging the receipt of "the Body of Husbandry and some Pamphlets," but complaining that WF had been remiss in writing his friends in Philadelphia. WF to Joseph Galloway, Dec. 28, 1759, Hist. Soc. Pa.

To David Hall LS: Independence National Historical Park, Philadelphia

Dear Mr. Hall   London, April 8, 1759

I have yours of Novr. 20. Decr. 5 and 8, and Jany. 18, with a Postscript of Feb. 5.[8] Your prudent Conduct in my Absence, with regard to the Parties, as well as in every other respect, gives me great Satisfaction. If I do not correspond so fully and punctually with you as you expected, consider the Situation and Business I am in, the Number of Correspondent I have to write to, the eternal Interruptions one meets with in this great City, the Visits one must necessarily receive and pay, the Entertainments or Amusements one is invited to and urg'd to partake of, besides the many Matters of Use and Importance worth a Stranger's while to enquire into who is soon to return to his own Country, and then if you make a little additional Allowance for the Indolence that naturally creeps upon us with Age, I think you will be more ready to excuse me.

I was surpriz'd to hear that the new Fount of Bourgeois was not got to hand, as I found by my Accounts that I had got it ready and order'd it to be shipt in September when I paid Caslon for it; but on Enquiry I find it was not shipt till November, and then on board the Rebeccah and Susannah, Capt. Nicholson; it was in two Boxes mark'd BF. No. 1, 2.[9] I must have sent you both the Bills of Lading, as I have neither of them by me. I hope long before this time it is got safe to hand. If you think another Fount of Brevier[1] necessary besides this, let me know. I wish I had known sooner that you would have chosen Brevier rather than Bourgeois.

I congratulate you on the Success of our Forces and Treaty in

8. For Hall's letters of November 20 and January 18, see above, pp. 174, 230–2. The others have not been found.

9. Bourgeois type, between Brevier and Long Primer in size, corresponds to 9-point type in the modern American point system. Under date of Sept. 29, 1758, BF recorded paying William Caslon £31 2s. "for Letter sent to my Office under D. Hall 311 lb. Bourgeois." Later he added to the entry: "sent per Rebecca and Susanna Capt. Nicholson." "Account of Expences," p. 41; *PMHB*, LV (1931), 114. The vessel was reported at Deal, outward bound, December 5. *London Chron.*, Dec. 5–7, 1758. Doubtless held up somewhere along the Channel awaiting a convoy, its arrival at Philadelphia was not reported in *Pa. Gaz.* until April 5, 1759, three days before BF wrote this letter.

1. Brevier type corresponds to 8-point in the modern American system.

driving the French from the Ohio, and establishing Peace with the Indians.[2] I hope this Year will finish our American War. The strong Fleet sent hence some time since for the Attempt on Quebec, is I imagine, before now arriv'd on your Side;[3] and the Troops embarking for that Service. God grant them Success, and deliver us for ever from those mischievous Neighbours.

You may remember you were always complaining, and justly, of the bad Pay of our Subscribers on the Post Roads, and urging me to fall on some Method of remedying the Evil for the future. The Instruction relating to the Carriage of Newspapers was form'd for that purpose; and I think must produce the Effect.[4] Some good Paymasters may possibly at first take Offence and decline the Paper; but when they consider the Equity as well as Necessity of the Thing, their Disgust must in Time wear off, and they will return to us again. The greatest Part of those that drop, are such as would never pay, and whose Custom therefore is not worth keeping; or rather we may consider them now as so many Benefactors, since they have remitted the expensive Tribute we us'd to pay 'em yearly in Paper and Printing. If we continue to print 18 Token,[5] and get paid for that Quantity, 'tis a very good

2. Forbes's capture of Fort Duquesne, Nov. 25, 1758, and the Indian treaty at Easton the preceding October.

3. On February 14 Rear Admiral Charles Holmes, with a squadron of 21 warships, sailed from Portsmouth escorting 60 transports to New York. Vice Admiral Charles Saunders' squadron of 18 warships followed, with Maj. Gen. James Wolfe aboard the flagship *Neptune*. They reached Halifax April 30 and joined the forces already there for the assault upon Quebec. *London Chron.*, Feb. 15–17, 17–20, 1759. On British preparations for this decisive campaign, see Gipson, *British Empire*, VII, 371–6.

4. BF and Hunter's instruction, March 10, 1758, required the local postmasters to deliver newspapers only to persons who would agree to pay them the subscription price of the papers and "a small additional Consideration" as a fee to the postriders for carrying them from one community to another. The postmasters were to distribute the "Consideration" among the riders concerned and send the subscription money to the printers once a year after deducting a 20 percent commission. See above, VII, 390–2. Hall may have questioned the desirability of this rule in one of the missing letters BF acknowledged above.

5. Token: A unit of presswork from one form. The number of impressions which constituted one token varied from place to place; in Great Britain and New York it was 250 impressions, while in Boston it was 500. Alternatively, the unit sometimes represented one hour's work on a hand press. How many

Thing and we may be contented. But then the Instruction must be stuck to, and no Papers sent but what are engag'd for, otherwise all is to no purpose; and I must leave it to you to contrive a better Method, having now done my best.

You are in the right not to be uneasy at the Number of Printing Offices setting up in Philadelphia.[6] The Country is increasing and Business must increase with it. We are pretty well establish'd, and shall probably with God's Blessing and a prudent Conduct always have our Share. The young ones will not be so likely to hurt us as one another.

I much doubt whether I shall be able to send you Copy for the Almanack: I thought I should surely have sent it last year, having collected many Materials which only wanted putting together, but Sickness at Times, other Business, and various Interruptions disappointed me. If you do not receive it by the Pacquet that sails from hence in May, shift without it one Year more as you did very well last year; and before another I hope to be at home.[7]

Parson Smith has been applying to Osborne for a large Cargo of Books, acquainting him that he could be of vast Service in selling great Quantities for him, as there was only one Hall at Philadelphia who demanded excessive Prices; and if another Shop was but open'd where People could be supply'd reasonably, all the Custom would run to it.[8] I know not whether he was to sell

copies of an average issue of *Pa. Gaʒ.* would equal 18 token in the minds of BF and Hall is not clear.

6. Here again BF seems to be responding to a comment in one of Hall's missing letters. Charles Evans, *American Bibliography,* III (Chicago, 1905), 186–245, 446–7, and Charles R. Hildeburn, *The Issues of the Press in Pennsylvania 1685–1784,* I (Phila., 1885), 327–45, list publications by four Philadelphia printing houses in 1758–59: Anton Armbrüster, in German only; William Bradford; James Chattin, bought out and succeeded by William Dunlap in 1758; and Franklin & Hall. Hall's comment, may have arisen from the aggressive printing and bookselling activities of Dunlap, DF's relative. BF had cautioned his wife to do nothing to encourage Dunlap as a printer "that may draw Reflections on me" because of BF's engagements to Hall. See above, p. 92.

7. There is no evidence that BF furnished material for any of the *Poor Richard* almanacs after the one for 1758, except possibly for that of 1765. See above, VII, 326 n.

8. William Smith was still in London awaiting judgment on his appeal, which was rendered on June 26, 1759; see above, pp. 87–8 n. On Thomas Osborne, the bookseller, see above, III, 318–19; VII, 176 n.

them himself or employ some other. He gave Osborne a Catalogue. Osborne came to me, and ask'd me if I knew him, and that he should be safe in trusting him. I told him I believ'd my Townsmen who were Smith's Creditors would be glad to see him come back with a Cargo of any kind, as they might have some Chance of being paid out of it; And so I could not in Conscience dissuade him from trusting him. "Oh, says he, is that the Case; then he shall have no Books of me I assure you: He persuaded me to trust him £10's worth of Books, and take his Note payable in Six Months. But I will have the Money immediately or the Books again."[9]

As soon as I saw the three Third-Bills I found my Mistake. I had indeed receiv'd the No. 276, and enter'd it in my Bills deliver'd my Banker, but having Bills from Mr. Parker which I receiv'd and deliver'd at the same Time, when I came to look over my List I was deceiv'd by the Date of that Bill, being at N. York, and suppos'd therefore that it had come from him, the Bill itself being out of my Hands, and no other Copy arriving, which would have given me an opportunity of looking at the Indorsement.[1] This was the Reason I did not give you Credit for it. I might have been set right if I had recurr'd to his and your Letters, but having no doubt I did not examine them. It was a Fault, and I am sorry it has given you so much Trouble. However, the Method I took of sending you a compleat and particular List of all the Bills I suppos'd I had receiv'd from you, has enabled you to take the Step that has clear'd up the Difficulty effectually, by sending me those three-Thirds as aforesaid.

I have receiv'd your Bill drawn by James Pemberton on D. Barclay & Son for £100. and since that, another of John Hunter

9. BF's report on Smith's financial credit was perhaps unduly severe, but it does not stand alone. Writing in 1770 to a New Jersey friend from whom Smith wished to rent a house in Philadelphia, William Logan warned: "I must do the Justice to tell thee that he is accounted So very bad a Pay Master that it may be difficult to get thy Rent from him—if his Character be true." Albert F. Gegenheimer, *William Smith Educator and Churchman 1727–1803* (Phila., 1943), pp. 149–50.

1. On the mix-up over Hall's remittances, see above, p. 230. Like Hall, James Parker sent BF bills of exchange from time to time; some were in payment for printing-office equipment and supplies, some as income of the American postal service of which he was comptroller.

on Messrs. Thomlinson &c. No. 290, for £100 also.[2] I must repeat my Thanks for your careful and regular Remittances.

There is all Appearance[3] that the ensuing Campaign will be a bloody one. The Powers at War on the Continent have exerted themselves to the utmost this Winter, to be able to bring vast Armies into the Field, and they are already in Motion. If the King of Prussia can stand his Ground this Year, 'tis thought his Enemies will be tired of so costly a War. And he bids fair for it, for he takes Field this Spring with as fine an Army as he has had since the War began, and hitherto he has very little burthen'd his own People for Supplies either of Money or Men, drawing both from his Enemies or Neighbours. But what the Event will be God only knows. Three great Monarchys the most powerful in Europe, besides the Swedes, all on his Back at once![4] No Magnamity [Magnanimity] but his own could think of bearing it; no Courage but his that would not sink under it, nor any less Bravery, Skill and Activity than his that would be equal to it. If he again should drub them all round, and at length obtain an honourable and advantageous Peace, his Renown will far exceed that of all the Heroes in History.

I am glad to hear Cousin Molly is better.[5] I hope her Health will be fully restored. My Love to her and the Children, in which and Compliments to all Friends Billy joins with Your affectionate Friend and humble Servant   B FRANKLIN

P. S. Send me the Votes, Treaties, and other public Things as you print them, for thro' waiting for the Seal, and other Causes, I am often long without them.[6] I wish you would also send me all Party

2. Receipt recorded in "Account of Expences," pp. 23, 24; *PMHB*, LV (1931), 115, 116.

3. Hall reprinted this paragraph in *Pa. Gaz.*, July 19, 1759, introducing it with: "By Captain Simpson, from London, a Gentleman there writes his Friend here as follows."

4. Frederick II of Prussia was opposed by France, Austria, and Russia; Sweden had occupied Pomerania in 1757. British troops and the forces of Hanover, Brunswick, and Gotha supported Frederick on the Continent, while other German states of the Empire joined with his enemies.

5. Mary Leacock Hall (F.2.2.3), David's wife and DF's second cousin.

6. Public papers which BF was to lay before the authorities in London required proper authentication, which took time and seems often to have been carelessly performed.

Papers, or of a publick Nature, tho' printed by others. I am often the last that see such Things, and oblig'd to other People here for the Favour. Send me also 2 of Mr. Scull's new Maps of the improv'd Part of Pensylvania.[7]

April 9. Since writing the above, I have receiv'd yours of Feby 27 per Finglass, with a Bill for £100 for which have given you Credit;[8] and as to the Affair you mention can only say, that as yet I have heard nothing of it, and you may depend on all the Candour you could wish from me on such Occasions.

Billy has sent you in the 2 Vessels which lately saild for Philadelphia 300 of the Enquirys, 50 of which are to be deliver'd to the Assembly, 25 to Messrs. Israel Pemberton and Charles Thomson, and the remaining 225 to be dispos'd of in Pensylvania and the neighbouring Governments.[9]

From Benjamin Wilson[1]   ALS: American Philosophical Society

Dear Sir   8 April 1759

I have been considering Mr. Coldens experiment[2] which we tried on Saturday last, and the appearances it affords seem not now so surprising, or indeed, curious, as I at first imagined. For the excited tube, you know, when opposed properly to the cork balls, attracts them a little: it must therefore electrify the balls plus, instead of minus: and not only the balls will be electrified plus, in some degree, but the threads by which they are suspended, together with the leaden covering of the vial. On bringing the ex-

7. Nicholas Scull's *Map of the Improved Part of the Province of Pennsylvania* (Evans 8489) was announced as ready for delivery to subscribers in *Pa. Gaz.*, Feb. 15, 1759.

8. For the letter, see above, p. 287. Receipt of the bill of exchange is recorded in "Account of Expences," p. 26; *PMHB*, LV (1931), 117.

9. See above, pp. 199–200, 297–8, 313.

1. On Benjamin Wilson, electrical scientist and portrait painter, see above, IV, 391 n, and this volume, pp. 239–63. The warm tone of this letter suggests the friendly relations existing between Wilson and BF before they came into sharp disagreement over the respective merits of rounded and pointed lightning rods.

2. The reference is probably to an experiment described in David Colden's paper sent to BF (for the second time) Oct. 26, 1758; see above, pp. 170–2.

cited tube nearer towards the balls they will be electrified plus to as great a degree as the tube, in such circumstances, is capable of doing it: and after that is effected, a repulsion will succeed between the balls and the tube: which must ever be the case when they are both equally electrified and by the same power.

I will endeavour to satisfy you that this is probably the fact by an experiment or two which are easily made when I see you next— in the meantime believe me Yours most affectionately B WILSON

Addressed: To Doctor Franklyn[3]

Endorsed: Mr. Wilson

To Deborah Franklin

ALS: American Philosophical Society

Pennsylvania Coffee house

My dear Child,   London April 12. 1759

Calling here just now, I find a Bag not taken away, and as my Letters are gone or going, part by the Ships now at Portsmouth[4] and part per Packet to be dispatch'd on Saturday, I write this Line to let you know we are well, and that you may not be uneasy at not having one Letter by this Ship.

Now I think on't; there was a Trunk sent last year by the Speedwell; it was shipt by Mr. Collinson and included in the same Bill of Lading with one for the Library Company; it was mark'd J.F No. 1, and should have gone to New York, being for Jemmy Franklin.[5] I cannot hear that he or you have receiv'd it; and sup-

3. The earliest surviving use in a letter of the title by which BF was regularly addressed during the remainder of his life.

4. On April 28 the warships *Norwich, Echo,* and *Lyon* sailed from Portsmouth convoying "the trade for North America." *London Chron.,* April 28–May 1, 1759. To judge by the published "Ship News," this convoy had been assembling for a considerable period.

5. BF recorded under date of May 19, 1758, "a Trunk of Books" sent to his nephew James Franklin (C.11.4) of Newport, valued in "Boston Lawful Money" at £48 19s. 9d. (£36 14s. 3d., sterling), which James was to sell at that price, retaining 20 percent as commission. At about the same time BF recorded sending DF in a trunk for the Library Co. a ream of writing paper, 200 large quills, and two lbs. superfine wax, to a total value of £1 9s., sterling. "Account of Expences," pp. 32, 17; *PMHB,* LV (1931), 111. He told DF, June 10, 1758, that these articles were a gift to Mrs. Samuel Preston Moore; see above, p. 91.

pose it lies in the Store of Mr. Neave's[6] Correspondent at Philadelphia waiting for somebody to claim it. Pray enquire about it; you can get the Bill of Lading of Mr. Morris, the Secretary to the Library Company;[7] and when you receive the Trunk, forward it to Jemmy. The Freight was paid here.

Tell Mr. Thomson that I have just heard the Proprietor is writing an Answer to his Book, and will pay off him and the Quakers.[8]

My Love to all Pensylvania. I am as ever Dear Debby, Your affectionate Husband   B FRANKLIN

P.S. I have sent you 2 Boxes, and a Leaden Case containing a Cheese: they are ship'd on board the Cornelia, Capt. Smith, by Mr. Neate; but no Bill of Lading was taken.[9] Enquire for them when the Ship arrives: They are mark'd BF No. 1, 2, 3. The Boxes contain Books and a Thermometer for Mr. Norris, Do. for Mr. James Wright; Barometer and Thermometer for Mr. Hughes. Books for Mr. Galloway. Cloaths for you and Sally; and sundry small Articles, of which you will have a particular Account per Pacquet.

Mr. Hunter is gone home to Virginia perfectly well![1] God be thanked.

Addressed: [*Torn*] / Mrs Franklin / at the Post Office / Philada.

6. Richard Neave, London merchant; see above, IV, 115 n.

7. Library Co. minutes show no one in Philadelphia holding office as secretary at this time. Joseph Morris (1715–1785) was treasurer, however, and reported, July 9, 1759, that he soon expected a shipment of books from Collinson.

8. Thomas Penn's copy of Charles Thomson's *Enquiry* (above, p. 199), with marginal notes in his hand, is in John Carter Brown Lib. "But as far as is known his intentions never got beyond the stage of exasperated annotation." Lawrence C. Wroth, *An American Bookshelf 1755* (Phila., 1934), pp. 18, 19.

9. See above, pp. 306–7. BF paid William Neate, London merchant (above, IV, 115 n), £3 2s. 5d. for the shipping charges. "Account of Expences," p. 38. Eddy omitted this entry from *PMHB*, LV (1931), 97–133.

1. William Hunter, BF's colleague as joint deputy postmaster general, arrived in Virginia on July 5, after a voyage of ten weeks. Hunter to DF, July 22, 1759, APS.

From Thomas Holme

ALS: Historical Society of Pennsylvania

Sir   Wellingborough April 12th. 1759.

I communicated your Last and Mrs. Morris's Letter[2] to Mr. Fisher at my Return from a Journey last Saturday, else you would have heard from me Sooner, however I now send you such a Discharge as will satisfie Mr. Fisher, which when you have executed please to return either to him or me by the Post, and he will directly remitt you the Money.[3] I am Sir Your very humble Servant   THO: HOLME.

Addressed: To / Mr. Benjamin Franklin / at Mrs. Stephensons in Craven Street / Strand / London

Endorsed: Revd Mr Holme April 12 59

2. For BF's letter of March 27, see above, p. 302. Eleanor Morris' letter has not been found; it probably concerned her request that her share of Mary Fisher's estate be paid to BF.

3. An undated entry (not later than May 30, 1759) in BF's "Account of Expences," p. 29 (summarized in *PMHB*, LV, 119–20), records in detail the distribution of Mrs. Fisher's estate. It begins by repeating *verbatim* the administratrix' account as transmitted by Holme to BF, March 17, 1759 (above, pp. 288–9), and then continues:

"Note, Mrs. Fisher's Effects were to be distributed among her Relations of equal Degree, which were as follows,

     Mrs. Ann Farrow Daughter of John Franklin
     Mrs. Eleanor Morris Daughter of
         Hannah Franklin
     Mr. Samuel Franklin of Boston Son of   all Children of
         Benja Franklin   Thomas Franklin
     Mrs. Elizabeth Dowse   whose Grandaughter
         Daughter of   Mrs. Fisher was
     Mr. Peter Franklin Son of   Josiah Franklin
     Mrs. Jane Mecom Daughter of
     and myself Son of

"I gave my Share to be divided between Mrs. Farrow and Mrs. Morris two poor ancient Women; the other Shares belonging to Relations in America are in my hands, viz.

Samuel Franklin's Share	11.	8.	4
Eliz Dowse's Share	11.	8.	4
Peter Franklin's Share	11.	8.	4
Jane Mecom's Share	11.	8.	4
in all £45	13	4"	

From Isaac Norris

Letterbook copy: Historical Society of Pennsylvania

April 12th. 1759

The above is Copy of a Message sent down by the Governor a few hours ago to which the House returned a Verbal Message "that they unanimously adhered to their Bill and were of Opinion that if the Bill should not receive the Governors Assent the ill Consequences he had pointed out must lye upon him."[4] Soon after I came from the House I received a few Lines from the Governor "that he would be glad to see me"—in Consequence of which I waited upon him and upon a long and free Conference I have the

4. On March 24, 1759, the Assembly passed a supply bill for £100,000 which provided for taxing the proprietary estates. Governor Denny returned it, March 29, proposing a separate bill under which, "on a fair and equal Taxation of their Quit-Rents and appropriated Tracts," any deficiency in the Proprietors' former grant of £5000 would be made up. Within half an hour the Assembly sent their bill back to Denny, having resolved "by a great Majority" to adhere to it. On the Council's unanimous advice, the governor responded, March 31, that he would not pass this bill but would approve one similar to that of the previous year which exempted the proprietary estates. On April 2 the House voted unanimously not to grant the exemption and "by a great Majority" agreed to prepare a new supply bill taxing the Proprietors "in their full Proportions of the sums already granted, and to be granted," giving credit for the previous free gift of £5000. Such a bill passed the House and went to the governor, April 5. Denny returned it two days later, objecting to taxing the Proprietors unless they had a share in naming the assessors, but the Assembly refused to change the measure. General Jeffery Amherst (see final footnote to this letter) arrived in Philadelphia on the 9th and Denny informed him of the *impasse*, whereupon the commander-in-chief conferred with Speaker Norris and other leading assemblymen and, "finding them Obstinate" (as Denny reported to the Council), th. atened to withdraw all the King's forces from the province. The House then sent a new message reporting this threat and calling on Denny, "as you regard your Duty to the King, and to the Province," not to insist on a separate bill on the proprietary estates, "a Mode unjust and unknown to a British Constitution." The Council urged him to "press the Assembly once more," so Denny sent the message here referred to, April 12, reviewing the history of the dispute, urging the House to yield, and placing on it the responsibility for the consequences of a failure to supply the necessary appropriations. *Votes*, 1758–59, pp. 46, 51–2, 55, 56–7, 58, 60–1; *Pa. Col. Recs.*, VIII, 301–3, 304, 318, 319–20, 323–31. Norris' paraphrase of the Assembly's reply differs slightly from the text in *Votes*, p. 61, and in *Pa. Col. Recs.*, VIII, 331.

Satisfaction to assure you that The Bill will receive his Assent,[5] tho' I think it will be against the Advice of his Council which is to be called to Morrow Morning.[6] This Bill taxes the Proprietary Estates and makes provision for the 5,000 formerly given to our £60,000 Act,[7] I cannot conceive the least danger of the Disapprobation of the Crown,[8] but by being early apprized of what may happen due Care may be taken there against all Events.

Please to present the inclosed Bill of Exchange drawn by Peter

---

5. Denny's change of heart can undoubtedly be attributed to the intervention of General Amherst. On April 11, 1759, the day after his interview with Norris and other assemblymen, Amherst wrote Denny a letter begging the governor to "Wave the Proprietary Instructions," as he had done before at Loudoun's urging (see above, VII, 152 n, 261), and to pass the supply bill. The general promised to "take the very first Opportunity of informing the King's Ministers with the Necessity of your so doing, that no Inconvenience may arise to you from the Same." *Pa. Col. Recs.*, VIII, 331–2. Denny was afraid of being sued by the Proprietors for breach of their instructions, thus risking forfeiture of a sizable bond. He did not formally notify the Assembly of his intention to pass the supply bill until April 16. The next morning the House ordered the bill engrossed and then, "taking into Consideration the Governor's Support, after some Debate thereon" voted him £1000 for the year. At the ceremony the same morning, when Denny had signed the Supply Act and another measure, Norris formally presented the governor with an order for payment of "his Support, which his Honour received very kindly, and was pleased to return his Thanks to the House for the same." *Votes*, 1758–59, pp. 62–3; *Pa. Col. Recs.*, VIII, 332–3.

6. There is no record of the Council members' sentiments on Denny's *volte-face*, but in the following June, when he told them General Stanwix had advised him to approve another obnoxious bill, they protested vigorously, declaring that "such Letters from General Officers would not authorize the Governor to give his Assent to Acts which were unjust in themselves, and hurtful to the People." Denny in turn admonished the councilors "to Remember that Loyalty and Obedience was due from them to the King, as well as regard to the Proprietaries." *Pa. Col. Recs.*, VIII, 353–62, esp. 354, 357.

7. On the 1759 bill as enacted, see *Statutes at Large, Pa.*, V, 379–96. For the £60,000 Act of 1755, see above, VI, 257 n.

8. The Proprietors petitioned the King in Council to disallow the Supply Act of 1759, and the Board of Trade reported in their favor. The Privy Council overruled the Board, however, on BF and Charles's pledge (Aug. 28, 1760) that the Pa. Assembly would assess and tax the Proprietors' property equitably. *Pa. Col. Recs.*, VIII, 529–35, 554–5.

Razor on R Partridge[9] which he may keep in his Hands on the publick Account tho' I have no Mony of theirs yet in my Possession. I am called upon for this to go by the Packet[1] and I write late at Night having spent the forepart of it with the Governor. Your Assured Friend   I N

Late the 12 April—the Man sets out at Six aClock to Morrow and is now waiting for this. The Man goes on W. Griffitts account[2] with a few Letters and my Notice of it was very late. General Amherst[3] was here Two Days only and returned to N. York yesterday.

To BF by the Packet

Endorsed: BF recd this ackd. June 9th. 1759

9. BF recorded the receipt of this bill (for £40) on May 19, 1759. "Account of Expences," p. 27; *PMHB*, LV (1931), 118.

1. The *General Wall*, Capt. Walter Lutwidge, sailed from New York on April 16, 1759. Its arrival at Falmouth in 25 days was reported in *London Chron.*, May 17–19, 1759.

2. On William Griffitts, Philadelphia merchant, see above, IV, 290; V, 285 n; *PMHB*, XLVI (1922), 253. BF was "extreamly concern'd," as well as surprised, by Griffitts' declaration of bankruptcy in 1760. BF to DF, June 27, 1760, APS.

3. Jeffery Amherst (1717–1797), entered the British Army in 1731. He served on the staffs of Gen. John Ligonier and the Duke of Cumberland in the War of the Austrian Succession and was Cumberland's commissary in Germany early in the Seven Years' War. Pitt promoted him to major general, 1758; he commanded the army that captured Louisbourg in July of that year, and in September he became commander-in-chief in North America. His victorious campaigns of 1759 and 1760 resulted in his being made Knight of the Bath in 1761. He held the governorships of Virginia, 1759–68, and of Guernsey, 1770, but never officiated in either position. In 1776 he was raised to the peerage as Baron Amherst and two years later, as a full general, he became commander-in-chief of all British forces in England. *DAB, DNB*. On his brief visit to Philadelphia, April 9–11, mentioned in Norris' postscript, he was accompanied by Governors DeLancey of New York and Bernard of New Jersey, as well as by several army officers. *Pa. Gaz.*, April 12, 1759.

From Pieter van Musschenbroek[4]

ALS and AD: American Philosophical Society[5]

In response to a request transmitted through an unidentified clerical intermediary, Musschenbroek sent Franklin a list of European writers on electricity known to him. But in the covering letter he urged Franklin to continue his own electrical experiments. Since the air of Pennsylvania seemed to be very full of electricity (*electricitatis plenissimus*), he hoped the American would follow up his kite experiment (*volante in altum serico*) with others in which he would take particular note of the time of year and the meteorological conditions when they were conducted, adding thereby similar beautiful Pennsylvania discoveries (*perpulcra inventa ... Pensylvanica*) to those he had already communicated through Collinson. Musschenbroek in turn would communicate other things to Franklin, as his aim was to promote physical and natural science as long as he should live.

Leydae 15. Aprilis 1759.
Vir Nobilissimo Amplissimoque Benjam. Franklino S P D
P: V: MUSSCHENBROEK

Vir reverendus, qui se ministerio Euangelico fungi profitebatur, me tuo nomine rogavit, ut indicarem Autores, qui de Electricitate scripserunt, mihique erant cogniti. Votis tuis lubenter[ius?] annui; ita addisces quid alii in Europa praestiterunt Eruditi, sed simul videbis neminem magis recondita mysteria Electricitatis detexisse Franklino; utinam modo pergas proprio marte capere experimenta, et alia incedere via, quam Europaei incesserunt, nam tum plura et alia deteges, quae seculorum spatio laterent Philosophos: Aer Pensylvanicus videtur esse electricitatis plenissimus; sed attende an per totum anni curriculum, an interdum pauperior sit:

4. Pieter van Musschenbroek (1692–1761), Dutch natural philosopher. After holding successively a professorship at Duisburg and the chairs of natural philosophy and mathematics and of astronomy at Utrecht, 1719–39, he became professor of mathematics at Leyden, where he remained until his death, although he received flattering offers of positions in other countries. He is best known for his discovery of the Leyden jar, 1746, an achievement which he must share, however, with Ewald Georg von Kleist, who had made a similar accidental discovery in Pomerania a year earlier.

5. In the early arrangement of the Franklin Papers at APS, the letter and its enclosure became widely separated; they are now found in that collection at I, 54, and XLIX, 43, respectively.

quibus anni diebus, quo flante vento, qua caeli constitutione: distingue nubes electricitatis plenas aut expertes, uti volante in altum serico incepisti detegere omnium primus: opto similia perpulcra inventa legere Pensylvanica, ac scripsisti in litteris ad Expertissimum Virum Collinsonum; sique mecum quaedam communicare digneris, Tecum alia communicabo, nam meus scopus est Scientiam physicam et naturalem promovere quam diu vivam. Tu sis amicissime salutatus a Tui benevolentissimo cultore, et vale.

Addressed: Monsieur / Benjamin Franklin / Maitre des postes &c. &c. / en Pensylvanie

[Enclosure]⁶

Schilling in Actis Berolin: tomo 4⁷
Wheler in philos. Trans: no. 453, 454, 462⁸
Hausenius novi profectus in Historia Electricitatis⁹
Waitsius Neuen Deckte phaenomena¹
Winklerus Abhandelingen von den Electricitaet 3 vol. philos. Trans. no. 482²

6. Titles and works in Musschenbroek's list are not always as full or as accurate as one might wish. They have been identified as far as possible in the footnotes with the aid of several published bibliographies, catalogues, and treatises, the most useful of which has been Sir Francis Ronalds, comp., *Catalogue of Books and Papers relating to Electricity, Magnetism, the Electric Telegraph, &c. Including the Ronalds Library* (London, 1880). It is possible that BF made this list available to Joseph Priestley for use in his *The History and Present State of Electricity* (London, 1767).

7. Johann Jacob Schilling [b. 1702], "Observationes et Experimenta de vi electrica vitri aliorumque corporum," *Miscellanea Berolinensia,* IV (Berlin, 1735), 334–43; V (1737), 109–12.

8. Granville Wheler [d. 1770], "Some Electrical Experiments Chiefly Regarding the Repulsive Force of Electrical Bodies," *Phil. Trans.,* XLI (1739–41), 98–111 (no. 453); "A Letter . . . Containing Some Remarks on the Late Stephen Gray, His Electrical Circular Experiment," *ibid.,* XLI, 118 (no. 454); "Two Letters from G.W. to the President Concerning a Rotary Motion of Glass Tubes about Their Axes," *ibid.,* XLIII (1744–46), 341–5 (no. 476). Musschenbroek's assignment of no. 462 to this paper in the *Abridgement* of *Phil. Trans.* appears to be in error.

9. Christian August Hausen [1693–1743], *Novus Profectus in Historia Electricitatis* (Leipzig, 1743).

1. Musschenbroek assigned the wrong author to this work; it should be Johann Gabriel Doppelmayr [1671–1750], *Neu-entdeckte Phaenomena der electrischen Kraft* . . . (Nurnberg, 1744).

2. This work should be credited, apparently, to the author Musschenbroek

Gordon Phaenomena Electricitatis exposita[3]
Kruger Zuschrift von der Electricitaet[4]
Bosius Commentarii de Electricitate
 Recherche sur la cause de l'Electricité[5]
Kratzensteinius Theoria Electricitatis[6]
Nollet Essais sur l'Electricite. Recherces sur l'Electricité, Lettres
 sur L'Electricite[7]
Watson Experiments and Observations 2 vol.
 Account of the Experiments. philos. Trans. no 489.[8]

---

assigned to that immediately above: Jacob Siegismund Waitz [1698–1777],
*Abhandlung: Von der Electricität und deren Ursachen; Zweite Abhandlung: Von
der Natur der Electricität; Dritte Abhandlung: Von den Eigenschaften, Wirkungen und Ursachen der Electricität* (Berlin, 1745). The purpose of the reference to *Phil. Trans.* here is not clear. Musschenbroek may also have intended
to include in the list Johann Heinrich Winkler [1703–1770], *Gedanken von den
Eigenschaften, Wirkungen und Ursachen der Electricität, nebst einer Beschrei-
bung ʒwo neuer elektrischen Maschinen* (Leipzig, 1774).

3. Andreas Gordon [1712–1751], *Phaenomena electricitatis exposita* (Erfurt
[Erford], 1774).

4. Johann Gottlob Krüger [1715–1759], *Zuschrift an seine Zuhörer, worinn
er ihnen seine Gedanken von der Elektricität mittheilet, und ihnen ʒugleich seine
kunftigen Lectionen bekannt macht* (Halle, 1744).

5. Georg Matthias Böse [1710–1761], [Commentarius Primus] *De Attrac-
tione et Electricitate Oratio Inauguralis. De Electricitate. Commentarius II:
Quo simul ad capessendos honores magisteriales, et lauream poeticam invitabatur,
3 Novembre. De Electricitate inflammante et beatificante. Commentarius III.* The
first two were separately published, Wittenburg, 1743, and the third Wittenburg, 1744; the first and the commencement of the second and third were
also published in *Tentamina Electrica in Academiis Regalis Londinensi et
Parisina primum . . .* (Wittenburg, 1744). Same author, *Recherches sur la cause
et sur la véritable théorie de l'Electricité* (Wittenburg, 1745).

6. Christian Gottlieb Kratzenstein [1723–1795], *Theoria electricitatis more
geometrico explicata* (Halle, 1746).

7. Jean-Antoine Nollet [1700–1770], *Essai sur l'Electricité des corps* (Paris,
1746); *Recherches sur les causes particulières des phénomènes électriques* (Paris,
1749); *Lettres sur l'Electricité* (Paris, 1753). On Nollet, and especially the
last work listed, see above, IV, 423–8.

8. William Watson [1715–1787], *Experiments and Observations Tending to
Illustrate the Nature and Properties of Electricity* and *A Sequel to the Experiments and Observations Tending to Illustrate the Nature and Properties of Electricity* constitute the first title cited. The papers were first printed in *Phil.
Trans.* in 1745 and then separately reprinted, London, 1746. The second
work cited is "An Account of the Experiments Made . . . in Order to Measure

Martin Essay on Electricité.[9]
Muller Schreiben von der Ursachen der Electricitaet[1]
Philosophical Transact: Vol: 47.[2]
Watkins peculiar account of Electricity[3]
Baker in Philos. Transact: No. 486.[4]
Jallabert Experiences sur L'Electricité[5]
Olivier de Villeneuve Essais sur l'Experiences de L Electricite:[6]
Suite du Memoire
Morin nouvelle dissertation sur l'Electricité[7]
Richmannus in Commentari petropol: Vol. XIV.[8]
Histoire Generale et particuliere de L'Electricité 3 Tomes.[9a]
Bohadsch dissertatio philosophica de utilitatione Electrisationis
in morbis[1a]

---

the Absolute Velocity of Electricity," *Phil. Trans.*, XLV (1748), 491 (no. 489).
On Watson, see above, III, 357 n.

9. Benjamin Martin [1704–1782], *An Essay on Electricity* (Bath, 1746). For
BF's receipt of a copy of this work, see above, III, 134.

1. Gerhard Andreas Muller [1718–1762], *Schreiben an einem guten Freund
von der Ursachen und dem Nutzen der Electricität* (Weimar, 1746).

2. This does not appear to be a reference to a paper by Muller but to the
volume of *Phil. Trans.* in which appeared several important letters, including
Mazéas' report on Dalibard's performance of BF's proposed experiment to
prove the identity of lightning and electricity. See above, IV, 315–17, 390–2,
467 n.

3. Francis Watkins [dates not known], *A Particular Account of the Electrical Experiments Hitherto Made Publick* (London, 1747).

4. Henry Baker [1698–1774], "Medical Experiments of Electricity," *Phil.
Trans.*, XLV (1748), 270–5 (no. 486).

5. Jean Jallabert [1712–1768], *Expériences sur l'électricité, avec quelques con-
jectures sur ses causes et ses effets* (Geneva, 1748).

6. Olivier de Villeneuve [dates not known], *Essai de Dissertation médico-
physique sur les expériences de l'électricité* (Paris, 1748). What Musschenbroek
intended by "Suite du Memoire" is not clear.

7. Jean Morin [1705–1764], *Nouvelle Dissertation sur l'électricité des corps*
(Chartres, 1748).

8. Georg Wilhelm Richmann [1711–1753], "De electricitate in corporibus
producenda nova tentamina," *Commentarii Academiae Scientiarum Imperialis
Petropolitanae*, XIV (1744–46 [printed 1751]), 299–324. On Richmann's death
by lightning, see above, V, 155 n, 219–21.

9a. [Abbé de Mangin, d. c. 1780], *Histoire générale et particulière de l'électricité* (3 vols., Paris, 1752).

1a. Johann Baptist Bohadsch [1724–1768], *Dissertatio de utilitate Electrisationis in Arte Medica* (Prague, 1751). The title is so given by Ronalds from

daniel Gralath versuche der Natur forsch[enden] geselschafft[2]
Bammacarus de Electricitate[3]

To the Lords Commissioners of the Treasury

ADS:[4] Public Record Office, London

Pursuant to William Pitt's promises, conveyed to the colonial governors
in letters of Dec. 30, 1757, and Dec. 9, 1758, that Parliament would be
urged "to grant a proper Consideration" to those colonies which had
vigorously supported the war effort against France (above, p. 291 n),
the chancellor of the Exchequer laid before the House of Commons,
April 26, 1759, a message from the King recommending appropriate
reimbursements. This message was referred to the committee of the
whole house, which resolved on April 30 that a sum not exceeding
£200,000 be granted to the several colonies. On the same day the
resolution was read a second time and "agreed to by the House."[5]

April 1759

To the Right Honourable the Lords Commissioners of His Majesty's Treasury.

The Memorial of Benjamin Franklin Agent for the Province
of Pensilvania

Sheweth,

That since the Beginning of the present War, the said Province
has expended (as appears by the annexed Account) the Sum of
£327,851 10s. 11d. Currency,[6] which reduc'd to Sterling Money

Volta's copy in the Ronalds Library; British Museum Catalogue and other
listings give variants.

2. Daniel Gralath [1739–1809], "Geschichte der Electricität," 3 articles in
Versuche und Abhandlungen der Naturforschenden Gesellschaft in Danzig, I
(1747), 175–304; II (1754), 355–460; III (1756), 492–556; and "Electrische
Bibliotheck," 2 articles in *ibid.*, II, 525–52; III, 265–328.

3. Niccolò Bammacaro [d. *c.* 1778], *Tentamen de vi Electrica eisque phaeno-
minis* (Naples, 1748).

4. The memorial and the endorsement are in BF's hand; the accompanying
account is in another hand.

5. *Votes of the House of Commons*, 1758–59, pp. 427, 436–7.

6. Pa. currency; throughout this petition BF assumed that the rate of exchange between it and sterling was 50 percent. On March 17, 1759, the rate at
Philadelphia was 55 percent; see above, p. 290.

is £218,567 14s. 0d. in Raising, Paying and Maintaining Troops, Building Forts, &c. for the Defence of the Province, Annoying his Majesty's Enemies, and other Purposes and Services recommended from time to time by His Majesty and his Ministers.

That the said Province being a Frontier to His Majesty's Province of New Jersey, the Province of Maryland, and the Government of the three lower Delaware Counties, and more immediately expos'd to the Incursions of the Enemy, has suffered extreamly itself while it was a Protection to those Provinces, has at length at its own Expence obtain'd a Peace with the Indians,[7] of great Advantage also to His Majesty's Provinces of Virginia and New York, and has not receiv'd, nor is likely to receive from any of those Provinces the least Contribution or Compensation in Consideration of the said Services and Expences.

That the said Province of Pensylvania has also suffered greatly by the Loss of its bought Servants taken into His Majesty's Service under the Authority of an Act of Parliament, and no Satisfaction made to the Masters of the Servants, according to the Directions of the said Act.[8]

That it being thought for His Majesty's Service to prevent by an Act of Parliament the Carrying of Provisions from the Colonies to Spain and Portugal and the Islands and Ports under their Government in Europe as well as America;[9] Pensilvania, which

7. The Treaty at Easton, Oct. 7–26, 1758; see above, pp. 176 n, 199–211.

8. This statute, 29 George II, c. 35 (May 1756), empowered recruiting officers to enlist indentured servants, but stipulated that upon application from their masters (within six months of their enlistment) the servants might, at the discretion of their commanding officers, be returned. If they were not returned, the masters, again upon application, were to receive such compensation as two local justices of the peace should direct "in Proportion to the original Purchase-money given by the said Owner, Proprietor, or Master, for the said indentured servant, and to the Time of Service, yet remaining to be performed in Consequence of his Indenture." The text of this statute was printed in *Pa. Gaz.*, Sept. 2, 1756; for a discussion of the problems arising from the enlistment of servants, and BF's attempts to get compensation from Loudoun, see above, VII, 141, 224–8.

9. To reinforce an order of the Board of Trade, Oct. 9, 1756, Parliament in 1757 passed an act (30 George II, c. 9) prohibiting the exportation of corn, grain, flour, beef, pork, and other provisions to foreign dominions. In 1758, BF had tried without success to have exceptions to this act made in Pa.'s favor; see above, VII, 373 n.

subsists by the Provision Trade, has suffer'd for these two Years past a Loss of between 30 and 40 per Cent. in the Price of their Produce; which has greatly distress'd the Inhabitants of that young Colony, who are chiefly Husbandmen in low or but moderate Circumstances, and many of them New Comers that have not as yet had time to acquire the Wealth that might enable them to bear such Burthens and such Losses.

That in Obedience to His Majesty's Commands signify'd by Mr. Secretary Pitt's Letters,[1] the Assembly of the said Province, notwithstanding the Debts and Distresses the Province was involv'd in, did, in Reliance on the Promises of Recommendation for Reimbursement contain'd in the said Letters, again exert themselves so far as to Raise, Pay and Cloath for the last Campaign, Two Thousand Seven Hundred Men, who were employ'd under General Forbes in the Reduction of Fort Duquesne; and at the Request of General Amherst have retain'd 1400 of the said Troops in the Service ever since the Reduction of the said Fort.

That the said Province having never to this Day from its first Settlement received any Assistance from the Crown, or put the Nation to any Expence, nor ever had any Assistance from the neighbouring Colonies, tho' on Occasion it has frequently assisted them,[2] hopes that in its present Distress it may be thought intitled to a greater Proportion of His Majesty's Bounty proposed to be distributed among the Colonies in pursuance of a late Vote of the honourable House of Commons. B FRANKLIN

ACCOUNT of sundry Sums of Money paid by the Province of Pensylvania for HIS MAJESTY's Service, since the Commencement of Hostilities by the French in North-America; Exclusive of the general Contingent Expences of the Government, which have from that Time increas'd very considerably.

1. *Pa. Col. Recs.*, VIII, 27–8, 272–3.
2. Pa. had contributed £4000 to the New England expedition against Louisbourg in 1745 (above, III, 195 n) and £10,000 to the Mass. expedition against Crown Point in 1755 (above, VI, 3–6).

Extracted from the Journals of the Assembly.

	Pensylvania Currency
1754 and 1755. For Provisions supplied the King's Troops under the Command of General BRADDOCK: For opening and clearing a Road towards the Ohio; and for Establishing a Post between Winchester in Virginia and Philadelphia, for the Use of the Army, at the Request of said General[3]	£ 8,195 14 8½
For Provisions supplied the New-England and New-York Forces under General Johnson[4]	10,000 0 0
For Cloathing sent the Forces under General Shirley	514 10 1
For Presents to the Six Nations and other Indians in Alliance with the Crown of Great-Britain, and the Expences attending Two Treaties held with them, for securing them to the British Interest.[5]	2,023 5 0
For Maintenance of the Ohio and other Western Indians who had taken Refuge in Pensylvania; French Deserters; Soldier's Wives belonging to Braddock's Army; Arms and Ammunition deliver'd to such of the Frontier Inhabitants as were not able to purchase any for their Defence; Relief and Support of sundry of said Inhabitants who were driven from their Plantations by the Enemy; and for Expresses and other Purposes for his Majesty's Service.	5,653 13 2¼

3. This sum represents the following expenditures: £5000 for provisions for Braddock's troops (above, VI, 3–6); £2985 0s. 11d. for cutting a road for him (above, V, 42, 65); £210 13s. 9½d. for the Philadelphia-Winchester post the Assembly had authorized BF to establish for military communications (above, VI, 3–4 n, 42).

4. On this and the next entry, see above, VI, 391; VII, 142.

5. *Votes,* 1754–55, pp. 185, 187–8, and 1755–56, pp. 165–6, contain re-

[The above Sums were paid out of the Treasury and Loan Office, and by Money borrow'd on the Credit of the House of Assembly, before the Governor could be prevail'd on to pass any Bills for granting an Aid to HisMajesty.][6]

1756. For raising, paying and maintaining Forces; building Forts; maintaining and treating with the King's Indian Allies; Support of French Neutrals sent from Nova Scotia; billetting and supplying with Necessaries the King's regular Forces; and other Purposes for His Majesty's Service as recommended by his Ministers. [By two Acts of Assembly —£60,000 and £30,000.][7]   90,000   0   0

1757. For Ditto, by another Act of Assembly[8]   100,000   0   0

1758. For Ditto, by Ditto [Note, 2700 Men were rais'd and employ'd this Year in His Majesty's Service, by the Province of Pensylvania, in Pursuance of Mr. Secretary Pitt's Letter][9]   100,000   0   0

For sundry Indian Expences, omitted in the above[1]   38   13   0

For Support of a Ship of War for Protection of Trade,[2] (by a Duty on Tonnage, &c.) for a Six Month's Cruise   6,425   15   0

ports of expenditures for the period here covered, but the details are not organized in such manner as to make possible now a statement of how BF arrived at the exact totals he reported in this and the next entry.

6. Brackets in the original here and in the first and third entries below.

7. See above, VI, 257 n, 515 n. The expenditures under these acts are recorded in *Votes,* 1755–56, pp. 167–72, but are there arranged under names of individual payees, not grouped according to particular purposes. For lists of those payments in which BF was concerned as a provincial commissioner, see above, VI, 395–6, 438–40; VII, 3–5, 25–8.

8. See above, VII, 121–32, 152–3 n.

9. See above, p. 54.

1. *Votes,* 1757–58, p. 114.

2. See above, VII, 262 n.

For Interest paid by the Province for Money borrow'd for his Majesty's Service on the Credit of the Assembly; The Charges attending the Printing and Signing the Paper Money; and collecting and paying the several Taxes granted His Majesty, to the Provincial Treasurer and Trustees of the Loan-Office, with their and the Provincial Commissioners Allowance for their Trouble, may at least be estimated at	5,000	0	0

£327,851 10 11¾

From which deduct One Third to reduce the Sum to Sterling Value; an English Shilling passing for 1s. 6d. in Pensylvania	109,283	16	11¾

Sterling   £218,567 14   0

Endorsed: Pensilvania. The Agent's Memorial and Account of Expence incurr'd by that Province to the End of the Campaign of 1758.

To Mary Stevenson

MS not found; reprinted from Smyth, *Writings*, III, 478–9.[3]

My dear Child,   Craven Street, Friday, May 4, 1759.
Hearing that you was in the Park last Sunday, I hop'd for the Pleasure of seeing you yesterday at the Oratorio in the Foundling Hospital;[4] but, tho' I look'd with all the Eyes I had, not excepting

3. Also printed in Jared Sparks, ed., *A Collection of the Familiar Letters and Miscellaneous Papers of Benjamin Franklin* (Boston, 1833), pp. 61–2, and in the general editions of Sparks and Bigelow. The Smyth text is used here because it follows BF's usage in capitalization, spelling, and punctuation, as the earlier printings do not. Smyth had access to the ALS in 1905, it being then in the possession of Dr. T. Hewson Bradford, a descendant of Mary Stevenson. The text as printed in Stan V. Henkels, *Catalogue*, No. 1262, July 1, 1920, pp. 1–2, when the letter was sold, corresponds almost exactly in form and wording to the Smyth version.

4. In 1749 George Frideric Handel presented the chapel of the Foundling Hospital with an organ, and the next year inaugurated the instrument with

even those I carry in my Pocket I could not find you; and this Morning your good Mama, has receiv'd a Line from you, by which we learn that you are return'd to Wanstead.[5]

It is long since you heard from me, tho' not a Day passes in which I do not think of you with the same affectionate Regard and Esteem I ever had for you. My not writing is partly owing to an inexcusable Indolence, which I find grows upon me as I grow in Years, and partly to an Expectation I have had, from Week to Week, of making a little Journey into Essex, in which I intended to call at Wanstead, and promis'd myself the Pleasure of seeing you there. I have now fix'd this Day se'nnight for that Journey, and purpose to take Mrs. Stevenson out with me, leave her with you till the next Day, and call for her on Saturday in my Return. Let me know by a Line if you think any thing may make such a Visit from us at that time improper or inconvenient. Present my sincere Respects to Mrs. Tickell, and believe me ever, dear Polly, your truly affectionate Friend and humble Servant,

B. FRANKLIN.

P.S. We have Company that dine with us to-day, and your careful Mama, being busied about many things, cannot write. Will did

the first of a series of eleven benefit performances of his masterpiece, "The Messiah," which in time brought the Hospital receipts of about £7000. Although totally blind by 1753, he continued to supervise the performances and to play the organ concerto included in the oratorio. *The Public Advertiser*, April 7, 1759, announced that he would direct "The Messiah" at the Foundling Chapel on May 3 at twelve noon, but on the evening of April 6 he had been taken ill at a performance of the same oratorio at Covent Garden. He died on the 14th (Easter Eve), but public announcements of the Foundling Chapel event were repeated, merely substituting the name of Handel's protégé, John Christopher Smith, organist of the chapel, as the conductor. This memorable occasion, which BF attended, took place thirteen days after Handel had been buried in the Poet's Corner of Westminster Abbey; it brought to the hospital receipts of £405 8s. In his will Handel bequeathed to the hospital a fair copy of the score and all parts of "The Messiah." Robert M. Myers, *Handel's Messiah A Touchstone of Taste* (N.Y., 1948), pp. 136–44, 151–3; R. H. Nichols and F. A. Wray, *The History of the Foundling Hospital* (London, 1935), p. 205.

5. Polly Stevenson resided most of the time with her mother's sister, Mrs. Tickell, in the London suburb of Wanstead. Neither Mrs. Tickell's first name nor that of her deceased husband is known, but in some of Polly's surviving correspondence a relationship is suggested to the poet Thomas Tickell (1686–1740). On Mrs. Tickell's death Polly inherited her estate.

not see you in the Park. Mr. Hunter and his sister are both gone.[6] God prosper their Voyage. My Compliments to Miss Pitt.[7]

To the Printer of the London Chronicle

Printed in *The London Chronicle: or, Universal Evening Post,* May 10–12, 1759.

Paul Leicester Ford first identified Franklin as the author of this paper in 1889, and Verner W. Crane established the matter definitely in 1950 by pointing out the similarity of thought and treatment in certain passages with others of Franklin's writings.[8] Bigelow printed it in *Works,* IV, 244-58, but with the incorrect date of May 9, 1769, and without any of Franklin's footnotes. Smyth reproduced it directly from Bigelow in *Writings,* V, 206-18, using the same incorrect date.

To the Printer of the CHRONICLE.   May 9, 1759.
Sir,
    While the public attention is so much turned towards America, every letter from thence that promises new information, is pretty generally read; it seems therefore the more necessary that care should be taken to disabuse the Public, when those letters contain facts false in themselves, and representations injurious to bodies of people, or even to private persons.
    In your paper, No. 310. I find an extract of a letter, said to be from a gentleman in General Abercrombie's army.[9] As there are

6. See above, p. 324 n.
7. Miss Pitt, probably a friend of about Polly's age, is mentioned several times in the correspondence. Apparently her home was in Jamaica, to which she returned in 1763, but she is not otherwise identified.
8. Paul L. Ford, *Franklin Bibliography. A List of Books Written by, or Relating to Benjamin Franklin* (Brooklyn, 1889), p. 283; Verner W. Crane, ed., *Benjamin Franklin's Letters to the Press 1758–1775* (Chapel Hill, [1950]), p. 9.
9. "Extract of a Letter from a Gentleman in General Abercrombie's army, dated Camp at Lake George, August 24," *London Chron.,* Dec. 21–23, 1758. After describing the situation of Ticonderoga and Crown Point, the unidentified author discussed at length the chief characteristics of New England and New York as he observed them. Writing to Col. Peter Schuyler, June 19, 1759 (below p. 408), WF stated his belief that the author was no army officer but Dr. Adam Thomson, a Scottish physician then living in New York; see above, IV, 80 n.

several strokes in it tending to render the colonies despicable, and even odious to the mother country, which may have ill consequences; and no notice having been taken of the injuries contained in that letter, other letters of the same nature have since been published, permit me to make a few observations on it.

The writer says, "New England was settled by Presbyterians and Independents, who took shelter there from the persecutions of Archbishop Laud;[1] *they still retain their original character, they generally hate the Church of England,*" says he. If it were true, that some resentment still remained for the hardships their fathers suffer'd, it might perhaps be not much wondered at; but the fact is, that the moderation of the present church of England towards Dissenters in *Old* as well as *New* England, has quite effaced those impressions; the Dissenters too are become less rigid and scrupulous, and the good will between those different bodies in that country is now both mutual and equal.

He goes on: *"They came out with a levelling spirit, and they retain it. They cannot bear to think that one man should be exorbitantly rich and another poor, so that, except in the seaport towns, there are few great estates among them. This equality produces also a rusticity of manners; for in their language, dress, and in all their behaviour, they are more boorish than any thing you ever saw in a certain Northern latitude."* One would imagine from this account, that those who were growing poor, plundered those who were growing rich to preserve this equality, and that property had no protection; whereas in fact, it is no where more secure than in the New England colonies, the law is no where better executed, or justice obtain'd at less expence. The equality he speaks of, arises first from a more equal distribution of lands by the assemblies in the first settlement than has been practised in the other colonies, where favourites of governors have obtained enormous tracts for trifling considerations, to the prejudice both of the crown revenues and the public good;[2] and secondly, from the nature of their occupation; husbandmen with small tracts of land, though they may by industry

---

1. William Laud (1573–1645), dean of Gloucester, 1616–21; bishop of St. David's, 1621–26; bishop of Bath and Wells, 1626–28; bishop of London, 1628–33; archbishop of Canterbury, 1633–45; chancellor of Oxford University, 1629–41. *DNB.*

2. Such abuses were particularly flagrant in New York.

maintain themselves and families in mediocrity, having few means of acquiring great wealth, especially in a young colony that is to be supplied with its cloathing, and many other expensive articles of consumption from the mother country. Their dress the gentleman may be a more critical judge of than I can pretend to be; all I know of it is, that they wear the manufactures of Britain, and follow its fashions perhaps too closely, every remarkable change in the mode making its appearance there within a few months after its invention here; a natural effect of their constant intercourse with England, by ships arriving almost every week from the capital, their respect for the mother country, and admiration of every thing that is British. But as to their language, I must beg this gentleman's pardon if I differ from him. His ear, accustomed perhaps to the dialect practised in the *certain northern latitude* he mentions,[3] may not be qualified to judge so nicely in what relates to *pure* English. And I appeal to all Englishmen here, who have been acquainted with the Colonists, whether it is not a common remark, that they speak the language with such an exactness both of expression and accent, that though you may know the natives of several of the counties of England, by peculiarities in their dialect, you cannot by that means distinguish a North American. All the new books and pamphlets worth reading, that are published here, in a few weeks are transmitted and found there, where there is not a man or woman born in the country but what can read: and it must, I should think, be a pleasing reflection to those who write either for the benefit of the present age or of posterity, to find their audience increasing with the increase of our colonies; and their language extending itself beyond the narrow bounds of these islands to a continent, larger than all Europe, and to a future empire as fully peopled, which Britain may probably one day possess in those vast western regions.

But the Gentleman makes more injurious comparisons than these: *"That latitude,"* he says, "has this advantage over them, that it has produced sharp, acute men, fit for war or learning, whereas the other are remarkably simple or silly, and blunder eternally. We have 6000 of their militia, which the General would willingly exchange for 2000 regulars. They are for ever marring some one or

3. Scotland.

other of our plans when sent to execute them. They can, indeed, some of them at least, range in the woods; but 300 Indians with their yell, throw 3000 of them into a panick, and then they will leave nothing to the enemy to do, for they will shoot one another; and in the woods our regulars are afraid to be on a command with them *on that very account.*" I doubt, Mr. Chronicle, that this paragraph, when it comes to be read in America, will have no good effect, and rather increase that inconvenient disgust that is too apt to arise between the troops of different corps, or countries, who are obliged to serve together. Will not a *New England Officer* be apt to retort and say, What foundation have you for this odious distinction in favour of the officers from your *certain northern latitude?* They may, as you say, be *fit for learning,* but, surely, the return of your first General, with a well appointed and sufficient force from his expedition against Louisbourg,[4] is not the most shining proof of his *talents for war.* And no one will say his plan was *marred by us,* for we were not with him. Was his successor, who conducted the blundering attack and inglorious retreat from Ticonderoga, a New England man, or one of *that certain latitude?*[5] Then as to the comparison between *Regulars* and *Provincials,* will not the latter remark, That it was 2000 New England *Provincials,* with but about 150 *Regulars,* that took the strong fort of Beausejour in the beginning of the war, though in the accounts transmitted to the English Gazette, the honour was claimed by the regulars, and little or no notice taken of the others.[6] That it was the *Provincials*

4. The Earl of Loudoun, a Scot, had abandoned his campaign against Louisbourg in the summer of 1757, after assembling an army of sixteen regiments of British regulars at Halifax. Pargellis, *Lord Loudoun,* pp. 236–43; Gipson, *British Empire,* VII, 102–16.

5. James Abercromby, another Scot and Loudoun's successor as commander-in-chief, led an expedition against Ticonderoga in the early summer of 1758. It consisted of some 12,000 men, about half of whom were newly recruited and untrained provincials. Abercromby's direct frontal attack on the fort, July 8, was premature, ill planned, and carried forward without waiting for the emplacement of his artillery. His most effective subordinate, Lord Howe, had been killed in a preliminary skirmish; many, but far from all, of the raw provincials behaved badly; the regulars suffered heavy casualties; and the greatly outnumbered French defenders gained a complete victory. Abercromby retreated to Lake George and abandoned the idea of a second attempt on Ticonderoga that year. Gipson, *British Empire,* VII, 212–35.

6. In June 1755 a force of 2000 New England volunteers and 250 British

who beat General Dieskau, with his *Regulars,* Canadians, and *"yelling"* Indians, and sent him prisoner to England.[7] That it was a *Provincial-born* Officer,* with American battoemen, that beat the French and Indians on Oswego river.[8] That it was the same Officer, *with Provincials,* who made that long and admirable march into the enemies country, took and destroyed Fort Frontenac, with the whole French fleet on the lakes, and struck terror into the heart of Canada. That it was a *Provincial* Officer,† *with Provincials* only, who made another extraordinary march into the enemy's country, surprized and destroyed the Indian town of Kittanning, bringing off the scalps of their chiefs.[9] That one ranging Captain of a few *Provincials,* Rogers, has harrassed the enemy

*Colonel Bradstreet.
†Colonel Armstrong of Pensilvania.

---

regulars from the Nova Scotia garrison, commanded by Lieut. Col. Robert Monckton, a British officer, captured Fort Beauséjour and the smaller Fort Gaspereau on the opposite side of the Chignecto Isthmus. *Ibid.,* VI, 226–33. BF had complained to Sir Everard Fawkener, July 27, 1756, about the failure of the British officers and newspapers to give the New Englanders any credit for their part in the victory. See above, VI, 473.

7. After an initial setback, Gen. William Johnson, with a mixed force of Indians and provincials, mostly from New England, defeated the French at the Battle of Lake George, Sept. 8, 1755, and captured the wounded French commander-in-chief in North America, Baron de Dieskau. Gipson, *British Empire,* VI, 163–75; above, VI, 218 n.

8. In spite of BF's emphatic statement, it is uncertain whether John Bradstreet (*c.* 1711–1774) was born in Nova Scotia or immigrated at an early age. He may have been the Jean-Baptiste Bradstreet who was born in 1714, the son of an officer in the 40th Regiment (stationed in Acadia after the British conquest) and Agathe de la Tour of a prominent Acadian family. He became an ensign in the 40th Regiment in 1745, served with distinction at Louisbourg, and became a captain in Pepperrell's regiment, 1746, though recommended for the lieutenant colonelcy. In charge of supplying the garrison at Oswego, 1755–56, he organized 2000 bateaumen, constructed boats, and moved large quantities of provisions there, despite the enemy's efforts to disrupt his communications. Pitt advanced him to the rank of lieutenant colonel and appointed him deputy quartermaster general in 1757. He commanded a force of about 3000 men, all but some 150 of whom were provincials, which attacked and captured Fort Frontenac (now Kingston, Ontario), Aug. 27, 1758. *DAB;* Pargellis, *Military Affairs,* p. 187 n; Gipson, *British Empire,* VII, 238–46.

9. For Col. John Armstrong's attack on Kittanning in September 1756, see above, VII, 262, and William A. Hunter, "Victory at Kittanning," *Pa. Hist.,* XXIII (1956), 376–407.

more on the frontiers of Canada, and destroyed *more* of their men, than the *whole* army of *Regulars*.[1] That it was the *Regulars* who surrendered themselves, with the Provincials under their command, prisoners of war, almost as soon as they were besieged, with the forts, fleet, and all the provisions and stores that had been provided and amassed at so immense an expence, at Oswego.[2] That it was the *Regulars* who surrendered Fort William Henry, and suffered themselves to be butchered and scalped with arms in their hands.[3] That it was the *Regulars,* under Braddock, who were thrown into a panick by the *"yells* of 3 or 400 Indians,"in their confusion shot one another, and, with five times the force of the enemy, fled before them, destroying all their own stores, ammunition, and provisions![4] These *Regular Gentlemen,* will the *Provincial rangers* add, may possibly be *afraid,* as they say they are, *to be on a command with us* in the woods; but when it is considered, that from all past experience the chance of our shooting them is not as one to an hundred, compared with that of their being shot by the enemy, may it not be suspected, that what they give as the *very account* of their fear and unwillingness to venture out with us, is only the *very excuse;* and that a concern for their scalps weighs more with them than a regard for their honour.

Such as these, Sir, I imagine may be the reflections *extorted* by such provocations from the Provincials in general. But the *New England Men* in particular will have reason to resent the remarks

1. The exploits of Robert Rogers (1731–1795) and his rangers have become almost legendary, and hardly need to be summarized here. Some of his most famous operations had not yet taken place when BF wrote. Rogers was born in Methuen, Mass., and grew up in New Hampshire. John R. Cuneo, *Robert Rogers of the Rangers* (N.Y., 1959).

2. Oswego surrendered to Montcalm, Aug. 14, 1756. Pargellis, *Lord Loudoun,* pp. 147–60; Gipson, *British Empire,* VI, 195–203.

3. Largely because Gen. Daniel Webb had failed to provide adequate reinforcements, Lieut. Col. George Monro, with about 740 regulars and 1200 provincials, was forced to surrender Fort William Henry to Montcalm and his besieging army of 7000 French and Indians, Aug. 9, 1757. Montcalm guaranteed to protect the prisoners against his Indian allies, but he provided an inadequate guard, the Indians attacked and killed at least 200, including sick and wounded, women and children, before Montcalm himself appeared to stop the massacre. Pargellis, *Lord Loudoun,* pp. 243–51; Gipson, *British Empire,* VII, 78–88.

4. On Braddock's defeat, July 9, 1755, see above, VI, 109.

on their reduction of Louisbourg. Your writer proceeds, "Indeed they are all very ready to make their boast of taking Louisbourg, in 1745; but if people were to be acquitted or condemned according to the propriety and wisdom of their plans, and not according to their success, the persons that undertook that siege merited little praise: for I have heard officers, who assisted at it, say, never was any thing more rash; for had one single part of their plan failed, or had the French made the fortieth part of the resistance then that they have made now, every soul of the New Englanders must have fallen in the trenches. The garrison was weak, sickly, destitute of provisions, and disgusted, and therefore became a ready prey; and, when they returned to France were decimated for their gallant defence. Where then is the glory arising from thence?" After denying his facts, "that the garrison was weak, wanted provisions, made not a fortieth part of the resistance, were decimated," &c. the *New England* men will ask this regular gentleman, If the place was well fortified, and had (as it really had) a numerous garrison, was it not at least *brave* to attack it with a handful of raw undisciplined militia? If the garrison was, as you say, "sickly, disgusted, destitute of provisions, and ready to become a prey," was it not *prudent* to seize that opportunity, and put the nation in possession of so important a fortress at so small an expence? So that if you will not allow the enterprize to be, as we think it was, both *brave* and *prudent,* ought you not at least to grant it was *either one* or *the other?* But is there no merit on this score in the people, who, tho' at first so greatly divided, as to the making or forbearing the attempt, that it was carried in the affirmative, by the small majority of *one* vote only; yet when it was once resolved on, *unanimously* prosecuted the design,* and prepared the means with

*"As the Massachuset's assembly at first entered into the expedition upon the *coolest deliberation,* so did they on the other hand exert themselves with *uncommon vigour* in the persecution of it. As soon as the point was carried for undertaking it, EVERY MEMBER which had opposed it *gave up his own private judgment* to the public voice, and *vied* with those who had voted for the expedition, in encouraging the enlistment of the troops, and forwarding the preparations for the attempt." *Memoirs of the last War,* p. 41.[5]

5. *Memoirs of the Principal Transactions of the Last War between the English and French in North America. From the Commencement of it in 1744, to the*

the greatest zeal and diligence; so that the whole equipment was completely ready before the season would permit the execution? Is there no merit of praise in laying and executing their plan so well, that, as you have confessed, not a *single part* of it failed? If the plan was destitute of "propriety and wisdom," would it not have required the *sharp acute* men of the *northern latitude* to execute it, that by supplying its deficiencies they might give it some chance of success? But if such "remarkably silly, simple, blundering *Mar-plans,*" as you say we are, could execute *this plan,* so that not a *single part* of it failed, does it not at least show that the plan itself must be laid with *some* "wisdom and propriety?" Is there no merit in the ardour with which all degrees and ranks of people quitted their private affairs, and ranged themselves under the banners of their King, for the honour, safety, and advantage of their country?†

†"The bounty, pay, and other encouragements, allowed by the Massachuset's government to both officers and men, especially the former, was but small; but the *spirit* which reigned thro' the province supplied the want of that; the complement of troops was soon inlisted; not only the officers, who served in this enterprize, were gentlemen of considerable property, but most of the non-commission'd officers, and many of the private men, had valuable freeholds,[6] and entered into the service upon the same principles that the old Roman citizens in the first Consular armies used to do." *Memoirs of the last War,* p. 41.

To which I may add, that instances of the same noble spirit are not uncommon in all the other colonies; where men have entered into the service not for the sake of the pay, for their own affairs in their absence suffer more by far than its value; not in hopes of preferment in the army, for the Provincials are shut out from such expectations, their own forces being always disbanded on a peace, and the vacancies among the Regulars filled with Europeans; but merely from *public spirit* and a sense of duty. Among many others, give me leave to name Col. PETER SCHUYLER of New Jersey;[7] who, though a gentleman of a considerable

Conclusion of the Treaty at Aix la Chapelle. Containing in Particular An Account of the Importance of Nova Scotia or Acadie and the Island of Cape Breton to both Nations (London, 1757). The authorship has sometimes been attributed to William Shirley. The italics and small capitals in the quotation are BF's.

6. "Farms" in the original *Memoirs*.

7. Peter Schuyler (*c.* 1710–1762), well-to-do member of the family long prominent in N.Y. and N.J. affairs, organized and commanded a regiment, the "Jersey Blues," in 1746 for the abortive expedition against Canada, and

Is there no merit in the profound secrecy guarded by a whole people, so that the enemy had not the least intelligence of the design, till they saw the fleet of transports cover the sea before their port? Is there none in the indefatigable labour the troops went thro' during the siege, performing the duty both of men and

---

independent fortune, has, both in the last and present war, quitted that domestic ease and quiet which such affluence afforded, to take upon him the command of his country's forces, and by his example animated the soldiery to undergo the greatest fatigues and hardships: And who when a prisoner in Canada for fifteen months, did, during the whole time, generously make use of his own credit to relieve such British subjects as unhappily fell into the hands of the enemy. Not to mention his advancing his own private fortune towards paying the forces, raised during last war in America by order of the crown; when, by the continued delays in sending the money from England for that purpose, it was generally doubted whether it would ever be sent, and the common soldiers were therefore, from necessity, on the point of quitting his Majesty's service in a body.[8] An event which must at that time have been attended with very fatal consequences; and would not have been prevented, had not he risqued so considerable a part of his substance.

another at the beginning of the next war. He and half of his men, who were part of the garrison at Oswego, were captured when that post fell to the French in August 1756. Taken to Canada, he was released on parole in order to effect an exchange, but being unable to do this within the time specified, he returned to Canada, where he remained until exchanged with some of his soldiers after the British took Fort Frontenac in August 1758. He then organized a new regiment and was with the British army under General Amherst which captured Montreal, Sept. 8, 1760. Charles H. Winfield, *History of the County of Hudson, New Jersey* (N.Y., 1874), pp. 536–41; George W. Schuyler, *Colonial New York Philip Schuyler and His Family* (N.Y., 1885), II, 207–12.

8. While stationed in Albany in May 1747, Schuyler's troops started to mutiny because their pay was withheld by the military authorities. The colonel quelled the disturbance by offering to pay the men from his own resources, an action which brought upon him a sharp rebuke from Gov. George Clinton of N.Y. on the extraordinary grounds that "the retaining the greatest part of the arrears due . . . is the most effectual method at present to prevent desertions." Later, when some money became available and Schuyler paid his men in full, Clinton complained to the Duke of Newcastle that this was "the principal reason why the greatest number of the other forces and chiefly those levied in this Province remain discontented and mutinous, and refuse to receive less than their whole pay." 1 *N.J. Arch.*, VI, 441–2, 451–2.

horses; the hardships they patiently suffered for want of tents and other necessaries; the readiness with which they learnt to move, direct, and manage cannon, raise batteries, and form approaches;* the bravery with which they sustained sallies; and finally in their consenting to stay and garrison the place after it was taken, absent from their business and families, till troops could be brought from England for that purpose, tho' they undertook the service on a promise of being discharged as soon as it was over, were unprovided for so long an absence, and actually suffered ten times more loss by mortal sickness, thro' want of necessaries, than they suffered from the arms of the enemy? The nation, however, had a sense of this undertaking different from the unkind one of this gentleman. At the treaty of peace, the possession of Louisbourg was found of great advantage to our affairs in Europe; and if the brave men that made the acquisition for us were not *rewarded,* at

*"The New England troops, within the compass of 23 days from the time of their first landing, erected five fascine batteries against the town, mounted with cannon of 42 lb. 22 lb. and 18 lb. shot, mortars of 13, 11, and 9 inches diameter, with some cohorns; all which were transported *by hand,* with incredible labour and difficulty, most of them above two miles; all the ground over which they were drawn, except small patches or hills of rocks, was a *deep morass,* in which, whilst the cannon were upon wheels, they several times sunk so deep, as not only to bury the carriages, but their whole bodies. Horses and oxen could not be employed in this service, but all must be drawn by men, up to the knees in mud; the nights, in which the work was done, were cold and foggy, their tents bad, there being no proper materials for tents to be had in New England at the outset of the expedition. But notwithstanding these difficulties, and many of the men's being taken down with fluxes, so that at one time there were 1500 incapable of duty, they went on *without being discouraged or murmuring,* and[9] transported the cannon over those ways, which the French had always thought impassable for such heavy weights; and besides this, they had all their provisions and heavy ammunition, which they daily made use of, to bring from the camp over the same way upon their backs." *Memoirs of the last war in America,* page 52.[1]

9. BF omitted from the quoted passage: "by the Help of Sledges."
1. Pp. 52–3. This pamphlet devotes pp. 31–71 (about two-fifths of the whole) to an account of the planning and carrying out of the Louisbourg expedition of 1745 and the problem of garrisoning the fortress after its capture.

least they were *praised*. *Envy* may continue a while to cavil and detract, but *public virtue* will in the end obtain esteem; and honest impartiality in this and future ages will not fail doing justice to merit.

Your *gentleman writer* thus *decently* goes on. "The most substantial men of most of the provinces are children or grandchildren of those that came here at the King's expence, that is, thieves, highwaymen, and robbers." Being probably a military gentleman, this, and therefore a person of nice honour, if any one should tell him in the *plainest* language, that what he here says is an absolute falsehood, challenges and cutting of throats might immediately ensue. I shall therefore only refer him to *his own account in this same letter,* of the *peopling* of New England, which he says, with more truth, was by Puritans who fled thither for shelter from the persecutions of Archbishop Laud. Is there not a wide difference between removing to a distant country to enjoy the exercise of religion according to a man's conscience, and his being transported thither by law as a punishment for his crimes? This contradiction we therefore leave the *gentleman* and *himself* to settle as well as they can between them. One would think from his account, that the provinces were so many colonies from Newgate. The truth is, not only Laud's persecution, but the other publick troubles in the following reigns, induc'd many thousand families to leave England, and settle in the plantations. During the predominance of the parliament, many royalists removed or were banished to Virginia and Barbadoes, who afterwards spread into the other settlements: The Catholics shelter'd themselves in Maryland. At the restoration, many of the depriv'd nonconformist ministers with their families, friends and hearers, went over. Towards the end of Charles the Second's reign and during James the Second's, the dissenters again flocked into America, driven by persecution, and dreading the introduction of popery at home. Then the high price or reward of labour in the colonies, and want of Artisans there, drew over many, as well as the occasion of commerce; and when once people begin to migrate, every one has his little sphere of acquaintance and connections, which he draws after him, by invitation, motives of interest, praising his new settlement, and other encouragements. The "most substantial men" are descendants of those early settlers; new comers not having yet had time to raise estates. The practice of sending convicts thither, is modern; and the same indolence of temper and habits of idleness that make people poor and tempt them to steal in England, continue with them when they are sent to America, and must there have the same effects, where all who live well owe their subsistence to labour and business, and where it is a thousand times more difficult than here to acquire wealth without industry. Hence the instances of transported thieves advancing their fortunes in the colonies are extreamly rare, if there *really is* a single instance of it, which I very much doubt; but of their being advanc'd there to the gallows the instances are plenty. Might they not as well have been hang'd at home? We call Britain the *mother* country; but what good mother besides, would introduce thieves and criminals into the company of her children, to corrupt and disgrace them? And how cruel is it, to force, by the high hand of power, a particular country of your subjects, who have not deserv'd such usage, to receive your outcasts, repealing all the laws they make to prevent their admission, and then reproach them with the detested mixture you have made. "The emptying their jails into our settlements (says a writer of that country) is an insult and contempt, the cruellest perhaps that ever one people offered another; and would not be equal'd even by emptying their jakes on our tables."[2]

The letter I have been considering, Mr. Chronicle, is follow'd by another, in your paper of Tuesday the 17th past, said to be *from an officer who attended Brigadier General Forbes in his march from Philadelphia to Fort Duquesne;* but wrote probably by the same gentleman who wrote the former,[3] as it seems calculated to

2. The quotation is slightly modified from a sentence in a longer passage, also placed within quotation marks, printed in *Pa. Gaz.*, April 11, 1751, at the end of a catalogue of felonies committed by indentured servants and others in Virginia, Maryland, and Pennsylvania. In the issue of the following May 9, BF had followed up that attack on the British policy of transporting felons to the colonies with his well-known satire in which he proposed gathering up in America, shipping to Britain, and releasing there quantities of rattlesnakes as "the highest *Returns* of Gratitude and Duty" the colonies could make to the mother country for the "tender *parental* Concern" she showed them in sending over her felons. See above, IV, 130–3.

3. "A Letter from an Officer who attended Brigadier General Forbes, in his March from Philadelphia to Fort Duquesne, (now Pittsburgh) Feb. 25, 1759,"

raise the character of the officers of the *certain northern latitude,* at the expence of the reputation of the colonies, and the provincial forces. According to this letter-writer, if the Pensilvanians granted large supplies, and raised a great body of troops for the last campaign, it was not obedience to his Majesty's commands, signified by his minister Mr. Pitt, zeal for the King's service, or even a regard for their own safety; but it was owing to the "General's proper management of the Quakers and other parties in the province."[4] The withdrawing of the Indians from the French interest by negotiating a peace, is all ascribed to the General, and not a word said to the honour of the poor Quakers who first set those negotiations on foot, or of honest Frederic Post that compleated them with so much ability and success.[5] Even the little merit of the Assembly's making a law to regulate carriages, is imputed to the General's "multitude of letters."[6] Then he tells us,

---

London Chron., April 14–17, 1759. This is a detailed account of the Forbes expedition. WF told Col. Peter Schuyler, June 19, 1759, that he thought the author was "Parson Smith of Philadelphia"; see below, p. 408. The two letters to which BF was replying in this paper occupy together approximately the same amount of space in the *Chronicle* as his defense of the provincials.

4. The Pa. Assembly, voted to raise 2700 men for the campaign, March 23, 1758, fifteen days after Governor Denny sent them Pitt's letter of Dec. 30, 1757; after the usual controversy over taxation of proprietary estates, the House yielded the point and on the afternoon of April 18 agreed to prepare a bill granting £100,000. General Forbes arrived in Philadelphia that evening. Denny put aside his objections to the commissioners named in the bill on April 22 and the measure became law the same day. Since Forbes's arrival in the city and his first conference with Denny seem not to have taken place until a few hours after the Assembly had made its important concession, it is not clear how he could have exercised any "proper management of the Quakers and other parties in the province" in securing the appropriation, except by persuading Denny to yield on the matter of the commissioners. *Votes,* 1757–58, pp. 50–1, 56–7, 77–80; Alfred P. James, ed., *Writings of General John Forbes* (Menasha, Wis.), p. 65.

5. See above, pp. 199, 230, 298.

6. Before the campaign began Forbes appears to have written only one letter to Denny (on March 23) on the need for an act regarding wagons and carriages for the army. The Assembly passed such a bill, April 1, and after consulting with Forbes's quartermaster general, Sir John St. Clair, Denny signed it, April 8. The wagons and teams provided under this act proved inadequate after the march had begun; Forbes appealed to Denny for an additional act, September 9, and also wrote to several provincial leaders; the Assembly received the request on the 13th; and Denny signed the resulting

"innumerable scouting parties had been sent out during a long period, both by the General and Colonel Bouquet,[7] towards Fort Duquesne, to catch a prisoner, if possible, for intelligence, but never got any." How happened that? Why, "It was the *Provincial troops* that were constantly employed in that service," and they, it seems, never do any thing they are ordered to do. *That,* however, one would think, might be easily remedied, by sending *Regulars* with them, who of course must command them, and may see that they do their duty. *No; The Regulars are afraid of being shot by the Provincials in a Panick.* Then send all Regulars. *Aye; That was what the Colonel* resolved *upon.* "Intelligence was now wanted (says the letter-writer). Col. Bouquet, whose attention to business was [only] very considerable [that is, *not quite so great* as the General's, for he was not of the *northern latitude*] was *determined* to send NO MORE Provincials a scouting."[8] And how did he execute this determination? Why, by sending "Major Grant[9] of the Highlanders, with *seven* hundred men, *three* hundred of them Highlanders, THE REST Americans, Virginians, and Pensilvanians!" No *blunder* this, in our writer; but a *misfortune;* and he is nevertheless one of those *"acute sharp"* men who are *"fit for learning!"* And how did this Major and seven hundred men succeed in catching the prisoner? Why, their "march to Fort Duquesne was *so conducted* that the *surprize* was *compleat.*" Perhaps you may imagine, gentle reader, that this was a surprize of the enemy. No such matter. They knew every step of his motions, and had, every man of them, left their fires and huts in the fields, and retired into the fort. But the Major and his 700 men, *they* were *surprized;* first to find no body there at

bill, September 20. James, ed., *Forbes Writings,* pp. 63, 206–8, 213; *Votes,* 1757–58, pp. 60, 62, 63, 98–9, 100, 101; *Pa. Col. Recs.,* VIII, 60-1, 69, 71, 77, 167–70, 171.

7. Lieut. Col. Henry Bouquet (see above, VII, 63 n) was second in command of the Forbes expedition.

8. The brackets in this sentence were inserted by BF to indicate his interpolations in the quotation.

9. James Grant (1720–1806) entered the British Army in 1741 and in 1757 was made major of the newly raised First Highland Battalion or Montgomery Highlanders (later the 77th Regiment). This unit was the nucleus around which Forbes's expedition was organized. Grant was governor of the province of East Florida, 1764–71, and served in the army in America again during the Revolution. He commanded the expedition which captured St. Lucia in the West Indies in 1778. *DNB.*

night; and next to find themselves surrounded and cut to pieces in the morning; two or three hundred being killed, drowned, or taken prisoners, and among the latter the Major himself. Those who escaped were also *surprized* at their own good fortune; and the whole army was *surprized* at the Major's bad management.[1] Thus the *surprize* was indeed *compleat;* but not the disgrace; for *Provincials were there* to lay the blame on. The *misfortune* (we must not call it *misconduct*) of the Major was owing, it seems, to an unnamed and perhaps unknown *Provincial* officer, who, it is said, "disobeyed his orders and quitted his post."[2] Whence a formal conclusion is drawn, "That a Planter is not to be taken from the plow and made an officer in a day." Unhappy *Provincials!* If *success* attends where you are joined with the Regulars, they claim all the honour, tho' not a tenth part of your number. If *disgrace*, it is all yours, though you happen to be but a small part of the whole, and have not the command; as if Regulars were in their nature invincible, when not mix'd with Provincials, and Provincials of no kind of value without Regulars! Happy is it for you that you were present neither at Preston-Pans nor Falkirk, at the faint attempt against Rochfort, the rout of St. Cas, or the hasty retreat from Martinico.[3] Every thing that went wrong, or did not go right,

1. On September 11 Bouquet, who commanded the advance units, sent Grant with nearly 800 men, about half of them regulars, ahead to feel out the strength of the enemy, take prisoners, and then retreat. By the 14th Grant was close enough to Fort Duquesne to send Major Andrew Lewis of Virginia with 300 regulars and 100 Virginians to attack the Indian encampment near the fort, but Lewis returned without accomplishing his mission because, as he said, his men could not find their way through the woods in the darkness. Later that day the French and Indians sallied from the fort and enveloped Grant's outnumbered troops. Partly because Lewis and Grant missed each other when they tried to join forces, the French gained a complete victory. The British lost 300 killed or missing (mostly regulars) and 44 others wounded; Grant and Lewis were both taken prisoner. Forbes later blamed both Bouquet and Grant for their rashness in this operation. James, ed., *Forbes Writings*, pp. 215–16, 217, 218; [Thomas Balch, ed.], *Letters and Papers Relating Chiefly to the Provincial History of Pennsylvania* (Phila., 1855), p. 139; Gipson, *British Empire*, VII, 268–70.

2. Apparently a reference to Major Lewis of the Va. regiment; see the preceding note.

3. Prestonpans (Sept. 21, 1745) and Falkirk Moor (Jan. 17, 1746) were Jacobite victories in the Rebellion of 1745. On the abortive expedition against Rochefort in the summer of 1757, see above, VII, 375 n. After an unsuccessful

would have been ascribed to you. Our commanders would have been saved the labour of writing long apologies for their conduct. It might have been sufficient to say, *Provincials were with us!*

But these remarks, which we only suppose may be made by the provok'd provincials, are probably too severe. The generals, even those who have been recall'd, had in several respects great merit, as well as many of the officers of the same nation that remain, which the cool discreet part of the provincials will readily allow. They are not insensible of the worth and bravery of the British troops in general, honour them for the amazing valour they manifested at the landing on Cape Breton, the prudence and military skill they show'd in the siege and reduction of Louisburg,[4] and their good conduct on other occasions; and can make due allowance for mistakes naturally arising where even the best men are engag'd in a new kind of war, with a new and strange enemy, and in a country different from any they had before experienc'd. Lord HOWE was their darling,† and others might be nam'd who are

† The assembly of the Massachusets-Bay have voted a sum of money for erecting a monument in Westminster-Abbey, to the memory of that Nobleman, as a testimony of their veneration for his virtues. A proof that their sense of merit is not narrow'd to a country.[5]

raid against St. Malo, Lieut. Gen. Thomas Bligh's troops were attacked by the French, Sept. 11, 1758, while attempting to reembark at the nearby port of St. Cas and suffered heavy losses, running into the hundreds as the British admitted, or the thousands as the French asserted. A combined military and naval expedition under Maj. Gen. Thomas Peregrine Hopson and Commodore John Moore undertook the capture of Martinique in January 1759, but finding stronger resistance and greater topographical difficulties than anticipated, abandoned the undertaking after minor assault operations and sailed for Guadeloupe, which was successfully reduced and surrendered May 2, 1759, although Hopson died during the campaign. News of the achievement at Guadeloupe, of course, had not yet reached London when BF wrote this sentence. On the St. Cas and Martinique operations, see Gipson, *British Empire*, VII, 135–7; VIII, 86–94.

4. At the contested landing operation with which Gen. Jeffery Amherst opened his attack upon Louisbourg, June 8, 1758, the troops of the "Red Division" under James Wolfe acquitted themselves with particular bravery and success. In spite of a stubborn defense against the British siege which followed, the French commander, the Chevalier de Drucour, was forced to surrender the stronghold, July 26, 1758. Gipson, *British Empire*, VII, 192–207.

5. George Augustus, 3d Viscount Howe (*c.* 1724–1758), brigadier general and second in command of Abercromby's expedition against Ticonderoga,

growing daily in their esteem and admiration. There are also among the regular officers, men of sentiments, concerning the colonies, more generous and more just than those express'd by these letter-writers; who can see faults even in their own corps, and who can allow the Provincials their share of merit; who feel pleasure as Britons, in observing that the *children* of Britain retain their native intrepidity to the third and fourth generation in the regions of America; together with that ardent love of liberty and zeal in its defence, which in every age has distinguish'd their progenitors among the rest of mankind. To conclude, in all countries, all nations, and all armies, there is, and will be a mixture of characters, a medley of brave men, fools, wisemen and cowards. National reflections being general, are therefore unjust. But panegyrics, tho' they should be too general, cannot offend the subjects of them. I shall therefore boldly say, that the English are brave and wise; the Scotch are brave and wise; and the people of the British colonies, proceeding from both nations—I would say the same of them, if it might not be thought vanity in Your humble servant, A NEW ENGLANDMAN.

Certificate of Nomination to the Royal Society

DS: The Royal Society, London

Franklin was elected a fellow of the Royal Society on April 29, 1756, and was formally admitted on Nov. 24, 1757.[6] He attended meetings regularly, was a frequent guest at dinners of the Royal Society Club,[7]

---

endeared himself to the troops, provincials and regulars alike, by his ability to adapt to the conditions of wilderness fighting in America and his willingness, rare in a British officer of his rank and station in life, to sacrifice personal luxuries to the exigencies of a campaign. He was killed at the start of a skirmish, July 6, 1758, which opened Abercromby's unsuccessful expedition. His younger brothers Richard and William became respectively naval and military commanders of British forces in the American Revolution. *DAB.* The monument in Westminster Abbey, voted by the Mass. General Court, Feb. 1, 1759, was "opened," July 10, 1762. It is described, with the text of the inscription, in *Gent. Mag.*, XXXII (1762), 340.

6. See above, VI, 375–6, for the certificate of his nomination and a summary of the Royal Society's rules on elections.

7. Archibald Geikie, *Annals of the Royal Society Club* (London, 1917), pp. 69 *et passim.*

and took an active part in the Society's business, being elected a member of the Council in 1760, 1766, 1767, 1772. Between 1759 and 1774 he joined in recommending at least thirty-seven persons for election as fellows, in some instances, like that of John Winthrop of Harvard, probably initiating the action, in others supporting nominations first made by friends. Several of these candidates had made contributions to electrical science or other subjects in which he was interested, and many have appeared or will appear often in the pages of this edition.

The first recommendation Franklin signed was for Edward Hussey Delaval of Cambridge University, who was proposed on May 17, 1759, and elected the following December 6. The text of his certificate is printed in full below. Other certificates that Franklin signed nearly always followed the same general form, although they often mentioned the candidates' particular fields more specifically. They will not be individually printed in this edition at their respective dates, but they are listed here in chronological order, showing their dates of nomination, not of election. All these nominating papers are in the archives of the Royal Society. Those in Franklin's hand, or in which his name leads the list of nominators, are marked with an asterisk (*); probably they relate to people in whom he was especially interested. So far as possible the dates of birth and death of the candidates and brief indications of residence and special activities and interests are supplied.

Edward Hussey Delaval (1729–1814). May 17, 1759
   Cambridge. Fellow of Pembroke College; chemist; electrician.
William Harrison (d. 1815). Feb. 7, 1765
   London. Mathematician; assisted father John with chronometer.
Domenico, Marchese Caraccioli (1715–1789). Feb. 28, 1765
   London. Ambassador of the Kingdom of the Two Sicilies to the British King; mathematician and physicist.
John Lewin. March 21, 1765
   London. Naturalist.
Richard Price (1723–1791). May 9, 1765
   London. Clergyman; political economist.
*John Winthrop (1714–1779). June 27, 1765[8]
   Cambridge, Mass. Astronomer, mathematician.
John Mills (d. 1784?). June 1765
   London. Agriculturist; author of *The New and Complete System of Agriculture*.

8. A draft is in APS. At the bottom a clerk has noted: "Benj: Franklin signed a Bond for him for his Contributions and paid his Admission fee in November 1767."

*Arthur Lee (1740–1792). Feb. 20, 1766[9]
    Williamsburg, Va. Physician.
Joseph Priestley (1733–1804). March 13, 1766
    Warrington, Lancashire. Clergyman; teacher; historian of electricity.
Anthony Tissington. June 19, 1766
    Stanwick, Derbyshire. Natural philosopher.
*Charles L'Epinasse. April 2, 1767
    London. Mathematician.
Father Joseph-Etienne Bertier (1702–1783). Aug. 10, 1767
    A father of the Oratory, Paris; professor of natural philosophy and chemistry at Mans and (later) Saumur.
M. [Louis-Joseph Plumard] de Dangeul (b. 1722). Feb. 26, 1768 (*Not elected*)[1]
    Paris. Political economist.
Edward Spry. June 2, 1768 (*Not elected*)[2]
    Totness, Devon. Physician; physicist.
Baron de Leutichauw. Nov. 11, 1768 (*Not elected*)[3]
    Copenhagen. Identified only as "a Danish Nobleman and Doctor of Laws in the University of Oxford."
Philipp Heinrich Seyberth. November 1768 (*Not elected*)[4]
    Göttingen. Professor of civil law; mathematician.
*Jan Ingenhousz (1730–1799). Feb. 13, 1769
    Vienna. Physician at the imperial court; physicist.
Timothy Lane. May 6, 1769
    London. Apothecary; electrician.

9. Clerk's notation at bottom: "Benjamin Franklin LLD signed a Bond for him for his Contributions and paid his Admission fee in December 1767."

1. This paper does not follow the usual form. It is written in French and dated "a Paris ce 26 fevrier 1768," and most of the nine signers were French members. Probably BF and the other resident members who signed did so as a courtesy. On the second page John Pringle (who had already signed) wrote "London 20 March 1768" and signed again. A further notation reads "Read Novr. 10. 1768," but the paper bears no record of the display at ten further meetings required before election might take place.

2. Notation following entry of the ten meetings at which a certificate was displayed: "Jany. 12. 1769 Ballotted and Rejected 23 A. 21 N." A two-thirds majority of those present and voting was necessary for election.

3. Possibly a phonetic version of the name of some member of the Levetzau family. The Oxford lists of degrees have no such name or variation. The certificate contains no record of the reading, display, or ballot on this nomination.

4. The certificate contains no record of the reading, display, or ballot on this nomination.

Charles LeRoy (1726–1779). Nov. 16, 1769
  Montpellier, France. Professor of medicine; chemist.
William Hewson (1739–1774). Dec. 7, 1769
  London. Anatomist and physiologist; Copley medalist, 1769.
James Welsh (d. 1778). Dec. 14, 1769
  Winchester. Physician.
John Arbuthnot. April 21, 1770
  Mitcham, Surrey. Agriculturist.
Robert Erskine. June 28, 1770
  London. Mathematician; engineer.
*Alexander Dalrymple (1737–1808). Nov. 8, 1770
  London. Mathematician; geographer.
George Walker (c. 1734–1807). Feb. 21, 1771
  Great Yarmouth, Norfolk. Clergyman; mathematician.
Alexander Aubert (1730–1805). May 16, 1771
  London. Merchant; astronomer.
Jean-Baptiste LeRoy (1720–1800). Sept. 5, 1772
  Paris. Philosopher; electrician.
*Patrick Brydone (1736–1818). Nov. 24, 1772
  Berwickshire. Electrician; traveler.
Edward Bancroft (1744–1821). Feb. 18, 1773
  London. Physician; author of *The Natural History of Guiana.*
*William Henley [Henly] (d. 1779). Feb. 18, 1773
  London. Linen-draper; electrician.
Alexander Garden (c. 1730–1791). March 4, 1773
  Charleston, S.C. Physician; botanist.
*John Coakley Lettsom (1744–1815). April 28, 1773
  London. Physician; philanthropist.
Pierre-Isaac Poissonier (1720–1798). Oct. 25, 1773
  Paris. Physician; chemist.
Anthony George [Anton Georg] Eckhardt. Nov. 15, 1773
  The Hague. Inventor.
John Mervin Nooth. Nov. 23, 1773
  London. Physician.
John Hyacinth de Magalhaens (1723–1790). Jan. 20, 1774
  London. Instrument maker.
Richard Twiss (1747–1821). March 3, 1774
  Norwich. Traveler; writer.

[17 May 1759.]

Edward Delaval M.A and Fellow of Pembroke Hall in Cambridge,[5] being personally known to us, and desirous of being

5. Edward Hussey Delaval (1729–1814), of an old Northumberland family.

elected into the Royal Society, we recommend him as a Gentleman extremely well qualify'd to become a valuable Member.

FRANCIS BLAKE[6]
B FRANKLIN
B: WILSON[7]

17 May 1759.
1 May 24.
2 —— 31.
3 June 14.
4 —— 21.
5 —— 28.
6 July- 5.
7 Novr.- 8.
8 —— 15.
9 —— 22.
10 —— 30.
Decr. 6. Ballotted and Elected

Remarks on Thomas Penn's Estimate of the Province

Printed in [Richard Jackson], *An Historical Review of the Constitution and Government of Pensylvania* ... London: Printed for R. Griffiths, in Paternoster-Row, 1759, pp. 431–8.

In the issue of May 26–29, 1759, *The London Chronicle* announced that *An Historical Review of the Constitution and Government of Pensylvania*

An accomplished classicist, he was also interested in chemistry and electricity. Benjamin Wilson, one of his nominators, had read to the Royal Society, March 22, 1759, a letter from Delaval to himself on electricity. *Phil. Trans.*, LI (1759), 83. In 1769 he was a member of a committee of the Society with BF to report on the protection of St. Paul's Cathedral from lightning. Later (1773) he sided with Wilson against BF in favor of using blunt instead of pointed lightning rods to protect buildings. He experimented with the use of various metals in making glass and received the Copley Medal, 1769, for a paper on this subject. *DNB*. BF saw and heard Delaval's set of musical glasses and was so "charmed with the sweetness of its tones" that, using the same principle, he invented a new musical instrument, the armonica, which enjoyed great vogue. BF to Giambatista Beccaria, July 13, 1762.

6. Francis Blake (1708–1780), F.R.S., 1746. His father Robert was a member of a family from Galway who by his marriage had acquired lands in Durham Co. The son devoted much of his time to mathematics and mechanics, and during the Rebellion of 1745 actively supported the government. He was created a baronet in 1774. *DNB*.

7. See above, IV, 391 n.

was "This day published." So appeared at last a work with which Franklin had been long and closely concerned.[8] The main part of the book consists of a 380-page narrative of the colony's political history from the granting of the royal charter to William Penn in 1681 to the end of September 1756. It includes, in full or in extract, many of the messages exchanged between the governors and the Assembly, organized and presented in such a way as to emphasize the allegedly selfish and arbitrary policies of the Proprietors and their deputies and to justify the Assembly's position in the long series of disputes that had taken place. At the end there appears, in sixty-four pages of fine print, an appendix "containing sundry Original Papers" relating to these controversies. Among these are the Proprietors' Answer to the Assembly's Representation and the Assembly Committee's Report on the Answer, Sept. 11, 1753 (above, V, 42–57); the Assembly Committee's eloquent Report on the Governor's Instructions, Sept. 23, 1756 (above, VI, 515–31); William Franklin's letter to *The Citizen*, Sept. 17, 1757 (above, VII, 258–63), and Thomas Penn's estimate of the value of the proprietary estates and revenues, with remarks on the estimate. The whole work was a major propaganda effort to win support, especially in Great Britain, for the Assembly in its protracted conflict with the Proprietors.

At the time and for many years afterwards, Franklin was generally regarded as the author of the *Historical Review*, but it has long been recognized that, although he and his son William supplied many of the materials, the actual writer was Richard Jackson. Franklin repeatedly denied authorship and was even a little apologetic to Norris for some of the expressions in the book, saying he "was not permitted to alter every Thing [he] did not fully approve."[9] In discussing it with David Hume, Sept. 27, 1760, he stated specifically that it "was not written by me, nor any Part of it, except the Remarks on the Proprietor's Estimate of his Estate, and some of the inserted Messages and Reports of the Assembly which I wrote when at home, as a Member of Committees appointed by the House for that Service; the rest was by another Hand."[1] The Assembly "Messages and Reports" to which he referred have all been printed in earlier volumes of this edition; the "Remarks on the Proprietor's Estimate" are printed below, preceded, in order to make them intelligible, by the Estimate itself.

The authenticity of the Penn Estimate has been sharply challenged. In a study of the proprietary system in Pennsylvania, William R. Shepherd pointed out that "No authentic document of this origin or

8. See above, VII, 374 n.
9. See below, p. 402.
1. ALS in Royal Society of Edinburgh.

nature is known to exist," and added that the only direct reference to it or to Franklin's remarks on it to be found among the Penn Manuscripts is in a letter from Thomas Penn to Richard Peters, May 18, 1767, in which the Proprietor declared: "It is quite impossible that Mr. Franklin's accounts can have any foundation." Shepherd strongly implied, but without directly saying so, that Franklin was guilty of outright forgery, and that he based the alleged Estimate either on his own knowledge of the procedures in the Pennsylvania Land Office or on information supplied by others in the colony. Shepherd pointed out, further, that the figures in the Estimate are greatly in excess of those found in other, more reliable records.[2]

The present editors have been unable either to prove or to disprove the authenticity of the Penn Estimate, though it is clear that if it was a forgery Franklin was not the author. Writing to Joseph Galloway, Sept. 16, 1758, he acknowledged receipt of the paper and declared that it would "be of good Use."[3] Isaac Norris knew it had been sent to Franklin and he referred to its contents in a letter written a few days after the *Historical Review* was published.[4] Obviously the paper was sent to Franklin from Pennsylvania as part of the "ammunition" his backers were supplying him for his assault on the Proprietors, and there seems no reason to believe that either Franklin or Jackson suspected its authenticity. Who wrote it, if it was a forgery, or how Franklin's Pennsylvania friends got hold of it, if it was genuine, remains unknown.[5] In any case, the remarks on the Estimate are clearly by Franklin and so are included here among his papers.

The Proprietaries have for a long Series of Years made a great Secret of the Value of their Estate and Revenue: By Accident the following authentic Paper is fallen into our Hands, and will serve as a Ground-work, on which the Reader may be enabled to form some Idea of the

2. William R. Shepherd, *History of Proprietary Government in Pennsylvania* (N.Y., 1896), pp. 84–9.

3. See above, p. 151.

4. See below, pp. 391–2.

5. It may be pointed out that soon after the publication of the *Historical Review* the book was violently attacked, both in general and on particular points, by the Proprietors or their supporters, but the editors have found no contemporary allegation, published or unpublished, that the Estimate itself was spurious, other than Penn's remark quoted above. See, for example, the hostile review in *The Critical Review: or, Annals of Literature*, VIII (1759), 108–15, and a long, anonymous criticism in what appears to be the same clerical hand that is found on several papers emanating from the office of Ferdinand J. Paris, APS.

Value of that Estate in Pensylvania. It is a Copy of an original Paper drawn by Mr. Thomas Penn himself many Years ago,[6] and endors'd "My Estimate *of the Province,* T PENN."

"ESTIMATE.

Pensylvania Curr.

"1 Lands granted since my Arrival are very near 270,000 Acres, of which not 10,000 have been paid for; more than of old Grants are remaining unpaid;[7] is } £ 41,850 0 0

"2 The Rent on the said Grants is £550 Sterling a Year, which at 20 Years Purchase, and 165 per Cent. Exchange,[8] is } 18,150 0 0

6. If the Estimate is authentic and BF's conclusion (in the first paragraph of his Remarks below) is correct that Penn drew up this Estimate while he was residing in Pa., it must have been prepared between 1732 and 1741, probably before 1735, when the Gilbert Manor was sold to Samuel McCall. *PMHB,* III (1879), 454.

7. The Proprietors derived revenue from the granting of land to individuals in two major ways: the original purchase money, and the annual quitrent (a fixed payment, theoretically in perpetuity, in commutation of all feudal dues to which the Proprietors might be entitled as lords of the soil). The rates stipulated for grants changed several times. Before 1713, though there were many individual variations, the purchase price was generally £5 per hundred acres and the quitrent (always payable in sterling or the equivalent in local currency) was one shilling per hundred acres. In 1713, or soon after, the purchase price was increased to £10 per hundred, and in 1719 the quitrent was raised to 2s. per hundred. In 1732 Thomas Penn advanced the purchase price to £15 10s. per hundred acres and the quitrent to a halfpenny per acre (4s. 2d. per hundred). These rates exceeded those of neighboring colonies and resulted in substantial emigration. The Penns made some reductions in the 1750s in the purchase price on new grants and in 1765 set it at £5 sterling per hundred acres but raised the quitrent to a penny per acre (8s. 4d. per hundred). Shepherd, *Proprietary Government,* pp. 34–5.

8. In this and the following entries dealing with properties on which the Proprietors were entitled to quitrents, the capital value of proprietary rights is calculated at twenty times the annual quitrent yield. In converting the sterling amounts into Pa. currency £100 sterling are equated to £165 Pa. currency, which BF conceded was "near the Medium," but see below, p. 378, for BF's comment on the proprietary receiver general's action in charging a landowner for many years at a much higher rate.

363

"3 The old Rent,⁹ £420 a Year Sterling, at ditto, is	15,246	0	0
"4 Lands granted between Roll and the first Article¹ are £570 a Year Sterling, which at 20 Years Purchase, and 165 per Cent. is	18,810	0	0
"5 To the Difference between £420 and £570 for Arrearages of Rents which may be computed at half the Time of the other Arrearages, that is 11 Years at 165 per Cent.²	2,722	10	0
"6 Ferries let on short Leases, the Rents being £40 a Year are worth³	1,000	0	0
"7 Lands settled in the Province for which no Grants are yet passed, except a few since the above Account was taken, not less than 400,000 Acres, which at £15 10s. od. amounts to	63,000	0	0
"The Rent at an Half-penny an Acre is £833 6s. 8d. a Year Sterling, reckon'd as above is	27,500	0	0
	£188,278	10	0

9. In 1706 James Logan, provincial secretary, prepared and sent to William Penn in England a quitrent roll of the province (referred to in the next entry). 2 *Pa. Arch.*, VII, 65. Probably the "old Rent" mentioned here represents the total shown on that roll.

1. That is, between 1706 and 1732.

2. The arithmetic of this calculation is simple: £150 (the difference between the annual rents mentioned in entries 3 and 4 above) multiplied by 11 years gives £1650 sterling, which, converted at 165 percent, equals £2722 10s. Pa. currency. It is not clear, however, what the *difference* between total annual rents due for lands granted during *two separate periods* has to do with arrearages, or what specific 22-year period is involved in "the Time of the other Arrearages," or why half that time should be used for such a computation.

3. Under the royal charter Penn had authority to provide ferries, though various Assemblies contested his exclusive control over them.

"Manors.[4]

		M. from the City,	Acres,	per H.			
"	1 Conestogoe,	65	13,400	at £40	5,360	0	0
"	2 Gilbert's,	25	3,200	70	2,240	0	0
"	3 Springfield,	12	1,600	75	1,200	0	0
"	4 Highlands,	35	2,500	30	750	0	0
"	5 Spring-tow[n],	37	10,000	35	3,500	0	0
"	6 Vincent's,	40	20,000	35	7,000	0	0
"	7 Richland's,	35	10,000	15	1,500	0	0
"	9 About 20 Tracts in the several Counties, mostly 500 Acres each; reckon'd 10,000 at £40				4,000	0	0
"	Springet's-bury		207 Acres at £5		1,035	0	0
" 8	On the North Side of the Town		50	30	1,500	0	0
	Back of the said Land		15	10	150	0	0
"	9 Lot in the Bank[5] at the North End of the Town, 200 Feet at £3				600	0	0

4. William Penn and his heirs retained for themselves numerous parcels of land, both large and small. They erected several into what they called manors and often leased out portions of these or other tracts to tenants for cultivation. The properties named in the list of holdings here recorded were located as follows: Conestoga, in Lancaster Co., near the town of Lancaster; Gilbert, in the present Montgomery Co., including parts of Pottstown and Pottsgrove; Springfield, in Montgomery Co., almost directly north of Philadelphia on Whitpaine's Creek; Highland, in Bucks Co., on the Delaware River in Upper Makefield Township; Springton, in northeastern Chester Co., on the east branch of Brandywine Creek; Vincent, in northern Chester Co., near the Schuylkill River; Richland, in northwestern Bucks Co., mostly in Richland Township; Springettsbury, probably the manor in the Fairmount area, now part of Philadelphia, not the large manor of the same name in York Co.; Streiper's Tract, in Bucks Co., on the Delaware River in Tinicum Township. A map showing the location of most of these Penn properties and many others not here listed, prepared by Fred J. Gorman, is in *PMHB,* LXVII (1943), 92.

5. When William Penn was granting lots in the city, he accorded special treatment to many of those on the bank of the Delaware between Front St. and the river. There were restrictions on the height of buildings and the quit-rent was to be increased at the end of every fifty years to an amount equaling one-third of the then rental value of the property. Charles P. Keith, *Chronicles of Pennsylvania* (Phila., 1917), I, 81; Shepherd, *Proprietary Government,* p. 37 n.

"10 A Front and Bank Lot between Vine and Sassafras Street, 102 Feet at £6			612	o	o
"11 Bank Lot between Cedar and Pine Street, 204 Feet at £3			612	o	o
"12 Front Lot on the Side of Cedar Street	102	3	306	o	o
"13 Ditto between Cedar and Pine Street	160	2	320	o	o
"14 Bank Lot between the same Streets	40	2	80	o	o
"15 Marsh Land near the Town	600 Acres at £3		1,800	o	o
"16 Ditto 200 Acres, at 1s. Sterling Rent, and 165 per Cent. is			330	o	o
"Lands within the Draft of the Town, at least 500 Acres.					
"250 nearest Delaware, at £15 per Acre			3,750	o	o
"250 nearest Schuylkill, at £10 per Acre			2,500	o	o
"17 Omitted.—Streiper's Tract in Bucks County, 35 Miles; 5,000 Acres at £25			1,250	o	o
"18 The Rents of the above Manors and Lands being 77,072 Acres at a Half-penny per Acre. 20 Years Purchase, and 165 per Cent. Exchange, is			5,298	12	o
			£233,972	2	o
"The Government to be calculated at no less than was to have been paid for it, viz. £11,000[6] at 165 per Cent. is			18,150	o	o
			£252,122	2	o

6. During the early years of the eighteenth century protracted negotiations took place between William Penn and the royal officials for the surrender of the government of Pa. to the Crown. In 1712 agreement was reached and a deed prepared by which Penn and his heirs were to yield all rights of government (but not the rights to the soil) in return for payment of £12,000 in four years. Penn received £1000 on account, but before he had formally executed the deed he suffered an incapacitating stroke. His continued ill health, the tangled state of his finances, and changes in the government prevented further action, and when the Whigs returned to power in 1714 the matter was

"In this Calculation no Notice is taken of the Thirds reserved on the Bank Lots (a Copy of the Patents J. Penn has by him to shew the Nature of them*) and nine Tenths of the Province remains undisposed of.

"Three Fifths of all Royal Mines is reserved in the Grants, and in all Grants since the Year 1732. One fifth Part of all other Mines, delivered at the Pits Mouth without Charge is also reserved.

"No Value is put on the Proprietor's Right to escheated Lands; and, besides these Advantages, several Offices are in the Proprietor's Gift of considerable Value.

"Register General,	about	£200
"Naval Officer,		£300
"Clerk of Philadelphia,		£400
" Chester,		£300
" Bucks,		£200
" Lancaster,		£200

"Besides several other Offices of less Value. These are only guessed at."

The above Paper has no Date, but by sundry Circumstances in it, particularly there being no Value put on the *Thirds* of the *Bank Lots,* because they were not then fallen in;[8] and by the *Valuation* put on the Lands (which is *very different* from their *present* Value) it must have been drawn while Mr. Thomas Penn resided in Pensylvania, and probably more than Twenty Years ago; Since which Time a *vast Addition* has been made to the *Value* of the

---

*By these Patents, at the end of 50 Years the *Proprietor* was to have *One Third* of the Value of the *Lots* and the *Buildings,* and other *Improvements* erected on them.[7]

---

dropped. Winfred T. Root, *The Relations of Pennsylvania with the British Government, 1696–1765* (N.Y., 1912), pp. 349–65.

7. BF's note. As indicated in the next note but one above, the quitrent was to be increased at the end of fifty years to one-third of the then current rental value.

8. For many of the "bank lots" the change in quitrent was to occur during the middle 1730s.

Reserved Lands, and a *great Quantity* of Land has been *disposed of,* perhaps equal to all preceding.

We must therefore *add* to the above Sum of £252,122 2s. 0d. the following Articles, viz.[9]

	Pensylvania Curr.
Brought over	£252,122 2 0
1. For the *increased Value* of the Lands of the Conestogoe Manor now valued at £400 *per* Hundred Acres, and in the above Estimate valued only at £40 *per* Hundred, the said increased Value being £360 *per* Hundred, on 13,400 Acres,	48,240 0 0
2. For the *increased Value* of Gilbert's Manor, now worth £400 *per* Hundred Acres,	10,560 0 0
3. For *Ditto* on Springfield Manor, now worth £500 *per* Hundred Acres,	6,800 0 0
4. For *Ditto* on Highland's Manor, now worth £350 *per* Hundred Acres,	8,000 0 0
5. For *Ditto* on Springtown, now worth £400 *per* Hundred Acres,	36,500 0 0
6. For *Ditto* on Vincent's Manor, now worth £300 *per* Hundred Acres,	53,000 0 0
7. For *Ditto* on Richland's now worth £450 *per* Hundred Acres,	43,500 0 0
9. For *Ditto* on the 20 Tracts, now worth £300 *per* Hundred Acres,	26,000 0 0
8. For *Ditto* on Springetsbury, &c. at least	2,685 0 0
9. For *Ditto* on all the Articles of *Lots* from No. 9 to 14. being *trebled* in Value,	5,060 0 0
15. For *Ditto* on the *Marsh Land,* now worth £20 *per* Acre,	10,200 0 0
16. For *Ditto* on the Value of Lands within the Draft of the *Town,* now worth one with another, £50 *per* Acre,*	18,750 0 0

*The Lots of Land within the Plan of the Town were originally

9. While it is impossible to suggest more accurate figures now, BF's estimates of the increased capital value of many of these properties during a period of twenty or twenty-five years seem excessive.

17. For *Ditto* on Streiper's Tract now worth £325 *per* Hundred. [On the next Articles for the *Reserved Rent*, and the *Value of the Government*, we add no Advance.]³	15,000	0	0
For the *Thirds* of the *Bank Lots* and *Improvements* on them, as they fell in after this Estimate was made; reckoning every 20 Feet of Ground with its Improvements, one with another, worth £480 the *Thirds* being £160 for each 20 Feet,	37,280	0	0
	573,697	2	0

promis'd to be *given* to the Purchasers of Land in the Country.¹ But that has been long since discontinued; and for many Years past the Proprietor has shut the Office, and forbid his Agents even to *sell* any more of them; intending to keep them all, till he can let them out on high Ground Rents, or on Building Leases. 500 Acres divided into House Lots, and dispos'd of in this Manner, will alone make a vast Estate. The old Proprietor likewise in his Plan of the City, laid out five large *Squares*, one in each Quarter, and one in the Centre of the Plan, and gave the same to the Inhabitants for *publick Uses*. This he publish'd in all his Accounts of the Country, and his Papers of Invitation and Encouragement to Settlers; but as no formal Deed or Conveyance of those *Squares* is now to be found, the present *Proprietor* has resum'd them, turn'd them again into *private Property* that the Number of his *Lots* may be increas'd; and his Surveyor General in his lately publish'd Plan of the City, has conceal'd all those *Squares* by running intended Streets over them.² A Proceeding equally odious to the People, and dishonourable to the Family!

1. In 1681 Penn offered each of the first purchasers who should buy or lease 500 acres a city lot of 10 acres, if there should be sufficient land. Many later purchasers thought that they were included in the offer and considerable dissatisfaction followed when the Proprietors denied their claims. Shepherd, *Proprietary Government*, pp. 18–25.

2. Possibly a reference to Nicholas Scull and George Heap's "A Map of Philadelphia and Parts Adjacent," reproduced in *Gent. Mag.*, XXIII (1753), 375, which shows only one public square in the conventional grid representation of the city.

3. Brackets in the original.

Thus far for the *present Value* of what was *then* estimated, But since that Time, very great Quantities of *Land* have been *sold,* and several *new Manors* laid out and *reserv'd;* one of which, viz. that of *Conedoguinet*⁴ is said to contain 30,000 Acres: The Quantity sold since the Estimate, must be at least equal to what was sold before, as the People are doubled, and the Manors probably equal in Quantity: We may therefore suppose, that a fair Estimate of the Lands sold, Rents and Manors reserved, and new Towns laid out into Lots, since the above Estimate, would be at least equal to it, that is another Tenth,⁵ and amount also to £573,697 2s. 0d.

573,697 2 0

For *Eight* of these Nine Tenths of the Province which were not dispos'd of at the Time of making the Estimate; *Note,* The Province Grant to William Penn is of three Degrees of Latitude, and five of Longitude; each Degree of Latitude contains 69½ Statute Miles, and each Degree of Longitude about Lat. 40 contains 53 Statute Miles; so the Dimensions of the Province are 265 Miles by 208½, which gives for its Contents 55,252½ square Miles or *Thirty five Millions, Three Hundred and Sixty-one Thousand, Six Hundred Acres;* Eight Tenths of this Quantity, is 28,289,280 Acres, which at £15 10s. per 100 Acres (the present selling Price) is⁶

4,384,838 8 0

4. On the west side of the Susquehanna River at Harris's Ferry; see above, VI, 254 n.

5. It is not clear how BF arrived at the conclusion that the lands disposed of up to the time of the Estimate and those disposed of since then each totaled one tenth of the total land in the province. According to his calculation in the next paragraph each tenth would amount to 3,536,160 acres.

6. In estimating the potential value of the remaining eight-tenths of Pa. and

For the yearly *Quitrent* on 28,289,280 Acres at a ⎫
    Halfpenny Sterling per Acre, is £58,936 ⎪
    per Annum, which at 165 per Cent. and 20 ⎬ 1,856,484   0   0
    Years Purchase, is ⎭

For the additional Value on *One Tenth* Part, *at* ⎫
    least, of those Eight Tenths, which being ⎪
    pick'd out of the best of the Lands after ⎪
    every Purchase from the Indians, before ⎪
    any private Person is allowed to take up ⎬ 8,486,784   0   0
    any,[7] and kept for 20 or 30 Years, is to be ⎪
    sold at a Medium for £300 per 100 Acres ⎪
    Advance; this on 2,828,928 Acres, is ⎭

For the *Three Fifths* of all *Royal Mines,* and One ⎫
    Fifth of all other Mines reserv'd to these ⎪
    Lords Proprietors, we can as yet estimate ⎪
    no Sum, and must leave it a Blank as we ⎪
    find it; but since in the Ridges of Moun- ⎬
    tains not yet settled, some very valuable ⎪
    Specimens of Ores have been found by ⎪
    Travellers, it is not unlikely this Article ⎪
    may in Time become considerable beyond ⎪
    Computation. ⎭

---

the potential capitalized value of the quitrent income to be derived from it, BF made two very dubious assumptions:

a. All the remaining area in the province—valleys, plateaus, mountains, river beds, and bodies of water—was equally salable at the set price of £15 10s. per hundred acres, regardless of its suitability for settlement.

b. All lands would yield quitrents at a halfpenny an acre, although it was common knowledge in Pa. that there were already a great many squatters occupying lands for which they had paid no purchase money or quitrent, in spite of the efforts of the proprietary agents to collect (Shepherd, *Proprietary Government,* pp. 49–53, 71–2). What BF could not know was that, when finally surveyed, the total area of Pa. has proved to be not 55,252.5 square miles, but only 45,302.33. Iris Richey, ed., *The Pennsylvania Manual, 1961–1962* (Vol. 95), p. 754.

7. According to Shepherd (*Proprietary Government,* p. 47) the surveyors often failed to set aside the proprietary tenths of new tracts before settlers swarmed in "and the proprietors had to content themselves with land which had been avoided by the settlers because of its worthlessness."

For the *Offices* we shall likewise make no Estimation, tho' they are greatly increas'd in Number and Value, with the Increase of People; as we believe the Proprietaries do not raise *immediate* Money from the Grants of those Offices at present, they being chiefly dispos'd of to bribe or reward their Partisans and Favourites; in which however they may find their Account.

For the *Escheats* we likewise add nothing; for tho' it is thought a valuable Article, we have no Information on which we can form any Judgment concerning its Value, it must however be continually increasing.

There is another Article, we are greatly at a Loss about, which is the *Interest* of Money arising to the Proprietors from Securities on Lands possess'd by Persons unable to make present Payment. These pay not only *Quitrent* for the Land but *Interest* for the *Purchase Money*. This Interest* is thought to be a very considerable Income, but we cannot estimate it.

The *Three Lower Counties* on Delaware, which are a distinct Territory and Government from the Province of Pensylvania, and held by a different Title, are also a *very valuable* Part of the Proprietary Estate; tho' what Value should be put on the same is at present difficult to say.

Total in Pensylvania Currency £15,875,500   12   0

In Sterling, about Ten Millions!

But on the whole, it appears pretty clearly, that deducting all the Articles containing the Valuation of Lands yet unsold, and unappropriated within their Patent, and the Manors and Rents to be hereafter reserv'd, and allowing for any small over-Valuations in their present reserv'd Lands and Incomes [tho' 'tis thought if any be it will not be found to exceed the under-Valuation in other

*See Fisher's Account hereafter.

Instances][8] there cannot remain less than a *Million* of Property which they *now at this Time* have in Pensylvania.

And in that Province there are but 20,000 Families, to each of which, one with another, there does not belong more than £300 of Property, if so much; which multiply'd by 20,000 gives £6,000,000 for the whole Property of the People there.

The Proprietaries then have in present Possession a Property there at least equal to one sixth of That of the People. They ought therefore to pay the same Proportion of the Taxes.

That the Reader may form some Judgment of the Profits made by this Monopoly of Land in America in Favour of the HOUSE OF PENN, we shall just mention, that the Land is first purchased of the Indians, and none but the *Proprietors* are allow'd to purchase of the Indians within the Limits of their Grant: The Indians of late Years have somewhat rais'd their Price; and for the last great Purchase in 1754,[9] which was of about *Seven Millions* of Acres, they demanded (how much do you think?) no less than 2000 Dollars amount at Seven and Sixpence Currency each, to *Seven Hundred and Fifty Pounds.*

Pensyl. Currency.

The Land so bought the Proprietor has the Moderation to sell (except the best of it serv'd in Manors for himself) at so low a Price as £15 10s. 0d. per Hundred Acres, which will produce   £1,085,000   0   0

Deduct the *Purchase Money*   750   0   0

Remains PROFIT   £1,084,250   0   0

Besides the *Profit* of a *Tenth* of the 7,000,000 Acres, reserv'd in *Manors* to be sold hereafter at an Advance of at least £300 per Hundred Acres[1]   2,100,000   0   0

And also the Quitrent to be reserv'd on 7,000,000 Acres at ½d. Sterling per Acre £14,583 6s. 8d. which at 165 per Cent. and 20 Years Purchase, is worth   £481,250   0   0

Profit, in all £3,665,500   0   0

8. Brackets in the original.

9. See above, v, 349–50 n, and map facing p. 225.

1. BF had already included this tenth among the lands to be sold at £15 10s. per hundred acres, mentioned in the entry immediately above.

But the Indian Council at Onondago not being satisfied with the sale of so much Land at once, the Proprietors have since been obliged to disgorge a Part of the Hunting Country *they had not paid for,* and reconvey the same to the Indians,[2] who, when they are dispos'd to sell it, may possibly demand 2000 Dollars more, for which the above Account must then have Credit.

One would think that where such good Bargains are bought of the poor Natives, there should be no Occasion for fraudulent Art to over-reach them, in order to take more than is granted: And that if a War occasion'd by such Injuries should be drawn upon the innocent Inhabitants, those who were the Cause of the War, if they did not, as in Justice they ought, bear the whole Expence of it, at least they would not refuse to bear a reasonable Part. Whether this has ever been the Case is now a Subject of Publick Enquiry.

But let us see how the Land bought in such *lumping Pennyworths* of the Natives by the Monopolist, is *huckster'd* out again to the King's Subjects. To give the Reader some Idea of this, after re-marking that £15 10s. 0d. per Hundred Acres for wild Land, is *three* Times dearer than the Proprietor of Maryland's Price, and *ten* Times dearer than his Majesty's Lands in Virginia and Carolina, both as good if not better Countries, we shall present him with a *genuine Account,* stated under the Hand of the Proprietor's Receiver General, obtain'd with *great Difficulty* by the Purchaser of two Tracts of Land, some Time *after* he had paid his Money; when on more particular Consideration of the Sum paid compar'd with the Quantity bought, he imagin'd he had paid too much. The Account is as follows, viz.[3]

2. See above, pp. 210–11.

3. For an understanding of the account and the discussion of it the following summary or the procedure in making land grants in Pa. may be helpful: The prospective buyer normally filed in the provincial secretary's office a claim for the land he desired, though often only the number of acres would be indicated, not the specific location within a general area. The secretary would issue to the surveyor general a warrant to lay out and survey the land in question. When the surveyor general or his deputies had performed this task he executed and returned a certificate of survey. After receiving this document and a certificate from the receiver general of payment of the purchase price, the commissioners of property (later the governor) would issue a patent under the great seal, which was recorded by the provincial secretary. In theory, these steps should follow each other in short order, but in practice many years often elapsed between them. The Proprietors intended that the

JOHN FISHER in Right of JACOB JOB   *Dr.*

"To Land 423 A. 53 Ps. in Pextang Township, Lancaster County, granted to said Job by Warrant of Mar. 19th, 1742   £65   12   1

"Interest from 1st March 1732[4] to 19th March 1742, is 10 Years 18 Days   39   11   2

                               105   3   3

"19th March 1742, paid[5]   15

                               90   3   3

"Int. from 19th March 1742 to 20th February 1747, is 4 Years, 11 Months, 1 Day   26   11   11

"Quitr. to next Month is 15 Years, £13 4s. 7d. *Sterl.* at 85 per Cent.[6]   24   9   6

                               141   4   8

"JOHN FISHER in Right of THOMAS COOPER   *Dr.*

"To Land 268 Acres in Pextang Township, Lancaster County granted by Warrant of 9th January 1743 to said Cooper   £41   10   9

"Interest from 1st March 1737[7] to 9th January 1743 is 5 Years, 10 Months, 8 Days   14   11   9

                               56   2   6

purchase price ("consideration money") should be paid at the time of the first application, but often the prospective grantee made only a partial down payment, or even none at all. The proprietary agents later assessed interest on the unpaid balance of the purchase price and on the stipulated quitrent from this earliest date in the transaction, though settlers believed they were not liable for either until the warrant for the survey was issued. Shepherd, *Proprietary Government*, pp. 26–38.

4. Apparently the date on which Jacob Job had initially filed for the land. Recomputation shows that in all entries in this account, and in the restatement which follows it, interest was charged at the rate of 6 percent per annum. It was calculated as simple interest for the period indicated in each entry but the receiver general compounded it from one period to the next.

5. Apparently Job (or Fisher if he had bought Job's interest by then) paid £15 down on the purchase price on the date the warrant for survey was issued.

6. Charged from the date of Job's initial application and converted to Pa. currency at a very high rate of exchange.

7. Apparently the date on which Thomas Cooper had initially filed for the land.

"9th January 1743 paid[8]	7	10	0
	48	12	6

"Interest from 9th January 1743 to 20th February⎫
1747 is 4 Years, 1 Month, 11 Days ⎬   11 19 10

"Quitr. to next Month is 10 Years, £5 11s. 8d. *Sterl.*
at 85 per Cent.[9]   10   6   7

                                         70 18 11

£141   4 8   20th February 1747.
  70 18 11

 212   3   7
     10   Transfer, &c.[1]

 212 13   7

                             Philadelphia, 23d February 1747.

"Received of John Fisher Two Hundred and Twelve Pounds, Three Shillings and Seven Pence, in full for 423 Acres in Pextang Township, granted by Warrant of 19th March 1742, to Jacob Job, and for 268 Acres in same Township, by Warrant of 9th January 1743 to Thomas Cooper, both in the County of Lancaster.

£212   3 7   For the Hon. Proprietaries,
  10   Fees

(   )

 212 13 7   LYNFORD LARDNER Receiver Gen.

       N. B. The Quitrent in full to 1st March 1747.

The Purchaser not being skill'd in Accounts, but amaz'd at the Sum, apply'd to a Friend to examine this Account, who stated it over again as follows,[2] *viz.*

"JOHN FISHER in the Right of JACOB JOB,   *Dr.*

1742.   "To 423 Acres, 50 Per. of Land, in Pex-⎫
19th   tang, County Lancaster, granted to said ⎬ £65 12 1
March.   Job by Warrant dated this Day   ⎭

                  "By Cash paid that Day   15   0   0

                             £50 12 1

8. Cooper's (or Fisher's) down payment at the time of the warrant.

9. Charged from the date of Cooper's initial application.

1. Perhaps the charge for recording the transfers of title to Fisher, although under Thomas Penn warrants specified the payment of one year's quitrent at every alienation. Shepherd, *Proprietary Government*, p. 33.

2. In this restatement the accountant eliminated all charges for interest and quitrents from the dates of the initial filings to the dates of issuance of the warrants for survey.

376

"To Interest on £50 12s. 1d. from the
19th March 1742 to 20th Feb. 1747,
being 4 y. 11 m. 1d. ⎫ 14 18 9

"To 5 Years Quitrent for said Land at One
Halfpenny Sterl. per Acre Ann. *viz.*
from March 1742, the Time the Land
was surveyed (for Quitrent *ought not* to
be paid before) to March 1747 amounting in the whole to £4 8s. 4d. Sterling
at 85 per Cent. the Exchange charg'd in
the Account delivered ⎫ 8 5 9

"20th Feb. 1747. Sum due on Job's Right £73 16 7

"JOHN FISHER, in Right of THOMAS COOPER.   *Dr.*

1743.   "To 268 Acres of Land in Pextang afore-
9th   said, granted said Cooper by Warrant £41 10 9
January, this day

"By Cash paid that Day   7 10

"9th Jan. 1743, Ballance due £34   0 9

"To Interest on £34 0s. 9d. from 9th Jan.
1743, to 20th Feb. 1747 being 4 y. 1 m.
11d. ⎫ 8 7 8

"To 4 Years and 2 Months Quitrent for
said Lands, *viz.* from Jan. 1743 to the
First March 1747, Amounting in the
whole to £2 6s. 6d. Sterling, at 85 per
Cent ⎫ 4 7 2¼

"20th Feb. 1747. Sum due on Cooper's
Right   £46 15 7¼

"In Feb. 1747, John Fisher obtained a Proprietary Patent for
the Lands above mentioned. But by the Accompts then exhibited
to him, and which he paid, he was charged on Job's Right £141
4s. 8d. which is £67 8s. 1d. more than the above Account, and also
was charged on Coopers Right, £70 18s. 11d., which is £24 3s.
3¾d. more than the above Accompt of Cooper's. So that by the
two Accompts it is supposed he has paid £91 11s. 4¾d. more than
could legally be received from him.

"The Reason of such great Difference in the Accompts are as follow, *viz.*

"1st That Interest has been charged on the Consideration Money for Job's Land, for 10 Years and 18 Days before the Land was survey'd.

"2d That Quitrent has also been charged for that Time at 85 per Cent.

"3d That the Principle and Interest to the Time of Warrant and Survey were added together, and that Interest was charged for that Total to the Time the Patent was granted.

"4th That Interest has been charged on the Consideration Money for Cooper's Land, for 5 *y*. 10 *m*. 8 *d*. before the Land was survey'd.

"5th That Quitrent has also been charged for that Time at 85 per Cent.

"6th That the Principle and Interest to the Time of Warrant and Survey were added, and Interest charged for that Total to the Time the Patent was granted, which is *compound Interest.*"

To these Remarks of the Accountant we shall only add, That the Price of Exchange between Philadelphia and London is not fix'd, but rises and falls according to the Demand for Bills; That 85 per Cent. charg'd for the Exchange in this Account is the *highest* Exchange that perhaps was ever given in Pensylvania, occasion'd by some particular Scarcity of Bills at a particular Time; That the Proprietor himself in his Estimate reckons the Exchange but at 65, which is indeed near the Medium, and this Charge is 20 per Cent. above it. That the Valuing the Currency of the Country according to the casual Rate of Exchange with London, is in itself a false Valuation, the Currency not being really depreciated in Proportion to an occasional Rise of Exchange; since every Necessary of Life is to be purchas'd in the Country, and every Article of Expence defray'd by that Currency (English Goods only excepted) at as low Rates after as before such Rise of Exchange; That therefore the Proprietor's obliging those who purchase of him to pay their Rents according to the Rate of Exchange is unjust, the Rate of Exchange including withal the Risque and Freight on remitting Money to England; and is besides a dangerous Practice, as the great Sums to be yearly remitted to him, put it in the Power of his own Agents to play Tricks with the Exchange at Pleasure, raise it at the Time of Year when they are to receive the Rents, by buying a few Bills at a high Price, and afterwards lower it by refraining to buy till they are sold more reasonably.

By this Account of the Receiver General's, it appears we have omitted two other Articles in the Estimation of the Proprietary Estate, *viz.*

> For the Quitrents *of Lands many Years* before *they are granted!* ____
>
> For the Interest *of the Purchase-Money many Years* before *the Purchases are made!* ____

On what Pretence these Articles of Charge are founded, how far they may be extended, and what they may amount to, is beyond our Knowledge; we are therefore obliged to leave them blank till we can obtain more particular Information.

Board of Trade to the Privy Council Committee

Copies (two): Historical Society of Pennsylvania[3]

On Feb. 2, 1759, the Privy Council referred Franklin's petition on behalf of Teedyuscung to its Committee on Plantation Affairs, which referred it in turn to the Board of Trade on April 12.[4] The Board conducted a hearing, May 15, attended by Franklin and his solicitor, Joshua Sharpe, and by the Proprietors with Paris.[5] The next day the Board ordered the preparation of a report. The draft, submitted on May 23, was considered on that day and again on May 29, when the Board agreed to it and ordered it to be transcribed. On June 1 the four members of the Board who were present signed it.[6]

Whitehall June 1st: 1759.

To the Right honourable the Lords of the Committee of His Majesty's most honourable Privy Council for Plantation Affairs.

My Lords

Pursuant to Your Lordship's Order dated the 12th. of April last, We have taken into Consideration the humble Petition of Ben-

3. Both copies are in the Penn Papers.

4. See above, pp. 264–76.

5. For BF's detailed account of the hearing, see below, pp. 397–8. Sharpe had also been BF's solicitor at the hearings on William Smith's petition the previous year. See above, pp. 5, 29.

6. *Board of Trade Journal,* 1759–63, pp. 36–7, 40–1, 42.

jamin Franklin Esquire Agent appointed by the Assembly of Pennsylvania relating to the differences subsisting, between his Majesty's Subjects, and the Indians bordering upon the said Province, concerning large Quantitys of Land, which the said Indians alledge, they have been deprived of without their Consent, or satisfaction made them for the same, particularly, of the Lands which are included within the Forks of the River Delaware, and also of other Lands, on both sides the said River.[7] And having been attended by the Petitioner, and also by the Proprietaries of Pennsylvania, and heard what each Party had to offer upon the occasion, We beg leave to acquaint Your Lordships.

That it appears, from many Letters and authentick Papers in the Books of our Office, that the extensive Purchases of Land made, not only by the Proprietaries of Pennsylvania, but in other Governments bordering on the Indian Country, have, long since, occasioned Disgusts, and Suspicions of Injury, in the Minds of the Indians, and that these Jealousies have been one Principal Cause of their Defection from the British Interest, and of the Hostilitys, which they have committed on the Frontiers of His Majesty's Colonies.

Sir William Johnson,[8] His Majesty's Agent for Indian Affairs in the Northern District of North America, has in many of his Letters, declared himself of this opinion in general, and in a Letter to Us, of the 10th. of September 1756,[9] he acquaints us, that he has the greatest Reason to believe, that the Hostilitys which Pennsylvania, in particular, had suffered from the Indians living on the Sasquehanna, had in great Measure, arisen from the large Purchase, made by that Government in 1754,[1] at which, tho' publickly consented to, and fairly paid for, at Albany, some of the Six Nations appeared to be disgusted, and others to repent of their having consented to it.

This Information, We thought it our Duty immediately to com-

7. The lands referred to here were those acquired by the Proprietors by the Walking Purchase of 1737 (above, pp. 267–70).

8. See above, VI, 139 n.

9. Printed in *N. Y. Col. Docs.*, VII, 127–30.

1. For the Albany Purchase of 1754, part of which was relinquished by the Proprietary agents at Easton in October 1758, see above, V, 225 (map), 349–50 n.

municate, to the Proprietaries of Pennsylvania,[2] who having in their Answer thereto,[3] made a proposal to appoint Commissioners to treat with the Indians in concert with Sir William Johnson, upon all Points relative to these Affairs, and to hear and determine any Complaints, which might be made, by any Indians, who had committed Hostilitys on the Frontiers of that Province, We transmitted the said Answer and Proposal to Sir Wm. Johnson, directing him to take such Measures as shou'd be most expedient, for carrying the said Proposal into execution.[4]

Accordingly, it appears, that, in July and August 1757, Mr. George Croghan,[5] being deputed by Sir Wm. Johnson for that purpose, did, in conjunction with Mr. Denny (the Proprietaries Deputy Governor) and certain Commissioners, chosen out of, and appointed by, the Assembly, hold a Treaty, with Teedyuscung, Chief of the Delaware Indians, the Complainant mentioned in Mr. Franklins Petition.[6]

From what passed, at the opening of these Conferences, it might reasonably have been hoped, that all Matters, in Dispute with the Delawar Indians, where Hostilitys had so long vexed the Middle Colonys, would have been happily, and speedily, adjusted. Teedyuscung, their Chief, declared himself well pleased with the appointment of Mr. Croghan to hear his Complaints, and willing to submit them to his Decision. But, upon his desiring that the Deeds, by which the Proprietaries hold the Lands, might be produced, read in publick, and examined, that it might be known, from what Indians, they had bought the Lands, and what was the real extent of the Purchase,[7] it appears that Mr. Denny, who, in the beginning, had told Teedyuscung that Mr. Croghan was expressly appointed by Sir Wm. Johnson, to hear and enquire into the Grievances he might have to complain of, now said, that Sir Wm.

2. The Board of Trade informed Thomas Penn of the allegations in Sir William Johnson's letter of Sept. 10, 1756, on Dec. 1, 1756. *Board of Trade Journal*, 1754–58, p. 278.

3. Delivered to the Board of Trade on Feb. 10, 1757. *Ibid.*, p. 278.

4. Board of Trade to Sir William Johnson, March 10, 1757, *N. Y. Col. Docs.*, VII, 221–2.

5. See above, v, 64 n.

6. For this treaty, held at Easton, July 25–Aug. 7, 1757, see above, p. 271. The text is in Van Doren and Boyd, *Indian Treaties*, pp. 189–212.

7. Teedyuscung made this request on July 28, 1757; see above, pp. 271–2.

Johnson was the Person, appointed to hear the particulars of his Charge, and the Proprietaries Defence, that Mr. Croghan had informed him, that he had no Power to suffer any Altercation upon the Complaint, that it must be referred to Sir Wm. Johnson, by whom, alone the Matter could be heard.[8]

This Declaration, put an end to all further proceeding towards an Enquiry into the Matter in Dispute. Teedyuscung refused to go to Sir William Johnson, for many Reasons, but principally, because some of the Indian Nations were there, who had been Instrumental to the Misunderstanding, in selling the Lands in Question.[9] The Deeds, however, were produced; And Teedyuscung then proposed to Mr. Denny, that Copys of them should be sent, to Sir Wm. Johnson, to be by him laid before his Majesty, and caused his own Clerk[1] to send Copies of them, to the Speaker of the Assembly of Pennsylvania, requesting that he, with the Assembly, would look into the Matter, and transmit Copys, to His Majesty, by his Ministers.[2]

Sir Wm. Johnson, in the Letter with which he transmitted to Us Copys of the Conferences held at this Treaty, observes, that as Teedyuscung had refused his Mediation, and made choice of the Quakers for his Advocates and Agents, he had not thought it advisable to press his Mediation upon these Indians any further. But he complains of the extraordinary Conduct of the Assembly, in appointing Members of their own House, to interfere, as Provincial Commissioners, in Indian Treaties, in providing and giving Presents, as from their own Body, distinct from those given by the Governor, and in procuring, by management, their Speaker and

8. Van Doren and Boyd, *Indian Treaties*, p. 199.

9. The reference is to land in northeastern Pa., claimed by the Delaware, but sold to the Proprietors by the Six Nations in 1749; see above, p. 264 n. For the complicated story, involving the control of the Iroquois over the Delaware, the removal of squatters from Indian lands, and the "more glaring deception" by omission of boundary lines on the map attached to the deed, see Van Doren and Boyd, *Indian Treaties*, pp. lvii–lxii, 231, 233, 237, 317.

1. Charles Thomson.

2. Thomson relayed to the House on Aug. 31, 1757, Teedyuscung's request that his minutes of the conference and copies of the deeds be submitted "to His Majesty, for His Royal Determination." The Assembly complied September 29 and sent the papers to the agents in London to lay before the King. *Votes,* 1756–57, pp. 147, 161.

themselves, to be appointed Agents, to sollicit Indian Complaints, before his Majesty and his Ministers.[3]

At a Treaty, in October 1758, between the Government of Pennsylvania, and the Delawar's, and Thirteen other different Nations of Indians,[4] Teedyuscung makes a further Declaration, concerning the Purchases complained of by the Delawars, but this Matter does not appear to have been much agitated; at that Treaty,[5] the principal object and result of which was, the Proprietaries of Pennsylvania relinquishing, to the Six Nations, that part of Land, purchased at Albany in 1754, which lyes to the Westward of the Mountains, and we cannot, without injustice to the Proprietaries, omit acquainting your Lordships, that full satisfaction was given, by them, to the Indians, with respect to this Purchase, which had been the cause of great disgust and discontent.

Having thus Stated, to your Lordships, such Facts as appeared to us to be necessary, for enabling you to form an Opinion, of the Matter in Judgement before You, We must beg leave to observe, that it is impossible to reflect, tho' but for a Moment, upon the unparalled Distresses, which have been suffered by his Majesty's Subjects, in the back Settlements of the Middle Colonies, from the cruel Hostilitys and Devastations of the Delaware and other Indians, without seeing the necessity there is, of steadily pursuing every Measure, which may have a tendency to redress and remove those Grievances and Complaints, which are alledged to have been the principal Cause of such Hostilitys; It was, with

3. Johnson to the Board of Trade, Sept. 28, 1757, *N. Y. Col. Docs.*, VII, 276–9.

4. See above, pp. 201–11, and Van Doren and Boyd, *Indian Treaties*, pp. 213–45, for the treaty at Easton, Oct. 7–26, 1758.

5. On October 18 Teedyuscung asserted again that his people had been defrauded of land "from Tohiccon as far as the Delawares owned," and reaffirmed his desire to have George II settle the dispute. The Board of Trade's statement that the "Matter does not appear to have been much agitated" at Easton is hardly borne out by the contemporary accounts. The Iroquois were much incensed at Teedyuscung's implication that they had sold lands belonging to the Delaware; to prevent a break between the Indians the proprietary agents made the most of their willingness to let the King hear the claims. Van Doren and Boyd, *Indian Treaties*, pp. 231–3, 237, 316–18. It would appear that the Board of Trade was now following the Proprietors' lead in playing down this dispute.

this Idea, and for this purpose, that we referred it, in 1757, to Sir William Johnson, to examine into the Grievances complained of, by the Delawar Indians; and, in pursuing this Method, we followed what we conceived to have been the view and object of Government, in appointing this Gentleman Sole Agent for Indian Affairs, who might manage and direct our Concerns with them, upon One uniform Plan, and thereby, put a stop to the Mischiefs so long complained of, arising from the irregular and unwarrantable Interferings of particular Provinces, and, in many Instances, of particular Persons.

The Part, which some Members of the Assembly of Pennsylvania appear to have had, in the Transactions with the Indians, in July and August 1757, does in our opinion, seem to be of this kind; and to have been one Principal Cause of the Failure of those Measures, which were taken to examine into, and redress the Complaints of the Indians, at this Meeting. Jealousies and Suspicions appear to have been raised, and excited, in the Minds of the Indians, and, in lieu of that Examination and Redress, which might have been expected, from the Disposition that appeared in all Parties, at the opening of the Conferences, no one essential point was settled, and the whole Result of the Treaty was a proposition made, and assented to, that the Deeds and Writings, concerning the Lands, should be transmitted to Great Britain, to be laid before his Majesty for his determination.

It is difficult to conceive, what Idea, the Indians (unacquainted, as they are, with the Forms of Business) might have, of the Efficacy and Propriety of this proposition, But it is impossible that, either, the Deputy Governor, or the Members of the Assembly, who assisted at the Conferences, should not know, that the proposition, of sending over the Deeds, was as irregular, as the Examination of, and Decision upon them, here, was impracticable.

The Circumstances of Fraud, suggested by the Indians, are, that, in some Cases, the Lands were purchased of Persons who had no Right to sell, and, in other Cases, that greater Quantitys of Land had been surveyed and taken up, than was expressed in the Deeds,[6] which are Circumstances, that can only be judged of, upon the Spot, and by those who are well acquainted with the

6. The references are to the purchase of 1749 and the Walking Purchase of 1737, respectively.

Persons, and Claims, of different Indians; and it is as impossible, in the Nature of Things, as it would be irregular, in the Course of Business, for the Crown, to judge, of a Matter of this kind, in the first Instance, and before a regular Examination and Report, in Consequence of such Examination, had been made, by the proper Officer.

The Members of the Assembly, who were present at the Treaty, seem clearly to have understood the Matter, in this light, for, altho' they accepted the proposition from Teedyuscung, and actually received from him, the Treaty and Deeds annexed, in Order to be by them transmitted, to be laid before his Majesty, yet, they never thought proper to transmit them, nor to interpose their Mediation, until the Application, now before your Lordships.

This being the State of the Case, We would humbly propose to your Lordships, that further and more express Orders should be sent, to His Majesty's Agent for Indian Affairs, to examine into the Complaints of the Delaware Indians, with respect to Lands, which, they alledge, they have been defrauded of, by the Proprietaries; and that, for this purpose, he should take the earliest opportunity of signifying to them, that he has, in consequence of what passed at the Conferences in July and August 1757, received his Majesty's Orders, to enquire into their Grievances, and press them to appoint such time and place as shall be most convenient to them, for that purpose, That he be directed to give timely Notice of such Meeting to the Commissioners appointed by the Proprietaries, to act on their part, to the End they may come properly instructed and prepared, to support the Claims of their Constituents; and that, when he shall have made a full and particular Enquiry, into the Circumstances of the Case, and heard what all Partys may have to offer, he do transmit his proceedings, in this Business, to be laid before his Majesty, together with his Opinion, of what may be proper to be done thereupon.[7]

Having stated to your Lordships the several Facts, respecting the particular Case, referred to our Consideration, together with our opinion, upon the whole, it is necessary, for us, before we close our Report, to take this opportunity of observing, to your Lord-

7. The Committee for Plantation Affairs endorsed these recommendations on July 19, 1759, and the Privy Council, meeting on August 29, ordered Sir William Johnson to act upon them. See below, pp. 432–3.

ships, That the Frauds and Abuses, with respect to Purchases, and Settlement of Indian Lands, properly so called, and the fatal Effects of such Abuses, are not confined to the Province of Pennsylvania, nor to this particular Tribe of Indians; They have been as much practiced, complained of, and almost as severely felt, in every other Province, and extend to almost every Tribe of Indians with whom we have any intercourse, and tho' other Nations may not have taken up the Hatchet against us, as the Delawares have done, yet they have not afforded us any effectual assistance in the War in which we are engaged; Their conduct in general has been at best doubtful and equivocal, And they have been more or less our Friends, as the Chances of War have been more or less, in our favour.

It is not to be wondered, that the Indians are tender and Jealous, in a Matter which so essentially concerns their Interest, nay, their very existence. Whilst our Settlements were confined to the Sea Coast, and those of the French to the lower Parts of the River St. Lawrence, the Indians entertained little Jealousy, and did not consider us in the light of Invaders. Their hunting Grounds lay higher up, in the interior parts of the Country, and they not only acquiesced, in our Settlements, but encouraged them, from the advantage they derived from them, in the supply of many wants, which our connections with them had introduced; But no sooner had the prodigious Increase of our People obliged us, and the discovery made of the richness and fertility of the interior parts of the Country, encouraged us, to extend our Settlements, and that Individuals were, from the want of a proper Plan for ascertaining the Mode of acquiring Property, left at Liberty to practice every Fraud and Abuse, in the obtaining excessive Tracts of Land from the Indians, then, they, at once, felt the Embarassment, and grew Jealous of the consequence, of such a Conduct.

In this Situation therefore, the five Nations, who were at the head of a Confederacy of almost all the Northern Nations, and in whom all their Interests were united, did in 1701, resolve upon a Measure, the most wise and prudent, with regard to their own Interest, and the most advantageous, with regard to ours, that could have been framed; they delineated upon Paper, in the most precise and exact manner the Limits of what they called their hunting Grounds, comprehending the great Lakes of Ontario and

Erie, and all the circumjacent Lands, for the distance of Sixty Miles around them; The sole and absolute property of this Country, they desired, might be secured to them, and as proof of perpetual alliance, and to support our Rights, against any Claims which the French might make, founded on the vague and uncertain pretence of unlimited Grants, or accidental local discovery, they declared themselves willing to yield to Great Britain, the Sovereignty and absolute Dominion of it, to be secured and protected by Forts, to be erected, whenever it shou'd be thought proper; a Treaty was accordingly enter'd into and concluded, upon these Terms, by Mr. Nansan, then Lieutenant Governor of New York, and a Deed of Surrender of the Lands expressing the Terms and Conditions, executed, by the Indians.[8]

The advantages of such a Concession on the Part of the Indians, were greater than our most sanguine hopes could have expected, and had the Judgement, Zeal and Integrity, of those, whose Duty it was faithfully to execute the conditions of the engagement, been equal, to those, of him, who made it, the Indians might have been for ever secured in our Interest, and all Disputes with France, about American Territory, prevented, but, by neglect of Government, on one hand, and the enormous abuses of Individuals, in the Purchase of Lands, on the other hand, all the solid advantages of this Treaty and Concession were lost, and, with them, the Memory even of the Transaction, itself. The Indians were disobliged and disgusted, and many of them joined with the Enemy in the War, which followed this Treaty,[9] and desolated our Settlements, whilst the French to whom this Transaction pointed out, what their Plan should be, took every Measure to get possession of the Country by Forts and Military Establishments, and altho' they were compelled, at the Treaty of Utrecht,[1] to acknowledge in express Terms, our Sovereignty over the Six Nations, yet, finding We took no Steps to avail ourselves of such a favourable declaration, either by a renewal of our engagements with the Indians, or taking Measures to support our Sovereignty by Forts erected in proper Parts of the Country, they ceased not to pursue

8. For this treaty, dated July 19, 1701, see *N. Y. Col. Docs.*, IV, 908–11. John Nanfan (d. 1716) was lieutenant governor of N.Y.

9. The War of the Spanish Succession or Queen Anne's War, 1702–13.

1. Concluded April 11, 1713.

that Plan, in which they had already made so considerable a progress, and it was not, till the year 1725, when they had by their Establishment at Niagara secured to themselves the possession of Lake Ontario, that we saw, too late, our Error, in neglecting the advantages which might have been derived from the Treaty in 1701.

Mr. Burnet,[2] who was then Governor of New York, applied himself, however, with great Assiduity, to recover the Interests and Affections of the Indians, as the only means of defeating the designs of the French, and such was the force of their Inclinations to live well with us, and to renew the antient Covenant Chain, as they express it, that they consented, notwithstanding all the ill Treatment they had suffered from us, to enter into the same Engagement; as they had enter'd into in 1701, and a Treaty was accordingly concluded upon the same Terms, and a new Deed, reciting the former, executed by them.[3]

The Experience We had had, of the Mischiefs which followed, from a want of a proper Regard and Attention to our Engagement in 1701, increased by the Danger which now threaten'd Our Colonies, from the Daily and Enormous Encroachments of the French, ought to have been a lesson to us, to have been, now, more careful of our Interests, but, yet, the same Avidity after Possession of Indian Land, aggravated by many other Abuses, stil remain'd uncheck'd and uncontrolled, by any permanent Plan; no Measures were taken to erect Forts, no proper Places to secure the sovereignty of the Country, and to protect it against the Attempts of our Enemys, And it is to the same Causes, producing the same Effects, that we are now to impute, not only the present unsettled and declining state of our Interests with the Indians, but also those Disputes with France concerning Limits and Territory, which have involved us in a most dangerous and critical War.

By the Success of His Majesty's Arms, in the late Expedition against Fort DuQuesne, a great and valuable part of the Country, included in the Deeds of 1701 and 1726, have been recovered, to the Dominions of the Crown of Great Britain. As no Circumstances relative to this Event, and the Negotiations with the Indians, in consequence of it, have been communicated to us, We

2. William Burnet; see above, I, 159 n.
3. For this deed, dated Sept. 26, 1726, see *N.Y. Col. Docs.*, V, 800–1.

cannot take upon us to say, what Measures it may be proper to
pursue, to secure the Dominion of this part of His Majesty's
Territorys, and fix the Indians in our Interest, but we have thought
it proper to trouble Your Lordships with this Narrative of Facts,
in order to shew how dangerous it may be, to make Grants and
Settlements of Indian Lands, which have been ceded for protection, and not Settlement, especially, when all the Political Advantages of such Cession may be obtained, without such Settlement. We are My Lords Your Lordships Most obedient and most
humble Servants

Signed   DUNK HALLIFAX
JAMES OSWALD
WM. SLOPER
SOAME JENYNS

Endorsed: Coppy of the Report of the Board of Trade on B Franklins Petition

From Isaac Norris

Letterbook copy: Historical Society of Pennsylvania

Dear Friend B Franklin   Fairhill June 4th. 1759.[4]
   The Bills of Exchange I have remitted are as follows—to wit—
+1 My Bill or Order on the Executors
  of Doctor Logan for   £200. o. o Sterling
+2 John Hunter on Messrs. Tomlinson
  Hanbury &c. No 732   300. o. o
    I have your Letter of the 18th of
    January acknowledging the Re-
    ceipt of these[5]
+3 Anthony Stoker on
  Geo. Campbell £200. o. o
  payable in London[6]

4. In the ALS sent to BF, Norris dated this letter June 14, not 4; see below,
p. 418.
5. For these two bills, see above, pp. 176, 177. BF's acknowledgement was
dated Jan. 19, 1759, not 18; see above, p. 236.
6. For three bills listed together here, see above, pp. 290, 303.

Ditto	On	Ditto	131.	8.	0		
Ditto	On	Ditto	30.	17.	2	362. 5. 2	

+4 John Hunter on Messrs. Tomlinson &c. No 1049[7] 200. 0. 0

5 Peter Razer On Richard Partridge protested since paid[8] 40. 0. 0

I shall send duplicates of No 3. 4 and 5 as hereunder £1102. 5. 2

Inclosed I likewise send First Bills of Exchange[9]

+6 Joshua Howell on Messrs. Wm. and Richard Baker. No. 5020 £1000. 0. 0

Ditto On Ditto 5021 1000. 0. 0

It will then stand thus That £3102. 5. 0

All these are Come to Hand { The Thirds Bills of Number Three / The Second Bill of Number Four / The Second Bill of Number Five and / The First Bills of Number Six i.e. N 5020 and 5021 / will be inclosed herewith.[1]

---

7. See above, p. 303.

8. See above, p. 327–8. The words "protested" and "since paid," in two different hands, which also appear in the margin, were clearly added later and at different times. The bill was protested because Partridge had died. BF recorded the resulting transactions in "Account of Expences," pp. 27, 50; *PMHB*, LV (1931), 118, 126.

9. BF recorded the receipt of these two bills on Aug. 2, 1759; "Account of Expences," p. 44; *PMHB*, LV (1931), 125.

1. Following this line in his letterbook Norris wrote later "See Page 101," referring to the page where he repeated this tabulation in his letter of July 31; see below, p. 422. He added the following memorandum, obviously not a part of the letter sent to BF: "B Franklin acknowledges the Receipt of all these Bills together with my Letter on the same date, page 99 [the rest of the present letter]. See B Franklins Letter of the 6th. July 1759 which came to my hands by the Packet Via N York and I received by Post October 10th. 1759." No letter from BF dated July 6, 1759, has been found; Norris probably should have written "August 6" (as in the marginal endorsement of this letter), but that letter does not survive. The *Earl of Halifax*, Capt. Bolderson, arrived in N.Y., Oct. 5, 1759, six weeks after leaving Falmouth. *N.-Y. Mercury*, Oct. 8, 1759.

There are unforseen Changes in consequence of this American War. In Philadelphia Houses[2] are high and Bills of Exchange easy to be procured and very considerably under Par which has tempted me to sell several of my Houses and every Thing else I could convert into Mony to invest them in Bills of Exchange.[3] But what I now transmit will not be wholly mine, and as soon as it can be done I will give Notice of what belongs to the Province. As the Bills are good, the Distinction is not so immediatly necessary, but for fear you might be in want of Mony for the Publick and the Province suffer on that Article I took the earlyest Opportunities I could find, at the Request of a considerable Number of the Members, to supply any Defect on that Head. Whilst the Issue of our Bill[4] was unknown and its Success almost dispaired of which must have involved us (in the Consequences of its failure) in the greatest Difficulties in Mony Matters, and no very small Ones in our Civil Affairs but by resolving to venture ev'ry Thing rather than subject our selves to that miserable Disease which preyd continually upon our Vitals we have at length procured that Justice of joining the Proprietary Estates with our Own towards defraying the Expence of the War, And I do not doubt that we shall chearfully exert our Selves in Our several Stations to extricate the Province from the Load of Debt brought upon us by the present War when we consider that the Property of all, contribute, under the present Law by an equal taxation to the general Defence.

But when I suppose that the Property of all is equally taxed, I need not distinguish to my Friend BF who is so well acquainted with our Situation and Affairs that even as the Law stands the Proprietary Estate cannot be equally taxed, since we do not touch their unlocated Lands which will be as much theirs as any other Part of their Property and may be sold whenever the Enemy is expelled and the Frontier once more considered as Safe and fit for Inhabitants as the Internal Parts of the Province. The Property thus excluded by our Law was not long since estimated by them-

2. After "Houses" Norris first wrote, then crossed out, "and Lots."
3. Writing to Richard Jackson, March 8, 1763, after his return to Philadelphia, BF commented on the enormous rise in prices caused by wartime inflation. Among other things, he reported, "Rent of old Houses, and Value of Lands" had "trebled in the last Six Years." APS.
4. The supply bill enacted April 17, 1759; see above, pp. 326–7.

selves to be nearly Nine Tenths of the Whole, as appears by an Estimate in your Hands.[5] But tho' by the Law thus circumstanced and by this Remark it may appear that the Proprietors cannot contribute their full proportion of the Expences, I should not think it Right to tax the unlocated Lands; And I believe the Assessors Will be careful in assessing those that are located so as by no Means to exceed the Proportions of the located Estates and property of the other Inhabitants which are to be defended (as far as we are able to defend them) at the common Charge of all.[6] I shall make this a Seperate Letter and close it and refer any further Advices to what I may have Occasion to inform you of when either my Self, or the Committee transmit the Laws for the Supplies and Indian Trade with the Minutes relating to them under the G[reat] Seal and the proof of the Clerk. I am &c.   I N

Please to put all the Bills (after using what you have Occasion for on the Public Account) into the Bank as by my former Orders. I N

Endorsed: B Franklin received this Letter V. his Letter dated The 6th August 1759. which I received 8th. 10th. 1759.

In the margin: Pd. to [*illegible*] for 6 Gallon 6 2 Qt. 12 Qt. 6 Pint Decanters and 12 Water Glasses from a Quart to half a Pint.[7]

5. "My Estimate of the Province, T. Penn," a copy of which Galloway had sent to BF in July 1758; see above, pp. 151, 360–7.

6. Distrust of the colonial assessors was one of the reasons for the Penns' opposition to the supply bill of 1759 before the King in Council. To secure its passage, BF and Robert Charles, at Lord Mansfield's suggestion, signed an agreement, Aug. 28, 1760, pledging to secure an act of the Assembly which would insure equitable assessment. According to BF, the Assembly did not think such an act necessary because it had appointed a "Committee to examine the Procedings of the Assessors" on which it had put "several particular Friends of the Proprietaries," who after "a full Enquiry" had "unanimously sign'd a Report that they found the Tax had been assess'd with perfect Equity." *Autobiog.* (APS-Yale edit.), pp. 265–6. For the report of the committee of the Assembly, see 8 *Pa. Arch.,* VI, 5216.

7. This notation probably relates to glassware Norris asked BF to buy and send him. In their accounts are records of two such shipments, neither itemized: one on Jan. 11, 1760, for £7 13s., the other on Feb. 20, 1761, for £9 3s. 11d. "Account of Expences," pp. 51, 59; *PMHB.* LV (1931), 126, 130; Norris' MS Account Book, 1735–1765, described above, pp. 147–8.

To William Heberden[8] ALS: Harvard College Library[9]

Tourmaline crystals, brought to Europe from the East by the Dutch early in the eighteenth century, began to attract the attention of electrical scientists when they found that, if heated, they had the power of attracting and repelling ashes and other light substances. The German scientist Aepinus began to study this pyroelectrical property and wrote a paper in 1756, in which he reported that, when a tourmaline was heated in boiling water, one side was electrified positively and the opposite side negatively, and that these charges could also be affected in various ways by other experimental treatments.[1] An Italian investigator, Giovanni Carafa, Duke of Noja, disputed these findings in a paper published in 1759.[2] Franklin's friend Dr. Heberden became interested in the matter, procured a set of tourmalines, and lent them to various English acquaintances for experimental purposes. Franklin's letter is the earliest known report on such investigations in England. Since it was not published for ten years, however, or read to the Royal Society, his friends John Canton and Benjamin Wilson, accounts of whose experiments became public later in 1759, gained general priority among English investigators of the subject.[3]

Dear Sir Thursday June 7. '59.

I have been so long in determining which to chuse of the two Tourmalines, that I fear you begin to think me unreasonable

8. See above, p. 281 n.

9. Printed as Letter XXXIV in *Exper. and Obser.*, 1769 edit., pp. 375–8, and 1774 edit., pp. 383–6.

1. "Mémoire concernant quelques nouvelles expériences électriques remarquables," *Histoire de l'Académie Royale des Sciences et Belles Lettres. Année MDCCLVI* (Berlin, 1758), pp. 105–21. An English summary was printed in *Gent. Mag.*, XXVIII (1758 supplement), 617–19. Franz Ulrich Theodor Aepinus (1724–1802) was born in Saxony, studied medicine and the physical sciences, was admitted to the Academy of Sciences in Berlin, and in 1757 settled in St. Petersburg, where he was made a member of the Imperial Academy of Sciences and professor of physics. In the course of his electrical work Aepinus introduced important modifications of BF's theories, which he nevertheless basically upheld.

2. *Lettre du duc de Noya-Caraffa sur la tourmaline à Monsieur de Buffon* (Paris, 1759).

3. *Gent. Mag.*, XXIX (1759), 424–5; *Phil. Trans.*, LI, pt. I (1759), 308–39. The fullest eighteenth-century account of this subject in English is in Joseph Priestley, *The History and Present State of Electricity* (London, 1767), pp. 314–26, 697–713. The second passage contains Priestley's account of his own experiments, made in 1766 with Heberden's tourmalines.

enough to keep them both. I now return the small one, and beg your Acceptance of my sincerest Thanks for the other, which tho' I value it highly for its rare and wonderful Properties, I shall ever esteem it more for the Friendship I am honour'd with by the Giver.

I hear that the Negative Electricity of one Side of the Tourmalin when heated, is absolutely denied, and all that has been related of it ascrib'd to Prejudice in favour of a System, by some ingenious Gentlemen abroad, who profess to have made Experiments on the Stone with Care and Exactness.[4] The Experiments have succeeded differently with me; yet I would not call the Accuracy of those Gentlemen in question. Possibly the Tourmalins they have try'd were not properly cut; so that the positive and negative Powers were obliquely plac'd, or in some manner whereby their Effects were confus'd, or the negative Part more easily supply'd by the positive. Perhaps the Lapidaries who have hitherto cut these Stones, had no Regard to the Situation of the two Powers, but chose to make the Faces of the Stone where they could obtain the greatest Breadth or some other Advantage in the Form. If any of these Stones in their natural State can be procur'd, I think it would be right to endeavour finding, before they are cut, the two Sides that contain the opposite Powers, and make the Faces there. Possibly in that Case the Effects might be stronger and more distinct. For tho' both these Stones that I have examin'd have evidently the two Properties, yet without the full Heat given by boiling Water they are somewhat confus'd; the Virtue seems strongest towards one End of the Face, and in the Middle or near the other End scarce discernible; and the Negative I find always weaker than the Positive.

I have had the large one new cut, so as to make both Sides alike; and find the Change of Form has made no Change of Power, but the Properties of each Side remain the same as I found them before. It is now set in a Ring in such a manner as to turn on an Axis that I may conveniently in making Experiments come at both Sides of the Stone. The little Rim of Gold it is set in has made no Alteration in its Effects. The Warmth of my Finger when I wear it, is suffi-cient to give it some Degree of Electricity, so that 'tis always ready to attract light Bodies.

4. The Duke de Noja had asserted that, when heated, both sides of the tourmaline were positively charged, but one side more than the other.

The following Experiments have satisfy'd me, that M. Epinus's Account of the positive and negative States of the opposite Sides of the heated Tourmalin, is well founded.

I heated the large Stone in boiling Water.

As soon as it was dry I brought it near a very small Cork Ball that was suspended by a silk Thread.

The Ball was attracted by one Face of the Stone, which I call A, and then repell'd.

The Ball in that State was also repell'd by the positively charg'd Wire of a Phial; and attracted by the other Side of the Stone B.

The Stone being fresh heated, and the Ball attracted by the Side B, was presently after repell'd by that Side.

In this second State it was repell'd by the negatively-charg'd Wire of a Phial.

Therefore, if the Principles now generally receiv'd, relating to Positive and Negative Electricity are true, the Side A of the large Stone, when the Stone is heated in Water, is in a positive State of Electricity, and the Side B in a negative State.

The same Experiments being made with the small Stone stuck by one Edge on the End of a small Glass Tube with Sealing Wax, the same Effects are produced.

The flat Side of the small Stone gives the Signs of positive Electricity; the high Side gives the Signs of negative Electricity.

Farther,

I suspended the small Stone by a Silk Thread.

I heated it as it hung, in boiling Water.

I heated the large one in boiling Water.

Then I brought the large Stone near to the suspended small one; which immediately turn'd its flat Side to the Side B of the large Stone, and would cling to it.

I turn'd the Ring, so as to present the Side A of the large Stone to the flat Side of the small one.

The flat Side was repell'd, and the small Stone turning quick, apply'd its high Side to the Side A of the large one.

This was precisely what ought to happen on the Supposition that the flat Side of the small Stone, when heated in Water, is positive, and the high Side negative; the Side A of the large Stone positive, and the Side B negative.

The Effect was apparently the same as would have been produc'd, if one Magnet had been suspended by a Thread, and the different Poles of another brought alternately near it.

I find that the Face A of the large Stone being coated with Leaf Gold (attach'd by the White of an Egg, which will bear dipping in hot Water) becomes quicker and stronger in its Effect on the Cork Ball, repelling it the Instant it comes in contact; which I suppose to be occasion'd by the united Force of different Parts of the Face collected and acting together thro' the Metal.

You have a Right to all the Experiments and Observations I have made or may make on this admirable Stone.[5] I therefore offer no Apology as giving you Trouble, when I only intend performing a Duty, which you may forbid whenever it becomes disagreable. With the greatest Esteem and Respect, I am, Dear Sir Your most obedient and most humble Servant B FRANKLIN

Dr. Heberden

To Isaac Norris

Duplicate:[6] Yale University Library

Dear Sir London June 9, 1759

It gives me great Pleasure to learn by yours of the 12th. of April,[7] that the Bill taxing the Proprietary Estate would pass. I believe he will not dare to oppose it here; but if he does, I think it will bring the Point to a Decision the shortest Way, and that it must in all Probability be decided against him.[8] The Firmness of the Assembly on this Occasion pleases me much.

5. BF is not known to have made further experiments with the tourmaline. Probably he felt that he could safely leave the matter in the hands of Canton and Wilson, who also confirmed Aepinus' findings.

6. In WF's hand but with a few additions and corrections and the signature by BF. Marked in the upper corner: "(Copy. Original per Pacquet) Capt. Lutwidge."

7. See above, pp. 326–8.

8. The Supply Act of 1759 was the eleventh measure passed by the Assembly in 1758 and 1759 which the Proprietors opposed at home. They initiated their campaign for repeal by petitioning the King in March 1760 to be "heard by their counsel against the said acts." The Board of Trade held hearings on this petition May 21, 22, 24, and June 3, 1760. Charles Pratt and Charles Yorke, respectively attorney and solicitor general, represented the Proprietors; Richard Jackson and William de Grey represented the Assembly. On June 24 the Board recommended to the Committee for Plantation Affairs that the King disallow seven of the acts, including the Supply Act. For

We had a Hearing on Tuesday the 15th. past at the Board of Trade, on the Petition relating to Indian Affairs, of which I formerly sent you a Copy.[9] Their Lordships at first seem'd inclin'd to refer the Enquiry to Commissioners to be appointed out of the Neighbouring Provinces, and indeed the Secretary[1] had previously told me they would do so, the Complaint of the Indians seeming too vague and their Claim too uncertain at present for their Lordships to judge of. Paris seeing this, and imagining from some Expressions I dropt in consequence of that Information, that I wanted to waive a present Enquiry, call'd out loudly to have it immediate; declaring his Readiness and Ability to justify the Proprietors instantly from any Charge that could be brought against them, and insisting much on the Hardship of any Delay when the Characters of such good worthy honest Gentlemen were injur'd by so black a Calumny, which he insinuated was forg'd by the Assembly, the Quakers, and your humble Servant, who had stir'd up the Indians to throw it on the Proprietors, with a great deal of more Abuse of the same kind on the Province, the Assembly and myself; and mov'd that Proofs of the Charges against the Proprietors should be immediately demanded of me. I then told their Lordships, that the Notice I had receiv'd to attend the Board, was, to verify the Allegations of the Petition; that the Allegations of the Petition were only these, That the Indians had at certain Treaties made such and such Complaints concerning certain Lands they suppos'd they had been wrong'd of; that at those Treaties it had been stipulated between them and the Proprietaries, that the Deeds by which the Proprietaries claim'd the controverted Lands should be laid before his Majesty, and the Disputes submitted to His Royal Determination; and the Prayer of the Petition was, that His Majesty would be pleased, for the future Safety of the Province, to take the Premises into Consideration, and do therein as to his Wisdom should seem meet: That I had accordingly

---

the agreement the Assembly agents signed August 28, which finally induced the Committee to permit the Supply Act to stand, see above, p. 392 n. *Board of Trade Journal*, 1759–63, pp. 108–12, 120; *Acts Privy Coun., Col.*, IV, 439–42; *Statutes at Large, Pa.*, V, 652–737. See also the next volume.

9. For documents relating to the Teedyuscung petition, see above, pp. 264–76, 379–89.

1. John Pownall.

verify'd those Allegations by producing the Treaties, and reading the Parts wherein it appear'd that such Complaints were made by the Indians and such Stipulation enter'd into by the Proprietaries; that this was all that seem'd incumbent on me to do, the Matter was now before their Lordships, and I imagin'd that on a little further Consideration the Indian Complaint would not be found so vague and uncertain as at first Sight it might appear. For that it appeared by the Treaty they had claim'd all the Land expressly between Tohickon Creek and the Kittochtiny Hills, as taken from them by Fraud; and when the Deeds were laid before their Lordships, they would be able by comparing the Descriptions of the Lands granted with the Plans of the Land Survey'd in consequence of those Grants, to judge whether such Lands were or were not really convey'd by such Grants. I thought therefore their Lordships might bring this Matter to a speedy Conclusion without sending to America to make further Enquiry; and that whenever they should think fit to direct my Attendance for that Purpose, I would readily furnish their Lordships with any Lights in my Power; and ended with moving that their Lordships would call upon Mr. Penn to lay before them his Deeds and the Plans of his Surveys. Paris rashly oppos'd this in Behalf of his Client, saying no Man should be oblig'd to produce his Deeds for his Adversaries to pick Holes in; that I had no other View in moving it, and a good deal more to this Purpose. But their Lordships who had heard me with great Goodness and Attention, were of a different Opinion; and Lord Halifax[2] said, Mr. Franklin only moves they should be laid before us for our Examination; he does not want to see them. No, my Lord, said I, I already have Copies of all that were deliver'd to the Indians, and here they are. Paris then objected to those Copies as not being certify'd under the Seal of the Province; but Lord Halifax observing that they were certify'd by Tedyuscung's Secretary[3] as true Copies examin'd by him, he said that was sufficient. We then withdrew. What Order their Lordships made on this Hearing is not yet known: As soon as I learn any Thing farther on this Head, I shall communicate it.[4]

2. President of the Board of Trade.
3. Charles Thomson.
4. Although the Board of Trade report was signed June 1, 1759, the Privy Council Committee report approving it was filed only on July 19, and the

On the 29th. I was again at the Board in pursuance of the Notice, a Copy of which I enclose. Their Lordships had conceiv'd
an Objection against the Indian Trade Act as prejudicial to the
Freedom of Trade, and a kind of Monopoly.[5] Mr. Penn was
present. I inform'd their Lordships, That this Act was fram'd in
Imitation of a Law of the same kind long in Use in New England,
and there found so advantageous as to be repeatedly renew'd:[6]
That the Enormities of private Traders made it necessary: That it
had been in force a Year, and none of the Inhabitants had complained of it, but all were I believ'd highly pleas'd with it, as
conducing to the Peace and Safety of the Province: That it was
not a Monopoly in favour of a private Company, but for the
Benefit of the whole Country; That were [where] exclusive Companies for Trade were form'd in England, the chief Reason to
justify the Exclusion of others, was, that the Company must be at
the Expence of maintaining Forts to secure the Trade: That the
same Reason held good in this Case; and more strongly: For as
the Country must suffer all the Loss and Expence of a War occasion'd by the Wickedness of private Traders, or must support
the Forts necessary to secure the Trade and awe the Indians to
Peace under all Provocations, it was just that the Public should
take the Trade into its own Hands, since all Regulations of it in
private Hands had hitherto been evaded, and were by Experience

---

resulting order in council was issued Aug. 29, 1759. *Acts Privy Coun., Col.,*
IV, 402–3.

5. On April 8, 1758, Denny signed the Indian Trade Bill which the Assembly had been trying for years to enact. To proprietary supporters the measure
had seemed to be one more example of the Assembly's continual encroachment on areas of control properly belonging to the executive. See above, VII,
175–6 n. The act as passed put the Indian trade under the supervision of commissioners appointed by the Assembly and excluded private traders from the
area beyond the Kittatinny Hills. Paris presented it, along with six other acts
passed in 1756–58, to the King in Council and they were referred to the
Board of Trade for report, Nov. 14, 1758. After receiving the opinion of
their counsel on the legal aspects of the Trade Act, the Board ordered the
Proprietors and the Assembly agents to attend a hearing on May 29, 1759.
Board of Trade Journal, 1754–58, p. 428; 1759–63, pp. 38, 41; *Statutes at
Large, Pa.,* V, 593–7.

6. BF had been interested in this matter for years and it was he who first
brought the Mass. Indian Trade Act to the attention of the Pa. Assembly.
See above, IV, 120; V, 79–80, 111–12.

found impracticable. That if it were still to continue open, tho' a fair Trade should be carried on at the Truck-houses, the private Traders would flock over the Mountains with Horse Loads of Whiskey, make the Indians drunk, and sweep all their Skins, so that they would have Nothing left to buy Goods with, and the old Mischiefs would be renew'd and continu'd; but by the Trade as now directed in this Act, the Indians having less Drink would be able to buy more British Manufactures; and the Lowness of the Price (the Province intending no Profit) would attach the Indians to our Interest in Preference to the French; and draw other Nations over from the French, to the great Increase of the Trade and Demand for English Goods, and Security of His Majesty's Dominions in those Parts. Mr. Charles observed, that it was but a temporary Act, and if any Inconveniencies were found they would end with the Act, and might be remedy'd in the next. I imagine it will not be disallow'd.[7]

While we were attending in one of the Chambers belonging to the Board of Trade, and were allow'd to search in the Press, containing the Plantation Acts, for the New-England Indian Trade Laws to show their Lordships, my Son cast his Eye on the manuscript Volumes of old Pensylvania Laws formerly transmitted home for Approbation, and found in the Vol. mark'd *Pensylvania Laws from 1701 to 1709,* the Law of the 4th. of Queen Anne, to ascertain the Number of Members of Assembly and regulate Elections, properly certify'd by the then Governor, and Secretary Logan.[8] He found also in another Volume the private Act for vest-

7. At the end of the hearing the Board of Trade agreed that the act "should lye by, until the further effect and operation of it might be known." *Board of Trade Journal,* 1759–63, p. 41.

8. The text of this act, passed Jan. 12, 1705/6, is in *A Collection of All the Laws of the Province of Pennsylvania: Now in Force* (Phila., 1742), pp. 67–75. It specified the declarations to be made by members of the Assembly. These were so framed as to exclude Roman Catholics but otherwise required, in matters of religion, only that each member formally "profess Faith in God the Father, and in Jesus Christ his eternal Son, the true God, and in the Holy Spirit, one God, blessed for evermore," and acknowledge the divine inspiration of the Old and New Testaments. These provisions, of course, enabled Quakers to serve, something they could not do at the time in England. Their opponents petitioned in 1756 to have them excluded by an act of Parliament, and argued that the act of 1706 was invalid because it had not been submitted to the Privy Council within the five years stipulated by the Pa. charter.

ing certain Lands in Geo. McCall, &c.⁹ So that 'tis certain both those Laws have been transmitted and laid before the Board in due Time after passing, and have never been disapprov'd. I saw them.

The Book relating to the Affairs of Pensylvania, is now pub-lish'd.¹ I cannot send you one per the Pacquet; but you will have

As directed, the Board of Trade had held a hearing on the petitions, and al-though nothing came of the proposal, BF was obviously gratified to be able to report to Norris two years later that the act of 1706 could not be disre-garded in this manner. *Acts Privy Coun., Col.*, IV, 326; *Board of Trade Journal, 1754–58*, pp. 215, 217, 218; Charles J. Stillé, "The Attitude of the Quakers in the Provincial Wars," *PMHB*, x (1886), 283–315, esp. 312–14. The gov-ernor who had certified the act was John Evans (fl. 1703–1731) and the secre-tary was James Logan (above, I, 191 n). On the basis of the validity of the act of 1706, see above, p. 62 n.

9. This sentence is pertinent to exchanges between the Assembly and two of the governors in September 1753 and January 1755. As far back as 1723 Gov. William Keith, together with governors of several other colonies, had received a royal instruction forbidding him to assent to any private act (that is, one concerning a particular person or persons rather than the public in general) unless it contained a clause suspending its operation until the King's pleasure should be known. Leonard W. Labaree, ed., *Royal Instructions to British Colonial Governors 1670–1776* (N.Y., 1935), I, 141. In spite of this injunction, still binding on Keith's successors, when George McCall, a Phila-delphia merchant, bought a large tract of land from John Penn in 1735, Gov. Patrick Gordon quickly approved, without a suspending clause, a private act confirming McCall's title to that land. The act was reviewed by the usual authorities in London and confirmed by the Privy Council, May 21, 1736. *Acts Privy Coun., Col.*, III, 850. When in September 1753 Gov. James Hamil-ton had refused to sign a bill for paper currency without a suspending clause, as required by another royal instruction of 1750, the House (with BF on the committee which prepared the report) promptly pointed out the disregard of the instruction of 1723 as a usable precedent, though without citing any specific violation of it. *Votes*, 1752–53, pp. 39–40, 41–7; *Pa. Col. Recs.*, V, 649–54; above V, 38–40. While BF was away from Philadelphia in the early winter of 1754–55, Gov. Robert Hunter Morris also used the instruction of 1740 as an important reason for rejecting a bill for paper currency. In response the Assembly once more brought up the instruction of 1723, this time citing specifically the McCall Act of 1735 as having been passed "in direct Contra-diction to that Instruction, without the least Mention of a suspending Clause." They added that they did not know whether the act had ever been sent to England for approbation. *Votes*, 1754–55, pp. 24–8, 31–4, 37–9, 56–8; *Pa. Col. Recs.*, VI, 192–3, 206–15, 232–6. WF's discovery that the act had indeed been sent to England and had not been rejected for its failure to include a suspending clause strengthened the precedent the Assembly had used.

1. Richard Jackson, *Historical Review*. See above, pp. 360–1.

them per Bolitho.[2] The Proprietor is enrag'd. When I meet him any where there appears in his wretched Countenance a strange Mixture of Hatred, Anger, Fear, and Vexation. He supposes me the Author, but is mistaken. I had no hand in it. It is wrote by a Gentleman said to be one of the best Pens in England, and who interests himself much in the Concerns of America, but will not be known. Billy afforded great Assistance, and furnish'd most of the Materials. The old Proprietor[3] and some others are set in a Light I could have wish'd not to have seen them in; but the Author contended for the Sacredness of Historical Truth, which ought not to be violated in Favour to one's Friends; and that it was Time we should all be weaned from a Family determin'd to oppress us, and which will every Day have it more and more in its Power, if our Attachment should continue. I look'd over the Manuscript, but was not permitted to alter every Thing I did not fully approve. And, upon the whole, I think it a Work that may be of good Use here, by giving the Parliament and Ministry a clearer Knowledge and truer Notion of our Disputes; and of lasting Use in Pensylvania as it affords a close and connected View of our Public Affairs, and may spread and confirm among our People, and especially in the rising Generation, those Sentiments of Liberty that one would wish always to prevail in Pensylvania. It is also a full Refutation of Smith's Brief State and Brief View,[4] without doing the Author the Honour of taking the least Notice of him or his Work. On these Accounts I agreed to encourage the Publication by engaging for the Expence.[5] I hope the Sale may pay great Part of it; to which End I wish it may be encourag'd by our Friends in Pensylvania.[6] Five hundred are sent over to D. Hall to be dispos'd

2. Norris received a copy on Nov. 22, 1759. It arrived on the *James and Mary*, Capt. James Friend. Norris MS Account Book, 1735–65, Lib. Co. Phila.; *Pa. Gaz.*, Nov. 22, 1759.

3. William Penn.

4. William Smith's *A Brief State of the Province of Pennsylvania* (London, 1755), and *A Brief View of the Conduct of Pennsylvania* (London, 1756), both bitterly anti-Quaker. See above, VI, 52 n, 213 n.

5. Paper and printing of 2000 copies and binding of 600 cost £154 5s., special leather binding of 40 copies, £3 12s., and packing and shipping of 500 copies to Pa., £7 8s. See below, p. 453.

6. David Hall wrote BF that the *Reviews* were not selling; the Quakers, he reported, did not "like them because of some Reflections they contain on the old Proprietary." See below, p. 448.

of; and I have order'd 50 for the Assembly, to be distributed where you may think proper.

Smith is still here, aiming I imagine from his late Publication of Sermons, to get into some Living or Preferment on this Side the Water.[7] The Loss of him on your Side, will not, I fancy, be much regretted. The Attorney and Solicitor General I am told will now soon make their Report on his Affair. What it will be I cannot say, but if prejudicial to our Privileges, we shall fight the Battle over again before the Council.[8] How his Finances will support a long Solicitation he best knows, but I believe his Expences must be considerable. He is very close with Mr. Hamilton, who it is said, is to be again our Governor.[9]

The Parliament have voted £200,000 to the Colonies, of which we may in Time expect a Share. I have lodg'd a Memorial in the Treasury, of which enclos'd is a Copy.[1] Both Houses being prorogu'd I shall now shortly make a Journey in to the Country for

7. The publication of William Smith's *Discourses on Several Public Occasions during the War in America* was announced in *London Chron.*, June 2–5, 1759. Smith returned to Philadelphia, Oct. 8, 1759, carrying a deed from Thomas Penn assigning to the Trustees of the College of Philadelphia "his fourth part of the manor of Perkasie in Bucks County containing Two Thousand Five hundred Acres." Montgomery, *Hist. Univ. Pa.*, p. 344.

8. For Smith's petition and his efforts to expedite it in England, see above, pp. 28–51, 295–6, 311. Soon after this letter was written the attorney and solicitor general submitted a report to the Committee for Plantation Affairs unfavorable, on the whole, to the Assembly. It held that the Assembly had no right to imprison Smith and proceed against him "for a Contempt to any former Assembly" and advised him that "as the Law provided sufficient remedy in all cases of illegal and Arbitrary Commitments," he should seek redress in the proper courts of justice in Pa. They were also of the opinion that "inferior Assemblys ... must not be compared, either in power or privileges, to the Commons of Great Britain" and that in denying Smith a writ of habeas corpus, the Assembly had committed "a high and unwarrantable Invasion" of the "Royal prerogative, and the Liberties of the Subject." The Committee adopted this report on June 26, 1759, and, in addition, recommended that the governor of Pa. should be "commanded to signify to the Assembly there, your majesty's high displeasure against all such unwarrantable proceedings and Oppression of the Subject." On the same day the Privy Council adopted these recommendations and drew up an order to enforce them. *Pa. Col. Recs.*, VIII, 438–46. *Acts Privy Coun., Col.*, IV, 375–85.

9. James Hamilton's commission as lieutenant governor, dated July 21, 1759, is in *Pa. Col. Recs.*, VIII, 409–11.

1. See above, pp. 333–8.

the better preserving my Health, as the great Offices are little attended in the Summer.[2]

The French threaten us hard with an Invasion.[3] Prudent Precautions are accordingly taking to defend the Coasts; but I do not find that much Danger is apprehended. It would seem an extreamly rash Undertaking for the Enemy to cross the Channel with an Army at a Time when we have so manifestly the Superiority at Sea; and, tho' they should land we may cut off their Supplies, or their Retreat if they should be worsted. The King of Prussia having succeeded early in the Campaign, in destroying many of the Magazines both of the Russians and Austrians, now turns the Fabius upon Marshal Daun, and hovers over him in the Mountains with his Armies. The French have been long on the Defensive but now begin to advance.[4] The Disputes between us and Holland are still unsettled. It is thought however that Means will be found to prevent a Rupture.[5]

I wrote to you largely by the last Ships to Philadelphia which left Portsmouth the 25th. of April, and I hope are safe arriv'd.[6] Be pleased to present my best Respects to the Assembly, and believe me, with sincere Esteem, Dear Sir, Your most obedient humble Servant   B FRANKLIN

Mr. Norris

2. See above, p. 430–1.

3. In the spring of 1759 the French planned a massive assault on Great Britain. One force of 20,000 men would sail around Ireland, capture Glasgow and Edinburgh, and invade England from the north with support from disaffected Scottish Highlanders and possibly a Swedish expeditionary army. Then the main French fleet would seek to gain at least temporary control of the English Channel, permitting two French corps to cross in flatboats, land on the south coast, and march on London. Capture of a letter to the French ambassador at Stockholm informed the British of the plan. Gipson, *British Empire*, VIII, 4–6.

4. For Frederick's campaigns during this spring, see *ibid.*, VIII, 31–2.

5. To prevent the neutral Dutch from supplying the French West Indies, Great Britain, invoking the famous Rule of 1756 and its corollary, the Doctrine of Continuous Voyage, had seized many Dutch merchantmen. In February 1759 the Dutch voted to arm twenty-five ships of the line to protect their trade, but there were no further incidents and the crisis passed. *Ibid.*, VIII, 72–8.

6. BF may be referring to his letter of March 19 (above, pp. 291–7), or to a letter written in April which has not been found.

Provincial Commissioners: Order to Pay Isaac Norris

DS: Historical Society of Pennsylvania

Philada. June the 12th 1759

Pay or Cause to be paid to Isaac Norris Esqr. the Sum of Two Thousand three Hundred and Sixty Two pounds Ten Shillings being the Amount of Fifteen Hundred pounds Sterling Advanced to Benjamin Franklin Esqr to Enable him to Solicit the Affairs of this province at the Court of Great Brittain in pursuance of the Resolves of a Late house of Assembly of this province.[7]

To the Trustees of the   JON HUGHES[8]
General Loan Office   JOS: FOX
                                   JOS. GALLOWAY
                                   THOS: CADWALADER
                                   WM: MASTERS

7. On April 3, 1757, BF received £750 sterling in bills of exchange, costing £1237 10s. Pa. currency, half of the £1500 sterling voted for expenses of his mission to England (above, VII, 166–7). On March 20, 1759, the Assembly formally declared that BF's expenses were "a Debt justly due from, and chargeable to this Province" and ought to be paid out of the proceeds of the next supply act; the House ordered that a certificate be prepared to this effect and Norris signed it immediately (*Votes*, 1758–59, p. 45). Governor Denny signed the pending £100,000 supply bill, April 17, 1759, and, as Norris explained in his letter to BF, July 31 (below, p. 418), he procured the present order to cover the full £1500 sterling previously voted for BF's expenses. In several letters (see above, esp. p. 176) Norris urged that, if necessary for public service, BF spend any part of the funds he, Norris, was sending to England from time to time for his own account. Although BF's "Account of Expences" does not show the matter clearly, he apparently acted on this basis, for after his return to Philadelphia his public account, submitted to the speaker Feb. 15, 1763, acknowledged that "Fifteen Hundred Pounds of the Public Money was at different Times put into my Hands, for which I ought to account" (Hist. Soc. Pa.). Meanwhile, on Oct. 18, 1760, Norris reported to the Assembly that he had advanced and remitted to BF £750 sterling, costing £1125 currency at 50 percent exchange, representing the second half of the £1500 originally voted for BF, and that he still had in hand £1237 10s. currency, representing the £750 sterling given BF before departure, for which the speaker stood accountable to the province. The Assembly directed him to pay this balance back to the trustees of the General Loan Office, and their accounts for 1760–61 show that he did so. 8 *Pa. Arch.*, VI, 5167, 5271.

8. These men were commissioners to "order and appoint the disposition of the moneys" arising from the Supply Act of April 17, 1759. *Statutes at Large, Pa.*, V, 393–4.

From David Hall   Letterbook copy: American Philosophical Society

Sir,   Philada. June 18. 1759.

Being just going to set off on a Journey to the Sea Side with my Wife,[9] for the Benefit of her Health, have only Time now to enclose you the first Copy of a Bill of Exchange for Two Hundred Pounds Sterling; for which you will give me Credit, as usual, and Advise, when paid.[1] This Letter I directed to the Care of Mr. Strahan, in case of your being set out for Philadelphia before it reached. The Exchange of this last 50. The Number of the Bill 1167. I am, Sir, Your very humble Servant   DAVID HALL

Sent by the William and Mary, Capt. Nicholson

NB. I have now sent you in all, exclusive of the protested Bill for One Hundred Pounds Sterling,[2] Fifteen Hundred and Forty-nine Pounds, Twelve Shillings, and Five-pence Sterling.

To Benjamin Franklin Esq:

William Franklin to Peter Schuyler

ALS: Morristown National Historical Park

Dear Sir   London June 19, 1759

If I am found among the last in congratulating Col. Schuyler and my Country on his Release from Canada,[3] my Distance must be my Apology. It cannot methinks be attributed to a Want of Regard for either, when 'tis recollected that for the Sake of the latter I last War serv'd as an Officer in its Service, and my Esteem for the former prompted me to become a Volunteer under him when his Regiment was order'd upon what was then deem'd a very hazardous March to Saratoga.[4] This War, 'tis true, I have not

9. Mary Leacock Hall (F.2.2.3), DF's second cousin.

1. BF recorded the receipt of this bill on Aug. 2, 1759. "Account of Expences," p. 44; *PMHB*, LV (1931), 123.

2. For the protested bill, see above, VII, 236.

3. See above, pp. 348–9 n.

4. For WF's services in King George's War, 1743–48, see above, III, 89 n, 233 n. After occupying Fort Clinton at Saratoga, N.Y., Schuyler's regiment was compelled to retire in the fall of 1747 for want of provisions. See George W. Schuyler, *Colonial New York Philip Schuyler and His Family* (N.Y., 1885), II, 209.

been much concern'd in the military Way, having only had the Direction of the Forces sent with my Father to erect some Forts on the Frontier of our Province.[5] But I can assure you, Sir, tho' I have not been personally engag'd, my Heart has ever accompany'd you and the other Gentlemen of America who have so nobly signaliz'd themselves in its Defence: Nor could I excuse myself to myself for not being one of the Number, were it not for the pleasing Reflection of having been in some Measure instrumental in defending my Country from intestine Foes as dangerous as its foreign Enemies.[6]

But how great soever may be the Proofs of Disinterestedness, and Public Spirit, given by the Gentlemen of N. America, it seems there are some residing among them, who from Jealousy, Envy, or other mean Motives, would rob them of all the Merit due to such Actions. Two flagrant Instances of this, among many others, have lately appear'd in the public Prints in England. One of them said to be a Letter from an Officer in General Abercrombie's Regiment, the other from an Officer in General Forbes's Army. The Tendency of these Letters was evidently to make the Provincial Forces in particular, and the Americans in general, appear in a very rediculous nay hateful Light to the Mother Country. It would therefore have been unpardonable if none of the Americans on the Spot where these Aspersions were publish'd, had not stood up in Behalf of the Colonies, and shewn how egregiously Facts had been misrepresented. This Fault, however, cannot be added to the others already laid to their Charge, as you will see by the inclos'd News-paper, which contains as full an Answer to those calumniating Letters as could be well publish'd in that Manner.[7]

To you, Sir, it may be deem'd necessary to make some Apology for the Mention made of your Name and Services on this Occasion: For you are one of those who, as the Poets says,

"Do good by Stealth, and blush to find it Fame."[8]

But the Author, 'tis to be suppos'd, thought that some Regard was

5. See above, VI, 381.
6. Probably a reference to his letter to *The Citizen*, Sept. 16, 1757 (above, VII, 255–63), and possibly also to help he may have given in preparing Jackson's *Historical Review*.
7. BF's letter in the *London Chron.*, May 10–12, 1759, in reply to the two letters here mentioned; see above, pp. 340–56.
8. Pope, *Epilogue to the Satires*, I, 136.

also due to his own Reputation. To speak of the meritorious Actions perform'd by the Inhabitants of N. America, and omit those of Col. Schuyler, would be an Omission not to be justify'd.

Tho' these Letters have some Appearance of being wrote by Officers of the Regulars, yet I have lately from several Circumstances had great Reason to think, that the first is the Production of Dr. Thompson of N. York,[9] and the second of Parson Smith of Philadelphia. Whether my Conjecture is justly founded or not, you will perhaps be able to determine by what you may hear among the Officers. This I certainly know, that they have on more Occasions than one express'd a very contemptuous Opinion of the Americans, and that they possess a large Share of that Vanity and Self-sufficiency which so particularly distinguishes the lower Class of the Scottish Nation.

We are extremely anxious here to know the Event of the Expedition against Ticonderoga and Quebeck, particularly the latter, which has been represented by those who are no Friends of Mr. Pitt's Measures as impracticable on Account of the Navigation. For my Part, I think there is nothing in that Objection, and that if any Thing prevents General Wolfe's Success it must be the Want of a sufficient Number of Men. If that should be the Case, whoever directed the carrying on an Expedition to Niagara, and another to Venango, at the same Time as the two grand Expeditions were on foot, will incur a great deal of Censure.[1] It will be

9. For Dr. Adam Thomson, see above, IV, 80 n.

1. British military plans for 1759 were drawn up by William Pitt. They called for Gen. James Wolfe to attack Quebec via the St. Lawrence River and for Gen. Jeffery Amherst to invade Canada "by Way of Crown Point or LaGalette" and to attack either Montreal or Quebec. Pitt also encouraged Amherst to attack Fort Niagara "if the great and main Objects of the Campaign shall permit." An assault against Fort Machault at Venango (now Franklin, Pa.), was not specifically mentioned, although the British commander in Pa. was expected to undertake "such offensive Operations" as were "most expedient for annoying the Enemy. . . ." Pitt to Amherst, Dec. 29, 1758, Gertrude S. Kimball, ed., *Correspondence of William Pitt* (N.Y. and London, 1906), I, 432–42. The issue of Wolfe's campaign is well known. With "somewhat less than nine thousand men" (he had been promised 12,000), he left Halifax on May 13, 1759, and by the end of June he was before Quebec. On September 13, his troops routed the French at the famous battle on the Plains of Abraham, in which both Wolfe and his opposite number, Montcalm, were killed, and made themselves the masters of Quebec.

ask'd, If the Taking of Quebec would not render all the others unnecessary? and if so, Should not the chief Part of our Forces have been directed to that Quarter? And certainly it does seem at first Sight, that the Provincial Forces, with a few Regulars, properly employ'd on the Frontiers of New York and Pensylvania would have been sufficient to have defended those Provinces from any Incursions which might be apprehended from Niagara and Venango; or even Ticonderoga, when the Enemy had Reason to expect an Attack upon Quebeck; and that therefore more Regulars should have been spar'd for the latter Service. From dividing the Forces so much, and sending them on so many different Expeditions, which must necessarily add greatly to the Expence of the Nation, some will be led to suspect it is done principally with a View of putting a profitable Job into the Hands of the particular Commanders, who must by this Means have much greater Emoluments arising to them than if they serv'd only in their respective Stations in the Army. Admiral Durell is blam'd for not being sooner in the River St. Lawrence, to prevent the French receiving any Reinforcements. It does not appear that he sent a single Ship there till Saunders's Arrival, altho' one of the principal Reasons for his wintering at Halifax was, that he might be there sooner than the French possibly could; and now we have Intelligence of several Store Ships being arriv'd there from Old France:[2]

General Amherst's forces got no farther than Lake Champlain. They did, however, capture Fort Ticonderoga (July 26) and Crown Point (July 31) and detachments from Amherst's force, joined by Sir William Johnson and 1000 Indians, took Fort Niagara on July 25, 1759. In attempting to take Fort Machault, the British suffered one of their few defeats in the otherwise glorious campaign of 1759. On March 28, 1759, a force under Col. Hugh Mercer, going from Pittsburgh against the fort, was defeated and compelled to give up the attempt. Gipson, *British Empire*, VII, 329–427; Hunter, *Forts*, pp. 162–3.

2. On Dec. 28, 1758, Pitt instructed Rear Adm. Philip Durell, who was wintering in North America with 14 warships, to sail as soon as the weather permitted to the island of Bic in the St. Lawrence and to intercept all French provision ships bound for Quebec. When Wolfe and Vice Adm. Sir Charles Saunders, commander of the naval forces of the expedition, arrived at Halifax on April 30, 1759, Durell was still there, shut in by bad weather. He reached Bic on May 22, but in the meantime a French convoy of sixteen ships had passed up the river to Quebec. According to Gipson, the weather and not Durell's want of vigilance should be blamed for this situation. Gipson, *British Empire*, VIII, 375–79.

Whether this Conduct of his, is the Result of a Concert between him and the Contractors, or Persons concern'd in fitting out his Majesty's Navy, who from Motives of Interest are extremely averse to the having any of the Men of War winter out of England, Time perhaps will discover.

I congratulate you on our Success at Guadulope. That Capitulation is, however, not much relish'd here; but I am well convinc'd that with a little prudent Management it may be made a very valuable Acquisition.[3] We have for some Time been threaten'd with an Invasion, but little Danger is apprehended, tho' much Pains seem to be taken for political Considerations to keep alive and increase our Fears.[4]

There's here a poor Woman of the Name of James,[5] in whose Prayers I believe you are never forgotten. Her Mouth is ever full of your Praises. She was taken Prisoner in the Year 1755 or 56 by the Indians on the Frontiers of Pensylvania, where she formerly liv'd in good Circumstances, and by them carried to Canada. After a Series of Hardships among them, she was taken to Montreal, where she says you purchas'd her Freedom. From thence she was sent to old France with some other Women in the same Situation. During her Stay there she likewise suffer'd greatly. At length she got over to England in a Cartel Ship, and was for some Time as much distress'd here as in her Captivity, not knowing she had any kind of Knowledge of a single Person in the Kingdom. By Accident she heard of my Father being here, and upon her applying to him, he reliev'd her, and intends sending her by the first Ship home to America.[6]

I have taken the Liberty to send you, by way of Philadelphia one of the Historical Reviews of the Constitution and Government of Pensylvania,[7] of which I desire your Acceptance. It is wrote in Defence of the Liberties of that Province, and I flatter myself will not prove unacceptable to One who has

3. After resisting for almost four months, the French forces in Guadeloupe capitulated to Maj. Gen. John Barrington on May 1, 1759. *Ibid.*, VIII, 94–105.

4. See above, p. 404 n.

5. Identified by BF as Mrs. Mary James; see next document.

6. BF advanced Mrs. James one guinea. "Account of Expences," p. 41; *PMHB.*, LV (1931), 120.

7. See above, p. 360–1.

so often risqu'd his Life to preserve the Liberties of America in general.

That this may find you sitting under your own Vine, enjoying the pleasing Satisfaction of having contributed greatly to the Reduction of that Country in which you were once a Prisoner, and which was so highly detrimental to the British Interest, is the ardent Wish of him who is with great Esteem and Respect, Dear Sir, Your most obedient and most humble Servant

WM: FRANKLIN

P.S. I happen not to have by me one of the News-Papers containing the Vindication of the Colonies, but I suppose you will see it printed in the American Papers. 'Tis sign'd *"A New England Man."*[8]

Col. Schuyler.

Endorsed: Wm Franklin Coll: Ptr: Schuyler London 19 June 1759

To James Wright[9]

LS: Yale University Library; transcript: John L. W. Mifflin, Middlebush, N.J. (1955)

Dear Sir   London July 9, 1759
    By the Cornelia Capt. Smith I sent you in a Box to Mrs. Franklin[1]

Norden's Egypt. cost	£4:	4:	0
Maintenon's Letters and a Book of Husbandry	0:	6:	0
A Thermometer[2]	1:	11:	6
	£6:	1:	6

which I hope are got safe to hand.

There has been at my House one Mary James[3] who was taken from Juniata about 3 Years and a half since, and carried by the

8. See above, p. 340–56.

9. See above, IV, 210–11 n.

1. See above, p. 306, for the books mentioned below. The brig *Cornelia,* Capt. Robert Patten, not Smith, arrived in Philadelphia June 19, 1759. *Pa. Gaz.,* June 21, 1759.

2. BF recorded this purchase on March 10, 1759; see "Account of Expences," p. 38.

3. See opposite page. She has not been otherwise identified. Several Indian attacks on settlers in the Juniata valley were reported in late 1755 and early

Indians to Canada, was redeem'd from them by Col. Schuyler, and got among the French; was sent with other Prisoners to old France; and after living there 15 Months, got over hither. She tells me she left two Children with you and your good Sister whom she is very desirous of seeing. I am endeavouring to procure a Passage for her.

I wrote to you some time since concerning the Silk Affair.[4] For public Matters must beg leave to refer you to my Letters to the Speaker,[5] having now only time to add, that I am, with affectionate Regards to all Friends at the River,[6] Your most obedient Servant   B FRANKLIN

Billy presents his Respects.

Mr. Wright

To James Wright[7]

Copy: William L. Clements Library

Sir,   London July 9; 1759

When Mr. Hunter[8] came to Town, I conferr'd with him on the Subject of Supporting a regular constant Post between Charles Town in South Carolina and Williamsburgh in Virginia, agreeable

---

1756, but few individuals were named in the accounts. 1 *Pa. Arch.*, II, 454, 458, 566, 568.

4. The cultivation of silk worms was one of the many interests of Wright's sister, Susanna (above, IV, 210–11 n). BF's letter "concerning the Silk Affair" has not been found.

5. See above, pp. 232–7, 291–7, 396–404.

6. The Wright family and their connections lived on both sides of the Susquehanna River.

7. James Wright (1716–1785), agent for South Carolina, 1757–61, was born in London but moved to Charleston as a boy with his parents. He entered Grey's Inn, 1741, was called to the bar, and subsequently became attorney general of South Carolina. He was appointed lieutenant governor of Georgia, 1760, and promoted to governor the next year, serving until expelled in 1776. He was generally credited with preventing the Georgia Assembly from sending delegates to the First Continental Congress. He returned to his post upon the British reoccupation in 1779 but was forced to leave again in 1782. He was created a baronet in 1772. *DNB*.

8. For William Hunter, BF's colleague as deputy postmaster general of North America, see above, V, 18 n. Hunter sailed for America in May 1759, after spending three years in England for his health. See above, p. 324.

to what Pass'd when I had the Pleasure of Meeting you at the General Post Office. He was Concerned to hear, that by the Death of Mr. Fareis[9] who we had appointed to Carry on that Post, and who had undertaken to Procure assistance from the Governments of both Carolinas to Support it, the same had been dropt. Mr. Hunter readily agreed to my Proposal, that we would appoint and Commission such Officers for the Purpose, as should be recommended to us by those Governments, at Charles Town, George Town, Cape Fear, and Edenton, or Such other Places as may be thought more Convenient for the Several Stages; which Officers should keep exact Accounts of all Expences Attending the Affair, Such as the Wages Paid to riders, Hire of Horses, Disbursements for Mails, Bags &ca. together with their own reasonable Salaries, or Allowances for their Care and Trouble in receiving and Dispatching the Mails, Delivering Letters, &ca. and also Accounts of the Sums they have received for the Postage of Letters, all which being fairly drawn, and attested upon Oath by the Officers, shall be yearly Submitted by us to the Inspection of any Persons to be appointed by the said Governments; Provided that those Governments will for the Encouragement and Support of this Post, agree to Pay only the Difficiency, or so much as the receipts shall appear to fall Short of the Expences.

What this Difficiency may be Mr. Hunter could not undertake to say, as he knew not at what rate riders and Horses might be had in those Parts, nor what the Postage of the Letters might amount to: But as Mr. Fareis had made Trial, and Carried on the Several Stages Some time before his Death, the Expence might be found in the Account he kept, which as yet had not been rendred to us.

Mr. Hunter was then going over to America, and Probably is now there. If this Proposal should be agreeable to those Governments he will immediately take the Proper Measures for carrying it into Execution, and we shall jointly use our best Endeavours to have it Conducted in the most Satisfactory and advantageous Manner to the Public.[1]

9. Not identified.

1. The establishment of a "regular constant Post" between Charleston, S.C., and Va. was not attempted until 1769, four years after the southern colonies had been made a separate postal department, administered first by

Whatever the Expence may be, it will Lessen yearly as People, Commerce and Correspondence Encrease, and in a few Years there is no Doubt but the Post will be able to Support itself. Each Government, besides the more easy and expeditious Dispatch of Publick Letters, Will Probably find otherways its Account in encouraging the Post; Since encreasing the Facility of Corresponding and the Opportunities of Sending Orders and receiving Advices is found to be a Means of Encreasing Mutual Commerce. With great Esteem, I am, Sir Your most Obedient Humble Servant

B FRANKLIN

To J. Wright Esqr: Marlborough Street.

To Jane Mecom

ALS: American Philosophical Society

Dear Sister, London, July 14. 1759

I received your kind Letter of Jany. 31.[2] You are very good in not resenting some Part of my Letter of September 16. which I confess was a little rude;[3] but you fatfolks can't bear Malice.

Our Cousin Fisher and her Husband are both dead since I saw them.[4] She surviv'd him but a few Days. What she had in her Disposal was but little; and it was divided into 7 equal Shares, among seven of us who were her Relations in equal Degree, viz. three here in England 1. Mrs. Ann Farrow Daughter of our Uncle John Franklin; 2. Mrs. Eleanor Morris, Daughter of our Aunt Hannah: 3. My self. And four in America, viz. 1. Cousin Samuel Franklin. 2. Sister Dowse. 3. Brother Peter. 4. Yourself. Each Share was just £11 8s. 4d. Sterling. I divided what came to me equally between Mrs. Farrow and Mrs. Morris, the two Cousins here, they being ancient Women and poor. The four American

---

Benjamin Barons and then by Peter DeLancey. Service between the two places was extremely irregular, however, until after the Revolutionary War. Ruth L. Butler, *Doctor Franklin Postmaster General* (N. Y., 1928), pp. 115–24.

2. Not found.

3. See above, pp. 152–5.

4. For Mary Franklin Fisher (A.5.2.1.1) and her husband, Richard, for BF's activities in connection with the distribution of Mrs. Fisher's estate, and for his English and American relatives mentioned in this letter, see above, pp. 221–5, 288–9, 302, 325.

Shares are paid into my Hands for the Parties, and I desire you
would let me know what will be most agreable to have it sent in.
I would have you also visit Sister Dowse, and read her this Letter,
and help her to contrive what I shall send hers in.[5] I can now only
add, that I am, Your ever Affectionate Brother   B FRANKLIN

To Ebenezer Kinnersley

MS not found; reprinted from *The Pennsylvania Magazine of History and
Biography*, XIII (1889), 247–8.

Dear Sir,   London, July 28, 1759.
I received your favour of Sept. 9[6] and should have answer'd it
sooner, but delay'd in Expectation of procuring for you some Book
that describes and explains the Uses of the Instruments you are at
a loss about. I have not yet got such a Book but shall make further
Enquiry. Does not Desaguliers in his Course explain them?[7] You
do not mention the Reasons of your being tired of your Situation
in the Academy.[8] And if you had, it would perhaps be out of my
Power at this Distance to remedy any Inconveniences you suffer
or even if I was present. For before I left Philadelphia, everything to be done in the Academy was privately preconcerted in a
Cabal without my Knowledge or Participation and accordingly
carried into Execution. The Schemes of Public Parties made it

5. Elizabeth Douse (C.1), eldest of Josiah Franklin's seventeen children,
died Aug. 25, 1759, aged 81, and it is uncertain whether this letter arrived in
time for her youngest sister, Jane Mecom, to read it to her. In a letter of Jan.
9, 1760, BF took note that Benjamin Mecom, who owed BF considerable
money, had advanced his mother's legacy to her since she wanted it immediately.

6. Not found.

7. John Theophilus Desaguliers, *A Course of Experimental Philosophy* (2
vols., London, 1734–44). Collinson had suggested this book as a possible
guide for the selection of instruments for the Academy; see above, IV, 3–4.

8. Kinnersley was at this time master of the English School and professor of
English and oratory in the College of Philadelphia. Personal illness; the
Trustees' neglect of the English School, the enrollment of which had dropped
more than half; and perhaps a realization that he was not as gifted a teacher as
his predecessor David James Dove had been, were probable factors in Kinnersley's disenchantment. He held his position, however, until 1772. Montgomery, *Hist. Univ. Pa.*, pp. 244–51, 342.

seem requisite to lessen my Influence whereever it could be lessened. The Trustees had reap'd the full Advantage of my Head, Hands, Heart and Purse, in getting through the first Difficulties of the Design, and when they thought they could do without me, they laid me aside.[9] I wish Success to the Schools nevertheless and am sorry to hear that the whole Number of Scholars does not at present exceed an hundred and forty.

I once thought of advising you to make Trial of Your Lectures here, and perhaps in the more early Times of Electricity it might have answer'd;[1] but now I much doubt it, so great is the general Negligence of every thing in the Way of Science that has not Novelty to recommend it. Courses of Experimental Philosophy, formerly so much in Vogue, are now disregarded; so that Mr. Demainbray,[2] who is reputed an excellent Lecturer, and has an Apparatus that cost nearly £2000, the finest perhaps in the World, can hardly make up an audience in this great City to attend one Course in a Winter.

I wonder your roughening the Glass Globe[3] did not succeed. I have seen Mr. Canton[4] frequently perform his Experiments with the smooth and rough Tubes, and they answered perfectly as he describes them in the Transactions.[5] Perhaps you did not use the same Rubbers.

There are some few new Experiments here in Electricity which

9. Richard Peters was elected president of the trustees, in BF's place, May 11, 1756; see above, VII, 12 n.

1. For Kinnersley's lectures in electricity, see above, IV, 192 n.

2. After lecturing on electricity in the British Isles and then in France in the 1740s and 1750s, Stephen Charles Triboudet Demainbray (1710–1782) returned to England and in 1754 became the tutor of the Prince of Wales in mathematics, experimental philosophy, and natural history. In 1768, his former pupil, now George III, appointed him astronomer at the royal observatory at Kew. *DNB*.

3. On Dec. 5, 1757, BF recorded the purchase of a globe for Kinnersley. "Account of Expences," p. 9; *PMHB*, LV (1931), 106.

4. For John Canton, F.R.S., English electrical experimenter, and twice winner of the Copley Medal, see above, IV, 390 n.

5. See *Phil. Trans.*, XLVIII (1754), 780–5. There Canton sought to demonstrate that "the positive and negative powers of electricity" could be "produced at pleasure" by altering the surface of a glass tube and by rubbing it with different substances. See also I. Bernard Cohen, *Franklin and Newton* (Phila., 1956), pp. 534–7.

at present I can only just hint to you. Mr. Symmer[6] has found that a new black Silk Stocking worn 8 or 10 Minutes on a new white one, then both drawn off together, they have, while together, no great Signs of Electricity; i.e. they do not much attract the small Cork Balls of Mr. Canton's Box; but being drawn one out of the other, they puff out to the full Shape of the Leg, affect the Cork Balls at the Distance of 6 Feet and attract one another at the Distance of 18 inches and will cling together; and either of them against a smooth Wall or a Looking Glass, will stick to it some time. Upon Trial, the black Stocking appears to be electris'd negatively, the white one positively. He charges Vials with them as we us'd to do with a Tube. Mr. Delavall has found that several Bodies which conduct when cold, or hot to a certain Degree, will not conduct when in a middle State.[7] Portland Freestone, for Instance, when cold, conducts; heated to a certain degree will not conduct; heated more it conducts again; and as it cools, passes thro' that Degree in which it will not conduct till it becomes cooler.

This with what you mention of your Cedar Cylinder, makes me think, that possibly a thin Cedar Board, or Board of other Wood, thoroughly dried and heated, might if coated and electrified, yield a Shock as glass Planes do. As yet I have not try'd it.[8]

But the greatest Discovery in this Way is the Virtue of the *Tourmalin* Stone, brought from Ceylon in the Indies which being heated in boiling Water, becomes strongly electrical, one side positive, the other negative, without the least Rubbing.[9] They are very rare but I have two of them and long to show you the Experiments.

Billy joins with me in Compliments to you and to good Mrs. Kinnersley and your promising Children. I am with much Esteem and Affection Dear Sir, Your most obedient Servant. B. FRANKLIN.

Mr. Kinnersley.

6. Robert Symmer (above, IV, 276–7 n) published four papers on the electrical properties of silk in *Phil. Trans.*, LI (1759), 340–89. In one of these (pp. 374–7) he mentioned that he had used BF's electrical apparatus and had conducted some experiments in his presence.

7. For these experiments by Edward Hussey Delaval, the first man BF helped to nominate for membership in the Royal Society (above, pp. 359–60), see *Phil. Trans.*, LI (1759), 83–8.

8. Kinnersley reported another experiment with cedar in his letter to BF of March 12, 1761.

9. See above, pp. 393–6.

From Isaac Norris

ALS: American Philosophical Society; letterbook copy: Historical Society of Pennsylvania; copy: American Philosophical Society[1]

Dear Friend Benjn Franklin   Fairhill, July 31th. 1759

Just on closing my last Letter which was on the 14th of June last I added a figure 1 before the 4 though it was actually wrote on the 4th of that Month[2] and being called off from adding a few lines to explain the difference Situation between those Dates it will be incorrect in some Points unless it is read upon its true time and considered in that Light, for about the 14th I got an Order from the Commissioners for Some publick Mony to be paid to Me for discharging the Agents Salarys as well as for a further Supply to your Self if there should be Occasion in pursuance of two Resolves of Assembly of the 3d of February and 1st of April 1757 which will appear by the Votes of that Year.[3]

General Amherst[4] came to Philadelphia on the 9th of April last, and the time for beginning the ensuing Campain pressing, he left us on the 11th before Noon. At his Request I had a long and free Conference with the General on the Tenth and on the same Day the Commissioners waiting upon him he entered immediatly into the Business of the Supplies for the ensuing Year, A Bill then lying before the Governor for that Purpose, the Issue of those Conferences will appear by General Amhersts Letter to our Governor a Copy of which the Governor favoured me with as well as some other Papers of Importance which I shall inclose.[5] No. 1 is a Duplicate of General Amhersts Letter on or rather previous to his

1. The postscript, not found with the ALS, and only in shortened form in the copy, is printed from the letterbook copy.

2. See above, pp. 389–92.

3. See above, p. 405, for the commissioners' order of June 12, 1759; the Assembly resolves are in *Votes*, 1756–57, pp. 78, 107.

4. Maj. Gen. Jeffery Amherst was British commander-in-chief in North America; see above, p. 328 n.

5. On April 11, 1759, Amherst wrote Denny that Norris and other Assembly leaders had obstinately refused his entreaties to pass a supply bill exempting the proprietary estates from taxation. He therefore urged Denny to waive his instructions and approve the bill as it stood. *Pa. Col. Recs.*, VIII, 331–2. For the general's efforts to get Pa. to enact a supply bill, see above, p. 326 n. The enclosures do not survive with Norris' ALS.

passing the Supply Bill. No. 2 is a Copy of a Letter from General Stanwix to pass the ReEmitting Act in the three Lower Counties.[6] No. 3 Gen. Stanwix to Governor Denny to pass Our ReEmitting Act &c.[7] No. 4 is a Letter From General Amherst in vindication of the Governors Conduct in passing The Bill for Reemitting our Mony and lending £50,000 to Colonel Hunter for the Use of the Crown[8] and No. 5 is the Speech Governor Denny made to the Council on resolving to pass the Act for Recording Warrants and Surveys &c.[9]

6. Upon the death of Forbes, March 11, 1759, Amherst appointed Brig. Gen. John Stanwix (above, VII, 45 n) to take his place as commander of British troops in Pa. *Pa. Col. Recs.*, VIII, 298. Stanwix wrote Denny (letter not found) urging approval of a Delaware act to reissue £20,000 in currency for a further sixteen years. *PMHB*, XLIV (1920), 120–1; J. Thomas Scharf, *History of Delaware. 1609–1888* (Phila., 1888), I, 142–3.

7. On June 9, 1759, the Pa. Assembly passed a bill (not to be confused with the Delaware act mentioned immediately above) providing for the reissue of bills of credit previously re-emitted, and for striking £36,650 to enable the Trustees of the Loan Office to lend £50,000 for six months to John Hunter, agent for the money contractors of the British forces in America. The Council objected strenuously to the measure on several counts, among them that it joined two separate matters in one bill, that it threatened to lower the value of the bills in circulation, and, above all, that by its terms it substantially reduced the amount in sterling the Proprietors would receive in payment of quitrents. Denny returned the bill, June 13, asking that the proprietary receipts be restored to their former level and that Hunter be allowed, as he had asked, an additional £25,000 loan and twelve months, instead of six, for repayment. The Assembly yielded on the duration of the loan to Hunter but refused the other proposed changes. On June 16 Denny produced to the Council a letter from Stanwix (not found) urging him to approve the bill and, in spite of a formal protest by the Council members, gave his assent on the 20th. The Assembly immediately presented him £1000. *Votes*, 1758–59, pp. 76, 77, 78, 80–1, 83, 87; *Pa. Col. Recs.*, VIII, 342–3, 350–2, 353–4, 356, 357–60, 362.

8. Amherst's letter in vindication has not been found.

9. This measure concerned the basic documents involved in transfers of land from the Proprietors to individuals. It shifted the final authority for recording such papers from the provincial secretary and surveyor general, officials responsible solely to the Proprietors, to a new officer, the recorder, responsible to the public at large. The Council and other proprietary supporters vigorously opposed the bill, but on July 7, 1759, Denny approved it, telling the Council that if the Board of Trade had any objections to it they would lay it before the King, "who is the most equal as well as Supreme Judge of the Rights of the Proprietaries and the People." As soon as the great seal was

As the Governor assured me that he would give his assent to our Supply Bill about Five or Six Days before he enacted it into a Law¹ I had the Opportunity of giving you very early intelligence of it by the E[arl] of Leicesters Packet Captain Morris who arrived in thirty Days² so that you very probably had Notice of it before the End of May.

The Law for Recording Warrants and Surveys &c. is in my Opinion a Just and equitable Law between the Proprietaries and the People and as it is not connected with any immediate Business or Interest of the Crown it may require more attention and well deserves all possible diligence and Care to get it confirmed by the King in which I think no reasonable Expence should be spared. The ReEmitting Act may have its Merit but all Circumstances considered, it passed the House without any concurrence of mine and I have no Share in it; but as it is a Law of the Province and the repeal of it would involve us in great Difficulties I cannot doubt you will use your best Endeavours to get it approved as well as the Act for the Relief of the Heirs Divisees and Assigns of Persons born out of the Kings Leigeance &c. which I think is a Righteous and valuable Law.³

The passing of these Acts, and the Confirmation of them at Home, will go a great way towards settling our Differences with the Proprietors and I hope bring them to a Sence of their true

---

affixed at the usual formal ceremony, Norris presented Denny an order for £1000, as he had done twice earlier that year, April 17 and June 20, on the passage of bills the Assembly wanted but the Council opposed. *Pa. Col. Recs.*, VIII, 333, 362, 375–6.

1. See above, pp. 326–7.

2. So the *Pa. Gaz.* reported on July 12, 1759. It appears, however, that Norris' letter of April 12, 1759, which contained the "very early intelligence" went by the *General Wall* packet, Capt. Walter Lutwidge. See above, p. 328 n.

3. On June 20, 1759, Gov. Denny signed an "Act for the Relief of the Heirs, Devisees and Assigns of Persons born out of the King's Ligiance . . ." which stated that unnaturalized persons might convey "lands, tenements, and hereditaments" by deed or will and that these conveyances were to be "taken to be as good, effectual and available in the law to all intents, constructions and purposes as if such persons so conveying and devising had been natural-born subjects within this province." This act, and the two last mentioned, were repealed by the King in Council on Sept. 2, 1760. See *Statutes at Large, Pa.*, V, 443–5.

Interest and may probably induce some of them once more to come among us; especially as the Governor assures me he has wrote to Secretary Pitt about ten Months ago to insist on the Proprietors' being sent over to be answerable for their Own Conduct for he could not under his present Instructions answer for his as a Governor either to His Majesty or the People committed to his Care.[4]

I am now to inform you That no Person whatever either had or could take a Copy of a free paragraph in One of your former letters relating to the Proprietors from me.[5] I know too well the Nature of such open Intelligence and the Ill use which might be made of it to suffer any Thing of the kind; but have been informed you wrote to the same Purport to One of the then Committee and if so it might have been obtained from thence, and yet I must not omitt to say that I thought it my Duty to shew it to the Comittee who had it in their Hands for some Time, but I can and do assure you no Copy was ever taken whilst it remained in My Possession nor at any other Time with my knowledge or Assent, This however may, and I presume will, have its effect upon all those who have a Right to see our publick Intelligences.

I will close this Letter with the Advice of two First Bills of Exchange now Transmitted. John Hunter on Messrs. Thomlinson & Company for £500. each[6] and refer to a further Account of the Bills of Exchange in a Separate Paper: and if any Thing material shall come to my Notice will continue to trouble you as Occasion and Opportunities present themselves. I am with great Respect your Assured Friend   ISAAC NORRIS

PS to the above Letter   By the Chippenham Captain Spain[7]

4. Denny's suggestion was ignored; he was succeeded by James Hamilton. Yet on June 18, 1763, Thomas and Richard Penn commissioned Richard's son, John Penn, lieutenant governor of Pa. He arrived in Philadelphia in October, 1763, and except for a two-year absence in England, 1771–73, governed Pa. until 1776. During his absence his brother Richard Penn served as lieutenant governor.

5. See BF's letter of Jan. 14, 1758, in which he compared Thomas Penn to a "low Jockey", above, VII, 360–4.

6. BF recorded the receipt of these bills on Nov. 6, 1759. "Account of Expences," p. 48; Eddy, in *PMHB*, LV (1931), 125, erroneously gives the date as Nov. 2, 1759.

7. On Aug. 16, 1759, the *Pa. Gaz.* recorded the clearance of the *Chippenham,*

An Account of the Bills of Exchange[8]			Sterling
1 My Order on the Executors of Doctor Logan			£ 200
2 John Hunter on Messrs. Thomlinson & Company			
No. 732			300 0
3 Anthony Stoker on George Campbell	£200	0	
Ditto on Ditto	131	8 0	
Ditto on Ditto	30	17 2	362 5 2
4 John Hunter on Messrs. Thomlinson & Company			
No. 1049			200 0
5 Peter Razor on Richard Partridge			40 0
6 Josha Howell on Messrs. Wm and Richard Baker			
No. 5020		£1000 0	
Ditto on Ditto No. 5021		1000 0	2000 0 0
7 John Hunter on Messrs. Thomlinson & Company			
No. 1492[9]		£ 500 0 0	
Ditto on Ditto No. 1493		500 0	1000 0 0
			£4102 5 2

Of These

> No. 1 and 2 are come to Hand per Advice
> 3 I have already Sent the First Second and Third
> 4 I now enclose the Third Bill sent two before
> 5 ——————— The Third Bill ut supra
> 6 I now Send the Second Bills
> 7 I send the First Bills herewith

I wrote the above Letter some Days ago we are now come to the 5th of August and have just received an Account of the Reduction of Niagara and Ticonderoga, and that the Forces are landed before Quebeck and are bombarding it, of which you will receive more particular Accounts from N York or directly by Express. This will make our Western Expedition unactive[?] and in all probability successful. 'Tis said that Six Hundred Prisoners were taken on the

Capt. Edward Spain, for London. She sprung a leak, however, and had to return to Philadelphia. Consequently, Norris sent this and his next two letters in the *Dragon*, Capt. Francis Hammett, which planned to sail for London on Aug. 23, 1759. See below, p. 427.

8. Through the first six items this account is identical with that in Norris' letter of June 4, 1759; see above, pp. 389–90.

9. Nos. 1492 and 1493 are the bills mentioned in the final paragraph of the main text of this letter.

surrender of Niagara. Col. Amherst sailed in the Packet a few Days ago with an Account of the taking of Ticonderogo. Niagara surrendred since on the 26th of July.[1]

    NB Niagara surrendered on the 24th of July

To Deborah Franklin   ALS: American Philosophical Society

My dear Child   London, Augt. 6. 1759
 I wrote to you already by this Ship,[2] but have since receiv'd yours and Sally's of June 18. and 21.[3] which gave me great Pleasure, as your Letters always do; and the greater as it was long that I had not heard from you. I have wrote you several long Letters this Year,[4] and suppose they got to hand at last, tho' it seems by yours they have been long by the Way: Ships often stay long for Convoy. I think some Letters I wrote in November did not leave England till February; the Pacquets are some times ordered away suddenly and unexpectedly; some Ships sail without my knowing it, (as I suppose the last from N York did without your knowing it, for I had no line from anybody by her;) and when several sail together it seems needless and endless for me to write or send Copies in all; so you must learn not to expect Letters from me every Month, nor by every Ship; and make your self easy if a Ship or Pacquet arrives without a Letter for you; considering it only as a Sign that you are to have a very long one in the next.
 You tell me that Smith's Vessel is arriv'd, but the Captain says there is no Box on board.[5] I suppose that to be only a Mistake, as he might not find them in the List of Bills Lading he had sign'd; the Case being this, the Ship was under Sail when Mr. Neat's People put those Boxes on board, and no Bill of Lading was taken; but they were certainly shipt, and I hope they were found soon after you wrote. My former Letters will tell you what there was.

1. See above, p. 408 n, for the progress of British arms during the summer of 1759. The version of this postscript in the copy omits the data on bills of exchange and contains only the final paragraph of news. It ends: "Niagara Surendred on the 24th of July" and omits the line correcting the date.
2. This letter has not been found.
3. Not found.
4. Only those of April 7–11, and of April 12, 1759, have been found.
5. See above, pp. 306–7, for the contents of the boxes sent by the *Cornelia*.

Inclos'd is a Bill of Lading for the 2 Boxes sent per this Ship; one of which is for Mr. Gambier at Providence,[6] and to be delivered by you to Messrs. Conyngham & Nesbit.[7] In another Letter[8] I have given you an Account of the Things contain'd in the other.

Being just setting out on my Journey,[9] I can only add, that I am, my dear Child, Your ever loving Husband   B FRANKLIN

P.S. Here is a Person who represents herself to be Wife of Mr. Henry Flower, Watchmaker of Philadelphia.[1] She tells me a very lame Story of her Husband's sending her over before him with two small Children, to prepare a Place for him, he intending to come here to settle. I cannot understand it; but as the Woman is in Distress, and ready to starve with her Children for want of Necessaries, I have out of Regard to my Townsman, furnish'd her with a little Money. Pray mention it privately to him, and enquire into the Matter, that I may know whether I ought to advance any more on his Account.[2]

When you get Mr. Dunlap[3] to direct your Letters, desire him not to put the Title *Honourable* before my Name; but direct plainly and simply to B. Franklin, Esqr. in Craven Street, London.

Mrs. Franklin

---

6. Probably John Gambier (above, VII, 325 n) of New Providence Island, where Nassau is situated in the Bahamas, or his brother Samuel, a lawyer and member of the council there.

7. A Philadelphia mercantile firm, founded in 1756, by Redmond Conyngham (d. 1785) and John Maxwell Nesbitt (c. 1730–1802).

8. Not found.

9. To the north of England and to Scotland.

1. Henry Flower had a shop in Philadelphia at Second Street near Chestnut. It is not certain whether he is the Henry Flower, an American who published a pamphlet in London in 1766 entitled *Observations on Gout and Rheumatism.* Brooks Palmer, *The Book of American Clocks* (N.Y., 1959), p. 193; J. Bennett Nolan, *Benjamin Franklin in Scotland and England* (Phila., 1938), p. 212.

2. On Aug. 8, 1759, BF recorded the loan of £3 13s. 6d. to Mrs. Flower. "Account of   Expences," p. 45; *PMHB*, LV (1931), 125. Henry Flower eventually wrote BF and told him that Mrs. Flower was an impostor and should be cut off. But BF concluded that he was lying and was, on that account, "a very bad man." BF to DF, March 28?, 1760, APS.

3. William Dunlap (above, VII, 168), DF's nephew by marriage and at this time postmaster of Philadelphia.

From Deborah Franklin

Extract: [4]Associates of the Late Rev. Dr. Bray

[August 9, 1759]

Extract of a Letter from Mrs Franklin in Philadelphia, to B F. in London, dated Aug. 9. 1759

"I went to hear the Negro Children catechised at Church.[5] There were 17 that answered very prettily indeed, and 5 or 6 that were too little, but all behaved very decently. Mr. Sturgeon exhorted them before and after the Catechising. It gave me a great deal of Pleasure, and I shall send Othello[6] to the School."

Endorsed: Extract of Letter from Mrs. Franklin Philadelphia Aug: 9: 1759

From Isaac Norris

ALS: American Philosophical Society; letterbook copy: Historical Society of Pennsylvania; copy: American Philosophical Society

Dear Friend Benja. Franklin   Fairhill August 11th. 1759

My Brother[7] just now brought me up your Letters of the 9th of June by the Packet[8] and promises to enquire whether any Passengers are yet to be met with by whom I might send this in addition to what I have already wrote so that in this uncertainty I shall only acknowledge the Receipt of those Letters and my

4. In BF's hand.

5. On plans of the Associates of Dr. Bray for opening a school for Negro children in Philadelphia, see above, VII, 100–1, 252–3, 356, 377–9. The school was opened Nov. 20, 1758. The schoolmistress took the children to Christ Church on Wednesdays and Fridays to be catechised by Rev. William Sturgeon (above, VII, 252 n), the assistant minister. *PMHB,* LVIII (1934), 7; LXIII (1939), 285–6.

6. Possibly a child of BF's "Negro Man Peter, and his Wife Jemima," the couple to be freed under his will of 1757 (above, VII, 203), or a "Negrow boy" for whom DF paid £41 10s. in June 1757; Memorandum Book, 1757–76 (described above, VII, 167–8).

7. Charles Norris, see above, II, 376 n.

8. See above, pp. 396–404. The *General Wall* packet, Capt. Walter Lutwidge, arrived in N.Y. on Aug. 6, 1759, after a passage of seven weeks from Falmouth. *N.-Y. Mercury,* Aug. 13, 1759.

perfect Satisfaction in your Conduct in lodging my Mony in the same manner with your own and can only beg you will excuse the trouble and continue to act in the same Friendly way with the Bills I have since remitted or may remitt to your care[9] of which I shall write more fully next Week when I am told a Vessel will sail for London. I refer to the Publick Papers for the important Articles they contain and the successful Expeditions Every where against the French. As they have reduced Niagara Ticonderoga and Crown Point we have the prospect of the same Success at Quebeck for our Forces are greatly Superior and the French intimidated by these rapid Conquests made upon them in their strongest Forts and important passes. I am my Dear Friend Your assured Friend   ISAAC NORRIS

Pray remember me affectionately to Billy.

Addressed: To / Benjamin Franklin Esqr / Agent for the Prov. of Pensylvania / in London

Endorsed: I Norris Esqr. Aug 11. 1759

From David Hall   Letterbook copy: American Philosophical Society

Dear Sir   Philada: Augt: [*c.* 14] 1759[1]
    I have only time now to own the receipt of Yours by Simpson,[2] for which I am obligded, Captain Spain going off a day or two sooner than I expected, And to inclose You the second Copy of a Bill of Exchange for two hundred Pounds Sterling, the first of which was sent You by the William and Mary, Capt: Nicholson.[3] I am glad the Affair of the Bill thought to be lost, is cleared up,[4]

9. For BF's investments on Norris' behalf, see above, p. 148; for Norris' remittances to BF, see above, p. 422.
    1. The day of the month is omitted, but the reference to the departure of Captain Spain puts it on or about August 14, since the *Chippenham*, Capt. Edward Spain, was reported to have cleared Philadelphia in *Pa. Gaz.* Aug. 16, 1759.
    2. Possibly BF's letter of April 8 (above, pp. 317–22); more probably one of later date, not found. The snow *James*, Capt. George Simpson, was reported as having arrived in Philadelphia in *Pa. Gaz.*, July 19, 1759, but its date of departure from England has not been determined.
    3. See above, p. 406.
    4. See above, p. 320.

shall write you fully by Hamet, who sails next Week. Remember me kindly to Your Son. Give You Joy of Niagara, Ticonderoga, and Crown Point, being Under English Colours and hope to do the same by Hamet with respect to Quebec, and in the mean time Am Dear Sir Yours very Affectionately   DAVID HALL

Copia Sent by the Snow Chippenham Capt: Spain

To B. Franklin

No. of the Bill 1167

From David Hall   Letterbook copy: American Philosophical Society

Sir: Philada: Augt. 21. 1759

In case of Miscarriages, I have sent You the third Copy of a Bill of Exchange for £200 Sterling the first Copy of which I sent You by the William and Mary Capt. Nicholson[5] and the Second by the Chippenham, Capt. Spain who had the Misfortune to spring a Leak at sea,[6] which will cause some Delay in her. But I am told she will sail again in ten days at farthest.

I am glad the Affair of the Bill thought to be lost, is Clear'd up[7] and am Sir Your humble Servant: D. HALL

Copia per Dragon. Hamit
To Mr. B. Franklin

From Isaac Norris

Letterbook copy: Historical Society of Pennsylvania; copy (first part only): American Philosophical Society

Dear Friend BF   Augt. 22d 1759.

I have already wrote and had sent my Letters by the Chippenham Captain Spain but the Ship sprung a Leak at Sea and my Brother informs me is again returned to Port so that these Letters will be forwarded by Captain Hamet who is to sail to morrow

5. See above, p. 406.
6. See above, p. 421 n.
7. See above, p. 320.

Morning:[8] This little Interval will give me an Opportunity of Returning my Thanks for the Care you have taken on my Account in Mony Matters and to request the continuance of these Friendly Offices if they are not too troublesome. I have acknowledged that I am entirely satisfied with what has been done on my Account in regard to the Mony already received and what more may come to your Hands during your Stay in England[9] but I desire You will use what is necessary for the Publick without the least Reserve. The Situation of the Publick Mony with me stands thus. Just before the last sitting of the Assembly ended I procured an Order from the Commissioners not only for the Mony which the House had Voted, whenever it should be wanted, but likewise for what Mony had been paid by the Trustees of the Loan Office for the Bills of Exchange purchased on your going over in Virtue of a Certificate signed by Order of the House before the passing our last Supply Bill so that this Order repays the Loan Office and provides a further Supply for your Use as Agent whenever it may become Necessary;[1] But the Assembly sitting long beyond the usual Time and the Members extreamly pressing to be at their Harvests[2] the House did not give any Orders for a further Supply but that ought not to make any difference or create any difficulty in the free use of such Sums [as] are necessary for carrying on the publick Business as it may be (no doubt) readily procured at our next sitting now near at hand and I will endeavour to take Care that it may not be then forgotten.

The Bills the Governor has passed this Year makes us all pretty good Friends here to outward appearance; How the Proprietary Countenance will behave on the Occasion you will have an Opportunity of remarking as the Laws come over.[3] The Act for Recording Warrants and Surveys &c. is in itself so just that I hope all imaginable Care will be taken to preserve it, as it guards us against the Iniquity of the Land Office which has Tyranized over

8. See above, pp. 421–2 n.

9. For bf's investments on Norris' behalf, see above, p. 148.

1. See above, p. 405 n.

2. The Assembly adjourned on July 7, 1759, having been in more or less continuous session since Feb. 5, 1759. *Votes,* 1758–59, p. 92.

3. For the acts referred to, see above, pp. 326–7, 418–21. The Proprietors opposed them before the King in Council; see above, p. 396 n.

this poor Colony so many Years without Controul, in My Opinion without Mercy and without Justice.

It gives me great Pleasure to find the Law of the Fourth of Q. Anne, "to ascertain the Number of Members of Assembly &c. has been duely transmitted as well as the private Act for the Sale of the Lands to Geo. McCall in which my private Fortune is so nearly concernd without having ever received the least Advantage to my Self from that Engagement.[4] You will find at the End of the Second Vol. of the Pensylvania Votes page 467[5] that upon a Message from the House of the 15th of January 1725 J Logan informs the then Assembly on the 18th. "that all the Laws of the Fourth of Q Anne that were printed at large (among which the above mentioned Act to Ascertain the Number of Members of Assembly you know was One) were confirmed and such as were repealed only the Titles were printed." But whether any formal Confirmation was sent over is more than I can Affirm tho' I have often searched for it among the Assembly Papers. 'Tis probable the present Council would not be very fond of publishing a Confirmation of that Law at this Time, tho' I do not dispair the Governor in his present Disposition may give me some Intelligence from the Council Minutes.

The Governors Finances being at present in good Order[6] he has retired to the Ferry by the Falls of Schuylkill which he bought of Garrigues where he now resides with his Family,[7] this looks like settling among us when he may be superseeded in the Government. As the Place from its Rural Situation among the Rocks and Fall of Waters struck his Fancy for Retreat, it became necessary

4. See above, pp. 400–1. In 1701 William Penn had granted the land in question to Isaac Norris, Senior, and two others, in trust for John Penn. Many years later, at the direction of the other Penn heirs, the present Isaac Norris, acting as successor trustee, had conveyed the land outright to John Penn. *Statutes at Large, Pa.*, IV, 286–90.

5. *Votes and Proceedings of the House of Representatives of the Province of Pennsylvania* [Collected Edition], II (Phila., 1753), 467.

6. In the preceding months the Assembly had given Denny £3000 after he had enacted legislation opposed by the Council. See above, pp. 419–20 n.

7. In the summer of 1759 Francis Garrigues sold Denny a forty-five acre plantation with a large two-story house near the falls of the Schuykill River. Charles R. Barker, "The Story of the Schuylkill," *PMHB*, L (1926), 362; Nicholas B. Wainwright, "Governor William Denny," *ibid.*, LXXI (1957), 194–5.

to drop the Ferry which was soon done and by this precaution all accidental or impertinent Visitors are pretty well shut out as I apprehend much to his Taste. He called two or three Days since at my House but I happend to be from Home which I am sorry for as I presume he had an Inclination to let me see his Intelligences by the last Packet, what they are I cannot tell but it is confidently reported in Town that James Hamilton is certainly to succeed him very soon,[8] tho' I think General Amhersts Letters may probably give some delay.[9] The General's Abilities and Successes in America must add great weight to his interposition, otherwise the contravening either Royal or even Proprietary Instructions (as they serve to catch a part of the Odium) would not be very agreeable to the Plan of extending those Instructions and making them Laws in America.[1] I am &c.   I N

by Captn Hamit

BF. recd this Letter ackd. Novr. 10th 1759[2]

To Deborah Franklin   ALS: American Philosophical Society

This letter is the first document connected with the long trip the Franklins took to the north of England and to Scotland in the summer and early autumn of 1759. The honors paid Franklin and the new friends he made mark this journey as one of the high points of his first mission to Great Britain. Documentation is inadequate to provide precise dates for the entire itinerary, but the following chronology shows, with most dates only approximate, the course of the Franklins' travels:[3]

8. Hamilton was commissioned lieutenant governor July 21, 1759. *Pa. Col. Recs.*, VIII, 409–11.

9. To encourage Denny to pass the supply bill, Amherst had promised to intercede with the King's ministers so that "no Inconvenience" might result to the governor; see above, p. 327 n.

1. A reference to BF's letter of March 19, 1759, in which he warned that certain powerful British politicians held that the King's instructions were "the Law of the Land" in the colonies; see above, p. 293.

2. BF's letter of Nov. 10, 1759, has not been found.

3. An extended account of this journey, though with some details necessarily supplied by reconstruction and with some differences from the present editors' interpretation of documents, is in J. Bennett Nolan, *Benjamin Franklin in Scotland and Ireland 1759 and 1771* (Phila., 1938), pp. 11–96.

August 8?: The two Franklins and servant Peter leave London.
August 10? to 29: In Derbyshire, Manchester, and Liverpool.
August 29: Leave Liverpool for Lancaster and the North.
September 1?: Arrive in Edinburgh.
September 1? to 17?: In Edinburgh.
September 5: Franklin admitted burgess and gild brother of city of Edinburgh.
September 8: William Strahan calls on Franklin in the morning.[4]
September 11: Dines with magistrates, the Duke of Argyll, Lord Lyttelton, Strahan, and others.
September 13: Breakfasts with Strahan; dines with Alexander Kincaid.
September 17?: Travels from Edinburgh to Glasgow.
September 17? to October 4?: In Glasgow, then traveling: through Dumbarton, Argyll (Inverary),[5] and Perth, and at St. Andrews in Fife.
September 19: Franklin admitted burgess and gild brother of the city of Glasgow.
October 2: Franklin receives freedom of the burgh of St. Andrews.
October 4?: Returns to Edinburgh.
October 6 to 12: Visits Sir Alexander and Lady Dick at Prestonfield.
October 12: Leaves Prestonfield to start return journey.
"Some weeks" spent on return, visiting Lord Kames in Berwickshire and traveling through Yorkshire and Lincolnshire, arriving in London by November 2.[6]

My dear Child,   Liverpool, Augt. 29. 1759

I wrote to you largely just before we left London;[7] we have been out now almost 3 Weeks, having spent some time in Derbyshire among the Gentry there to whom we were recommended, as also at Manchester and this Place. We shall set out to day for Lancaster. The Journey agrees extremely well with me; and will probably be many ways of use to me. Billy presents his Duty, and

4. This and the next two entries are based on William Strahan's diary, APS.
5. After returning to London Strahan reported to David Hall that when he left Edinburgh September 25, the Franklins "were gone to Inverary [seat of the Duke of Argyll] from whence they talked of returning in about ten Days." To Hall, Oct. 6, 1759, APS.
6. BF to Sir Alexander Dick, Jan. 3, 1760, N.Y. Pub. Lib.; to Lord Kames, Jan. 3, 1760, Scottish Record Office. In his "Account of Expences" BF made three entries dated August 7, then left two pages blank (probably with the intention of recording later what he had spent on the journey) and dated the next London entry November 2 (p. 48).
7. Probably a reference to his letter of August 6 (above, pp. 423–4).

Peter. I am not certain whether we shall continue our Route to Scotland or return thro' Yorkshire and Lincolnshire to London but expect to meet Letters at Lancaster that will determine me. I long much to hear from you and shall endeavour to return early next Spring. My Duty to Mother, and Love to Sally and all Friends. I am, as ever, my dear Debby, Your affectionate Husband

B FRANKLIN

Addressed: To / Mrs Franklin / at the Post Office / Philadelphia / via New York / per Two Sisters / Capt Pollard

The Privy Council: Order on Franklin's Petition

Two copies: Historical Society of Pennsylvania[8]

At the Court at Kensington the 29th: day of August 1759.
Present
The Kings most Excellent Majesty

Arch Bishop of Canterbury	Earl of Hardwicke
Lord Keeper	Viscount Falmouth
Lord President	Viscount Barrington
Duke of Ancaster	Lord Berkeley of Stratton
Earl of Cholmondeley	Mr. Secretary Pitt.

WHEREAS Benjamin Franklin Esquire, Agent appointed by the Assembly of Pensilvania, did some time since present his humble Petition to His Majesty at this Board, relating to the Differences subsisting between His Majestys Subjects, and the Indians bordering upon the said Province, concerning large Quantitys of Land, which the said Indians alledge they have been deprived of, without their Consent, or Satisfaction made them for the same, particularly of the Lands which are included within the Forks of the River Delawar, and also of other Lands on both Sides the said River.[9] His Majesty having taken the same into Consideration, and received the Opinion of the Lords Commissioners for Trade

8. The one endorsed in Ferdinand J. Paris' hand as "Office Copy" has been used here.

9. For the background of the petition, the preliminary draft, and the final text as presented and as referred to the Privy Council Committee, Feb. 2, 1759, see above, pp. 264–76.

432

and Plantations,[1] and also of a Committee of the Lords of His Majestys most Honourable Privy Council thereupon,[2] is pleased, with the Advice of His Privy Council, to Order as it is hereby Ordered, that His Majestys Agent for Indian Affairs, do examine thoroughly into the Complaints of the Delawar Indians, with respect to Lands which they alledge they have been defrauded of by the Proprietaries, and that for this Purpose he do take the earliest Opportunity of signifying to them, that he has, in Consequence of what passed at the Conferences in July and August 1757, received His Majestys Orders to enquire into their Grievances, and press them to appoint such time and Place, as shall be most convenient to them for that purpose; That he do likewise give timely Notice of such Meeting to the Commissioners appointed by the Proprietaries to act on their Part, to the End they may come properly instructed, and prepared, to support the Claims of their Constituents, and that when he shall have made a full and particular Enquiry into the Circumstances of the Case, and heard what all Partys may have to offer, he do transmit his Proceedings in this Business to the Lords Commissioners for Trade and Plantations, in order to be laid before His Majesty, together with his Opinion of what may be proper to be done thereupon. And the said Lords Commissioners for Trade and Plantations are to signify the same to His Majestys said Agent for Indian Affairs accordingly.[3]

Endorsed: 29. Augt. 1759 Office Copy Order of Councill on Benja. Franklins Peticon for the Indians agt. the Pensilva proprietrs

1. For the Board of Trade report, June 1, 1759, see above, pp. 379–89.

2. *Acts Privy Coun., Col.,* IV, 402–3, indicates that the Privy Council Committee report of July 19 concurred in the Board of Trade's recommendations.

3. On March 1, 1760, Johnson asked Teedyuscung to set a date for a conference, but the chief declined, saying that he was about to set off "to the Wiandot Nation." *N.Y. Col. Docs.,* VII, 436–7. For two years Teedyuscung made no effort to bring his case to a hearing. Irritated, Johnson wrote again in February 1762, threatening to complain to the Crown unless a conference were arranged. *Johnson Papers,* III, 639. This letter resulted in a meeting at Easton, which began June 18, 1762. Teedyuscung still insisted that his people had been cheated at the Walking Purchase of 1737, but declared that if the governor would not help the true owners they would "leave their Right to be settled when they both appear before the Judge above that knows they are wrong'd." The Indian announced that he would "bury under Ground all

433

City of Edinburgh: Admission
as Burgess and Gild-Brother

DS: American Philosophical Society; two copies: Yale University Library[4]

Edinburgh The Fifth day of September One Thousand Seven hundred and fifty nine Years

The Which Day In Presence of The Rt. Honorable George Drummond Esquire Lord Provost of the City of Edinburgh,[5] George Lind, Andrew Simpson, John Learmouth and John Mansfeild Baillies of the said City John Carmichaell Dean of Gild and the Gild Councill BENJAMIN FRANKLIN Esquire L.L.D. of Philadelphia in Pensylvania in North-America, Compearing,[6] was and hereby Is admitted a Burges and Gild:brother of this City, as a Mark of the affectionat Respect which the Majestrats and Councill, have to a Gentleman, whose amiable Charecter, greatly Distinguished for usefulness to the Society which he belongs to, and Love to all mankind, had Long ago, reach'd them, Across the Atlantick Ocean. EXTRACTED furth[7] of the Records of the Councill

---

Controversies about Land" and was ready to sign a release for all the lands in dispute. *Ibid.*, pp. 780, 786. Johnson reported this outcome to the Board of Trade, and on March 3, 1763, the Board advised the Privy Council that, since the affair had been happily concluded, no further action was necessary. *Acts Privy Coun., Col.*, IV, 555–6. Thus ended the proceedings set in motion by BF's petition of Feb. 2, 1759.

4. The Yale copies are in the Stiles Papers and the College Records, respectively.

5. George Drummond (1687–1766) served six two-year terms as lord provost of Edinburgh between 1725 and 1764. During this period the university was under the control of the city and Drummond was largely responsible for its growth and development and particularly for the establishment of its medical faculty. He led in the founding of the Royal Infirmary and brought about many municipal improvements. During the Rebellion of 1745 he actively supported the Hanoverian cause. *DNB.* The four bailies had functions similar to those of aldermen in English cities and presided in rotation over the Bailie Court with jurisdiction in municipal causes. The dean of gild and the gild council regulated the construction, maintenance, and repair of buildings in the city. Hugo Arnot, *The History of Edinburgh* (Edinburgh, 1788), pp. 499–502.

6. Scottish legal terminology for "appearing," as in a court of law. *OED.*

7. From; out of.

434

of Edinburgh by me Mr. William Forbes, Clerk thereof. Likeas[8]
the seall of the said City is hereto Affix'd   WILL FORBES

For / Benjamin Franklin Esqr. / Burges and Gild:brother of
Edinburgh / 1759[9]

To William Strahan   ALS: Yale University Library

Dear Sir   Edinburgh, Sept. 6. 59
   Your agreable Letter of the 4th August,[1] is just come to hand,
being sent back to me from London hither. I have been a Month
on my Journey; but the first Thing I did after my Arrival here was
to enquire at Mr. Kincaid's[2] whether you were yet in Scotland.
He told me he believ'd you were out of Town, but not return'd
to England, and might be heard of at Mrs. Scot's.[3] We went there
immediately, in hopes at least to have seen Rachie but were disappointed. We left a Note of our Inn; but having now taken
Lodgings, I write this Line to inform you that we are at Mrs.
Cowan's in Miln Square,[4] where I hope soon for the very great
Pleasure of seeing you: being Dear Friend, Yours affectionately
                                             B FRANKLIN

   8. In the same way as.
   9. At the same time George, Lord Lyttelton (1709–1773), his son Thomas,
WF, and two other persons were similarly honored. J. Bennett Nolan, *Benjamin
Franklin in Scotland and Ireland 1759 and 1771* (Phila., 1938), pp. 51–2, 214.
   1. Not found. Writing to David Hall, Oct. 6, 1759, Strahan said he had
recently returned to London after a ten-week excursion to Scotland, spending
part of the time in the Highlands, where he had left his daughter "Rachie" to
recover her health. Later he had met the Franklins in Edinburgh. APS. See
also above, p. 431 n.
   2. Alexander Kincaid was an Edinburgh bookseller and friend of Strahan.
J. Bennett Nolan, *Benjamin Franklin in Scotland and Ireland 1759 and 1771*
(Phila., 1938), p. 43.
   3. Possibly the wife of William Scott, bookbinder. *Ibid.*, p. 44.
   4. Milne Square was on the north side of the Canongate.

City of Glasgow: Admission as Burgess and Gild-Brother

Two copies: Yale University Library[5]

At Glasgow the nineteenth Day of September one thousand seven hundred and fifty nine years:

The which day in Presence of the Right honourable John Murdoch Esquire Lord Provost[6] of the said City Archibald Ingram Walter Brisbane and John Robertson Baillies thereof Colin Dunlap Dean of Gild and sundry of the Gild Council of said City BENJAMIN FRANKLIN ESQUIRE DOCTOR OF LAWS is admitted and received BURGES and GILD BROTHER of the said City and the whole Liberties Privileges and Immunities belonging to an Burges and Gild Brother thereof are granted to him in most ample form who gives his Oath of Fidelity as Use Extracted furth of the Gild Books of the said City by

ARCHIBALD MCGILCHRIST Dep.

From Isaac Norris

Letterbook copy: Historical Society of Pennsylvania

My Dear friend B Franklin   Sept 25th 1759
I was Unwell with a lurking fever all the While I was writing the above letters,[7] but they were no sooner Dispatched, than I was laid up with a very severe attack, which has Confind me al-

---

5. In the Stiles Papers and College Records, respectively. BF undoubtedly supplied Stiles with the text, along with records of his other honors, July 11, 1763, at Stiles's request. Stiles Papers, Yale Univ. Lib. BF's own copy does not survive.

6. John Murdoch, of a mercantile family prominent in the government of Glasgow in the middle of the eighteenth century, was chosen lord provost six times between 1746 and 1759. Robert Renwick, ed., *Extracts from the Records of the Burgh of Glasgow with Charters and Other Documents*, VI, *A.D. 1739–1759* (Glasgow, 1911), p. 602.

7. A four-page sheet survives containing copies of his letters of July 31 and August 11 and the first part of the one of August 22. Probably a second sheet, now lost, contained the rest of the letter of August 22 and the whole ALS of this one.

most ever since, and hinderd me from attending the Assembly, both as it was Calld by the Governor, and as it is now seting.[8] This is the first Time I have been able to set up long enough to write, and even that must be as Laconick as Possible, till I Can gather More strength, which I have now a good Prospect of. I shall enclose such Bills of Exchange as I have no Advice of and a first Bill which I purchased Yesterday drawn By Joshua Howel on Messrs Wm and Richard Baker in London No 2001 for £200 Sterl:[9] and as you write, and poor Rasor Informs me Richard Partridge Executors have (or has if but One Executor) Paid or Accepted his Bill.[1] I Shall add it to the List herewith sent. Will You Excuse the trouble I am Continualy Pressing upon You, To apply to Sylvanus or Timothy Bevan for an Asortment of family Med'cines, I suppose a Guinea or Two, was what I have formerly had of Them at a Time, That they may Continue fresh but I hope they will not forget A Q S, as they Call it of the best Bark.[2] I Cannot find but this must be my febrifuge, I am Your Assured frd

I NORRIS

If I Can write more will make it a
seperate letter.

Bills Exchange[3] No. 1 my order on
the Executors of Dr Logan   £200
No. 2, John Hunter on Messrs.
Thomlinson &c. No. 732   300

8. The Pa. Assembly convened, Aug. 29, 1759, and because of Norris' "Indisposition" elected Thomas Leech "Speaker, pro Tempore." *Votes*, 1758–59, p. 93.

9. BF recorded the receipt of this bill on Nov. 13, 1759. "Account of Expences," p. 49; *PMHB*, LV (1931), 125.

1. Because of Partridge's death on March 6, 1759, this bill had been protested; see above, p. 390 n.

2. Sylvanus and Timothy Bevan (above, V, 291 n), wealthy Quaker apothecaries in London, had in the past supplied the Pa. Hospital with medicines. On June 18, 1760, Norris recorded the payment of £2 7s. 8d. to Sylvanus Bevan. Norris MS account book, 1735–1765, p. 5, Lib. Co. Phila. The "best Bark" was, of course, quinine; Q.S.: *quantum satis*, hence, enough, or the usual quantity. In his letter of October 8 (below, p. 441) Norris indicated he wanted at least two pounds.

3. Except for item no. 8, this list is identical with the one appended to Norris' letter of July 31, 1759, above, p. 422.

3 Anthony Stoker on Geo.
Campbel, Three Bills 362 5 2

4 John Hunter on Messrs.
Thomlinson &c. No. 1049 200

5 Peter Razor on Richard
Partridge Protestd but since
paid, I have your Account of
these being come to Hand 40

£1102 5 2 £1102 5 2

6 Joshua Howel on Messrs.
Wm. and Richard Baker

No. 5020 £1000
No. 5021 1000

£2000 0 £2000 0 0

7 John Hunter on Messrs.
Thomlinson &c.

No. 1492 £500
No. 1493 500

£1000 £1000 0 0

8 Joshua Howel on Wm and
Richard Baker payable to } £200
Wm Henderson endorsed
payable to me No. 2001

£4302 5 2

I now Inclose Third Bills of No. 6
Second Bills of No. 7 £4302 5 0
first Bill of Number 8 (Intendd by Capt Buden)

[*In margin*] By Captn Budden[4]
BF. recd this Letter ackd. Decembr the 8th 1759[5]

---

4. *Pa. Gaz.*, Oct. 4, 1759, records the clearance of the *Philadelphia Packet*, Capt. Richard Budden. *London Chron.*, Nov. 10–13, 1759, records its passing Gravesend, inbound, November 12.

5. No letter from BF to Norris of Dec. 8, 1759, has been found.

The Burgh of St. Andrews: Freedom of the Burgh[6]

DS: American Philosophical Society; two copies: Yale University Library[7]

[October 2, 1759]

Apud Civitatem Sancti Andreae Secunda die mensis Octobris anno partus Salutiferi Millesimo Septingentesimo quinquagesimo nono.[8]

Quo Die Magistratuum illustris ordo et Honorandus Senatorum Coetus Inclitae Civitatis Sancti Andreae Indebiti amoris et affectus tesseram Erga virum valde generosum Benjaminum Franklin Armigerum LLD. de Philadelphia Immunitatibus praefatae Civitatis Societatis etiam ac Fraternitatis Aedilitiae privilegiis Solenni Interveniente Sacramenti de omnibus a Cive necessario exigendis ac praestandis Dona[ve]runt possessione Inaugurali ab Honorabilibus viris Jacobo Lumsdaine de Rennyhill Armigero, Praeposito,[9] Roberto Key Aedili, Jacobo Robertson, Laurentio Gib Mr. Joanne Morison et Davide Rymer Praetoribus Concessa ex fori Judicialis Sancti Andreae Codicibus Extractum per

PATR[ICU]M WILSON Cl[ericu]m

Admissio / Benjamini Franklin / Armigeri / 1759

Endorsed: St. Andrews 2d Oct. 1759

6. For the award of an honorary degree to BF by the University of St. Andrews, Feb. 12, 1759, see above, pp. 277–80.

7. In the Stiles Papers and College Records, respectively.

8. This record may be somewhat freely translated as follows: "The burgh of St. Andrews, on the 2d day of October in the 1759th year of the Redemption. On which day the distinguished company of magistrates and the honorable body of the Senate, in the gratitude of love and affection, have given to a very eminent man, Benjamin Franklin Esquire of Philadelphia, admission to the immunities of the aforementioned company of the burg, as well as to the privileges of the communal brotherhood, entering into the customary obligation required by the civil authority of all who are singled out and honored, installation in this possession being granted by the honorable persons: [*names here follow*]. Extracted from the records of the judicial bench by PATRICK WILSON Clerk."

9. James Lumsdaine of Rennyhill was provost of the burgh of St. Andrews, 1753–60. C. J. Lyon, *History of St. Andrews, Episcopal, Monastic, Academic, and Civil* (Edinburgh, 1893), II, 415. Robert Key was dean of guild and the next four named were bailies. Morison was probably a St. Andrews graduate (M.A., 1722), hence the "Mr." before his name. The designation "Clm" after the name of Patrick Wilson at the end was not strictly accurate

To Sir Alexander Dick[1]

ALS: Mrs. Ailsa Joan Mary Dick-Cunyngham, Prestonfield, Edinburgh (1955)

Miln Square, Friday morning, [October 5, 1759][2]
Dr. Franklin and his Son present their respectful Compliments
to Sir Alexander Dick, and shall attend him to Preston-field[3] to-

---

but was often used by town clerks and other similar persons. Wilson's name
is entered somewhat more formally in the Borrowing Register of the university as "scriba Andreapolitanus." The identifying information has been
kindly supplied by R. G. Cant, Keeper of the Muniments at the University
of St. Andrews.

1. Sir Alexander Dick (1703–1785), who became one of BF's warmest friends
in Scotland, was a younger son of Sir William Cunyngham of Caprington,
Bart., and his wife Janet, only child and heiress of Sir James Dick of Preston-
field, Bart. By the terms of its creation the Dick baronetcy passed in 1746 to
Alexander Cunyngham, who thereupon assumed the surname of Dick. (The
Cunyngham baronetcy descended through Sir William's eldest son, but in
1829 it passed through a failure of direct heirs to Sir Alexander's son Sir
Robert Keith Dick, who changed his name in 1845 to Dick-Cunyngham.)
Alexander studied medicine at Leyden, receiving the M.D. there in 1725 and
again at St. Andrews in 1727. He practised in Edinburgh and traveled extensively on the Continent with the painter Allan Ramsay. He was president
of the College of Physicians of Edinburgh, 1756–63, a member of the Philosophical Society of Edinburgh, and was one of the founders of the Royal
Society of Edinburgh, 1783. In 1774 he received the gold medal of the Society
of Arts "for the best specimen of rhubarb." He married in 1736 Janet, daughter of his cousin Alexander Dick of Edinburgh; she died Dec. 26, 1760, leaving
two daughters, and in 1762 he married Mary, daughter of David Butler of Pem-
brokeshire. *DNB;* G. E. C[okayne], *Complete Baronetage,* IV (Exeter, England, 1904), 273–4, 445–6; Mrs. Atholl Forbes, *Curiosities of A Scots Charta
Chest 1600–1800* (Edinburgh, 1897), pp. 76–321.

2. Known dates during BF's Scottish tour establish that this letter could
have been written only on Friday, September 7, or October 5. If the former,
then this letter must refer to a short, week-end visit to Prestonfield, which was
followed in October by a second, longer stay, because subsequent correspondence indicates that the Franklins left for London immediately after a visit at
Prestonfield. See below, pp. 443–4, and BF to Sir Alexander Dick, Jan. 3,
1760, N.Y. Pub. Lib. The weight of the evidence is in favor of only a single
visit from Saturday, October 6, to about Friday, October 12. It was at this
time that BF introduced the Dicks to his "Parable against Persecution"; see
above, VI, 114–24.

3. Prestonfield House, which Dick inherited with his baronetcy, is about
two miles southeast of the center of Edinburgh and almost directly south of
Arthur's Seat.

morrow with great Pleasure. They are extreamly oblig'd to Sir Alexander for his kind Invitation to spend some Days at his Seat in the Country, but doubt the short Stay they must make in these Parts will not allow them that Advantage.

Addressed: To | Sir Alexander Dick | Preston Field

From Isaac Norris

Letterbook copy: Historical Society of Pennsylvania

Dear Friend B Franklin   Pensylva Octobr 8th. 1759

I have been recovering slowly from a Tedious lurking Fever for some Time tho I do not venture to go much abroad. The frequent bile I have lately been subject to made me think it my Duty to request the Electors of this County to chuse some other person in my stead but tho' I thot it very reasonable under my present Circumstances I have not been able to prevail and can therefore stand more excused if my ill health should oblige me to discharge my Duty to the publick with more Interruptions than I could wish or desire.[4] I write this chiefly to inclose two Bills of Exchange via Leverpoole and intend to make the publick Business the Subject of a Letter independant of my private Affairs. I shall only add to the trouble I gave you in my last of the 25 Septr.[5] that as I then wrote for a quantity of the best Bark to be joined to a small Quantity of Family Medicines I think it cannot be less than Two pounds which I would have in Powder as they have their Sieves and Utensils better than we have them here. I believe the Electors have gone generally for the Old Members tho' I have not heard from some of the Back Counties. I am &c.   I N

I am just told that J Hamilton is arrived in a Packet at N.Y. with a Commission for this Government—not much credited.[6] A Law

4. On Sept. 20, and again on Sept. 27, 1759, *Pa. Gaʒ.* published a letter from Norris to the "Freeholders and Electors of the City and County of Philadelphia" begging to be acquitted from "farther Attendance" in the Assembly and recommending that "some other Person" be chosen in his stead. On Oct. 1, however, the voters of Philadelphia Co. elected him to serve another term. *Pa. Gaʒ.,* Sept. 20, 27, Oct. 4, 1759.

5. See above, pp. 436–8.

6. The ship on which Hamilton was rumored to have arrived was probably

has passed to authorize the Agent to receive any Mony which has been given by the Parliament for this Province. The Clerk informs me he has sent it under the G[reat] Seal—with the other Laws.[7]

3d Bill[8] Jno Hunter on Mr. Thomlinson &
    Co N 1492. £500.
        ditto on ditto 1493. 500.

£1000 – –

2d Bill Joshua Howell on Wm. and
Richard Baker N 2001 payable to Wm. } 200 – –
Henderson endorsed payable to me.

Via Liverpoole
B F receivd this Akd. Febry. 1760[9]

From Lady Dick

AL: American Philosophical Society

Prestonfild Octobr 12th [1759]
Lady Dicks Compliments to Doctor Franklen a good Journy to father and son, a happy meeting with Mrs. Franklin and Miss at Philadelphia,[1]

the *Earl of Halifax* packet, Capt. Bolderson, which reached N.Y. on Oct. 5, 1759. *N.-Y. Mercury,* Oct. 8, 1759. Hamilton, however, did not arrive in N.Y. until sometime after the first of November and then aboard H.M.S. *Mercury.* He reached Philadelphia on Nov. 17, 1759. *Pa. Gaz.,* Nov. 15, 22, 1759.

7. On Sept. 19, 1759, the Pa. Assembly appointed a committee to prepare a bill authorizing its agents to receive Pa.'s share of the £200,000 voted by Parliament to reimburse the colonies for their war expenditures (above, p. 330). The bill, presented on Sept. 25, empowered BF "to have, take and receive" the parliamentary grant and directed him to deposit it in the Bank of England. It passed the next day and Denny signed it on Sept. 29, 1759. *Votes,* 1758–59, pp. 99–103.

8. For this and the following bill, see above, p. 438.

9. No letter written by BF to Norris in February 1760 has been found.

1. BF had probably told the Dicks of his hope to return to Philadelphia in a few months, as soon as his business pending before the Privy Council should be finished.

442

I send this Empty purse to you.
  and wish it May be always fou,[2]
My Pythagorean Honest John[3]
  with us regrits you when your gone.

Addressed: To | Doctor Franklen

Endorsed: Lady Dick with a Purse

To Sir Alexander and Lady Dick: Joys of Prestonfield Adieu!

Copy: Mrs. Ailsa Joan Mary Dick-Cunyngham, Prestonfield, Edinburgh (1955)

[October 15–20?, 1759][4]

Verses by Doctor Franklin to Sir Alexander and Lady Dick many years ago wrote at Coldstream on his return to England. ——October 1759

I

Joys of Prestonfield Adieu!
Late found, soon lost, but still we'll view
The' engaging Scene—oft to these eyes
  Shall the pleasing Vision rise!

2

Hearts that warm towards a friend,
Kindness on kindness without end,
Easy converse—sprightly wit
  These we found in *Dame* and *Knight.*

2. Scots for "full." In his letter of Jan. 3, 1760, to Sir Alexander Dick BF sent his respectful compliments to Lady Dick and asked him to "assure her I have great faith in her parting-Prayers, that the Purse she honour'd me with will never be quite empty." N.Y. Pub. Lib.

3. John Williamson of Moffat; see below, p. 445 n.

4. The exact date when BF composed and sent these verses cannot be determined, but it was probably during the third week of October 1759. After leaving Edinburgh about the 12th he and WF spent a few days at Kames, near the Tweed in Berwickshire, with Henry Home, Lord Kames, during which time they took several rides together, to or along the river. BF to Lord Kames, Jan. 3, 1760, Scottish Record Office. One of these excursions may have taken them to Coldstream (12 miles up the Tweed from Berwick), or the Franklins may have stopped there after leaving Kames and before crossing over into Northumberland.

3

Chearfull meals, balmy rest,
Beds that never buggs molest,
Neatness and Sweetness all around
These at *Prestonfield* we found.

4

Hear O Heaven a strangers prayer,
Bless the hospitable pair!
Bless their sweet Bairns, and very Soon
Give these a *Brother*—Those a *Son*.[5]

Verses addressd to Lady Dick by Robert Alexander Esquire[6]—
October 1759

1

What Franklin writes appears so fine,
I wish his thoughts and words were mine,
Why then so cruel coudst thou be,
As send his sprightly lays to me?

2

Alas! I'm of such Jealous mettle
That ever since I ne'er could settle,
Whate'er he feels he can express,
I silent stand—but feel no less.

3

Our prayers and sentiments the same
I love the *Knight*—adore the *Dame*
Unlike alone in this our Vow,
He prays for *one* Son—I for *two*.

4

But see what's all he pleased to say
Thy Beauty could not make him stay
A lover gone you'll understand,
Is not so good as—one at hand.

5. A second daughter, Anne, had been born to the Dicks the previous May
15. Lady Dick died, Dec. 26, 1760, and Sir Alexander's hopes for a son and
heir were not fulfilled until after his second marriage. *The Scots Magazine,*
XXI (1759), 272; XXII (1760), 670.

6. Robert Alexander (d. 1774), Edinburgh merchant and banker, was probably a house guest at Prestonfield during BF's visit there. He and his brother
William were sons of William Alexander, who had been lord provost of Edin-

From John Williamson[7]

ALS (fragment):[8] American Philosophical Society

[October, 1759]

[*First part missing*] of the Innocent Sort in pensylvany or the plantations will be very acceptable as also an account of what books and Tracts They have write your or Their Correspondence in This particulars will be very acceptab

Let me know how I coud Send letters or Tracts to you and I shall be ready to do it an I think Them worthy and woud be glad that you or any of the above persons of the Innocent way of thinking and living viz. Innocent Towards men and animals; woud do the Same. I rest Sincerly yours &c.   JOHN WILLIAMSON

Endorsed: Memorial To Mr. Franklane octor 1759.

---

burgh, 1751–52, and with whom they were associated in the firm of William Alexander & Sons. Robert Alexander and BF became good friends; in about 1766 Alexander asked for and received BF's advice on certain "important papers," and to commemorate the event he commissioned David Martin to paint for him the famous "Thumb Portrait" of BF. The painting descended to Alexander's niece Mariamne, wife of Jonathan Williams, Jr., BF's grandnephew; in 1962 it was presented to the White House, where it now hangs. *The Scots Magazine,* XXXVI (1774), 503; Charles C. Sellers, *Benjamin Franklin in Portraiture* (New Haven, 1962), pp. 75–80, 328–31.

7. John Williamson of Moffat, originally the tenant of a sheep farm, became a convert to the theories of Pythagoras and a believer in the transmigration of souls. As a vegetarian he forbade the buyers of his sheep and lambs to slaughter them and his landlord therefore deprived him of the property but gave him a small annuity. He read widely in some of the more esoteric branches of philosophy, became an amateur mineralogist, and wandered about in search of useful metals. His discovery of a mineral spring, the Hartfield Spa, added somewhat to his income. Though he advocated polygamy, he never married. John Ramsay of Ochtertyre, who knew him described his eccentricities at some length, commenting: "It was plain that John had a mist in his brain; but it was fortunate that it neither spoilt his morals nor diminished his goodwill to man." *Scotland and Scotsmen in the Eighteenth Century,* Alexander Allardyce, ed. (Edinburgh and London, 1888), II, 327–35.

8. Only the lower half of a single sheet has survived.

A Description of Those, Who, at Any Rate, Would Have a Peace with France

Printed in *The London Chronicle: or Universal Evening Post,* November 22–24, 1759.

A Description of those, who, at any rate, would have a Peace with FRANCE.[9]

London, Nov. 24. [1759]

The two prevailing motives among us, which strongly bias great numbers of people, at this time, to wish for a peace with France, let the terms be ever so dishonourable, ever so disadvantageous, or likely to prove of ever so short a duration, are Power and Self-interest.

As to the First, there is a set of men, who have been so long used to Power, that it is become part of their constitution; and if they cannot preserve it, they and their Dependents must linger and pine away. They find plainly, that whatever they have undertaken has succeeded so ill, that, instead of their gaining the people's Applause and Confidence, They become every day more and more Obnoxious and Contemptible: And they perceive, on the other hand, that such part of the Administration, in which they have had no share, has been so well understood and conducted, that such general Satisfaction has been given throughout the whole kingdom, as reflects highly on the want of Integrity and Capacity in those who have gone before. No wonder therefore, if such men should be desirous of peace at any rate, so it lasts their time; that the frequent scenes of Honour to others, and Dishonour to themselves, may not haunt them any more: And, especially being sensible the National Credit has been strained to such a degree by their extravagant plan of Dissipation, as to render it necessary for the Publick Accounts being taken, as was so frequently and honestly done during the reigns of King William and Queen Anne, even at the Minister's own desire.

The latter are those who are engaged in our Public Funds, and are impatient to have them rise, AND THOSE (IN NO SMALL NUMBER)

---

9. Verner W. Crane first identified BF as the author of this piece. See his *Benjamin Franklin's Letters to the Press 1758–1775* (Chapel Hill, [1950]), pp. 11–13.

WHO HAVE SO INFAMOUSLY LENT THEIR MONEY TO THE FRENCH GOVERNMENT: Merchants who are concerned in branches of Commerce and of Business, which they imagine will improve upon their hands, in case of a Peace: other Mercantile People, who have their prospects of advantage, upon the conclusion of a Peace; such for example, who think we shall hold some of our conquests, which of course will give room for new Settlements; and some who have prospects of Places in such new Settlements: Some who have formed to themselves agreeable plans, for striking into new Branches of Trade: Many Country Gentlemen and others, who wouldn't perhaps be sorry for a Peace, in hopes of being eas'd in their taxes: And lastly, there are very few Roman Catholicks in the Kingdom, but would rejoice at a Peace, at any rate.

It is a melancholy Reflection, that there should be among us such selfish wretches, and such enemies to their Country, who had rather see it sink, a while hence, and its bitterest enemies triumph, than that their present lust for Power, and their sordid Views, should not be gratified; And that there should be those, who are striving to diminish the Importance of every conquest we make, that the people mayn't grow too fond of keeping them; and even go so far, as to propagate the very Nonsensical Language of MAU-BERT;[1] viz. THE ENGLISH *will persevere in their conquests till they draw all the Powers of Europe upon their backs*.

Such is the true Picture of those, who, on such infamous Terms, would sell advantages their Country has obtained, at the expence of so much blood and treasure, over their most Inveterate and most Treacherous enemies.

---

1. Probably Jean-Henri Maubert de Gouvest, or Gouvert (1721–1767), a renegade monk, an author of some repute (his *Political Testament of Cardinal Alberoni* brought him to the attention of Bolingbroke), and a wanderer who was once suspected of being a French spy and at one time or another was imprisoned in many of the countries of Europe. He is depicted as a complete scoundrel in a colorful memoir in *London Chron.*, June 28–30, July 5–7, 12–14, 1759.

From David Hall

Letterbook copy: American Philosophical Society

Sir, Philada. December 15. 1759.

I received yours by Captain Friend,[2] and the Reviews sent by him, in good Order, but I shall never sell them. The Half of the first Parcel you sent me, are yet on my Hands.[3] The Quakers, I am told, don't like them because of some Reflections they contain on the old Proprietary, which I believe has prevented their Sale.[4]

Inclosed you have now the first Copy of a Bill of Exchange for £200 Sterling, which you will please credit me for, and advise of its being paid, when you have received the Money.[5] This makes in all Seventeen Hundred and Forty-nine Pounds, Twelve Shillings, and Five Pence Sterling, remitted you by me since you left Philadelphia.[6]

I am glad to know that we shall have the Pleasure of seeing you early in the Spring,[7] when, I hope, we shall get our long standing Accounts brought to some Sort of Settlement. Have sent you Poor Richard's and the Pocket Almanack, and shall be glad if you are pleased with them;[8] and I flatter myself that my Conduct, in general, since you left me, is satisfactory to you, for I can, with great Truth, say, I have never done any thing, either with respect to public or private Business, but with a View to please all Parties; and if I have not altogether succeeded in it, I am sorry for it; it must be imputed to an Error of my Judgment, not of my

2. This letter, not found, must have been written early in August 1759. Hall to BF, April 18, 1760.

3. It is not certain when Hall received the first shipment of the *Historical Review* (above, p. 360). The book was first advertised in the *Pa. Gaz.* on Oct. 4, 1759.

4. BF himself was unhappy with Jackson's delineation of William Penn in the *Historical Review*. See above, p. 402.

5. BF recorded the receipt of this bill on Jan. 31, 1760. "Account of Expences," p. 51; *PMHB*, LV (1931), 126.

6. For a complete list of Hall's remittances to BF, see above, VII, 235–6.

7. So apparently BF had told Hall in his letter by Captain Friend.

8. *Poor Richard's Almanack* for 1760 was advertised in the *Pa. Gaz.* as "just published" on Oct. 4, 1759; the *Pocket Almanack* for 1760 was first advertised on Oct. 25, 1759.

448

Will. Remember me kindly to your Son, and believe me to be,
Dear Sir, Yours very affectionately   D. HALL
To. B. Franklin Esq;
By the James and Mary, Capt. Friend.[9]

Humourous Reasons for Restoring Canada[1]

Printed in *The London Chronicle: or, Universal Evening Post,* December
25–27, 1759.

News of the British victory on the Plains of Abraham, Sept. 13, 1759,
and of the capitulation of Quebec five days later reached London
October 16.[2] Together with British victories in other theaters of
operation in recent months, this conquest seemed to many observers
to promise an end to the war in the near future. Discussion soon began
to appear in the public prints about the terms on which Great Britain
should make peace. Franklin's major contribution to that debate was
the so-called "Canada Pamphlet," published in April 1760, which will
be reprinted in the next volume of this edition. The present letter to *The
London Chronicle* is, in Verner W. Crane's words, "a preliminary and
ironic sketch of arguments" more fully developed in that pamphlet.[3]

Mr. Chronicle,   [December 27, 1759]
We Britons are a nation of statesmen and politicians; we are
privy councellors by birthright; and therefore take it much amiss
when we are told by some of your correspondents, "that it is not
proper to expose to public view the many good reasons there are
for restoring Canada," *(if we reduce it.)*[4]

9. *Pa. Gaz.,* Dec. 20, 1759, records the clearance of the *James and Mary*
from Philadelphia, and *London Chron.,* Jan. 29–31, 1760, reports its arrival in
the Downs after a passage of thirty-four days.

1. This caption was assigned to the letter when it was reprinted in *The
Grand Magazine,* II (Dec. 1759), 682–3. In *Gent. Mag.,* XXIX (1759 Suppl.),
620–1, it was captioned more soberly as "Reasons for restoring Canada to
the French." BF's authorship was first indicated in Paul L. Ford, *Franklin
Bibliography* (Brooklyn, 1889), p. 285. This was probably one of the compositions BF referred to when he wrote Lord Kames, Jan. 3, 1760, that he was
sending his Scottish friend "some little Sketches that have been printed in
the Grand Magazine." Scottish Record Office.

2. *London Chron.,* Oct. 16–18, 1759.

3. *Benjamin Franklin's Letters to the Press 1758–1775* (Chapel Hill, [1950]),
p. 13.

4. This quotation does not appear in any communication to *London Chron.*

I have, with great industry, been able to procure a full account of those reasons, and shall make no secret of them among ourselves. Here they are. Give them to all your readers; that is, to all that can read, in the King's dominions.

1. We should restore Canada; because an uninterrupted trade with the Indians throughout a vast country, where the communication by water is so easy, would encrease our commerce, *already too great*, and occasion a large additional demand for our manufactures,* *already too dear*.

2. We should restore it, lest, thro' a greater plenty of beaver, broad-brimmed hats become cheaper to that unmannerly sect, the Quakers.

3. We should restore Canada, that we may *soon* have a new war, and another opportunity of spending two or three millions a year in America; there being great danger of our growing too rich, our European expences not being sufficient to drain our immense treasures.

4. We should restore it, that we may have occasion constantly to employ, in time of war, a fleet and army in those parts; for otherwise we might be too strong at home.

5. We should restore it, that the French may, by means of their Indians, carry on, (as they have done for these 100 years past even in times of peace between the two crowns) a constant scalping war against our colonies, and thereby stint their growth; for, otherwise, the children might in time be as tall as their mother.†

*Every Indian now wears a woollen blanket, a linnen shirt, and cloth stockings; besides a knife, a hatchet and a gun; and they use a variety of other European and Indian goods, which they pay for in skins and furs.

†This reason is seriously given by some who do not wish well to the Colonies: But, is it not too like the Egyptian Politics practised by Pharoah, destroying the young males to prevent the increase of the children of Israel?

during the last half of 1759. It may, however, be an allusion to a brief summary in the issue of November 3–6 of an article in the *Westminster Gazette*, Nov. 3, 1759, containing "hints at the terms upon which we ought to make peace." The summary concludes: "7. Quebec should be restored, to give Europe a proof of English moderation—The reasons why it is not for the interest of England to keep Quebec, the author reserves till another opportunity."

6. What tho' the blood of thousands of unarmed English farmers, surprized and assassinated in their fields; of harmless women and children murdered in their beds; doth at length call for vengeance; —what tho' the Canadian measure of iniquity be full, and if ever any country did, that country now certainly does, deserve the judgment of *extirpation:*—yet let not us be the executioners of Divine justice;—it will look as if Englishmen were revengeful.

7. Our colonies, 'tis true, have exerted themselves beyond their strength, on the expectations we gave them of driving the French from Canada; but tho' we ought to keep faith with our Allies, it is not necessary with our children. That might teach them (against Scripture) to *put their trust in Princes:* Let 'em learn to trust in God.

8. Should we not restore Canada, it would look as if our statesmen had *courage* as well as our soldiers; but what have statesmen to do with *courage?* Their proper character is *wisdom.*

9. What can be *braver,* than to show all Europe we can afford to lavish our best blood as well as our treasure, in conquests we do not intend to keep? Have we not plenty of Howe's, and Wolfe's, &c. &c. &c. in every regiment?[5]

10. The French‡ have long since openly declar'd, *"que les Anglois et les François sont incompatible dans cette partie de l'Amerique;"* "that our people and theirs were incompatible in that part of the continent of America:" *"que rien n'etoit plus important à l'etat, que de delivrer leur colonie du facheux voisinage des Anglois;"* "that nothing was of more importance to France, than delivering its colony from the troublesome neighbourhood of the English;" to which end, there was an avowed project on foot *"pour chasser premierement les Anglois de la Nouvelle York;"* "to drive the English in the first place out of the province of New York;" *"et apres la prise de la capitale, il falloit* (says the scheme) *la* BRULER *et* RUINER *le pays jusqu' à Orange;"* "and after taking the capital, to *burn it,* and *ruin* (that is, *make a desart* of) the whole country, quite up to Albany." Now, if we do not fairly leave the French in Canada, till they

‡Histoire Generale de la Nouvelle France, par Charlevoix. Liv. XII.[6]

5. George Augustus Howe, 3d Viscount Howe (above, p. 355 n,) killed at Ticonderoga, July 6, 1758, and Brig. Gen. James Wolfe, killed at Quebec, Sept. 13, 1759.

6. Pierre F.-X. de Charlevoix, *Histoire et Description générale de la Nouvelle France* (3 vols., Paris, 1744), I, 559–62.

have a favourable opportunity of putting their *burning* and *ruining* schemes in execution, will it not look as if we were afraid of them?

11. Their historian, Charlevoix, in his IVth book, also tells us, that when Canada was formerly taken by the English, it was a question at the court of France, whether they should endeavour to recover it; for, says he, *"bien de gens douterent si l'on avoit fait une veritable perte;"* "many thought it was not really a loss." But tho' various reasons were given why it was scarce worth recovering, *"le seul motive* (says he) *d'empecher les Anglois de se rendre trop puissans—étoit plus que suffissant pour nous engager a recouvrer Quebec, a quelque prix que ce fût;"* "the single motive of preventing the increase of *English* power, was more than sufficient to engage us in recovering Quebec, *what price soever it might cost us."*[7] Here we see the high value they put on that country, and the reason of their valuing it so highly. Let us then, *oblige them* in this (to them) so important an article, and be assured they will *never prove ungrateful.*

I will not dissemble, Mr. Chronicle; that in answer to all these reasons and motives for restoring Canada, I have heard one that appears to have some weight on the other side of the question. It is said, that nations, as well as private persons, should, for their honour's sake, take care to preserve a *consistence of character:* that it has always been the character of the English to fight strongly, and negotiate weakly; generally agreeing to restore, at a peace, what they ought to have kept, and to keep what they had better have restored: then, if it would really, according to the preceding reasons, be prudent and right to restore Canada, we ought, say these objectors, to keep it; otherwise *we shall be inconsistent with ourselves.* I shall not take upon myself to weigh these different reasons, but offer the whole to the consideration of the public. Only permit me to suggest, that there is one method of avoiding fairly all future dispute about the propriety of *keeping* or *restoring* Canada; and that is, *let us never take it.* The French still hold out at Montreal and Trois Rivieres, in hopes of succour from France. Let us be but *a little too late* with our ships in the river St. Laurence, so that the enemy may get their supplies up next spring, as they did the last, with reinforcements sufficient to enable them to recover Quebec, and there is an end of the question. I am, Sir, Yours, &c.   A. Z.

7. *Ibid.,* pp. 173–4.

William Strahan: Bill and Receipt

ADS: Historical Society of Pennsylvania

Printed for Benjamin Franklin Esq; by Wm. Strahan

	£	s.	d.
1759. Enquiry concerning the Indians,[8] 11¾ Sheets			
March No. 1000 at £1 3s.	13	16[9]	
For 23½ Reams of Paper for Do. at 13s.	15	5	6
Working Description of the Map		7	6
Additional Sheet to the Pamphlet on Innoculation[1]			
No. 2000	1	8	
Four Reams of Paper for Do.	2	14	
Review of the Constitution of Pensylvania,[2] 29½			
Sheets			
No. 2000, viz. 24½ Sheets large Pica, at			
£1 14s. 0d.	41	13	
4 Sheets Appendix at £3 2s. 0d.	12	8	
1 Sheet Contents, &c. at £1 18s. 0d.	1	18	
For 118 Reams of Paper for Do. at 13s.	76	14	
Frederick Post's 2d Journal,[3] 4½ Sheets, No. 500			
at 17s.	3	16	6
For 4½ Reams of Paper for Do. at 13s.	2	18	6
Paid for Binding 600 Reviews at £3 12s. 0d. per 100	21	12	
For 3 Trunks for packing 500 Do. for Pensylvania	1	18	
For Freight and Shipping Charges of Do.	5	10	
For 1 Reem 12 Quires Writing Medium for Do.	2	14	6
Paid Binder for Hot pressing 25 Do.		8	6
Binding 6 Do. in Morocco	1	4	
19 Do. Gilt and Lettered	1	4	
25 Do. Calf Lettered	1	4	
	208	14	

8. Charles Thomson's *An Enquiry into the Causes of the Alienation of the Delaware and Shawanese Indians from the British Interest;* see above, p. 199.

9. This total shows that Strahan charged for a full 14 sheets.

1. BF's preface to William Heberden's *Some Account of the Success of Inoculation for the Small-Pox in England and America;* see above, pp. 281–6.

2. Richard Jackson's *An Historical Review of the Constitution and Government of Pensylvania;* see above, pp. 360–1, 402.

3. *The Second Journal of Christian Frederick Post, on a Message from the Governor of Pensilvania;* see above, p. 298 n.

Decr. 31. 1759. Received the Contents of the above Bill in full of all Demands   WILL: STRAHAN

Endorsed: Decr. 31. 1759 Wm. Strahan—Acct. for Printing & Binding £208 14*s*. 0*d*.[4]

List of Franklin Birthdays   AD: Historical Society of Pennsylvania

[1759][5]

The Birthdays of the Children of Josiah and Ann Franklin

Eliz. Franklin,	Mar. 2. 1677/8.	Died Aug. 25. 1759.
Samuel	May 16. 1681	Mar. 30. 1720
Hannah	May 25. 1683	April 3. 1723
Josiah	Aug. 23. 1685	Went to Sea, never heard of
Ann	Jan. 5. 1686/7	June 16. 1729
Joseph	Feb. 6. 1687/8	Died 11th of same Month
Joseph	June 30. 1689	Died July 15. 1689

Ann Franklin the first wife of Josiah Franklin died July 9. 1689.
Josiah Franklin and Abiah Foulger married Nov. 25. 1689

John Franklin born.	Dec. 7. 1690	Died
Peter Franklin	Nov. 22. 1692	
Mary	Sept. 26. 1694	
James	Feb. 4. 1696/7	
Sarah	July 9. 1699.	
Ebenezer	Sept. 20. 1701	Died Feb. 5. 1702/3

4. In BF's hand. In submitting an account of his expenses to the Pa. Assembly on Feb. 15, 1763, he reported that on this day he paid £213 13*s*. "for Printing sundry Pieces in Defence of the Province." The discrepancy between these two totals is accounted for by his payment to Thomas Jefferys of £4 19*s*. on May 11, 1759, for engraving the "Indian Map" for Thomson's *Enquiry.* "Account of Expences," p. 40; *PMHB*, LV (1931), 118.

5. The first entry in this record indicates its earliest possible dating; BF could hardly have received the news of his half-sister Elizabeth's death until after returning to London from his Scottish tour at the beginning of November 1759. He referred to the loss in a letter to Jane Mecom, Jan. 9, 1760. Just when he compiled the list, however, or for what purpose, remains uncertain. For additional information about BF's brothers and sisters, see the genealogical tables and charts, above, I, lvi–lxii, lxxii–lxxv.

Thomas   Dec. 7. 1703   Aug 17. 1706
Benjamin   Jan. 6. 1705/6
Lydia   Aug 8. 1708
Jane   Mar. 27. 1712
Sarah Daughter of Benjamin born at Philadelphia Aug 31. 1743.

To Mary Stevenson   ALS: Library of Congress[6]

Cravenstreet, Saturday Evening past 10. [1759][7]
At length I have found an Hour, in which I think I may chat with my dear good Girl; free from Interruption.

The Attention you have always shown to every thing you think agreable to me, demands my most grateful Acknowledgements. I have receiv'd the Garters you have so kindly knit for me; they are of the only Sort that I can wear, having worn none of any kind for 20 Years, till you began to supply me; but besides their Usefulness, these appear to me the finest, neatest and prettiest that were ever made![8] Accept my heartiest Thanks, and be assured that I shall think as often of you in the Wearing, as you did of me in the Making, them.

The Question you ask me is a very sensible one, and I shall be glad if I can give you a satisfactory Answer. There are two Ways

6. Printed, with the omission of the first two and the final paragraphs and the complimentary close, as Letter LV in *Exper. and Obser.*, 1769 edit., pp. 461–3. BF's cancellations of the omitted passages and his "To the same" for the heading and "I am &c." in place of the complimentary close remain on the MS and show how he intended the letter to appear in that edition. Sparks (*Works*, VI, 324–6) and Bigelow (*Works*, IV, 287–8) reprinted it from *Exper. and Obser.*, both under the date of 1769. Smyth (*Writings*, V, 234–5) printed the letter under the same year date, using the original MS then in the possession of Polly Stevenson's descendant, Dr. T. Hewson Bradford. Smyth included the opening paragraphs but deliberately omitted the final one, saying in a footnote, "A paragraph of no importance is omitted."

7. The reference to BF's Scottish trip in the final paragraph shows that this letter must have been written within a few weeks after his return at the beginning of November 1759. It could not have been written following his second trip to Scotland in 1771 for "Miss Stevenson" became "Mrs. Hewson" on July 10, 1770. The mention of Miss Pitt, who returned to Jamaica in 1763, supports the earlier date.

8. Polly Stevenson had previously knit garters for both BF and DF; see above, VII, 381–2.

of Contracting a Chimney; one by contracting the Opening *before* the Fire; the other, by contracting the Funnel *above* the Fire.[9] If the Funnel above the Fire is left open in its full Dimensions, and the Opening before the Fire is contracted; then the Coals, I imagine, will burn faster, because more Air is directed through the Fire, and in a stronger Stream; that Air which before pass'd *over* it, and on each side of it, now passing *thro'* it. This is seen in narrow Stove Chimneys, when a Sacheverell[1] or Blower is used, which still more contracts the narrow Opening. But if the Funnel only *above* the Fire is contracted, then, as a less Stream of Air is passing up the Chimney, less must pass thro' the Fire, and consequently it should seem that the Consuming of the Coals would rather be check'd than augmented by such Contraction. And this will also be the Case, when both the Opening *before* the Fire, and the Funnel *above* the Fire are contracted, provided the Funnel above the Fire is more contracted in Proportion than the Opening before the Fire. So you see I think you had the best of the Argument; and as you notwithstanding gave it up in Complaisance to the Company, I think you had also the best of the Dispute. There are few, tho' convinc'd, that know how to give up, even an Error, they have been once engag'd in maintaining; there is therefore the more Merit in dropping a Contest where one thinks one's self right; 'tis at least respectful to those we converse with. And indeed all our Knowledge is so imperfect, and we are from a thousand Causes so perpetually subject to Mistake and Error, that Positiveness can scarce ever become even the most Knowing; and Modesty in advancing any Opinion, however plain and true we may suppose it, is always decent, and generally more likely to procure Assent. Pope's Rule

9. One of the virtues of BF's "Sliding Plate" was that it could be made to contract either opening; see above, pp. 195–8.

1. In *Oeuvres de M. Franklin* (Paris, 1773), II, 302, Barbeu Dubourg identifies a "Sacheverell" as "A kind of blower [which] takes its name from a famous seditious preacher, who was the greatest firebrand in England." This was Henry Sacheverell (1674?–1724), whose impeachment and conviction in 1710 for inflammatory attacks on Whig dissenters and the Revolutionary settlement produced great disturbances and an overthrow of the Whig ministry. *OED* cites BF's passage as an example of the use of "Sacheverell" in this specialized sense.

To speak, tho' sure, with seeming Diffidence,[2]
is therefore a good one; and, if I had ever seen in your Conversation the least Deviation from it, I should earnestly recommend it to your Observation.

Depend upon it, my dear Girl, your Letters always give me Pleasure. You say you do not mean to beg a Compliment; and I suppress every thing I think of them lest I should seem to be writing Compliments. You made me very happy with a Letter when I was in Scotland.[3] I thank you for the Care and Pains you took in my Affairs when I was absent; you manag'd very well in collecting my Letters; but it was imposing rather too much on yourself, to go to the Coffee House; for me. Present my best Respects to your good Aunts,[4] and to Miss Pitt, and believe me to be, with the sincerest Regard and Esteem, Dear Child, Your affectionate Friend and most obedient Servant   B FRANKLIN

Miss Stevenson

From Peter Collinson   ALS: Historical Society of Pennsylvania

Tuesday Noone [1759?–1762][5]
Lett not my Dear Friend Forgett that I expect Him and his Son to Morrow being Wednesday to drink Tea and afterwards to spend the Evening which will oblige his sincere friend
P COLLINSON

Doctor Frankland

2. Alexander Pope, *Essay on Criticism,* line 567.
3. Not found.
4. Polly spent most of her time in Wanstead with two elderly aunts, Mrs. Tickell (above, p. 122 n) and Mrs. Rooke.
5. Certainly written during BF's first mission to England because of the mention of WF. If the "Doctor Frankland" is contemporary, the note was written after BF's honorary degree from the University of St. Andrews, Feb. 12, 1759, but the name does not appear to be in Collinson's hand, the spelling "Frankland" is not characteristic of Collinson's other letters, and it is written slantingly across the lower part of the page as if it might have been a later addition. For the editorial procedure in placing these undated papers during BF's English years, see above, VII, 316.

From———⁶ AL (fragment): Historical Society of Pennsylvania

[1759–1775]⁷
[*First part missing*] Franklyn for the Favor of his Invitation, sho'd have answer'd his Card sooner but has been kept at Westminster the whole Day, begs Leave now to say, that He will wait on the Doctor, and in the mean Time begs his Acceptance of his most respectful Compliments.

Boswell Court Monday 8 o Clock

6. The writer has not been identified, though the handwriting bears a slight resemblance to that of Richard Jackson. The mention of Westminster (probably Westminster Hall, not the Houses of Parliament) and the address "Boswell Court" (Carey Street, Lincoln's Inn Fields) suggest that the writer was a lawyer, but so far as can be determined Jackson lived throughout these years in King's Bench Walk, Inner Temple.

7. The reference to BF as "Doctor" places this note after Feb. 12, 1759. It might have been written at any later date during either of BF's two missions to England.

Index

Compiled by Helene H. Fineman

Chattin, James: in Smith-Moore case, 35; sells printing house, 92; mentioned, 319 n

Cheese, sent to DF, 324

Cherokee Indians: to be set against Six Nations, 74; against Venango, 76; turn away from British, 77 n; Forbes's difficulties with, 79; send friendly message to Delaware, 104; terrorizing Pa., 104 n; sent to Pa. by Atkin, 104 n; join in Fort Duquesne action, 107; leave Fort Duquesne, 107 n; Penns try to set against Delaware, 113 n

Chew, Benjamin: tries to protect Hockley, 65 n; journal on Easton Treaty, 176 n; quoted, 211 n; Penn informs of bypassing BF, 187 n; represents Council at Easton, 202

Chihohocki Indians, chiefs at Easton, 200

Child, James, witnesses declaration, 205

Chillaway, Job, reports on scalps and skirmishes, 71–2

Chimneys: drafts in, 197–8; as "air conditioner," 197–8; useful for miners, 198; control of drafts in, 456

Chippenham (snow): arrives in Phila., 78 n; carries mail, 421, 427; disabled at sea, 427

Cholmondeley, Earl of, at Privy Council, 432

Christ Church, Phila., Negro school at, 425 n

Church of England: still hated in New England, 341; relations with Dissenters improving, 341

Cider, excellence of, in Va., 155–6

Citizen, The, WF letter in, 361, 407 n

Civil War, English, interrupts entries in registers, 116

Clevland, John, BF discusses guard ships with, 316

Clifford, George, identified, 86 n

Clifford, Thomas: identified, 86 n; orders instruments from Titley, 86

Clinton, Fort, Schuyler occupies, gives up, 406 n

Clinton, George, rebukes Schuyler in mutiny affair, 348 n

Clock, showing tides: Ferguson devises, 220 n; BF has made, 220 n

Clock, three-wheel: devised by BF, 216; produced in England, 216; Ferguson improves BF model, 216; illustrated, 217

Colden, Alexander, to confer with BF on D. Colden paper, 171

Colden, Cadwallader: electrical researches of, 170; D. Colden sends papers to, 172 n; comments on Wilson treatise, 263 n

Colden, David: electrical researches of, 170; letter to BF lost, 170 n; asks BF advice on paper, 170–1; BF praises work of, 172 n; "New Experiments in Electricity" published, 172 n; experiment of, discussed, 322; letter from, 170–2

Coldstream, Berwickshire, BF writes verses at, 443

Cole, Hannah Franklin (C.3): mentioned, 135 n; birth and death, 454

Coleman, William, unlikely subject of Roberts' pun, 83 n

Collinson, Peter: sends black silk to DF, 93; to deliver D. Colden paper to A. Colden, 171 n; receives mail for BF, 287, 301; ships trunk to J. Franklin, 323; mentioned, 240, 329; letter from, 171–2 n (quoted), 457; letters to, mentioned, 190 n

Committee of Correspondence, Pa., letters to, 60–9; 87–90

Commons, House of: cases of contempt cited, 30; BF buys journals for Pa., 169

Condensation of atmospheres, effect of, on repulsion, 246–7

Conductors, of electricity, glass, silk, cedar, tourmaline, 417

Conedoquinet Manor, increased value of, 370

Conestoga Indians, confirm Wright's report, 73 n

Conestoga, treaty at, mentioned, 199

Conestoga Manor, value of, 365, 368

Connecticut: Quakers support aid to, 41; Jackson owns land in, 309 n

Conoy Indians, chiefs at Easton, 200

Convicts: sent to America, 351; BF satire on, 351 n

Conyngham, Redmond, identified, 424 n

Conyngham & Nesbitt, DF to deliver box to, 424

Cooper, Thomas, in Penn land sale, 374–8

Cooper, William, bill drawn by, protested, 98

Cork balls, charged, experiments with 245–8

Corn, effects of harvest on embargo, 89–90

Cornelia (brig): carries mail, 174; goods shipped on, 306, 324, 411

Council, Md., attitude in taxation of proprietary estate, 166

Council, Pa.: seek Denny's removal, 56; relations with Denny, 57; weak defense of "Walking Purchase," 158; Lardner sole signer of report, 158; instructed on Penn's wishes, 234 n; disagrees with Denny on Supply Act, 327 n

Courts, Pa., tenure of judges omitted from Heads of Complaint, 232

Cowan, Mrs., BF lodges with, 433

royal charter for, rumored, 97; Indian treaty at, 113; success of inoculation in, 283; smallpox epidemics in, 283–4 n; can support new printing offices, 319; value of Penn land in, 365–6; policy on lots in, 368–9

Philadelphia (ship), cleared for Liverpool, 80 n

Philadelphia Packet, carries mail, 438 n

Philadelphia-Winchester post: Quaker support for, 44; account of Pa. aid to, 336

Philadelphische Zeitung, prints Moore libel, 32

Philidor, A.D., BF buys chess book of, 169, 170 n

Pisquetumen, brings letter from Allegheny country to Easton, 203

Pitt, William: war plans of, 54, 408; and reimbursement of colonial war expenses, 56 n, 311, 333, 335; inaccessible to BF, 67 n; Sharpe reports Forbes's impatience to, 101; high hopes for administration of, 106–7; Louisbourg victory solidifies position, 151; advice on arming Md. disregarded, 166; informed of progress of Duquesne expedition, 191; Fort Duquesne renamed for, 212 n; orders reports sent from Pa., 291; "friend to Liberty," 294; directs war, 294 n; enemies try to undermine, 316; letter from, mentioned, 337; Denny asks, to send Proprietor to Pa., 421; at Privy Council, 432; mentioned, 352

Pitt, Miss: identified, 340 n; greetings to, 340, 457

Pitt (schooner), clears for England, 112 n

Pittsburgh: Fort Duquesne renamed, 212 n; goods for Indians arrive at, 213 n; must not be left to French, 298, 312

Plains of Abraham, Wolfe victory at, 408 n, 449

Pocket Almanack, sent to BF, 448

Poissonier, Pierre-Isaac, nominated to Royal Soc., 359

Pollard, Capt., commands *Two Sisters,* 432

Pontchartrain, Fort, taking of, would secure Twightwee, 193

Poor Richard's Almanack: BF to send copy for, 98; Hall prepares, 98 n; BF unable to send copy for, 319; Hall sends to BF, 448

Pope, Alexander, quoted, 407, 456–7

Portland freestone, conductivity of, 417

Portraits: of Sarah Franklin, 91, 92 n; of DF, 91, 92 n; of BF, 91, 92 n, 445 n; of "Franky," 91, 92 n; of B. Lay, 92

Portsmouth, England, convoy sails from 323 n

Portugal, embargo on colonial goods to, 334

Post, Christian Frederick: on missions to Indians, 77 n, 104 n, 199; accompanies Indians to Wyoming, 114; journals of, 199, 230, 230 n, 297–8, 453; misdirects Indian message, 203; Norris on importance of journal, 230; contribution ignored, 352

Post Office, American: instructions on newspaper service discussed, 318; Phila.-Winchester route set up, 336; Charleston-Williamsburg post plans, 413

Post Office, Philadelphia, moved to Dunlap's house, 92–3

Potter, Mr., BF recalls talks with, 67 n

Potts, Henry, to receive newspapers for BF, 99

Potts, Stephen: death of, 84; characterized, 159–60

Pownall, John, identified, 315 n

Pownall, Thomas, mentioned, 315 n

Pratt, Charles: biographical note, 3 n; Penns ask opinion on Heads of Complaint, 3; hearings on Smith petition, 40–1, 51 n, 60–2, 87; away from London on holiday, 69; delays report on Smith petition, 87, 149, 295–6, 311; delivers opinion, 88 n, 403 n; defends Md. tax bill defeat, 166 n; delays opinion on Heads of Complaint, 178 n, 234–5; inclined to favor colonies, 294; angry at Privy Council and Smith, 295–6; represents Penns at Board of Trade hearing, 396 n; decision in Smith case due, 403

Prerogative, royal: Penns adamant on, 185; Parliament not to meddle with, 296; Presqu'Isle: French hold until surrender of Niagara, 191 n; securing of, urged, 191–2

Prestonfield, BF and WF visit, 431, 440–1

Prestonpans, Scotland, battle of 354

Price, Richard, nominated to Royal Soc., 357

Priestley, Joseph: *History of Electricity* quoted, 240 n; may have used BF list, 330 n; nominated to Royal Soc., 358; experiments with tourmalines, 393

Prince Edward (frigate), privateering on Del. coast, 220 n

Pringle, John, signs Royal Soc. nomination, 358 n

Printing: shortage of workers for, 6; offices numerous in Phila., 319; supplies sent to B. Mecom, 152 n. *See also* Type